the Third Reich at War

This bibliography was conceived and compiled from the periodicals database of the American Bibliographical Center by editors at ABC-Clio Information Services.

Lance Klass and Susan Kinnell, project coordinators

Pamela R. Byrne
Gail A. Schlachter

the Third Reich at War

a historical bibliography

ABC-Clio Information Services

Santa Barbara, California
Denver, Colorado
Oxford, England

Library of Congress Cataloging in Publication Data
Main entry under title:

The Third Reich at war: a historical bibliography.

    Includes index.
    1. World War, 1939-1945–Germany–Bibliography.
2. Germany–History–1933-1945–Bibliography.
I. ABC-Clio Information Services. II. Series.
Z6207.W8T46 1984 [D757] 016.94053 83-27168
ISBN 0-87436-393-4

Copyright©1984 by ABC-Clio, Inc.

All rights reserved. No part of this publication may be reproduced, stored in a retrieval system, or transmitted, in any form or by any means, electronic, mechanical, photo-copying, recording, or otherwise, without the prior written permission of ABC-Clio, Inc.

ABC-Clio Information Services
2040 Alameda Padre Serra, Box 4397
Santa Barbara, California 93103

Clio Press Ltd.
55 St. Thomas Street
Oxford 0X1 1JG, England

Printed and bound in the United States of America

ABC-CLIO RESEARCH GUIDES

The ABC-Clio Research Guides are a new generation of annotated bibliographies that provide comprehensive control of the recent journal literature on high-interest topics in history and related social sciences. These publications are created by editor/historians and other subject specialists who examine every article entry in ABC-Clio Information Services' vast history database and select abstracts of all articles published during the past decade on the particular topic of study.

Each entry selected from this database—the largest history database in the world—has been reedited to ensure consistency in treatment and completeness of coverage. The extensive subject profile index (ABC-SPIndex) accompanying each volume has also been reassessed, specifically in terms of the particular subject presented, to allow precise and rapid access to the entries.

The titles in this series are prepared to save researchers, students, and librarians the considerable time and expense usually associated with accessing materials manually or through online searching. ABC-Clio's Research Guides offer unmatched access to significant scholarly articles on the topics of most current interest to historians and social scientists.

ABC-CLIO RESEARCH GUIDES

Gail Schlachter, Editor
Pamela R. Byrne, Executive Editor

1.
World War II from an American Perspective
1982   ISBN 0-87436-035-8

2.
The Jewish Experience in America
1982   ISBN 0-87436-034-x

3.
Nuclear America
1983   ISBN 0-87436-360-8

4.
The Great Depression
1983   ISBN 0-87436-361-6

5.
Corporate America
1983   ISBN 0-87436-362-4

6.
Crime and Punishment in America
1983   ISBN 0-87436-363-2

7.
The Democratic and Republican Parties
1983   ISBN 0-87436-364-0

8.
The American Electorate
1983   ISBN 0-87436-372-1

9.
The Weimar Republic
1984   ISBN 0-87436-378-0

10.
The Third Reich, 1933-1939
1984   ISBN 0-87436-379-9

11.
The Third Reich at War
1984   ISBN 0-87436-393-4

12.
American Family History
1984   ISBN 0-87436-380-2

13.
The Sino-Soviet Conflict
1984   ISBN 0-87436-382-9

CONTENTS

LIST OF ABBREVIATIONS x
INTRODUCTION xi
1. WARTIME GERMANY 1
2. WARTIME TRADE AND DIPLOMACY. 58
3. THE INVASION AND OCCUPATION OF POLAND. 82
4. AT WAR WITH WESTERN EUROPE 95
5. AT WAR IN EAST AND SOUTHEAST EUROPE 121
6. AT WAR WITH RUSSIA 141
7. THE HOLOCAUST 165
   SUBJECT INDEX 223
   AUTHOR INDEX 266

LIST OF ABBREVIATIONS

A.	Author-prepared Abstract	*Illus.*	Illustrated, Illustration
Acad.	Academy, Academie, Academia	*Inst.*	Institute, Institut-.
Agric.	Agriculture, Agricultural	*Int.*	International, Internacional, Internationaal, Internationaux, Internazionale
AIA	Abstracts in Anthropology		
Akad.	Akademie		
Am.	America, American	*J.*	Journal, Journal-prepared Abstract
Ann.	Annals, Annales, Annual, Annali	*Lib.*	Library, Libraries
Anthrop.	Anthropology, Anthropological	*Mag.*	Magazine
Arch.	Archives	*Mus.*	Museum, Musee, Museo
Archaeol.	Archaeology, Archaeological	*Nac.*	Nacional
Art.	Article	*Natl.*	National, Nationale
Assoc.	Association, Associate	*Naz.*	Nazionale
Biblio.	Bibliography, Bibliographical	*Phil.*	Philosophy, Philosophical
Biog.	Biography, Biographical	*Photo.*	Photograph
Bol.	Boletim, Boletin	*Pol.*	Politics, Political, Politique, Politico
Bull.	Bulletin	*Pr.*	Press
c.	century (in index)	*Pres.*	President
ca.	circa	*Pro.*	Proceedings
Can.	Canada, Canadian, Canadien	*Publ.*	Publishing, Publication
Cent.	Century	*Q.*	Quarterly
Coll.	College	*Rev.*	Review, Revue, Revista, Revised
Com.	Committee	*Riv.*	Rivista
Comm.	Commission	*Res.*	Research
Comp.	Compiler	*RSA*	Romanian Scientific Abstracts
DAI	Dissertation Abstracts International	*S.*	Staff-prepared Abstract
		Sci.	Science, Scientific
Dept.	Department	*Secy.*	Secretary
Dir.	Director, Direktor	*Soc.*	Society, Societe, Sociedad, Societa
Econ.	Economy, Econom-.		
Ed.	Editor, Edition	*Sociol.*	Sociology, Sociological
Educ.	Education, Educational	*Tr.*	Transactions
Geneal.	Genealogy, Genealogical, Genealogique	*Transl.*	Translator, Translation
		U.	University, Universi-.
Grad.	Graduate	*US*	United States
Hist.	History, Hist-.	*Vol.*	Volume
IHE	Indice Historico Espanol	*Y.*	Yearbook

INTRODUCTION

In the pre-dawn hours of Friday, 1 September 1939, the armed forces of the Third Reich crossed the western and northern frontiers of Poland in a surprise invasion which was to plunge the world into its second major conflagration in less than a quarter century. Soon the Nazi forces were driving against the Russians in the East, overrunning the Low Countries and France and threatening England with invasion, sweeping through the Balkans, Denmark, and North Africa, and pushing forward on an ever-widening battlefield that threatened to permanently transform the political and social fabric of world civilization.

Since the final days of World War II a multitude of studies have been published that have sought to give the researcher and student insight into almost every aspect of the war. These studies, in turn, have given rise to bibliographies and research guides which have tended to view the war from a Western, or Allied, perspective, focusing more on Allies strategies, assaults, and successes than on the German involvement in the war. *The Third Reich at War: A Historical Bibliography* represents a different, complementary approach to the historiography of World War II insofar as it focuses solely on the actions of Nazi Germany from 1939 through mid-1945. This volume is a compendium of scholarship that gives a comprehensive picture of the Third Reich at war with the world. It brings into focus the strategies, diplomacy, and tactics of the German leadership and war machine, the nature of Nazi occupation policies and activities, and the terrible drive for racial hegemony which swept up the unwanted peoples of Europe into a holocaust of death and despair.

The Third Reich at War: A Historical Bibliography is the eleventh volume in the ABC-Clio Research Guides series. It contains 1,069 abstracts of journal articles selected from ABC-Clio Information Services' vast database—the largest history database in the world. This database includes abstracts of articles from more than 2,000 journals in 42 languages, published in 90 countries. In order to create this unique bibliographic volume, the editors reviewed the many thousands of abstracts of articles written during the decade 1973-1982 and selected every abstract that related to the Third Reich at war. Thus, this volume offers an in-depth representation of the scholarship published in the world's journal literature on the subject of the Third Reich in World War II, and far exceeds what one could expect to find through an online search of the database or even through a manual search of the subject index for the ABC-Clio Information Services' history database as a whole.

The abstracts are divided into seven chapters. The variance in the size of these chapters represents not any predisposition on the part of the editors, but rather the amount of scholarship on each topic that was published in the journal literature during the decade covered by this volume. The first chapter, *Wartime Germany,* covers a broad range of topics that is not limited to the specific subjects covered in detail in the next six chapters. Chapter two, *Wartime Trade and Diplomacy,* deals specifically with Nazi Germany's wartime diplomacy with Axis, neutral, and even hostile countries, and with German attempts to maintain trade in strategic materials necessary for the maintenance of the German war machine. Chapter three, *The Invasion and Occupation of Poland,* focuses on the 1 September 1939 invasion of Poland, its military aftermath, and the years of Nazi occupation of that country. The emphasis here, as in the rest of the book, is on what the Nazis did, rather than on the response of those subjugated peoples whose lives were so dramatically affected by the events of the war. Chapter four, *The War in Western Europe,* presents the entirety of the German invasion of the West, including studies of the war in Belgium, Holland, and France, the assault on Britain, the invasion of Denmark and Norway, and the war in North Africa. Chapter five, *The War in East and Southeast Europe,* gives the same attention to Nazi war activities in Hungary, Czechoslovakia, and the Balkans. Chapter six, *At War with Russia,* includes abstracts of articles which describe the German assault on the Soviet Union, the continuing efforts of the Nazi armies to wear down the Russian defense forces, and the later attempts of the Nazis to hold off the burgeoning counteroffensive of the Russian forces until the final days of the Battle of Berlin. Chapter seven, *The Holocaust,* includes studies which deal directly with the Nazi program to exterminate the Jews and other unwanted groups. This chapter exceeds the scope of the other chapters of this book in that it includes studies of the various resistance movements which arose among those peoples targeted for extermination, as well as studies of the effects of the Holocaust on its victims and on European society. For that reason, studies of the Warsaw Ghetto uprising and other Jewish defensive actions are included in this chapter.

These chapters are followed by ABC-SPIndex—one of the most advanced and comprehensive indexing systems yet developed. The editors have taken great care to eliminate inconsistencies that might have appeared in the subject index as a result of combining a decade of database material on this special subject. ABC-SPIndex thus allows fast, analytical, and pinpoint access by linking together the key subject terms and historical period of each abstract to form a composite index entry that provides a complete subject profile of the journal article. Each set of index terms is then rotated so that the complete profile appears in the index under each of the subject terms. Thus, the number of access points is increased severalfold over conventional hierarchical indexes, and irrelevant material can be eliminated early in the search process. Additional cross-references have been added to ensure fast and accurate searching.

1

WARTIME GERMANY

1. Aronsfeld, C. C. WHITEWASHING HITLER: "REVISIONIST" HISTORY DISTORTERS AT WORK. *Patterns of Prejudice [Great Britain] 1980 14(1): 16-23.* Attacks attempts by some German academicians and others to refute Adolf Hitler's responsibility for World War II and Jewish genocide.

2. Baird, Jay W. L'EXPERT EN BOLCHEVISME DU DR GOEBBELS [Dr. Goebbels' expert on Bolshevism]. *Rev. D'Hist. de la Deuxième Guerre Mondiale [France] 1974 24(96): 13-36.* Dr. Eberhard Taubert gained the attention of Paul Goebbels shortly after joining the Nazi Party in 1931. Two years later he organized the *Gesamtverband deutscher antikommunistischer Vereinigungen*. Later he directed the bureau for East European and anti-Bolshevik affairs in the propaganda ministry under Goebbels. After the war, Taubert continued under Adenauer and Erhard to work as a professional anti-Communist, but his fortunes declined when Willi Brandt initiated his Ostpolitik. After the Hitler-Stalin pact, Taubert remained anti-Bolshevik. He led the struggle against Alfred Rosenberg to retain control of propaganda in the occupied eastern territories and took measures on behalf of Goebbels to end the use by the SS of a brochure called *Der Untermensch* (The Subhuman). Taubert also constructed an organization called Vineta to support the morals of eastern workers and gain collaborators. 14 notes. G. H. Davis

3. Bajohr, Stefan. WEIBLICHER ARBEITSDIENST IM "DRITTEN REICH": EIN KONFLIKT ZWISCHEN IDEOLOGIE UND ÖKONOMIE [Women's Labor Service in the Third Reich: conflict between ideology and economy]. *Vierteljahrshefte für Zeitgeschichte [West Germany] 1980 28(3): 331-357.* The Women's Labor Service, established in 1932 to stem unemployment, was transformed by the Nazis into an organization to instill preindustrial values and return young women to the countryside and domestic service. The growing labor demands of rearmament and the war, however, led to an increasing conflict between this antimodern ideology and the requirements of the economy, and by 1942 the labor service had turned into a labor reservoir for the armaments industry. Based on Labor Service publications and memoirs, Bundesarchive Koblenz and Freiburg; 183 notes. D. Prowe

4. Bald, Detlef. THE GERMAN OFFICER CORPS: CASTE OR CLASS? *Armed Forces and Soc. 1979 5(4): 642-668.* In view of the traditional caste-like philosophy and behavior, and the policy of exclusive social recruitment of military officers, explores the extent to which the social structure of the officer corps

has been able to maintain itself since the end of the Prussian-German army, how professional and vocational mobility has affected the traditional elitist pattern, and how higher education has influenced officer recruitment. Statistical studies reveal a marked decline in the proportion of the nobility or upper middle class previously considered desirable recruitment sources. Since the mid-1960's, education has contributed significantly to the reduction of social inequality. 6 tables, 30 notes. R. V. Ritter

5. Baldwin, P. M. CLAUSEWITZ IN NAZI GERMANY. *J. of Contemporary Hist. [Great Britain] 1981 16(1): 5-26.* Two ideas of Karl von Clausewitz may be regarded as particularly significant to Nazi policy: the notion of war as a continuation of politics and the concept of absolute war. On the first point, Clausewitz is ambiguous because death interrupted the completion of his study. He did speak of absolute war but certainly not in the sense of total war of annihilation. German opposition generals admitted that war required reason and a sense of responsibility with the goal of "an honorable and equal peace." Neither damnation nor exoneration of Clausewitz is convincing. The Nazis used his name and phrases for their own purposes which would have remained the same had Clausewitz never existed. Primary sources; 64 notes. M. P. Trauth

6. Barkas, Janet. FACE TO FACE WITH THE PLANNER OF THE THIRD REICH. *Contemporary Rev. [Great Britain] 1973 222(1285): 72-77.* An interview with Albert Speer (b. 1905) discussing his career in Adolf Hitler's Germany.

7. Herzstein, Robert E.; Becker, Peter and Barrett, Michael, commentary. FROM GREATER GERMAN REICH TO GREAT REGION ECONOMY: WERNER DAITZ AND NAZI POSTWAR PLANNING, 1939-1944. *Pro. of the South Carolina Hist. Assoc. 1981: 142-155.* Examines the career of Werner Daitz, who hoped to receive a high position in Nazi Germany with detailed plans for a postwar economy. Reaching his greatest influence in 1942, he was undermined by a combination of military defeat and the machinations of Martin Bormann two years later. Based primarily on German documents; 13 notes. Commentary, pp. 171-180. J. W. Thacker

8. Becker, Peter W. THE GERMAN ECONOMY DURING WORLD WAR II: PETROLEUM. *Pro. of the South Carolina Hist. Assoc: 1975: 16-29.* Analyzes the German petroleum supply during World War II, the source of which was importation, production from domestic oil fields, and synthesis of petroleum products from coal. When the war started, Germany anticipated that the conquest of Russian oil fields would provide them with needed petroleum; but when this failed, Hitler was forced to depend more heavily on synthetic supplies and rationing. Bombing of manufacturing installations in mid-1944 ended most German petroleum production. Based on German documents and the Strategic Bombing Survey; 6 tables, 50 notes. J. W. Thacker, Jr.

9. Becker, Peter W. THE ROLE OF SYNTHETIC FUEL IN WORLD WAR II GERMANY: IMPLICATIONS FOR TODAY? *Air U. Rev. 1981 32(5): 45-53.* Discusses the production of synthetic fuel derived from coal as an alternative energy source and Germany's synthetic fuel development during World War II.

10. Benditer, J. SITUAȚIA INTERNĂ A CELUI DE AL TREILEA REICH, OGLINDITĂ ÎN DIRECTIVELE LUI GOEBBELS [The internal situation in the Third Reich as seen in Goebbels's directives]. *Anuarul Institutului de Istorie și Arheologie "A. D. Xenopol" [Rumania] 1974 11: 145-153.* Surveys Joseph Goebbels's attitudes about German domestic affairs during World War II. Although the war was presented to the people as bringing great advantages, it actually brought great difficulties. The state used terrorist measures, when faced with military defeats, to overcome the disaffection of the masses. Based on published accounts; 75 notes. F. Kellogg

11. Benser, Günter. DAS JAHR 1945. VOM ANTIFASCHISTISCHEN WIDERSTAND ZUR ANTIFASCHISTISCH-DEMOKRATISCHEN UMWÄLZUNG [The year 1945: from antifascist resistance to antifascist-democratic upheaval]. *Zeitschrift für Geschichtswissenschaft [East Germany] 1980 28(4): 311-323.* The transition of the Communist Party of Germany from an illegal to a legal political party of the masses consisted of three phases: the final period of resistance, quasilegality after the liberation, and the start of new political life with the formation of the Communist Party in the open. The presence of the Soviet army in one part of Germany and the imperialist occupation of the other parts enduringly influenced Germany's political development. The Soviet liberation freed the working class for revolutionary action. Primary and secondary sources; 47 notes. G. E. Pergl

12. Bezymenski, L. KAK ROZHDAIUTSIA VOINY [How wars are born]. *Mirovaia Ekonomika i Mezhdunarodnye Otnosheniia [USSR] 1980 (11): 121-128.* Reviews Volume 1 of M. Messerschmidt's *Das Deutsche Reich und der Zweite Weltkrieg* (1979).

13. Biddiss, Michael D. FROM ILLUSION TO DESTRUCTION: THE GERMANIC BID FOR WORLD POWER, 1897-1945. *British J. of Int. Studies [Great Britain] 1976 2(2): 173-185.* Reviews Fritz Fischer's *Griff nach der Weltmacht: Die Kriegszielpolitik des kaiserlichen Deutschland, 1914-18* (Düsseldorf, 1961), *Weltmacht oder Niedergang: Deutschland in Ersten Weltkrieg* (Hamburg, 1965), and *Krieg der Illusionen: Die deutsche Politik von 1911 bis 1914* (Düsseldorf, 1969), recent works by John Moses on Fischer's revolutionary place in the national historiographical tradition and works by Norman Rich on German aims associated with World War II.

14. Billson, Marc K., III. A CONVERSATION WITH ALBERT SPEER. *Dalhousie Rev. [Canada] 1978 58(1): 17-29.* Interview with the former Minister of the Third Reich, commenting on his experiences in Spandau Prison and their influence on his writing of *Spandau Diaries* and *Inside the Third Reich.* C. H. Held

15. Billson, Marcus K., III. INSIDE ALBERT SPEER: SECRETS OF MORAL EVASION. *Antioch Rev. 1979 37(4): 460-474.* Results of the author's 1977 interview with Albert Speer on the subject of Speer's memoirs, 1930's-60's, *Inside the Third Reich* and *Spandau: The Secret Diaries.*

16. Binion, Rudolph. FOAM ON THE HITLER WAVE. *J. of Modern Hist. 1974 46(3): 522-528.* Analyzes recent biographical treatments of Hitler's life: W. Maser's *Adolf Hitler: Legende, Mythos, Wirklichkeit* (Munich, 1971);

I. C. Fest's *Hitler: Eine Biographie* (Frankfurt-am-Main, 1973); and E. Duerlein's *Hitler: Eine politische Biographie* (Munich, 1969). 32 notes.

P. J. Beck

17. Binion, Rudolph. HITLER LOOKS EAST. *Hist. of Childhood Q. 1975 3(1): 85-102.* An exploration of Adolf Hitler's two primary themes, eastern expansionism and anti-Semitism. The expansionist theme was drawn from German history, while Hitler superimposed anti-Semitism on German culture. Both themes were integrated through the concept of national unity; the removal of the Jews would lead to unity and conquest. After the tripartite formula was fixed in the mass unconscious, Hitler could mute those aspects which would foster critical foreign attention, emphasizing only unity. But in emphasizing unity, the other two aims were constantly reinforced in the unconscious. Primary sources; 76 notes.

R. E. Butchart

18. Bird, Eugene K. LE MYSTÈRE RUDOLF HESS [The Rudolf Hess mystery]. *Nouvelle Rev. des Deux Mondes [France] 1980 (4): 110-117.* Discusses the motives for Rudolf Hess's 1941 flight to Scotland and advocates Hess's discharge from Spandau prison. Based on confidences received from Hess by the author, American director of Spandau.

19. Blankestein, Herbert and Turkenburg, Wim C. ATOOMENERGIE IN HET DERDE RIJK [Atomic energy in the Third Reich]. *Spiegel Hist. [Netherlands] 1981 16(12): 690-697.* Discoveries in atomic research in the 1930's raised fears of German development of atomic weapons. Germany's failure to do so was the result not of resistance or even misgivings from within the German scientific community, but a lack of high-level scientific manpower, a serious shortage of funds, a scarcity of important materials such as heavy water, and setbacks from a series of accidents. The roles of Werner Heisenberg and Ernst von Weizsächer are discussed. Primary sources; 10 illus.

C. W. Wood, Jr.

20. Blankestein, Herbert and Turkenburg, Wim. C. DE BEWEGING VOOR ARISCHE NATUURKUNDE [The movement for Aryan science]. *Spiegel Hist. [Netherlands] 1981 16(11): 627-633.* The rise of Nazism in Germany led to the establishment of "Aryan science," an ideological accompaniment of the new order. The new racist, politicized science undoubtedly had adverse effects, but they were not decisive. The great tradition in theoretical physics continued undeflected. Primary sources; 7 illus. Article to be continued.

C. W. Wood, Jr.

21. Bleistein, Roman. HITLERS JÜNGSTE SOLDATEN [Hitler's youngest soldiers]. *Stimmen der Zeit [West Germany] 1982 200(1): 61-63.* After 15 February 1943, tens of thousands of German students were used as anti-aircraft artillery assistants, their combat status never being clear, as the 15 to 17-year-olds were subject to the authority of the military, the Nazi party, and the Hitler Youth.

22. Boelcke, Willi A. DAS "SEEHAUS" IN BERLIN-WANNSEE. ZUR GESCHICHTE DES DEUTSCHEN "MONITORING-SERVICE" WÄHREND DES ZWEITEN WELTKRIEGES [The "Seehaus" in Berlin-Wannsee: the German monitoring service during the Second World War]. *Jahrbuch für die Geschichte Mittel- und Ostdeutschlands [West Germany] 1974 23: 231-269.* Evaluates German monitoring of foreign radio broadcasts as a source of intelli-

gence on the enemy assessment of the war situation, on conditions in enemy countries, and for propaganda purposes. In contrast to Britain, German monitoring was extremely rudimentary at the outbreak of World War II. By mid-1940 the foreign office had created an extensive organization employing nearly 700 people and housed at a former restaurant in Wannsee. This was accomplished despite conflicts over competency, especially between Goebbels and Ribbentrop, and an increasing fear of the role of foreign broadcasts in spreading defeatism. As the reliability of espionage agents and friendly neutrals as intelligence sources diminished, broadcasting played an increasingly important part in the war effort. Based on documentary sources and secondary works; 80 notes.

J. A. Perkins

23. Bond, Brian. LIDDELL HART AND THE GERMAN GENERALS. *Military Affairs 1977 41(1): 16-20.* Examines the assertions of several World War II German generals that they were influenced by B. H. Liddell Hart. His prewar publications were translated and widely read in Germany. But so were the publications of other writers, such as J. F. C. Fuller and Giffard Martel. Heinz Guderian, in particular, found Liddell Hart's ideas useful, especially the concept of deep strategic penetrations when he was gaining practical field experience. Guderian provided the most important of the postwar credit to Liddell Hart. 21 notes.

A. M. Osur

24. Bowers, Ray L. AFTER THIRTY YEARS: CONVERSATIONS ON THE AIR WAR. *Aerospace Hist. 1974 21(2): 65-69.* US and German airmen discuss their experiences in Europe during World War II, 1942.

S

25. Braubach, Max. VOM ERSTEN BIS ZUM ENDE DES ZWEITEN WELTKRIEGES. BERICHT UBER VERÖFFENTLICHUNGEN DER JAHRE 1971-1974 [From the First to the Second World War: report on publications 1971-74]. *Hist. Jahrbuch [West Germany] 1974 94: 247-332.* A review of 52 German and French publications under the following headings: the struggle for the new order and for democracy; the "Hitler-Renaissance"; collaborators and enemies of Hitler; new primary sources on contemporary history; monographs on political and military history. 81 notes.

G. Bassler

26. Brecht, Alfred. ERINNERUNGEN AUS 60 JAHREN URACHER SEMINARGESCHICHTE [Memoirs of 60 years of the Urach Seminary's history]. *Blätter für Württembergische Kirchengeschichte [West Germany] 1977 77: 149-160.* Personal recollections of the development of this Protestant theological seminary, which reflect Brecht's view of German Protestantism during World War I, the Weimar republic, World War II, and the postwar period.

27. Browning, Christopher R. *UNTERSTAATSSEKRETAER* MARTIN LUTHER AND THE RIBBENTROP FOREIGN OFFICE. *J. of Contemporary Hist. [Great Britain] 1977 12(2): 313-344.* Hitler's vassals functioned like assassin barons, each with a supporting underlord to share the burden and the guilt. Such were the Himmler-Heydrich alliance and, considered here, the duet of Joachim von Ribbentrop and Under-State-Secretary Martin Luther (1895-1945). Luther headed Ribbentrop's Party Liaison Office and blocked rivals by such maneuvers as monopolizing party correspondence. Luther began to break with Ribbentrop in 1941 and to accuse him privately of megalomania and incom-

petence. Dissatisfaction with his superior grew into disillusionment with the whole Nazi system and, "amoral realist" though he was, Luther began to favor a compromise peace. Betrayed by Himmler, Luther was arrested in 1943 and condemned to be shot, but the sentence was commuted to internment at Sachsenhausen. Here he was treated relatively well and was released as the Russians closed in on Berlin. Shortly after the end of the war, he died of a heart attack. Archival sources; 61 notes. M. P. Trauth

28. Caspar, Gustav-Adolf. DIE KRIEGSLAGE VOM HERBST 1943 BIS ZUM WINTER 1944/45 UND DAS ENTSTEHEN DER VEREINBARUNGEN ÜBER DIE GRENZEN DER BESATZUNGSZONEN IN DEUTSCHLAND [The war situation of fall 1943 through the winter 1944-45 and the emergence of arrangements over the boundaries of occupation zones in Germany]. *Militärgeschichtliche Mitteilungen [West Germany] 1979 (2): 173-183.* Describes the development of Allied occupation policy for Germany as its collapse approached. The possible rectifications of boundaries enlarging the western zones were nullified by setbacks at Arnhem, Aachen and the Ardennes at the end of 1944. In any event the German government learned of occupation plans too late to shift defensive preparations to save territory from Soviet occupation. Based upon published sources; 44 notes. K. W. Estes

29. Charisius, Albrecht and Moritz, Erhard. ZUR FUSION DES OKW-AMTES AUSLAND ABWEHR MIT DEM SICHERHEITSDIENST (SD) 1944 [On the fusion of the German high command's Abwehr with the Sicherheitsdienst (SD) in 1944]. *Militärgeschichte [East Germany] 1977 16(1): 44-57.* Provides insight into the amalgamation process of the two most important intelligence services of Nazi Germany in 1944. Documentation shows that after the turn in World War II brought about by the Soviet army, the fascist ruling circles wanted to adjust intelligence activity to the strategic defensive. These circles hoped to escape total defeat through a higher effectiveness of espionage. The documents refute the legend of imperialist historiography about the forced amalgamation of the military Abwehr with the Sicherheitsdienst of the SS.
J/T (H. D. Andrews).

30. Charnitzky, Jürgen. STRUTTURA E POLITICA DEL TERZO REICH [Structure and politics of the Third Reich]. *Studi Storici [Italy] 1982 23(1): 205-213.* Reviews *Der "Führerstaat": Mythos and Realität. Studien zur Struktur und Politik des Dritten Reiches,* edited by G. Hirschfeld and L. Kettenacker (1981). 41 notes. E. E. Ryan

31. Cluet, Marc. DANGER AÉRIEN ET ARCHITECTURE DU IIIe REICH [Aerial danger and Third Reich architecture]. *Rev. Hist. des Armées [France] 1980 (4): 147-174.* Between the wars, Germany, although deprived by the Versailles Treaty of the right to possess an air force, was engaged in an intensive study of the conduct of air warfare. Giulio Douhet's *Mastery of the Air* (1921) had foretold that air attacks would not be limited to the enemy's armed forces but would extend to the sources of his strength, including civilian populations. The German military applied these ideas to offensive and defensive planning. The article studies the defensive aspect of their thinking in organizational and architectural terms. The aim of the planners was to diffuse or dilute urban construction and to armor it. 8 plates, 100 notes. J. V. Coutinho

32. Cogniot, Georges. LA LUTTE ANTIFASCISTE DES COMMUNISTES ALLEMANDS PENDANT LA GUERRE 1939-1945 [The antifascist struggle of the German communists during World War II, 1939-45]. *Pensée [France] 1974 (174): 112-116.* On 28 September 1943, members of the Manouchian group shot Julius von Ritter, the representative of Fritz Sauckel (1894-1946) in France. This was but one episode of the German Communist resistance to Nazism, begun in Germany, transferred to Spain during the Spanish Civil War, and later moved to occupied France. At its Bern Conference (January-February 1939) the German Communist Party developed a program for a new democratic republic which helped unite opposition forces in an antifascist popular front. In July 1943, a national committee for a free Germany was established in the Soviet Union, and shortly thereafter, the Comité national "Allemagne libre" pour l'ouest (CALPO) with the journals *Volk und Vaterland* and *Unser Vaterland* in France. Publication of *Resistance* (Berlin: Dietz Verlag, 1973), which includes the memoirs of 34 participants in the anti-Nazi movement, should publicize the German Communist contribution. A. W. Novitsky

33. Cole, C. Robert. A. J. P. TAYLOR AND THE ORIGINS OF THE SECOND WORLD WAR. Parker, Harold T., ed. *Problems in European History,* (Durham, N.C.: Moore Publ., 1979): 267-282. A. J. P. Taylor's *The Origins of the Second World War* (1961), represented a rejection of the "Nuremberg Thesis," i.e., of the notion that Hitler was personally responsible for the war and that consequently the governments of Western Europe and the German people were both substantially innocent and could present a morally unassailable front against a Soviet threat much analogous to the former Nazi one. Taylor saw World War II as in the long run inevitable thanks to Versailles and in detail the result of accidents and blunders in which all were more or less equally at fault. F. H. Hinsley accused Taylor of ignoring the role of long-range plans and of conscious choice between available alternatives, and a host of critics found his thesis morally unacceptable. Some of his ideas have been supported by subsequent scholarship. Refs. L. W. Van Wyk

34. Collotti, Enzo. STORIA MILITARE E STORIA POLITICA IN ALCUNE RECENTI OPERE SULLA SECONDA GUERRA MONDIALE [Military and political history in recent works on World War II]. *Studi Storici [Italy] 1974 15(4): 985-1000.* Reviews B. H. Liddell Hart's *Storia militare della seconda guerra mondiale* (Milan, 1970), Gordon Wright's *L'Europe en guerre 1939-1945* (Paris, 1971; transl. *The Ordeal of Total War 1939-1945),* H. A. Jacobsen's *Nationalsozialistische Aussenpolitik 1933-1938* (Frankfurt, 1958), and Lothar Gruchmann's *Der Zweite Weltkrieg. Kriegführung und Politik* (Munich, 1971). 18 notes. E. J. Craver

35. Constantiniu, Florin. PERIODIZAREA CELUI DE AL DOILEA RĂZBOI MONDIAL [Periodization of World War II]. *Rev. de Istorie [Rumania] 1974 27(7): 1039-1047.* A new periodization of World War II according to military strategic criteria: the blitzkrieg between September 1939 (the invasion of Poland) and April-May 1942 (the battle for Moscow) divided by the retreat at Dunkirk and the attack on the Soviet Union into two subperiods; the period of strategic equilibrium, from April-May 1942 (the battle for Moscow) to July 1943 (the battle of Kursk) which is, in its turn, divided in two by the Stalingrad battles; and the period of the Allies' strategic initiative, July 1943 - September

1945. Three major crises of July-August 1944 mark this latter period: the Allies' landing in France, the collapse of the Center army group on the eastern front, and Rumania's withdrawal from the anti-Soviet war. RSA (12:414)

36. Conway, J. S. REVIEW ARTICLE: HERMANN RAUSCHNING AS HISTORIAN AND OPPONENT OF NAZISM. *Can. J. of Hist. [Canada] 1973 8(1): 67-78.* Discusses four books dealing with the works of Hermann Rauschning, with particular emphasis on his *Hitler Speaks* (1940), which contains observations on Adolf Hitler's personality.

37. Conway, John S. A GERMAN NATIONAL REICH CHURCH AND AMERICAN WAR PROPAGANDA. *Catholic Hist. Rev. 1976 62(3): 464-472.* In 1941 American sources obtained a secretly circulated pamphlet from Germany outlining a plan to abolish Christianity and substitute a National Reich Church complete with Nazi symbols, liturgies, and ideology. Franklin D. Roosevelt used this for his propaganda campaign, designed to attack Nazi Germany and to denounce the persecution of the churches. He assumed that this plan was an official Nazi proposal and used it to win over opponents, particularly American Roman Catholics. In fact, Gestapo reports showed that the proposal stemmed from a pro-Nazi fanatic. But, the anti-clerical and anti-Christian aspects of the program closely resembled the Gestapo's own plans. A

38. Creveld, M. van WAR LORD HITLER: SOME POINTS RECONSIDERED. *European Studies Rev. [Great Britain] 1974 4(1): 57-79.* Reconsiders aspects of Adolf Hitler's conduct in World War II, with particular reference to his attitudes toward war.

39. Csikos, Stefan. DER MINENKRIEG AUF DER DONAU [Mine warfare on the Danube]. *Marine Rundschau [West Germany] 1975 72(8): 464-477.* Describes the German Danubian minesweepers during World War II, especially those connected with the Yugoslavian campaign in the spring of 1941 and the war with Russia. These units later countered Allied minelaying actions until the end of the war. 3 photos, 2 appendixes. G. E. Pergl

40. Csöppüs, István. A MAGYARORSZÁGI MEZŐ- ÉS ERDŐGAZDASÁGI IDÉNYMUNKÁSOK NÉMETORSZÁGI MUNKAVÁLLALÁSA (1937-1944) [Hungarian agricultural and forestry seasonal workers employed in Germany, 1937-44]. *Magyar Tudományos Akadémia Filozófiai és Történettudományok Osztályának Közleményei [Hungary] 1978 27(1-3): 187-237.* Due to the slow industrial development of Eastern Europe, the idea of temporary employment in Germany was well received by the large surplus of agricultural workers in Hungary. As the war progressed, inadequate housing, food, and wages caused severe hardship to the workers. Employers and merchants took advantage of several large groups, sometimes with the assistance of government officials. 21 tables, 162 notes. T. Kuner

41. Dar, E. H. U-BOATS AT WAR: A STUDY IN LEADERSHIP. *Army Q. and Defence J. [Great Britain] 1978 108(2): 208-219.* Analyzes the abilities of German submarine commanders during World War II.

42. Defrasne, J. UN INSTRUMENT CARACTÉRISTIQUE DE L'ARME PSYCHOLOGIQUE: LES UNITÉS DE PROPAGANDE DE LA WEHRMACHT [A characteristic instrument of the psychological arm: the propaganda units of the Wehrmacht]. *Rev. Hist. des Armées [France] 1980 (1): 111-130.* Psychological warfare existed before the name, but its techniques have progressed. The German army, exposed during World War I to the impressive Allied propaganda, had created several innovations on the eve of World War II. It had assembled several military units of propaganda troops, whose origins, organization, and procedures are examined. Document, 6 plates, 6 tables, 3 charts, 6 notes, biblio. J. V. Coutinho

43. Delmas, J. LA SERVICE HISTORIQUE DE L'ARMÉE DE TERRE ET LA DEUXIÈME GUERRE MONDIALE [The Historical Service of the Army and World War II]. *Rev. d'Hist. de la Deuxième Guerre Mondiale [France] 1978 28(110): 113-121.* The Historical Service of the French army has inherited the oldest archives in France, functioning continuously since 1688. The service maintains and updates these archives, while publishing works on military history, including the history of World War II. In addition, the service operates the Military History Center at the Château of Vincennes, with a library of 300,000 volumes, a periodical room with military reviews of the 19th and 20th centuries, and a German language library of 25,000 volumes, largely dedicated to World War II. The University of Paris has installed its own Center for Military History there, in order to take advantage of the rich resources for scholars. 4 notes.
J. C. Billigmeier

44. DeLuca, Anthony R. "DER GROSSMUFTI" IN BERLIN: THE POLITICS OF COLLABORATION. *Int. J. of Middle East Studies [Great Britain] 1979 10(1): 125-138.* Analyzes the collaboration of the Mufti of Jerusalem, Haj Muhammad Amin al- Hussein, with the German government during World War II. The Mufti linked his offers of collaboration with German guarantees of Arab independence and recognition of his leadership of the Arab world. The Mufti was eager to lend the prestige of his position and the influence of his office to the Axis cause in World War II. Based on German Foreign Office documents and secondary sources; 47 notes. R. B. Orr

45. Demps, Laurenz. ZAHLEN ÜBER DEN EINSATZ AUSLÄNDISCHER ZWANGSARBEITER IN DEUTSCHLAND IM JAHRE 1943 [Statistics on the use of foreign forced labor in Germany in 1943]. *Zeitschrift für Geschichtswissenschaft [East Germany] 1973 21(7): 830-843.* Publication of two German government documents of 1943 which deal with the use of forced labor in the German armaments industry.

46. DeWitt, Thomas E. J. THE ECONOMICS AND POLITICS OF WELFARE IN THE THIRD REICH. *Central European Hist. 1978 11(3): 256-278.* Analysis of the public welfare system in Germany inherited by the Nazis. Hitler had to maintain the welfare to keep the masses satisfied, but he needed some of the money expended on welfare to finance his rearmament. He was able to use propaganda and increased private welfare, especially by the party, to reduce public expenditures for welfare and to carry out his foreign policy. "Nazi welfare policies failed because they were intertwined with politics and economics, and soon became their handmaiden." However, the failure did not seriously affect the Nazi regime. Based on primary sources. 77 notes. C. R. Lovin

47. Diephouse, David J. THE "GERMAN CATASTROPHE" REVISITED: CIVIL RELIGION IN THE THIRD REICH. *Fides et Historia 1975 7(2): 54-74.* While the Nazi Party rejected Christianity, its ability to command respect and loyalty from the masses lay in its exploitation of the traditional symbols of German civil religion. Support for Hitler was provisional, based on traditions. That support existed independent of the barbaric ethics of Nazism. Primary and secondary sources; 67 notes. R. E. Butchart

48. Dow, James Elstone. COUNT VON STAUFFENBERG AND THE TWENTIETH OF JULY. *Modern Age 1976 20(2): 206-213.* Claus von Stauffenberg (1907-44) and his friends were heroic and romantic. They were aristocrats and as such they failed in executing the July 20 Plot. Hitler's power in Germany before and after 20 July, 1944 was the measure and the symbol of their failure. Secondary sources; 43 notes. M. L. Lifka

49. Drechsler, Karl; Groehler, Olaf; and Hass, Gerhart. POLITIK UND STRATEGIE DES FASCHISTISCHEN DEUTSCHLANDS IM ZWEITEN WELTKRIEG [Politics and strategy of fascist Germany in World War II]. *Zeitschrift für Geschichtswissenschaft [East Germany] 1976 24(1): 5-23.* While the blitzkrieg strategy secured the initiative for the Germany army in World War II until 1942, Russian advances after Stalingrad and US and British bombing forced the German general staff to change to the strategic defensive. Based on documents in the Bundesarchiv/Militärarchiv Freiburg, Bundesarchiv Koblenz, National Archives, Washington, Zentrales Staatsarchiv Potsdam, printed documents and secondary sources; 38 notes. R. Wagnleitner

50. Drechsler, Karl; Drobisch, Klaus; Hass, Gerhard; and Schumann, Wolfgang. ZWANGSAUSSIEDLUNGEN UND GERMANISIERUNG IN DEN KRIEGSZIELPLANUNGEN DER FASCHISTISCHEN DEUTSCHEN MONOPOLBOURGEOISIE. FUNKTION UND TÄTIGKEIT DER DEUTSCHEN UMSIEDLUNGS-TREUHAND-GESELLSCHAFT MBH [Forced evacuations and Germanization in planning war aims by the fascist German monopolistic bourgeoisie. Function and activities of the German Resettlement Fiduciary Company]. *Zeitschrift für Geschichtswissenschaft [East Germany] 1974 22(2): 208-218.* The German Resettlement Fiduciary Company was founded in November 1939 to aid in transferring Germans to newly occupied areas, a program which reached its high point in the "General Plan East" of 1941. The company was financed by a consortium of German banks, including the Dresdner Bank and the Deutsche Bank. Its main function was to provide loans to the German settlers, but it was also involved in fascist crimes, such as the confiscation of the property of those driven out of their homelands. Based on archival research, printed primary sources, and secondary works; 52 notes. J. T. Walker

51. Drobish, K. ANTIFASHISTSKAIA GRUPPA "BELAIA ROZA" (NOVYE MATERIALY) [The antifascist group Weisse Rose: new material]. *Novaia i Noveishaia Istoriia [USSR] 1979 (3): 91-107.* The German antifascist underground group Weisse Rose began in January 1943 at Munich University. One of its first activities was leafleting the students decrying the loss of life at Stalingrad. Brother and sister Hans and Sofie Sholl led the group, whose main tactics were leafleting, small meetings and slogans on the walls of buildings.

During the battle for Stalingrad in December 1942, they issued a manifesto to the German people which called for peace. On 18 February 1943, Hans and Sofie Sholl and another member of the group, Christophe Probst, were arrested, tried and sentenced to death. They were executed on 22 February. Other antifascist groups sprang up in Berlin and elsewhere. Thus the spirit of the Weisse Rose lived on. 64 notes, diaries. — L. J. Seymour

52. Droz, Jacques. LA RÉSISTANCE ALLEMANDE À L'HITLÉRISME [German resistance to Hitler]. *Histoire [France] 1980 (27): 99-101.* Discusses the diversity of the German resistance movement—Communists, Social Democrats, the bourgeoisie, aristocracy, students, and military—to Adolf Hitler's Nazism from 1933 to the final defeat of the resistance after 20 July 1944.

53. Dülffer, Jost. DAVID IRVING, DER WIDERSTAND UND DIE HISTORIKER [David Irving, the Resistance, and the historians]. *Geschichte in Wissenschaft und Unterricht [West Germany] 1979 30(11): 686-690.* During a lecture tour through West Germany, David Irving revealed the views behind his book on Field Marshal Erwin Rommel. Irving sees Rommel as a victim of the members of the German Resistance, who sacrificed him although he was not one of their number. But Rommel was a member of the Resistance in the sense that he no longer followed Hitler and wanted peace. Irving criticizes and even slanders the Resistance, because he does not believe that they preferred defeat to Nazism. He attacks German historians for presenting a false picture of the Third Reich, but it seems that Irving now shares the views of the extreme right wing and serves neo-Nazi aims. — H. W. Wurster

54. Dunk, H. W. von der. ADOLF HITLER EN DE HISTORICI [Adolf Hitler and historians]. *Kleio [Netherlands] 1977 18(9): 749-765.* Analysis of selected diverse and contradictory historiographical interpretations concerning Hitler's background, personality, policies, ideology, and his role in the Nazi movement. An objective evaluation of the Hitler phenomenon is still impossible because "historians now react irritatingly against each other's irritations." 32 notes. — R. C. Alltmont

55. Eichholtz, Dietrich. DIE KRIEGSZIELDENKSCHRIFT DES KOLONIALPOLITISCHEN AMTES DER NSDAP VON 1940: STECKBRIEF EINES DOKUMENTS [The war aims memorandum of the Colonial Political Office of the Nazi Party of 1940: Warrant for a document]. *Zeitschrift für Geschichtswissenschaft [East Germany] 1974 22(3): 308-324.* The memorandum of 1940, outlining war aims in Africa and in the Pacific, was prepared by Kurt Weigelt of the Deutsche Bank, who was associated with the Colonial Political Office of the party as well as the "Deko group," an association of German imperialist firms. Although the memorandum itself has not yet been located, its broader features can be seen in other documents. Weigelt envisioned a middle African colonial empire which, in the short run, was to provide raw materials for the war effort. Based on primary and secondary sources; 57 notes, 4 documents. — J. T. Walker

56. Eichholtz, Dietrich. DIE VORGESCHICHTE DES "GENERALBEVOLLMÄCHTIGEN FÜR DEN ARBEITEINSATZ" (MIT DOKUMENTEN) [The historical background of the Plenipotentiary for Labor

Allocation, with documents]. *Jahrbuch für Geschichte [East Germany] 1973 9: 339-383.* On 21 March 1942, Hitler appointed Fritz Sauckel, governor of Thuringia, as Plenipotentiary for Labor Allocation. Under his authority, mass deportations of citizens of occupied countries were organized, and the deportees put to work in the German industrial war machine, as well as in agriculture and mining. The historical background of Sauckel's appointment has been little researched. There is much documentation to show that the use of foreign forced labor, including that of Soviet and other prisoners of war, was being planned throughout 1941, in accordance with Hitler's statement of 10 March 1941 that the whole European continent must be utilized for Germany's war economy. The author blames many people and institutions for this policy, including Albert Speer. 6 documents, 108 notes.　　　　　　　　　　　　　　　J. C. Billigmeier

57. Eichholtz, Dietrich. "GROSSGERMANISCHES REICH" UND "GENERALPLAN OST": EINHEITLICHKEIT UND UNTERSCHIEDLICHKEIT IM FASCHISTISCHEN OKKUPATIONSSYSTEM [Greater German Empire and General Plan East: uniformity and diversity in the fascist system of occupation]. *Zeitschrift für Geschichtswissenschaft [East Germany] 1980 28(9): 835-841.* The Greater German Empire and its corollary General Plan East were racial and ideological slogans aimed at securing the territories Germany had acquired through imperial expansion. To be sure, Heinrich Himmler and the Nazi leadership took these slogans seriously, but these also served to obscure the regime's anticommunism and anti-Sovietism as well as its desire to destroy humanism and democracy. Based on films in the Central State Archive at Potsdam; 8 notes.　　　　　　　　　　　　　　　　　　　　J. T. Walker

58. Ellis, Donald W. THE PROPAGANDA MINISTRY AND CENTRALIZED REGULATION OF MUSIC IN THE THIRD REICH: THE "BIOLOGICAL AESTHETIC" AS POLICY. *J. of European Studies [Great Britain] 1975 5(3): 223-238.* Nazi views on racial causes for musical achievement developed from the concept of a "genetic aesthetic" which certain German academics formulated in the 1920's. The Nazi propaganda ministry developed its policy from this concept in the 1930's: it propagated the belief that German musical achievements were characteristic of the Nordic race, issued a list of prohibited composers, and prescribed commandments for German musicians. Alfred Rosenberg (1893-1946) and Joseph Goebbels (1897-1945) contributed greatly to the development of Nazi doctrine on music. Primary and secondary sources; 53 notes.
　　　　　　　　　　　　　　　　　　　　　　　　　　　N. Dejevsky

59. Ernst, Volker; Kaun, Anita; and Zeidler, Hans-Jürgen. NEUERSCHLOSSENE BESTÄNDE IM MILITÄRARCHIV DER DDR (ZEITRAUM 1920-1945) [Recently opened holdings in the Military Archives of East Germany for the years 1920-45]. *Militärgeschichte [East Germany] 1981 20(1): 95-97.* Describes the provenance of about 13,000 documents from the years 1920 to 1945 that were opened in 1979.　　　　　　　　　　　　　　H. D. Andrews

60. Finker, Kurt. BOMBA V "VOLCH'EM LOGOVE": ZAGOVOR 20 IULIA 1944 G. V GERMANII [The bomb in the wolf's den: the July 20 Plot of 1944 in Germany]. *Novaia i Noveishaia Istoriia [USSR] 1974 (6): 127-147; 1975 (1): 119-137.* Bourgeois writers claim that the essentially conservative and reactionary officers' plot to kill Adolf Hitler in 1944 was the only antifascist

opposition in Germany, and take no notice of the Communist-led anti-Nazi workers' movement. Some of the 1944 plotters wanted to replace Hitler with monopolists or militarists, but others, headed by Claus von Stauffenberg, were more progressive. Whereas the right-wing group wanted to conclude a separate treaty with Britain and the United States in order to check the Soviet attack from the East, the more progressive plotters were anxious to collaborate with the USSR. The plot's failure and the execution of its leaders and accomplices are described. The plot of these aristocratic officers could not hope to reflect the true aspirations of the German people. 94 notes. S

61. Fjaerli, Eystein O. 20. JULI-OPPRØRET MOT HITLER: LITT OM DETS BAKGRUNN OG ASPEKTER [The 20 July rebellion against Hitler: some aspects and a little about its background]. *Norsk Militaert Tidsskrift [Norway] 1977 147(12): 559-561.* Examines the attempt, 20 July 1944, to assassinate Adolf Hitler, asserting that this and previous attempts indicate that the attitude of the professional German army was anti-Nazi.

62. Fleischer, Hans-Otto. EINIGE BEMERKUNGEN ZUR BESONDEREN ROLLE DER SS INNERHALB DES SYSTEMS DER FASCHISTISCHEN ORGANISATIONEN (1933-1945) [The special role of the SS in the system of fascist organizations, 1933-45]. *Jenaer Beiträge zur Parteiengeschichte [East Germany] 1976 37-38: 74-94.* The continuous growth of the power of the SS (Schutzstaffel) after 1933, its tendencies to independence, and the frequent tensions with the Nazi Party were not the result of personal rivalries between the Nazi leaders, but the effect of the SS's role—to secure law and order when the mass base of the party was in decline.

63. Forišković, Aleksandar. PRILOG ANTROPOLOGIJI NACIZMA [A contribution to the anthropology of Nazism]. *Zbornik za Istoriju [Yugoslavia] 1979 (20): 229-237.* Review article on Polish lawyer and journalist Kazimierz Moczarski's *Conversation with an Executioner,* which describes 225 days he spent as a political prisoner in a Warsaw prison with SS officer Jürgen Stroop in 1949. J. Bamber

64. Fröhlich, Elke. DIE KULTURPOLITISCHE PRESSEKONFERENZ DES REICHSPROPAGANDAMINISTERIUMS [The Reich Propaganda Ministry's press conference on cultural policy]. *Vierteljahrshefte für Zeitgeschichte [West Germany] 1974 22(4): 347-381.* Beginning with the Olympics in the summer of 1936, the German Propaganda Ministry regularly staged special press conferences on cultural policy. These were apparently not primarily instruments of censorship, but represented an attempt to cover up the failure of a specifically Nazi art and literature and the severe shortage of talent due to suppression and emigration. Obliging journalists gave relatively extensive and frank information and communicated a sense of dynamics by dwelling on the positive, extolling the famed artists, and encouraging art among the people. Based on Fritz Sänger's press conference notes at the Institut für Zeitgeschichte, Munich; 216 notes. D. Prowe

65. Galen, Clemens August von and Volk, Ludwig, ed. SCHWEIGEN ODER BEKENNEN? (EINGELEITET UND KOMMENTIERT VON LUDWIG VOLK S. J.) [To be silent or to testify? (Introduction and commentary by

Ludwig Volk, S. J.)]. *Stimmen der Zeit [West Germany] 1976 194(4): 219-224.* Reprints a previously unpublished letter of 26 May 1941, from the Bishop of Münster to a fellow bishop, prior to the sermons of July and August 1941 in which he spoke out against the Hitler regime. A *cri de coeur* reciting Nazi aggressions against the Catholic Church and lamenting the Church's passivity, the letter cites Thomas More as an example of the courage to denounce crimes of state at the risk of martyrdom. Notes. R. Stromberg

66. Galitsan, A. S. KRUSHENIE FASHISTKOGO BLITSKRIGA [The collapse of the fascist blitzkrieg]. *Voprosy Istorii [USSR] 1981 (12): 18-33.* The article discusses the Blitzkrieg theory of aggressive wars elaborated by the German militarists in the early 20th century and the fascist strategy in World War II based on it. With a wealth of factual material, the author reveals its fallacious and adventuristic character, demonstrates its failure at the very beginning of the war against the USSR, and notes its utter collapse after the rout of the German fascist troops in Moscow, which was the turning point in the war. Virtually alone, the Soviet Union blocked the way to fascist aggression and prevented its spread to other countries and continents, thereby imbuing in the peoples of the world confidence in the final victory over fascism. J

67. Genri, Ernst. PROSHLOE—V NASTOIASHCHEM [The past and the present]. *Mirovaia Ekonomika i Mezhdunarodnye Otnosheniia [USSR] 1980 (5): 110-116.* Examining documents and memoirs published in the last 30 years, the author suggests that World War II, except for the cowardice of the capitalist West, could have been avoided. The lessons of the Munich years 1938-39, if applied today, could forestall a third world war. Based on published documents and memoirs and secondary sources; 24 notes.

68. Gessner, Klaus. ZUR ORGANISATION UND FUNKTION DER GEHEIMEN FELDPOLIZEI IM ZWEITEN WELTKRIEG [On the organization and function of the Geheime Feldpolizei (Secret Field Police) during World War II]. *Rev. Int. d'Hist. Militaire [France] 1979 (43): 154-166.* Determines the place and the function of German Secret Military Police in wartime Germany. The organization of this secret executive power in the German Wehrmacht was based on close cooperation with the Gestapo, the SS Sicherheitsdienst, and other Nazi police agencies. Its activities were mainly directed after 1941 toward crushing the Soviet partisans. Between 1 July 1942 and 31 March 1943 its units killed 21,000 persons in occupied Soviet Russia. Based on military documents; 2 illus., 36 notes. G. E. Pergl

69. Glatz, Ferenc. A MÁSODIK VILÁGHÁBORÚS HISTORIÓGRÁFIAI KONFERENCIA FŐBB VITAKÉRDÉSEI [Vital points of debate at the conference on the historiography of World War II]. *Törtenelmi Szemle [Hungary] 1973 16(3-4): 468-487.* A summary of the issues raised in September 1973 at this conference in Budapest, devoted to World War II, and especially the national and territorial problems connected with the hostilities.

70. Grammdorf, Gerda. ZUR SOZIALEN GLIEDERUNG DER BEVÖLKERUNG IN DER STADT ROSTOCK UNTER DEN BEDINGUNGEN DER KAPITALISTISCHEN PRODUKTIONSVERHÄLTNISSE IN DEN JAHREN VON 1939 BIS 1945 [The social structure of the population

of Rostock under conditions of the capitalist relations of production, 1939-45]. *Wissenschaftliche Zeitschrift der U. Rostock. Gesellschafts- und Sprachwissenschaftliche Reihe [East Germany] 1973 22(7): 669-673.* Before 1939 the social organization of Rostock was primarily dominated by the lower middle classes. The growth of the airplane industry at Rostock during World War II brought a large number of workers to the city, which changed its social structure completely. Based on documents in the Stadtarchiv Rostock and secondary literature; 7 tables, 20 notes. R. Wagnleitner

71. Gritschneder, Otto. RECHTSPRECHUNG IM DIENST DER DIKTATUR [Justice in the service of dictatorship]. *Stimmen der Zeit [West Germany] 1977 195(2): 136-138.* Reviews two scholarly studies of jurists who served in high posts under Hitler. Franz Gürtner (1881-1941), minister of justice in 1932-41, and Erwin Bumke, president of the supreme court, who committed suicide in 1945, were forced to bend the law to the dictator's will. Biographies of Gürtner by Ekkehard Reitter (Berlin, 1976) and of Bumke by Dieter Kolbe (Karlsruhe, 1975) thoroughly document the prostitution of justice under the Third Reich. R. Stromberg

72. Grobelný, Andělín. NĚMECKÉ BÁDÁNÍ O VÝCHODNÍ A JIHOVÝCHODNÍ EVROPĚ 1938 AŽ 1945 (SE ZAMĚŘENÍM NA JEHO CENTRUM VE SLEZSKU) [German research on Eastern and Southeastern Europe from 1938 to 1945 (focusing on its center in Silesia)]. *Průmyslové Oblasti [Czechoslovakia] 1975 (5): 5-74.* Reviews the development of German research institutions, created mainly in response to the expansionism of German imperialism and to support its economic and political goals before and during World War II. Based on documents; 175 notes. G. E. Pergl

73. Grobelný, Andělín. PROJEKT DÁLKOVÉHO PLYNOVODU H. SLEZKO-OSTRAVSKO-VÍDEŇ V HOSPODÁŘSKÉ POLITICE NACISTŮ V LETECH 1940-1944 [The project for a long-distance gas pipeline between the Upper Silesia and Ostrava region and Vienna in Nazi economic policy, 1940-44]. *Průmyslové Oblasti [Czechoslovakia] 1980 7: 201-264.* The Ostrava and Upper Silesia region became an important part of German plans to construct a connection for natural gas deliveries to Vienna. The accompanying integration of industry would have eliminated Czechs in Bohemian-Moravian industry and the Polish in Upper Silesia, leading to the collapse of Czech and Polish industrial structures as raw materials were diverted to industry around Vienna. The long-range projects of the Nazi regime involved enormous investment of funds and scientific and technical know-how. The pipeline project fell victim to war events, manpower shortages, and the Soviet offensive. 2 tables, 4 documents, 148 notes.
G. E. Pergl

74. Grobosch, Werner. ENTSTEHUNG UND ROLLE DES DEUTSCHEN VOLKSSTURMS [The development and role of the German *Volkssturm*]. *Militärgeschichte [East Germany] 1978 17(2): 180-192.* Sketches Germany's military and domestic policy goals in formulating the local militia, the *Volkssturm*, the last manpower resource for defense of German territory during World War II and a domestic support for the Nazi regime. Considers the battle deployment of the *Volkssturm* units. Based on extensive archive material; 4 photos, 3 sketches, 41 notes. J/T (H. D. Andrews)

75. Groehler, Olaf. DIE ENTWICKLUNG DER LUFTKRIEGSTECH-NIK WÄHREND DES ZWEITEN WELTKRIEGES [The development of the technology of air warfare during World War II]. *Militärgeschichte [East Germany] 1975 14(3): 337-346.* Discusses the development of the following airplanes between 1939 and 1945: the Soviet BI-1, the German ME 163, the American Lockheed XP-80, the Japanese Mitsubishi J8 M1, the German ME 262, the British Gloster Meteor 1, the Soviet MiG-9 and Yak 15 and the American Bell X-1.

76. Groehler, Olaf. DIE "HOCHDRUCKPUMPE"(V3)-ENTWICKLUNG UND MISERE EINER "WUNDERWAFFE" [The High Pressure Pump, or the V3: development and misfortunes of a "wonder weapon"]. *Militärgeschichte [East Germany] 1977 16(6): 735-744.* Investigates the relationship between Hitler and the German war industry, with special reference to the development of the V3 in Poland. In January 1943 August Coenders and Hermann Röchling gave Hitler the idea of building this artillery weapon, consisting of 50 connecting pipes capable of shooting up to 10,000 shots a month. Originally designed from a French prototype of 1918, it was to be installed near Calais, in order to fire upon London. Despite setbacks, Röchling wanted to continue the development of the weapon even in December 1944, but it was eventually shown to be inadequate for the purpose. Based on archives; 31 notes.   A. Alcock

77. Groehler, Olaf. STÄRKE, VERTEILUNG UND VERLUSTE DER DEUTSCHEN LUFTWAFFE IM ZWEITEN WELTKRIEG [Strength, distribution, and losses of the German air forces in World War II]. *Militärgeschichte [East Germany] 1978 17(3): 316-335.* The activities of the German air forces during World War II and the losses suffered on the various fronts. The chief concentration of forces was on the Russian front, and it was there that the Germans suffered their greatest losses and most decisive defeats. Based on newly discovered statistical sources; 23 tables, 19 notes.   J/T (H. D. Andrews)

78. Groehler, Olaf and Moritz, Erhard. ZUR KADERAUSLESE DES FASCHISTISCHEN GEHEIMEN MELDEDIENSTES 1944-45 [Personnel selection for the Fascist Secret Service in 1944-45]. *Militärgeschichte [East Germany] 1978 17(5): 582-594.* Although the political and military leaders of Germany knew the futility of prolonging the war, they nevertheless undertook considerable efforts to increase the personnel and enhance the effectiveness of their secret service. The documents published disclose that these efforts had two special goals: first, the end of the war should be postponed as long as possible; second, the leadership sought to assure their own survival and the continuation of the foundations of German imperial power. Moreover, the documents offer insight into the methods and "arguments" of the personnel recruiting of the secret service.
J/T (H. D. Andrews)

79. Gruchmann, Lothar. DOKUMENTATION: AUSGEWÄHLTE DOKUMENTE ZUR DEUTSCHEN MARINEJUSTIZ IM ZWEITEN WELTKRIEG [Documentation: selected documents relating to the German naval courts in World War II]. *Vierteljahrshefte für Zeitgeschichte [West Germany] 1978 26(3): 433-498.* A presentation and analysis of documents of German naval courts during World War II showing general legal procedures, the relationship between judges and supervising officers, the limited degree of judicial inde-

pendence from the army, government, and Nazi Party, and individual judges' limited opportunities for ignoring or modifying prescribed sentences, especially in cases of desertion in the last days of the war. Based on West German Federal Kornelimünster and Freiburg Military archives; 98 notes.   D. Prowe

80. Hamerow, Theodore S. WOMEN, PROPAGANDA, AND TOTAL WAR. *Rev. in Am. Hist. 1979 7(1): 122-127.* Review essay of Leila J. Rupp's *Mobilizing Women for War: German and American Propaganda, 1939-1945* (Princeton, N.J.: Princeton U. Pr., 1978) and Allan M. Winkler's *The Politics of Propaganda: The Office of War Information, 1942-1945* (New Haven, Conn.: Yale U. Pr., 1978).

81. Hammond, Keith. GUDERIAN—THE HONOURABLE INNOVATOR. *Army Q. and Defence J. [Great Britain] 1981 111(3): 310-314.* Discusses the strategic theory of German Colonel General Heinz Guderian implemented in World War II.

82. Hammond, Mason. "REMEMBRANCE OF THINGS PAST": THE PROTECTION AND PRESERVATION OF MONUMENTS, WORKS OF ARTS, LIBRARIES, AND ARCHIVES DURING AND AFTER WORLD WAR II. *Massachusetts Hist. Pro. Soc. 1980 92: 84-99.* The nature of World War II and the advance planning by Allied monument officers and the German Kunstschutz helped minimize the damage done to Europe's cultural treasures. While the air war devastated some British and German cultural centers, such as the German Kaiser Friedrich Museum, swift land maneuvers actually helped to preserve much of the art and architectural preservation facilities. The northern European centers in France, Belgium, Norway, Denmark, and the Netherlands suffered little or no damage, and the overall damage to Italian centers was slight. Allied monument officers instructed troops to respect the cultural facilities in order to minimize looting and discourage careless destruction. Much of the art looted by the Germans was restored to the proper public and private collections.
G. A. Glovins

83. Hanlon, Lindley P. FILM DOCUMENT AND THE MYTH OF HORST WESSEL: A SAMPLER OF NAZI PROPAGANDA. *Film & Hist. 1975 5(3): 16-18.*

84. Hanson, John H. NAZI AESTHETICS. *Psychohistory Rev. 1981 9(4): 251-281.* Nazi art provides insight into the processes by which the Nazi era was part of a cultural continuum. Psychoanalytic theory offers explanations for Nazi abhorrence of modernist art and architecture. Often overlooked by students of Nazism, Nazi art demonstrates the intentions of Nazi leaders to merge individual interests into the life of the state. Films and mass rallies were seen by nonleaders as art whose purpose was to create a total state. Secondary sources; 78 notes.
J. M. Herrick

85. Harris, James F. RECENT USES OF QUANTIFICATION IN GERMAN HISTORY: A REVIEW ESSAY. *Hist. Methods 1978 11(3): 123-128.* Reviews Peter H. Merkl's *Political Violence Under the Swastika: 581 Early Nazis,* (1975), citing several bibliographic items which illustrate Merkl's statistical weaknesses. The problem turns on the nature of the research data: the use of 581 autobiographies on deposit at the Hoover Institute does not constitute a solid

statistical base from which to study the rank and file Nazi. Merkl also used psychological and psychohistorical language and conclusions which weakened his quantitative approach. Understandably, Merkl's dislike of Nazism influenced his conclusions which were not fully developed from his unique use of collective autobiographical data. 15 notes. D. K. Pickens

86. Hass, Kurt. LITERATURKRITIK IM DRITTEN REICH. AUFGABEN, MASSTÄBE UND ORGANIZATION [Literary criticism in the Third Reich. Tasks, standards, and organization]. *Frankfurter Hefte [West Germany] 1974 29(1): 52-60.* Reviews the attitudes and policies of the Nazi leadership toward literature and literary criticism and describes the Nazi apparatus for controlling literature. Nazi ideology viewed literature as a means for furthering the political goals of the state. Standards were purely political, and no clear artistic or aesthetic criteria were formulated. Content, not form, determined the acceptability of literature. The author cites popular themes in Nazi literature. Based on contemporary journals and secondary works; 41 notes.

J. B. Street

87. Hauner, Milan. DID HITLER WANT A WORLD DOMINION? *J. of Contemporary Hist. [Great Britain] 1978 13(1): 15-32.* Newer historiography on Adolf Hitler only confirms what he himself said in *Mein Kampf* about the master race and Lebensraum theory: he indeed meant to conquer the world for Germany. 51 notes. M. P. Trauth

88. Heider, Paul. PROBLEME DER MILITÄRPOLITIK DER KOMMUNISTISCHEN PARTEI DEUTSCHLANDS (1919-1945) [Problems of the military policy of the Communist Party of Germany (KPD), 1919-45]. *Militärgeschichte [East Germany] 1982 21(1): 5-28.* Summarizes the extensive source material and literature and sketches the basic outlines of the development and execution of the military policy of the KPD. Describes the changing relations between the concrete situation in the Weimar Republic and under the fascist dictatorship and the policy responses of the KPD and traces the continuity in the struggle of the KPD against imperialism, militarism, armaments, and war and for peace, democracy, and socialism. 86 notes. J/T (H. D. Andrews)

89. Herzstein, Robert E. GOEBBELS ET LE MYTH HISTORIQUE PAR LE FILM (1942-1945) [Goebbels and historical myth in films, 1942-45]. *Rev. d'Hist. de la Deuxième Guerre Mondiale [France] 1976 (101): 41-62.* Joseph Paul Goebbels (1897-1945) created many historical myths in his propaganda to activate the German people and armed forces, especially through the use of film. In *The Great King* he glorified and exaggerated the hardness and courage of Frederick II (1712-86) in the hopes of inspiring the German people to accept the hardships of war. In the film *Kolberg* Goebbels glorified the ideals of the 1813 War of Liberation and distorted the career of August von Gneisenau (1760-1831). One of five articles in a special edition on propaganda. 49 notes.

G. H. Davis

90. Herzstein, Robert Edwin. LA DÉCOUVERTE DU JOURNAL DE GOEBBELS: QUEL EST SON INTÉRÊT HISTORIQUE? [The discovery of Goebbels's journal: what is its historical value?]. *Rev. d'Hist. de la Deuxième Guerre Mondiale [France] 1980 30(120): 49-58.* Fragments of Joseph Goebbels's

diaries were published in 1947 and 1961 but the rest was believed to have been destroyed in 1945. In 1978 Hugh R. Trevor-Roper published *Final Entries: The Diaries of Joseph Goebbels* (New York, 1978), which appears to be authentic. Its value lies in the analysis of Goebbels's remarkable mind, which was enslaved by his worshipful attitude toward Hitler. 19 notes. G. H. Davis

91. Hildebrand, Klaus. HITLER'S WAR AIMS. *J. of Modern Hist. 1976 48(3): 522-530.* Reviews Norman Rich's two-volume study, *Hitler's War Aims* (New York: W. W. Norton, 1973-74). Through examination of invasion policy and war aims, the author seeks to understand Hitler's long-term plans as well as the contradictions and inconsistencies in his policy.

92. Hildebrand, Klaus. LE FORZE MOTRICI DI POLITICA INTERNA AGENTI SULLA POLITICA ESTERA NAZIONALSOCIALISTA [The driving forces of internal politics acting on National Socialist foreign policy]. *Storia Contemporanea [Italy] 1974 5(2): 201-222.* Examines various theories as to the internal forces driving Nazi foreign policy toward aggressive expansionism. One key reason was Adolf Hitler himself. Germany's dictator was not guided by the usual preoccupation of diplomats—the maintenance of the social system and political self-preservation—but rather with destruction of the status quo and with it the whole social, political, and ethnic structure of the Eurasian continent and the world. His program was one of all or nothing, triumph or defeat. 29 notes, biblio. J. C. Billigmeier

93. Hildebrand, Klaus. NATIONALSOZIALISMUS OHNE HITLER [Nazism without Hitler]. *Geschichte in Wissenschaft und Unterricht [West Germany] 1980 31(5): 289-304.* Summarizes the proceedings of a conference of historians from Great Britain, Canada, the United States and West Germany organized by the German Historical Institute in London, 10-12 May 1979. Protagonists of a new picture of Adolf Hitler and the Third Reich opposed the prevailing image, but could not produce a convincing overall interpretation. 26 notes. H. W. Wurster

94. Hillgruber, Andreas. DIE "ENDLÖSUNG" UND DAS DEUTSCHE OSTIMPERIUM ALS KERNSTÜCK DES RASSENIDEOLOGISCHEN PROGRAMMS DES NATIONALSOZIALISMUS [The Final Solution and the German eastern empire as nucleus of the race-ideological program of National Socialism]. *Vierteljahrshefte für Zeitgeschichte [West Germany] 1972 20(2): 133-153.* Discusses the ideological basis of Nazism: Adolf Hitler's fusion of the goals of biological anti-Semitism (the Final Solution) and conquest of a world empire. During the Russian campaign, military conquest and the Final Solution increasingly merged in practice with the overlapping functions of the Army and the SS, anti-partisan warfare, and the growing role of military men in atrocities and genocide. Based on Nuremberg trial and German military documents, and secondary sources; table, 59 notes. D. Prowe

95. Hillgruber, Andreas. LITERATURBERICHT: INNEN- UND AUSSENPOLITIK DEUTSCHLANDS 1933-1945 [Literature report: German domestic and foreign policy, 1933-45]. *Geschichte in Wissenschaft und Unterricht [West Germany] 1973 24(9): 571-580.* Reviews 18 new publications on German foreign and domestic policy between 1933 and 1945 including the annexation of

Austria, the creation of the independent Croatia, British appeasement toward Germany, the history of the Nazi party, and German strategy in World War II.

96. Hillgruber, Andreas. LITERATURBERICHT: INNEN- UND AUSSENPOLITIK DEUTSCHLANDS VON 1933-1945 [Review of literature; internal and foreign policy of Germany, 1933-45]. *Geschichte in Wissenschaft und Unterricht [West Germany] 1976 27(8): 509-520.* Reviews new publications on the foreign and domestic policy of the Third Reich, 1933-45. 36 notes.
R. Wagnleitner

97. Hillgruber, Andreas. LITERATURBERICHT: INNEN- UND AUSSENPOLITIK DEUTSCHLANDS 1933-1945 [The domestic and foreign policy of Germany, 1933-45]. *Geschichte in Wissenschaft und Unterricht [West Germany] 1974 25(4): 239-256.* Reviews 50 new publications on various aspects of Germany policy between 1933 and 1945, including the ideological background of national socialism, the relationship between German industrialists and national socialism, the German resistance, and the Anschluss.
R. Wagnleitner

98. Hillgruber, Andreas. TENDENZEN, ERGEBNISSE UND PERSPEKTIVEN DER GEGENWÄRTIGEN HITLER-FORSCHUNG [Tendencies, interpretations, and perspectives: current Hitler research]. *Hist. Zeitschrift [West Germany] 1978 226(3): 600-621.* Recent historical literature on Adolf Hitler falls into four main categories: detailed collections of previously unknown facts; psychohistorical interpretations; revisionist studies based on social history, which concentrate on Hitler's function within the movement and the system; and a goal-oriented interpretation based on Hitler's architectural ideals. 63 notes.
G. H. Davis

99. Hoffmann, Marhild. MÖGLICHKEITEN UND BEDINGUNGEN DES WIDERSTANDES [Possibilities and conditions of resistance]. Meyers, Peter and Riesenberger, Dieter, ed. *Der Nationalsozialismus in der historisch-politischen Bildung* (Göttingen: Vandenhoeck & Ruprecht, 1979): 120-146. Examines methods of resistance in general and particular instances in Germany, 1933-45.

100. Hoffmann, Peter. THE LIFE OF HITLER. *Queen's Q. 1975 82(2): 266-270.* Reviews Joachim C. Fest's *Hitler* (New York: Harcourt Brace Jovanovich, 1974). Fest contends that Hitler was a great man who did more to change the world in a short period of time than any other man of the century, and argues that the policy of exterminating Jews was not tied directly to Hitler. Fest's argument is weak; he quotes primarily from secondary sources, fails to consider the massive loss of life under Hitler, and at times confuses or misinterprets facts. The book is valuable as a presentation of one point of view, but certainly is not the definitive work which the world still awaits.
V. L. Human

101. Hofman, J. and Stam, A. DE LEVENSLOOP VAN RUDOLPH HESS [The career of Rudolf Hess]. *Spiegel Historiael [Netherlands] 1977 12(3): 150-157.* Rudolf Hess (b. 1894) abandoned his business education to study history, economics, and geopolitics in 1920. He joined an anti-Marxist Freikorps and regarded the Germans as a sick people that a coming dictator would cure. Adolf Hitler soon enlisted him, and he became a prominent Nazi leader. Hess went to prison with Hitler, where he served as secretary during the writing of *Mein*

Kampf. Hess's greatest influence was in the development of the Hitler personality cult. After 1939, he lost his former status as Hitler's sole confidant and began displaying neurotic tendencies. His political career ended in May 1941, when he made his secret flight to Scotland and authorities in Germany declared him mentally disturbed. He remained under psychiatric care in England until he was brought before the International Military Tribunal at Nuremburg in 1945. He was sentenced to life imprisonment. 10 illus.
J. E. Snellen

102. Homze, Edward L. THE LUFTWAFFE'S FAILURE TO DEVELOP A HEAVY BOMBER BEFORE WORLD WAR II. *Aerospace Hist. 1977 24(1): 20-26.* Compares the explanation of Erhard Milch with that of Theo Osterkamp and Franz Bocher for Germany's failure to develop a heavy bomber. Appointed state secretary in the Air Ministry in 1933, Milch claims that Hermann Goering decided not to proceed with heavy bomber development in order to reduce Milch's influence in the Luftwaffe. In their *Tragödie der Luftwaffe? Werk von Irving/Milch* (Neckargemund, 1971), Osterkamp and Bocher argue that Milch not only knew of Göring's decision but also supported it. The general staff, the technical staff, and the aviation industry shared in the decision, which was more than a mere dispute between Göring and Milch. Lack of sufficient labor, capital, and raw materials in the 1930's contributed to the failure. The author reviews the development of Luftwaffe aviation. Based on official sources; 11 photos, 27 notes.
C. W. Ohrvall

103. Horn, Daniel. THE DIARIST REVISITED: THE PAPERS OF SEAMAN STUMPF. *J. of the Rutgers U. Lib. 1978 40(1): 32-48.* Richard Stumpf's impressions of German history, 1914-54. A seaman in the Imperial German Navy, Stumpf's edited and translated wartime diary describes the rise of Nazism, Germany during World War II, the Soviet occupation, the early days of the East German state, and the development of contemporary Germany. Based on the Richard Stumpf Papers at Rutgers University Library; 41 notes.
R. Van Benthuysen

104. Horn, Daniel. THE HITLER YOUTH AND EDUCATIONAL DECLINE IN THE THIRD REICH. *Hist. of Educ. Q. 1976 16(4): 425-448.* Waging a war of chaos and destruction against the traditional German educational structure, the Hitler Jugend (under the leadership of men who had no background in either education or youth organization) was primarily responsible for the demise of the educational system in Germany, 1933-45.

105. Horn, Daniel. YOUTH RESISTANCE IN THE THIRD REICH: A SOCIAL PORTRAIT. *J. of Social Hist. [Great Britain] 1973 7(1): 26-50.* A review of youth resistance to the German Nazi regime. Historians have tended to discount the influence of these "wild gangs," but their numbers continued to grow and their influence to spread until the regime fell. The gangs, composed of sons of the rich and the poor, were not very political and were primarily interested in avoiding regimentation. Neither the Hitler Youth nor the Gestapo could suppress them. Had not defeat in war terminated the regime, dissident youth may in time have produced the same result. 78 notes.
V. L. Human

106. Isby, David C. PANZER BATTLES: THE EVOLUTION OF MECHANIZED WARFARE, 1939-79. *Strategy and Tactics 1979 (73): 4-15.* Examines tank warfare focusing on World War II battles.

107. Jacobsen, H. A. ZUR GESCHICHTSSCHREIBUNG DES 2. WELTKRIEGES IN DER BUNDESREPUBLIK DEUTSCHLAND: EIN ÜBERBLICK [The historiography of World War II in West Germany: an overview]. *La Seconda Guerra Mondiale nella prospettiva storica a trent'anni dall'epilogo* (Como: Casa editrice Pietro Cairoli, 1977): 243-258. A detailed bibliographical essay on the treatment by West German historians of World War II.
J. C. Billigmeier

108. Jaeger, Harald and Rumschöttel, Hermann. DAS FORSCHUNGSPROJEKT "WIDERSTAND UND VERFOLGUNG IN BAYERN 1933-1945": EIN MODELL FÜR DIE ZUSAMMENARBEIT VON ARCHIVAREN UND HISTORIKERN [The research project, Resistance and Prosecution in Bavaria, 1933-45: a model for cooperation between archivists and historians]. *Archivalische Zeitschrift [West Germany] 1976 72: 209-220.*

109. Jaeger, Harald. PROBLEMATIK UND AUSSAGEWERT DER ÜBERLIEFERUNGSGESTÖRTEN SCHRIFTGUTBESTANDE DER NS-ZEIT [Problems of displaced archival documents of the Nazi era]. *Archivar [West Germany] 1975 28(3): 275-291.* Discusses the problems connected with the collecting of documents covering German history, 1933-45, caused by the postwar division of Germany.

110. Janner, William, Jr. NATIONAL SOCIALISTS AND SOCIAL MOBILITY. *J. of Social Hist. 1976 9(3): 339-368.* Proposes upward social mobility as incentive to support Nazism, especially among those with limited prospects under the pre-Nazi educational system with its emphasis on classical and legal studies. The author offers data on the backgrounds of middle level Nazi appointees to party, local, and national positions to show that their age, class and educational status differed from those of Weimar and Bonn era appointees. This is important now that older views of the Nazis as 1) tools of big business, 2) anti-socialists, 3) totalitarians, and 4) antimodernists are being challenged. Struggles within the party over the degree to which educational requirements for educational and civil service positions would stay loosened, or be further loosened, increased over the years. Several kinds of schools were developed to offer more widespread entry for loyal Nazis on the basis of their zeal and personal drive. All this was in keeping with a long tradition of leveling efforts in European societies.
M. Hough

111. Jonca, Karol. AUX ORIGINES JURIDIQUES DE LA GRANDE ALLEMAGNE [The juridical origins of Greater Germany]. *Rev. d'Hist de la Deuxième Guerre Mondiale [France] 1974 24(96): 1-12.* The principle architect of new Nazi principles of international law based on völkisch-racist assumptions was Carl Schmitt (b. 1888). Rejecting other principles, Schmitt, Gustav Walz, and others developed concepts of national groups *(Volksgruppen),* space *(Raum)* allocated to racial communities, and *Reich.* Other German writers on Germany's position in Europe and the German-speaking minority groups in eastern Europe applied the terminology developed by Schmitt and Walz. 26 notes.
G. H. Davis

112. Jukes, Geoffrey. AHEAD AT HALF-TIME? HITLER'S GENERALS. *A.N.U. Hist. J. [Australia] 1977 13: 61-67.* Reviews Richard Brett-Smith's *Hitler's Generals* (London: Osprey, 1976) which assesses Germany's World War II effort and the military strategy of the German High Command, 1938-44.

113. Jung, Dieter. SPÄHSCHIFFE [Spy ships]. *Marine Rundschau [West Germany] 1974 71(6): 356-363.* Describes the activities of German reconnaissance ships, first revealed in World War II during the battleship *Bismarck* engagement in 1941. These spy ships masqueraded as common merchant vessels during World War II actions. 6 illus., appendix. G. E. Pergl

114. Kafka, John S. ADOLF HITLER: A FAMILY PERSPECTIVE. *Psychiatry 1978 41(2): 221-225.* This review article, prompted by *Adolf Hitler: a Family Perspective,* by Helm Stierlin (New York: Psychohistory Pr., 1976), centers on the assertion, pivotal to much of Stierlin's book, that Hitler believed his mother to have been killed by a Jewish doctor, her physician Eduard Bloch. Points out that Hitler, after his mother's death, sent Bloch warmly worded postcards, and later arranged special privileges for him when restrictions were being placed on Jews. Discusses a 1973 article by Rudolph Binion which served as the basis of Stierlin's thesis involving Bloch, who was the reviewer's uncle and guardian. 3 notes. L. W. Van Wyk

115. Kahn, David. LE RÔLE DU DÉCRYPTAGE ET DU RENSEIGNEMENT DANS LA STRATÉGIE ET LA TACTIQUE DES ALLIÉS [The role of cryptography and intelligence in Allied strategy and tactics]. *Rev. d'Hist. de la Deuxième Guerre Mondiale [France] 1978 28(111): 73-85.* In the late 1920's Germany began using an electric rotor encipherment machine based on a commercial machine called Enigma for transmitting secret messages. Polish cryptographers analyzed the German system and developed decipherment machines which they shared with England and France in the summer of 1939. Americans also developed a similar technique so that British and American intelligence services were able to read many—but not all—high-level German and Japanese messages throughout the war. The office of British military intelligence called Ultra controlled distribution of intercepted messages to the Allies. Contrary to writings by Frederick Winterbotham, Anthony Cave Brown, and William Stevenson, Winston Churchill did not sacrifice the city of Coventry to protect the secrecy of Ultra. To what extent did decipherment win the war? It was a factor but not the only one. 24 notes. G. H. Davis

116. Kam'a N'dumbe III, Alexandre. LES BUTS DE GUERRE DE L'ALLEMAGNE HITLÉRIENNE EN AFRIQUE [The war aims of Hitler's Germany in Africa]. *Rev. d'Hist. de la Deuxième Guerre Mondiale [France] 1977 27(106): 37-60.* Adolf Hitler had definite plans for North Africa, black Africa south of the Sahara, and South Africa. He announced these in his first two books. Major German political parties, colonial associations, and powerful capitalists supported a strong African policy before World War II, and the military sought posts there. Nazi racial theory was applied as a pseudoscience to African conditions and colonial policy. The defeat of Nazi Germany weakened the color line by demonstrating that white people *per se* are not invincible and encouraged colonial people to fight for liberty after the war against imperialist powers as they had done against the dictators during the war. Based mostly on German archives; 51 notes. G. H. Davis

117. Karczowa, Halina. NAGRANIA NIEMIECKIE Z LAT 1938-1945 Z ROZGŁOŚNI RADIA RZESZY, DZIAŁAJĄCYCH NA OKUPOWANYCH ZIEMIACH POLSKICH I NIEMIECKIEJ CZĘŚCI ŚLĄSKA [Recordings of German broadcasting stations operating on Nazi-occupied territories, 1939-45]. *Archeion [Poland] 1972 57: 107-114.* A number of German radio recordings from World War II can be found at the Warsaw Mechanical Documentation Archives. These recordings were made on Polish territories, and in the German part of Silesia. In addition to these recordings, a large number of photographs have been saved; they depict various official German celebrations and daily life. The author classifies these materials into several groups, and describes in detail the most characteristic recordings and photographs. J

118. Karner, Stefan. BEMÜHUNGEN ZUR AUSWEITUNG DER LUFTRÜSTUNG IM DRITTEN REICH 1940/41: DIE FLUGMOTORENWERKE OSTMARK UND IHR MARBURGER ZWEIGWERK 1941-45 [Efforts to expand air force armaments in the Third Reich, 1940-41: the Ostmark Aircraft Motor Works and its Marburg branch, 1941-45]. *Zeitgeschichte [Austria] 1979 6(9-10): 318-345.* Discusses the development of the Ostmark branch factory in Maribor (Marburg, Styria) and its importance for Germany's air force as the only branch to reach full-scale production. The Marburg factory was switched from propeller manufacture to construction of general airplane machinery in 1942, when it was incorporated into the United German Metalworks Frankfurt a/M. and became the Aeronautical Works Styria, Inc. It reached its goal of full production in spite of labor problems and the low morale of its poorly paid and housed Slovenian work force, increasing partisan terrorism, and aerial bombings. Primary sources; 2 tables, 141 notes, 3 appendixes.
G. Herritt

119. Karner, Stefan. DER PLAN EINER GESCHLOSSENEN UMSIEDLUNG DER GRÖDNER IN DIE STEIERMARK 1941 [The plan for a complete resettlement of the population of the Gröden valley in Styria 1941]. *Zeitschrift des Hist. Vereines für die Steiermark [Austria] 1978 69: 113-123.* In 1940 and 1941 German SS leaders worked out plans to transfer the whole population of the Gröden valley in the South Tyrol to the Styrian Hochschwab area.
R. Wagnleitner

120. Kárný, Miroslav. GENERÁLNÍ PLÁN VÝCHOD [General Plan East]. *Československý Časopis Hist. [Czechoslovakia] 1977 25(3): 345-382.* The German conquest of Poland and annexation of ethnically Polish territories in 1939 gave rise to a program of complete Germanization through resettlement, and started the displacement of racially unacceptable or unassimilable populations. This period gave the Germans initial practice in methods of depopulation and extermination. After the assault on the USSR, between July 1941 and May 1942, two offices under Heinrich Himmler worked out competing versions of a "General Plan East" to Germanize much of Eastern Europe and to subject the rest. Reckoning with the prior elimination of the Jews, these plans became increasingly adventurous, setting ever closer target dates and involving progressively larger numbers of Slavic victims. Some 31 million people were earmarked for removal when the Soviet victories of 1942-43 put a stop to this particular type of planning. Based on archival material and published primary sources; 165 notes.
R. E. Weltsch

121. Kárný, Miroslav. "KRUH PŘÁTEL ŘÍŠSKÉHO VŮDCE SS" (PŘÍSPĚVEK K VÝZKUMU VZTAHŮ NĚMECKÉ MONOPOLISTICKÉ OLIGARCHIE A SS) [The "friends' circle of the *Reichsführer SS*": an exploratory contribution on relations between the German monopolist oligarchy and the SS]. *Československý Časopis Hist. [Czechoslovakia] 1980 28(5): 669-702.* From 1930 through World War II, Nazism represented the class interests of German monopoly capital. The "friends" circle" grouped around SS (Schutzstaffel) leader Heinrich Himmler finally comprised 44 business leaders, some of them SS officers, who hoped to get favors, and perhaps a measure of control, out of this affiliation. Though not all major industrialists joined the Himmler circle, and though its proceedings remain obscure, the context bears out the Marxist contention that the locus of Nazi power and responsibility for Nazi crimes must be found among German big businessmen, who prosper in West Germany today. Based on German and Czechoslovak archival sources and published studies; 157 notes. Russian and German summaries.

R. E. Weltsch

122. Kater, Michael H. ANTI-FASCIST INTELLECTUALS IN THE THIRD REICH. *Can. J. of Hist. [Canada] 1981 16(2): 263-277.* A consideration of the role of intellectuals in Nazi Germany. Certainly intellectuals were not early and articulate opponents of the regime, nor were they ever comfortable with it, perhaps because it denied to them the roles to which they had become accustomed. Some intellectuals fled voluntarily; others fled because they had to. Many stayed, but the Nazi regime had already dismantled their forums. After the war came a sense of guilt for not having done more to prevent the catastrophe. 51 notes.

V. L. Human

123. Kater, Michael H. HITLER IN A SOCIAL CONTEXT. *Central European Hist. 1981 14(3): 243-272.* The literature on Adolf Hitler has "failed to classify Hitler properly from a sociological or sociohistorical perspective." In his attempt to increase understanding of Hitler's "personality and preeminence by analyzing the social conditions that surrounded his adolescence and supported his rise to and stay in power," the author discusses his classlessness, his antipathy for certain social groups, his reading habits, and his charisma. Based primarily on secondary works; 58 notes, biblio.

C. R. Lovin

124. Kater, Michael H. HITLERJUGEND UND SCHULE IM DRITTEN REICH [Hitler Youth and the schools in the Third Reich]. *Hist. Zeitschrift [West Germany] 1979 228(3): 572-623.* The style of the Hitler Youth organization expressed in part the prejudices of Hitler and others against teachers. The students took these attitudes for their own struggles against teachers' authority and caused severe difficulties in the schools. The *Nationalsozialistischer Lehrerbund* [National Socialist Teachers League] tried to use Hitler Youth agitation to strengthen its position among teachers. Social analysis of teacher affinity to the Nazi Party suggests that the Teachers League was much less secure than the Hitler Youth and was itself manipulated. After 1943 the Teachers League was dissolved and the Hitler Youth and the Nazi Party came into complete domination of the schools. Based on archival and published documents and secondary works; 191 notes.

G. H. Davis

125. Kessel, Joseph. MISIUNEA "DOCTORULUI" KERSTEN ["Doctor" Kersten's mission]. *Magazin Istoric [Rumania] 1977 11(1): 57-61, (2): 57-61, (3): 57-61, and (4): 50-53.* Reproduces extracts from Joseph Kessel's *Mains miraculeuses,* describing the efforts of Felix Kersten, Heinrich Himmler's Finnish masseur, to use his influence for victims of Nazism, particularly through his connection with the Dutch resistance. Also publishes extracts which describe Kersten's role in convincing Himmler of Germany's inevitable defeat.

126. Kibata, Kazuko. NACHISU DAISAN TEIKOKU-KA NO KOKUEI KIGYŌ: HERUMANN GÖRING TEIKOKU KŌGYŌ-SHO NO SEIRITSU TO HATTEN [The government enterprises under the Third Reich: the establishment and development of the Reichswerke AG Hermann Göring]. *Rekishi Hyōron [Japan] 1980 (367): 43-58.* An attempt to reveal an aspect of the power structure of the Third Reich through analyzing the formation of the Hermann Göring Works and its expansion. West German leftists' alliance-theory, which contends that the party and the capitalists entered into an alliance with each other in that the Reichswerke sometimes gained profits through cooperating with private enterprises although it was established in rivalry with them. Based on documents of the trials of War Criminals at Nuremberg and records in the Bundesarchiv Koblenz; 45 notes. Y. Imura

127. Kirste, Peter. WIRTSCHAFTSPOLITIK UND ANTIIMPERIALISTISCHE UMWÄLZUNG. ZUR ERARBEITUNG WESENTLICHER GRUNDSÄTZE DER WIRTSCHAFTSPOLITISCHEN KONZEPTION DER KPD FÜR DIE ANTIFASCHISTISCH-DEMOKRATISCHE UMWÄLZUNG (FEBRUAR 1944-APRIL 1945) [Economic policy and antiimperialist upheaval: the development of the basics of the economic policy conceptions of the KPD for the anti-fascist democratic upheaval, February 1944-April 1945]. *Jahrbuch für Geschichte [East Germany] 1976 14: 235-286.* The German Communist Party spent 1944 and early 1945 preparing itself for a dominant role in the political life of postwar Germany. KPD groups in the USSR, France, Great Britain, Switzerland, Sweden, and Mexico kept in close touch and laid their plans carefully. Germany was first to be an antifascist-democratic state, where small and middle-sized entrepreneurs would still be permitted to operate; only big capitalists would be nationalized. Later all means of production were to be socialized. 146 notes. J. C. Billigmeier

128. Klemperer, Klemens von. GLAUBE, RELIGION, KIRCHE UND DER DEUTSCHE WIDERSTAND GEGEN DEN NATIONALSOZIALISMUS [Faith, religion, church, and the German resistance against Nazism]. *Vierteljahrshefte für Zeitgeschichte [West Germany] 1980 28(3): 293-309.* In their reaction to Nazism, leaders of the German conservative resistance shared with their adversary the reaction of "outraged tradition" against secularization and a "neognostic" search for religious knowledge. The sources of their search for a new piety were, however, personal and national political-moral distress. They were ecumenically oriented, only loosely linked to the established churches, and believed in the importance of the "courageous deed" rather than regular prayer and orthodox theology. Based on papers and memoirs of the resistance; 89 notes. D. Prowe

129. Koonz, Claudia. MOTHERS IN THE FATHERLAND: WOMEN IN NAZI GERMANY. Bridenthal, Renate and Koonz, Claudia, eds. *Becoming Visible: Women in European History* (Boston: Houghton Mifflin Co., 1977): 445-473. Nazism saw woman as restorer of the traditional family. However, its policy toward women altered according to the political and economic situation. Before 1933, women were considered men's equals in the struggle for Nazi ascendancy. They were allowed organizational and ideological autonomy to organize other women, but in 1933 early leaders and writers were retired and replaced by bureaucratic women who emphasized feminine virtues, marriage, and childbirth. As Germany prepared for war, large numbers were incorporated into the public sector. By 1943, all women were required to register with the employment office. Despite this major policy change, wages remained unequal and women were denied positions of leadership or control. Based on local histories of women's organizations, government sources, and secondary sources; 15 notes.
S. Tomlinson-Brown

130. Korthals Altes, A. PARIJS, 20 JULI 1944 [Paris, 20 July 1944]. *Spiegel Hist. [Netherlands] 1981 16(5): 279-288.* A discussion of events in Paris related to the assassination attempt against Adolf Hitler, 20 July 1944 in East Prussia based on manuscript memoirs of Gotthard Freiherr von Falkenhausen, Walter Bargatzky, and Friedrich Freiherr van Teuchert and conversations with eyewitnesses Hans Speidel and Max Horst. The plot had strong support among German officers in Paris, and the officers' revolt on 20 July proceeded further there than elsewhere. Based on manuscript sources; 11 illus. C. W. Wood, Jr.

131. Kozeński, Jerzy. KREISAUER KREIS—ODŁAM NIEMIECKIEJ OPOZYCJI PRAWICOWEJ W III RZESZY [The Kreisau Circle: a segment of German right-wing opposition in the Third Reich]. *Przegląd Zachodni [Poland] 1978 34(1): 127-143.* Outlines the program for the future of Germany following the collapse of Nazism, by the right-wing underground group, the Kreisau Circle, 1938-44. The group believed in the complete reeducation and democratization of the German people and punishment for all those implicated in Nazi crimes. A federal system, large-scale nationalization and state control of industry, and European unity were points in their program. Lack of national support and lack of Allied support with the arrest of many of the group's members brought activities to an end in mid-1944. 42 notes. M. A. Zurowski

132. Kozeński, Jerzy. O ZAMACHU STANU STAUFFENBERGA Z DNIA 20 LIPCA 1944 R. [On the Stauffenberg coup of 20 July 1944]. *Przegląd Zachodni [Poland] 1979 35(5-6): 68-103.* Many groups in Germany planned unsuccessfully to eliminate Hitler. From the old party opposition arose an attempt by Römer with the cooperation of the Robert Uhrig group. The military opposition was peculiarly inept. From the opposition centered in the Evangelical Church arose the Kreisau Circle, the first to raise the deeper problem of what direction Germany should take after Hitler. The military allied themselves with Carl Friedrich Goerdeler and hoped that elimination of Hitler might preserve not only Germany but even Hitler's conquests. After Stalingrad and the Allied landing in Normandy such hopes were clearly vain. At that time Lieutenant Colonel Claus von Stauffenberg decided to kill Hitler personally. The military in Berlin were then supposed to assume power under the code name of Operation Valkyrie. Stauffenberg failed and the military opposition was quickly eliminated. Primary sources. M. Krzyzaniak

133. Krammer, Arnold. FUELING THE THIRD REICH. *Technology and Culture 1978 19(3): 394-422.* Having suffered in World War I from a dearth of fuel, Germany developed by the early 1930's the hydrogenation techniques necessary to convert its abundant coal into high grade liquid fuels. From 1934 the Nazis pushed the building of these synthetic fuel plants, especially by I. G. Farben. Beginning World War II with only a few months' fuel reserves, Germany acquired vast oil resources by its European conquests. But in 1944-45 the German military machine slowed and then collapsed: defeat on the eastern front had deprived it of natural oil and Allied bombing had disrupted transport of synthetic fuel produced in Germany. Based on German documents now in the National Archives; 8 illus., 38 notes. C. O. Smith

134. Krantz, G. T. DET TYSKA MILITÄRVETERINÄRVÄSENDET UNDER ANDRA VÄRLDSKRIGET [The German army's veterinary service during World War II]. *Kungliga Krigsvetenskaps Akademiens Handlingar och Tidskrift [Sweden] 1974 178(4): 81-105.* Examines the organization of Germany's veterinary service, 1932-45, and its role in several battles after the 1939 mobilization. Describes its units and army horses, and mentions the use of other animals in this service as well as in the air force and navy and by the police. Gives brief attention to the separate veterinary service within the SS, and considers the role of the army's veterinary service in North Africa. Based on Wilhelm Zieger's *Das deutsche Heeresveterinärwesen im Zweiten Weltkrieg* (Freiburg: Verlag Rombach). B. Jacobsen

135. Krasuski, Jerzy. THE GERMAN REICH AND THE BALANCE OF POWER IN EUROPE. *Polish Western Affairs [Poland] 1973 14(1): 33-48.* Chronicles the impact of Germany, in its various empires, unifications, and divisions, 1800-1945, on the balance of power in Europe.

136. Krause, Michael D. HITLER: TWO VIEWS. *Air U. Rev. 1978 29(4): 84-88.* Presents a review of David Irving's *Hitler's War* (Viking Press, 1977) and Bradley F. Smith's *Reaching Judgment at Nuremberg* (Basic Books, 1977). Irving presents a controversial and revisionist interpretation of Hitler and his policies, maintaining, for instance, that Hitler was against killing the Jews and that Himmler and others were responsible. Smith's book is a detailed study of the personalities and policies at work at the Nuremberg Trials.
J. W. Thacker, Jr.

137. Kreidel, Hellmuth. DER UMGANG MIT DER ZIVILBEVÖLKERUNG IN DEN VON DEN DEUTSCHEN WEHRMACHT IM 2. WELTKRIEG BESETZTEN OSTGEBIETEN [Relations between the civilian population and the German army in the eastern occupied territories in World War II]. *Rev. Militaire Générale [France] 1972 (10): 499-507.* In spring 1942, Germany's army received the assignment of governing the territory which extended from the Baltic Sea to the Black Sea. Civilians had some sympathy for and confidence in the Germans, which helped the military government gain substantial cooperation from them. In the winter of 1942-43, however, Adolf Hitler's forced recruitment of workers strained relations and played into the hands of the partisan forces. J. S. Gassner

138. Kren, George M. PSYCHOHISTORIANS CONTRA THE THIRD REICH. *Psychohistory Rev. 1976 5(2): 34-40.* A review of several psychohistorical works on Nazism and Nazi atrocities just prior to and during World War II.

139. Kren, George M. PSYCHOHISTORICAL INTERPRETATIONS OF NATIONAL SOCIALISM. *German Studies Rev. 1978 1(2): 150-172.* Surveys the major psychohistorical interpretations of Nazism, including those concentrating on the national leadership and those seeking to understand "followership" and the passivity of the concentration camp victims. This approach proves to be particularly appropriate due to the "large irrational component of National Socialism which traditional historiography has not been able to handle adequately." 55 notes. R. V. Ritter

140. Krieger, Leonard. NAZISM: HIGHWAY OR BYWAY? *Central European Hist. 1978 11(1): 3-22.* Deals with the relationship of Nazism to 20th-century culture. Outlines "the four main features of the composite Nazi portrait that is beginning to emerge": planned chaos; the homogeneity of Nazism through time; the permanence of the martial mentality; the Nazi ideal. Discusses the revolutionary elements in Nazism and affirms that the "unforgettable evil" of the Nazis is "their legacy to all mankind." 23 notes. C. R. Lovin

141. Kuckhoff, Greta. VOSPOMINANIIA UCHASTNITSY ANTIFASHISTSKOGO SOPROTIVLENIIA [Memoirs of a participant in the antifascist resistance]. *Novaia i Noveishaia Istoriia [USSR] 1977 (3): 79-90, (4): 91-100.* Part I. The memoirs of a member of the Schulze-Boysen-Harnack organization, a German Communist resistance group which engaged in anti-Hitler propaganda and sabotage until nearly all its members were arrested and executed in 1943. The author provides character sketches of her companions. Conditions were too severe for mass opposition to materialize. The group collected photographs of atrocities to expose the SS (Schutzstaffel), but these were seized. It supported the Nazi-Soviet Pact as a necessary part of Soviet defense strategy. Part II. The author describes her arrest in August 1942, imprisonment, and interrogation, and the execution of several group members, including her husband, in 1943. She was condemned to death but her sentence was eventually commuted to imprisonment. 12 notes. D. N. Collins

142. Kühnrich, Heinz and Pech, Karlheinz. NEUE, BEDEUTSAME MATERIELEN ÜBER DIE POLITISCH-THEORETISCHE TÄTIGKEIT DER ILLEGALEN OPERATIVEN LEITUNG DER KPD IN DEUTSCHLAND 1944 [Significant new materials on the political-theoretical activity of the outlawed leadership of the Communist Party of Germany in Germany 1944]. *Beiträge zur Geschichte der Arbeiterbewegung [East Germany] 1979 21(1): 26-41.* Several recently discovered documents concerning the Communist Party of Germany and its leadership in 1944 reveal the widespread activities of the resistance to Hitler. Illegal since 1933, the Party gave form and unity to many opponents of fascism, ranging from soldiers to concentration camp inmates, and including the Free Germany movement. Especially noteworthy are several items analyzing the final phase of the war and planning for the postwar period. 19 notes. G. H. Libbey

143. Kühnrich, Heinz. ZUR ERFORSCHUNG UND DARSTELLUNG DER DEUTSCHEN ANTIFASCHISTISCHEN WIDERSTANDSBEWEGUNG WÄHREND DES ZWEITEN WELTKRIEGES. ERGEBNISSE UND AUFGABEN [The German anti-Fascist resistance movement during World War II: research results and tasks]. *Beiträge zur Geschichte der Arbeiterbewegung [East Germany] 1975 17(2): 260-281.* Reviews and analyzes current research on the German anti-Fascist movement during World War II. The existence of the Soviet Union gave German socialists a viable alternative to a return to the bourgeois capitalist system which had enabled Adolf Hitler to rise to power during the period between wars. The Communist Party of Germany and brother parties throughout Eastern Europe were united and well-organized in their opposition to the Hitler dictatorship. East German historians need to study the resistance movement as part of the international class struggle against imperialism. Secondary materials; 34 notes, biblio. G. H. Libbey

144. Kührich, Heinz and Pech, Karlheinz. AM BEGIN DER LETZTEN PHASE DER KRIEGES: EIN NEUES, BEDEUTSAMES DOKUMENT AUS DEM ILLEGALEN KAMPF DER KPD IN DEUTSCHLAND 1944 [At the beginning of the last phase of the war: a new, important document on the illegal struggle of the Communist Party in Germany, 1944]. *Beiträge zur Geschichte der Arbeiterbewegung [East Germany] 1979 21(3): 402-425.* Reprints a document on the resistance of the Communist Party during World War II, which evaluated the war effort and observed that the political fronts were active. It called for further clandestine operations by the Party and detailed lines of action.

G. E. Pergl/S

145. Kulak, Zbigniew. THE ANTI-NAZI RESISTANCE MOVEMENT IN THE THIRD REICH AND POLAND. *Polish Western Affairs [Poland] 1978 19(1): 144-147.* Describes a conference on the anti-Nazi movement in the Third Reich and Poland, 2-4 June 1977 at Lancut, Poland, the first of a series of annual conferences to be held alternately in Poland and West Germany according to the terms of the UNESCO Commission for History and Geography Schoolbooks.

M. Swiecicka-Ziemianek

146. Kulikov, V. G. INTERNATSIONALNAIA POMOSHCH SOVIETSKIKH VOORUZHENNIKH SIL NARODAM EVROPY V 1941-1945 [The Soviet armed forces' international aid to the peoples of Europe in 1941-45]. *Novaia i Noveishaia Istoriia [USSR] 1974 (1): 22-47.* Examines the growth of fascism in Germany from 1933, the outbreak of World War II in Europe, and the involvement of the USSR after Hitler's invasion of Soviet territory in 1941. Discusses the liberation of Poland, Hungary, and Austria, and events in the Baltic region. 66 notes. L. Smith

147. Łagodziński, Stanisław. STALAG I B HOHENSTEIN (W ŚWIETLE ZEZNAŃ ŚWIADKÓW) [Stalag I B Hohenstein according to eyewitness testimony]. *Komunikaty Mazursko-Warmińskie [Poland] 1977 (3-4): 403-426.* Most of the records of the camp located in Olsztynek (Hohenstein, East Prussia), 1939-45, were destroyed during its evacuation. Polish, French, Soviet, Italian, and Belgian soldiers and Polish civilians were among its approximately 45,000 prisoners. Most prisoners were used in agricultural, industrial, forestry, and transportation work. Typhus epidemics, starvation, and executions claimed many lives. Based on archival material and eyewitness reports; table, 99 notes.

R. Seitz

148. Lakowski, Richard. ZUR AUSRÜSTUNG DES DEUTSCHEN HEERES MIT TECHNISCHEN KAMPFMITTELN IM ZWEITEN WELTKRIEG [The technical outfitting of the Germany Army in World War II]. *Militärgeschichte [East Germany] 1975 14(3): 311-322.* Publication of statistical material on production and losses of tanks, artillery, and other equipment of the German infantry between 1939 and 1944.   R. Wagnleitner

149. Langbein, Herrmann. ÜBERBLICK ÜBER NEONAZISTISCHE LITERATUR [Survey of neo-Nazi literature]. *Zeitgeschichte [Austria] 1975 2(9/10): 236-242.* Analyzes neo-Nazi propaganda literature and pamphlets in West Germany and Austria on World War II war crimes and concentration camps. Based on neo-Nazi works, newspapers, and pamphlets; 50 notes.
R. Wagnleitner

150. Lange, Dieter. ÜBER HISTORISCHE FORSCHUNGEN ZUR GESCHICHTE DES ZWEITEN WELTKRIEGES IN DER DEUTSCHEN DEMOKRATISCHEN REPUBLIK [Historical research on World War II in East Germany]. *La Seconda Guerra Mondiale nella prospettiva storica a trent'anni dall'epilogo* (Como: Casa editrice Pietro Cairoli, 1977): 259-267. An account of the historiography of World War II in East Germany, stressing the correctness of its Marxist-Leninist approach and emphasizing the role of the Communist Party in the resistance against the Nazis. 16 notes.
J. C. Billigmeier

151. Lange, Wolfgang. DIE TRANSPORTFLIEGERKRÄFTE DER FASCHISTISCHEN LUFTWAFFE UND IHRE WICHTIGSTEN FLUGZEUGTYPEN [The air transport forces of the fascist air force and its most important airplane types]. *Militärgeschichte [East Germany] 1978 17(3): 337-350.* Construction of air transport forces before World War II played a subordinate role in German armaments plans because of the blitzkrieg military strategy. To be sure, units had been utilized in the Spanish Civil War and the occupation of Austria to transport troops. When the blitzkrieg conception shattered on the realities of the Russian front, the German air leadership belatedly realized the significance of air transport of supplies and replacement of parts, but mass production of new types of planes was not achieved until 1943-44 and organizational regrouping to gain greater efficiency in action floundered on fuel scarcity. Eleven types are described. 15 illus., 12 notes.   H. D. Andrews

152. Langenberg, William H. THE GERMAN BATTLESHIP *TIRPITZ*: A STRATEGIC WARSHIP? *Naval War Coll. Rev. 1981 34(4): 81-92.* While it may seem unrealistic, perhaps farfetched before the advent of nuclear weapons, to categorize a single warship as strategic, one ship can rightfully be so described: the German battleship *Tirpitz,* the "Lonesome Queen" of the north during World War II, which by her mere existence influenced the balance of seapower in every ocean.   J

153. Langenberg, William H. WHAT PRICE VIGILANCE? THE *KORMORAN-SYDNEY* BATTLE. *Naval War Coll. Rev. 1980 33(1): 78-84.* Discusses the 19 November 1941 World War II naval battle 150 miles off the west coast of Australia between the German merchant raider *Kormoran* and the Australian cruiser *Sydney,* which left both ships on fire and crippled. The *Kor-*

moran was scuttled, its 393 officers and men dead or imprisoned by the Australians until 1947. The *Sydney* sailed from view and was never seen again. 22 notes.
S

154. Laqueur, Walter. INTRODUCTION. *J. of Contemporary Hist. [Great Britain] 1981 16(1): 1-4.* The historiography of World War II, "most important event of this century," has been attacked by both right revisionists who try to prove that the Nazis and the Japanese were egged on by a bellicose West or that Hitler fought a preventive war against the Soviet Union, and by left revisionists who maintain that the Allies were mainly trying to protect their economic and imperial interests. In more recent years, newer questions about war have been raised: the role of Nazi Fifth Columns, the military "benefits" of the Munich agreement, the impact of intelligence, the real turning-point of the war, the importance of the air offensive against Germany and of the North African theater. These current investigations are typified in this special issue of the *Journal of Contemporary History* [16 (1) January, 1981], to be followed by another in summer, 1981. M. P. Trauth

155. Larson, Arthur D. THE SECRET SIDE OF WAR: ANGLO-AMERICAN AND GERMAN INTELLIGENCE IN WORLD WAR II. *J. of Pol. & Military Sociol. 1980 8(1): 121-124.* Review article of David Kahn's *Hitler's Spies: German Military Intelligence in World War II* (New York: Macmillan, 1978) and Anthony Cave Brown's *Bodyguard of Lies* (New York: Harper and Row, 1975).

156. Lee, Asher. THE BUILDING OF THE LUFTWAFFE. *J. of the Royal United Services Inst. for Defence Studies [Great Britain] 1974 119(2): 78-79.* A review article of David Irving's *The Rise and Fall of the Luftwaffe: The Life of Erhard Milch* (London: Weidenfeld and Nicolson, 1974). Milch "was second only to Hermann Goering in influencing the course of German air power from 1933 to 1945." Milch, however, tended to underestimate the need for large numbers of fully trained pilots and decided too late to press for high production of fighter aircraft; his belief that defensive air power could save Germany reveals that "few air leaders have a true sense of proportion." D. H. Murdoch

157. Lehmann, Joachim. FASCHISTISCHE AGRARPOLITIK IM ZWEITEN WELTKRIEG. ZUR KONZEPTION VON HERBERT BACKE [Fascist agrarian policy in World War II: the concepts of Herbert Backe]. *Zeitschrift für Geschichtswissenschaft [East Germany] 1980 28(10): 948-956.* With the introduction of the Four Year Plan in 1936 Herbert Backe was appointed chief of the *Geschäftsführung Ernährung,* which eventually allowed him to supersede his old chief Walther Darré, the Reichsminister of Nutrition and Agriculture. Unlike Darré, Backe was free of Nazi agrarian ideological concepts, such as "Blut und Boden"; instead, he advocated pragmatic measures to improve agrarian conditions. Backe also promoted a continental European agrarian system, dominated by Germany, and helped plan the agrarian exploitation of Russia. 50 notes. J. T. Walker

158. Lehmann, Joachim. ZUR MOBILISIERUNG DEUTSCHER ARBEITSKRÄFTE FÜR DIE LANDWIRTSCHAFT IN DEN JAHREN 1942-1945 [On the mobilization of German workers for agriculture between 1942 and

1945]. *Wissenschaftliche Zeitschrift der U. Rostock. Gesellschafts- und Sprachwissenschaftliche Reihe [East Germany] 1974 23(9): 551-561.* Between 1942 and 1945 German agricultural leaders were not able to make up for workers lost to mobilization for war. Although war industry used forced labor from occupied countries, the industrial sector became a strong competitor for agricultural labor and absorbed the much-needed rural labor force. Based on documents in the Zentrales Staatsarchiv, Potsdam, Staatsarchiv Weimar, and secondary sources; 3 tables, 80 notes.   R. Wagnleitner

159. Levy, Paul M. G. LES CONDITIONS DE PAIX DE LA RADIO NAZIE [The conditions of peace of Nazi radio]. *Cahiers d'Hist. de la Seconde Guerre Mondiale [Belgium] 1980 6: 5-20.* After their victory in the West in summer 1940, the Germans planned the future penetration of Europe by radio in the following pattern: 1) to create a European Radio Union out of the French, Belgian, Dutch, Norwegian, and Balkan networks, centralized in Germany; 2) to denationalize the French state network into a joint stock company with majority German shares; and 3) to standardize the pattern and capacity of all French receivers and transmitters so that German transmissions could readily penetrate and any other radios be the more easily controlled. The plans were not realized as the war did not go as expected and other departments objected for various reasons. Based on German Propaganda Ministry archives; 5 facsimile reproductions of documents, map, 12 notes.   M. K. Palat

160. Lukens, Nancy. ADAM VON TROTT: RESISTANCE AND CONTEMPLATION: A WORK ETHIC IN NAZI GERMANY. Ryan, Michael D., ed. *Human Responses to the Holocaust: Perpetrators and Victims, Bystanders and Resisters* (New York: Edwin Mellen Pr., 1981): 169-201. Examines the role of Adam von Trott (d.1944), an official in Germany, in opposing Nazism from 1929 until his execution in 1944 after the unsuccessful assassination attempt against Hitler, and focuses on the moral evolution of von Trott as manifested in his correspondence and writings from 1929 to 1944.

161. Luttwak, E. N. THE OPERATIONAL LEVEL OF WAR. *Int. Security 1980-81 5(3): 61-79.* The German Blitzkrieg of 1939-42 and Finnish plans for the defense of Lappland against Soviet aggression provide models of functioning at the operational level and of the rational maneuver style of warfare, which avoids confronting the enemy where it is strongest and, instead, relies on deception.

162. MacDonald, William W. ADOLF HITLER AND THE PSYCHOHISTORIANS. *Res. Studies 1978 46(2): 117-139.* Discusses Adolf Hitler's personality from the viewpoint of psychohistory, an approach sparked by Walter C. Langer's wartime (1943) study *The Mind of Adolf Hitler: The Secret Wartime Report* (New York, 1972).

163. MacDonald, William W. THE *HITLER WELLE:* THE HISTORIANS' SEARCH FOR ADOLF HITLER. *Res. Studies 1978 46(1): 54-68.* Examines the waves of books on Adolf Hitler and the failure of biographers, particularly Eugene Davidson, David Irving, and John Toland, to explain him fully.

164. Madajczyk, Czesław. TYPOLOGY OF OCCUPATIONS. *Polish Western Affairs [Poland] 1980 21(1): 129-140.* Discusses the concept of *occupatio bellica* as described in the Hague Convention of 1907 and the violations of these provisions by the Nazis and the Fascists during World War II. The Nazis identified three types of military occupation—1) occupation by annexation, 2) colonial occupation, and 3) supervisory occupation—but all three were intended to destroy through terror the social, economic, and political structures of the occupied countries. Based on *The Occupation Systems of the Axis Powers in Europe* and numerous primary sources; table, 15 notes.
D. S. Lloyd

165. Madej, W. Victor. EFFECTIVENESS AND COHESION OF THE GERMAN GROUND FORCES IN WORLD WAR II. *J. of Pol. and Military Sociol. 1978 6(2): 233-248.* Motivational explanations of German perseverance, notably Shils' and Janowitz' classic study of the German army, are questioned here because they tend to overlook technical variables such as military skill and efficiency. This paper traces the characteristics of the German participation in World War II. Data established that the ground war began mainly in the summer of 1941, and was decisively concluded in the summer of 1944. Over 80 per cent of unit commitment and casualties occurred on the eastern front. Certain German societal values may well have fostered military effectiveness but the importance of psychological factors was overshadowed by the impact of modern weaponry.
J

166. Mainuš, František. ŽIVOT CIZINCŮ V NĚMECKU ZA DRUHÉ SVĚTOVÉ VÁLKY [The life of foreigners in Germany during World War II]. *Časopis Matice Moravské [Czechoslovakia] 1977 96(1-2): 87-98.* Discusses the living and working conditions of the 10 million foreigners put to work in Germany during World War II, including prisoners of war, civilians imported from occupied countries, and immigrants from friendly countries, like Italy. Sufferings were of a psychological as well as a physical nature. Among the prisoners of war the Soviets were the worst and the British the best treated. The British were able to make the highest percentage of escape attempts because of the treatment they received, and working conditions for civilians doing hard labor were atrocious. Based on military archives and secondary sources; 33 notes.
M.-M. Petrzilkova

167. Makhrov, N. SLUCHAINOST' V RESHENII KOMANDIRA [Chance in the decisions of a commander]. *Morskoi Sbornik [USSR] 1980 (3): 15-19.* Discusses various examples of chance in the experience of German, American, and Japanese navies in World War II such as failure of torpedoes to explode, running into a typhoon at a critical moment, and the delay of crucial intelligence information. The naval commander should try to take into account the favorable and unfavorable workings of chance when making decisions and correct his original plans as quickly as possible when chance factors intervene. 7 notes.
C. J. Read

168. Mann, Golo. "BAYERN IN DER NS-ZEIT" [Bavaria during the National Socialist era]. *Schweizerische Zeitschrift für Geschichte [Switzerland] 1980 30(3-4): 427-432.* Review of the first two volumes of a projected six-volume history of Bavaria during the era of National Socialism published by the Munich Institute for Contemporary History in 1977 and 1979. The project's real goal "has

been grandiosely achieved: they fill with real life the framework built long ago by theory or general history." H. K. Meier

169. Mann, Golo. HELMUTH JAMES VON MOLTKE. *J. of European Studies [Great Britain] 1974 4(4): 368-389.* Discusses the thoughts and fate of Helmuth James von Moltke relying primarily on Gerrit van Roon's *Neuordnung im Widerstand* (1967). A cosmopolitan member of the German upper class, Moltke dissented against the Nazi regime, joined the Kreisau Circle, and was executed as a traitor in 1944.

170. Mann, Golo. HITLER—FOR THE LAST TIME? ON JOACHIM FEST'S NEW BIOGRAPHY. *Encounter [Great Britain] 1974 42(6): 56-65.* Reviews the new English translation by Richard and Clara Winston of Joachim Fest's *Adolf Hitler* (Harcourt Brace Jovanovich, 1975), focusing on Hitler and the question of historical greatness.

171. Mann, Reinhard. WIDERSTAND GEGEN DEN NATIONAL-SOZIALISMUS [Resistance to National Socialism]. *Neue Politische Literatur [West Germany] 1977 22(4): 425-442.* Although Communist and Socialist resistance groups carried on about 80% of all resistance activities against Nazism in Germany, the West German historical literature and the public consciousness still identify antifascist resistance with the group of 20 July 1944.

R. Wagnleitner

172. Mason, T. W. IL NAZIONALSOCIALISMO E L'EREDITÀ DEL 1918 [National socialism and the 1918 heritage]. *Storia Contemporanea [Italy] 1973 4(1): 3-25.* Focuses on Nazi labor policy toward the German working class during World War II from the perspective of the social causes (both real and assumed) of the November 1918 revolution, and deriving from its analysis some elements for a better explanation of the Nazi expansionist dynamic. The wisest Nazi leaders realized that the conflict would impose greater sacrifices on Germans than in 1914-18. They also realized that, in order to succeed in temporarily shifting the people's interest from material things to great ideals, it was necessary that the required sacrifices were not too heavy and that the achievement of those ideals truly bore concrete advantages to the people. Hence their effort toward high productive levels for consumption goods even until 1943 and their consideration for working class needs. Therefore, there was the need to structure the German economy along lines unrelated to war, a need that for a long time prevented rational war production and led to economic instability. A change took place in 1942-43 when Germany was fighting a desperate defensive war under fear of invasion. J/S

173. Mason, Tim. WOMEN IN GERMANY: 1925-1940: FAMILY, WELFARE, AND WORK. *Hist. Workshop J. [Great Britain] 1976 (1): 74-113, (2): 5-32.* Part I. World War I forced many German women onto the labor market and into various jobs. The ensuing economic depression limited career opportunities for them, and the Nazi insistence that a woman's place was in the home further limited their professional prospects. The Nazi policy in this case was based primarily on a desire to raise Germany's birth rate. 6 photos, 92 notes. Part II. By the late 1930's, Germany was experiencing a shortage of labor power which became acute with the outbreak of World War II. Nazi policy had to be altered,

and women came to be recruited and conscripted into German industry instead of being consigned to the home. 67 notes. A. J. Evans

174. Mason, Tim. ZUR FRAUENARBEIT IM NS-STAAT [Working women in the Third Reich]. *Archiv für Sozialgeschichte [West Germany] 1979 19: 579-584.* Reviews Dörte Winkler's *Frauenarbeit im Dritten Reich* (Hamburg, 1977). It is the first substantial inquiry into the Nazi policy toward German women's labor during World War II. H. W. Wurster

175. McKale, Donald. THE MAN WHO DISOBEYED HITLER. *Res. Studies 1973 41(1): 52-56.* Recounts a 1942 incident in which chief judge Walter Buch led a Party trial to overrule Hitler's decision to expel a local Party leader. Buch retained his position, though the expulsion order was effected. S

176. McKale, Donald M.; Becker, Peter and Barrett, Michael, commentary. PURGING NAZIS: THE POSTWAR TRIALS OF FEMALE GERMAN DOCTORS AND NURSES. *Pro. of the South Carolina Hist. Assoc. 1981: 156-170.* Studies the careers of three women convicted of war crimes—physicians Oberherser and Flocker and a nurse named Huber. Concludes with some remarks about the war crimes trials in general. Based primarily on the records of the War Crimes Tribunal and German documents; 26 notes. Commentary, pp. 171-180.
J. W. Thacker

177. Mensch, Terry G. PSYCHOHISTORY OF THE THIRD REICH: A LIBRARY PATHFINDER AND TOPICAL BIBLIOGRAPHY OF ENGLISH LANGUAGE PUBLICATIONS. *J. of Psychohistory 1979-80 7(3): 331-354.* A library pathfinder and topical bibliography to all levels of published, English-language psychohistorical research and synthesis about the people and events of the Third Reich. This compilation includes material written from a variety of approaches and interpretations, and is intended to serve as a bibliographic aid for serious students of Nazism in Germany from 1933 to 1945.
J. Powell

178. Mertsalov, A. N. ZAPADNOGERMANSKAIA BURZHUAZNAIA ISTORIOGRAFIIA NATSIZMA [West German bourgeois historiography of Nazism]. *Novaia i Noveishaia Istoriia [USSR] 1974 (6): 158-169.* Though studies of West German historiography of Nazism have been published in the USSR, little attention has been paid to the basic principles upon which this historiography is based. The lack of unity in approach among West German historians arises from their being bourgeois, liberal, or social democratic, and from political fluctuations inside West Germany. Explanations of Nazism in ideological terms without Marxist content, or in terms of psychological abnormality, exemplify the resulting confusion. Those books which place the blame on Hitler alone are attempts to protect the real culprits, the imperialist bourgeoisie. Also unacceptable are explanations in terms of mass culture, which stress the support given to the Nazi Party by the German people, and the concept of a Nazi revolution. Marxist historians have shown that all the aims of the Nazis corresponded with the aims of capitalists. 112 notes. D. N. Collins

179. Messerschmidt, M. LA STRATÉGIE ALLEMANDE (1939-1945): CONCEPTION, OBJECTIF, COMMANDEMENT, RÉUSSITE [German strategy, 1939-45: conception, objective, command, and success]. *Rev. d'Hist. de*

la Deuxième Guerre Mondiale [France] 1975 (100): 1-26. The German military strategy of Blitzkrieg included the use of diplomatic and economic instruments as well as the tactical deployment of air and armored forces to isolate the enemy. In the case of Norway, Hitler underestimated the risks. Yugoslavia became an unexpected campaign because of political miscalculation, and Hitler became overcommitted in North Africa to support an earlier commitment to Mussolini. After the French campaign, the Russian invasion dominated war planning but Hitler refused to adjust his plan because Britain remained a force at his rear. After the Russians stopped the German advance in late 1941, the war was lost and the Germans could seek only local initiatives. After 1943 Germany was completely on the defensive and from 1944 until the end of World War II Hitler's actions were mainly to prolong the hostilities. 29 notes. G. H. Davis

180. Meyer, Michael. THE NAZI MUSICOLOGIST AS MYTH MAKER IN THE THIRD REICH. *J. of Contemporary Hist. [Great Britain] 1975 10(4): 649-665.* Denunciation of Jewish composers, disparagement of Christian influences, condemnation of modern atonality and jazz, and the overriding canonization of Richard Wagner, marked National Socialist musicology. Music was especially prepared for Nazi pageantries and rallies as were special song books for popular singing. All music was supposed to express something generally and eternally German—that elemental joy in combat characteristic of Nordic man. Yet, as late as 1943, commentators had to admit that there really was no such thing as National Socialist music. Based on contemporary periodical literature; 15 notes. M. P. Trauth

181. Mitchell, Alan. NAZI OCCUPATION POLICIES AND THE RESPONSE OF POLISH, DUTCH, AND FRENCH ELITES. *Wiener Lib. Bull. [Great Britain] 1979 32(49-50): 34-40.* Accommodation to Nazi hegemony was determined not by the desire or lack of desire to cooperate, but by the economic needs and racial notions of the Nazi state. Thus, the Polish elite was wiped out, whereas the Netherlands was to be brought into the Reich. The Dutch, however, opted to be treated as an occupied enemy. With the French, the Nazis had conceptual difficulties, for they were neither subhuman nor Aryan. The prevailing attitude of French elites was to favor collaboration, as a way of restoring traditional values that had been weakened by the Third Republic. French leaders cooperated in handing over large numbers of Jews to the Nazis, although they filled their "quotas" in so far as possible with nonnative Jews. 25 notes.
R. V. Layton

182. Moltke, Helmuth von. VAINE REVOLTE? LE SORT DE LA RESISTANCE À HITLER [A vain revolt? The outcome of the Hitler resistance]. *Documents [France] 1974 29(6): 44-54.* In a rare uncensored letter to a British friend, explains the spirit of the German masses in 1943, their ignorance and isolation from the outside world, their preoccupation with material need, and the anti-Hitler spirit which was to lead to the assassination attempt by the resistance the following year.

183. Mommsen, Hans. BEGRIFF UND PROBLEMATIK DES DEUTSCHEN WIDERSTANDS GEGEN HITLER IN DER ZEITGESCHICHTLICHEN FORSCHUNG [Concept and problems of the German resistance to Hitler in contemporary research]. *Int. Jahrbuch für Geschichts- und Geogra-*

phieunterricht [West Germany] 1977-78 18: 280-287. Describes current research concerning resistance to Adolf Hitler within the Third Reich, which resulted in the 26 July 1944 attempt on his life. Considers the differing interpretations of British, and West and East German historians based in large part on their differing views of Fascism, and traces connections with the Weimar Republic. Based on a paper presented to the 10th UNESCO German-Polish Historians' Schoolbook Conference, Lancut, Poland, 2-5 June 1977; 22 notes.

J. L. Colwell

184. Morozov, V. POLITICS AND WAR. *Soviet Military Rev. [USSR] 1975 (11): 6-8.* Examines the extent to which foreign and domestic politics affected Germany's aggression in Europe which led to World War II, 1938-45.

185. Mulholland, Virginia. THE PLOT TO ASSASSINATE HITLER, 1938-44. *Strategy and Tactics 1976 (59): 4-15.* Discusses assassination attempts and plots on the life of Adolf Hitler and members of the Nazi hierarchy in Germany, 1938-44; emphasizes the conspiratorial efforts of Claus von Stauffenberg.

186. Müller, Rolf-Dieter. DIE DEUTSCHEN GASKRIEGVORBEREITUNGEN 1919-1945. MIT GIFTGAS ZUR WELTMACHT? [The German chemical warfare preparations 1919-45: toward world power with poison gas?]. *Militärgeschichtliche Mitteilungen [West Germany] 1980 (1): 25-54.* Details German research, stockpiling, and planning for chemical warfare after World War I. The German army planned the use of military gas as the only way to fight a major war under the Versailles limitations. Experimental stations in Russia subverted Versailles prohibitions, and these activities were transferred to Germany in 1933 with the Nazi seizure of power. Major production planned by chemical officers and industrialists did not synchronize with the Blitzkrieg economy and military operations, and proposals for a nerve gas wonder weapon late in the war were thwarted by lack of defensive measures and raw materials and the Allied advance. Based upon documents of the Military Archives, Freiberg; 5 tables, 45 notes.

K. W. Estes

187. Müller, Rolf-Dieter. INDUSTRIELLE INTERESSENPOLITIK IM RAHMEN DES "GENERALPLANS OST" [The policy of industrial interests in the framework of "general plan east"]. *Militärgeschichtliche Mitteilungen [West Germany] 1981 (1): 101-141.* Documents the rivalry between various factions of the Nazi leadership over the direction of economic exploitation of the eastern occupied countries. The aims of the heavy industry concerns of Rhineland-Westphalia collided with political and racial concepts of the Himmler faction. Efforts of the *Oberkommando der Wehrmacht* (OKW) to clarify roles were mooted by the deterioration of the military situation in the eastern front. Based on documents in the Military Archive, Freiburg; 11 documents, 203 notes.

K. W. Estes

188. Murray, Williamson. THE LUFTWAFFE BEFORE THE SECOND WORLD WAR: A MISSION, A STRATEGY? *J. of Strategic Studies [Great Britain] 1981 4(3): 261-270.* The Luftwaffe's conception both of itself and its mission before World War II was quite different from the generally held historical view. It did consider a strategic bombing role as well as other functions, and close air support was not considered its chief mission. "The real war of 1939 and 1940

was not the war for which most of the Luftwaffe had prepared, but it was a war —in its initial stages—to which the Luftwaffe could and did adapt, and to which the Luftwaffe could in the final analysis apply air power in cooperation with the army to gain a devastating strategic victory." Based on German and other primary sources; 37 notes. A. M. Osur

189. Murray, Williamson. THE STRATEGY OF THE "PHONEY WAR": A RE-EVALUATION. *Military Affairs 1981 45(1): 13-17.* Examines the overall strategic situation of Germany during the first months of World War II, Allied strategy toward Germany, and the possibilities that existed for Allied strategy to unbalance Germany's strategic equilibrium. During this "phoney war" only the most cursory skirmishing took place between the forces of the Western powers and Nazi Germany. Yet, German economic documents reveal an economy facing extraordinary problems under the pressure of blockade. The Western powers failed to place enough pressure on the German war machine or to unbalance the German economic and strategic situation. Primary sources; 48 notes.
A. M. Osur

190. Nelson, H. N. LOYALTIES AT SWORD-POINT: THE LUTHERAN MISSIONARIES IN WARTIME NEW GUINEA, 1939-45. *Australian J. of Pol. and Hist. [Australia] 1978 24(2): 199-217.* Examines the fate of Lutheran missionaries in New Guinea in World War II. German-owned property had been given up after 1914 and control vested in the United Evangelical Lutheran Church in Australia and the Evangelical Lutheran Synod of Iowa. By 1939 most missionaries were Australian or American but there were 87 Germans. With other mission employees there were 473 Germans in New Guinea. Known Nazis were arrested. A few stayed behind with the missions during the Japanese occupation. Some detail on Adolph Wagner, killed by the Japanese, is given. Comments on Australian prejudice and the problem of getting missionaries back after the war. Based on Australian archives; 77 notes. W. D. McIntyre

191. Nelson, Otto M. *SIMPLICISSIMUS* AND THE RISE OF NATIONAL SOCIALISM. *Historian 1978 40(3): 441-462.* Focuses on Germany's most prominent satirical-political journal and its evolving attitudes toward Adolf Hitler and the National Socialist movement in the 1920's and 1930's. Many of the journal's concerns reflected the political attitudes and reactions of the liberal middle classes of Germany. The Munich-based journal presented many of its perceptions and criticisms of Hitler and his movement in the form of political cartoons. Under extreme political pressure *Simplicissimus* became little more than Nazi propaganda and ceased publication in 1944. M. S. Legan

192. Noakes, Jeremy. HITLER. *Hist. Today [Great Britain] 1980 30(July): 22-27.* Traces the political and economic developments, beginning about 1928 in Germany, which provided the milieu for the rise of Adolf Hitler and Nazism in the early 1930's; discusses Hitler's contributions to 20th-century history: his responsibility in causing World War II in 1939, the slaughter of millions of Jews, and the results of World War II on world superpowers, national boundaries, and economics.

193. O'Donnell, James P. CONVERSATIONS WITH SPEER. *Encounter [Great Britain] 1976 47(4): 6-16.* Exposes, through personal interviews, Albert Speer's involvement with Adolf Hitler and Nazism in Germany, his reflections on the 1945 Nuremberg trials, and his 20-year imprisonment at Spandau, where he wrote his memoirs.

194. Olsson, Sven-Olof. THE DOCUMENTS OF "ZENTRALE PLANUNG" AS A BASIS FOR RESEARCH ON THE GERMAN WAR ECONOMY. *Scandinavian Econ. Hist. Rev. [Denmark] 1976 24(1): 45-59.* The central file of documents on the German economy, called Zentrale Planung, furnishes the best source for industrial conditions after 1942, when Albert Speer took control of the economy. Transcripts of discussions on central directions and decisions are available in these documents where the main themes are supplies of iron and steel, other metals, coal, labor, and transport. The transcripts reveal the relationship between leaders, the problems that they faced during the war, and the accomplishments of German industry. Only Alan Milward and Martin Fritz have made use of the documents to any degree, although the US Strategic Bombing Survey had access to them for its study immediately after the war. Appendix.
R. E. Lindgren

195. Oppen, Beate Ruhm von. HELMUTH JAMES VON MOLTKE: A CHRISTIAN WITNESS. Ryan, Michael D., ed. *Human Responses to the Holocaust: Perpetrators and Victims, Bystanders and Resisters* (New York: Edwin Mellen Pr., 1981): 145-167. Discusses the role of Helmuth James von Moltke (1907-45) in the German anti-Nazi opposition from 1940 to 1945, and compares his attitude toward the attempted assassination of Adolf Hitler with that of Dietrich Bonhoeffer.

196. Orlov, A. S. OPYT PRIMENENIIA BALLISTICHESKIKH I KRYLATYKH PAKET V GODY VTOROI MIROVOI VOINY [The use of missiles and ballistic missiles in World War II]. *Voenno-Istoricheskii Zhurnal [USSR] 1974 (5): 86-91.* Examines the use of missiles by the German army, 1944-45, and explains their failure to prevent the Allied victory.

197. Oseraner, Michail. DEUTSCHE ANTIFASCHISTEN IN DER PARTISANENBEWEGUNG IM SÜDEN DER UDSSR UND IN POLEN [German antifascists in the partisan movement of the southern USSR and Poland]. *Militärgeschichte [East Germany] 1977 16(1): 58-64.* Reports about the participation of German opponents of Adolf Hitler in the antifascist resistance in the USSR, Poland, and Czechoslovakia. This evaluation of individual actions and individual destinies, which are integrated into the larger relationships of the antifascist liberation struggle, is a contribution to deepening our knowledge about the prehistory of the alliances of peoples and states of the socialist community. Based on memoirs of Soviet partisans.
J/T (H. D. Andrews).

198. Overy, R. J. FROM "URALBOMBER" TO "AMERIKABOMBER": THE LUFTWAFFE AND STRATEGIC BOMBING. *J. of Strategic Studies [Great Britain] 1978 1(2): 155-178.* Survey of the development of strategic thinking and aircraft in the Luftwaffe from 1934 to 1945. Germany was committed to the idea of building up a strategic bomber force, but never could switch from the Luftwaffe's roles of ground support and medium-bombing. The failure was

a product of the Nazis' inability to translate intention readily into reality when the strategic gains from an air offensive held such high potential. For Germany the strategic air war was lost before it started. Based on German records; 2 tables, 89 notes. A. M. Osur

199. Overy, R. J. HITLER AND AIR STRATEGY. *J. of Contemporary Hist. [Great Britain] 1980 15(3): 405-421.* Hermann Göring has been blamed for the misuse of German airpower during World War II, but the guilt really lay with Adolf Hitler who made decisions either without consultation with Luftwaffe personnel or in spite of them. Hitler was actually ignorant of air affairs, even though he talked glibly about them. He did not coordinate the Luftwaffe with the other branches of service. He did not plan in terms of continuous massive quantity and quality in the number of planes or in their offensive use. He thought in terms of defense or of secret, magic weapons for one massive, catastrophic blow. Based on published primary sources; 57 notes. M. P. Trauth

200. Overy, R. J. HITLER'S WAR AND THE GERMAN ECONOMY: A REINTERPRETATION. *Econ. Hist. Rev. [Great Britain] 1982 35(2): 272-291.* It is sometimes stated that Hitler planned a *Blitzkrieg* economy, with only partial mobilization of the economy for war purposes, 1939-41. Actually, Hitler did not expect war in 1939 and its outbreak caught him with the plans for a large-scale military economy for world conquest only partly completed. Early military successes convinced him that such conquest was possible earlier than planned, but more rapid conversion to the appropriate economy was frustrated by such factors as Hitler's personality, lack of planning, reluctance of industrialists, and the role of the military leaders. B. L. Crapster

201. Patrick, Stephen B. PARATROOP: A HISTORY OF AIRBORNE OPERATIONS. *Strategy and Tactics 1979 (77): 4-13.* Sketches the evolution of airborne troops and provides a detailed description of Allied and Axis paratroop action during World War II.

202. Peša, Václav. PŘÍČINY, PRŮBĚH A VÝSLEDKY DRUHÉ SVĚTOVÉ VÁLKY 1939-1945 [The causes, course, and results of World War II, 1939-45]. *Časopis Matice Moravské [Czechoslovakia] 1980 99(3-4): 206-230.* Western imperialism allowed the emergence of fascism and the policy of noninterference and appeasement turned the thrust of fascism against the socialist USSR, which played the major part in crushing fascism. Other states also contributed, their coalition with the USSR demonstrating the possibility of cooperation despite differences of system. The war resulted in the crushing of the fascist bloc, the creation of favorable conditions for revolutionary movements in capitalist states, the decline of colonial empires, and the growth of the international influence of the USSR. 40 notes. L. Short

203. Peters, Jan. DIE LANDESORGANISATION DER KPD IN SCHWEDEN IM GEMEINSAMEN KAMPF MIT SCHWEDISCHEN ANTIFASCHISTEN (1933-1943) [The organization of the Communist Party of Germany in Sweden in its common struggle with Swedish antifascists, 1933-43]. *Beiträge zur Geschichte der Arbeiterbewegung [East Germany] 1976 18(6): 1070-1086.* Sweden's physical proximity to Germany and its neutrality after 1940 enabled German Communists to use Sweden as a center for illegal operations. The

negative attitude of Swedish authorities would have made these operations impossible; the personal and material assistance of Swedish antifascists facilitated Communist activities. Based on documents in the archives of the Institute of Marxism-Leninism, Berlin, and secondary literature; 63 notes.

R. Wagnleitner

204. Petersen, Jürgen. JOURNALIST IM DRITTEN REICH [Journalist in the Third Reich]. *Frankfurter Hefte [West Germany] 1981 36(3): 41-49, (4): 41-48.* Part I. LEHRJAHRE IN DARMSTADT UND BERLIN [Apprenticeship in Darmstadt and Berlin]. Personal recollections of work on the *Darmstädter Tagblatt,* his training in the *Reichspresseschule* at Berlin (including paramilitary training with the SA) and his work for the *Berliner Tagblatt* between 1936-38. Part II. AN DER *DEUTSCHEN ALLGEMEINEN ZEITUNG* [At the *Deutsche Allgemeine Zeitung*]. Frankfurter Hefte [West Germany] 1981 36(4): 41-48. Recollections of work for the *Deutsche Allgemeine Zeitung.* Describes attempts at journalistic self-censorship during World War II.

205. Peukert, Detlev. RUHR MINERS UNDER NAZI REPRESSION, 1933-1945. *Int. J. of Oral Hist. 1980 1(2): 111-127.* Discusses the attitudes and problems of Ruhr miners active in the resistance to Nazism in Germany from 1933 to 1945. Based on interviews.

206. Popescu-Puțuri, Ion. PROPAGANDA ÎN ANII CELUI DE-AL DOILEA RĂZBOI MONDIAL: METODE, OBIECTIVE, REZULTATE [Propaganda in the years of World War II: methods, aims, achievements]. *Anale de Istorie [Romania] 1980 26(1): 84-98.* Examines the role of propaganda during World War II, describing the organization and dissemination of propaganda by the Axis powers and the Allies. Aims and methods varied according to whether the propaganda was directed at the people of the disseminating nation, its enemies, or the occupied countries. The role of propaganda in the war was crucial, especially by radio and the clandestine press. 42 notes.

R. O. Khan

207. Potra, George G. POLITICA ASASINATELOR POLITICE [The policy of political assassinations]. *Magazin Istoric [Rumania] 1978 12(12): 41-44.* Examines the involvement of Nazi Germany in political assassinations. Pays particular attention to the Nazis' relations with fascist groups in other countries and to their antipathy toward the Rumanian foreign minister Nicolae Titulescu.

208. Pożywiłek, Michał. WSPÓLNIE Z NIEMIECKIMI KOMUNISTAMI [With the German Communists]. *Z Pola Walki [Poland] 1975 18(2): 161-172.* Reminiscences of a Polish Communist (b. 1916), who was captured and then imprisoned in Germany in 1939 and conspired with German Communists during his enforced stay in Germany.

209. Quinnett, Robert L. THE GERMAN ARMY CONFRONTS THE NSFO. *J. of Contemporary Hist. [Great Britain] 1978 13(1): 53-64.* After Stalingrad, Hitler established a new system of political officers, the National Socialist Leadership Officers, who were expected to make Nazi fanatics out of the German soldiers. The High Command of the Armed Forces resisted the program and had no respect for its chief, General Hermann Reinecke. The ensuing infighting and hostile atmosphere sabotaged the program. Based on archival sources; 31 notes.

M. P. Trauth

210. Rabinbach, Anson G. THE AESTHETICS OF PRODUCTION IN THE THIRD REICH. *J. of Contemporary Hist. [Great Britain] 1976 11(4): 43-74.* The attempt to legitimize political rule through aesthetic symbolism is perhaps the decisive characteristic distinguishing 20th-century fascist regimes from other forms of authoritarian domination. Under Nazism, aesthetics and politics were integrated not only in mass festivals and public architecture, but in the sphere of production as well. Both the interior and the exterior of the German industrial plant were to be beautiful, while social harmony and political transformation were to be achieved through "aestheticization of labour relations." In 1937, the Bureau of Beauty of Labor also inaugurated a "Beautiful Village" campaign. The movement eventually included daycare centers, holiday homes, sports and entertainment facilities and "Hot Meals in the Plant." The crowning achievement for Beauty of Labor was to be the *Wunderauto Volkswagen* plant near Fallersleben, envisioned as the heart of a new model city. War halted the project. Primary and secondary sources; 150 notes. M. P. Trauth

211. Rauchensteiner, Manfried. BEMERKUNGEN ZUM KONZEPT EINER GESAMTDARSTELLUNG DES ZWEITEN WELTKRIEGES [Notes on a concept of a comprehensive description of the Second World War]. *Zeitgeschichte [Austria] 1974 2(2): 50-55.* Discusses the attempts by German, American, and British historians to approach a comprehensive history of World War II which can be encompassed within a world-historical theory. Points out the major shortcomings of past attempts and the major problems still to be resolved. Based on secondary works; 42 notes. J. B. Street

212. Rempel, Gerhard. GOTTLOB BERGER AND WAFFEN-SS RECRUITMENT 1939-1945. *Militärgeschichtliche Mitteilungen [West Germany] 1980 (1): 107-122.* Details the efforts of Himmler's military recruiter Gottlob Berger to fashion an independent private army within the Third Reich against bureaucratic opposition of the party, General-SS, and armed forces. Eroding fortunes of war provided the opportunity to gain favorable concessions from Hitler, wresting more control from the competition until almost a million men had been placed under arms. Based on German documents filmed by the National Archives; 78 notes. K. W. Estes

213. Riemenschneider, Rainer. L'ENSEIGNEMENT DE L'HISTOIRE, EN ALLEMAGNE, SOUS LE IIIe REICH [History teaching in Germany under the Third Reich]. *Francia [France] 1979 7: 401-428.* Examines the history textbooks authorized by the Nazis, with excerpts from the works of Dietrich Klagge and Moritz Edelmann, and focuses on major features of the "new" history taught in first through eighth grades. The history textbooks, revised in 1938 by historians close to the government and for material profit, were introduced into classrooms between 1941 and 1945 and propagandized the main tenets of Adolf Hitler's *Mein Kampf*: the continuity of Germany's historical evolution to justify Hitler's regime and interpretation of the heroic past to serve the political ends of the Third Reich. Based mostly on Edelmann's *Volkwerden der Deutschen* (Leipzig: Teubner, 1943), and Klagge's *Volk und Führer* (Frankfurt am Main, 1941); 48 notes, 6 appendixes. G. Herritt

214. Robbins, Michael. THE THIRD REICH AND ITS RAILWAYS. *J. of Transport Hist. [Great Britain] 1979 5(2): 83-90.* Reviews Eugen Kreidler's *Die Eisenbahnen im Machtbereich der Achsenmächte während des Zweiten Weltkrieges,* Studien und Dokumente zur Geschichte des Zweiten Weltkrieges, vol. 15 (Göttingen: Musterschmidt, 1975), and Alfred B. Gottwaldt's *Deutsche Kriegslokomotiven 1939-1945* (Stuttgart: Franckh, 1974). Kreidler considers the development of the German railroads between the wars and the preparations for World War II. Gottwaldt discusses the relationship of the railways to Germany's wartime economy.
E. J. Adams

215. Roberts, Geoffrey. HITLER: THE POLITICAL PERSPECTIVE. *Government and Opposition [Great Britain] 1974 9(4): 510-514.* Reviews Geoffrey Pridham's *Hitler's Rise to Power: the Nazi Movement in Bavaria 1923-33* (New York: Harper & Row, 1973) and Robert Payne's *The Life and Death of Adolf Hitler* (New York: Praeger, 1973), focusing on the need for political scientists to study Hitler as a politician.

216. Rohwer, Jürgen. VORLÄUFIGE BEMERKUNGEN ZUR FRAGE DER SICHERHEIT DER DEUTSCHEN SCHLÜSSELMITTEL [Provisional notes on the security problem of the German code system]. *Marine Rundschau [West Germany] 1975 72(9): 527-533.* Traces the history and development of the modern code system, Enigma, known since 1928 and used by the Germans during World War II. From the autumn of 1941 the Allies were able to decode German submarine messages but fell behind in the spring of 1943 when the German Navy took delivery on the new M-4 code machine. 5 notes.
G. E. Pergl

217. Rossetto, L. SKORZENY'S TESTAMENT. *Army Q. and Defence J. [Great Britain] 1981 111(4): 421-436.* Sketches the military career of Otto Skorzeny, Chief of Germany's Special Troops in World War II, including his rescue of Mussolini, attempted abduction of Tito, and infiltration of Allied forces during the Battle of the Bulge, with special attention to the general strategy behind these missions and how it might be employed by the Warsaw Pact.

218. Rothfeder, Herbert P. AMT SCHRIFTTUMSPFLEGE: A STUDY IN LITERARY CONTROL. *German Studies Rev. 1981 4(1): 63-78.* The Nazi party organization Amt Schrifttumspflege [Office for the Propagation of Literature] was subordinated to Alfred Rosenberg's Beauftragter des Führers für die Überwachung der Gesamten Geistigen und Weltanschaulichen Schulung und Erziehung der NSDAP (BUE). The primary task of the Amt Schrifttumspflege was the promotion of Nazi literature. To this end, it published book reviews of both acceptable and unacceptable books, prepared lists of ideologically approved books, published an index of Jewish authors, and attempted to eliminate unsuitable books from local libraries. 41 notes.
J. T. Walker

219. Ruge, Friedrich. THE PROGRESS OF THE GERMAN OFFICIAL HISTORIES. *Military Affairs 1974 38(4): 151-154.* Lists, with a general introduction, the published and projected studies of the Militärgeshichtliches Forschungsamt [Office of Military Historical Research] of the Federal Republic of Germany. These will cover German military history from 1648 to the present.
K. J. Bauer

220. Rühle, Jürgen. UNSER UMGANG MIT DEM ÜBERLIEFERTEN PROZESSMATERIAL ÜBER DEN 20. JULI 1944. [Coping with materials from the trial of the 20 July 1944 conspirators]. *Geschichte in Wissenshchaft und Unterricht [West Germany] 1980 31(7): 399-402.* The West German Broadcasting Corporation has acquired newly discovered films showing the trials against the unsuccessful conspirators of 1944. They allow the younger generation to understand emotionally and to identify with the situation of the time.
H. W. Wurster

221. Rupp, Leila J. "I DON'T CALL THAT *VOLKSGEMEINSCHAFT*": WOMEN, CLASS, AND WAR IN NAZI GERMANY. Berkin, Carol R. and Lovett, Clara M., ed. *Women, War & Revolution* (New York: Holmes & Meier, 1980): 37-53. Discusses the failure of the Nazis to mobilize women for the war effort into the labor force, focusing on women's responses to mobilization based on class. Nazi propaganda failed to persuade women to work in the spirit of sacrifice; rather, they avoided work because of low wages, poor conditions, and long hours. However, working-class and lower-middle-class women favored conscription in general while middle- and upper-class women opposed it. S

222. Rupp, Leila J. WOMAN'S PLACE IS IN THE WAR: PROPAGANDA AND PUBLIC OPINION IN THE UNITED STATES AND GERMANY, 1939-1945. Berkin, Carol Ruth and Norton, Mary Beth. *Women of America: a History* (Boston: Houghton Mifflin Co., 1979): 342-359. Compares US and German exhortations for women to join in the war effort. Though both societies encouraged women to participate, neither altered traditional concepts of women's roles. The American female labor force increased by 32% during the war, the German only 1%, although many women were mobilized before the war. Both countries took a patriotic approach, particularly seen in the American Office of War Information campaigns. Primary sources; 12 notes.
K. Talley

223. Rupp, Leila J. WOMEN, CLASS AND MOBILIZATION IN NAZI GERMANY. *Sci. and Soc. 1979 43(1): 51-69.* The Nazis did not successfully mobilize middle- and upper-class German women for the war effort. The burden of industrial and other war connected work fell to working-class women. Based on their security service reports, the Nazis realized that a total mobilization of female labor during World War II would be very unpopular among the middle and upper classes. Working-class members bitterly resented the exemption from labor of their middle- and upper-class equivalents as well as the latter's easy evasion of work regulations that were imposed. Based mainly on German language primary sources.
N. Lederer

224. Saint-Jours, Frédéric. CHRONIQUE DU CINEMA: ASPECTS D'UN CINEMA OCCUPÉ (1940-1944) [Chronicle of the cinema: aspects of the cinema during the German occupation, 1940-44]. *Écrits de Paris [France] 1974 (342): 106-112.* Even during World War II, films were produced and seen in both Germany and France which contributed significantly to the art of filmmaking in general.

225. Scheel, Heinrich. DDR—ERFÜLLUNG DES VERMÄCHTNISSES DER KÄMPFER GEGEN FASCHISMUS UND KRIEG [East Germany, fulfillment of the heritage of the fighters against fascism and war]. *Beiträge zur Geschichte der Arbeiterbewegung [East Germany] 1979 21(5): 657-662.* The antifascist resistance struggle of German Communists and Socialists between 1933 and 1945 is an important basis for the ideological and political understanding of the East German state. The ideas of the popular front and proletarian internationalism were tried to the limit under Nazism, but finally emerged victorious. Based on published documents and secondary literature; 5 notes.

R. Wagnleitner

226. Scheel, Klaus. FASCHISTISCHE KULTURPROPAGANDA IM ZWEITEN WELTKRIEG: IHR EINSATZ ZUR IRREFÜHRUNG DES DEUTSCHEN VOLKES WÄHREND DER ERSTEN KRIEGSJAHRE (1939-1941) [Fascist cultural propaganda in World War II: its employment for misleading Germans during the first war years 1939-41]. *Jahrbuch für Volkskunde und Kulturgeschichte [East Germany] 1979 22: 99-119.* Attempts to ascertain the extent to which popular culture in Nazi Germany became a Nazi propaganda tool. The preparations for it were made soon after January 1933 at the Ministry of Enlightenment and Propaganda with cooperation of the Council for the Defense of the Reich. All mass media were subordinated and used to create total obedience for the war efforts. 63 notes.

G. E. Pergl

227. Schnapp, Alain; Vigne, Eric, interviewer. QUAND LES NAZIS SE FAISAIENT ARCHÉOLOGUES: UN ENTRETIEN AVEC ALAIN SCHNAPP [When the Nazis turned archeologists: an interview with Alain Schnapp]. *Histoire [France] 1982 (43): 82-84.* Interviews Schnapp, a researcher at the Institut d'Art et d'Archéologie (University of Paris I), about the Nazi takeover of archaeology in Germany during the 1930's.

228. Schöllgen, Gregor. DAS PROBLEM EINER HITLER-BIOGRAPHIE [The problem of a Hitler biography]. *Neue Pol. Literatur [West Germany] 1978 23(4): 421-434.* Predominantly psychoanalytical explanations of Adolf Hitler's political development cannot explain the social, political, cultural, and economic traditions and tendencies that were reflected in the political actions and decisions of the German Nazi leader.

229. Schreiber, Gerhard. DER MITTELMEERRAUM IN HITLERS STRATEGIE 1940 [The Mediterranean Sea and area in Hitler's strategy, 1940]. *Militärgeschichtliche Mitteilungen [West Germany] 1980 (2): 69-99.* Although Hitler's planning of the war after the fall of France took on a global character and featured far-reaching initiatives and hypothetical campaigns, the fateful decision to settle the issue with the USSR emerged as the decisive program. Advocates of a peripheral strategy concentrating on the Mediterranean to force England out of the war could not offer objectives of a weight competitive with those of the Russian campaign. The Mediterranean strategy developed into a stabilization of Italian operations to secure the southern flank of the Russo-German War. Based on documents in the Military Archives, Freiburg and published sources; 193 notes.

K. W. Estes

230. Schumann, Wolfgang. DIE WIRTSCHAFTSPOLITISCHE ÜBERLEBENSSTRATEGIE DES DEUTSCHEN IMPERIALISMUS IN DER ENDPHASE DES ZWEITEN WELTKRIEGES [The strategy of economic and political survival of German imperialism in the final phase of World War II]. *Zeitschrift für Geschichtswissenschaft [East Germany] 1979 27(6): 499-513.* High functionaries of the SS (Schutzstaffel), the Reich ministries, and industrial monopoly organized committees to prepare for the economic future of postwar Germany. Among these groups were the Planungs-Stab Europa, (later Europa Kreis), formed by the Reich Ministry for Armaments and War Production, and the Arbeitskreis für Aussenwirtschaftsfragen, organized by the Reich Economics Ministry. These groups planned for a postwar European Economic Community and an increase in German exports. Doubts that the alleged Strassburg Secret Conference of 10 August 1944 on postwar planning ever took place. Based on archival sources; 51 notes.   J. T. Walker

231. Schumann, Wolfgang. POLITISCHE ASPEKTE DER NACHKRIEGSPLANUNGEN DES FASCHISTISCHEN DEUTSCHEN IMPERIALISMUS IN DER ENDPHASE DES ZWEITEN WELTKRIEGES [Political aspects of postwar planning by fascist German imperialism in the final phase of World War II]. *Zeitschrift für Geschichtswissenschaft [East Germany] 1979 27(5): 395-408.* German bankers and industrialists, supported by the government and the SS, began as early as 1943 to plan for the transition from fascism to a peacetime imperialist regime. Initially the Europakreis, a committee organized by the Ministry for Armaments and War Production, began such planning, but by late 1944 it was superseded by the Arbeitskreis für Aussenwirtschaftsfragen. Also important was the Reichsgruppe Industrie, which financed the Institut für Industrieforschung in Nuremberg, headed by Ludwig Erhard. Based on archival sources; 45 notes.   J. T. Walker

232. Selzer, Michael. ON NAZIS & NORMALITY. *Psychohistory Rev. 1977 5(4): 34-36.* After reviewing the psychological evidence, the author questions the methodology and the conclusion of Molly Harrower, "Were Hitler's Henchmen Mad?" *Psychology Today* (July 1976). Nazi war criminals were normal individuals.   R. V. Ritter

233. Seydewitz, Ruth and Seydewitz, Max. RĂZBOIUL TABLOURILOR [The art war]. *Magazin Istoric [Romania] 1979 13(1): 57-61, (2): 35-40, (3): 34-37.* Part I. Recounts German seizures of French works of art during the years 1940-44. Part II. The occupation of Holland and western Russia, 1940-45, were the occasion for massive seizures of art collections and libraries. Part III. Italy, though a German ally, lost many art treasures to Germany during World War II. Extracts from the authors' *Die Dame mit dem Hermelin* (Berlin: Henschel, 1963).

234. Shamir, Haim. "ANKLAGE GEGEN DEN VOLKSVERDERBER HITLER": EIN BEITRAG ZUR GESCHICHTE DER OPPOSITION IM DRITTEN REICH (MIT DOKUMENTENANHANG) ["Accusations against the destroyer of the nation": a contribution to the history of the opposition in the Third Reich]. *Jahrbuch des Inst. für Deutsche Geschichte [Israel] 1976 5: 449-466.* Reprints a 1943 handbill attacking Adolf Hitler and his regime and demanding his downfall. The author concludes that it is a remaining sample of

brochures sent out to prepare for the Beck-Goerdeler attempt to assassinate Hitler in 1943. Describes in some detail the last stages of preparation of the plot and its failure. Based on government document preserved in Würzburg; 36 notes.
M. Faissler

235. Sims, Amy R. INTELLECTUALS IN CRISIS: HISTORIANS UNDER HITLER. *Virginia Q. Rev. 1978 54(2): 246-262.* Explains why German university intellectuals, and historians in particular, failed to lead opposition to the Nazis. Historians did not perceive Hitler as a real threat, and their elitist background and nationalistic convictions and loyalties induced inaction. The author analyzes Germany's leading historians with special emphasis on Friedrich Meinecke.
O. H. Zabel

236. Sobczak, Kazimierz et al. DYSKUSJA NAD *ENCYKLOPEDIA II WOJNY SWIATOWEJ* [Discussion of the *Encyclopedia of World War II*]. *Nowe Drogi [Poland] 1976 (9): 159-192.* A group of Polish military historians discuss the *Encyclopedia II Wojny Swiatowej* [Encyclopedia of World War II] (Warsaw: M.O.N., 1975).

237. Spangenberg, Max. ANTIFASCHISTISCHER KAMPF DEUTSCHER KOMMUNISTEN IN DÄNEMARK [The antifascist struggle of German Communists in Denmark]. *Beiträge zur Geschichte der Arbeiterbewegung [East Germany] 1977 19(4): 617-635.* A summary report of the antifascist activities of German emigrant Communists in Denmark, 1933-45. Until the German occupation of Denmark in 1940 the German emigrants tried to coordinate the antifascist efforts throughout northern Germany. During the occupation German Communists worked with other German emigrants and antifascist Danes, aiming especially at winning over German soldiers of occupation. Describes the underground publications and organizations of the Communist-led resistance in Denmark. Based on the author's recollections, documents in the archives of the Institute for Marxism-Leninism, Berlin, and secondary works; 15 notes.
J. B. Street

238. Spivey, Delmar T. and Durad, Arthur A. SECRET MISSION TO BERLIN. *Air Force Mag. 1975 58(9): 115-120.* Recounts the secret mission of two American prisoners of war, who were sent by their German captors to Berlin in a secret conspiracy to overthrow Adolf Hitler and end the war in the West.

239. Stam, A. HITLER ALS PATIENT [Hitler as patient]. *Spiegel Historiael [Netherlands] 1973 8(2): 88-95.* Reviews various interpretations of Adolf Hitler's death. Hitler suffered from Parkinson's disease and, as a child, probably had encephalitis. The dictator suffered from some kind of neurosis, and one source concludes that Hitler was sado-masochistic. The SS doctor Röhr contends that Hitler was poisoned by Dr. Morell who administered overdoses of the wrong medication. Biblio.
G. D. Homan

240. Stang, Werner. ORGANE UND MITTEL DER MILITÄRISCHEN FÜHRUNG DES FASCHISTISCHEN DEUTSCHLANDS ZUR MEINUNGSMANIPULIERUNG BESONDERS DER SOLDATEN DES HEERES 1939-1943 [Organs and means of fascist Germany's military command in manipulating opinion, particularly of the soldiers of the army, 1939-43]. *Militärgeschichte [East Germany] 1980 19(1): 53-66.* Although supported by the Propa-

ganda Ministry and the Nazi Party, political and ideological influence on soldiers was the responsibility of the Wehrmacht, specifically superior officers of a unit. Certain army units supervised internal propaganda as well as the means—civilian newspapers and magazines, field editions of books, radios and radio programs, troop information publications, instruction manuals for officers, illustrated army magazines and journals, and finally the *National Socialist Guidance Officer*—by which propaganda was disseminated. The effort was successful, for the troops continued to fight despite clear signs of impending military defeat. Central State Archives, Potsdam; Military Archives of the German Democratic Republic; 3 charts, 42 notes. H. D. Andrews

241. Stang, Werner. ZAHLENMATERIAL ZUR MATERIELLEN LAGE DER FASCHISTISCHEN WEHRMACHT IM ZWEITEN WELTKRIEG [Statistics on the fascist army's materiel in World War II]. *Militärgeschichte [East Germany] 1975 14(1): 61-80.* Statistics on German army materiel and technical equipment, including ammunition, cars, losses of ships and airplanes, and the use of gasoline between 1941 and 1945.

242. Stegemann, Bernd. HITLERS ZIELE IM ERSTEN KRIEGSJAHR 1939/40: EIN BEITRAG ZUR QUELLENKRITIK [Hitler's aims in the first year of the war, 1939-40: a critical study of the sources]. *Militärgeschichtliche Mitteilungen [West Germany] 1980 (1): 73-105.* Reviews Hitler's war aims at various points of the early Blitzkrieg period. Options of collaboration with Russia or Great Britain against the other were entertained before the final attack against the USSR. The historical consensus of expansion by stages is sound, although Hitler never assumed any rigidity in program. Based upon published documents and monographs; 65 notes. K. W. Estes

243. Steinert, Marlis G. L'ÉVOLUTION DES IMAGES NATIONALES EN ALLEMAGNE PENDANT LA DEUXIÈME GUERRE MONDIALE [The evolution of national images in Germany during World War II]. *Relations Int. [France] 1974 (2): 213-232.* After defining the image of a people and explaining the factors which condition such an image, analyzes the respective German masses' and Adolf Hitler's images of other nations during World War II. Examines the evolution of German public opinion of their enemies and their allies. Even after consideration of Nazi propaganda, the author reveals a remarkable agreement between Hitler and the German public. 52 notes. G. P. Cleyet

244. Stephenson, Jill. MIDDLE-CLASS WOMEN AND NATIONAL SOCIALIST "SERVICE." *History [Great Britain] 1982 67(219): 32-44.* The German Nazi Party's efforts to enlist middle-class women in national service met with only slight success. Service schemes remained only piecemeal, centering on the NS-Frauenschaft (National Socialist Women's Groups) and the subordinate German Women's Enterprise (DFW). NSF remained an organization of clerical workers, school teachers, and civil servant's wives, few of whom were active members. DFW held no mass appeal for working-class women and even fell out of favor with the middle class when its work was reoriented to meet the demands of the regime rather than its members. Based largely on Nazi party and government archives and correspondence and on contemporary publications; 87 notes.
R. P. Sindermann, Jr.

245. Stephenson, Jill. REICHSBUND DER KINDERREICHEN: THE LEAGUE OF LARGE FAMILIES IN THE POPULATION POLICY OF NAZI GERMANY. *European Studies Rev. [Great Britain] 1979 9(3): 350-375.* The Reichsbund der Kinderreichen, formed in Germany in 1920, was not a Nazi invention, but a product of various pro-natalist groups. Only in 1935 when the Nazi Party took it over, did it perform a specific role in Nazi policy and propaganda, emphasizing racial and political purity, rather than size. With the outbreak of war a higher birth rate was more essential, but the impact of the association was weakened by the lack of sufficient financial incentives offered, in terms of child allowances and tax reliefs. Based on various German archival materials and secondary sources; 110 notes. E. J. Adams

246. Stich, Karl. DIE BALLISTISCHE RAKETE A4 (V2)—ENTWICKLUNG UND EINSATZ [The ballistic rocket A4 (V2): development and operation]. *Militärgeschichte [East Germany] 1980 19(2): 210-217.* Describes the development and operation of one of the "wonder weapons" of fascist Germany with which a turning point in the course of the war was supposed to be brought about. Describes the construction, testing, composition, and military operation of this first ballistic rocket and shows the limits of its effectiveness. Provides numerous technical details as well as precise data on the number of A4's manufactured, rockets launched, and targets struck. 3 photos, map, 3 tables, 27 notes.
J/T (H. D. Andrews)

247. Šuica, Nada. KLIZO LANOV—LISTOVI IZ ZAROBLJENIŠTVA [Cluseau Lanauve: the graphic art works from prisoner of war camps]. *Vesnik Vojnog Muzeja-Beograd [Yugoslavia] 1976 (21-22): 105-118.* The French graphic artist and painter Cluseau Lanauve was a prisoner of war in Stalag XII and in Limburg in Westerwald from July 1941 to October 1942. Here he witnessed the arrival of Yugoslav prisoners of war who were incarcerated near the French and Belgian prisoners who gave them help and shared their food and cigarettes. Cluseau recorded camp life in pen, India ink, water color, and tempera. The Military Museum Art Collection owns 19 figural pieces and one copper etching which are of incomparable value as documents as well as for their figural character. 6 illus., 6 notes. A. C. Niven

248. Sydnor, Charles W., Jr. LA DIVISION S.S. "TOTENKOPF" [The SS Death's Head division]. *Rev. d'Hist. de la Deuxième Guerre Mondiale [France] 1975 98: 57-76.* The elite "Totenkopf" (Death's Head) division of the Nazi *Waffen-SS* was formed in 1939 at Dachau by Theodor Eicke. Except for participation in the 1940 invasion in France, the elite division saw military service only on the eastern front. There it distinguished itself for cruelty and fanatic adherence to Hitler's "no retreat" policy. It was the most formidable example of the Nazi military ideal. 56 notes. G. H. Davis

249. Takashi, Saito. LA FIN DE LA DEUXIÈME GUERRE MONDIALE DANS LES PUISSANCES DE L'AXE: ESSAI DE THÉORIE COMPARATIVE [The Axis powers and the end of World War II: a comparative theoretical essay]. *Rev. d'Hist. de la Deuxième Guerre Mondiale [France] 1973 23(89): 79-88.* Comparisons of the events leading to the defeat of Japan, Italy, and Germany provide significant insights into the postwar history of each country. Benito Mussolini was overthrown by a courtly uprising by the fascist leadership.

Germany called for peace after the effective destruction of the state, when no bargaining was possible. The futile uprising against Adolf Hitler, in June 1944, was designed to negotiate with the West to avoid Soviet invasion and the destruction of capitalism. Japan had no domestic opposition to the war and peace was recommended by imperial councillors to avoid the destruction of the imperial system. The United States used the atomic bomb and compromised with the imperial system in order to conclude the war before the USSR could become involved. In the case of Italy, no strife developed between the western Allies and the USSR although Hitler hoped for such a rupture until the end.

G. H. Davis

250. Teppe, Karl. ZUR SOZIALPOLITIK DES DRITTEN REICHES AM BEISPIEL DER SOZIALVERSICHERUNG [Social insurance: an instance of social policy in the Third Reich]. *Archiv für Sozialgeschichte [West Germany] 1977 17: 195-250.* Analyzes the social security system and how the Nazis used it. The Ministry of Labor reorganized social security after its near-collapse during the Depression. The Deutsche Arbeitsfront (DAF) sought a new system under its control, and in the subsequent quarrel with the Ministry of Labor the DAF increased its influence, and social security services deteriorated. Its capital was used to finance armament and war and was exhausted by 1945. The Nazis used social security for the discipline of workers and the exploitation of their labor. Based on the Federal Archive Koblenz, social security archives in Frankfurt and Berlin, and secondary works; 4 tables, 261 notes. H. W. Wurster

251. Thälmann, Ernst; Stanca, Horia, transl. RĂSPUNS LA SCRISORILE UNUI TOVARĂŞ DE ÎNCHISOARE [Reply to an imprisoned comrade's letters]. *Magazin Istoric [Romania] 1979 13(10): 49-52.* Romanian translation of a letter secretly written to a fellow prisoner in early 1944 by the German Communist Ernst Thälmann, who was afterwards executed by the Nazis.

252. Tiefel, Hans. USE AND MISUSE OF LUTHER DURING THE GERMAN CHURCH STRUGGLE. *Lutheran Q. 1973 25(4): 395-411.* Evaluates the interpretations of Luther and his doctrines by the German Christians who supported Hitler's National Socialism as an extension of Lutheran ideology, and by their opposition, represented by Asmussen, Iwand, and Bonhoeffer, who saw the Nazi movement as a destructive ideology. S

253. Tilford, Earl H., Jr. SEENOTDIENST: EARLY DEVELOPMENT OF AIR-SEA RESCUE. *Air U. Rev. 1977 28(2): 36-53.* Discusses the early development of air-sea rescue operations, emphasizing the role of *Seenotdienst,* the German air-sea rescue operations of World War II. Although some air-sea rescue efforts were made during World War I, it was the organization of the German air force in the period 1937-41 that marked the beginning of modern air-sea rescue techniques. The equipment, major developments, and successes and failures of the *Seenotdienst* are also discussed. Based on published sources; 24 illus., 55 notes.

J. W. Thacker, Jr.

254. Timokhovich, I. KHARAKTER I SPOSOBY BOR'BY ZA GOSPODSTVO V VOZDUKHE [The character and means of the struggle for air superiority]. *Voenno-Istoricheskii Zhurnal [USSR] 1980 22(7): 26-34.* Its World War I role was minor, but aviation in World War II had strategic significance,

becoming not only a matter of destroying enemy aircraft but also involving attacks on industry, fuel supplies, etc. Analysis of several World War II operations shows the importance of air superiority. The Germans were vulnerable because they imported much of their oil from Romania, but the US and Great Britain withheld their attacks to avoid any premature weakening of German forces in Russia. Soviet attacks on Ploeşti and Romania's withdrawal from the war finally had an effect. Today air superiority requires complex means and careful analysis of the enemy. Based on Soviet archival and published materials, including translations of works by Western military analysts such as Liddell-Hart; 21 notes.

P. R. Taylor

255. Todd, Douglas. SYNTHETIC RUBBER IN THE GERMAN WAR ECONOMY: A CASE OF ECONOMIC DEPENDENCE. *J. of European Econ. Hist. [Italy] 1981 10(1): 153-165.* Germany developed a synthetic rubber industry in the 1930's because of the experience of World War I. In 1938 an order was issued requiring all bicycle tires to be made of synthetics. While synthetic rubber was never price or quality competitive with the natural product, the German war machine functioned primarily on synthetic rubber. Thus German foresight in developing and protecting the infant synthetic rubber industry during peacetime served the country well during the war. 6 tables, 29 notes.

D. S. Rockwood

256. Tracey, Donald R. THE DEVELOPMENT OF THE NATIONAL SOCIALIST PARTY IN THURINGIA, 1924-30. *Central European Hist. 1975 8(1): 23-50.* Presents the development of the Nazi party in Thuringia as a model for understanding its development in Germany as a whole. The party strife, the early, amateurish Nazi efforts, the coalition with *völkisch* elements, and the maturing, parliamentary phase are all described in detail. The first coalition government which included Nazis was in Thuringia. Based largely on unpublished German sources; 140 notes.

C. R. Lovin

257. Unger, Manfred. DOKUMENTE EINES ANTIFASCHISTEN [Documents of an antifascist]. *Archivmitteilungen [East Germany] 1977 27(6): 205-207.* Describes the document collection of Georg Sacke, now held in the Leipzig State Archive. Sacke, an antifascist, was engaged in Communist Party resistance work in the Hamburg shipyards, 1942-44; he was murdered by the SS in 1945.

258. Voitsekhovski, Marian. KONSERVATIVNAIA OPPOZITSIIA V GITLEROVSKOI GERMANII I POL'SHE (1933-1944) [The conservative opposition in Hitler's Germany and in Poland, 1933-44]. *Sovetskoe Slavianovedenie [USSR] 1978 (3): 23-28.* Adolf Hitler preserved the Weimar state and military apparatus and its personnel virtually intact, and hence the conservative opposition came mainly from within their ranks. Examples are Ulrich von Hassell and Carl Goerdeler. Their programs for a post-Nazi Germany, worked out in 1940-43, are characterized by a wish to preserve German hegemony in Europe, probably in conjunction with Britain. Their attitude to the problem of Poland, envisaged as a bulwark against Communist Russia, and subordinated to German domination, indicates their failure to appreciate the new realities in Europe. 19 notes.

A. Herford

259. Volkmann, Hans-Erich. ZUR ANSIEDLUNG DER DEUTSCH-BALTEN IM "WARTHEGAU" [On the settlement of the Baltic Germans in the Warta region]. *Zeits. für Ostforschung [West Germany] 1981 30(4): 527-558.* The settlement of the German-Balts in the Warta River region during World War II offers the last possibility to study a relatively closed national minority as a group before its reassimilation in Germany and the Eastern annexation policy of the Third Reich. The material circumstances of the evacuees and the ideological conditions that the Third Reich desired in the Warthegau have to be taken into account. The new territory was supposed to become a granary important for the supply of Germany. Moreover, because of the National Socialist racial theory, the people settled here were supposed to form a human boundary against the Slavic peoples and at the same time to become a germ cell of the blood renewal of the German people. The annexed territory was supposed to be an experimental field, where Germany intended to perform a systematic alteration in all spheres of life according to National Socialist conceptions of nationality and spatial arrangement, in order to avoid rural exodus and the negative results of urbanization.
J/S

260. Volkov, N. IDEOLOGICHESKAIA OBRABOTKA DOPRIZYVNOI MOLODEZHI I VOENNOSLUZHASHCHIKH V TRET'EM REIKHE I FRG [Political education of preconscription youth and soldiers in the Third Reich and West Germany]. *Voenno-Istoricheskii Zhurnal [USSR] 1978 (7): 72-77.* Establishes a link between Nazi propaganda and West Germany's program of military indoctrination, the connection being anticommunism and anti-Sovietism. Right-wing forces such as the Christian Democrats, led by F. Strauss, and neo-fascist groups are important in German politics and a number of leading figures in the West German media spent their formative years working for Joseph Goebbels. 22 notes.
V. Sobeslavsky

261. Vosske, Heinz and Nitzsche, Gerhard. STRANITSY ZHIZNI I BOR'BY VIL'GEL'MA PIKA (1939-1945 GG.) [The life and struggle of Wilhelm Pieck, 1939-45]. *Novaia i Noveishaia Istoriia [USSR] 1978 (1): 79-97.* Elaborates on the political fight of Wilhelm Pieck while living in exile in the USSR during World War II to strengthen the Comintern and regenerate the Communist Party of Germany. He set up a German radio station in exile, which appealed to all antifascist factions in Germany to sabotage Hitler's war effort. In collaboration with the Central Committee of the Communist Party of the USSR, he organized the National Committee "Free Germany" in July 1943. In August 1944, German Field Marshal Friedrich von Paulus, then a prisoner of war after his 1943 defeat at Stalingrad, joined the committee. Pieck returned to Berlin in June 1945 after Germany's liberation. 42 notes.
N. Frenkley

262. Waite, Robert G. L. INTERDISCIPLINARY APPROACHES TO THE STUDY OF MODERN GERMANY: PSYCHOANALYSIS AND THE STUDY OF HITLER. *Europa [Canada] 1981 4(1): 133-138.*

263. Waite, Robert G. L. REVIEW. *Central European Hist. 1974 7(1): 90-94.* Werner Maser's *Adolf Hitler. Legende—Mythes—Wirklichkeit* (Munich: Bechtle Verlag, 1972) is more a collection of unusual facts than a biography. His second work, *Hitlers Briefe und Notizen. Sein Weltbild in Handschriftlichen Dokumenten* (Düsseldorf: Econ Verlag, 1973) has little source material that is new. Specialists will find some interesting tidbits in these works.
C. R. Lovin

264. Wall, Donald D. THE CONFESSING CHURCH AND THE SECOND WORLD WAR. *J. of Church and State 1981 23(1): 15-34.* Discusses the relationship between the Confessing Church pastors and Nazism—cooperation to 1939, resistance after that. Emphasizes their refusal to support war before 1939. Political necessity led them to do so after that but to interpret their support as Christian witness. Describes the guilt felt within the church following the war's end. Based on material in the Berlin archives and some printed materials; 77 notes. E. E. Eminhizer

265. Wegner, Bernd. AUF DEM WEG ZUR PANGERMANISCHEN ARMEE: DOKUMENTE ZUR ENTSTEHUNGSGESCHICHTE DES III. ("GERMANISCHEN") SS-PANZERKORPS [The road to the pan-German army: documents on the history of the origins of the 3d ("Germanic") SS Panzer Corps]. *Militärgeschichtliche Mitteilungen [West Germany] 1980 (2): 101-136.* The formation of foreign legions and multinational military units in the Waffen-SS circumvented the armed forces conscription limitations on the size of Himmler's army. The concept of forging large-scale formations from this collection of units originated among the administrators and field commanders of these units. Ultimately, the separatist national feelings and German errors in recruiting and training limited their potential. Based on documents in the National Archives, Berlin Document Center, and Military Archives, Freiburg; 14 documents, 172 notes. K. W. Estes

266. Wegner-Korfes, Sigrid. DER 20. JULI 1944 UND DAS NATIONALKOMITEE "FREIES DEUTSCHLAND": AUS PERSÖNLICHEN UNTERLAGEN DER FAMILIE VON OBERST RITTER ALBRECHT MERTZ VON QUIRNHEIM [20 July 1944 and the National Committee "Free Germany": from the private family papers of Colonel Albrecht Mertz von Quirnheim]. *Zeitschrift für Geschichtswissenschaft [East Germany] 1979 27(6): 535-544.* On 20 July 1944 Colonel Albrecht Mertz von Quirnheim and his long-time friend Count Claus von Stauffenberg were executed for their part in the Officers' Plot against Hitler. Mertz von Quirnheim's brother-in-law Otto Korfes was a member of the National Committee "Free Germany" (NKFD) in Russia. Although Mertz von Quirnheim had been unable to contact the NKFD, the Officers' Plot strengthened the resolve of that organization to create a new Germany. Based on archival documents; 42 notes. J. T. Walker

267. Weinberg, Gerhard L. ZUR DOTATION HITLERS AN GENERALFELDMARSCHALL RITTER VON LEEB [On Hitler's endowment to Field Marshal Ritter von Leeb]. *Militärgeschichtliche Mitteilungen [West Germany] 1979 (2): 97-99.* Documents the efforts of Field Marshal Wilhelm von Leeb (1876-1956) upon retirement using his 250,000-Reichsmark gift from Adolf Hitler. Additional aid from Hitler and Finance Minister Hans Lammers proved necessary to secure suitable land, and additional funds totaled 888,000 Reichsmarks. Based upon Leeb papers published by the Military History Research Office, Freiburg; 21 notes. K. W. Estes

268. Weissbecker, Manfred. SIE KÄMPFTEN UND STARBEN, ABER SIE WERDEN NIEMALS VERGESSEN SEIN. (GEDANKEN ZUM 30. JAHRESTAG DER ERMORDUNG VON HANS UND SOPHIE SCHOLL AM 22. FEBRUAR 1943) [They fought and died, but they will never be

forgotten. (Thoughts on the 30th anniversary of the murder of Hans and Sophie Scholl on 22 February 1943)]. *Jenaer Beiträge zur Parteiengeschichte [East Germany] 1974 (36): 4-27.* Commemorates the lives of Hans and Sophie Scholl, executed by Hitler in 1943. The growing horrors of Nazism and the teachings of Kurt Huber in Munich forced Hans Scholl and his circle into active resistance, which they expressed in a series of pamphlets. Hans Scholl is honored in East Germany for believing that German power politics must give way to a new social order in which the workers have the right to the fruits of their labor. Published by the historical section of the Friedrich-Schiller University (Jena); 25 notes.

M. Faissler

269. Weissbecker, Manfred and Gottwald, Herbert. ZUR ROLLE DER FÜHRER BÜRGERLICHER PARTEIEN: BIOGRAPHISCHE ASPEKTE IN DER GESCHICHTE DER POLITISCHEN PARTEIEN DES DEUTSCHEN IMPERIALISMUS VON DER JAHRHUNDERT-WENDE BIS 1945 [The role of bourgeois party leaders: biographical aspects of the history of German imperialist political parties from the turn of the century until 1945]. *Zeitschrift für Geschichtswissenschaft [East Germany] 1979 27(4): 299-315.* Presents several hypotheses concerning bourgeois party leaders, a topic which has hitherto been neglected in Marxist historiography. These leaders had freedom of action only within their own economic, political, social, and ideological milieu. Successful leaders have had the following characteristics: deep insights into the interests of the ruling class, and a mastery of the tactics needed in the class struggle; ability to exploit the weaknesses of their class opponents; and skill in manipulating the masses. 83 notes.

J. T. Walker

270. Weisstein, Ulrich. LE TERME ET LE CONCEPT D'AVANT-GARDE EN ALLEMAGNE [The term and concept of avant-garde in Germany]. *Rev. de l'U. de Bruxelles [Belgium] 1975 (1): 10-37.* Although the term "avant-garde" was used for literary and artistic descriptions in France, Italy, and England early in the 20th century, in Germany the term did not become common until the 1930's. This is because the Germanic movement of Expressionism was not conceived as a unified movement at first, nor did it see itself making a distinct break with the past. The Expressionists felt themselves part of an international movement rather than isolated, and in Germany the avant-garde in art and politics were distinct. After 1940, when the term was used in Germany, it has become a term of derision and criticism associated with bourgeois decadence and materialism. 77 notes.

J. Buschen

271. Wilhelm, Hans-Heinrich. DER SD UND DIE KIRCHEN IN DEN BESETZTEN OSTGEBIETEN 1941/42. [The *Sicherheitsdienst* (SD) and the churches in the occupied eastern territories, 1941-42]. *Militärgeschichtliche Mitteilungen [West Germany] 1981 (1): 55-99.* The expectations for a short war against the USSR in 1941 influenced the initial draconian approach of the SD, involving strict supervision and infiltration of all religious activity to prevent wider organization of church groups and to ferret out Bolshevik sympathizers. A toleration policy followed in 1942 in the face of the strength of religious activity, but the SD still handled the groups as political splinter groups, with few positive accomplishments or preventive successes. Based on documents in the Military Archives, Freiburg; 73 notes.

K. W. Estes

272. Wilhelmus, Wolfgang. VORBEREITUNGEN DER FACHISTISCHEN WEHRMACHT ZUR BESETZUNG SCHWEDENS [Preparations by the fascist army to occupy Sweden]. *Zeitschrift für Geschichtswissenschaft [East Germany] 1975 23(9): 1032-1040.* In December 1942, the German High Command, motivated by fear of an Allied invasion of Scandinavia and increasing Swedish reluctance to cooperate with Germany, ordered the Chief of the General Staff of the Army in Norway, General Rudolf Bamler, to draw up plans for the invasion of Sweden. However, the plans produced by Bamler's staff were never used, chiefly because of German defeats in Russia and other military setbacks. 50 notes. J. T. Walker

273. Willig, Kenneth C. H. THE BAR IN THE THIRD REICH. *Am. J. of Legal Hist. 1976 20(1): 1-14.* Discusses the gradual elimination of the lawyers' role in Germany, 1933-45, and of the confrontation between the German Bar association and Nazism. The modern German Bar, created in 1878, was not only a professional organization, but also the central element in the traditional German power structure. The once prosperous members of the Bar, suffering from social and economic dislocation by 1933, proved susceptible to the Nazi movement. By 1943 the Bar had become extinct as an organization composed of "servants of justice"; instead, its remaining members had become simply servants of the state. Based on government documents and reports; 68 notes.
L. A. Knafla

274. Winkler, Dörte. FRAUENARBEIT VERSUS FRAUENIDEOLOGIE. PROBLEME DER WEIBLICHEN ERWERBSTÄTIGKEIT IN DEUTSCHLAND 1930-1945 [Working women vs. the image of woman: the problems of women at work in Germany, 1930-45]. *Archiv für Sozialgeschichte [West Germany] 1977 17: 99-126.* Analyzes the development of a female labor force and party policy in the Third Reich. After the Great War, many women worked, most at unskilled, poorly paid jobs. The government tried to reduce their numbers after 1929. The Nazis saw women primarily as mothers and opposed their working. When war came, half-hearted labor programs affected lower-class women only. This angered many working women, and production declined. Despite several campaigns, millions of able women from the middle and upper classes never worked. Based on the state archives in Freiburg and Koblenz, and other primary and secondary works; 3 tables, 119 notes, appendix. H. W. Wurster

275. Witthöft, Hans Jürgen. SCHIFFBAU IN RAHMEN DES HANSABAUPROGRAMM [Shipbuilding in the Hansa construction program]. *Marine Rundschau [West Germany] 1973 70(8): 462-482.* The history of the German merchant fleet during World War II, especially the system of construction in the Hansa company since 1942. G. E. Pergl

276. Woche, Klaus. DIE SOLDATEN DER FELDHERRNHALLE [The soldiers of the Feldherrnhalle regiment]. *Zeitschrift für Heereskunde [West Germany] 1977 41(272-273): 98-103.* Recalls the contributions of members of the SA (Sturmabteilung) regiment Feldherrnhalle to the Wehrmacht's war effort during World War II.

277. Zumpe, Lotte. ZWEI AUTOBIOGRAPHIEN UND IHR AUSSAGEWERT FÜR DIE ERFORSCHUNG DES DEUTSCHEN FASCHISMUS: UNTER BESONDERER BERÜCKSICHTIGUNG STAATSMONOPOLISTISCHER ASPEKTE [Two autobiographies and their testimonial value for research on German fascism: with special regard for state monopoly aspects]. *Jahrbuch für Wirtschaftsgeschichte [East Germany] 1979 (3): 137-153.* Review article on the memoirs of Count Lutz Schwerin von Krosigk, German finance minister, 1932-45, and Hans Kehrl, a top crisis manager for the Nazis. Both were sentenced at the Nuremberg Trials, Krosigk to 10 years, Kehrl to 15, and freed by an American gesture of mercy in 1951. 40 notes.
G. E. Pergl

278. —. [THE AFTERMATH OF ANSCHLUSS]. *Austrian Hist. Y. 1978 14: 129-186.*
Williams, Maurice. THE AFTERMATH OF *ANSCHLUSS:* DISILLUSIONED GERMANS OR BUDDING AUSTRIAN PATRIOTS?, *pp. 129-144.* Analyzes the effect of the Anschluss on Austria, 1938-39. By the end of 1938, all segments of the population had become disillusioned with German rule, and their dissatisfaction was reflected in vocal complaints and outright resistance and sabotage. Thus, a spirit of Austrian nationalism was engendered. 41 notes.
Bernbaum, John A. THE NEW ELITE: NAZI LEADERSHIP IN AUSTRIA, 1938-45, *pp. 145-160.* Examines the leadership of Austria, 1938-45, and attempts to determine what part of the leadership was Austrian and what part German. Austrians dominated the municipal and provincial levels of government, and were used extensively in other Nazi-occupied areas. 48 notes, appendix.
Burian, Peter. COMMENTS, *pp. 159-160.* Criticizes Williams for his neglect of some of the economic factors contributing to resistance. Agrees with most of Bernbaum's major ideas.
Steiner, Herbert. COMMENTS, *pp. 161-163.* Agrees with the major conclusions of both articles.
Hanisch, Ernst. COMMENTS, *pp. 164-166.* Criticizes the weakness of Williams's source which allow him to "make generalizations that can hardly be supported." 3 notes.
Botz, Gerhard. COMMENTS, *pp. 167-182.* Adds factual material to both articles, but does not disagree with their conclusions. 43 notes.
Williams, Maurice and Bernbaum, John. A REPLY, *pp. 183-186.* The authors defend their articles.
J. W. Thacker, Jr./S

279. —. BIBLIOGRAFIJA STRANE ISTORIOGRAFIJE O DRUGOM SVETSKOM RATU (1971-1974) [Bibliography of foreign historiography on World War II, 1971-74]. *Vojnoistorijski Glasnik [Yugoslavia] 1980 31(1): 322-330.* Lists foreign books on the history of World War II published 1971-74, by author, letters L-N.
J. Bamber

280. —. NAZIS VERSUS NATIONALISTS. *Patterns of Prejudice [Great Britain] 1978 12(2): 5-8.* Although anti-Semitic and nationalistic, Germany's National People's Party supported a return to monarchy and resisted association with the Nazis, 1925-44.

2

WARTIME TRADE AND DIPLOMACY

281. Bezymenski, L. A. TAINAIA DIPLOMATIIA PRINTSA GO-GENLOE (IZ ISTORII ZAKULISNYKH PEREGOVOROV MEZHDU GIT-LEROVSKOI GERMANIEI I ZAPADNYMI DERZHAVAMI) [Prince Hohenlohe's secret diplomacy: secret negotiations between Hitler's Germany and the Western powers]. *Novaia i Noveishaia Istoriia [USSR] 1980 (1): 123-138, (2): 136-150.* Part I. The anticommunist nature of international power politics is shown by the secret negotiations carried on both before and during World War II by representatives of the United States and Hitler's Germany. Details meetings between Allen Dulles and Prince Maximilian Hohenlohe-Langenburg. The latter had already figured in prewar talks with Great Britain in 1938, and was in close contact with important American businessmen. He was also involved in the Vatican's machinations with Hitler. Part II. Discusses secret talks in Switzerland between the emissaries of Hitler's Germany and the United States at the beginning of 1943. In particular, meetings between Allen Dulles and Prince Hohenlohe. Examines questions touched on during their meetings. The archives of Prince Hohenlohe include various notes and drafts of conversations during the meetings, which extended from 1939 to 1944. Based on the Hohenlohe papers, archives in London and Prague, and documents in German, Russian, and English; 107 notes. D. N. Collins/S. R. Gudgin

282. Botz, Gerhard. WIEN UND OSTEUROPA NACH DEM AN-SCHLUSS. DIE ROLLE DES WIENER BÜRGERMEISTERS IN DER NATIONALSOZIALISTISCHEN AUSSENPOLITIK DES JAHRES 1938 [Vienna and Eastern Europe after the Anschluss. The role of the mayor of Vienna in National Socialist foreign policy in 1938]. *Österreichische Osthefte [Austria] 1974 16(2): 113-122.* During 1938-40 the national socialist mayor of Vienna, Hermann Neubacher, maintained friendly contacts with British politicians and industrialists. Although Neubacher fully supported the aims of Nazism, he did not accept all of its methods. Neubacher and his friends tried to mediate in Great Britain during the Sudeten crisis. Based on documents in Austrian and German archives, printed documents, secondary literature and newspapers; 32 notes.
R. Wagnleitner

283. Boyd, Carl. THE BERLIN-TOKYO AXIS AND JAPANESE MILITARY INITIATIVE. *Modern Asian Studies [Great Britain] 1981 15(2): 311-338.* The creation of a Berlin-Tokyo political and military axis between 1934 and 1940 owed much to the initiatives of Oshima Hiroshi. As military attaché in

Berlin he was instrumental in the making of the Anti-Comintern Pact of 1936, and after 1938, as ambassador, he had the support of the military and pro-Axis Japanese in aligning Japan with Germany and Italy, despite the misgivings of some elements in the Japanese government. He both represented and expressed military and totalitarian tendencies in Japanese society, helping them to reach dominance in Japan by 1940. Based on naval records in the National Archives, Washington, D.C., the International Military Tribunal for the Far East, and secondary sources; 71 notes. D. J. Nicholls

284. Breccia, Alfredo. LE POTENZE DELL'ASSE E LA NEUTRALITÀ DELLA JUGOSLAVIA ALLA VIGILIA DELLA SECONDA GUERRA MONDIALE (FEBBRAIO-SETTEMBRE 1939) [The Axis powers and the neutrality of Yugoslavia on the eve of World War II, February-September 1939]. *Riv. di Studi Politici Int. [Italy] 1974 41(2): 225-251.* Discusses relations between Yugoslavia and the Axis Powers in 1939, a formative period for Yugoslavia's ultimate role in World War II.

285. Brügel, Johann Wolfgang. DAHLERUS ALS ZWISCHENTRÄGER NACH KRIEGSAUSBRUCH [Dahlerus as middleman after the outbreak of war]. *Hist. Zeitschrift [West Germany] 1979 228(1): 70-97.* The Swedish engineer Jean Birger Essen Dahlerus (1891-1957) wrote in 1945 of his role as a personal messenger between British authorities and Hermann Goering immediately before the outbreak of World War II. This article shows he continued this activity after the outbreak of war in the hope that Goering might influence Hitler to accept a peaceful arrangement with Great Britain. Dahlerus was not taken seriously in the British Foreign Office after he made some unrealistic suggestions. However, the British did not break off the exchanges through Dahlerus until December 1939, which must have influenced Hitler's thinking. 49 notes. G. H. Davis

286. Ceva, Lucio. L'INCONTRO KEITEL-BADOGLIO DEL NOVEMBRE 1940 NELLE CARTE DEL GENERALE MARRAS [The Keitel-Badoglio meetings in November 1940 in the letters of General Marras]. *Risorgimento [Italy] 1977 29(1-2): 1-45.* General Luigi Marras, who was military attaché to Marshal Pietro Badoglio, 1928-33, and representative of the Italian military in Germany, 1936-43, has donated his archives pertaining to the period to the Ufficio Storico of the Stato Maggiore. This article contains the memorandum of meetings held between Badoglio and Marshal Wilhelm Keitel in Innsbruck, 14-15 November 1940. E. J. Craver

287. Choldkovskij, Victor M. DIE POLITIK HITLERDEUTSCHLANDS GEGENÜBER FINNLAND AM VORABEND UND WÄHREND DES ZWEITEN WELTKRIEGES [The policies of Hitler's Germany toward Finland on the eve of, and during, World War II]. *Nordeuropa [East Germany] 1976 9: 47-64.* Analyzes the many changes of Hitler's policy toward Finland, with reference to the non-aggression pact between Germany and Russia. Hitler subsequently requested Finland's help, but later betrayed his ally.

288. Ciuikov, V. I. BERLIN, 1 MAI 1945. GENERALUL KREBS ÎNCEARCĂ SĂ CÎȘTIGE TIMP [Berlin, 1 May 1945. General Krebs tries to gain time]. *Magazin Istoric [Rumania] 1975 9(4): 15-18, 32.* Describes negotiation attempts by German General Hans Krebs during General Vasili Chuikov's assault on Berlin. 4 notes.

289. Constantiniu, Florin. ASPECTE ALE CRIZEI REGIMULUI ANTONESCIAN ÎN AJUNUL INSURECȚIEI NAȚIONALE ARMATE ANTIFASCISTE ȘI ANTIIMPERIALISTE [Aspects of the crisis facing the Antonescu regime on the eve of the armed national antifascist and antiimperialist insurrection]. *Rev. de Istorie [Romania] 1979 32(7): 1305-1313.* Analyzes the crisis of Ion Antonescu's regime in its relations with the Third Reich immediately before the insurrection of August 1944. The political and military situation forced Ion Antonescu to suggest, in conversations with German representative Karl Clodius between 24 July and 4 August, that he be given "freedom of action" for his country. However, in his last meeting with Hitler, 5-6 August 1944, he was bluntly asked whether he and Romania would follow Germany to the very end, and agreed to do so. Also examines other accounts and aspects of the last days of Antonescu's relations with Nazi Germany. Based on unpublished documents from British and German sources; 29 notes. R. O. Khan

290. De Felice, Renzo. LA QUESTIONE DELL'ALTO ADIGE NEI RAPPORTI ITALO-TEDESCHI DALL' "ANSCHLUSS" ALLA FINE DELLA SECONDA GUERRA MONDIALE (1938-1945) [The question of the South Tyrol in Italo-German relations from the *Anschluss* to the end of World War II, 1938-45]. *Storia e Politica [Italy] 1974 13(1-2): 146-226.* Ever since, by the Treaty of St. Germain (1919), the largely German-speaking South Tyrol had become the Italian province of Alto Adige, its recovery by a German state had been the dream of German nationalists. Hitler, however, as early as 1926, stated that the South Tyrol would have to be sacrificed in order for Germany to gain a badly needed ally: Italy. When he seized Austria in 1938, Hitler applied this doctrine; German-speaking Tyrolese could "opt" for Germany and leave for the greater Reich. When Mussolini fell, however, German forces occupied the area, annexed it to the Reich, and carried out an extensive re-Germanization program. 139 notes. J. C. Billigmeier

291. Dupeux, Louis. HISTORIOGRAPHIE RÉCENTE DU "TROISIÈME REICH" [Recent historiography of the "Third Reich"]. *Rev. d'Allemagne [France] 1978 10(2): 275-292.* Continued from a previous article. The works of about 100 contemporary historians, mostly German, but also some European and American, are cited with brief critical and descriptive comments. All deal with some aspect of the foreign policy of the Third Reich, including its relation to that of preceding German governments, the relations of Nazi Germany with other European states and the United States, the strategy and tactics of World War II, and the administration of Nazi-occupied countries. Article to be continued. Primary sources; 4 notes. J. S. Gassner

292. Durand, Yves. 1940: VICHY JOUE L'ALLEMAGNE [1940: Vichy bets on Germany]. *Histoire [France] 1981 (30): 10-19.* While allusions have been made to the double game played by the Vichy Regime, French and German records show that as early as 1940 Vichy was negotiating with Germany. J

293. Durand, Yves. 1940: VICHY JOUE L'ALLEMAGNE [1940: Vichy bets on Germany]. *Histoire [France] 1981 (31): 121-128.* Reprints entire article correcting pagination errors [see preceding entry].

294. Eckert, Rainer. DIE LEITER UND GESCHÄFTSFÜHRER DER REICHSGRUPPE INDUSTRIE, IHRER HAUPT- UND WIRTSCHAFTSGRUPPEN(I):DOKUMENTATION ÜBER IHRE STELLUNG IN MONOPOLEN, MONOPOLISTISCHEN VERBÄNDEN UND BEI DER STAATSMONOPOLISTISCHEN WIRTSCHAFTSREGULIERUNG [Leaders and managers of the Reichsgruppe Industrie, its main groups and its economic associations, part I: documentation on their position in monopoly systems and associations and on state-monopoly regulation of the economy]. *Jahrbuch für Wirtschaftsgeschichte [East Germany] 1979 (4): 243-277.* After Hitler's takeover in Germany, January 1933, the bourgeois democracy lost its power in the state to a fascist state apparatus and the monopolies. The author examines the history, development, function, and war activities of one of the most important instruments of state-monopoly regulation of the economy in the Third Reich, the so-called Reichsgruppe Industrie (there were also Reich groups for commerce, manual labor, banks, insurance, energy, economy and tourism in post-1933 Germany). Based on newly discovered papers; 70 notes, biblio., index. Article to be continued. G. E. Pergl

295. Eichholtz, Dietrich. DAS MINETTE-REVIER UND DIE DEUTSCHE MONTANINDUSTRIE. ZUR KRIEGSZIELSTRATEGIE DER DEUTSCHEN MONOPOLE IM ZWEITEN WELTKRIEG (1941-42) [The Minette district and the German mining industry: the war aims of German monopolies in World War II, 1941-42]. *Zeitschrift für Geschichtswissenschaft [East Germany] 1977 25(7): 816-838.* A commission of officials of the German mining industry, chaired by Hugo Klein, was organized in 1941 to advise the government on the disposition of mines and related facilities in the occupied territories. The Klein Commission recommended the annexation of Briey, Longwy, and Nancy. Its report demonstrates that German monopoly promoted the annexation of the same territories during both world conflicts, thus providing further proof that there was long-term continuity in the striving of the German government and monopolies for world hegemony. Based on documents from the Central State Archives, Potsdam, and secondary sources; 32 notes, 6 documents. J. T. Walker

296. Espinosa, Manuel. MEMORIAS DE UN AGREGADO NAVAL: DOS VUELOS ACCIDENTADOS [Memoirs of a naval attaché: two eventful flights]. *Rev. General de Marina [Spain] 1978 195(Oct): 273-281.* The Spanish naval attaché in Berlin, 1938-45, recounts the experiences and difficulties encountered in flying between Spain and Germany late in World War II. Map.
W. C. Frank

297. Facon, Patrick and Ruffray, Françoise de. APERÇUS SUR LA COLLABORATION AÉRONAUTIQUE FRANCO-ALLEMANDE (1940-1943) [Observations on Franco-German aeronautical collaboration, 1940-43]. *Rev. d'Hist. de la Deuxième Guerre Mondiale [France] 1977 27(108): 85-102.* In August 1940 at Wiesbaden, Germany offered economic advantages to the French aircraft industry in return for production of military aircraft for the German war effort. The Vichy regime did not approach the matter in a servile way, but attempted to preserve some bargaining power in a compromised situation. The Vichy government negotiated in good faith with the Germans even though self-interest was at the root of its discussions. Based on French sources, this article

complements Peter F. Klemm's "La production aéronautique française de 1940 à 1942"; table, 53 notes.
G. H. Davis

298. Feldenkirchen, Wilfried von. FERNOSTGESCHÄFTE DER FELTEN & GUILLEAUME CARLSWERK AG BIS ZUM BEGINN DES ZWEITEN WELTKRIEGES [Far Eastern business of the Felten & Guilleaume Carlswerk Co. up to the beginning of World War II]. *Zeitschrift für Unternehmengeschichte [West Germany] 1977 22(2): 91-108.* An exploration of the business relationship between Felten & Guilleaume and its affiliate the North German Ocean Cable Works and Japan, China, and the Dutch East Indies from the end of the 19th century to the outbreak of World War II. Until 1914 German firms enjoyed profits from an expanding market. From 1914 to 1925 competition grew and markets diminished. From 1925 to 1939 individual German firms reaped large profits in the wire and cable trade. The electrical industry did not benefit greatly by Far Eastern markets. The author analyzes the meaning of the Far Eastern markets for the development of German wire and cable industries. Based largely on unpublished archival material; 6 tables, 85 notes. Article to be continued.
M. A. Butler

299. Förster, Jurgen. RUMANIENS WEG IN DIE DEUTSCHE ABHÄNGIGKEIT. ZUR ROLLE DER DEUTSCHEN MILITÄRMISSION 1940/41 [Romania's course under German dependency: the role of the German military mission 1940-41]. *Militärgeschichtliche Mitteilungen [West Germany] 1979 (1): 47-77.* Romania's earlier dependency upon the Western democracies for security collapsed with the fall of Poland and defeat of France by mid-1940, leaving Romania alone to suffer partial annexation under Russian and German pressure. Romania's realignment in the German orbit brought an extremely large German military mission and cadre with the triple tasks of training Romanian armed forces, preparing future operations against Russia, and securing Romanian oil fields. The efforts of the mission prepared Romania for war long before a military and political alliance was struck for that purpose. Based on sources in Bonn, Freiburg, and London archives; 177 notes.
K. W. Estes

300. Fritz, Martin. LES RELATIONS ÉCONOMIQUES GERMANO-SUÉDOISES DURANT LA SECONDE GUERRE MONDIALE [German-Swedish economic relations during World War II]. *Rev. d'Hist. de la Deuxième Guerre Mondiale [France] 1978 28(109): 33-58.* Though Sweden avoided Nazi control and maintained its neutrality during World War II, it was one of Germany's leading trading partners during that conflict. The Third Reich imported lumber, paper, foodstuffs, and above all iron from Sweden, and exported coal, textiles, and industrial products. The Germans paid high prices for Swedish products, but the main reason for the close commercial ties was Sweden's fear of invasion or blockade. When Allied victory became ineluctable, the Swedes refused to renew their trade treaty with the Reich, and iron exports to Germany ceased. 13 tables, 54 notes.
J. C. Billigmeier

301. Fritz, Martin. SWEDISH BALL-BEARINGS AND THE GERMAN WAR ECONOMY. *Scandinavian Econ. Hist. [Denmark] 1975 23(1): 15-35.* Interest in the German-Swedish ball-bearing traffic has been mainly focused on its diplomacy. The real question is whether it affected German production or influenced the economy in any way. With the outbreak of World War II, Swe-

den's exports to Germany and the continent jumped immediately because outside markets were cut off. The Allies pressured Sweden into limiting exports, and then through purchases themselves, cutting off exports. Despite a decline in exports, neither German production nor supply declined because SKF, the Swedish producer, shifted to exporting steel to its German subsidiary, VKF, and other German factories, and the export of machines to produce ball bearings. This kept Germany happy and Swedish trade relatively stable. Furthermore, German industry was little affected by American strategic bombing raids, and German production and supply in 1944 equaled that of earlier years.

R. E. Lindgren

302. Fritz, Martin. SWEDISH IRON ORE AND GERMAN STEEL 1939-40. *Scandinavian Econ. Hist. R. [Denmark] 1973 21(2): 133-144.* Reviews debate in the *Scandinavian Economic History Review* on the importance of Swedish iron ore in German steel production, involving contributions from Rolf Karlbom, Alan S. Milward, Jörg-Johannes Jäger, Mathias Riedel, and others. German annual steel production declined to an average of 1.75 million tons, approximately 20 percent below the pre-1914 average because of shortages of coke, closure of the Saar district blast furnaces, lack of labor, scrap iron and other materials, and problems of transport. The reduced supply of iron ore can be attributed to the end of imports from France, North Africa, Newfoundland, and other foreign sources, but not particularly to the Swedish imports. Shipments from Sweden and Luleå rose sharply in 1940, when Narvik was closed because the British navy threatened closure of the passage through Norwegian waters. The Germans formulated alternative plans to cut the deficit if Swedish ore were not available. The major value of Swedish sources was that they provided accessible, cheap, and good quality ore.

R. E. Lindgren

303. Groehler, Olaf and Schumann, Wolfgang. ZU DEN BÜNDNISSBEZIEHUNGEN DES FASCHISTISCHEN DEUTSCHLANDS IM ZWEITEN WELTKRIEG [Fascist Germany's alliances during World War II]. *Zeitschrift für Geschichtswissenschaft [East Germany] 1980 28(7): 624-639.* The problem of the fascist system of alliances and the war efforts of the Axis powers is among the most important questions in World War II research. German ruling and military circles valued alliances only for how much they might contribute to Germany's power and influence. For example, during the German attack on the Soviet Union all allies were to be totally exploited and finally subjected to the planned New European Order in which Germany would be master. Based on published materials and documents; 52 notes.

G. E. Pergl

304. Gyllenstierna, Ebbe. TYSKTÅGEN UNDER ANDRA VÄRLDSKRIGET [German trains in Sweden during World War II]. *Kungliga Krigsvetenskaps Akademiens Handlingar och Tidskrift [Sweden] 1974 178(6): 148-155.* During 1940-43 German trains were allowed to pass through Sweden to Norway and Finland, though Sweden closely controlled the transit. This caused protests from Great Britain, Norway, and the USSR, but Sweden feared German attack and wished to preserve its steel exports to Germany. The Swedish dilemma was that Germany was unable to supply the country with oil, which made Sweden dependent on Great Britain. Not until 1943, when the situation in Europe had changed in favor of the Allies, did Sweden denounce the agreement with Ger-

many. Based on Rune Karlsson's *Så Stoppades Tysktågen* (Stockholm: Allmänne Förlaget, 1974). U. Bartels/S

305. Hanisch, Ernst. VATIKAN—DEUTSCHER EPISKOPAT—DRITTES REICH [The Holy See, the German Episcopacy, and the Third Reich]. *Zeitgeschichte [Austria] 1976 4(3): 99-108.* Surveys current literature on the relations between the Vatican and Nazi Germany. Noting three phases in the development of German thought on this subject, the author analyzes each briefly and cites key works and authors. The notes comprise a useful bibliography. 62 notes. G. H. Libbey

306. Hillgruber, Andreas. ENGLAND IN HITLERS AUSSENPOLITISCHER KONZEPTION [England in Hitler's foreign policy conception]. *Hist. Zeitschrift [West Germany] 1974 218(1): 65-84.* Three basic interpretations of Hitler's foreign policy are: 1) it was unplanned and subordinated to domestic policy; 2) its ultimate aim was dominance of Eastern Europe, 3) its ultimate aim was world conquest. Hitler had a three-phase plan: 1) to dominate the continent while allied with Britain; 2) to gain world-power status after a confrontation with England; 3) to attain world predominance after forcing English cooperation against America. Describes Hitler's implementation of his policy after 1933. From address to the Anglo-German Group of Historians, Cologne, December 1972; translated in the *Journal of Contemporary History* 1974 9(1): 5-22. 51 notes. G. H. Davis

307. Hillgruber, Andreas. GRUNDZÜGE DER NATIONALSOZIALISTISCHEN AUSSENPOLITIK 1933-45. [Essential elements of national socialist foreign policy 1933-45]. *Saeculum [West Germany] 1973 24(4): 328-345.* Although Hitler after 1933 no longer publicly mentioned his basic aim of creating a German empire stretching to the Urals, this concept remained a key point of orientation with him. While affecting only the goal of drastic revision of the Versailles Treaty, his consistent intention was to accomplish his "grand design" through an alliance with Great Britain, which would also serve as the political and military basis for a final conflict with the United States. The Rome-Berlin Axis was only a temporary and often embarrassing solution. Hitler's invasion of the USSR was designed not only to destroy that country and carve up its territory together with Japan but also to menace British India and induce Britain to join Germany in a "world Blitzkrieg" against America. After his failures in Russia, Hitler was determined to force one of two alternatives: establishment of his German world empire in the face of all adversity, or Germany's complete destruction. Biblio. C. F. Latour

308. Hirschfeld, Yair. IRANS BEDEUTUNG FÜR DIE DEUTSCHE KRIEGSWIRTSCHAFT: VOM BEGINN DES ZWEITEN WELTKRIEGES BIS ZUR ANGLO-RUSSISCHEN BESETZUNG IRANS IM AUGUST 1941 [Iran's importance to the German war economy: from the beginning of World War II to the Anglo-Russian occupation of Iran, August 1941]. *Jahrbuch des Inst. für Deutsche Geschichte [Israel] 1978 7: 421-445.* When war began in 1939 the Germans sought foodstuffs and minerals from Iran. Statistics indicate a steady stream of Iranian exports to Germany until 1941, but in fact Iran provided no real contribution to the German war effort. Transportation was unbelievably difficult, Iranian officials were sometimes unfriendly, and Iranians themselves

competed for goods the Germans needed. Most important, Nazi officials used what they received from Iran to maintain luxury living for the German elite. 5 tables, 92 notes.   M. Faissler

309. Johnson, Ronald W. THE GERMAN-AMERICAN BUND AND NAZI GERMANY: 1936-1941. *Studies in Hist. and Soc. 1975 6(2): 31-45.* The activities of the German-American Bund were directed by Fritz Kuhn, a fervent pro-Nazi who attempted to organize US support for Adolf Hitler's government. Two visits to Germany led to a brief interview with Hitler in 1936 and to rejection by one of Hitler's aides in 1938. Kuhn's leadership was an embarrassment to the German foreign ministry and to German-Americans who opposed the Nazi regime. The Bund achieved none of its intended goals of aiding the rise of a new German fascist empire. Primary sources; 75 notes.   G. H. Libbey

310. Jokipii, Mauno. LAPIN VÄLIRAUHAN AJAN TIERAKENNUKSET JA NIIDEN SUURPOLIITTINEN TAUSTA [Road building in Lapland during the armistice and its background in great power politics]. *Scripta Hist. [Finland] 1977 5: 224-269.* Describes road and railway construction plans and activity in Finnish Lapland from March 1940 to June 1941. Under Soviet pressure a railroad link was built to the Soviet-Finnish border. In consultation with the Germans, several major roads were begun to link Finland with northern Norway, though these were completed only after the German attack on the USSR in 1941. The new transport routes were symptomatic of the new role of Finnish Lapland in great power politics which continued also after 1945. Based on Finnish archives and European monographs; 3 maps, 119 notes.   R. G. Selleck

311. Juhász, Gyula. KÉT TÁRGYALÁS 1943 TAVASZÁN (FELJEGYZÉSEK KÁLLAY MIKLÓS 1943, ÁPRILIS 1-I RÓMAI ES HORTHY MIKLÓS 1943 ÁPRILIS 16-17-I KLESSHEIMI TÁRGYALÁSAIRÓL) [Two negotiations during the spring of 1943: Miklós Kallay's in Rome on 1 May, and Miklós Horthy's in Klessheim on 16-17 April]. *Történelmi Szemle [Hungary] 1973 16(3-4): 488-530.* Publishes five documents concerning Kalley's meeting with Benito Mussolini and Horthy's with Adolf Hitler during World War II. The leaders of both Axis powers were by then already informed of the Hungarian government's secret peace approaches to the Allies and made their displeasure quite clear. Commentaries accompany the documents. 55 notes.

H. Szamuely/S

312. Karner, Stefan. ÖSTERREICHS RÜSTUNGSINDUSTRIE 1944: ANSÄTZE ZU EINER STRUKTURANALYSE [The Austrian armaments industry 1944: approach to a structural analysis]. *Zeitschrift für Unternehmensgeschichte [West Germany] 1980 25(3): 179-206.* Nazi economic policies have left a deep imprint on Austria's economic structure. A computer-assisted analysis of all 716 Austrian armaments factories in existence in 1944 attempts to determine their characteristics and long-run development and the effects of political measures on the armaments industry. Most of the firms were privately owned; less than a quarter of them were joint-stock companies. The relatively few large firms, however, employed almost half the approximately 500,000 people working in the industry. The incorporation of Austrian industry into war production for the Third Reich took place gradually, most of the firms being converted into armaments enterprises in the years 1939 and 1941. Most of

the firms had been in existence for less than 25 years in 1944. A fourth were founded during the Nazi period. Investments, financed mainly by government loans, led to lasting structural changes that persisted even after 1945, especially in western Austria. Vienna, Linz, and the Inn valley of Tirol were the centers of the armaments industry. J/S

313. Kaslas, Bronis J. THE LITHUANIAN STRIP IN SOVIET-GERMAN SECRET DIPLOMACY, 1939-1941. *J. of Baltic Studies 1973 4(3): 211-225.* A secret protocol of 28 September 1939 revised the Russo-German Nonaggression Pact of 23 August 1939. One provision transferred Lithuania from the German to the Soviet sphere of interest, excepting a strip of territory along Lithuania's southwest frontier. In July-August 1940 the USSR occupied and then annexed this strip along with the rest of Lithuania. In compensation Germany accepted 7.5 million gold dollars, paid by the USSR in February-April 1941. Based on archival and published sources; 37 notes. E. W. Jennison, Jr.

314. Kasper, Hanns-Heinz. DAS ERDÖL IN DEN RAUBPLÄNEN DES DEUTSCHEN FASCHISMUS IN VORBEREITUNG UND BEI DER DURCHFÜHRUNG DES ZWEITEN WELTKRIEGES [Petroleum in the rapacious designs of German fascism for the preparation and conduct of World War II]. *Jahrbuch für Wirtschaftsgeschichte [East Germany] 1976 (3): 55-77.* The Nazi Four Year Plan emphasized the development of oil sources in the economic preparations for war. After September 1939, the oil resources of occupied territories were systematically exploited for the benefit of the German war economy. The agency of control was the Kontinentale Oel AG, which received a 99-year monopoly over Russian oil fields in 1941. West German historians state that the cutting off of oil imports was the critical factor in crippling the German war effort; more important was the defeat of the Nazi military machine by the Red Army. Primary and secondary sources; 5 tables, 93 notes.
R. J. Bazillion

315. Kludas, Arnold. HUNDERT JAHRE BLOHM & VOSS [The 100th anniversary of the firm Blohm & Voss]. *Marine Rundschau [West Germany] 1977 74(4): 153-167.* Describes the history of the largest private shipyard in Hamburg, Germany, the Blohm & Voss firm, which celebrated its 100th year of existence in April 1977. The author shows the humble beginnings of the enterprise, its road to gradual expansion and success, the world wars and present situation of this most efficient of German shipyards. 36 illus., fig.
G. E. Pergl

316. Koch, H. W. THE SPECTRE OF A SEPARATE PEACE IN THE EAST: RUSSO-GERMAN "PEACE FEELERS," 1942-1944. *J. of Contemporary Hist. [Great Britain] 1975 10(3): 531-549.* A series of meetings took place during 1942-44 involving Germany's Dr. Peter Kleist, a specialist in international law and honorary member of the SS, and a certain Edgar Clauss, a middleman for the USSR. Both agents allegedly acted unofficially in putting forth feelers for a separate peace. The negotiations failed because of mutual distrust and the changing military situation. Based on archival sources; 34 notes.
M. P. Trauth

317. Kováts, Lajos. ADATOK A MAGYAR LÉGIERŐ ANYAGI-TECHNIKAI ÁLLAPOTÁRÓL 1938-1944 [Information about the material and technical state of the Hungarian air force between 1938 and 1944]. *Hadtörténelmi Közlemények [Hungary] 1979 26(3): 462-485.* Provides figures on the number of pilots and the types of airplanes in operation in the wartime Hungarian air force. Developments after 1938 led Hungary to place orders with Italy and Germany. By 1942 Germany had replaced Italy as the major supplier of airplane materials and components. Primary sources; 3 tables, 108 notes, ref. Gy. Foxcroft

318. Krammer, Arnold. LE JAPON ENTRE MOSCOU ET BERLIN (1941-1945) [Japan between Moscow and Berlin, 1941-45]. *Rev. d'Hist. de la Deuxième Guerre Mondiale [France] 1976 26(103): 1-11.* Japan attempted on several occasions to act as a mediator for a separate peace between Germany and the USSR during World War II. Although Hitler repudiated such efforts, he was ambiguous and encouraged Japanese optimism. Hitler doubted that Stalin would enter any such peace arrangements, but his intentions are difficult to interpret. Japan hoped to release Germany from its quarrel with Russia so it could defeat England and isolate the United States. Based on German, Japanese, and English sources; 27 notes. G. H. Davis

319. Krimper, Ronald L. THE DIPLOMATIC PRELUDE TO THE DESTRUCTION OF YUGOSLAVIA. *East European Q. 1973 7(2): 125-147.* A factual account of the diplomatic activities of Germany, Italy, Yugoslavia, England, and the United States early in 1941, emphasizing the difficult decision Yugoslavia had to make concerning its future relations with Germany. Based almost entirely on vol. 12 of *Documents on German Foreign Policy;* 73 notes.
C. R. Lovin

320. Kumlin, Ragnar and Carlgren, W. M., ed. SMÅSTATSDIPLOMATI I STORMAKTSKRIG: PROMEMORIOR FRÅN KRIGSÅREN [Small state diplomacy in great power wars: memoranda from the war years]. *Hist. Tidskrift [Sweden] 1977 (4): 436-452.* Publishes memoranda, 1941-43, of Ragnar Kumlin, assistant head of the Swedish foreign affairs ministry's political department. Though written on his own initiative and not authorized as official memoranda, they were used both within the department and between the department and the embassies as basis for discussions. Revealing what information the foreign ministry had and how it was assessed, these memoranda supplement the ministry's official documents. They contain a rare description of the foreign ministry's attempts through knowledge of the Germans' code to influence reports from the German legation in Stockholm in ways favorable to Swedish interests.
P. A. Hegstad

321. Lammers, Karl Christian. NYERE FORSKNING OM TYSKLANDS UDENRIGSPOLITIK 1933-1945 [Newer research on Germany's foreign policy, 1933-45]. *Hist. Tidsskrift [Denmark] 1974 74(1): 313-341.* Studies and bibliographies on Nazi foreign policy are rich because of the unusual availability of documentary collections and access to films of captured German documents. Gerhard L. Weinberg and Klaus Hildebrand have made important additions to the field. East German historians stress the role of monopoly capitalism (fascist and imperialist) during the Nazi period with its expansionism toward the East. Many monographs study individual aspects of foreign policy within the context

of the Third Reich: Axel Kuhn (eastward expansion), Dietrich Aigner (public opinion), F. A. Krummacher and H. Lange (Soviet-German relations), Hans-Jürgen Schröder (US-German relations), etc. R. E. Lindgren

322. Lehmann, Hans Georg. LEITMOTIVE NATIONALSOZIALISTISCHER UND GROSSJAPANISCHER WIRTSCHAFTSPOLITIK [Leitmotifs of National Socialist and Greater Japanese economic policy]. *Zeitschrift für Politik [West Germany] 1974 21(2): 158-167.* The conversations of Walther Funk, Reich Minister for the Economy, with Japanese Foreign Minister Yosuke Matsuoka, which took place on 28 March 1941, showed how much the two empires had in common in structure and in their autarkic economic plans.

323. Levine, Herbert S. THE MEDIATOR: CARL J. BURCKHARDT'S EFFORTS TO AVERT A SECOND WORLD WAR. *J. of Modern Hist. 1973 45(3): 439-453.* A study of Carl Jacob Burckhardt's (1891-) single-handed attempt to prevent World War II, in his role as high commissioner of the League of Nations in the free city of Danzig from 1937. His ultimate failure should not obscure his significance as a liaison between Britain and Germany. The British always paid some note to his opinions, but the Nazis regarded him as a suitable instrument for exploiting British weakness. 69 notes. R. V. Ritter

324. Lutzhöft, Hans-Jürgen. DEUTSCHLAND UND SCHWEDEN WÄHREND DES NORWEGENFELDZUGS (9. APRIL-10. JUNI 1940 [Germany and Sweden during the Norwegian campaign, 9 April-10 June 1940]. *Vierteljahrshefte für Zeitgeschichte 1974 22(4): 382-416.* German-Swedish relations during the Nazi campaign in Norway required delicate diplomatic balance by both sides. Eager for Swedish ore shipments, Germany had no specific plan of attack, but pressed for a benevolent Swedish attitude. The Swedish government, bent on averting war and protecting its sovereignty, steered a cautious course of preserving neutrality while making limited concessions to Germany for transit of food, medicine, and shipwrecked sailors and reacting with great circumspection to territorial violations. Based on sources at the German Foreign Office and Freiburg Military Archive, German and Swedish published documents, and secondary works; 205 notes. D. Prowe

325. Mal'kov, Viktor Leonidovich. SPETSSLUZHBY SSHA I "MIRNAIA INITSIATIVA" FON PAPENA V 1943 G. [US Special Services and von Papen's "peace initiative" in 1943]. *Novaia i Noveishaia Istoriia [USSR] 1980 (3): 122-140.* Toward the end of World War II anti-Soviet movements in England and the United States became increasingly influential. In 1943 US agents met emissaries of the Third Reich in Turkey. Franz von Papen, German ambassador to Turkey, saw his mission as the division of the anti-Nazi coalition, and the formation of alliances of Great Britain, the United States, and Germany against the USSR. Such an alliance was advocated in the United States by George Earle. The author bases his claim on an intelligence report from Istanbul (declassified in the United States in 1976) which records the US-Nazi meeting, and which is here reproduced in full (in Russian translation). Uses archival sources in the Franklin D. Roosevelt Library, including recently declassified documents; 76 notes.
J. S. S. Charles

326. Manninen, Ohto. LUDWIG WEISSAUER I HEMLIGA UPPDRAG 1940-1943 [The secret missions of Ludwig Weissauer, 1940-43]. *Historisk Tidskrift för Finland [Finland] 1975 60(3): 177-193.* Describes activities during 1940-43 of Dr. Ludwig Weissauer, an agent of the SD (Sicherheitsdienst) of Nazi Germany, insofar as these concerned Finland and Sweden. In July 1940 Weissauer visited Helsinki and Stockholm to ascertain Finnish and Swedish views on Finland's military future. In September 1940 he visited Stockholm in an abortive attempt to open secret peace discussions with England. In January 1941 he asked the Finnish businessman Henrik Ramsey (1886-1951) to investigate peace sentiment in England. His contacts with Finnish officials continued into 1943. Based on Finnish, Swedish, and German archives; 38 notes. R. G. Selleck

327. Melka, R. L. MAX FREIHERR VON OPPENHEIM: SIXTY YEARS OF SCHOLARSHIP AND POLITICAL INTRIGUE IN THE MIDDLE EAST. *Middle Eastern Studies [Great Britain] 1972 9(1): 81-94.* Max von Oppenheim (1860-1946), a German diplomat and self-taught archaeologist, worked covertly to foster Arab sympathy for the German government in World War II. In the interwar period, Oppenheim excavated many sites, and gained an international reputation and many influential friends among the Arabs of Syria. He returned to Germany in 1939 and was dismayed at his government's desultory efforts to harass the Allies through Arab revolts. Using his friends among the Arabs, German archaeologists, and foreign diplomatic missions, Oppenheim tried to infiltrate agents into Vichy Syria and British Palestine. Although few of his efforts succeeded, Oppenheim's career illustrates a curious blend of lasting scholarship and futile political meddling. Based on filmed archival materials from the German Foreign Office, published primary material, and secondary sources; 55 notes. J. W. Leedom

328. Melka, Robert L. DARLAN BETWEEN BRITAIN AND GERMANY 1940-41. *J. of Contemporary Hist. [Great Britain] 1973 8(2): 57-80.* Admiral Jean Darlan (1881-1942), convinced of an ultimate German victory, and distrustful of Great Britain, verged on undertaking naval war against Britain after the armistice of June 1940. As a high-ranking official in the Vichy government, he repeatedly offered Hitler active military cooperation against Britain. Hitler, however, distrusted France and preferred it to remain neutral while he attacked Russia. After the British conquest of Syria in 1941 and Hitler's failure to defeat Russia quickly, Darlan moved away from his policy of collaboration. Based on primary and secondary sources; 79 notes. B. A. Block

329. Mel'nikov, D. E. and Chernaia, L. B. NEKOTORYE PROBLEMY ISTORII GERMANSKOGO FASHIZMA [Problems of the history of German fascism]. *Novaia i Noveishaia Istoriia [USSR] 1973 (6): 68-84.* Studies two problems of German fascism as presented in West German and Soviet historiography: the early phase of Nazi foreign policy; and the interrelationship between Hitler's regime and German financial capitalism. The authors counter the bourgeois emphasis on the peaceful aspects of Adolf Hitler's early foreign policy by examining its geopolitical basis. They also refer to *Mein Kampf* to illustrate Hitler's basic strategy, his false protestations of peace in the 1930's, his rearmament policy, and his use of referenda and terrorism. In addition they illustrate the interdependence of Hitler and German monopolies by examining Hitler's record of concessions to industry, his 1934 reorganization of the economy, and his economic policy, 1939-45. Table, 41 notes. C. R. Pike

330. Menger, Manfred. DAS MILITÄRPOLITISCHE VERHÄLTNIS ZWISCHEN DEUTSCHLAND UND FINNLAND IM HERBST 1944 [The military-political relations between Germany and Finland in the Autumn of 1944]. *Militärgeschichte [East Germany] 1979 18(3): 297-307.* The elimination of Finland from the fascist bloc and its consequences for the military situation in North Europe have heretofore scarcely been investigated in the historical scholarship of East Germany. The author can depict in detail for the first time how the German military sought to maintain a position in this area. But a different policy was pursued temporarily by parts of the Finnish army command, and the author shows that in the population and army of Finland a change to an antifascist attitude took place that expressed itself in action against German troops. Based on extensive documentary material from Finnish archives; map, 4 illus., 81 notes.
J/T (H. D. Andrews)

331. Menger, Manfred; Petrick, Fritz; and Wilhelmus, Wolfgang. GRUNDZÜGE IMPERIALISTISCHER DEUTSCHER NORDEUROPAPOLITIK BIS 1945 [Basic features of imperialist Germany's Northern Europe policies to 1945]. *Zeitschrift für Geschichtswissenschaft [East Germany] 1973 21(9): 1029-1044.* During the 20th century Northern Europe and Scandinavia became increasingly important to Germany as a market for exports, a source of raw materials, and an area for investment. In World War I and World War II Scandinavia was of great strategic and economic importance, especially after the German invasion of the USSR. Secondary literature; 56 notes.
R. Wagnleitner

332. Minei, Nicolae. DIPLOMATUL NAZIST ŞI PONOASELE SPIONAJULUI "NECONVENABIL" [The Nazi diplomat and the drawbacks of "unsuitable" spying]. *Magazin Istoric [Rumania] 1977 11(7): 48-51.* Reproduces an extract from *Les Archives secrètes de Wilhelmstrasse* Vol. 9 books 1 and 2 (Paris, 1960), preceded by comments on the difficult position of the German chargé d'affaires in Washington in 1940 because of the agents sent to the United States by Wilhelm Canaris and Heinrich Himmler.

333. Musat, Mircea and Bobocescu, Vasile. ÎMPOTRIVA UNEI NEDREPTĂŢI ISTORICE: 40 DE ANI DE LA MARILE MANIFESTAŢII POPULARE ÎMPOTRIVA DICTATULUI FASCIST DE LA VIENA [Against historical injustices: 40 years since the great popular demonstrations against the fascist Vienna diktat]. *Anale de Istorie [Romania] 1980 26(3): 75-104.* Describes the background to the award of the Vienna conference of August 1940 dictated by the Axis powers and the consequences for Romania. Although Romania was forced to cede territory to Hungary and effectively accept Axis control, the government only accepted these conditions because of the unfavorable international situation. The Romanian people, including numerous politicians, remained firmly opposed to the concessions and voiced their protests in various ways, especially demonstrations, which influenced international opinion. 146 notes.
R. O. Khan

334. Overy, R. J. THE LUFTWAFFE AND THE EUROPEAN ECONOMY 1939-1945. *Militärgeschichtliche Mitteilungen [West Germany] 1979 (2): 55-78.* The German air force participated in the economic exploitation of occupied territories during World War II in the form of seizures of aircraft, parts, and

production facilities. It competed with other German agencies for these assets as well as a share of the foreign labor pool. The Allied bombing of Germany disrupted the exploitation of foreign assets in the homeland, producing a curious reversal of policy through the dispersal of production back to the occupied territories to escape attack. Based on documents in the Military Archives, Freiburg as well as US and British archives; 134 notes. K. W. Estes

335. Pavlović, Konstantin. ZABELEŠKA O RAZGOVORIMA IZMEDJU FIRERA I POGLAVNIKA U ZAMKU KLESHAJM (KLESSHEIM), 27. APRILA 1943 GODINE [Note of conversations between the Führer and the Governor in Klessheim Castle, 27 April 1943]. *Vojnoistorijski Glasnik [Yugoslavia] 1980 31(3): 320-324.* Translation of original German record of talks between Adolf Hitler and Ante Pavelić, head of the Independent State of Croatia. Principal subjects of discussion were the strengthening of the Croatian army, attempts to crush the partisans and establish order in Croatia, and German economic interests. F. A. K. Yasamee

336. Pavlović, Konstantin. ZABELEŠKA O RAZGOVORU IZMEDJU HITLERA I POGLAVNIKA (ANTE PAVELIĆA) U FIREROVOM GLAVNOM STANU "VERVOLF" (WERWOLF), 24.SEPTEMBRA 1942 [Note of a conversation between Adolf Hitler and the Governor (Ante Pavelić) in the Führer's Werewolf Headquarters, 24 September 1942]. *Vojnoistorijski Glasnik [Yugoslavia] 1980 31(3): 315-320.* Translation of original German record of discussion between Hitler and the head of the Independent State of Croatia. Subjects discussed are military cooperation in suppressing the partisans, relations with Italy, German economic interests, and the Jews. F. A. K. Yasamee

337. Pavlović, Konstantin. ZABELEŠKA O RAZGOVORU IZMEDJU FIRERA I PREDSEDNIKA VLADE NDH MANDIĆA U ZAMKU KLESHAJM (KLESSHEIM) I. MARTA 1944. GODINE [Note of a conversation between the Führer and Prime Minister Mandić of the Independent State of Croatia in Klessheim Castle on 1 March 1944]. *Vojnoistorijski Glasnik [Yugoslavia] 1980 31(3): 324-327.* Translation of original German record of talks which turned principally on the question of suppressing the partisans, Mandić's complaints about German support for the Chetniks, and Hitler's criticisms of the Italians. F. A. K. Yasamee

338. Pommerin, Reiner. ÜBERLEGUNGEN DES "DRITTEN REICHS" ZUR RÜCKHOLUNG DEUTSCHER AUSWANDERER AUS LATEINAMERIKAS [Consideration in the Third Reich about recalling German emigrants from Latin America]. *Jahrbuch für Geschichte von Staat, Wirtschaft und Gesellschaft Lateinamerikas [West Germany] 1979 16: 365-377.* Hitler's intention to use the German emigrants in Latin America to support his foreign policy is well known, but he also thought of using these German emigrants more generally to support German imperial expansion. For example, the special abilities and experiences gained in Latin America were to be used to obtain colonial space in Africa and for the settlement of the Eastern European areas which Hitler envisioned in his continental expansion policy. Based upon manuscript and printed materials; 49 notes. T. D. Schoonover

339. Radandt, Hans. HERMANN J. ABS—BANKIER IM GEHEIMAUFTRAG GÖRINGS [Hermann J. Abs: banker under secret orders from Göring]. *Jahrbuch für Wirtschaftsgeschichte [East Germany] 1974 (4): 27-55.* Refutes the assertion of Fritz Seidenzahl in *100 Jahre Deutsche Bank 1870-1970* (Frankfurt/Main, 1970) that Hermann J. Abs, a member of the board of directors of the Deutsche Bank, was under Nazi suspicion. Quite to the contrary, Abs enjoyed a special relationship of trust with Hermann Göring's (1893-1946) Office for the Four-Year Plan and conducted a number of important financial operations for Göring in 1940. Based on documents from the Zentrales Staatsarchiv Potsdam (Historical Division I) and the US National Archives; 45 notes, appendix.
J. D. Hunley

340. Reimaa, Markku. FINLAND OCH DET TYSKA ANFALLET PÅ NORGE [Finland and the German attack on Norway]. *Hist. Tidskrift för Finland [Finland] 1977 62(1): 18-34.* During 1940 the Finnish government generally followed a policy of strict neutrality in the German-Norwegian conflict in the interests of maintaining good communications with Germany. Based on Finnish, Swedish, and German archival material; 55 notes. R. G. Selleck

341. Roche, Emile. L'AMBASSADEUR BURCKHARDT CHEZ LE CHANCELIER HITLER A BERCHTESGADEN [Ambassador Burckhardt with Chancellor Hitler at Berchtesgaden]. *Nouvelle Rev. des Deux Mondes [France] 1979 (3): 579-590.* Text of a conversation in Berchtesgaden between Ambassador Carl Jacob Burckhardt, High Commissioner at Danzig, and Hitler on 10 August 1939.

342. Salewski, Michael. STAATSRÄSON UND WAFFENBRÜDERSCHAFT. PROBLEME DER DEUTSCH-FINNISCHEN POLITIK 1941-1944 [Reason of state and brethren-in-arms: problems of German-Finnish relations, 1941-44]. *Vierteljahrshefte für Zeitgeschichte [West Germany] 1979 27(3): 370-391.* Reviews the course of German-Finnish relations during World War II from Finnish-German military cooperation as "brethren-in-arms" in 1942 to the open conflict and German scorched earth policy in Lappland after the Finnish surrender in August 1944. For Finland cooperation with Hitler's genocidal war against the USSR and betrayal of the common war effort in 1944 were motivated by the *ethos* and *kratos* of national pride and survival. Based on German ambassadorial telegrams and notes in the German Foreign Office Political Archive, memoirs and secondary works; 49 notes. D. Prowe

343. Schärer, Martin R. LA REPRESENTATION DES INTERETS BELGES PAR LA SUISSE [The representation of Belgian interests by Switzerland]. *Cahiers d'Hist. de la Seconde Guerre Mondiale [Belgium] 1976 4: 221-228.* During World War II, Switzerland undertook to represent the interests of various belligerents. In the Belgian case Switzerland had two possible roles: to represent the London-based Belgian government-in-exile in the various Axis countries, and to represent the Allied powers in Brussels. The author concentrates on the representation of the London-based Belgian government-in-exile in Germany. Diplomatic moves were made, but the Reich rejected such diplomatic representation during both the period of the occupation of Belgium until 1944 and thereafter when Belgium was liberated. Based on German and Swiss archives; 37 notes.
M. K. Palat

344. Schieder, Theodor. DAS DOKUMENTENWERK ZUR DEUTSCHEN AUSWÄRTIGEN POLITIK 1918-1945 [Documentary work on German foreign policy 1918-45]. *Hist. Zeitschrift [West Germany] 1974 218(1): 85-95.* The great collection entitled *Akten zur Deutschen Auswärtigen Politik* [Documents on German foreign policy] grew out of a 1947 agreement between Britain and France to publish German foreign office documents. Divided into five series: A:1919-24; B:1925-33; C:1933-37; D:1937-41; E:1941-45. Parts of series C and D published in English translation. Includes information on personalities and domestic political issues.   G. H. Davis

345. Schreiber, Gerhard. LES STRUCTURES STRATÉGIQUES DE LA CONDUITE DE LA GUERRE DE COALITION ITALO-ALLEMANDE AU COURS DE LA DEUXIÈME GUERRE MONDIALE [The strategic structures for the conduct of Italian-German coalition warfare during World War II]. *Rev. d'Hist. de la Deuxième Guerre Mondiale [France] 1980 30(120): 1-32.* The personal rivalry between Adolf Hitler and Benito Mussolini and the fact that the two allies never coordinated their activities reflect the negative motivations which brought about the alliance. Analysis of the industrial raw materials base and the military organizations show that Italy and Germany did not complement each other. They were not natural allies. Based on German documents in the Bundesarchiv-Militärarchiv, Freiburg, publications of the Militärgeschichtliches Forschungsamt and in G. Bocca's *Storia d'Italia nella guerra fascista 1940-1943* (Rome, 1973); 84 notes.   G. H. Davis

346. Schröder, Josef. LA GERMANIA E I SUOI ALLEATI NELLA SECONDA GUERRA MONDIALE. UN CONTRIBUTO SULLA POLITICA DEGLI OBIETTIVI BELLICI DI HITLER [Germany and its allies during World War II: the politics of Hitler's war objectives]. *Storia Contemporanea [Italy] 1976 7(4): 751-781.* Adolf Hitler's war aims included the destruction of the USSR, German territorial expansion, and Great Power status for the Reich, alongside Great Britain, Japan, and the United States. His allies in Europe—Fascist Italy, democratic Finland, clerical Slovakia, feudal Hungary, military-ruled Rumania, for example—not only diverged ideologically from each other and from the Reich, but had far more limited objectives. The rapid defection of these allies as World War II began to swing against the Axis can be attributed to the lack of common ideology and war objectives. 111 notes.

J. C. Billigmeier

347. Schumann, Wolfgang. DAS SCHEITERN EINER ZOLL- UND WÄHRUNGSUNION ZWISCHEN DEM FASCHISTISCHEN DEUTSCHLAND UND DÄNEMARK 1940 [The failure of the proposed customs and monetary union between Nazi Germany and Denmark in 1940]. *Jahrbuch für Geschichte [East Germany] 1973 9: 515-566.* Though the Wehrmacht swept over Denmark in April 1940, Danish leaders offered no resistance. The German occupiers therefore did not treat Denmark as a conquered territory, allowing its constitutional government to remain in power. The Nazi government, backed by leading German industrialists, was trying to build a customs and monetary union which would include the Reich plus the Netherlands, Belgium, Luxembourg, Norway, and, if possible, Denmark. The other nations, treated as vanquished foes, could be coerced; Denmark had to be persuaded. The Germans hoped that economic pressures would induce Denmark to join. In this they were disappointed. Most

Danish political and business leaders feared being swallowed by Germany. The Germans, having enough enemies, and other means to gain their economic ends in Denmark, acquiesced. 13 documents, 33 notes.　　　　　　J. C. Billigmeier

348. Schustereit, Hartmut. DIE MINERALÖLLIEFERUNGEN DER SOWJETUNION AN DAS DEUTSCHE REICH 1940/41 [Oil shipments of the USSR to Nazi Germany, 1940-41]. *Vierteljahrschrift für Sozial- und Wirtschaftsgeschichte [West Germany] 1980 67(3): 334-353.* After initial transportation difficulties the volume of Soviet oil shipments to Nazi Germany was determined by political decisions reflecting the course of World War II. Soviet oil deliveries remained hesitant in the first months after the Molotov-Ribbentrop Pact of August 1939, they rose drastically following Hitler's blows against the West in Scandinavia and France (March-August 1940), dropped with the conclusion of German alliances with the Balkan states, Finland, and Japan (September 1940-March 1941), rose again after the quick defeat of Yugoslavia in April 1941 and gradually fell thereafter. Based on Bundesarchiv-Militärarchiv (Freiburg), Politisches Archiv, Auswärtiges Amt (Bonn), printed documents and secondary works; 5 tables, graph, 76 notes.　　　　　　　　　　　　　D. Prowe

349. Schützle, Kurt. DIE MISSACHTUNG DES STATUS NEUTRALER STAATEN DURCH DAS IMPERIALISTISCHE DEUTSCHLAND [The disregard of the status of neutral states by imperialist Germany]. *Militärgeschichte [East Germany] 1977 16(6): 693-699.* Argues that Blitzkrieg warfare and disregard for other countries' neutrality began to develop in Germany in the late 19th century; in 1899 Germany disregarded the neutrality of Belgium and Luxembourg and in 1907 the Hague Agreement. From 1939 to 1945 Germany merely continued to follow these precedents. The main disadvantage for Germany of invading neutral countries was that they expanded the theater of war thereby taxing German resources. Based on secondary works; 26 notes.　　A. Alcock

350. Sergeev, F. OPERATSIIA "VOSKHOD SOLNTSA" [Operation Sunrise]. *Novaia i Noveishaia Istoriia [USSR] 1976 (3): 125-144, (4): 115-129.* Examines the secret negotiations (nicknamed "Operation Sunrise" in America and "Crossword" in Britain) in the spring of 1945 in Switzerland between one of the leaders of the American Secret Service, Allen Dulles, and Karl Wolff, the spokesman for the SS (Schutzstaffel) in the German army stationed in Italy, concerning the conditions of surrender for the German troops in Italy. 73 notes.
　　　　　　　　　　　　　　　　　　　　　　　　　　　R. Permar

351. Shamir, Haim. DER DEUTSCHE EINFLUSS IN AFGHANISTAN 1940.-EIN BEITRAG ZUR GESCHICHTE DES EINDRINGENS DEUTSCHLAND IN DEN MITTLEREN OSTEN [The German influence in Afghanistan 1940: A monograph on the history of German penetration in the Middle East]. *Jahrbuch des Instituts für Deutsche Geschichte [Israel] 1975 4: 479-483.* Presents a memo of a conversation 30 September 1940 between the state secretary of the Reich foreign ministry, Ernst von Weizsäcker, and the ambassador from Afghanistan. German involvement with Afghanistan began before World War I. Afghanistan was particularly friendly to Germany during the late 1930's and 1940's because of Germany's opposition to England and Russia. Afghanistan hoped to take India up to the Indus river if the Axis powers won the war. The ambassador told the secretary of these hopes and of Afghanistan's

friendship and support of Germany. The secretary in turn informed the ambassador that Germany would keep in mind Afghanistan's goals. E. F. Stocker

352. Simion, A. and Ştefan, M. AUGUST 1940. DICTATUL DE LA VIENA—EXPRESSIE A POLITICII DE FORȚĂ [August 1940. The Vienna Diktat: instance of the politics of force]. *Magazin Istoric [Rumania] 1975 9(8): 17-22.* Reviews the Axis partition of Transylvania in favor of Hungary.

353. Simion, A. LES CONDITIONS POLITIQUES DU DIKTAT DE VIENNE (30 AOÛT 1940) [The political conditions of the Vienna Diktat 30 August 1940]. *Rev. Roumaine d'Hist. [Rumania] 1972 11(3): 447-472.* On 30 August 1940, representatives of Rumania were forced to cede the northern half of Transylvania to Hungary. Discusses the political conditions which allowed this to happen: the total dominance of Nazi Germany, now at the height of its power after its defeat of France, and the weak attitude of Rumania's political leaders, who capitulated to the dictation of Germany without attempting any resistance. 67 notes. J. C. Billigmeier

354. Sjøqvist, Viggo. MINISTER MOHRS REFERATER AF SAMTALEN MED AMBASSADØR RITTER DEN 18. JULI 1940 [Undersecretary Mohr's accounts of his conversation with ambassador Ritter, 18 July 1940]. *Historie [Denmark] 1973 10(3): 426-432.* Discusses the authenticity of the two versions by Otto Mohr, under-secretary in the Danish foreign office, of his negotiations in Berlin with German ambassador Ritter about Danish-German trade cooperation, 18 July 1940.

355. Stuhlpfarrer, Karl. IL PROBLEMA ALTOATESINO DELL' "ANSCHLUSS" ALLA FINE DELLA SECONDA GUERRA MONDIALE [The South Tyrol problem from the *Anschluss* to the end of World War II]. *Storia e Politica [Italy] 1974 13(1-2): 127-145.* When Nazi Germany seized Austria in 1938, it desired to reassure its new ally, Fascist Italy, that it did not want to alter the frontier on the Brenner and annex the German-speaking region of South Tyrol, the Italian province of Alto Adige. A scheme was worked out by which those German-speaking South Tyrolers who wished could "opt" for Germany; they were to be settled in conquered territory: Sudetenland, Slovenia, the Crimea. Actually, most of the "opting" Tyrolese stayed where they were. After the fall of Mussolini in 1943, the Germans moved in and annexed the South Tyrol. 70 notes. J. C. Billigmeier

356. Talpeş, Ioan. ROMÂNIA ÎN FAȚA EXPANSIUNII GERMANIEI NAZISTE ŞI A ATACURILOR REVIZIONISTE (30 SEPTEMBRIE 1938-13 APRILE 1939) [Rumania confronted with the expansion of Nazi Germany and revisionist attacks, 30 September 1938-13 April 1939]. *Rev. de Istorie [Rumania] 1976 29(9): 1297-1323.* Reacting to the 1938 Munich agreement, Rumania tried to strengthen its economic, political, and military relations with Britain, France, Poland, and the Balkan Entente, but fear of German aggression and lack of unconditional Franco-British support led to the economic agreement with Germany.

357. Thies, Jochen. PEUT-ON QUALIFIER HITLER DE "DICTATEUR FAIBLE"? ESSAI D'ANALYSE DES THÈSES DE LA POLITIQUE EXTÉRIEURE NATIONAL-SOCIALISTE [Can one characterize Hitler as a

feeble dictator? An analytical essay on National Socialist foreign policy]. *Rev. d'Hist. de la Deuxième Guerre Mondiale [France] 1980 30(120): 33-48.* Recent popular histories by Joachim Fest and John Toland assemble facts about Adolf Hitler's life, while David Irving creates controversy by asserting that Hitler did not know of the extermination of the Jews. Wolfgang Schieder attempts to reconcile the different points of view concerning Nazi foreign and domestic policy. Martin Broszat finds that Hitler's social motivations, philosophy, and events and policies are so contradictory that Hitler's ideas could not have been the controlling factor in foreign policy. Hans Mommsen finds Nazi foreign policy fluid and indecisive. Andreas Hillgruber and Klaus Hildebrand believe that Hitler proclaimed his plans in *Mein Kampf* and his second book for a phased world conquest; subsequent policy shifts were merely tactical adjustments. Jochen Thies calls attention to the career of Albert Speer and the grandiose construction plans Hitler ordered him to make. These were based on world domination and enslavement of the manpower of conquered territories and included a plan to exterminate the Jews. Based on published works and the German Bundesarchiv at Koblenz and Freiburg; 56 notes. G. H. Davis

358. Thulstrup, Åke. GUSTAV V'S ROLL UNDER MIDSOMMARKRISEN 1941 [Gustavus V's role in the Midsummer crisis 1941]. *Historisk Tidskrift [Sweden] 1972 92(1): 72-79.* Cites German documentary evidence that King Gustavus V of Sweden (1858-1950) threatened to abdicate on 22 June 1941 unless the Swedish government agreed to German demands for transit rights across Swedish territory. 12 notes. R. G. Selleck

359. Treue, Wilhelm. DREIMAL 50 JAHRE GOTHAER LEBENSVERSICHERUNG [150 years of the Gotha Life Insurance Company: a report on the past 50 years, 1927-77]. *Zeitschrift für Unternehmensgeschichte [West Germany] 1977 Beiheft(10): 1-63.* From its founding in 1827 under Ernst Wilhelm Arnoldi (1778-1841) as the first German life insurance company, the Gotha Life Insurance Company has played a leading role in Germany's business history. Chronicles the company's fortunes since 1927, shedding light on the effects of inflation, depression, and war on the insurance business. 5 illus., 2 figs., note.
M. A. Butler

360. Uola, Mikko. YKSITYISTÄ ULKOPOLITIIKKAA "AJOPUUSYKSYLTÄ" [Private foreign policy during the "driftwood autumn"]. *Hist. Aikakauskirja [Finland] 1980 78(3): 232-239.* An account of a visit to Germany in October 1940 by Rauno Kallia (1901-48), a leader of Finland's right-wing IKL party. The Germans with whom he spoke were surprisingly sympathetic to Finland, indicating the shift in German foreign policy which was implemented in November 1940. Based on Kallia's private papers and on Finnish monographs; 40 notes. R. G. Selleck

361. Vago, Bela. THE INTELLIGENCE ASPECTS OF THE JOEL BRAND MISSION. *Yad Vashem Studies on the European Jewish Catastrophe and Resistance [Israel] 1974 10: 111-128.* The intelligence aspects of the Joel Brand mission (Eichmann's proposal to exchange Jewish lives for war materials) overshadowed its other features in May and June 1944. Examines the intelligence task of Bandi Grosz, Brand's companion and a notorious double-agent connected with the intelligence forces of Germany, Hungary, Britain, the United States, and

the Jewish Agency. Grosz was to inform the Allies of those Hungarian elements willing to surrender to the Allies on condition that Russia not enter Hungary, and of the desire of the *Sicherheitsdienst* to discuss a separate peace with the Western Allies. Based on archival and published sources; 40 notes. J. P. Fox

362. Vanwelkenhuyzen, Jean. LA CONFERENCE DIPLOMATIQUE DU 5 AVRIL 1940 [The diplomatic conference of 5 April 1940]. *Cahiers d'Hist. de la Seconde Guerre Mondiale [Belgium] 1974 (3): 85-101.* Analysis of the conference of 5 April 1940 of Belgium's prime minister, foreign minister, and ambassadors to London, Paris, The Hague, Berlin, and Rome. Surveying the international situation, they clearly saw Belgium's helpless position, but determined to keep its foreign policy options open even while remaining committed to neutrality. The details of the conference were revealed to the German ambassador in Brussels, apparently in order to show the Germans that Belgian foreign policy had not changed. Based on German and Belgian archives and memoirs; 57 notes.
M. K. Palat

363. Vedovato, Giuseppe. L'ADESIONE DELLA JUGOSLAVIA AL PATTO TRIPARTITO [Yugoslavia's signing of the Tripartite Pact]. *Riv. di Studi Pol. Int. [Italy] 1978 45(4): 554-558.* Reviews Alfredo Breccia's *Jugoslavia 1939-1941. Diplomazia della neutralità* (Milano: Giuffrè, 1978), examining historiographical interpretations of diplomacy between the Yugoslavian government and the Axis powers, 1939-41.

364. Volkmann, Hans-Erich. L'IMPORTANCE ÉCONOMIQUE DE LA LORRAINE POUR LE IIIe REICH [The economic importance of Lorraine to the Third Reich]. *Rev. d'Hist. de la Deuxième Guerre Mondiale [France] 1980 30(120): 69-93.* The mining industry of Lorraine played a special role in the actual war economy of Nazi Germany and in the plans for a postwar European economy under German domination. Part of Lorraine was annexed to Germany and the rest—the department of Meurthe-et-Moselle—remained technically a part of German-occupied France. Although Lorraine produced more iron ore than Germany itself by 1943, the ore was more difficult to process and production fell drastically in 1944 because of the extreme labor shortage. Based on documents in the German Bundesarchiv, Koblenz and Freiburg; 5 tables, 69 notes.
G. H. Davis

365. Warner, Geoffrey. FROM PEARL HARBOUR TO STALINGRAD: GERMANY AND ITS ALLIES IN 1942. *Int. Affairs [Great Britain] 1978 54(2): 282-292.* Briefly surveys the publication of German diplomatic documents on the period 1918-45 in the light of the appearance of the first volumes to be edited by West Germans, while also stressing the need to read the documents deriving from one government department in the context of the complex nature of German policymaking. Examines the evidence on the difficulties of coordinating German and Japanese strategy in 1942 and stresses Japan's reluctance to become involved against Russia. The documents also throw light on German-Italian relations over North Africa and on the possibility of an Axis alliance with Vichy France. Based on *Akten zur deutschen Auswärtigen Politik 1918-1945. Serie E: 1941-1945,* vol. 1-4 (Göttingen, 1969-75); 47 notes. P. J. Beck

366. West, John M. THE GERMAN-SWEDISH TRANSIT AGREEMENT OF 1940. *Scandinavian Studies 1978 50(1): 76-99.* Explains the acquiescence by Sweden to German demands for transit permission to Norway. This request was almost inevitable after the invasion of Norway in April 1940. It was especially needed when Germany lost control of the sea route to Narvik. The Swedes at first refused and prepared for invasion. Tension rose through May, heightened by the Allied capture of Narvik, only to lessen with German successes on the Continent and Allied withdrawal from Norway. Sweden was now more isolated and thus further under the influence of Germany. On 18 June the Swedish cabinet agreed to the German demands. This was the price Sweden paid for peace. Based on official sources; 73 notes. C. W. Ohrvall

367. Wilhelmus, Wolfgang. DAS SCHWEDISCHE ECHO AUF DIE FASCHISTISCHEN "NEUORDNUNGS"—PLÄNE IM ZWEITEN WELTKRIEG [The Swedish response to fascist New Order plans in World War II]. *Jahrbuch für Wirtschaftsgeschichte [East Germany] 1975 (1): 35-46.* Recounts Nazi efforts to draw Sweden into the "greater German economic sphere" following the invasion of Denmark and Norway in 1940. Sweden vigorously defended its neutrality and resisted German economic pressure. Throughout the war Sweden ignored Germany's blandishments, supplying strategic raw materials to the Reich only with great reluctance. By September 1944 the Swedish government had virtually discontinued trade between the two countries. Primary and secondary sources; 52 notes. R. J. Bazillion

368. Wilhelmus, Wolfgang. DIE BEDEUTUNG DES SCHWEDISCHEN EISENERZES FUR DIE FASCHISTISCHE KRIEGSWIRTSCHAFT [The significance of Swedish iron ore for the fascist war economy]. *Jahrbuch für Wirtschaftsgeschichte [East Germany] 1973 (4): 37-56.* Swedish iron ore played a dominant role in Germany's Scandinavian policy. The support of the USSR until 1941, the involvement of the German army in the east from 1941, and Swedish readiness to compromise preserved Sweden's neutrality. Germany's capacity to meet Sweden's import needs, especially of coal and armaments, as much as German political power, controlled the volume of ore exports, which declined in the early years of the war and peaked in 1943. Based on secondary and archival materials; 3 maps, 9 tables, and 72 notes. J. A. Perkins

369. Wilhelmus, Wolfgang. SCHWEDEN UND DAS FASCHISTISCHE DEUTSCHLAND IM ZWEITEN WELTKRIEG [Sweden and fascist Germany in World War II]. *Zeitschrift für Geschichtswissenschaft [East Germany] 1973 21(7): 791-809.* Between 1939 and 1943 Sweden, which remained neutral during World War II, became subjugated to German economic pressure because of its isolation after the German victories in Scandinavia. Only after the defeat of the German armies before Moscow was Sweden able to return to full neutrality. In the final stages of the war it developed close relations with the antifascist coalition. Based on documents in the Deutsches Zentralarchiv Potsdam, printed documents, and secondary literature; 95 notes. R. Wagnleitner

370. Wilhelmus, Wolfgang. ZU DEN BEZIEHUNGEN ZWISCHEN DEM FASCHISTISCHEN DEUTSCHLAND UND SCHWEDEN NACH DEM ÜBERFALL AUF DIE SOWJETUNION [Relations between fascist Germany and Sweden after the attack on the Soviet Union]. *Zeitschrift für Geschichtswis-*

senschaft [East Germany] 1978 26(8): 687-699. Shortly before the German attack on Russia in June 1941 the Germans asked the Swedes to cooperate with them, pointing out that Finland was already helping Germany. The Germans were allowed to transport men and equipment through Sweden from 24 June 1941 onwards. Subsequently the Germans wrested many concessions from the Swedes, to such a degree that Sweden was forced to revise its "neutrality." Nonetheless, Sweden never fully cooperated in the anti-Soviet Front. Archive sources; 54 notes.
A. Alcock

371. Zetterberg, Kent. LE TRANSIT ALLEMAND PAR LA SUÈDE DE 1940 À 1943 [German transit via Sweden, 1940-43]. *Rev. d'Hist. de la Deuxième Guerre Mondiale [France] 1978 28(109): 59-80.* Though ostensibly neutral, Sweden felt itself constrained, in the years 1939-43, to allow the Germans transit rights on Swedish railroads. Millions of German troops travelled in this way through Sweden, and it was through that country that German forces were sent to Finland before the attack on the Soviet Union, 22 June 1941, and thereafter. Petroleum and other vital products went to Finland and the northern part of the Eastern Front through Sweden. In August 1943 the transit agreement, as constituted, was terminated at Swedish initiative. Germany was losing the war, and could not bring sufficient pressure on Sweden to preserve it. After this, German use of Swedish railroads declined rapidly, and was stopped altogether for petroleum. 50 notes.
J. C. Billigmeier

372. Zinsser, Christian. DIPLOMATISCHE MISSION IN HONDURAS [Diplomatic mission in Honduras]. *Jahrbuch für Geschichte von Staat, Wirtschaft und Gesellschaft Lateinamerikas [West Germany] 1975 12: 434-455.* Written about 1961, this memoir recounts a seven month period when the author was German chargé d'affaires in Tegucigalpa during late 1940 and early 1941. Describes the diplomatic community, the Honduran political figures, and the basis for his dismissal as *persona non grata* from Honduras and later from Guatemala, assigning chief responsibility for these dismissals to US influence.
T. D. Schoonover

373. —. [FINLAND'S FOREIGN POLICY, 1940-41].
Jokipii, Mauno. VUODENVAIHDE 1940-1941 UUDESSA VOLOSSA [The turn of the year 1940-41 in a new light]. *Hist. Aikakauskirja [Finland] 1977 75(1): 3-17, (2): 77-95.* Finnish military leaders became interested in military cooperation with Germany during August 1940 when a Soviet attack on Finland seemed imminent. Both Finnish arms purchases from Germany and German army transit rights through Finland were then negotiated. In November 1940, Finnish leaders learned of the proposal by Soviet Foreign Minister Vyacheslav Molotov to liquidate Finland. During December the Finnish commander-in-chief Carl Gustav Mannerheim (1867-1951) raised with both Sweden and Germany the question of military support in case of Soviet attack. 74 notes. Part II. When negotiations for Swedish-Finnish military cooperation collapsed in January 1941, the Finnish commander-in-chief Carl Gustav Mannerheim (1867-1951) turned to Germany as a last resort. On 30 January 1941, Finnish and German military officers held the first explicit conversations about military cooperation against the USSR, earlier than was previously assumed. The context indicates that Mannerheim's motive was defense against a Soviet attack, not a war of

revenge. Mannerheim then pressured Finnish President Risto Ryti (1889-1956) into accepting his German policy and rejecting the conciliatory policy advocated by the Finnish diplomat Juho Kusti Paasikivi (1870-1956). Based on Finnish and German memoirs and archives; 75 notes.

Manninen, Ohto. UUDEN VALON VARJOT: VAIHTOEHTOJA VUODENVAIHTEEN 1940-1941 TULKINTOIHIN [Shadows of a new light: alternative interpretations of the turn of the year 1940-41]. *Hist. Aikakauskirja [Finland] 1977 75(3): 234-253.* Finnish foreign policy leaders had already shifted to a pro-German line in the summer of 1940. What occurred in early 1941 was a shift of German planning towards a policy of active support for Finland, which facilitated Finnish-German cooperation. 52 notes.

Myllyniemi, Seppo. KÄÄNNEKÖ HELMIKUUSSA 1941? [A turning point in February 1941?]. *Hist. Aikakauskirja [Finland] 1977 75(3): 253-255.* Argues that Jokipii has drawn too sharp a line between foreign policy alternatives perceived by Finnish leaders in the spring of 1941.

Jokipii, Mauno. VANHAN VALON VARJOTTOMUUS [Old light unshaded]. *Hist. Aikakauskirja [Finland] 1977 75(3): 255-265.* Rebuts Manninen's detailed critique, accepts some factual corrections, finds Myllyniemi vague, and sees no reason to revise his basic argument.

Manninen, Ohto. VALON JA VARJON LEIKKIÄ [The play of light and shadow]. *Hist. Aikakauskirja [Finland] 1977 75(4): 348-360.* Differs from Jokipii on several points: 1) the proffered resignation of the Finnish commander, Carl Gustav Mannerheim (1867-1951), in February 1941 was not a turning point; 2) Finnish experts did not contribute to the formation of Germany's Barbarossa plan for attack on the Soviet Union; and 3) the Finnish-German negotiations for a transit agreement in August 1940 were kept secret at the wish of Germany, not Finland. 20 notes.

R. G. Selleck

374. —. HITLEROVI RAZGOVORI SA PRETSTAVNICIMA NEZAVISNE DRŽAVE HRVATSKE [Hitler's talks with representatives of the Independent State of Croatia]. *Vojnoistorijski Glasnik [Yugoslavia] 1980 31(1): 281-291.* Reprints four documents on contacts between Adolf Hitler and representatives of the puppet state of Croatia, 1941-42. The documents from the Akten zur Deutschen auswartigen Politik, Series E, record Hitler's conversation with Ustaši leader Ante Pavelic on 6 June 1941; talk with Marshal Slavko Kvaternik at Hitler's headquarters in July 1941; audience granted to the Croatian Minister for Foreign Affairs Mladen Lorkovic, on 27 November 1941; and reception of the newly appointed Croatian Ambassador Milo Budak at the New Office of the Reich on 14 February 1942. 68 notes.

J. Bamber

375. —. [O. C. MOHR CONVERSATION IN BERLIN]. *Historie [Denmark] 1975 11(3): 309-364.*

Brunn, Hans Henrik. MOHR-SAGEN—FORSØG PA ET OVERBLIK [The Mohr case—an attempted overview], *pp. 309-360.* Examines the authenticity of minister O. C. Mohr's account of his 18 July 1940 conversation in Berlin with Ambassador Ritter. Evaluates Minister Mohr's actions, and reviews the available source material and the controversy on the question. The sources do not provide enough evidence to say that the 18 July report is of later construction. The author discusses the particular ethical problems which arise for historians of modern events and establishes rules with which they must comply. J/S

Sjøqvist, Viggo. SVAR TIL UNIVERSITETSADJUNKT H. H. BRUUN [Reply to university lecturer H. H. Brunn], *pp. 361-364.* Clarifies how the conflict about the Mohr reports came into being, and responds to a series of Brunn's critical comments about this issue. J/S

3

THE INVASION AND OCCUPATION OF POLAND

376. Bednarski, Hanna J. WARSAW UNIVERSITY LIBRARY, A HISTORY OF WARTIME SURVIVAL. *Canadian Lib. J. 1975 32(1): 34-39.* A history of Warsaw University Library's survival through wars and occupations for 600 years. Emphasizes the Nazi occupation and efforts of librarians to preserve collections from fire and intentional destruction. The present collection numbers three million volumes. Describes library administrative structure and departmental functions. 3 notes. L. F. Johnson

377. Beumer, P. M.; Lukkes, J. R.; and Renner, H. J. KATYN: EEN ONOPGELOST RAADSEL? [Katyn: an unsolved mystery?]. *Spiegel Hist. [Netherlands] 1979 14(9): 476-484.* The massacre of 4,500 Polish officers at Katyn in the USSR at the beginning of World War II has been charged against the Nazis. Recent investigation makes it almost certain that the mass execution was carried out by the Stalinist government. Primary sources; 12 illus. C. W. Wood

378. Bieda, Tadeusz. ZRÓDŁA HISTORYCZNE DO DZIEJÓW OKUPACJI HITLEROWSKIEJ W ZBIORACH ARCHIWALNYCH WOJEWÓDZTWA RZESZOWSKIEGO [Nazi archival documents in Rzeszów Province Archives]. *Archeion [Poland] 1976 64: 105-115.* Describes the political value and significance of materials in the Rzeszów provincial archives in the eastern part of present-day Poland, which contain documents produced by German authorities during World War II that they had no time to destroy. Compares these documents with Polish documents that give a complementary testimony of German war crimes in the province. J/S

379. Cygański, Mirosław. NAZI PERSECUTIONS OF POLISH NATIONAL MINORITIES IN THE RHINELAND-WESTPHALIA PROVINCES IN THE YEARS 1933-1945. *Polish Western Affairs [Poland] 1976 17(1-2): 115-138.* The years during World War II were the most difficult in the history of Polish emigrants in the Rhineland-Westphalia provinces. The Nazis deprived them of all possibilities of cultivating their national life in organized form. Nevertheless, Poles living in emigrant areas in the Rhineland-Westphalia region effectively opposed Nazi persecutions and the vehement denationalization action. M. Swiecicka-Ziemianek

380. Czubiński, Antoni. POLAND'S PLACE IN NAZI PLANS FOR A NEW ORDER IN EUROPE IN THE YEARS 1934-1940. *Polish Western Affairs [Poland] 1980 21(1): 19-46.* Discusses Hitler's plans to incorporate the Polish territories and establish central Europe as a sphere of German influence. Hitler's designs included "a new settlement of ethnographic relations" for the purpose of removing non-German elements from the area and the extermination of Polish society as such. Based on Hitler's books and writings, works of A. Rosenberga as well as on documents pertaining to German-Polish prewar negotiations; 107 notes. D. S. Lloyd

381. Drewniak, Bogusław. ORGANIZACJA NIEMIECKIEGO ŻYCIA TEATRALNEGO NA OBSZARACH POLSKI WCIELONYCH DO RZESZY W LATACH II WOJNY ŚWIATOWEJ [The organization of German theatrical life in the Polish territories incorporated into the Reich during World War II]. *Przegląd Zachodni [Poland] 1978 34(4): 55-65.* Describes the varied German theatrical and musical life which was financed by Joseph Goebbels's Propaganda Ministry in those Polish territories incorporated into Germany during World War II. A variety of theaters, some traveling, as well as orchestras, choirs, and ballet companies were introduced in such cities as Gdańsk, Poznań, Toruń, Katowice, Grudziądz and Łódz. 52 notes. M. A. Zurowski

382. Frank, Hans. HANS FRANK NAPLÓJÁBÓL [From the diary of Hans Frank]. *Világtörténet [Hungary] 1979 (4): 132-143.* Excerpts from the 11,000-page personal diary of Hans Frank, German governor of occupied Poland during World War II. 3 notes. R. Hetzron

383. Freundlich, Elisabeth. "AN SICHEREM ORT." DIE ERMORDUNG DER LEMBERGER HOCHSCHULPROFESSOREN (JULI 1941) ["An Sicherem Ort": The murder of the professors of Lemberg University (July 1941)]. *Zeitgeschichte [Austria] 1977 4(11-12): 398-409.* Describes and authenticates the Nazi murder of 25 Polish professors of Lemberg University and some of their relatives in July 1941. Based on oral reports and recollections; 7 notes.
J. B. Street

384. Giesinger, Adam, transl. THE TREK OF THE ETHNIC GERMANS FROM VOLHYNIA, GALICIA, AND THE NAREW RIVER REGION. *J. of the Am. Hist. Soc. of Germans from Russia 1978 1(1): 13-19.* Official report of the activities and organization of the 307-man force formed on the orders of Hitler that oversaw the repatriation of Germans living in eastern regions of Poland annexed by the USSR after the Nazi-Soviet Pact, 1939-40.

385. Golczewski, Frank. DEUTSCHE BESATZUNGSPOLITIK IN POLEN IM ZWEITEN WELTKRIEG [German occupation policy in Poland during World War II]. Meyers, Peter and Reisenberger, Dieter, ed. *Der Nationalsozialismus in der historisch-politischen Bildung* (Göttingen: Vandenhoeck & Ruprecht, 1979): 164-184. Examines the German invasion of Poland and treatment of this subject in history teaching in West Germany today.

386. Gollert, Friedriech. POWSTANIE WARSZAWSKIE 1944: SPRAWOZDANIE KOŃCOWE GUBERNATORA DYSTRYKTU WARSZAWSKIEGO GRUPPENFÜHRERA SA DR. LUDWIG'A FISCHERA DO GENERAŁ-GUBERNATORA MINISTRA RZESZY DR. FRANKA [The

Warsaw Uprising 1944: the final report of the governor of the Warsaw district Gruppenfuhrer SA Dr. Ludwig Fischer to governor-general minister of the Reich Dr. Frank]. *Zeszyty Hist. [France] 1978 (43): 182-205.* Analyzes the causes of the Warsaw Uprising in 1944 stressing its inevitability, and appraises its effect on gaining the support of the Poles for the German policy in Poland.

387. Gruggel, Bogumila. L'INIZIO DELLA SECONDA GUERRA MONDIALE: LA BATTAGLIA DI WESTERPLATTE [The beginning of World War II: the battle of Westerplatte]. *La Seconda Guerra Mondiale nella Prospettiva Storica a Trent'Anni dall'Epilogo* (Como: Casa Editrice Pietro Cairoli, 1977): 349-358. Ten years of exhaustive research have enabled the author to amass a comprehensive bibliography of the events concerning the battle of Westerplatte. The German attack on Danzig, or the península of Westerplatte, on 1 September 1939, is of particular significance to the Poles because of its heroic defense led by Major Sucharski.   M. T. Wilson

388. Heike, Otto. DAS STADTARCHIV IN LODZ, INSBESONDERE WÄHREND DER JAHRE 1939-1945 [The city archives of Łódz, especially during the years 1939-45]. *Zeitschrift für Ostforschung [West Germany] 1978 27(1): 86-111.* The author, a German of Polish birth, was editor of an anti-Nazi German newspaper when German forces took Łódz in September 1939. His newspaper was banned, but he was appointed director of the city archives because he knew Polish and Russian as well as German. In this office he was able, during the years of World War II, to save valuable documents not only from Łódz, but also from neighboring towns, including documents relating to Polish and Jewish communities that zealous Nazis would have done away with had they found them. When the German forces retreated, Heike aided in the preservation of the archives of the German occupation authorities. 15 notes, 6 appendixes (letters).
J. C. Billigmeier

389. Hoover, Karl D. THE BALTIC RESETTLEMENT OF 1939 AND NATIONAL SOCIALIST RACIAL POLICY. *J. of Baltic Studies 1977 8(1): 79-89.* Racism more than anti-Soviet motives led to the Nazi transfer in late 1939 of some 60,000 ethnic Germans from Estonia and Latvia to occupied Polish territory contiguous with Germany. 20 notes.   E. W. Jennison, Jr.

390. Horn, Maurycy. CENTRALNY PUNKT DLA VOLKSDEUTSCHÓW [Central Station for Volksdeutsche]. *Biuletyn Żydowskiego Inst. Hist. w Polsce [Poland] 1976 97(1): 89-92.* German occupation forces created an office to regulate the affairs of the *Volksdeutsche,* persons of German origin recruited from the local population. One of the tasks of such stations was seizure of Jewish property.   J/S

391. Jacobmeyer, Wolfgang. DIE POLNISCHE WIDERSTANDSBEWEGUNG IM GENERALGOUVERNEMENT UND IHRE BEURTEILUNG DURCH DEUTSCHE DIENSTSTELLEN [The Polish Resistance in the General Government and its assessment by German agencies]. *Vierteljahrshefte für Zeitgeschichte [West Germany] 1977 25(4): 658-681.* An analysis of World War II Polish resistance against German military occupation of Poland based on German reports. The two main forms of Polish resistance, harrassment of German administration and, increasingly, partisan warfare, were significantly

shaped by the policy and practice of the occupation, whose early espousal of extreme methods and goals left it little flexibility and drove Poles into similarly uncompromising methods of resistance. Based on document collection at the Institute for Contemporary History (Munich); 108 notes. — D. Prowe

392. Karchmer, Naphtali. BASHEVI HAGERMANI 'IM TSAVA POLANI MUVAS [In German captivity with a defeated Polish army]. *Yalkut Moreshet Periodical [Israel] 1981 (31): 117-131.* Relates the bitter experiences of the prisoners of war and of the Jews caught in the course of Germany's military occupation of East Prussia. Serving in the 1st Division of the regular Polish Army, the author was captured early. He managed to conceal his Jewish origin and was sent, with other Poles, to do forced labor on German farms. — R. Hetzron

393. Karp, Hans-Jürgen. GERMANISIERUNG ODER SEELSORGE? ZUR TÄTIGKEIT REICHSDEUTSCHER PRIESTER IN DEN DEM DEUTSCHEN REICH EINGEGLIEDERTEN GEBIETEN POLENS 1939-1945 [Germanization or religious welfare? The activities of German national priests in the parts of Poland being annexed by the German Reich, 1939-45]. *Zeitschrift für Ostforschung [West Germany] 1981 30(1): 40-74.* The National Socialist policy concerning church and racial questions in those parts of Poland annexed by the German Reich aimed at the extermination of the Polish intelligentsia, the clergy in particular, and at the Germanization of the Catholic population, partly by appointing German priests. There were differences in the manner of realizing the policy of Germanization in the several parts of the country, and the need for priests coming from the Reich and the number of clergymen actually working in these regions varied accordingly. — J/S

394. Konieczny, Alfred. WIĘZIENIE KARNE W KŁODZKU W LATACH II WOJNY ŚWIATOWEJ [The penal institution in Kłodzko during World War II]. *Śląski Kwartalnik Hist. Sobótka [Poland] 1974 29(3): 369-388.* Discusses records of prisoners held during 1903-45 at the prison in Kłodzko, and the prisoners detained there by the order of civil, military, and police courts during 1939-45. Many of them were held at the request of the Breslau Gestapo, at whose request prisoners were sent to concentration camps. Among some of the political prisoners held in Kłodzko were 39 members of a Polish resistance group in Silesia, the White Eagle Union; 18 were sentenced to death. Based on sources in the archives of the city and the province of Wrocław (Breslau).
— C. M. Nowak

395. Korotyński, Henryk. W ROCZNICĘ WRZEŚNIA 1939 R [On the anniversary of September 1939]. *Nowe Drogi [Poland] 1974 (9): 65-72.* Reflects on the many domestic problems and the misguided foreign policy of interwar Poland, which left it without effective allies in 1939.

396. Kozmiński, Maciej and Juhász, Gyula. HUNGARY AND POLAND IN 1939. *New Hungarian Q. [Hungary] 1980 21(80): 105-110.* The Hungarian government's refusal to grant permission for German troops to use its railway lines in September 1939 did little to prevent the fall of Poland, but, by retaining control of their common border, it did enable Polish refugees to escape to Hungary. Both self-interest and moral principle motivated Hungary to aid the Poles, despite the pro-Axis policy of Prime Minister Teleki. The Poles later played an

important role in Hungary's 1943 secret negotiations with Great Britain and in the Hungarian resistance. Based on *Hungarian Foreign Policy Documents 1936-1945*, Vol. IV, and other primary sources. E. L. Keyser

397. Krakowski, Shmuel. THE FATE OF JEWISH PRISONERS OF WAR IN THE SEPTEMBER 1939 CAMPAIGN. *Yad Vashem Studies on the European Jewish Catastrophe and Resistance [Israel] 1977 12: 297-334.* Between 34,000 and 64,000 Jewish soldiers were captured by the Germans in the September 1939 blitzkrieg of Poland. According to the testimony of former prisoners of war, the Nazis abused all their captives, but evidence presented here suggests that mistreatment of Polish Jews was particularly cruel. Documentation covers all phases of incarceration, from transit camps to *stalags* to the release of those Jewish soldiers who survived the overcrowded and unsanitary accommodations, meager rations, and systematic brutality. Officer camps were more endurable until the closing months of World War II. Based mainly on archival documents; 100 notes. B. Reiner

398. Krakowski, Shmuel. "POLICY OF THE THIRD REICH IN CONQUERED POLAND." *Yad Vashem Studies on the European Jewish Catastrophe and Resistance [Israel] 1973 (9): 225-245.* A detailed critique of Professor Czeslaw Madajczyk's two-volume work, *Polityka III Rzeszy w okupowanej Polsce* (Warsaw, 1970). While admitting that this is the most successful attempt made by a Polish historian to examine synthetically various aspects of Polish history during World War II, the author asserts that Madajczyk has produced a distorted evaluation of the Polish-Jewish tragedy as a result of the lines laid down for historians in Poland by the official propaganda machine, which required presentation of the Polish-Jewish tragedy in minimal dimensions, minimizing the scope of the Jewish resistance and exaggerating the help given by the Poles and concealing the part played by Poles in anti-Jewish activity. Based on archival and published sources; 32 notes. J. P. Fox

399. Król, Eugeniusz, C. GRABIEŻ POLSKICH SZKÓŁ WYŻSZYCH W OKRESIE OKUPACJI HITLEROWSKIEJ [The looting of Polish universities during the Hitlerite occupation]. *Przegląd Hist. [Poland] 1979 70(3): 475-497.* From the beginning of World War II, as part of the Tannenberg plan to eliminate intellectual and leadership centers in Poland, Hitler ordered the robbing and looting of Polish universities. Several German entities responsible for looting universities as well as arresting and deporting professors in Poznań, Cracow, and Lublin are described in detail. Based on German archives (AAN), documents of the International Military Tribunal (Nürnberg), Deutsches Zentralarchiv Potsdam (DZA), Bundesarchiv Koblenz (BK); 70 notes. Russian and French summaries. I. Lukes

400. Krzyżanowski, Jerzy R. and Saroka, Waclaw W. THE POLISH UNDERGROUND RESISTANCE IN THE LUBLIN AREA: A DUOLOGUE. *Polish Rev. 1975 20(4): 145-156.* The two volume *Związek Walki i Armia Krajowa w Okręgu Lubelskim, 1939-1944* (Union for Armed Struggle and the Home Army in Lublin Province, 1939-1944) is a welcome addition to the history of the Polish Resistance in World War II. Though marred by some errors of fact and the necessity of omitting some unsavory incidents regarding the Russian liberation of Poland, it is nevertheless a valuable book. It contains archival material hitherto inaccessible in the West. E. M. McLendon

401. Kwiatkowska, Celestyna. ZACHOWANE W ARCHIWUM PAŃSTWOWYM WE WROCŁAWIU MATERIALY Z LAT 1939-1945, DOTYCZACE JEŃCĆW WOJENNYCH I OEOZÓW JENIECKICH [Archival materials dating from the Second World War years, pertaining to prisoners of war, kept at the Wroclaw Voivodeship State Archives]. *Archeion [Poland] 1974 (61): 123-137.* The Wroclaw Voivodeship State Archives maintain fragments of records of the German occupation in World War II, which the authorities had no time to destroy prior to their withdrawal. These materials contain information on prisoners sent to Silesia from various fronts, including work, conduct, escapes, death rates, and causes of death. The materials are especially significant as they contain specifications of prisoners' names and nationalities. J/S

402. Liman, Stefan. POLACY W BERLINIE W SZACUNKOWYCH UJĘCIACH XIX I POCZĄTKACH XX W. ORAZ W SPISACH LUDNOŚCI Z LAT 1945 I 1946 [Poles in Berlin in estimates for the 19th and the beginning of the 20th centuries and in censuses for the years 1945 and 1946]. *Przegląd Zachodni [Poland] 1979 35(2): 64-83.* Poles were attested in Berlin for nearly 200 years, at first as students. After 1871 workers and artisans immigrated, and by 1889 there were 60,000 Poles in Berlin, by 1914, over 100,000. They were highly organized, with Polish banks, cooperatives, a trade union, newspapers, and parliamentary representation. After World War I many Poles repatriated, but still numbered 37,000 in 1927. The prisoners of war and forced laborers who came during World War II were massively repatriated after the war. The Allies ordered a census for August 1945, but it suffered from definitional problems. Better data were obtained in the census of October 1946, which counted 1,548 Polish citizens, of which 593 were Germans. There were 4,573 persons of Polish descent. Based on primary sources and publications. M. Krzyzaniak

403. Madajczyk, Czeslaw. DIE INTERNATIONALE BEDEUTUNG DES VON POLEN IM JAHRE 1939 GEFÜHRTEN VERTEIDIGUNGSKRIEGES [The international importance of the defensive war waged by Poland in 1939]. *Jahrbuch für Gesch. [East Germany] 1981 23: 305-313.* Poland paid heavily for its resistance against Germany in 1939, but it stopped the appeasement policy which had previously permitted Hitler to expand his territory without having to pay for it, thus making later resistance against him ever more costly. 9 notes. A. Schuetz

404. Madajczyk, Czesław. THE INTERNATIONAL IMPORTANCE OF POLAND'S DEFENSIVE WAR IN 1939. *Polish Western Affairs [Poland] 1980 21(1): 68-75.* Discusses Hitler's attack on Poland on 1 September 1939 and his attempt to isolate Poland from its French and British allies. Poland's rejection of Hitler's demands for incorporating Gdańsk into the Third Reich and the building of an extraterritorial highway across Pomerania was the first major step against Hitler's expansionist plans, without which the Allies would have had a harder time defeating fascism. Based on primary sources such as personal war diaries and Polish documents pertaining to World War II; 9 notes. D. S. Lloyd

405. Madajczyk, Czesław. KULTURA WARSZAWY W LATACH WOJNY I OKUPACJI [Warsaw's culture during the war and occupation]. *Kultura i Społeczeństwo [Poland] 1978 22(1-2): 21-32.* During World War II,

Warsaw was the cultural center of Poland. The German occupation in 1939 attempted to destroy cultural life in Warsaw and eliminate its influence in other parts of Poland. Polish writers, painters, actors, musicians, and scholars actively participated in the resistance. The struggle to preserve the culture of the capital instilled in its people the strength, vitality, and knowledge required to rebuild the city in the postwar years. M. Swiecicka-Ziemianek

406. Małczużyński, Karol. WARSZAWA: CASUS KARTAGINA [Warsaw: the fate of Carthage]. *Nowe Drogi [Poland] 1975 (8): 75-85.* Describes the Nazi plans since 1939 to destroy the city of Warsaw, an operation that was carried out ruthlessly and methodically in 1944 and which continued until Warsaw's liberation in January 1945.

407. Marczewski, Jerzy. POLAND IN NAZI CONCEPTIONS OF EXPANSION. *Polish Western Affairs [Poland] 1980 21(1): 106-120.* Discusses the Nazi policy of eastward expansion and the plan for the extermination of the native population of Poland and the colonization of the Slavic East with native Germans. Hitler conceived these plans in *Mein Kampf.* Based on official government documents, Hitler's speeches, and books; 57 notes. D. S. Lloyd

408. Miąso, Józef. CLANDESTINE EDUCATION IN POLAND IN THE YEARS OF THE NAZI OCCUPATION. *Polish Western Affairs [Poland] 1978 19(1): 104-112.* As a result of the closing of Polish schools, clandestine secondary schools were organized and assumed definitely established forms in 1940-41. Despite the persecution, even the Jagiellonian University began secret activities in 1941. The level of clandestine teaching was high, and the continuity of Polish schooling was maintained through the five-year occupation despite Nazi plans to liquidate it. M. Swiecicka-Ziemianek

409. Michta, Norbert. DZIELNICA GL-AL "MNISZEK" I SPRAWA "AUGUSTA II" [The People's Guard of the Mniszek District, the People's Army, and the matter of Augustus II]. *Z Pola Walki [Poland] 1972 15(2): 255-266.* The People's Guard and the People's Army of the Polish underground were active in the Mniszek district of the Miechów region near Cracow during the German occupation of Poland. The partisan with the code name Augustus II was actually a German agent. 33 notes. L. A. Krzyzak

410. Modrzewska, Krystyna. PAMIĘTNIK Z OKRESU OKUPACJI [Memoir of the Nazi occupation]. *Biuletyn Żydowskiego Instytutu Historycznego [Poland] 1959 (32): 65-78; 1960 (33): 105-124.* Continued from a previous article. Part II. Memoirs of a Jewish girl describing her ordeals posing as an Aryan during the Nazi occupation of the Lublin province. Covers the period from August 1942. Part III. As a clerk in a German office, district of Garwolin, she describes the miserable life in a small town under the occupation and the local Nazi officials who were afraid to go to the front line. Relates the echoes of the heroic Warsaw Ghetto uprising and the Nazi atrocities against Jews, which had reached the Lublin Province. Describes the intensified activity of local guerrillas and the last days of occupation and the first moments after the liberation. Note.
J/T. N. Cieplak

411. Nazarewicz, Ryszard. DIE MITWIRKUNG POLNISCHER AUFKLÄRER AN DER BEFREIUNG DEUTSCHLANDS VOM FASCHISMUS [The assistance of Polish scouts in the liberation of Germany from fascism]. *Militärgeschichte [East Germany] 1975 14(1): 53-60.* Personal recollections of the cooperation of the Polish resistance movement with German antifascists and the Red Army between 1944 and 1945. R. Wagnleitner

412. Olszewski, Marian. THE POLICY OF EXTERMINATING POLISH INTELLECTUALS DURING THE NAZI OCCUPATION. *Polish Western Affairs [Poland] 1980 21(1): 121-128.* Discusses Hitler's systematic plan to exterminate Polish intellectuals as a scheme to solve the Polish population problem. Hitler's speeches in 1939 and numerous Nazi documents address themselves specifically to the issue. According to the *Report on Polish War Losses and Damages Suffered in the Years 1939-1945,* 48,000 of 280,000 intellectuals perished. Based on numerous primary sources of the Nazi era such as Martin Bormann's protocol of 2 October 1940, Walter Daree's plan of 1939, the Erhard Wetzel and Gustav Hecht *Generalplan Ost 1941-43,* and others.
D. S. Lloyd

413. Pallas, Ladislav. K NACISTICKÉ NÁRODNOSTNÍ POLITICE NA HORNÍM SLEZSKU VČETNĚ TĚŠÍNSKA V LETECH 1938-1945 [The Nazi nationalities policy in Upper Silesia, except in Těšín, 1938-45]. *Slezský Sborník [Czechoslovakia] 1981 79(4): 261-286.* In Upper Silesia, the Germans executed their nationalities policy from the beginning of the war. Polish residents were transferred to Poland proper; the majority of the 81,000 went into special detention camps for Polish workers, intellectuals, older women, and children. Young men were sent to factories all over the Reich. This population was replaced with 38,000 Germans from the east. These early actions were meant to coerce many Silesians to claim German nationality in future census "volklists." Schooling was restricted to German nationals. 110 notes. B. Reinfeld

414. Pallas, Ladislav. NACISTICKÁ NÁRODNOSTNÍ POLITIKA NA HORNÍM SLEZSKU V L.1939-1945 [The Nazi nationality policy in Upper Silesia in the years 1939-45]. *Slezský Sborník [Czechoslovakia] 1981 79(1): 27-67.* In Upper Silesia the Nazi regime introduced a racist nationalities policy as it had done in Poland, but it tried to prove that Upper Silesia had had a predominantly German population before the war. The Deutsches Volkliste, a census carried out in the first two years, divided those claiming to be Germans into four categories which entitled those individuals to varied rights and privileges, such as joining the Nazi Party and attending German schools. Although the Volkliste showed that 80% of the population claimed German nationality, Germanization in Upper Silesia did not succeed. Many of those able to claim German nationality did it only for self-preservation; sometimes they were also members of the underground. Therefore, at the conclusion of the war, Upper Silesia remained Polish. 166 notes.
B. Reinfeld

415. Perski, Jakub. MATERIAŁY DO HISTORII ZŁOCZEWA (OKUPACJA HITLEROWSKA) [Materials concerning the history of Złoczów during the Nazi occupation]. *Przegląd Zachodni [Poland] 1975 31(4): 238-246.* A detailed report of the persecution endured by the inhabitants of the town, especially Jewish population, under German military occupation during World War II.

416. Pospieszalski, Karol Marian. DZIENNIK OKUPACYJNEGO BURMISTRZA PODDĘBIC K. ŁODZI JAKO ZRÓDŁO HISTORYCZNE [A diary of an occupying mayor of Poddębice near Łódz as a historical source]. *Przegląd Zachodni [Poland] 1978 34(2): 92-106.* Analyzes the diary of Franz Heinrich Bock, German mayor of Poddębice, near Łódz, Poland, December 1940-July 1942. Bock was well disposed to individual Jews and Poles, was respected by the local population, and tried to save one or two individuals, unsuccessfully, from the secret police. However, because of his background and Nazi Party indoctrination, he viewed Poles as culturally inferior and destined for Germanification. He also ignored mass atrocities such as the rounding-up and deportation of local Jews to a nearby death camp. 21 notes. M. A. Zurowski

417. Pospieszalski, Karol Marian. W SPRAWIE STRAT NIEMIECKIEJ MNIEJSZOSCI W POLSCE PRZED WYBUCHEM WOJNY I WE WRZEŚNIU 1939 [Losses among the German minority in Poland before the outbreak of the war and during September 1939]. *Przegląd Zachodni [Poland] 1980 36(2): 206-209.* The German news magazine *Stern* (47) of 15 November 1979 published photographic evidence, collected by an unknown Gestapo member, of German atrocities in Poland. To justify the acts it was claimed the Poles had exterminated 58,000 Germans prior to Gestapo revenge. The author of the article in *Stern* understands that the figure is immensely exaggerated, and contrasts it with a figure of 5,437 Volksdeutsche dead according to the German Foreign Affairs Department. Contrary to some German claims, such deaths as occurred took place only after the outbreak of war. The German card system for the burials of Volksdeutsche in 1942 showed 3,453 dead and 2,239 missing, but that included German partisans (Fifth Column), Germans who died from German bombing, and even some Poles, Russians, and Ukrainians. Many cards do not mention the cause of death. Losses due to Polish actions are probably much lower than the Germans claim. Based on vol. 7, *Documenta Occupationis* and other primary sources. M. Krzyzaniak

418. Przychodzki, Michal. LEKARZE POZNANSCY W LATACH HITLEROWSKIEJ OKUPACJI 1939-1945 [Poznan physicians during the Nazi occupation, 1939-45]. *Przegląd Zachodni [Poland] 1977 33(1): 106-139.* In 1938 there were 886 practicing doctors in Poznan. With the advent of Nazi rule most of them were denied the right to practice, and were sent to concentration camps or removed to other parts of Poland. The Nazis aimed at totally depriving the native Polish population of medical care to weaken the biological fabric of the Polish race. By 1940 only 70 Polish doctors were left; by 1945 over a hundred had died. 48 notes, biblio. W. Kowalski

419. Robertson, James C. THE OUTBREAK OF THE SECOND WORLD WAR. *Hist. J. [Great Britain] 1978 21(4): 1001-1007.* David Hoggan's thesis of British blame for the outbreak of war over Poland is questioned and partially substantiated on the basis of four monographs. Hoggan had argued that Britain was following a traditional policy of upholding the European balance of power against any single power that threatened to dominate the continent. Although the historical judgment that Germany was solely responsible for the immediate diplomatic origins of World War II is not called into serious question, Polish obduracy and Anglo-French adherence to outmoded balance-of-power doctrines in the Polish crisis, coupled with the previous pusillanimity of London and Paris, contributed to the outbreak of war. 6 notes. L. J. Reith

420. Rostowski, Dieter. SS-VERBRECHEN AN VERWUNDETEN DER 2. POLNISCHEN ARMEE ENDE APRIL 1945 [SS crimes against the wounded of the 2d Polish Army at the end of April 1945]. *Militärgeschichte [East Germany] 1980 19(4): 454-460.* As wounded Polish soldiers were being transported to the rear, the convoy was attacked at the town of Horka on 26 April 1945 and many of the wounded were killed and buried. Statements of six witnesses are appended. 24 notes. H. D. Andrews

421. Rutowska, Maria and Serwański, Edward. STRATY OSOBOWE ŚRODOWISKA TEATRALNEGO W LATACH 1939-1945: Z PROBLEMATYKI MARTYROLOGII I EKSTERMINACJI INTELIGENCJI W CZASIE DRUGIEJ WOJNY ŚWIATOWEJ I OKUPACJI HITLEROWSKIEJ W POLSCE [Human losses in the world of theater, 1939-45: the martyrology and extermination of the intelligentsia in Poland under the Nazi occupation during World War II]. *Przegląd Zachodni [Poland] 1976 32(1): 60-114.* Provides brief biographical details of 342 intellectuals in the Polish theater who perished during the German military occupation, relying on evidence in the Central File for the Losses of the Polish Intelligentsia, compiled by the Commission for the Investigation of Nazi Crimes in Poland.

422. Salecki, Jerzy A. 100 SECUNDE PENTRU FRANZ KUTSCHERA [100 seconds for Franz Kutschera]. *Magazin Istoric [Romania] 1979 13(7): 48-51.* Describes the work of Franz Kutschera as an SS general in German-occupied Warsaw, and the successful plan adopted for his assassination by the Polish resistance on 1 February 1944.

423. Schickel, Alfred. DIE POLNISCHEN KRIEGSVERLUSTE 1939-1945 [Poland's losses in World War II, 1939-45]. *Zeitschrift für Politik [West Germany] 1978 25(3): 279-296.* Although the majority of Polish people killed during World War II were victims of the German military, recent research has shown that Allied warfare was responsible for higher Polish casualties than has so far been estimated.

424. Serwański, Edward and Walczak, Maria. HITLEROWSKI TERROR I DYSKRYMINACJA NAUCZYCIELSTWA WIELKOPOLSKIEGO W LATACH 1939-1945 [The Nazi terror and discrimination against teachers in the Poznań region, 1939-45]. *Przegląd Zachodni [Poland] 1973 29(4): 262-307.* Describes the various kinds of persecution suffered by Polish teachers in this region, and documents 3,141 individual cases of injustice.

425. Sobczak, Janusz. NIEMCY WOBEC PRYMASA POLSKI AUGUSTA HLONDA W OKRESIE II WOJNY ŚWIATOWEJ [Germany's attitude toward August Hlond, primate of Poland, during World War II]. *Przegląd Zachodni [Poland] 1980 36(1): 135-145.* According to German consulates in Poznań and Katowice, August Hlond was an extreme Polish chauvinist unfriendly to Germany. Similar views may be found in secret reports by a German canon at the Poznań capitulary. After the German invasion of Poland Hlond found refuge at the Vatican. When he tried to return to his see at Poznań, the German authorities refused permission. He left the Vatican for Lourdes in unoccupied France. When the Germans occupied the rest of France they believed the Cardinal had escaped to Spain, when in fact Hlond was still hiding in Lourdes. Later

he found refuge in the Benedictine Abbey at Haute Combe, department of Savoie. In 1944 the Gestapo found and confined him in a cloister at Bar-le-Duc. After D-Day he was removed to the cloister of the Sisters of Charity at Wiedenbrück, Paderborn bishopric, where he was liberated by the US Army on 2 April 1945. Based on various German archives and primary sources. M. Krzyzaniak

426. Sobczak, Janusz. POLISH AFFAIRS IN THE FOREIGN POLICY OF NAZI GERMANY DURING THE SECOND WORLD WAR. *Polish Western Affairs [Poland] 1980 21(1): 76-105.* Discusses the Third Reich's policy of silence in reference to the Polish affairs of 1939 and its sophisticated propaganda campaign. An international team omitted the entry "Poland" from a collective work entitled *Akten zur Deutschen Auswärtigen Politik 1918-1945*, yet Polish historians have discovered numerous documents preserved by the German Foreign Office pertaining to this period. Based on numerous primary sources such as telegrams, messages, and documents to German ambassadors and envoys; 130 notes. D. S. Lloyd

427. Spyra, Bronisława. AKTA Z OKRESU OKUPACJI NIEMIECKIEJ Z LAT 1939-1945 W ARCHIWUM PAŃSTWOWYM W PSZCZYNIE [Records of the German occupation years in the Pszczyna State Archives]. *Archeion [Poland] 1975 63: 45-58.* After World War I, Pszczyna was turned over to Poland. During World War II, the Germans again occupied Upper Silesia and liquidated the Polish offices and institutions which operated there. In leaving, the Nazis did not succeed in taking all their records with them. What they did not take, and did not burn, has found its way to the Pszczyna Archives. These records consist of the records of the German state administration, records of the Nazi police, and economic records, mostly pertaining to mining. This entire collection of documents illustrates the German policy of annihilation of the Polish nation.
J/S

428. Stachiewicz, Wacław. MEMOIRS [Memoirs]. *Zeszyty Hist. [France] 1979 (50): 5-323.* Memoirs of the Polish Chief of Staff during the September 1939 campaign. The book covers the events in 1939 that led to the outbreak of World War II, the overall strategy of the army prior to the outbreak of hostilities, and a detailed account of the events that led to the collapse of Poland. The author presents an apologia for the military establishment of the time, their planning and tactics during the campaign. He is critical of French policy during this period. 10 maps, 7 tables, diagram, 140 notes, index. M. A. Zurowski

429. Strzembosz, Tomasz. 1859 DNI WARSZAWY [Eighteen hundred fifty nine days of Warsaw]. *Kwartalnik Hist. [Poland] 1978 85(2): 419-425.* A review of Władysław Bartoszewski's *1859 days of Warsaw*, (Cracow: Znak, 1974), which describes chronologically Warsaw during the German occupation, including not only political events, but also the daily life of the population. 5 notes. H. Heitzman-Wojcicka

430. Swianiewicz, Stanislaw. THE KATYN AFFAIR. *Survey [Great Britain] 1979 24(4): 188-198.* The responsibility for the 1943 Katyn massacre—the execution of about a third of the 15,000 Polish officers, noncommissioned officers, and police constables taken as prisoners of war by the Soviets and removed to Smolensk in 1939—clearly rests on the People's Commissariat of Internal Affairs

(NKVD), but a number of mysteries remain, most notably the fate of the rest of the prisoners and the Soviet motive in carrying out the massacre.

V. Samaraweera

431. Szarota, Tomasz. GERMANS IN POLISH EYES, 1939-1945. *Polish Perspectives [Poland] 1978 21(2): 36-47.* During World War II Poles had an extremely negative view of Germans, but fear of German soldiers and officials caused a near paralysis. Polish underground propaganda ridiculed Germans as bumbling idiots in an attempt to overcome this paralyzing fear.

432. Szarota, Tomasz. POLAND AND THE POLES IN GERMAN EYES DURING WORLD WAR II. *Polish Western Affairs [Poland] 1978 19(2): 229-254.* The stereotyped picture of Poland and the Poles which the Nazi authorities presented to German society from the spring of 1939 on exerted an influence on German public opinion. The objective of the propaganda was to implant attitudes in keeping with the principles and plans of the Nazi regime.

M. Swiecicka-Ziemianek

433. Terej, Jerzy Janusz. INTER ARMA *NON* SILENT MUSAE. *Polish Perspectives [Poland] 1977 20(12): 51-58.* Discusses the importance of aesthetic production in art, drama, and literature for the Nazi-occupied countries of Europe, especially Poland, during World War II; from a 1977 symposium organized by the Polish Commission for the History of World War II on the subject "War and Culture, 1939-45."

434. Wachowiak, Stanislaw. WSPOMNIENIA [Memoirs]. *Zeszyty Hist. [France] 1975 31: 143-157.* An affectionate, nostalgic, and humorous memoir of wartime Warsaw with many anecdotes of struggles against the Gestapo, by a Chairman of the Central Union of the Polish Industry. From this position of influence, his policy was to exploit the differences among the Germans. These were significant enough for him to oppose the indiscriminate assassinations of even Gestapo chiefs. He recounts several brilliantly successful bank robberies by the Underground and suggests that, banking having been in Polish hands throughout, it played an important role in protecting Poland in some degree from German rapacity. However, he does not substantiate this important point, and recommends it as a fruitful research topic. M. K. Palat

435. Wittram, Heinrich. AUFBRUCH INS UNBEKANNTE. ORIENTIERUNGSVERSUCHE UND STELLUNGNAHMEN DEUTSCHBALTISCHER GEISTLICHER 1939-1945 [Departure for the unknown: attempts at orientation and comments of Baltic German clergymen 1939-45]. *Zeitschrift für Ostfurschung [West Germany] 1978 27(4): 616-639.* In 1939 the Baltic German Church was removed from Latvia and Estonia by the National Socialists to the Warta and Vistula territories. The clergy initially supported the removal but came to oppose it and integrated into the Church of Poznań (and Łódz) against Nazi wishes, as there was little chance of succeeding in establishing separate Baltic German settlements. The Church of Poznań respected their differences, 1940-44. Primary sources; 69 notes. J/S

436. Wynot, Edward D., Jr. WORLD OF DELUSIONS AND DISILLUSIONS: THE NATIONAL MINORITIES OF POLAND DURING WORLD WAR II. *Nationalities Papers 1979 7(2): 177-196.* Considers the problems of

Poland's Ukrainians, Belorussians, Lithuanians, Jews, and Gypsies in responding to the German and Soviet occupation of Poland in the course of World War II.

437. Zawodny, J. K. HOW TO CAPTURE A CITY BY INSURGENCY AND HOW TO COMBAT INSURGENTS FIGHTING FOR SUCH A CITY: TWO COMBAT REPORTS FROM WORLD WAR II. *Terrorism 1979 3(1-2): 147-155.* Examines two operations reports, German and Polish, which pertain to the Warsaw Uprising of 1944.

438. Zeleński, Władysław. JAWNE SZKOLNICTWO WYŻSZE POD OKUPACJĄ NIEMIECKĄ WE LWOWIE [Open higher education under German occupation in Lvov]. *Zeszyty Hist. [France] 1977 (39): 221-229.* Examines the creation, by the Germans in 1942, of medical, technical, pharmaceutical, and agricultural university courses for the Ukrainians and Poles. This was against Nazi doctrine but the measures were taken for practical reasons and proved valuable for Poland after World War II.

439. Zyśko, Wojciech. NIEMIECKI URZĄD ARCHIWALNY (AR-CHIVAMT) W LUBLINIE W LATACH 1939-1944 I JEGO NADZÓR NAD DZIAŁNOŚCIĄ ARCHIWUM PAŃTSWOWEGO [Record of Nazi archival authorities kept at the Lublin Provincial State Archives]. *Archeion [Poland] 1975 63: 19-44.* After German troops invaded Poland in 1939, Nazi archival authorities organized in the occupied territories a German Board of Archives, called Archivamt, and subordinated all Polish archives to it, the Lublin Voivodeship State Archives included. A substantial quantity of records of this Archivamt has been preserved there, among them copies of the correspondence and reports sent to the central archival authorities in Berlin. The author describes these materials and quotes from them. J/S

4

AT WAR WITH WESTERN EUROPE

440. Andersen, William D. THE GERMAN REMOVAL OF THE DANISH CABINET IN 1943. *Scandinavian Studies 1977 49(4): 439-451.* Considers Germany's military occupation of Denmark during World War II, by which Denmark changed from a "model protectorate" and "free country" to the status of an occupied country. British propaganda broadcasts, German economic exploitation, and the increased pressures of German military and political representatives after 1941 resulted in the change of occupation status. Convinced by 1943 that Germany would lose the war, Danish resistance became commonplace. Rejection by the Danish cabinet of Germany's ultimatum of 28 August 1943, which instituted the death penalty, led on the next day to German dissolution of the cabinet, the imposition of martial law, and later a German-controlled civil government. 58 notes. C. W. Ohrvall

441. Andrae, Anders J. DE ALLIERADES MILITÄRA PLANER MOT NORDEN FRÅN SEPTEMBER 39 INTILL DEN 9. APRIL 1940 [The military plans of the Allies against the Scandinavian countries from September 1939 to 9 April 1940]. *Kungliga Krigsvetenskaps Akademiens Handlingar och Tidskrift [Sweden] 1972 176(8-9): 255-292.* Considers the resources, organization, and military strategy of the Allies concerning Scandinavia; Germany's motives for occupying Scandinavia; and the military intelligence information available to both sides relating to their respective plans during World War II. The Allies' resources were limited, their organizational methods produced delays, and their decision to lay mines along the Norwegian coast was only taken shortly before 9 April. They did not consider that the Nazis' war aims warranted an Allied invasion of Scandinavia. Germany wished to preserve its steel supply from Sweden, and Hitler wanted to support the Finns against the USSR. 72 notes.
U. Bartels/S

442. Auphan, Admiral. UN MENSONGE INCREVABLE: "LES ALLEMANDS À DAKAR" [A persistent lie: "the Germans at Dakar"]. *Écrits de Paris [France] 1974 (332): 11-15.* Shows that the Germans were not present in Dakar on 22 September 1940, contrary to statements in the recent edition of *Souvenirs de Guerre* by Admiral Thierry d'Argenlieu.

443. Avakoumovitch, Ivan. LE PCF VU PAR LE COMMANDEMENT DES TROUPES D'OCCUPATION ALLEMANDES (AOÛT 1940-MAI 1941) [The French Communist Party as viewed by the High Command of the German occupation forces in France, August 1940-May 1941]. *Mouvement Social*

[France] 1980 (113): 91-99. This paper is based upon the monthly reports issued by the German High Command of the occupation forces in France from August 1940 to May 1941. They have been kept in the National Archives at Washington since 1945. They show how the German military hierarchy analyzed the policy and the actions of the French Communist Party. They considered it altogether as an organization hostile to their authority.   J

444. Beauquier, J. P. L'ACTIVITÉ ÉCONOMIQUE DANS LA RÉGION MARSEILLAISE EN 1943 [Economic activity in the Marseilles region in 1943]. *Rev. d'Hist. de la Deuxième Guerre Mondiale [France] 1974 24(95): 25-52.* The German military occupation in November 1942 began a terrible year for Marseilles. In addition to intense political repression by the Germans, shipping, fishing, and industry declined drastically. Unemployment rose sharply early in the year but was reduced by conscription of workers for Germany by the Service du Travail Obligatoire (S.T.O.). The chamber of commerce, however, supported efforts to improve the tourist trade. Although individuals suffered greatly, the class structure survived through paternalism. 13 tables, graph, 28 notes.
G. H. Davis

445. Bennett, Neville. THE MYTH OF THE BATTLE OF BRITAIN. *Hist. News [New Zealand] 1979 (39): 10-16.* The Battle of Britain in 1940, in which the German Luftwaffe failed to defeat the British Navy, was not necessarily the turning point of World War II.

446. Berberova, Nina; Wilson, Craig A., transl. THE END OF THE TURGENEV LIBRARY. *J. of Lib. Hist. 1981 16(3): 509-516.* Personal recollections of the author, a Russian emigré writer, on the removal of the Turgenev Library from Paris to Germany during World War II. Removed in 1940, the books and other materials were apparently largely destroyed during a bombing raid while still in transit. The Russian emigrés who had used the library since the 19th century ranged from Lenin in the prerevolutionary era to anti-Bolsheviks of the postrevolutionary period. 11 notes.
J. S. Coleman

447. Bianchi, Gerardo. FIGURE DI PARTIGIANI SULLA LINEA GOTICA [Partisans on the Gothic Line]. *Civitas [Italy] 1980 31(9): 23-32.* Explores the activity of partisan commanders Manrico Ducceschi, Leandro Puccetti, and Viola Bertoni who during World War II fought on the Gothic Line, the Germans' final defensive line in Italy on the border of the Tuscan provinces, and faced events with firmness and moral strength.

448. Binoche, Jacques. L'ALLEMAGNE ET LE GÉNÉRAL DE GAULLE (1940-1945) [Germany and General de Gaulle, 1940-45]. *Rev. d'Hist. de la Deuxième Guerre Mondiale [France] 1974 24(94): 1-27.* The German press comment on General Charles de Gaulle followed several patterns. He was presented as an instrument of British policy, as a person of weak character, and as a Bolshevik agent. Hitler was interested in his 1934 book, *Vers l'armée de métier* (Toward a professional army), but he did not regard him seriously as a leader. After the fall of France, Hitler became suspicious that de Gaulle was plotting with Henri Pétain and Pierre Laval for control over North Africa. This affected his negotiations with Spain for an assault on Gibraltar. Propaganda minister Paul Goebbels created a special press campaign to dramatize quarrels between de

Gaulle and General Giraud. The German press criticized and ridiculed de Gaulle's Free French army for having African troops, his government for being a parliamentary farce, his 1944 arrival in France as traitorous, and his pact with the USSR as communistic. Only a few days before the end of the war, sampled German newspapers praised him for a statement that Germany should not be destroyed. 144 notes. G. H. Davis

449. Borgen, Thom G. EN STUDIE AV FELTMARSKALK ERWIN J. ROMMEL [A study of Field-Marshal Erwin J. Rommel]. *Norsk Militaert Tidsskrift [Norway] 1973 143(3): 119-126; 143(4): 181-194; 143(5): 247-254.* Part I. Describes Erwin Rommel's military career, 1911-43, considering also his relationship with Albert Kesselring during the defense of Italy in World War II. Part II. Covers Rommel's period of responsibility for defense against invasion, with particular reference to the Allied invasion of Normandy, and describes his relations with family, superiors, and subordinates, and with Adolf Hitler. Part III. Examines Rommel's views of his opponents and their views of him, his military strategy and his aims in the desert war.

450. Boussard, Isabel. LES NÉGOCIATIONS FRANCO-ALLEMANDES SUR LES PRÉLÈVEMENTS AGRICOLES: L'EXEMPLE DU CHAMPAGNE [Franco-German negotiations on agricultural confiscations: the example of champagne]. *Rev. d'Hist. de la Deuxième Guerre Mondiale [France] 1974 24(95): 3-24.* Efforts to mitigate the demands of the Germans during the period of Vichy and the military occupation sometimes had favorable results. But regarding their demands for champagne, the Germans were adamant and granted virtually no concessions. One of four articles on economic aspects of the German occupation of France. 68 notes. G. H. Davis

451. Brinkmann, August, Jr. STRIDEN PÅ STANGHELLE 1940, SETT MED TYSKE ØYNE [The battle at Stanghelle 1940 seen through German eyes]. *Norsk Militaert Tidsskrift [Norway] 1976 146(5): 205-211.* Describes a Norwegian-German military engagement on the Oslo-Bergen railway line in April 1940.

452. Carter, Carolle J. THE SPY WHO BROUGHT HIS LUNCH. *Éire-Ireland 1975 10(1): 3-13.* Günther Schütz, a German espionage agent air-dropped into Ireland in 1941, was immediately arrested and imprisoned and subsequently abandoned by the German government in the belief that he had Irish Republican Army connections, 1942.

453. Chabert, Henry. A POSSIBLE HISTORICAL MISTAKE: THE CAUSES OF THE ALLIED MILITARY COLLAPSE IN MAY 1940. *Military Rev. 1974 54(9): 80-91.* Discusses the military and strategic reasons for Germany's relatively easy conquest of Luxembourg, the Netherlands, Belgium, and France in 1940.

454. Chabert, Henry. A POSSIBLE HISTORICAL MISTAKE: THE CAUSES OF THE ALLIED MILITARY COLLAPSE IN MAY 1940. *Pro. of the Ann. Meeting of the Western Soc. for French Hist. 1973 (1): 379-390.* The backwardness of the French generals' concepts was not the primary cause of their subsequent defeat. Resistance was not impossible, although the war occurred in the middle of their rearmament program. German and Allied gener-

als employed some of the same tactics the French had been castigated for using. The only logical choice was to enter Belgium. The unexpected suddenness of the German successes meant that "the battle was lost before having been fought because all reinforcements were henceforth bound to arrive too late. . . . The collapse was really caused by the lack of fighting spirit of a few divisions located side by side at a key point in a crucial moment." Based on primary and secondary material; 48 notes. L. S. Frey

455. Collotti, Enzo. L'OCCUPATION ALLEMANDE LA RÉSISTANCE, LES ALLIÉS: ESSAI D'HISTORIOGRAPHIE [The German occupation, the resistance, the Allies: historiographical essay]. *Rev. d'Hist. de la Deuxieme Guerre Mondiale [France] 1973 23(92): 21-36.* Since the 1959 colloquium on Italian resistance in World War II, a number of significant works have been published on the German military occupation, the politics and activities of resistance, and the Allied response to the resistance. The establishment of special research institutes and the opening of archival collections have been especially helpful. 42 notes. G. H. Davis

456. Dahlgren, Tore. SVERIGE OCH DE TYSKA KRIGSPLANERNA OMKRING ÅRSSKIFTET 1941-1942 [Sweden and German war plans, 1941-42]. *Kungliga Krigsvetenskaps Akademiens Handlingar och Tidskrift [Sweden] 1973 177(6): 165-172.* At the end of 1941 the USSR, the United States, and Great Britain threatened Germany on several fronts. English raids on the Norwegian coast necessitated the continual presence of German troops and ships in the area to defend the harbors. Previously the Germans had planned to attack Sweden, and the German press had criticized Swedish policy. But in January 1942 such planning suddenly stopped, probably because Germany did not have the military strength to expand the war. 15 notes. U. Bartels/S

457. Datner, Szymon. UDZIAŁ ŻYDÓW W BELGIJSKIM RUCHU OPORU W ŚWIETLE MATERIAŁÓW HITLEROWSKICH [Participation of Jews in the Belgian resistance movement based on German materials]. *Biuletyn Żydowskiego Instytutu Hist. w Polsce [Poland] 1980 (1): 51-57.* Jews took considerable part in the resistance movement of Belgium, where they constituted barely one percent of the population. J. L. Charles and F. Dasney's *Secret Files of the German Police in Belgium* contains reports of the German Secret Field Police (Geheime Feldpolizei—GFP), engaged chiefly in combatting the resistance movement. The reports, covering 1940-42, contain evidence of Jewish participation. J/S

458. Davis, Frank. SEELÖWE, THE GERMAN PLAN TO INVADE BRITAIN, 1940. *Strategy & Tactics 1973 (40): 20-33.* Discusses the formulation between 1939 and 1940 of Operation Sea Lion, Germany's plan for the invasion of Great Britain during World War II.

459. Davis, Frank. WOLFPACK: THE GERMAN SUBMARINE WAR IN THE ATLANTIC, 1939-1943. *Strategy and Tactics 1974 (47): 5-24.*

460. Dehnert, Hans. DIE TAKTISCHE ÜBERASCHUNG BEI NARVIK 1940 [A tactical surprise at Narvik in 1940]. *Marine Rundschau [West Germany] 1975 72(11): 681-684.* Examines the military actions of German submarines (U-51, U-46) in the coastal waters around Narvik at the beginning of the

German invasion of Norway, 10-13 April 1940, and presents some new facts about this operation using newly discovered documents. 3 notes.

G. E. Pergl

461. DeJonghe, Albert. LA LUTTE HIMMLER-REEDER POUR LA NOMINATION D'UN HSSPF À BRUXELLES: ÉVOLUTION D'OCTOBRE 1942 À OCTOBRE 1943 [The Himmler-Reeder struggle for the appointment of a HSSPF in Brussels: October 1942-October 1943]. *Cahiers d'Hist. de la Seconde Guerre Mondiale [Belgium] 1978 5: 5-172.* Continued from a previous article. Describes the conflict between the military administration's attempt, led by Eggert Reeder, to retain total control of occupied Belgium and Heinrich Himmler's efforts to appoint his own senior SS and police chief (HSSPH). Himmler's main argument was the growing menace of the resistance and the army's feeble response. Himmler further sponsored his own collaboration movements, the De Vlag in Flanders, and the Rexists under Léon Degrelle in Wallonia. Both parties appealed to Hitler, who preferred to retain the status quo. Traces the maneuvers by all parties. 757 notes, appendix. Article to be continued.

M. K. Palat/S

462. DeJonghe, Albert. LA LUTTE HIMMLER-REEDER POUR LA NOMINATION D'UN HSSPF A BRUXELLES (1942-1944) [The Himmler-Reeder struggle for the appointment of a HSSPF in Brussels, 1942-44]. *Cahiers d'Hist. de la Seconde Guerre Mondiale [Belgium] 1974 3: 103-173, 1976 4: 5-160.* Part II. Heinrich Himmler wanted to appoint his own senior SS and police chief (HSSPH) in occupied Belgium but met with army resistance, especially from Eggert Reeder, chief of military administration in Belgium and northern France. Consequently, Himmler and the army promoted their respective collaboration movements. Himmler sponsored the Algemene SS-Vlanderen and De Vlag, a cultural exchange group of the 1930's revived by the SS to combat the army and the army-supported Vlaams National Verbond (VNV). De Vlag fully accepted the German annexation of Belgium. The army sponsored the rival VNV, a nationalistic and Catholic group opposed to incorporation into the Reich. The author documents the four-cornered struggle among these German and collaborationist groups. Based on German and Belgian archives and memoirs; 869 notes, appendix containing the decree of 2 January 1941 with 15 notes, table of abbreviations. Article to be continued.

M. K. Palat

463. Dejonghe, Etienne. LE NORD ISOLÉ: OCCUPATION ET OPINION (MAI 1940-MARS 1942) [The isolated north: occupation and opinion, May 1940-March 1942]. *Rev. d'Hist. Moderne et Contemporaine [France] 1979 26(Jan-Mar): 48-97.* Because the 1940 German-French peace settlement enabled Germany to control the government and normal means of communication, French public opinion was fragmented. This was accentuated by sectional, social, and cultural differences, as well as the severity of the occupation. Weaknesses in the interwar French political and socioeconomic structure were also made more apparent by German rule. Frenchmen in the north increasingly looked to England to oust the Germans. At the same time they became hostile to the Vichy government and came to see the south as collaborationist. Based on National Archives, Departmental Archives, and secondary works; 78 notes.

F. C. Bohm

464. DiNolfo, Ennio. L'OPERAZIONE "SUNRISE": SPUNTI E DOCUMENTI [Operation Sunrise: beginnings and documents]. *Storia e Politica [Italy] 1975 14(3): 345-376, (4): 501-522.* Part I. Operation Sunrise, or Operation Crosswords, as the British Army called it, is the code name for the Allied effort to secure the surrender of German forces in North Italy during the last year of the war. The German High Command knew the war was lost; the Catholic Church and the Swiss were seeking to use their good offices to arrange a swift termination of hostilities. Negotiations were carried on between representatives of the German commanders Field Marshal Albert Kesselring and Colonel General Karl Wolff and American OSS and British SOE men. A leading concern of the Anglo-Saxons (and of the Church) was to avoid a situation in which the Communists could seize power in North Italy. 15 documents, 46 notes. Part II. Follows negotiations between Wolff and other German generals and Allen Dulles of the OSS and the British representatives for the surrender of German forces in North Italy. Dulles met with Wolff on March 8 in Switzerland. These negotiations aroused Soviet suspicions; the Russians feared that the Germans would surrender on all fronts only to the Allies and not to them. Stalin does not seem to have cared about the position of the Italian Communists, whose drive to power the Allies hoped to thwart by arranging an orderly surrender of German troops. 7 documents; 81 notes. J. C. Billigmeier

465. Doenecke, Justus D. PROTEST OVER MALMEDY: A CASE OF CLEMENCY? *Peace and Change 1976 4(2): 28-33.* Examines the role of Frederick J. Libby of the National Council for the Prevention of War during the war trial of German soldiers responsible for the Malmédy massacre of 1944; Libby campaigned for justice for the Germans, maintaining that the US should apply the same rules to the Axis powers as it did to itself.

466. Douglas, Alec. THE NAZI WEATHER STATION IN LABRADOR. *Can. Geog. [Canada] 1982 101(6): 42-47.* Describes the operations of a German automatic land weather station that was set up by a German U-boat in Labrador in 1943; its remains were discovered in 1981.

467. Driss, Rachid. LA TUNISIE SOUS L'OCCUPATION ALLEMANDE (NOVEMBRE 1942-MAI 1943) [Tunisia under the German occupation, November 1942-May 1943]. *Cahiers de Tunisie [Tunisia] 1979 27(109-110): 455-471.* Recalls political and military events in Tunisia under the German military occupation, up to the entrance of Allied troops in May 1943.

468. Etzold, Thomas H. THE (F)UTILITY FACTOR: GERMAN INFORMATION GATHERING IN THE UNITED STATES, 1933-1941. *Military Affairs 1975 39(2): 77-82.* In spite of their volume and scope, German intelligence service operations in the United States, 1933-41, were not particularly effective, and they contributed little to the formulation and conduct of an operative policy. Internal failings doomed German intelligence work from the outset. Primary and secondary sources; 26 notes. A. M. Osur

469. Fonde, J.-J. L'AGONIE D'UNE PANZERBRIGADE. DOMPAIRE, 13 SEPTEMBRE 1944 [The destruction of a Panzer brigade: Dompaire, 13 September 1944]. *Rev. Hist. des Armées [France] 1979 (1): 177-207.* In September 1944 the US Third Army was advancing to France's German border. The

French 2d Armored Division under General Jacques Philippe Leclerc, covering the Third Army's southern flank, was moving across the Marne and the Meuse toward the Moselle River. As the Langlade Tactical Group of the 2d Armed Division moved toward Châtel-Thaon north of Epinal, it encountered the 112th Panzer Brigade in front of Dompaire (Vosges). In the battle that followed, the German armored unit counterattacked, the Langlade Tactical Group called for and received three separate air strikes by US and British fighter-bombers, and by 14 September the 112th Panzer Brigade ceased to exist. Extracts from the journal of the German Nineteenth Army's chief of staff describe the same battle from the point of view of German strategy. 8 illus., 3 maps, 15 notes.

J. S. Gassner

470. Galbraith, John Kenneth. AFTER THE AIR RAIDS. *Am. Heritage 1981 32(3): 65-80.* Excerpted from Galbraith's memoirs, *A Life in Our Times*, the article discusses the efforts of the US Strategic Bombing Survey conducted in Germany in 1945. Seeking information as to what the bombers had accomplished over Germany, Galbraith and his staff interviewed key figures in the economic life of the Third Reich. Their report, which concluded that strategic bombing had not won the war in Europe, was not accepted enthusiastically by the Army Air Force. 14 illus.

J. F. Paul

471. Gelber, Yoav. PALESTINIAN POWS IN GERMAN CAPTIVITY. *Yad Vashem Studies on the European Jewish Catastrophe and Resistance [Israel] 1981 14: 89-138.* Describes the experiences of the over 1,500 Palestinian Jewish prisoners of war, volunteers for service in the British armed forces. Most were captured in Greece early in 1941 and spent most of the war years in the Lamsdorf prisoner of war camp in Germany. On their journey to the camp, many managed to escape. Once interned at Lamsdorf, they were accorded equal treatment with the non-Jewish inmates, in stark contrast to the fate of East European Jews in nearby concentration camps. Based mainly on archival materials in Germany, Great Britain, and Israel; 3 illus., 149 notes.

B. Reiner

472. Gemzell, Carl-Axel. TYSK MILITÄR PLANLÄGGNING UNDER DET ANDRA VÄRLDSKRIGET: FALL SVERIGE [German military planning in World War II: the case of Sweden]. *Scandia [Sweden] 1975 41(2): 199-248.* An account of the development of German military planning against Sweden during three critical phases. During 1939-40 and 1942-43 German military planning included, though not unanimously, *Blitzkrieg* followed by invasion. After the Swedish attitude toward Germany hardened, the 1944-45 German attack plans included the use of V1 and V2 rockets. 92 notes.

U. G. Jeyes

473. Goldberg, Eric. DESCENT ON CRETE. *Strategy and Tactics 1978 (66): 25-34.* Describes the attack by Luftwaffe General Kurt Student's airborne troops on Crete, which would have been an even greater German disaster, although it was officially a German victory, had British General Bernard Cyril Freyberg's troops been better equipped by experience, imagination, and morale to defend the island against the airborne invasion.

474. Gollotti, Enzi. L'OCCUPATION ALLEMANDE, LA RÉSISTANCE, LES ALLIÉS: ESSAI D'HISTORIOGRAPHIE [The German occupation, the resistance, the Allies: historiographical essay]. *Rev. d'Hist. de la Deuxième*

Guerre Mondiale [France] 1973 23(92): 21-36. Since the 1959 colloquium on Italian resistance in World War II a number of significant works have been published on the German military occupation, the politics and activities of resistance, and the Allied response to the resistance. The establishment of special research institutes and the opening of archival collections has been especially helpful. 42 notes.

G. H. Davis

475. Gordon, Bertram. UN SOLDAT DU FASCISME: L'ÉVOLUTION POLITIQUE DE JOSEPH DARNAND [A soldier of fascism: the political evolution of Joseph Darnand]. *Rev. d'Hist. de la Deuxième Guerre Mondiale [France] 1977 27(108): 43-70.* Joseph Darnand was a celebrated hero of the French army during World War I and World War II. His disappointment at being excluded from the officer corps contributed to his right-wing antirepublicanism during the 1920's and 1930's. Always a man of action, he withdrew from Action Française in 1928 because it was too theoretical. With the fall of France Darnand's anticommunism, his respect for Henri Philippe Pétain, powerful elites, and authoritarian government, and his personal resentment led him into collaboration with Germany. He developed and commanded the *Milice,* which began as an unarmed organization to protect the Vichy government and became an antiresistance corps. The *Milice* committed a number of notorious atrocities before the Allies liberated France in 1944. Neither the Germans nor the Laval government trusted Darnand at first. He gained support, however, by joining the French unit of the Waffen SS. In 1944 he withdrew to Germany where he worked for Heinrich Himmler. He was executed for treason in 1945. 39 notes.

G. H. Davis

476. Gotovitch, José. BELGIQUE: ÉGLISE ET SYNDICAT SOUS L'OCCUPATION 1940-1942 (NOTE DOCUMENTAIRE) [Belgium: church and labor unions under the occupation (documentary note)]. *Rev. du Nord [France] 1978 60(238): 581-588.* During the first two years of German occupation of Belgium (1940-42), the Confédération des syndicats chrétiens (CSC) suffered deep crises, ending in its breakup and replacement by the UTMI, a Nazi-controlled union. Divergences among its membership originated from its espousing the causes of one of the opposing communities of the Walloons or the Flemish, a division also experienced by the membership of the socialist Confédération Générale du Travail (CGTB). However, the arguments developed were not formulated, or thought out in terms of community interests, but of general political and moral principles. Based on archival documents deposited at the Centre de la Seconde Guerre Mondiale; 6 notes, 3 appendixes.

G. P. Cleyet

477. Gounand, Pierre. L'INVASION DE LA BOURGOGNE EN JUIN 1940: DIJON VILLE OUVERTE [The invasion of Burgundy in June 1940: Dijon as an open city]. *Rev. d'Hist. de la Deuxième Guerre Mondiale [France] 1981 31(123): 3-16.* Dijon was a regional city with little military significance in 1939. During the *drôle de guerre* [Phoney War] from September 1939 to June 1940 Dijon experienced slight restrictions because of military actions. Superior German numbers made the defense of Dijon and the Canal de Bourgogne untenable. The city was surrendered on the condition that the French garrison be allowed to withdraw on June 17, 1940. Based on materials in Côte-d'Or departmental and Dijon municipal archives; 51 notes and citations.

G. H. Davis

478. Groehler, Olaf. DIE AUSWIRKUNGEN DER NIEDERLAGEN IM SOMMER 1944 AUF DIE KAMPFMORAL DER FASCHISTISCHEN STREITKRÄFTE IN WESTEUROPA [The effects of the defeats in the summer of 1944 on the fighting morale of the fascist forces in Western Europe]. *Militärgeschichte [East Germany] 1976 15(4): 418-426.* The massive defeats of German forces in the East and West in June and July 1944, the long-term setbacks in the East, and the transfer of disillusioned forces from the East to the West led in August and September 1944 to a collapse of the fighting morale of German forces in the West. Strenuous efforts only temporarily halted the disordered German retreat in the West and allowed the Germans to offer final resistance to the anti-Hitler coalition. Based on documents in various East and West German archives and secondary works; 43 notes. J. B. Street

479. Groehler, Olaf. DIE SCHLACHT UM AACHEN (SEPTEMBER/OKTOBER 1944) [The battle for Aachen, September-October, 1944]. *Militärgeschichte [East Germany] 1979 18(3): 321-333.* The delay of defeat at Aachen, together with the parrying of the Allied breakthrough attacks at Arnheim and in Alsace, contributed to the German command's temporarily stabilizing the front, organizing and equipping its forces anew, and thus compelling a transition to a protracted war of position. The U.S. 1st Army lost the possibility of being able to take the West Wall and push through to the Cologne lowlands area. Nevertheless, the German intention to make the defense of Aachen into a major symbol of fanatic resistance failed as well. The author describes in detail the intended aims and initial situation of both sides as well as the actual course of the struggle. Based on voluminous unpublished archive material; 2 maps, 48 notes. J/T (H. D. Andrews)

480. Groeneveld, Eduard G. DUTCH HISTORIOGRAPHY AND THE SECOND WORLD WAR 1945-75. *La Seconda Guerra Mondiale nella prospettiva storica a trent'anni dall'epilogo* (Como: Casa editrice Pietro Cairoli, 1977): 269-287. In the 30 years since the end of World War II Dutch historians have produced an impressive number of books on war and occupation in the Netherlands and on World War II in general. The author gives an overview under such headings as military operations, German and Dutch Nazi policy, social and economic history, resistance movement, and espionage and secret communications. J. C. Billigmeier

481. Hackman, W. Kent. THE 1940 BOMBING OF FREIBURG: FULLER AND THE WRITING OF MILITARY HISTORY. *Aerospace Hist. 1978 25(3): 155-158.* On 10 May 1940 the German government claimed that three Allied bombers had dropped bombs on Freiburg, Germany, killing 24 civilians. In actuality the bombing was done by lost German aircraft. In spite of the facts which have been documented, the late J. F. C. Fuller, distinguished British soldier, author, and military historian, recorded the falsehood as fact in *The Second World War, 1939-45* (New York: Meredith Pr., 1963) and *The Conduct of War, 1789-1961* (New Brunswick: Rutgers U. Pr., 1961). The author discusses the reasons why he did this. It is a classic example of how an emotional involvement blinded an author. Secondary sources; photo, 17 notes. C. W. Ohrvall

482. Hautecler, Georges. LA VIE RELIGIEUSE DES PRISONNIERS DE GUERRE BELGES (1940-1945). COMPLEMENTS. [The religious life of Belgian prisoners of war, 1940-45: addendum]. *Cahiers d'Hist. de la Seconde Guerre Mondiale [Belgium] 1976 4: 229-232.* The author complements his study on Catholic prisoners of war (see following abstract) with this article on Protestants among Belgian POW's. Gives precise figures on Protestants in different camps. The Protestants generally organized their religious life more successfully than the Catholics, perhaps because of their experience as a minority community in Belgium. Among the Protestants, the officers were better organized than the ranks. Based on published documents; note. M. K. Palat

483. Hautecler, Georges. LA VIE RELIGIEUSE DES PRISONNIERS DE GUERRE BELGES (1940-1945). FAITS ET DOCUMENTS. [The religious life of Belgian prisoners of war, 1940-45: facts and documents]. *Cahiers d'Hist. de la Seconde Guerre Mondiale [Belgium] 1974 (3): 49-64.* Nazi Germany was fundamentally anti-Christian and hindered the religious observances of prisoners of war. Most chaplains of the Belgian army were repatriated to Belgium, and the chaplaincy failed to insist on remaining with the prisoners of war or to organize a voluntary service as the army medical service had done. Consequently, it has been much criticized by prisoners who had to turn to French chaplains wherever available. German authorities never permitted prisoners to attend services for the German civilian population. Based on archives and memoirs; 21 notes.
M. K. Palat

484. Herzstein, Robert E. LE PARTI NATIONAL-SOCIALISTE FACE À LA FRANCE: APPRÉCIATION ET PROPAGANDE DANS LES INSTITUTIONS DU PARTI 1939-1945 [The National Socialist Party with regard to France: appreciation and propaganda in party institutions, 1939-45]. *Rev. d'Hist. de la Deuxième Guerre Mondiale [France] 1981 31(124): 69-96.* Nazi justification for its policies of occupation in France was based on a vision of the past which writers such as Friedrich Grimm had popularized. The mission of Nazi Germany was to overcome the past and replace French power and culture. Propaganda for the benefit of Nazi leaders revealed envy, cultural hostility, and lack of comprehension. A central theme was France's history of aggression toward Germany and the necessity to force France to cooperate in reconstructing Europe. Based on documents of the Nazi Party, German Foreign Office, Propaganda Ministry, the Nazi Auslands-Organisation; 109 notes. G. H. Davis

485. Herzstein, Robert Edwin. LE NAZISME ET LA FRANCE (1939-1942): POPULATION ET RACISME [Nazism and France, 1939-42: population and racism]. *Rev. d'Hist. de la Deuxième Guerre Mondiale [France] 1979 29(115): 1-25.* The attitudes of leading Nazis toward France were contemptuous. The Nazis asserted that France had been penetrated by Jews, that the French could not understand the Jewish problem, and that France had introduced Negroes into Europe. Hitler had no intention of returning Alsace-Lorraine to France after 1940 and supported a racially conceived Breton autonomy movement, while putting the Flemish population under German protection. Fantastic schemes and brutal policies characterized the military occupation of France. Based on microfilmed documents of the *Deutsches Auslandsinstitut.*
G. H. Davis

486. Hofsten, Gustaf von. DEN ITALIENSK-TYSKA PLANLÄGGNINGEN AV AN LANDSTIGNING PÅ MALTA 1942 [The Italian-German planning of a landing on Malta, 1942]. *Aktuellt och Historiskt [Sweden] 1975: 27-80.* Operation Hercules was the code name for the proposed German-Italian occupation of Malta. Conceived by the Italians in 1935-36, the Germans became interested in 1940. By mid-January 1942 German air forces began heavy raids on the island forcing withdrawal of British naval support. The plan was cancelled due to Hitler's hesitancy at costs, Field Marshall Rommel's opposition, and even Mussolini's ambivalence, although he was a minor figure. English summary.

R. E. Lindgren

487. Holmén, Hans. TEKNISK TRIUMF—STRATEGISKT MISSLYCKANDE: HISTORISKA OCH SKÖNLITTERÄRA FRAMSTÄLLNINGAR OM JAKTEN PÅ SLAGSKEPPET BISMARCK DEN 18-27 MAJ 1941 [Technical triumph, strategic failure: historical and literary descriptions of the hunt for the battleship *Bismarck*, 18-27 May 1941]. *Militärhistorisk Tidskrift [Sweden] 1980: 97-130.* A comparative analysis of several more or less scientific studies and two historical novels dealing with the naval warfare operations in the North Atlantic 18-27 May 1941 that led to the crippling and eventual sinking of the German battleship *Bismarck,* describing their interpretations of the *Bismarck* operation, its strategic background and aims, its execution, and the end result. The interpretations of the naval action itself largely agree, and all sources deal with it extensively, but most neglect to examine the end result and the reaction in Germany.

T. Parker

488. Huan, Claude. U-BOOT-OPERATIONEN AM PQ.13 UND DAS SCHICKSAL VON "U-585" [German submarine operations on PQ13 and the destiny of *U-585*]. *Marine Rundschau [West Germany] 1977 (1): 18-20.* Reviews the story of the German submarine attack on Great Britain's convoys PQ13 and QP9, March 1942, and sheds a new light on the mysterious loss of *U-585.* This German submarine, damaged by HMS *Fury* during the action, was later sunk by a floating German mine. Map, 2 notes.

G. E. Pergl

489. Hürten, Heinz. IM UMBRUCH DER NORMEN: DOKUMENTE ÜBER DIE DEUTSCHE MILITÄRJUSTIZ NACH DER KAPITULATION DER WEHRMACHT [In the upheaval of standards: documents on German military justice after the surrender of the armed forces]. *Militärgeschichtliche Mitteilungen [West Germany] 1980 (2): 137-156.* Details through documents the continuing functioning of the German military command in Norway after the unconditional surrender. Allied forces remained too small to handle the approximately 350,000 German troops as POW's, hence German commands handled their own surrender and repatriation. Wartime military regulations continued to govern discipline, with maximum punishments and definition of offenses limited by British occupation authority. Based on documents in the Military Archives, Freiburg and Royal Archive, Oslo; 16 documents, 49 notes.

K. W. Estes

490. Kelly, John Joseph. INTELLIGENCE AND COUNTER-INTELLIGENCE IN GERMAN PRISONER OF WAR CAMPS IN CANADA DURING WORLD WAR II. *Dalhousie Rev. [Canada] 1978 58(2): 285-294.* About 40,000 German prisoners of war and civilian internees were held at 25 different sites in Canada on behalf of the British government, 1940-47. The decision to

establish a Psychological Warfare Committee in Canada in 1943 followed obviously well-organized riots in camps at Ozada, Alberta, and Espanola, Ontario. Gestapo elements within the camps were responsible for many of the problems experienced in Canada. One of the major goals of the Canadian authorities was to reeducate the young, physically fit, thoroughly indoctrinated Nazis before they were returned to Germany following the war. During the war, murder, even mass murder, plotted by the Gestapo, was one of the major worries of Canadian officials. 15 notes. C. Held

491. Kirwin, Gerald. WAITING FOR RETALIATION—A STUDY IN NAZI PROPAGANDA BEHAVIOUR AND GERMAN CIVILIAN MORALE. *J. of Contemporary Hist. [Great Britain] 1981 16(3): 565-583.* In the latter half of World War II, the promise of *Vergeltung* (retaliation) against Britain was a major theme of German propaganda. New, long-distance missiles were promised by the end of 1943. The six-month delay in the fulfillment of this expectation was marked by increasing disbelief in the eventuality of any superweapon. The resumption of bombing over Britain did not knock out the enemy or raise morale in Germany. D-Day, 6 June 1944, arrived with no effective *Vergeltung* and thus began the crisis of confidence that lasted until the end. Based on archival sources; 83 notes. M. P. Trauth

492. Koch, Karl W., Jr. THE LUFTWAFFE AND MALTA: A CASE OF "HERCULES" CHAINED. *Aerospace Hist. 1976 23(2): 94-100.* In the fall of 1941 British air and sea forces based at Malta sank over half of the supplies destined for Rommel's Africa Korps. The Luftwaffe was assigned the task of neutralizing Malta. Their plan, Operation Hercules, could have worked but it was never implemented because of Hitler's preoccupation with Russia. The author discusses the war in the Mediterranean generally and the German attempts to neutralize Malta. The task of keeping the Mediterranean sea lanes from Italy open proved exhausting and wasteful of resources. Hundreds of German airmen were sacrificed needlessly in the debilitating effort to protect the supply arteries to Africa. Secondary sources; 3 photos. C. W. Ohrvall

493. Krier, Emile. LE REXISME ET L'ALLEMAGNE 1933-1940: UNE DOCUMENTATION [Rexism and Germany, 1933-40: documentary evidence]. *Cahiers d'Hist. de la Seconde Guerre Mondiale [Belgium] 1978 5: 173-220.* Demonstrates the close relationship between the Rexist Party, it leader Léon Degrelle, and Hitler's Germany, despite disclaimers from both sides. The Germans expected much from the Rexists, gave them propaganda support, and in 1936 arranged a meeting between Hitler and Degrelle. However, after the electoral successes of 1936 Rexism declined sharply with much public criticism of its German connection. On the outbreak of World War II Belgian opinion turned so hostile to Germany that propaganda for Belgian neutrality was instituted by the Germans and Rexism once again became useful for this purpose. Based on German archives and memoirs; 92 notes, appendix. M. K. Palat

494. Laurens, André. LE S.T.O. DANS LE DÉPARTEMENT DE L'ARIÈGE [Service du Travail Obligatoire (S.T.O.) in the department of Ariège]. *Rev. d'Hist. de la Deuxième Guerre Mondiale [France] 1974 24(95): 53-74.* During 1942-44 the Germans required the Vichy French government to provide thousands of conscripted workers for service in German factories, mines, etc., by

establishing the *Service du Travail Obligatoire* (S.T.O.). Although the proportions of the total working population conscripted from the department of Ariège was less than in the north of France, the results were very grave. Long-term economic damage was accompanied by intense political resentment which favored the resistance movement. Map, 2 tables, 3 graphs, 46 notes.
                                                                G. H. Davis

495. Lévy, Claude. L'AFFICHE ROUGE [The Red Poster]. *Histoire [France] 1979 (18): 22-30.* The *L'Affiche Rouge* affair was a striking aspect of the psychological campaign launched in 1944 by German and Vichy regime propagandists, on the occasion of the trial and execution of 24 foreign Resistance "terrorists," most of them Jews, in an attempt to discredit the French Resistance by playing on feelings of xenophobia.   J/S

496. L'Huillier, Fernand. STRASBOURG SOUS L'OCCUPATION ALLEMANDE ET SA LIBÉRATION EN 1944 [Strasbourg under German rule and its liberation in 1944]. *Rev. Hist. des Armées [France] 1981 (3): 131-150.* When the German forces took possession of Strasbourg in 1940, they found a nearly deserted city which they proceeded to repopulate with Germans. Their policy was to Germanize and Nazify the city. French resistance was severely punished by special tribunals, but otherwise life was normal, except for three aerial bombardments. In 1944, the allied forces liberated the city in a move spearheaded by the French 2d Armored Division under General Jacques Philippe Leclerc, who sent seven armored columns through the German defenses in the Vosges. Between the 17th and 23d of November, Leclerc's division took more than 12,500 prisoners, killed over 2,000 of the enemy, and lost only 150 men. Based partly on eyewitness accounts; 3 illus., 5 photos, map, 6 notes.
                                                                J. S. Gassner

497. L'Huillier, Fernand. SUR LA NAZIFICATION DE L'ALSACE [On the Nazification of Alsace]. *Rev. d'Hist. de la Deuxième Guerre Mondiale [France] 1980 30(120): 59-68.* An extended evaluation and summary of the French edition of Lothar Kettenbacher's *Nationalsozialistische Volkstumspolitik in Elsass* (Stuttgart, 1973). The French translation, *La politique de Nazification en Alsace* appeared in *Saisons d'Alsace* 1978 [France] (65 and 68). Nazi policy developed slowly after the conquest of France in 1940. Only gradually did Germanization plans become apparent. Restrictions against the use of the French language and names were followed by large deportations to the East for colonization purposes and for labor in Himmler's concentration camp enterprises. Ultimately Alsace was intended for colonization by immigrants from neighboring Baden. 26 notes.   G. H. Davis

498. Loewald, K. G. A *DUNERA* INTERNEE AT HAY, 1940-41. *Hist. Studies [Australia] 1977 17(69): 512-521.* The hilarious memoirs of a nine-month stay in the internment camp at Hay by a young German refugee from the Nazis, who had been interned in England on 28 June 1940 and transported to Australia in the *Dunera*.   W. D. McIntyre

499. Loock, Hans-Dietrich. WESERÜBUNG—A STEP TOWARDS THE GREATER GERMANIC REICH. *Scandinavian J. of Hist. [Sweden] 1977 2(1-2): 67-88.* Although it regarded the Nordic area as a marginal interest, the

German government was anxious in 1939 to secure the region's neutrality, thus ensuring, for example, vital imports of iron from Sweden. The outbreak of the Winter War in December 1939, by causing the risk of a clash between the Western powers and Russia, threatened German policy, and came at a time of crisis in Germany's political and military leadership. Various operational possibilities were examined culminating in the issue of a directive, *Weserübung,* in January 1940: before starting an offensive in the West, the northern flank had to be in German hands. The invasion of Denmark and Norway, which began in April, was partly a matter of military conquest, but it was also seen in ideological terms, that is, as a step towards a greater Germanic Reich based upon the racial principle. Based mainly on German and Scandinavian primary and secondary sources; 32 notes. P. J. Beck

500. Ludlow, Peter. DOKUMENTATION: PAPST PIUS XII., DIE BRITISCHE REGIERUNG UND DIE DEUTSCHE OPPOSITION IM WINTER 1939/40 [Documentation: Pope Pius XII, the British government and the German opposition in the winter of 1939-40]. *Vierteljahrshefte für Zeitgeschichte [West Germany] 1974 22(3): 299-341.* The Pope's first intervention (January 1940) in the British-German contacts was later than believed, owing chiefly to German hesitance to involve the Pope personally, and that both the Pope and the key makers of foreign policy in England looked favorably on the German opposition and the specter of a negotiated peace with a German coup government. Based on reminiscences in the Institut für Zeitgeschichte Archive, 13 dispatches between the British Mission at the Vatican and the Foreign Office from the British Archives (reprinted), and secondary works; 140 notes. D. Prowe

501. Lunt, J. D. OPERATION MARKET-GARDEN. *Army Q. and Defence J. [Great Britain] 1975 105(1): 22-24.* Reviews Cornelius Ryan's *A Bridge Too Far* (New York: Simon & Schuster, 1974) on the German defeat of the Allied airborne operation near Arnhem in the Netherlands in 1944.

502. Luther, Craig. THE LIMITS OF A HITLER ORDER: GENERAL HUBERT LANZ AND THE ITALIAN CAPITULATION, SEPTEMBER 1943. *Army Q. and Defence J. [Great Britain] 1982 112(1): 80-91.* Four weeks before the Italians surrendered to the Allies in September 1943, Lieutenant General Hubert Lanz arrived in Salonika, Greece to command the XXII Mountain Corps which was "to take control of the 1 Mountain and 104 Light (Jager) divisions in northwestern Greece (Epirus) upon receipt of the code word Axis." Lanz disobeyed a "Hitler Order" and singlehandedly negotiated the disarmament and surrender of the Italians without force.

503. Mandell, Richard D. CARL DIEM ON SPORT AND WAR. *Can. J. of Hist. of Sport and Physical Educ. 1974 5(1): 10-13.* Translation of Carl Diem's June 1940 article in *Reichsportsblatt* entitled "The Battle Charge Through France." S

504. Marsh, Patrick. CENSORSHIP IN FRANCE DURING THE GERMAN OCCUPATION. *Theatre Res. Int. [Great Britain] 1978 4(1): 27-31.* Studies some of the censored passages from the prompt copies used at the Comédie-Française 1939-45, showing how the Germans erased patriotic or political lines. Based on the Comédie-Française's prompt copies and secondary sources; note. A. Armstrong/S

505. Martres, M. LES TROUPES ALLEMANDES DANS LE MASSIF CENTRAL [German troops in the Massif Central]. *Cahiers d'Hist. [France] 1977 22(4): 405-420.* Study of the German troops in the Massif Central, 1942-44. Discusses the nature of the administration, security units, troops attached to divisions, and police and SS units. Considers the military operations undertaken in 1944 in detail. Based on German archival material, especially at the Freiburg military archives; 2 maps. R. Howell

506. Matthews, Kenneth. THE STRANGE CASE OF RUDOLF HESS. *Blackwood's Mag. [Great Britain] 1978 323(1952): 486-492.* Recounts events following the strange surrender of Nazi Party leader Rudolf Hess, when, in 1941, he parachuted into Scotland, was imprisoned, and found to be mentally incompetent.

507. Menger, Manfred; Petrick, Fritz; and Wilhelmus, Wolfgang. NORDEUROPA UNTER DER VORHERRSCHAFT DES FASCHISTISCHEN DEUTSCHEN IMPERIALISMUS 1940-1945 [Northern Europe under the dominance of fascist German imperialism 1940-45]. *Zeitschrift für Geschichtswissenschaft [East Germany] 1976 24(5): 516-529.* The North Europe policy of the German fascists was a result of the expansionist force of German imperialism all over Europe. The fascist policy used Scandinavia for strengthening the strategic position of Germany in its fight against the USSR. Based on documents in the Zentrales Staatsarchiv, Potsdam, Politisches Archiv des Auswärtigen Amtes, Bonn, Riksarkiv, Oslo, printed documents and secondary literature; 37 notes.
R. Wagnleitner

508. Merglen, Albert. SOLDATS FRANÇAIS SOUS UNIFORMES ALLEMANDS 1941-1945: LVF ET "WAFFEN-SS" FRANÇAIS [French soldiers in German uniforms, 1942-45: the LVF and the French Waffen-SS]. *Rev. d'Hist. de la Deuxième Guerre Mondiale [France] 1977 27(108): 71-84.* During World War II about 10,000 French volunteers served in the German armed forces. The Légion des Volontaires Français contre le Bolchevisme (LVF) was initiated immediately after the German invasion of the USSR at the request of Jacques Doriot, Marcel Déat, and several other leaders of the French fascistic Right. Although neither Adolf Hitler nor the German military leadership favored it, the LVF recruited a unit which became the 638th Wehrmacht infantry regiment. The LVF performed poorly under fire and was kept out of action after its first engagement. The establishment of the French Charlemagne division in the Waffen SS was more important. Begun in 1943, this unit incorporated all French military volunteers in Germany, including the LVF, and fought effectively but with great loss against the Russians. Overall, French volunteer units played an insignificant role. 17 notes. G. H. Davis

509. Meyer-Brenkhoff, Heinz-Jürgen. DIE OPERATION PQ.13/QP.9 [Operation PQ13/QP9]. *Marine Rundschau [West Germany] 1977 74(1): 10-17.* Describes tactical development and final stage of the first World War II convoy battle in the North Sea, 1942, involving planes, submarines, and destroyers. 9 photos, 2 maps, biblio. G. E. Pergl

510. Meyers, Willem C. M. LA *VLAAMSE LANDSLEIDING,* UN "GOUVERNEMENT" D'EMIGRES EN ALLEMAGNE APRES SEPTEMBRE 1944 [The *Vlaamse Landsleiding,* an emigre "government" in Germany after September 1944]. *Cahiers d'Hist. de la Seconde Guerre Mondiale [Belgium] 1972 2: 211-269.* As the Allies began their final offensive, Belgian collaborators fled into Germany and began projects for a future "liberated" Belgium. The *Vlaamse Landsleiding,* under Dr. Jef Van de Wiele, led in this unrealistic activity. It sought, after September 1944, to unite all Belgians in Germany for the welfare of Belgian refugees there. By October, however, it turned itself into a Belgian government-in-exile. It held fast to the idea of a Third Reich with the Walloons and Flemings occupying an equal place with the Germans but sought to preserve a minimal Belgian identity. Their hopes rose during the final German offensive in December 1944; after its failure, the organization rapidly disintegrated. Throughout, the other important Belgian collaborator group, the Vlaams National Verbond (VNV) under Dr. Elias, refused to participate in such unrealistic plans. Based on Belgian and German sources; 313 notes. M. K. Palat

511. Meyers, Willem C. M. LES COLLABORATEURS FLAMANDS DE FRANCE ET LEURS CONTACTS AVEC LES MILIEUX FLAMINGANTS BELGES: LES VISÉES TERRITORIALES SUR LA FLANDRE FRANÇAISE PENDANT LA SECONDE GUERRE MONDIALE [The Flemish collaborators in France and their contacts with the Belgian Flemish-speaking circles: the territorial claims on French Flanders during World War II]. *Rev. du Nord [France] 1978 60(237): 337-346.* Since the 1840's the Flemings of Belgium have constantly shown interest in French Flanders. This interest was echoed in the actions of the Comité Flamand de France. During World War I Flemish activists asked the Germans to incorporate French Flanders in the Flemish State. After the war, the Abbé Gantois created the *Vlaamsch Verbond voor Frankrijk,* which aimed at cultural ends but yielded more and more to Flemish nationalist influence. This influence brought him in 1940, with France occupied, to ask Hitler for the incorporation of French Flanders into a United Netherlands. Publications of Flemish nationalists and speeches by VNV leaders justified their claim on the grounds of common culture, economics, and the need for living space. In 1942, however, the Germans forbade the use of the term of "United Netherlands." This idea no longer fit with the German conceptions of the new Europe. J/S

512. Mievre, J. L'ÉVOLUTION POLITIQUE D'ABEL BONNARD (JUSQU'AU PRINTEMPS 1942) [The political evolution of Abel Bonnard until the spring of 1942]. *Rev. d'Hist. de la Deuxième Guerre Mondiale [France] 1977 27(108): 1-26.* There were significant changes in Abel Bonnard's political views between 1928, when they were close to those of Charles Maurras, and April 1942, when he took office as minister of education in the Vichy regime. By that time Bonnard accepted much more of the Nazi ideology. His vigorous collaboration with the Germans grew out of this ideological evolution. 136 notes.
G. H. Davis

513. Moritz, Erhard. PLANUNGEN FÜR DIE KRIEGFÜHRUNG DES DEUTSCHEN HEERES IN AFRIKA UND VORDERASIEN [Plans for the German army's warfare in Africa and the Middle East]. *Militärgeschichte [East Germany] 1977 16(3): 323-333.* Five documents from the Army's Supreme Com-

mand dated from April to July 1941 provide evidence of the origins of plans for military campaigns in Afghanistan and North Africa after the defeat of the Soviet Union. These plans were designed to challenge Great Britain in India and to prepare for conflict with the United States by control of West African territory. 5 documents, 4 notes. H. D. Andrews

514. Munthe-Kaas, O. U. FELTTOGET I NORD-NORGE 1940: EN OVERSIKT [The campaign in Northern Norway in 1940: a survey]. *Norsk Militaert Tidsskrift [Norway] 1975 145(2): 59-68.* Describes the battles in Narvik and Nordland in April-May 1940, maintaining that lack of established coordinated command over the Allied and Norwegian forces and German superiority in the air caused the German victory.

515. Munthe-Kaas, Otto H. and Hauge, Andreas. TYSK LISTIGHET MISLYKTES [German cunning failed]. *Norsk Militaert Tidsskrift [Norway] 1977 147(6): 243-249.* Studies the battles at Narvik in 1940 and the Norwegian evacuation, comparing the reports by Otto H. Munthe-Kaas and Hans Schleebrügge, chief of the First German battalion.

516. Nanteuil, Hughes de and Levy, Gilles. LA REDDITION DE LA COLONNE ELSTER [The surrender of the Elster Column]. *R. Historique des Armées [France] 1974 3(3): 62-85.* On 16 August 1944, Adolf Hitler ordered his army occupying France to withdraw to a defensible line running from Montpellier through Clermont-Ferrand to Orleans. This study reveals the circumstances under which 19,200 Germans commanded by General Elster, and comprising the rear guard of the retreating army, were obliged by the forces of the French Resistance to surrender to the Americans on 10 September 1944. Based on captured German military records housed at France's Service Historique de l' Armée and private papers of General Elster; photo, 14 maps, 8 notes.
A. Blumberg

517. Natali, Jacques. L'OCCUPANT ALLEMAND A LYON DE 1942 À 1944 D'APRÈS LES SOURCES ALLEMANDES [The German occupation in Lyons, 1942-44, from German sources]. *Cahiers d'Hist. [France] 1977 22(4): 441-464.* Reviews the nature of the administration and occupying forces, particularly the impact on young, discouraged soldiers of an active anti-Nazi propaganda campaign. Based mainly on documents in the Freiburg military archives; 6 notes.
R. Howell

518. Neigert, Marcel. LA RÉPRESSION ALLEMANDE EN MOSELLE (1940-1945) [German repression in the Moselle, 1940-45]. *Rev. d'Hist. de la Deuxième Guerre Mondiale [France] 1977 27(105): 79-100.* The Moselle department suffered great losses from military operations and Germanization policies. Over 2,500 persons were killed in the fighting, 100,000 expelled, 10,000 deported to Germany, 15,000 conscripted into the German army; 7,760 were arrested because of the resistance. Of these 151 were executed and 5,812 deported to Germany (of which 3,056 failed to return). Farms, factories, and businesses were ruined and 16,766 buildings destroyed. One of five articles in a special edition on Lorraine during World War II. 12 notes. G. H. Davis

519. Nicault, Maurice. LA CAPITULATION DE LA COLONNE ELSTER [The surrender of the Elster column]. *Rev. d'Hist. de la Deuxième Guerre Mondiale [France] 1975 (99): 91-99.* The German *Marschgrupp Süd* under the command of General Elster withdrew from Bordeaux in three columns on 28 August 1944. They moved into the department of Indre and under harassment of "Jedburgh group" leadership units sent in from England, they surrendered in Issoudun in September. This is one of five articles in a special edition on aspects of the French resistance. 16 notes. G. H. Davis

520. Nofi, A. A. THE DESERT FOX: ROMMEL'S CAMPAIGN FOR NORTH AFRICA, APRIL 1941-DECEMBER 1942. *Strategy & Tactics 1981 (87): 4-15.* Describes the North African campaign fought by General Erwin Rommel in Egypt and Libya during World War II. Of tremendous strategic importance, it was the last honorably conducted campaign in modern times.

521. Nofi, Albert A. PANZERARMEE AFRIKA AND THE WAR IN THE DESERT JUNE 1940—DECEMBER 1942. *Strategy & Tactics 1973 (40): 4-19.* Describes the military campaign between the Axis powers and Great Britain in North Africa during World War II.

522. Nofi, A. A. SICILY: THE RACE FOR MESSINA, 10 JULY-17 AUGUST, 1943. *Strategy & Tactics 1981 (89): 7-12.* Surveys the Allied invasion of Sicily in the summer of 1943 and the subsequent conduct of operations by both Allied and Axis commanders.

523. Oberdörfer, Lutz. MILITÄRISCHE PLÄNE UND AKTIVITÄTEN DER EUROPÄISCHEN WESTMÄCHTE UND DEUTSCHLANDS GEGENÜBER NORDEUROPA WÄHREND DES "SELTSAMEN KRIEGES" [Military plans and activities of the West European powers and Germany vis-à-vis northern Europe during the Phoney War]. *Militärgeschichte [East Germany] 1982 21(4): 430-442.* During the Phoney War Northern Europe was a priority object of the belligerent powers. The preparation of the German invasion of Norway and Denmark was a clearly aggressive step of German imperialism toward the attainment of domination in Europe. For the Allies it was a question of using the North for channeling the war against the USSR as well as for improving their own position vis-à-vis Nazi Germany within the framework of their general concept of warfare. 103 notes. J/T (H. D. Andrews)

524. Palm, Thede. SCHWEIZ OCH "FALL GELB" [Switzerland and Case Yellow]. *Kungliga Krigsvetenskaps Akademiens Handlingar och Tidskrift [Sweden] 1973 177(6): 159-164.* The 1940 Nazi invasion of France, Case Yellow, was preceded by the occupation of Belgium to prevent a major assault across the Franco-German border and the Maginot line. Because of the concentration of troops along the German-French-Swiss border the Swiss feared being drawn into the war. However, because Germany was involved in hostilities on two fronts, the number of German troops near Switzerland did not represent a serious danger to Swiss neutrality, although many did not realize this. Based on Christian Vetsch's *Aufmarsch gegen die Schweiz. Der deutsche Fall Gelb— Irreführung der Schweizer Armee 1939/40* (Walter Verlag, 1973). U. Bartels/S

525. Patrick, Stephen B. THE ARDENNES OFFENSIVE: THE BATTLE OF THE BULGE, DECEMBER 1944. *Strategy & Tactics 1973 (37): 4-21.* Discusses the World War II Battle of the Bulge in Western Europe between Germany and the Allies in 1944.

526. Patrick, Stephen B. BATTLE FOR GERMANY: THE DESTRUCTION OF THE REICH, DECEMBER 1944-MAY 1945. *Strategy and Tactics 1975 (50): 5-20.* Discusses the final Allied assaults on Nazi Germany, German countermeasures, and the weapons and strategies of the participants. S

527. Patrick, Stephen B. WESTWALL: FOUR BATTLES TO GERMANY. *Strategy & Tactics 1976 (54): 4-14.* Describes four battles fought in the Netherlands and western Germany in 1944 and 1945.

528. Pertz, Erik. LA MISE AU TRAVAIL DES COURTRAISIENS EN ALLEMAGNE (1940-1945) [The employment of Kortrijkers in Germany, 1940-45]. *Cahiers d'Hist. de la Seconde Guerre Mondiale [Belgium] 1976 4: 181-200.* A local study, confined to Kortrijk in Belgium, on the problem of drafting labor from occupied areas to Germany during World War II. Considers the administration of the call-up and concentrates on the statistics and tempo of labor supplied to Germany. Although an obligatory labor service was instituted on 6 October 1942, the number of volunteers always exceeded the number of deportees, and the former varied directly with the rate of unemployment in Belgium. Based on Belgian Health Ministry archives and censuses; 4 tables, 4 graphs, 33 notes. M. K. Palat

529. Peschanski, Denis. LA DEMANDE DE PARUTION LÉGALE DE *L'HUMANITÉ* (17 JUIN 1940-27 AOÛT 1940) [The request for legal publication of *Humanité*, 17 June-27 August 1940]. *Mouvement Social [France] 1980 (113): 67-89.* Two documents on discussion between French Communist Party leaders and the German authorities early in the occupation of France concerning the legal publication of the French Party newspaper, *l'Humanité;* the daily relation of events by lawyer R. Foissin and selections from the notebook of Maurice Thorez. The details provided here emphasize the duration of the discussions and throw light on the legalist strategy of the French party in 1940.
J/S

530. Picard, Roger and Racault, Gaston. LA VIE ÉCONOMIQUE DANS LA VIENNE (1940-1944) [Economic life in the Vienne Department, 1940-44]. *Rev. d'Hist. de la Deuxième Guerre Mondiale [France] 1980 30(119): 17-44.* It is difficult to examine the economy of a single French department. In general Vienne exhibited all the characteristics of a wartime economy while under German occupation. Confiscations and shortages of needed materials reduced the income of artisans and caused industrial problems. Economic planning caused a large bureaucracy to intervene in the economy. Transportation, especially automobiles, was restricted by tire shortages. Horse-related farm activities were undermined by confiscations for the use of the German army. Based on departmental archives; map, 16 tables, 3 graphs. G. H. Davis

531. Pitt, Barrie. TOBRUK. *British Heritage [Great Britain] 1981 2(6): 20-31; 1981-82 3(1): 32-45.* Continued from an earlier article. See abstract 533. Part 2. Describes the 1941 siege of Tobruk during World War II, focusing on

defense of the port by Australian troops under Major-General Leslie Morshead and the operations of assorted British and Indian troops against German and Italian forces under General Erwin Rommel. Part 3. Describes the June 1942 battle of Tobruk, in which General Erwin Rommel defeated the British forces, taking the fort which had resisted attack for more than a year. Article to be continued. See following abstract.

532. Pitt, Barrie. TOBRUK. *British Heritage [Great Britain] 1982 3(2): 38-51, (4): 36-47.* Continued from an earlier article. See preceding abstract. Part 4. Focuses on Rommel's Afrika Korps' raid on the Tobruk fortress in 1942, which resulted in defeat for the British under Major-General H. B. Klopper. Part 5. Focuses on the plan under the command of Lieutenant Colonel John Haselden, Operation Daffodil, which started with a small group of men whose mission was to blow up the main fuel storage tanks in Tobruk but soon became a bigger operation whose "success was negligible while its cost, especially to the Navy, was disastrous."

533. Pitt, Barrie. TOBRUK. *British Heritage [Great Britain] 1981 2(5): 34-45.* Part 1. History and significance of Tobruk, Libya, and the fighting there during World War II, 1939-43. Article to be continued. See abstract 531.

534. Pushkin, A. BOEVYE DEISTVIIA NEMETSKIKH PODVODNYKH LODOK PROTIV AVIANOSTSEV V PERIOD VTOROI MIROVOI VOINY [German submarine operations against aircraft carriers during World War II]. *Morskoi Sbornik [USSR] 1980 (6): 20-29.* During World War II the German navy dramatically increased its number of submarines, from 57 in 1939 to 1,131 in 1945 and German harassment of enemy, mostly British, aircraft carriers steadily increased. Secondary sources; 2 tables, 6 notes. J. Mamtora

535. Rastelli, Achille. I MEZZI NAVALI PER LA *OPERAZIONE SEELÖWE* [Naval vessels for Operation Sealion]. *Riv. Marittima [Italy] 1981 114(3): 65-78.* Describes preparations for the German invasion of Great Britain, summer 1940.

536. Riel, H. van. AANTEKENINGEN NAAR AANLEIDING VAN L. DE JONG, *HET KONINKRIJK DER NEDERLANDEN IN DE TWEEDE WERELDOORLOG* [Notes with reference to L. de Jong, *The Kingdom of the Netherlands during World War II*]. *Bijdragen en Mededelingen betreffende de Geschiedenis der Nederlanden [Netherlands] 1978 93(3): 483-501.* Review article of Louis de Jong, *Het Koninkrijk der Nederlanden in de Tweede Wereldoorlog*, 8 vols. (The Hague, 1969-78). The work is thorough and masterful. There is too much emphasis on the resistance movement, heroic deeds, and the persecution of the Jews. De Jong writes from the standpoint of a revisionist socialist, although his objectivity increases as the story unfolds. G. D. Homan

537. Roslyng-Jensen, Palle. RUSSERNE I DANMARK 1943-1945 [Russians in Denmark, 1943-45]. *Historie [Denmark] 1975 11(3): 392-416.* Analyzes the voluntary participation of Russian prisoners of war in the German occupation army in Denmark during World War II. The German policy of using Soviet citizens as reserve troops underwent several dramatic shifts. During the military occupation's last phase they were used in such large numbers that the German defense capability in Denmark was substantially affected. A series of episodes

before and after 5 May 1945 demonstrated that the reserve troops were willing and able to point arms against their German superior officers. J/S

538. Rössler, Eberhard. ENTWICKLUNG UND ERPROBUNG VON DEUTSCHEN UNTERWASSER-SCHLEPPKÖRPERN FÜR DEN VERSORGUNGSEINSATZ IM ZWEITEN WELTKRIEG [The design and testing of German towed submersible containers as supply vessels in World War II]. *Marine Rundschau [West Germany] 1977 74(1): 25-28.* To help in the logistic support of German and Italian troops in Northern Africa, 1943, the idea of submerged supply containers, towed by surface ships or by submarines, began actual testing procedures. Called submarine lighters, the apparatus showed positive results, but in late summer 1944 the plans were given up due to the strategic situation. Drawing. G. E. Pergl

539. Rousseau, Michel. DOUAI PENDANT LA SECONDE GUERRE MONDIALE, 1939-1945, DE LA IIIÊME À LA IVÊME RÉPUBLIQUE [Douai during World War II, 1939-45: from the Third to the Fourth Republic]. *Rev. du Nord [France] 1979 61(241): 475-497.* Under German occupation, War Committees and the Special Delegation replaced the bodies elected under the Third Republic, in Douai and Nord-Pas-de-Calais. Later on, the necessities of the war weakened German administration and enabled the Vichy regime to establish its own administrative structures. The first municipal elections after the Liberation brought to the Town Hall a majority of new men coming from the Resistance and moved by a new spirit. J/S

540. Schofield, B. B. THE DEFEAT OF THE U-BOATS DURING WORLD WAR II. *J. of Contemporary Hist. [Great Britain] 1981 16(1): 119-129.* The key factor in almost every military operation in World War II was the availability of shipping. Nevertheless the British Admiralty underestimated the threat posed by the German navy's 57 U-boats at the outbreak of war, a threat intensified by the shortage of convoy escort vessels for British ships. American Lend-Lease in 1940, the interception and deciphering of German coded messages, and the technique of fueling at sea made through-escort possible by May 1941 for transatlantic convoys. The new advantage suffered, however, after the United States entered the war and the vulnerability of the American east coast led to the loss of 526 British ships in the first six months of 1942. The situation was gradually redeemed in 1943 by increased American help and conflict within the German high command. 7 notes. M. P. Trauth

541. Scholliers, Peter. L'EVACUATION MASSIVE DES PRISONS SS EN BELGIQUE: LES CONVOIS DES 8 ET 23 MAI 1944 A DESTINATION DU CAMP DE CONCENTRATION DE BUCHENWALD [The mass evacuation of SS prisons in Belgium: the convoys of 8 and 23 May 1944 to the Buchenwald concentration camp]. *Cahiers d'Hist. de la Seconde Guerre Mondiale [Belgium] 1980 6: 115-144.* A statistical study of Belgians deported to German concentration and labor camps. The majority were industrial workers while professionals were surprisingly few; they were equally from Brabant and Wallonia, but slightly fewer from Flanders; and the vast majority had been arrested for resistance activity. The labor camps of Harzungen, Ellrich, and Dora took more than the concentration camps like Buchenwald; the criterion of distribution among them was manpower requirement and capacity for work; and the death rates were

higher in Ellrich and Dora than in Buchenwald. There are also figures on age-classification, the German agency, place, and date of arrest, place of internment in Belgium, resistance affiliations, and last minute evacuation before Allied liberation. Based on Belgian and German archives; 15 tables, 27 notes, 4 appendixes.

M. K. Palat

542. Schröder, Josef. LES PRÉTENTIONS ALLEMANDES À LA DIRECTION MILITAIRE DU THÉÂTRE ITALIEN D'OPERATIONS AU COURS DE L'ANNÉE 1943 [German intentions to assume military control of the Italian theater of operations during the year 1943]. *Rev. d'Hist. de la Deuxième Guerre Mondiale [France] 1974 24(94): 28-46.* Both Admiral Karl Doenitz and General Alfred Jode regarded the military reverses in Sicily as the fault of the Italian high command and took advantage of every opportunity to retain military and naval command over all German units as well as some Italian ones and to establish a unified command under German dominance. Hitler, however did not support these proposals before the fall of Mussolini in July 1943. 42 notes.

G. H. Davis

543. Selleslagh, F. LA K.A.J. CLANDESTINE EN ALLEMAGNE (1942-1944) [The KAJ underground in Germany, 1942-44]. *Cahiers d'Hist. de la Seconde Guerre Mondiale [Belgium] 1972 (2): 271-297.* Describes the activities of the Christian Workers Youth organization, founded in Belgium in 1925 to win the working class to Christianity. During World War II it turned to the welfare of Belgian workers transported to Germany through passive resistance to the Gestapo and Belgian collaboration. It created 25 districts with at least 1,800 members in Germany, and probably many more unregistered sympathizers. It was organized in a highly decentralized structure despite efforts by the Berlin branch to centralize it in 1943. Most of its leadership was arrested in September 1944, but by the end of the year it became active in repatriation to Belgium. Based on Belgian sources; 58 notes, appendix.

M. K. Palat

544. Shea, William L. and Pritchett, Merrill R. THE WEHRMACHT IN LOUISIANA. *Louisiana Hist. 1982 23(1): 5-19.* During World War II, over 20,000 Axis prisoners, mostly from Germany's Afrika Corps, were held in four Louisiana prison camps and 35 branch work camps. Well treated, they engaged in sports, musical and dramatic activities, handicrafts, and educational programs. Many worked under contract on farms, in lumbering, and on civic works, alleviating the acute shortage of civilian labor. Fanatical Nazis tried to dominate other prisoners, but were gradually identified and removed. At war's end, public outcry over the "coddling" of prisoners brought a harsher regime until the last camp closed in 1946. Based on government documents, Red Cross and YMCA reports, and newspapers; map, 23 notes.

R. E. Noble

545. Smirnov, V. P. OSVOBOZHDENIE PARIZHA OT GITLEROVSKIKH OKKUPANTOV [Freeing Paris from Hitler occupation]. *Novaia i Noveishaia Istoriia [USSR] 1974 (5): 119-131, (6): 111-126.* Describes the liberation of Paris toward the end of World War II, stressing the Allies' lack of success and good faith in this operation. The Allies, like the Germans, feared Communist influence among the Parisians and preferred not to have a Communist-led uprising help them drive the Germans from the city. The population of Paris played a leading role in emancipating the city by undermining German rule there

through strikes and armed resistance. The citizens' resilience was more instrumental in expelling the Nazis than were Western military operations. 170 notes.
D. N. Collins

546. Sobczak, Janusz. PROPAGANDA HITLEROWSKA WOBEC WOJSKA POLSKIEGO I POLSKICH SIŁ ZBROJNYCH NA ZACHODZIE [German propaganda regarding the Polish army and Polish armed forces in the West]. *Przegląd Zachodni [Poland] 1979 35(3): 37-56.* German war propaganda defamed Polish forces as cruel, unruly and cowardly. When Polish forces in Italy distinguished themselves, Hitler in 1944 ordered increased effort. Leaflets and a radio voice called "Wanda" addressed the Polish troops. Poles were pitied for discrimination, called poor mercenaries for the British, and urged to desert. Only two desertions from a Polish regiment were noted, but Wanda also advised where the Polish forces were, and thousands of Poles forcibly drafted into Wehrmacht deserted to join the Polish forces in Italy. Based on records in the Bundesarchive, Koblenz, and secondary sources.
M. Krzyzaniak

547. Speer, Albert. AZ AMERIKAI-ANGOL BOMBATÁMADÁSOK HATÁSÁRÓL 1944-BEN [On the effect of the Anglo-American air raids in 1944]. *Világtörténet [Hungary] 1979 (3): 106-109.* Excerpts from the memoirs of Albert Speer. The Allied bombing raids of 28-29 May 1944 proved Hermann Goering's optimism wrong, and Speer took over administration of air armaments.
R. Hetzron

548. Stich, Karl. DIE BRITISCHE V-WAFFEN-ABWEHR 1944/5 [The British V-weapon defense, 1944-45]. *Militärgeschichte [East Germany] 1978 17(6): 694-710.* Surveys German objectives in the use of V-weapons in 1944-45, and Great Britain's aims, organization, methods, and the results of its V-weapon defense. The V-weapons failed not because of their out-of-date conception and amateurish employment, but because of the persistent and successful struggle of the British V-weapon defense. 9 illus., 2 tables, 23 notes. H. D. Andrews

549. Suttorp, L. C. UIT EEN SCHOOLARCHIEF IN DE OORLOGSJAREN [From a school archive during the war years]. *Kleio [Netherlands] 1980 21(6): 199-203.* Records kept from 1940 to 1944 by the Higher Middle School, The Hague, reveal the attention paid to Dutch schools by the German occupation forces. Characterized by excessive attention to detail, the authorities' regulations affected pupils and all school personnel, interfering with daily schedules. They concerned not only the expulsion of all Jews, the education of youth to moral, positivistic attitudes, and punishment by arrest for any moral or political infractions, but minutiae like the behavior during air raid alerts and the exact furnishings of shelters. Based on the archive of the Hogereburgerschool, The Hague; table.
G. Herritt

550. Swint, William A. MAY 14, 1940, REVISITED: THE GERMAN AIR ATTACK ON ROTTERDAM. *Aerospace Hist. 1974 21(1): 14-22.*

551. Tugwell, Maurice A. J. DAY OF THE PARATROOPS. *Military Rev. 1977 57(3): 40-53.* The successful conquest of Crete in May 1941, by the use of General Kurt Student's paratroopers, represented both the high point and the last major use in battle of the airborne assault. Adolf Hitler considered that its surprise element and hence its effectiveness was gone. Subsequent Allied attempts

to use it had limited success in Operation Overlord, total disaster in Operation Market Garden. Subsequently, there has been little attention paid to its potential as an instrument of coercion in conditions short of fullscale war.

G. E. Snow

552. Umbreit, Hans. LA STRATEGIE DEFENSIVE DE L'ALLEMAGNE SUR LE FRONT DE L'OUEST EN 1944 [The defensive strategy of Germany on the western front in 1944]. *Rev. Hist. des Armées [France] 1974 1(4): 122-138.* A study based on a paper read to a colloquium at Paris in October 1974, devoted to the 30th anniversary of the liberation of France. Based largely upon unpublished documents drawn from German military archives and the published texts of Hitler's own analyses of the military situation; 45 notes. A. Blumberg

553. Umbreit, Hans. LES SERVICES D'OCCUPATION ALLEMANDS ET LES ÉGLISES CHRÉTIENNES EN FRANCE [The German occupation authorities and the Christian churches in France]. *Rev. du Nord [France] 1978 60(237): 299-309.* Among the numerous German services which settled in occupied France, the military administration, the embassy, and the SS were the main ones concerned with religious questions. Whereas the army mostly saw to it that churches and clergymen neither jeopardized internal security nor opposed their methods of exploiting the conquered territory, the SS regarded the Christian religion as an ideological adversary. For the embassy, the Catholic Church appeared as a moral force apt to contribute to a renewal of France and French nationalism. But the Germans did not interfere much with the internal affairs of the churches. They were content to keep a careful watch over them. The Churches enjoyed a period of relative freedom as long as the carrying out of the war did not permit establishment of the New Order. J/S

554. Underwood, G. L. SOVIET THREAT TO THE ATLANTIC SEA LINES OF COMMUNICATIONS: LESSONS LEARNED FROM THE GERMAN CAPTURE OF NORWAY IN 1940. *Naval War Coll. Rev. 1981 34(3): 43-47.* Examines the German invasion of Norway in 1940 and the importance of control of Norway for early German successes in World War II and argues that in Soviet-NATO conflict control of Norway and North Atlantic shipping and communications would be similarly vital.

555. Van Crefeld, M. ROMMEL'S SUPPLY PROBLEM, 1941-42. *J. of the Royal United Services Inst. for Defence Studies [Great Britain] 1974 119(3): 67-73.* Historians have tended to assume that Adolf Hitler's refusal to support Rommel in a thrust from Libya to the Persian Gulf was based on strategic considerations. Doubts can be raised about the feasibility of such an objective in terms of supply problems. An analysis of Rommel's difficulties indicates that the central issue was the length of his supply line rather than simply inadequate supplies of fuel. North Africa was lost to the Axis because of Rommel's "impossibly long lines of communication inside Africa," not the Axis failure to win the air-naval struggle on the Mediterranean, nor Hitler's failure to support him since "Rommel in fact got all the forces that could be maintained in Africa." Based on German military sources; 111 notes. D. H. Murdoch

556. Vanwelkenhuyzen, Jean and Van der Wee, Herman. A PROPOS DE L'ÉCONOMIE BELGE AU COURS DE LA SECONDE GUERRE MONDIALE [Notes on the Belgian economy during World War II]. *Rev. Belge de Philologie et d'Hist. [Belgium] 1979 57(2): 394-409.* Two reviews of John Gillingham, *Belgian Business in the Nazi New Order* (Ghent, 1977) which hypothesizes that the Belgians collaborated with the Nazis. Rejects Gillingham's scholarship although he has touched on some vital issues in the economic history of Belgium. 12 notes. B. S. Fetter

557. Vanwelkenhuyzen, Jean. AVERTISMENTELE VIN DE LA BERLIN [The warnings come from Berlin]. *Magazin Istoric [Romania] 1979 13(9): 44-48.* Describes German preparations for the April 1940 invasion of Belgium, and explains how Belgium heard rumors of an attack in October 1939.

558. Vanwelkenhuyzen, Jean. LA BELGIQUE ET LA MENACE D'INVASION 1939-1940: LES AVERTISSEMENTS VENUS DE BERLIN [Belgium and the menace of invasion 1939-40: intelligence reports from Berlin]. *Rev. Hist. [France] 1980 264(2): 375-395.* In October and November 1939 and in April 1940 the Belgian military attaché in Berlin, Colonel Georges Goethals, received warning from the Dutch military attaché that Germany intended to invade Belgium. The source of the information—at that time unknown—was Colonel Hans Oster, a close associate of Admiral Wilhelm Canaris and an anti-Hitler conspirator. Oster hoped to encourage Belgian resistance so that Hitler's offensive would be stalled, thus providing a favorable situation for a *Putsch* against him. Based on a reconstruction of communications between Goethals, the Dutch attaché and Oster through documents in Belgian archives and elsewhere; note.
G. H. Davis

559. Viault, Birdsall S. THE LOW COUNTRIES AND THE QUEST FOR A NEGOTIATED PEACE, 1939-1940. *Pro. of the South Carolina Hist. Assoc. 1979: 28-40.* Discusses the attempts by Belgium and the Netherlands to secure a negotiated peace with Germany September 1939-March 1940. Negotiations went on not only with Germany but also with the Allies in a search for terms that would satisfy both. In the end, they failed because Hitler was unwilling to limit his ambitions and the Allies could not make peace on Germany's terms. Based on government documents and published works; 37 notes.
J. W. Thacker, Jr.

560. Voorhis, Jerry L. A BIBLIOGRAPHIC NOTE ON OCCUPIED DENMARK, 1940-1943. *Scandinavian Studies 1980 52(3): 289-298.* Discussion of the literature of the occupation, divided by language of publication. Writers in each language have focused on areas of particular interest to their own countries, resulting in gaps that need to be filled. Paper presented at the annual meeting of the Society for the Advancement of Scandinavian Study, Seattle, May 1977.
C. W. Ohrvall

561. Wilt, Alan F. AN ADDENDUM TO THE ROMMEL-RUNDSTEDT CONTROVERSY. *Military Affairs 1975 39(4): 176-181.* Analyzes the Rommel-Rundstedt controversy concerning how best to defeat the expected Allied invasion of France. Actually, Gerd von Rundstedt did not tie himself exclusively to one solution, and the real dispute was between Field Marshal Erwin Rommel

and General Geyr von Schweppenburg, the head of German Panzer Forces in the West. Von Rundstedt failed to reconcile the two positions, forcing the German troops to fight the invasion battle from two contradictory plans. The author compares the leadership styles of Rommel and von Rundstedt. Primary and secondary sources; 41 notes. A. M. Osur

562. Wilt, Alan F. THE SUMMER OF 1944: A COMPARISON OF OVERLORD AND ANVIL/DRAGOON. *J. of Strategic Studies [Great Britain] 1981 4(2): 187-195.* Operations Overlord and Anvil/Dragoon against Normandy and southern France in June and August 1944 were closely linked for more than a year before they were launched. Although Operation Overlord was by far the larger and more complex operation, Operation Dragoon was also a considerable undertaking, and both military campaigns demonstrated overwhelming Allied naval and air superiority. While the Germans were surprised by the Normandy landing, they knew the date and approximate location of the French Riviera assault, but in the latter case their defensive posture had deteriorated to such an extent that they could do little about it. German reaction was much stronger in the north than in the south, where the Allies advanced rapidly up the Rhône River valley. But Anglo-American forces could not sustain the brilliant summer offensives into the fall of 1944; the pace had been too hectic and the distances for supply too great. Primary sources; 2 tables, 26 notes. A. M. Osur

5

AT WAR IN EAST AND SOUTHEAST EUROPE

563. Arndtova, Veronika. KRACH FAŠISTICKÉ AGRÁRNÍ A NÁRODNOSTNÍ POLITIKY NA SEVERNÍ MORAVĚ [The failure of the fascist agrarian and nationalist policy in Northern Moravia]. *Slezský Sborník [Czechoslovakia] 1976 74(2): 110-117.* Nazi plans for evacuation of Czech farmers and Germanization of the remaining "suitable" population did not succeed after the outbreak of World War II due to a number of factors: opposition of the Czechs, want of people and material, and general chaos created by the Nazis themselves. 38 notes.
B. Kimmel

564. Ballvora, Shyqri. LE RÉGIME D'OCCUPATION NAZIE EN ALBANIE ET LA LUTTE CONTRE LUI (SEPTEMBRE-NOVEMBRE 1943) [The Nazi occupation regime in Albania and the fight against it, September-November 1943]. *Studia Albanica [Albania] 1977 14(2): 61-91.* Discusses the Nazi policy in the Balkans and the German invasion of Albania following the capitulation of Italy in 1943. Examines the resistance campaign by the partisans and the consolidation of the national liberation front, relations between the various partisan groups, the Communist Party leadership of the liberation army and the mobilization of the people, and the German tactics for crushing the resistance. Based on wartime documents; 70 notes.
P. J. Taylorson

565. Ballvora, Shyqri. VENDOSJA E REGJIMIT NAZIST TË PUSHTIMIT NË SHQIPËRI (SHTATOR-NËN-TOR 1943) [The installation of the Nazi occupation regime in Albania, September-November 1943]. *Studime Hist. [Albania] 1977 31(2): 33-66.* Describes the military occupation of Albania by Germany in September 1943, shortly after the collapse of Fascist Italy. The Nazis set up a government made up of Albanian reactionary politicians who had not collaborated with the Italian administration. Although the Nazis claimed that they recognized Albanian sovereignty, all power was retained by the German army. One of the effects of the German occupation was to deepen the divisions between the Albanian Communist and non-Communist resistance forces. The Communists had to wage war on two fronts: against the Germans and against the Albanian nationalists who sided with the Communists, hoping to dominate the situation after Germany's defeat. Based on German and Albanian official sources; 70 notes.
A. Logoreci

566. Bantea, Eugen. LES ACTIONS MILITAIRES ROUMAINES SUR LA CÔTE DE LA MER NOIRE PENDANT L'INSURRECTION NATIONALE ANTIFASCISTE D'AOÛT 1944 [Rumanian military actions on the Black Sea coast during the national antifascist insurrection of August 1944]. *Rev. Roumaine d'Hist. [Rumania] 1974 13(1): 43-61.* Summarizes the historical, military, and geographic context of Rumanian military operations against the Wehrmacht on the Black Sea littoral. Captured soldiers, guns, and batteries, and the destruction of the German *Admiral Schwarzes Meer* and *Marine-Gruppe Süd* were crucial in driving Nazi forces out of Rumanian territory between the Danube and the Black Sea. The entrance of Soviet forces into this region was thus little more than a "strategic march." All this took place against the background of the seizure of power in Bucharest by the progressive Communist forces, who directed the turning of Rumanian arms against the Germans. Based on Rumanian Ministry of Defense archives, German and Soviet documentary material; map, 86 notes.
G. J. Bobango

567. Bantea, Eugen. L'INSURRECTION ROUMAINE D'AOÛT 1944 DANS LE CONTEXTE DE LA SITUATION POLITIQUE SUD-EST EUROPÉENNE [The Rumanian insurrection of August 1944 in the context of the southeastern European political situation]. *Rev. des Études Sud-Est Européennes [Rumania] 1975 13(3): 343-346.* The 1944 Rumanian uprising against Germany, in addition to its international implications, influenced and was influenced by the immediate political situation in southeastern Europe. Four bodies of evidence are cited in support of this claim: the simultaneous uprising in Yugoslavia, the modification of Hitler's military strategy in the Balkans, the reduction of Germany's forces in the area, and the apparent revision in Hitler's assessment of the political importance of Croatia. It is to the credit of all southeastern European countries that they threw off the yoke of Nazi tyranny. Secondary sources; 14 notes.
A. Howell

568. Bantea, Eugen. POSSIBILITÉS D'UN DÉBARQUEMENT ALLIÉ AUX BALKANS DANS LA VISION DU COMMANDEMENT ALLEMAND DE LA ZONE À L'ÉTÉ DE 1944 [The possibilities of an Allied landing in the Balkans in the planning of the German Regional Command in the summer of 1944]. *Rev. Roumaine d'Hist. [Romania] 1980 19(4): 701-728.* German intelligence and presumptions embraced by the Wehrmacht High Command made an Anglo-American invasion somewhere in the Balkan zone seem a real enough possibility following the Normandy landings to justify strategic, tactical, and logistic preparations. The central Dalmation coast and Istria were seen as especially logical targets for American forces moving across from Italy. As late as October 1944 a British assault through Greece was still envisioned in Berlin. Based on the *Kriegstagebuch des Oberkommandos der Wehrmacht,* specifically the Operations Journal of the Commandant of Southeast Army Group F, entries between 2 July and 8 August 1944, Romanian State Archives, and secondary studies; 60 notes.
G. J. Bobango

569. Bartoš, Josef. OKUPOVANÉ POHRANIČÍ A ČESKÉ OBYVATELSTVO 1938-1945 [Occupied borderlands of Czechoslovakia and the Czech population there, 1938-45]. *Acta U. Palackianae Olomucensis [Czechoslovakia] 1978 (19): 5-198.* Occupied by Germany following the 1938 Munich Agreements, the borderlands of Czechoslovakia were made part of the Reich. The Czech

population encountered hardship at every level of life, from Germanization pressure, political terror and economic extortion to slave labor for Hitler's war goals. Primary sources; 19 appendixes.   G. E. Pergl

570. Bartoš, Josef. STRUKTURA OBYVATELSTVA V TZV. VÝCHODNÍCH SUDETECH V LETECH 1938-1945 [Living conditions in so-called Eastern Sudetenland, 1938-45]. *Acta U. Palackianae Olomucensis: Hist. [Czechoslovakia] 1979 (20): 113-128.* In 1938 Germany occupied a large part of Czechoslovakia's border area in North Moravia and Silesia, creating from these territories a component of the Sudetenland. The Czech population was oppressed by German officials and the German population; poor economic and social conditions in the region resulted from Nazi rule, and many other misdeeds (especially in the Opava area) were committed by the masters and their helpers among the Sudeten Germans. The outbreak of World War II made the life of Czechs in this part of occupied Czechoslovakia even worse. Map, 40 notes.
G. E. Pergl

571. Bogdanović, Rade. BRITANSKA TAJNA DOKUMENTA O VAZDUŠNOM DEŠANTU NA DRVAR 25. MAJA 1944. GODINE [A British secret document about the parachute attack on Drvar, 25 May 1944]. *Istorijski Glasnik [Yugoslavia] 1977 (1-2): 157-164.* A document on the Nazi parachute attack on Josip Tito's headquarters prepared by the deputy chief of the British Mission to the Yugoslav partisans, Lieutenant Colonel Street. It analyzes partisans' capabilities and war aims.   P. J. Adler

572. Bojić, Mehmedalija. LES OPERATIONS ALLEMANDE "WEISS" ET "SCHWARTZ" [The German operations Weiss and Schwartz]. *Rev. Int. d'Hist. Militaire [France] 1981 (51): 173-205.* During the winter of 1942-43, after severe reverses on the Russian front and in North Africa, the Germans feared an Allied landing in the Balkans. For that reason they launched two campaigns, coded White and Black to annihilate the Yugoslavian national liberation army and what they called Tito's state. Several German divisions were involved in the operations which failed to achieve their objectives. Based on primary material in Yugoslav State archives; 35 notes.   J. V. Coutinho

573. Bošnjak, Ljubomir. MJERE OKUPATORA I KVISLINGA ZA ZAŠTITU PRIVREDNIH OBJEKATA I KOMUNIKACIJA 1941-1942. GODINE NA PODRUČJU JUGOSLAVIJE [The measures taken by the occupiers and quislings for the protection of industrial buildings and communications in Yugoslavian territory, 1941-42]. *Vojnoistorijski Glasnik [Yugoslavia] 1979 30(1): 95-116.* Discusses measures the occupying forces—Germans, Italians, Hungarians, and Bulgarians—took to protect their supplies of food, raw materials, and factories, but above all their communication lines. Since all these were targets of guerrilla warfare, the enemy forces had to coordinate their efforts among themselves and with collaborators, mainly the Ustaši and the Chetniks. In spite of the manpower involved (e.g., in July 1942, approximately 11,000 Italian soldiers were used to transport gasoline between Zagreb and Rijeka), none of the measures employed succeeded, and by the end of 1942 the Axis forces had resorted to a strategic defensive. 71 notes.   S. Košak

574. Brandes, Detlev. DIE DEUTSCHE REAKTION AUF DIE PRAGER DEMONSTRATIONEN IM HERBST 1939 [The German reaction to the Prague demonstrations, autumn 1939]. *Vierteljahrshefte für Zeitgeschichte [West Germany] 1975 23(2): 210-218.* Historians have interpreted German brutality against the Czech demonstrators as a turning point in German occupation policy in Czechoslovakia, but the background to that policy has been unclear. Czech records now reveal that behind the back of Constantin von Neurath and in cooperation with Heinrich Himmler, German police chief Karl Hermann Frank provoked the students in order to force a shift to a tough military occupation policy. Based on documents in the Archiv Ministerstva Spravedlnosti, Prague; 44 notes. D. Prowe

575. Branica, Vinko. NJEMAČKA OPERACIJA "ŠAH" OD 22. DO 30. MAJA 1944. GODINE [The German Operation Schach, 22-30 May 1944]. *Vojnoistorijski Glasnik [Yugoslavia] 1978 29(1): 41-55.* A chronology of German military operations against the Yugoslav partisans in western Bosnia and Croatia in May 1944. The main goal was to liquidate the Supreme Headquarters of the Yugoslav National Liberation Army at Drvar. The Germans failed to achieve this aim, but successfully implemented Operation Schach which restricted units of the fourth Corps of the Liberation Army to the Kordun and Banija regions, thus preventing them from relieving the besieged Supreme Headquarters. Based on documents in the Yugoslav Institute of Military History and other primary sources; map, 22 notes. J. Bamber

576. Columbeanu, Sergiu; Bantea, Eugen; and Ionescu, Mihail E. NOI DOCUMENTE INEDITE DIN ARHIVE STRĂINE DESPRE IMPORTANȚA INSURECȚIEI ROMÂNE DIN AUGUST 1944 [New unpublished documents from foreign archives on the importance of the Rumanian insurrection of August 1944]. *Magazin Istoric [Rumania] 1978 12(8): 7-12.* Presents three German military documents on tactics in the Prahova valley, Rumania, after the uprising of 1944, followed by an American report on the strategic effect of Germany's loss of Rumania.

577. Constantiniu, Florin. ANUL 1943 ȘI PERIODIZAREA ISTORIEI CELUI DE AL DOILEA RĂZBOI MONDIAL [The year 1943 and the periodization of the history of World War II]. *Studii și Articole de Istorie [Rumania] 1973 (22): 76-82.* Discusses the significance of 1943 as a turning point in the war. Points out the military and political events which gave the strategic initiative completely to the Allies. RSA 11:435

578. Csonkaréti, Károly. ADALÉK MAGYARORSZÁG NÉMET MEGSZÁLLÁSÁNAK TÖRTÉNETÉHEZ [A contribution to the history of the German occupation of Hungary]. *Hadtörténelmi Közlemények [Hungary] 1979 26(2): 275-280.* Hungarian historiographers agree that the occupation by the Germans on 19 March 1944 "apart from the resistance of the Újvidék garrison and some scattered shooting, went smoothly." The author describes the day in question in Újvidék (now Novi Sad in Yugoslavia), whose garrison was previously *not* instructed *not* to resist the invasion. Both the officers and soldiers, without a single exception, reacted in accord with their military duties to defend the entrusted railway bridge as well as their barracks by using their weapons against their former comrades in arms. 14 notes. E. Soos

579. Faitys, Antonin. A CSEHSZLOVÁK TÖRTÉNETÍRÁS ÉS A CSEH HATÁRMENTI TERÜLETEK TÖRTÉNETE 1938-1945 [Czech historiography and the Czech borderlands, 1938-45]. *Történelmi Szemle [Hungary] 1973 16(3-4): 406-410.* Recent Czech historiography has concentrated on the country's border regions during World War II, and the relationship between Germans, Czechs, and foreign workers there.

580. Fekete, Edit and Gyarmati, György. NEMZETKÖZI KONFERENCIA A KÖZÉP-ÉS DÉLKELET-EURÓPA FELÉ IRÁNYULÓ MÁSODIK VILÁGHÁBORÚS PROPAGANDÁRÓL [International conference on propaganda in Central and Southeast Europe during World War II]. *Történelmi Szemle [Hungary] 1979 22(3-4): 552-561.* Summarizes the discussion at the 1978 Budapest conference. The Germans wanted to keep both the satellite and occupied Southeast Europeans at peace with one another and productive for the Nazi war machine. Anglo-American propaganda initially supported a postwar confederation of the area's countries, but later dropped it to avoid Soviet suspicions. Hungarian press, radio, and film propaganda, while at first clumsily offensive, after March 1944, defensively claimed that "we did not want this war." The conference agreed that historiography both in Hungary and abroad is still in an initial stage of researching the problems of propaganda. E. Soos

581. Ferenc, Tone. KRASOSLOVEC IN JAMAR, POLKOVNIK IN ZLOČINEC [Specialist on the Karst (Kras) area and speleologist, colonel and criminal]. *Goriški Letnik [Yugoslavia] 1979 6: 191-216.* Dr. Hans Brand was a German specialist on the Karst (Kras) mountain plateau region and commanded occupation troops in the area during World War II.

582. Ferenc, Tone and Ževart, Milan. NEKATERE ZNAČILNOSTI IN POSEBNOSTI FAŠISTIČNE OKUPACIJE TER NARODNOOSVOBODILNEGA BOJA IN REVOLUCIJE NA SLOVENSKEM ŠTAJERSKEM [Some characteristics and peculiarities of the fascist occupation and of the national liberation war and revolution in Slovene Styria]. *Časopis za Zgodovino in Narodopisje [Yugoslavia] 1979 15(1-2): 448-461.* Describes peculiarities of the World War II military occupation of Slovenia and traces the progress of the national liberation war in Lower (Slovene) Styria. J/S

583. Ferenc, Tone. OKUPACIJSKA CIVILNA UPRAVA NA SLOVENSKEM IN NJENO GRADIVO [Civil administration in Slovenia under the occupation and its archives]. *Prispevki za Zgodovino Delavskega Gibanja [Yugoslavia] 1980 20(1-2): 31-56.* The first, more extensive part of the article examines some of the fundamental characteristics of the German, Italian, and Hungarian occupation of Slovenia (the dismemberment of the Slovene national territory, annexationism, and denationalization): the establishment of the occupation civil administration in individual provinces and its organization at provincial, district and communal level are described next. The second, less extensive part deals with the Yugoslav and foreign archives of the civil administration organs under occupation. J

584. Ferenc, Tone. SPOMENICE O NEMSKIH OZEMELJSKIH ZAHTEVAH V SLOVENIJI LETA 1940 [Memoranda concerning German territorial claims in Slovenia in 1940]. *Zgodovinski Časopis [Yugoslavia] 1975 29(3-4):*

219-246. Discusses the genesis and purpose of the 1940 memoranda containing German claims to Slovene territories in Yugoslavia. The memoranda were sent to Berlin from the office of the National Socialist Party in Klagenfurt, Austria, and from the Südostdeutsches Institut in Graz, Austria. They were part of a broader scheme dealing with German plans for reorganization of Southeast Europe. The territorial claims in Slovenia were based largely on the *Lebensraum* argument. Based on archival sources in Bonn and Koblenz; 65 notes.

T. Hočevar

585. Fiedor, Karol. POLITYKA TRZECIEJ RZESZY WOBEC SERBOŁUŻYCZAN (1933-1945) [The policies of the Third Reich toward Lusatian Sorbs, 1933-45]. *Śląski Kwartalnik Hist. Sobótka [Poland] 1976 31(2): 361-367.* Outlines the development of the 150,000-strong Sorb community in Upper Lusatia and describes Nazi Germanization policies toward them, 1933-45, especially through the Bund Deutscher Osten, 1933-39.

586. Fishta, Iljaz and Toçi, Veniamin. EKONOMIA E SHQIPËRISË NËN PUSHTETIN GJERMAN (SHTATOR 1943-NËNTOR 1944) [The economy of Albania under the German occupation: September 1943-November 1944]. *Studime Hist. [Albania] 1980 34(1): 91-114.* Following Italy's capitulation the Germans occupied Albania, pretending to reestablish its independence. This promise did not prevent them from exploiting the country in support of their war effort. They appropriated Albanian gold (over eight million gold francs) and currency (over 120 million Albanian francs) deposited in Rome. They appropriated the mineral resources of the country, especially oil and chrome. The occupying troops lived in the country, depriving the people of food. Industries were destroyed and unemployment increased. Production in the mines and agriculture decreased. An economic crisis was created from which only collaborating landowners and big merchants profited—taking 1.34 billion Albanian francs. Based on German army documents, the Official Gazette, Central State Archives, and secondary sources; chart, 97 notes. French summary. G-D. L. Naci

587. Frolow, B. BEGEGNUNGSSCHLACHTEN VON PANZERARMEEN IN ANGRIFFSOPERATIONEN DES GROSSEN VATERLÄNDISCHEN KRIEGES [Tank encounters during World War II]. *Militärgeschichte [East Germany] 1978 17(3): 287-296.* Discusses the conduct of tank warfare on the Eastern front during World War II.

J/T (H. D. Andrews)

588. Gibbons, Robert. ALLGEMEINE RICHTLINIEN FÜR DIE POLITISCHE UND WIRTSCHAFTLICHE VERWALTUNG DER BESETZTEN OSTGEBIETE [General guidelines for the political and economic administration of the occupied areas in the east]. *Vierteljahrshefte für Zeitgeschichte [West Germany] 1977 25(2): 252-261.* A reprint and analysis of a June 1941 memorandum by Otto Bräutigam, the deputy head of the political department of the Nazi Ministry for Occupied Eastern Territories *(Ostministerium).* He promoted a military occupation policy for the USSR designed to gain the sympathy of non-Russian peoples. The document reflects the conflict between the politically and ideologically oriented forces in Alfred Rosenberg's *Ostministerium* and those around Hermann Goering. The latter group pressed for maximum economic exploitation through centralized administration of Russia. Based on documents

in the National Archives, Nuremberg documents, secondary sources, and correspondence with Otto Bräutigam; 32 notes.

D. Prowe

589. Grobelný, Andělín and Pallas, Ladislav. K POSTAVENÍ OSTRAVSKÉ A HORNOSLEZSKÉ PRŮMYSLOVÉ OBLASTI ZA NACISTICKÉ OKUPACE 1939-1945 [The Ostrava and Upper Silesian industrial region during the Nazi occupation, 1939-45]. *Slezský Sborník [Czechoslovakia] 1980 78(1): 1-15.* During the occupation of Ostrava and Upper Silesia, the German press disseminated the racist theories of the Nazi ideology and emphasized that both regions belonged to ancient German lands about to be rightfully reclaimed. Private enterprises were bought out by the Germans. Although output and the mining of coal increased, productivity clearly decreased by 1943 due to the morale of the labor force. In their program of Germanization, the Germans argued that only Upper Silesian soil was German, the population was not to be converted, but destroyed. In Ostrava the Germans fully accepted that the Czechs would become Germanized, and their treatment was better than the Poles were receiving. This ideology dealt a blow to any nationalist philosophy and brought about the emergence of socialism in both regions after the war. 13 notes.

B. Reinfeld

590. Grobelný, Andělín. K VÝVOJI ZEMĚDĚLSTVÍ V ZÁPADNÍM SLEZSKU A NA SEVERNÍ MORAVĚ ZA NACISTICKÉ OKUPACE [Agricultural policy in western Silesia and in northern Moravia during the Nazi occupation]. *Průmyslové Oblasti [Czechoslovakia] 1978 6: 183-254.* Comparison of Czechoslovak agriculture before and after the German military occupation shows an enormous decline in productivity and inventory. The author explores German methods of exploitation of the entire population and the systems of confiscation, forced labor, and resettlement. Map, 13 tables, 97 notes.

G. E. Pergl

591. Grobelný, Andělín. PĚT NĚMECKÝCH DOKUMENTŮ O SLOVENSKÉM NÁRODNÍM POVSTÁNÍ [Five German documents about the Slovakian National Uprising]. *Slezský Sborník [Czechoslovakia] 1974 72(4): 245-258.* Describes the German occupation of Slovakia and details the contents of five letters by German authorities about the resistance movement. The first document by Dr. Beck from Bratislava describes the activities of partisans in the summer of 1944, suggesting that most of Eastern and Central Slovakia was in their hands. Subsequent letters further describe the military situation and recommend German counterattacks against the partisans. The final document, dated 27 October 1944, is a telegram from President Tiso thanking Hitler for assistance and declaring the fall of the Czechoslovak underground a victory for the German race and European culture. 11 notes.

B. Kimmel

592. Grobelný, Andělín. ŠKOLSKÁ OTÁZKA V OKUPOVANÉM POHRANIČÍ 1938-1945 [The question of education in the occupied border regions 1938-45]. *Slezský Sborník [Czechoslovakia] 1975 73(2): 100-119.* Konrad Henlein (1898-1945) announced in November 1938 that the national rights of the Czech population in the Sudetenland would be protected; but in reality an educational plan was worked out before the Munich agreement which stressed the liquidation of the Czech language in the border regions. Czech students were not allowed to register in German secondary schools, whether their citizenship fell

under the Third Reich or the Protectorate. Although officially all Czech primary schools were closed, in purely Czech towns this decree was never carried out. In mixed areas the Nazis began to choose children that were racially acceptable for admittance to German primary schools. Much depended on the zeal of the officials in charge in particular towns. After January 1943 a more aggressive policy toward Czechs in the frontier regions was advocated, such as the transfer of entire Czech town populations. Racial discrimination was also introduced into trade schools. Wherever Czech schools were retained, it was with the idea of ideological instruction in the Nazi philosophy. 53 notes. B. Kimmel

593. Grobelný, Antonín. NACISTICKÁ NÁRODNOSTNÍ POLITIKA A VÝKON OKUPAČNÍHO PRÁVA NA TĚŠÍNSKU 1939-1945 [Nationalities policy of the Nazis and the achievement of occupational rights in Těšín, 1939-45]. *Slezský Sborník [Czechoslovakia] 1977 75(1): 23-38.* After the World War II occupation of Teschen in 1939 the Germans settled as many Germans there as they could, adding to the original German minority. The scale of social status in occupied Teschen rose from Poles to Czechs, to *volksliste* Germans (one German parent), to Germans from the Reich. The Poles were subject to Polish occupation law which effectively cut them off from political and cultural life, which in turn fed their anti-Nazi feelings and actions. The Nazis retaliated by reducing food rations periodically on the slightest charge. The German occupation forces fell under a different set of laws; usually punishment for misdemeanors was postponed to after the war. Harsh interrogations, torture, and camps were reserved only for the Slav population. When labor productivity declined, a directive for better treatment of Poles and Eastern workers was received (1942), but remained a dead letter. 41 notes. B. Kimmel

594. Grobelný Andělín. PRŮMYSLOVÁ OBLAST SEVEROZÁPADNÍCH ČECH A JEJÍ NÁSILNÉ ZAČLENĚNÍ DO TŘETÍ ŘÍŠE V LETECH 1938-1945 [The northwestern industrial region of Bohemia and its integration into the Third Reich, 1938-45]. *Slezský Sborník [Czechoslovakia] 1981 79(4): 241-260.* According to the Munich agreement of 1938, the northwestern industrial region of Bohemia was forcibly integrated into the economy and administration of the Third Reich, as it was technically part of the Sudetenland. Along with these changes, an intensive nazification campaign was conducted among the German population, especially the young people. The political power of the Germans diminished after 1943 when most of the effort of the government in the region, especially in the center, Ústí nad Labem, was directed toward the protection of cultural valuables in the face of Soviet invasion. 40 notes, 3 maps.

B. Reinfeld

595. Herget, Toni. CHRONOLOGIE DER EREIGNISSE IM SUDETENLAND 1945 [Chronology of the events in the Sudetenland, 1945]. *Sudetenland [West Germany] 1975 17(4): 273-278.* Describes the Allied occupation of the Sudeten German areas and the beginning of anti-German measures in 1945.

596. Hladký, Ladislav. K VÝVOJI TEXTILNÍHO PRŮMYSLU V NÁCHODSKÉ OBLASTI ZA NACISTICKÉ OKUPACE [Development of the textile industry in the Náchod region during the Nazi occupation]. *Slezský Sborník [Czechoslovakia] 1980 78(4): 295-300.* The textile industry in the Náchod region was severely damaged by the Nazi occupation; it was disrupted even before

that by the Munich agreement, because many industries had branches in the Sudetenland. After the occupation of Czechoslovakia, many factories were converted to war industries. Much machinery was either destroyed or stored for the duration of the war. Only a few industrialists remained in textiles throughout the Nazi occupation, but they suffered from labor and raw material shortages. Though thus crippled, after the war the textile mills of Náchod were able to start operating again because of the successful cooperation of the National Council and the industrial boards representing the manufacturers. Secondary sources; 52 notes. B. Reinfeld

597. Horejsek, Jaroslav. TRAGÉDIE CESKEHO MALÍNA [The tragedy of Czech Malín]. *Slovanský Přehled [Czechoslovakia] 1973 59(3): 268-271.* Recollects the events of 13 July 1943, when the Ukrainian village of Czech Malín, a colony of Czech farmers, was totally destroyed along with its 500 inhabitants by German troops. The author concludes that this massive homicide was a thoroughly planned and executed action just as were many other similar German atrocities in occupied Soviet Russia. Secondary sources. G. E. Pergl

598. Ilel, I. VSTUPLENIE SOVETSKIKH VOISK V BOLGARIIU V 1944 GODU—OB'EKTIVNAIA NEOBKHODIMOST' [The entry of Soviet troops into Bulgaria in 1944: an objective necessity]. *Voenno-Istoricheskii Zhurnal [USSR] 1978 20(9): 83-86.* The true reasons for Soviet intervention in Bulgaria have been consistently falsified in the West. Bulgaria, ruled by a monarcho-fascist clique, occupied a pivotal position in Germany's Balkan strategy. By the summer of 1944, Bogdan Filov (1883-1945), head of the pro-German Bulgarian government, was about to declare war on the USSR. The entry of Soviet troops into Bulgaria in September 1944, coinciding with antifascist uprisings led by the Bulgarian Workers' Party (Communists), weakened Germany's hold on the Balkans and prevented a civil war as ruling Bulgarian circles had begun negotiations for an Anglo-American occupation of Bulgaria. 18 notes. N. Frenkley

599. Jonca, K. À *VÖLKERRECHTLICHE GROSSRAUMORDNUNG* ELMÉETE KÜLÖNÖS TEKINTETTEL A DUNAI ÉS A BALKÁN ÁLLAMOKRA [The ideology of the *völkerrechtliche Grossraumordnung* with special references to the Danube and Balkan states]. *Történelmi Szemle [Hungary] 1973 16(3-4): 372-375.* A discussion of the legalistic aspects of Hitler's expansionist policy in the Balkans.

600. Kaiser, Hans. DIE DEUTSCHEN UND DIE SLOWAKEI 1944 PROBLEM ZEITGESCHICHTLICHER EDITIONSTECHNIK IN DER CSSR [The Germans and Slovakia, 1944: problems of modern historical editorship in the CSSR]. *Jahrbücher für Geschichte Osteuropas [West Germany] 1973 21(3): 419-422.* An overview of archival holdings dealing with German rule in Slovakia, focusing on 1944. Describes some of the SS and SD materials useful to historians studying the effects of Nazi policies in occupied Czechoslovakia. Discusses the contribution made by Dr. Vilem Precan (before his dismissal in 1968) in cataloging the Prague holdings, *Cesta ke kvetnu* (2 vols., 1965). 3 notes.
J. R. Goldman

601. Kalbe, Ernstgert. ZU DEN ETAPPEN DER BALKANPOLITIK DES FASCHISTISCHEN DEUTSCHEN IMPERIALISMUS [The stages of the Balkan policy of Nazi imperialism]. *Rev. des Études Sud-Est Européennes [Rumania] 1975 13(3): 347-351.* Nazi German imperialism unfolded its plans to dominate the Balkan Peninsula in stages from 1933 to the outright invasion and occupation in April 1941. There were many conflicts with Germany's Italian, Hungarian, and Bulgarian allies, but although it made small concessions, Germany never gave up its predominant position in the Balkans. 9 notes.
J. C. Billigmeier

602. Karner, Stefan. DIE AUSSIEDLUNGEN DER SLOWENEN IN DER UNTERSTEIERMARK [The emigrations of the Slovenes in Lower Styria]. *Österreich in Geschichte und Literatur [Austria] 1978 22(3): 154-174.* The southern third of the province of Styria was assigned to Yugoslavia by the 1919 Treaty of St. Germain. After the German attack on Yugoslavia in 1941 this and neighboring territories were reunited with Styria. German racial policy called for the "re-Germanization" of Lower Styria. Thousands of Slovenes were deported, some to Germany and some to Yugoslavia. Germans from southeastern and Eastern Europe then settled these lands. After the war Yugoslavia reclaimed Lower Styria. Based on microfilmed and other official German documents, published Nuremberg documents, and secondary works; map, 5 tables, 69 notes, 3 appendixes.
J. B. Street

603. Kozeński, Jerzy. SOUTH-EASTERN EUROPE IN NAZI EXPANSIONIST PLANS. *Polish Western Affairs [Poland] 1980 21(1): 47-57.* Discusses Germany's hope and plans to profit from the rich raw materials of Southeastern Europe and to control the area politically. It was part of a general economic expansion of Germany into that area. Based on numerous primary documents; 31 notes.
D. S. Lloyd

604. Kozeński, Jerzy. SYTUACJA NA POGRANICZU AUSTRIACKO-JUGOSŁOWIAŃSKIM (1940-1945) [The situation in the border area between Austria and Yugoslavia, 1940-45]. *Przegląd Zachodni [Poland] 1973 29(3): 65-84.* Examines the political and social conditions in Steiermark during World War II. Based on the court records from Graz, now part of the Federal Archives in Koblenz.

605. Kráčmarová, Hana. ČESKÉ VYSOKOŠKOLSKÉ STUDENTSTVO V REVOLUČNÍCH UDÁLOSTECH NA JAŘE 1945 [Czech university students in the revolutionary events of spring 1945]. *Československý Časopis Hist. [Czechoslovakia] 1975 23(4): 502-518.* The German occupation closed Czech universities in November 1939 as a part of a planned spiritual and economic liquidation of the Czech nation. Eighteen thousand university students engaged in national resistance, participated in the Prague revolution of 1945, and worked toward consolidation in the first months of liberation when Czechoslovak universities were reopened. Secondary sources; 72 notes.
G. E. Pergl

606. Král, Václav. V PŘEDVEČER PRAŽSKÉHO POVSTÁNÍ [On the eve of the 1945 Prague Uprising]. *Slovanský Přehled [Czechoslovakia] 1975 61(2): 81-106.* Describes and examines the events preceding the May 1945 Prague Uprising. Outlines the German-collaborationist anti-Soviet intrigues during the

last weeks of occupied Czechoslovakia, the behind-the-scene diplomacy of the Western Allies—primarily the US military leadership's desire to capture Bohemia and exclude the USSR—and the internal politics of the Czech underground. Based on documents and printed material; 82 notes. G. E. Pergl

607. Latas, Branko. ČETNICI IZ LIKE U SLUŽBI NEMACA NA PODRUČJU HRVATSKOG PRIMORJA I U ITALIJI (1943-1944. GODINE) [Chetniks from Lika in German service in the Croatian littoral and in Italy, 1943-44]. *Vojnoistorijski Glasnik [Yugoslavia] 1979 30(1): 191-214.* Up to 1943, there were no major Chetnik units in the Croatian littoral with the exception of Rijeka, Sušak, and Opatija, where they acted under the auspices of General Grignola of Italian 2d Army Intelligence. They organized their troops in Lika in order to support German and Italian actions against the partisans. After the capitulation of Italy, they first retreated to Losinj Island and from there to Italy. There they joined the German forces in Bologna and Padua, where they were entrusted with guarding British prisoners of war. Primary sources; 69 notes.
S. Košak

608. Latas, Branko. ČETNIČKO-NEMAČKI SPORAZUMI O SARADNJI U SRBIJI (1943-1944) [The Chetnik-German agreements on cooperation in Serbia, 1943-44]. *Vojnoistorijski Glasnik [Yugoslavia] 1978 29(2): 113-138.* Examines agreements of military cooperation signed by Chetnik leaders and the German occupation forces, 1943-44, resulting mainly from Hitler's decision to engage nationalist and quisling groups as allies. Under the agreements, the Chetniks ceased operations against the Germans and engaged the partisans, in return for ammunition. Based on documents in the Yugoslav Institute of Military History archives, and secondary sources; 83 notes. J. Bamber

609. Leci, Thanas. LA POLITIQUE DE TERRORISME ET DE MASSACRES DES OCCUPANTS ITALO-ALLEMANDE EN ALBANIE [The Italian and German occupation forces' policy of terrorism and massacre in Albania]. *Studia Albanica [Albania] 1974 11(2): 137-146.* Through their policy of terrorism and massacre in Albania, 1939-44, the Italian and German occupation forces caused massive damage and human loss. Infiltration, arbitrary arrest, deportation to concentration camps, torture, imprisonment, rape, and murder formed part of the Fascist and Nazi policy. 25 notes. P. J. Taylorson

610. Madajczyk, Czesław. HITLEROVSKÁ OKUPÁCIA VO SVETLE POROVNÁVACÍCH VÝSKUMOV [Hitlerian occupation in the light of comparative observations]. *Hist. Časopis [Czechoslovakia] 1976 24(3): 335-357.* Compares fascist occupation systems in Europe during World War II, focusing on the political and organizational principles of the Nazi occupation. Analyzes the antifascist resistance as it affected the intensity of the occupation. J/S

611. Mainuš, František. PŘÁTELSKÉ VZTAHY ČESKOSLOVENSKÝCH A SOVĚTSKÝCH OBČANŮ V LETECH DRUHÉ SVĚTOVÉ VÁLKY [Friendly relations between Czechoslovak and Soviet citizens during World War II]. *Sborník Prací Filosofické Fakulty Brněnské University: Řada Historická [Czechoslovakia] 1976-77 25-26(23-24): 7-20.* Shows how Czechoslovaks doing forced labor in Germany aided Soviet prisoners of war, and how Czechs and Slovaks aided Soviet escapees from concentration camps as they headed back

eastward. Subsequently those who escaped joined the partisans in Eastern Czechoslovakia and became involved in the Slovak National Uprising.

612. Marcu, Paraschiv, ed. FROM THE CHRONICLE OF THOSE HEROIC DAYS. *Romania [Romania] 1979 4(2-3): 236-257.* Chronicles in some detail the events of 1 May to 31 August 1944 and the expulsion of the German occupation army, setting the stage for a socialist Romania.

613. Marjanović, Jovan. A JUGOSZLÁV TÖRTÉNETÍRÁS A HÁBORÚRÓL ÉS A FORRADALOMRÓL [Yugoslav historiography on the war and the revolution]. *Történelmi Szemle [Hungary] 1973 16(3-4): 402-405.* Examines Yugoslav studies of World War II and the Communist takeover in Yugoslavia produced since the mid-1950's, including a large number of documents which have been published during this period.

614. Merinsky, Karl. DAS KRIEGSENDE 1945 UND SEINE AUSWIRKUNGEN IM RAUM VON ZWETTL [The war's end in 1945 and its impact in Zwettl area]. *Unsere Heimat [Austria] 1975 46(3): 145-152.* Hugy Jury, gauleiter of Lower Austria, was able to control Zwettl until 1945 because neither the Russian nor the American army tried to occupy all of Lower Austria until the German capitulation.

615. Milak, Enes. HITLEROVI STAVOVI PREMA JUGOSLAVIJI SEPTEMBAR 1939-APRIL 1941 GODINE [Hitler's stand on Yugoslavia, September 1939-April 1941]. *Vojnoistorijski Glasnik [Yugoslavia] 1973 24(2-3): 185-200.* Describes Adolf Hitler's attitudes toward Yugoslavia from 1939 until Yugoslavia's entry into the war in April 1941: his views were largely governed by a desire to control the country's resources and strategic position.

616. Miletić, Antun. KONCEPCIJA VRHOVNE KOMANDE NEMAČKIH ORUŽANIH SNAGA ZA GUŠENJE NARODNOOSLOBODILAČKOG USTANKA 1941 GODINE [The plan by the Supreme Command of the German armed forces for quelling the national liberation uprising in 1941]. *Vojnoistorijski Glasnik [Yugoslavia] 1977 28(1): 211-238.* Realizing very early in World War II that the people's liberation uprising could not be contained by a strict policing system, the German Supreme Command brought combat troops into Yugoslavia in August 1941.

617. Miletić, Antun. TITO U OČIMA NEMAČKOG OKUPATORA 1941-1944. GODINE [Tito in the eyes of the German occupier, 1941-44]. *Vojnoistorijski Glasnik [Yugoslavia] 1977 28(2-3): 285-301.* Summarizes the various assessments of, and assumptions about, Josip Tito's personality as seen from documents of the German armed forces.

618. Milošević, Slobodan. KVISLINŠKE SNAGE U BANATU U SLUŽBI NEMAČKOG OKUPATORA 1941-1944. GODINE [Quisling forces in Banat in the service of the German occupiers, 1941-44]. *Vojnoistorijski Glasnik [Yugoslavia] 1979 30(1): 139-153.* Germany occupied Banat as a buffer zone between Hungary and Romania, both allied to the Axis. All key posts in the regional administration were given to the Volksdeutsche (ethnic Germans), although Banat was formally a province of Serbia, then ruled by Germany with the help of the Council of Commissars led by Milan Nedić. For this reason the Serbian

Chetniks had little influence in Banat, and their efforts to create a stronger foothold there were countered by the organizations of other, mutually hostile, ethnic groups—Hungarian, Romanian, and Slovak—encouraged by the Germans. Primary sources; 49 notes. S. Košak

619. Milova, Chr. and Toshkova, Vitka. A BOLGÁR TÖRTÉNETÍRÁS ÉS A DÉLKELET-EURÓPAI NEMZETKÖZI KAPCSOLATOK KÉRDÉSE, VALAMINT BULGARIA KÜLPOLITIKÁJA A MÁSODIK VILÁGHÁBORÚ ALATT [Bulgarian historiography on the problem of Bulgaria's foreign policy and international relations in Southeastern Europe during World War II]. *Történelmi Szemle [Hungary] 1973 16(3-4): 394-401.* Shows how postwar Bulgarian historians have concentrated on the events of 1944, when the country was invaded by Soviet troops and a Communist coup d'etat caused Bulgaria to terminate its Nazi alliance and side instead with the Allies. Secondary sources; 21 notes. H. Szamuely/S

620. Mîndru, Costachi. UN GENERAL HITLERIST CAPTURAT DE UN PLUTONIER ROMÂN [A Hitlerist general captured by a Rumanian warrant officer]. *Magazin Istoric [Rumania] 1975 9(8): 9-13.* The capture of the commandant of "Koruck 593."

621. Mirnić, Josip. A BÁCSKAI NÉMETEK A MAGYARORSZÁGI NÉMETEK NÉPI SZÖVETSÉGE KERETEIBEN [The Germans of Bac within the framework of the Hungarian German People's Association]. *Történelmi Szemle [Hungary] 1973 16(3-4): 443-467.* The *Volksbund* of Hungarian-occupied Bac was the largest and the strongest German minority group in Europe. It was strongly pro-Nazi and provided many recruits for the SS. Based on published documents of German groups in Central Europe, documents in the Archives of the Institute of Party History of Croatia, and secondary sources; 165 notes. H. Szamuely/S

622. Muşat, Mircea and Arimia, Vasile. O ZI BINE DEFINITĂ ÎN ISTORIA RĂZBOIULUI [A well-marked day in the history of the war]. *Magazin Istoric [Romania] 1979 13(8): 50-52.* Selects passages from German reports and memoirs to show how serious a blow was the Romanian uprising in August 1944.

623. Nejedlý, Miloslav. PLÁNY NACISTICKEHO WEHRMACHTU A PROSTOR ČESKOSLOVENSKA 1944-1945 [Plans of Nazi Wehrmacht and the Czechoslovak strategic space]. *Hist. a Vojenství [Czechoslovakia] 1978 27(5): 120-136, (6): 40-57.* Part I. Investigates strategic planning and actual use of Czechoslovak territory by the German General Staff and High Command in the last months of World War II. Examines the battles for the natural barrier of the East and South Carpathians. Based on military documents; 17 notes. Part II. Reviews operations of the German armed forces in southern and central Europe in developing defense lines against advancing Soviet troops, especially the use of the Army Group Süd, the strongest contingent facing the Soviets at the outset of 1945. War events on Czechoslovak soil then became an interrupted chain of battles and a defensive action by the German Army Group Mitte until the end of the war. Based on military documents; 14 notes. G. E. Pergl

624. Pawlowitch, Stevan K. "IL CASO MIROŠEVIĆ." L'EXPULSION DU MINISTRE DE YOUGOSLAVIE AU VATICAN PAR LE GOUVERNEMENT FASCISTE EN 1941 ["The Mirošević case": the expulsion of the Yugoslav ambassador at the Vatican by the fascist government in 1941]. *Balkan Studies [Greece] 1978 19(1): 105-137.* Surveys a complicated case of the Royal Yugoslavian representative at the Holy See of Pope Pius XII in 1941, when his country was overrun by Germans and thus became a target of combined intrigue of Croatian fascists and occupying forces of the Axis. After many entangled diplomatic actions, Niko H. Mirošević-Sorgo found asylum in Switzerland. 108 notes.
G. E. Pergl

625. Pliacheko, P. OSOBYE ZADANIIA: V OGNENNOM KOL'TSE [Special tasks: in the ring of fire]. *Voenno-Istoricheskii Zhurnal [USSR] 1980 22(6): 44-51.* Considers German occupation of Budapest and the Soviet liberation of Hungary 1944-45. Primary sources; note.
N. H. Foxcroft/S

626. Radandt, Hans. DER WIRTSCHAFTSBERATER DER DEUTSCHEN GESANDTSCHAFT IN BRATISLAVA—EIN VERTRETER DER INTERESSEN DEUTSCHER KONZERNE IM SYSTEM DES STAATS-MONOPOLISTISCHEN KAPITALISMUS [The economic adviser of the German embassy in Bratislava: a representative of German interests in the system of state-monopoly capitalism]. *Jahrbuch für Wirtschaftsgeschichte [East Germany] 1972 (1): 75-94.* Analyzes the correspondence of Erich Gebert, an Austrian representative of German state-monopoly capitalism who served as commercial attaché at Bratislava from December 1939 and as adviser to the Slovakian Ministry of Economics from September 1940. He gave orders as well as advice, exercising considerable influence over legislation and administration favoring the German war economy and interests. Based on primary sources in the State Archives in Bratislava; 106 notes.
J. A. Perkins

627. Radandt, Hans. EIN MITTLERES KAPITALISTISCHES UNTERNEHMEN IN BULGARIEN IM DIENSTE DEUTSCHER KONZERNE WÄHREND DES ZWEITEN WELTKRIEGES [A medium-sized capitalist enterprise in Bulgaria in the service of German big business during World War II]. *Jahrbuch für Wirtschaftsgeschichte [East Germany] 1980 (2): 249-264.* Case study of the Erz mining corporation of Sofia, Bulgaria. Examines stock ownership, marketing agreements, and credit relations; major German firms, such as the German Bank, Krupp, and I. G. Farben, had direct influence on the establishment and development of middle-sized industrial firms in Bulgaria during World War II. Control was exercised directly and through German subsidiaries in Bulgaria. Based on official archives in Sofia and secondary sources; 54 notes, 2 tables, appendix.
E. L. Turk

628. Romano, Jaša. PRILOG IZUČAVANJU ZLOČINA OKUPATORA I NJIHOVIH SLUGU NAD RANJENICIMA I SANITETSKIM OSOBLJEM NOV I POJ U TOKU NOR-A [A contribution to the study of the crimes committed by the occupation forces and their lackeys against the wounded and the medical personnel of the National Liberation Army and the partisan detachments of Yugoslavia during the National Liberation War]. *Vojnoistorijski Glasnik [Yugoslavia] 1980 31(1): 125-158.* In contravention of the Geneva Convention of 1929 protecting the wounded, the sick, and medical personnel in

wartime, the German occupation forces and the Yugoslav quisling groups systematically attacked and destroyed convoys of wounded partisans, hospitals, and ships carrying the wounded. Analyzes reasons behind these criminal acts, gives a detailed chronology of such attacks, and lists casualty figures for the period 1941-45. Based on documents from the Archives of the Institute for Military History, Belgrade and secondary sources; 315 notes. J. Bamber

629. Scheel, Klaus. DIE FASCHISTISCHE DEUTSCHE KRIEGSPROPAGANDA IN DEN BESETZTEN LÄNDERN SÜDOSTEUROPAS [German fascist war propaganda in occupied southeastern Europe]. *Jahrbuch für Geschichte der Sozialistischen Länder Europas [East Germany] 1980 24(1): 69-83.* Propaganda was a high priority for Nazi Germany. Radio, movies, and newspapers were used. Exaltation of German things, anti-Judaism, anti-Marxism, and protection of bourgeois property and moral values were the major themes, as was the inevitability of Germany's eventual victory, especially over the divided nationality groups. 65 notes. D. R. Stevenson

630. Scheel, Klaus. A NÉMET HÁBORÚS PROPAGANDA DÉLKELETEURÓPA MEGSZÁLLT ORSZÁGAIBAN [German war propaganda in the occupied countries of Southeast Europe]. *Történelmi Szemle [Hungary] 1979 22(3-4): 436-453.* Hitler's *Mein Kampf* recommended spreading war propaganda, and the ministry of propaganda, established in 1935, contemplated the establishment of Greek, Serbian, Bulgarian, and Romanian language broadcasts. In 1939 and progressively after 1941, Yugoslavia and Greece became the targets of psychological warfare as Germany acquired majority shares in or purchased local national transmitters, and Nazi radio stations in Bohemia and Austria broadcast propaganda. During the defeats of 1944-45 the high command of the Wehrmacht intensified its propaganda in Hungary and Bulgaria, stressing the "danger of Europe's destruction by the Reds." The 20-kilowatt portable "Prince Eugen Battle Transmitter" stayed on the air until the evening of 8 May 1945. 76 notes. E. Soos

631. Schönfeld, Roland. DEUTSCHE ROHSTOFFSICHERUNGSPOLITIK IN JUGOSLAWIEN 1934-1944 [German policy of securing raw materials in Yugoslavia, 1934-44]. *Vierteljahrshefte für Zeitgeschichte [West Germany] 1976 24(3): 215-258.* In 1938 40% of Yugoslavian exports went to Germany; France and Britain owned many metal mines but did little to prevent the export of metals necessary for the armaments industry to Germany. By 1939 Germany was the principal shareholder in the General Yugoslavian Bank Association and during the occupation, of Yugoslavia, Germans maintained normal business relations. German money financed Croatian Shell, which imported crude oil from Rumania. However, the Yugoslav resistance movement became active in 1942, and by 1944 the Allies had bombed Belgrade. Based on material in the Federal Archives in Koblenz (BAK) and from the Economic Ministry of the Reich (RWM-R7), parliamentary papers D, and secondary works; 312 notes.
A. Alcock

632. Schumann, Wolfgang and Wappler, Anke. MÁSODIK VILÁGHÁBORÚS TÖRTÉNETI IRODALOM AZ NDK-BAN [Literature on World War II in East Germany]. *Történelmi Szemle [Hungary] 1973 16(3-4): 356-371.* East German military historians dealing with World War II have concentrated

on publishing documents concerned with the Southeast European theaters of operation. Some of these publications are discussed here. 78 notes.

H. Szamuely/S

633. Sirkov, Dimităr. CONSÉQUENCES DIRECTES DE L'ADHÉSION DE LA BULGARIA AU PACTE TRIPARTITE [Direct consequences of Bulgaria's adherence to the Axis pact]. *Études Balkaniques [Bulgaria] 1975 (4): 27-37.* Analyzes the consequences of Bulgaria's adherence to the Axis, stressing its role as a Nazi satellite. Entry into the pact paralyzed Bulgarian-Soviet relations and left Bulgaria isolated internationally, particularly after the Axis attack on Greece and Yugoslavia. The German occupation had little effect on Bulgaria's sociopolitical structure since the government retained internal sovereignty, but it created an atmosphere of terror and repression that led to the ultimate rejection of the fascist regime. Based on military historical archives, central state archives, archives of the Ministry of the Interior, central party archives, and secondary sources; 40 notes.

C. E. King

634. Sládek, Oldřich. PLAN ALRZ A JEHO VLIV NA DOCHOVANOST ARCHIVÁLIÍ Z OBDOBÍ NACISTICKÉ OKUPACE ČESKOSLOVENSKA [The ARLZ plan and its influence on the survival of records from the period of the Nazi occupation of Czechoslovakia]. *Sborník Archivních Prací [Czechoslovakia] 1978 28(2): 356-409.* On 6 September 1944 the German High Command issued its directive No. 06850/44 preparatory to the ARLZ plan, designed to obliterate evidence of German wartime activity and to cripple economically important enterprises and installations. Reichsprotektor K. H. Frank and General R. Toussaint, for the civil and military domains respectively, received the directive on 13 September 1944. The plan was in four phases, A= Auflockerung (relocation of major documents), R=Räumung (removal of office and other equipment), L=Lähmung (removal of vital machine components), and Z=Zerstörung (destruction of entire installations). Stage A was first put into operation on 25 February 1945 in Moravia, and by March was also being applied in Bohemia. Subsequent adaptations of the original plan and contradictory directives led to chaos in its execution. Surviving documentary evidence describes what kind of records were destroyed and where, and witnesses' accounts show where some material was last seen, although its ultimate whereabouts is not known. Relatively few records of the ARLZ plan survive because the retreating Germans did not have time to carry out the plan fully. The Gestapo and Sicherheitsdienst were most efficient in destroying evidence. 102 notes.

L. Short

635. Sládek, Zdeněk and Tejchman, Miroslav. HOSPODÁŘSKÉ PRONIKÁNÍ NACISTICKÉHO NĚMECKA DO ZEMÍ JIHOVÝCHODNÍ EVROPY V LETECH 1933-1940 [The economic penetration of Southeast European countries by Nazi Germany, 1933-40]. *Slovanské Historické Studie [Czechoslovakia] 1976 11: 175-207.* Nazi Germany's massive agricultural purchases rescued the economies of Southeastern Europe, but made them dependent on German trade. By maintaining passive balances Germany also forced these poorest of European nations into a creditor role, building up its own war potential at their expense. The Anglo-French policy of appeasement facilitated German domination of the region well before the outbreak of World War II. Published sources; 17 tables, 83 notes.

R. E. Weltsch

636. Steflea, Ilie and Gîrbea, Titus. MEMORII INEDITE: DOI GENERALI IȘI AMINTESC [Unpublished memoirs: two generals remember]. *Magazin Istoric [Romania] 1979 13(8): 31-39.* General Steflea, chief of staff of the Romanian army 1942-44, describes maneuvers during German domination to preserve the army as an effective force. General Gîrbea's diary for March-August 1944 shows that he supplied information to the Romanian resistance while on liaison with the German high command.

637. Suppan, Arnold. BENEŠ, JAKSCH UND DIE VERTREIBUNG DER SUDETENDEUTSCHEN [Beneš, Jaksch, and the expulsion of the Sudeten Germans]. *Österreichische Osthefte [Austria] 1973 15(4): 445-448.* Reviews the correspondence between Wenzel Jaksch, the chairman of the Sudeten German Social Democrats, and Eduard Beneš, published as *Wenzel Jaksch—Edvard Beneš: Briefe und Dokumente aus dem Londoner Exil 1939-1943. Herausgegeben von Friedrich Prinz* (Köln, 1973). The letters and other documents show the continuous deterioration of the relations between Jaksch and Beneš in the first period of World War II. 2 notes.   R. Wagnleitner

638. Suško, Ladislav. POČIATKY HOSPODÁRSKEJ EXPLOATÁCIE SLOVENSKA NACIZMOM (MAREC 1939-JÚL 1940) [The beginnings of Nazi economic exploitation of Slovakia: March 1939-July 1940]. *Československý Časopis Hist. [Czechoslovakia] 1977 25(5): 682-714.* In the first year after the destruction of Czechoslovakia, the German government assured itself of complete economic preponderance in the Slovak state which it had helped to create. The secret protocol on economic and financial cooperation of 23 March 1939 geared Slovak economc development to Germany's needs and virtually put Slovak forestry, mining, arms industries, and communications at Germany's disposal. Diplomatic pressure, clearing arrangements, and German control of major stocks brought about Slovakia's dependence. Based on archives in Bratislava and Potsdam; 104 notes.   R. E. Weltsch

639. Suško, Ladislav. SYSTEM PORADCOV V NACISTICKOM OVLÁDÁNÍ SLOVENSKA V ROKOCH 1939-1941 [The system of advisers in the Nazi domination of Slovakia, 1939-41]. *Historicke Štúdie [Czechoslovakia] 1979 23: 5-25.* At first of minor influence, the German advisers in Slovakia became an important link in the system of Nazi domination, especially after the Salzburg Agreements of 1940. The advisers influenced crucial decisions in all branches of political, economic, and military life. Based on archival sources; 61 notes.   G. E. Pergl

640. Tejchman, Miroslav. ŘECKO-ITALSKÁ VÁLKA 1940-1941 [The Greek-Italian war, 1940-41]. *Slovanský Přehled [Czechoslovakia] 1980 66(5): 443-448.* Although Mussolini boasted that he would present an occupied Greece to Hitler, the Italians were unable to take the country easily because of the British expeditionary forces, including the Royal Air Force, who defended the Greek coastline. Only after Hitler directed the massive use of German tanks and troops and sent a number of divisions into the Balkans in the spring of 1941 was the will of the Greeks broken and British and Greek divisions evacuated to Egypt. 20 notes.   B. Reinfeld

641. Thackrah, J. R. THE ITALIAN INVASION OF GREECE AND ITS EFFECT ON ALLIED AND AXIS POLICY, 1940-41. *Army Q. and Defence J. [Great Britain] 1979 109(3): 337-349.* The failure of the Italian invasion of Greece forced Adolf Hitler to undertake a great deal more responsibility in Southeastern Europe and Africa in the war against Great Britain, but the consequent delay in the campaign against Russia and the failure to attack Malta, despite the defeat of the British in the Balkans, led to the failure of overall Axis strategy.

642. Uzelac, Dušan. NEMAČKI PROTIVUDAR U ISTOČNOJ BOSNI OD 19. DO 31. MARTA 1945. GODINE (OPERACIJA "MAIGEWITTER") [The German counterattack in eastern Bosnia, 19-31 May 1945: Operation Maigewitter]. *Vojnoistorijski Glasnik [Yugoslavia] 1978 29(1): 23-38.* Describes chronologically the two stages of the German counteroffensive against the second Yugoslav Army in eastern Bosnia in March 1945. The Germans employed surprise tactics and inflicted heavy losses on the second Army, but did not succeed in destroying it. Based on the archives of the Yugoslav Institute of Military History and other primary sources; map, 74 notes. J. Bamber

643. Vasdravelles, I. TRAGIKAI SELIDES TES ISTORIAS TES MAKEDONIAS KATA TON B' PANGOSMION POLEMON. ENGATASTASIS ELEŌ GERMANŌN VOULGARIKOU STRATOU EIS TEN KENTRIKEN MAKEDONIAN [Tragic pages in the history of Macedonia during World War II: the installation of a Bulgarian army in central Macedonia by permission of the Germans]. *Makedonika [Greece] 1973 13: 316-324.* While Greece was under military occupation, the Germans suddenly decided in 1943 to cut off German-occupied Macedonia and the Aegean islands from the rest of Greece and make them a German province. Dr. Merten, the economic and political counselor of the German military administration in Salonika, announced that Germany would station Bulgarian troops in Macedonia. This decision caused great worry to Christos Tendzos, the Greek secretary general, who was aware of the political consequences. Based on a document in dialogue form between Merten and Tendzos in the possession of the author; notes. Summary in French. V. Aldrich

644. Višnjić, Petar. BORBE 1. PROLETERSKE DIVIZIJE U SANDŽAKU (AVGUSTA 1944. GODINE) [The battles of the 1st Proletarian Division in Sanjak, August 1944]. *Vojnoistorijski Glasnik [Yugoslavia] 1979 30(1): 55-80.* In August 1944 the 1st Proletarian Division, which includes (among others) the Italian Garibaldi and Matteotti Volunteer Partisan Brigades, stopped on its march from Bosnia toward Serbia in Sanjak, where it was to join forces with the 6th Proletarian Division. The author analyzes the German counterattack, 13-17 August 1944, which used parts of the 7th (Prinz Eugen) SS Division and the Brandenburg Division reinforced by Bulgarian and quisling forces (Chetniks and Moslem volunteers). The 1st Proletarian Division avoided all major battles, outmaneuvered the enemy, and entered Serbia along the Lim River, whence it began the final offensive in Serbia. Primary sources; 48 notes. S. Košak

645. Wette, Wolfram. NÉMET PROPAGANDA ÉS A CSATLÓSORSZÁGOK: MAGYARORSZÁG, ROMÁNIA ÉS BULGÁRIA (1941-43) [German war propaganda in the satellite states of Hungary, Romania, and Bulgaria, 1941-43]. *Történelmi Szemle [Hungary] 1979 22(3-4): 454-483.* Analyzes

the concerted propaganda activities of the foreign and propaganda ministries and the army. The strategic desire "to push the Soviets beyond the Urals" was tactically documented in the Wehrmacht magazine *Signal.* Hitler considered broadcasting the most efficient propaganda vehicle. There were, however, few wireless sets in the Balkans. Each of the countries had revisionist claims against the neighbors, but Nazi propaganda took no sides; instead it tried to unite them against Bolshevism. 175 notes. E. Soos

646. Zelenin, V. V. OPERATSIIA KHOD KONEM [Operation Rösselsprung]. *Sovetskoe Slavianovedenie [USSR] 1974 (3): 86-99.* Describes preparations for Operation Rösselsprung, the Germans' advance of 25 May 1944 against the headquarters of the People's Liberation Army of Yugoslavia in Drvar. The unachieved objective of the three-week operation was to destroy the chiefs of staff of the People's Liberation Army and to kill or capture Josip Tito. The offensive began with an hour-long bombing, followed by the descent of parachutists, and an infantry attack from all directions. The Yugoslav high command was forced to move to Pototsi at the beginning of the offensive and finally escaped in a Soviet-supplied plane as did the British and US mission leaders. The offensive ended with heavy German losses. Describes distortions of this operation in the fascist press. 6 notes. L. Kalinowski

647. Ževart, Milan. IZGUBE OSVOBODILNEGA GIBANJA V SALEŠKI DOLINI OD KONCA MARCA DO ZAČETKA OKTOBRA 1942 [Losses of the liberation movement in the Šalek Valley from the beginning of March until October 1942]. *Časopis Za Zgodovino In Narodopisje [Yugoslavia] 1975 11(1): 142-153.* During the spring and summer of 1942 German persecutions of resistance groups in Styria and Slovenia caused heavy human losses. The author offers personal remembrances of 72 men and women from the Šalek Valley who were executed in Maribor and Celje during this period. Additional victims died in German concentration camps. 54 notes. T. Hočevar

648. Zografski, Dancho. MACEDONIA AND THE BALKAN POLITICS OF THE THIRD REICH. *Macedonian Rev. [Yugoslavia] 1975 5(2): 121-131.* Examines Germany's policy toward Macedonia, 1878-1945, emphasizing Hitler's position on the Macedonian question during World War II.

649. —. [HISTORIOGRAPHY OF WORLD WAR II IN EAST CENTRAL EUROPE]. *Történelmi Szemle [Hungary] 1973 16(3-4): 289-329, 437-439.*
Ránki, György. KELET-KÖZÉP-EURÓPA MÁSODIK VILÁGHÁBORUS TÖRTÉNETI IRODALMÁNAK KÉRDÉSEI [Issues of historical literature on World War II in East Central Europe], *pp. 289-311.* Argues for a regional, rather than general approach to the history of World War II. Relying on new sources, the author reexamines the relationship of the Danubian lands with Germany, and the effect of changing Allied policy on them. 71 notes.
Juhász, Gyula. POLITIKAI ÉS DIPLOMACIA-TÖRTÉNETI IRODALOM MAGYARORSZÁG MÁSODIK VILÁGHÁBORÚS TÖRTÉNETÉRŐL [Political and historical literature about Hungary's role in World War II], *pp. 312-329.* Examines the relation between Hungary's foreign and domestic policies during World War II, and its effect on Miklós Horthy's leadership. 14 notes.

Macartney, C. A. HOZZÁSZÓLÁS A RÁNKI GYÖRGY ÉS JUHÁSZ GYULA ELŐADÁSÁRÓL POLYTATOTT VITÁHOZ [Notes on the debate over Ranki's and Juhasz's papers], *pp. 437-439.* Outlines the British view of the problem of the Danubian lands during World War II, denying that the British government was intent on buttressing the Horthy regime.

H. Szamuely/S

6

AT WAR WITH RUSSIA

650. Achkasov, V. MINNO-ZAGRADITEL'NYE DEISTVIIA NA BALTIKE V NACHAL'NYI PERIOD VELIKOI OTECHESTVENNOI VOINY [Minelaying activity in the Baltic in the beginning period of World War II]. *Morskoi Sbornik [USSR] 1977 (6): 19-25.* Details German and Soviet minelaying operations and their results in June-July 1941, and discusses the Soviet shortcomings in countering German magnetic mines.

651. Amort, Čestmír. PLÁNY HITLEROVSKÉHO NĚMECKA NA ZNIČENÍ SOVĚTSKÉHO SVAZU [Plans of Hitler's Germany to destroy the Soviet Union]. *Slovanský Přehled [Czechoslovakia] 1981 67(4): 273-294.* Adolf Hitler's plans for the destruction of the Soviet Union were laid early in his regime. In 1934 Herman Göring justified the buildup of the military precisely because a confrontation with the USSR was inevitable. The diplomat Erich Kordt commented in his memoirs that Hitler's intention to destroy the USSR was not weakened by the Nazi-Soviet Pact. A number of other leading Nazi figures are quoted to support the details of the plans for the conquest of Russia and future plans. In leaflets handed out to the soldiers involved in Operation Barbarossa the racial characteristics of the Russian and Asiatic population are singled out as the main reason for ruthless persecution and suppression in order to maintain the racial purity of the Germans in their eastward expansion. 50 notes.
                                                                                                B. Reinfeld

652. Antsiz, B. IZ OPYTA DOSTIZHENIIA NEPRERYVNOSTI NASTUPLENIIA V VISLO-ODERSKOI OPERATSII [The experience of attaining an uninterrupted offensive in the Vistula-Oder campaign]. *Voenno-Istoricheskii Zhurnal [USSR] 1979 21(1): 26-32.* Modern war requires uninterrupted offensives. The continuous advance of the First White Russian Front of January-February 1945 is an example. For the breakthrough, tanks and artillery as well as infantry were concentrated, and special transport and signal measures were taken. On the first day of the operation, 14 January, a breakthrough was attained. As the Germans began to retreat toward the protection of several small rivers the pace of the offensive had to be stepped up to prevent the enemy from regrouping. Desperately, the Germans tried to prepare the line of the Oder for a last stand. Consequently the attackers had to speed their advance without pausing for resupply or reinforcements, so that they could force the great river barrier and seize beachheads on the west bank before the German reserves assembled. Despite a growing fuel shortage and heavy losses, the effort succeeded. Based on Soviet

archival material, Marshal Zhukov's memoirs, and published material; 14 notes.
P. R. Taylor

653. Ark, O. I. TYSK ETTERRETNINGSTJENESTE UNDER FELTTOGET MOT SOVETUNIONEN 1941-1945 [The German intelligence service during the campaign against the USSR, 1941-45]. *Norsk Militaert Tidsskrift [Norway] 1974 144(3): 99-112.* Outlines briefly the history of the German intelligence service since ca. 1800, and examines its contribution to Operation Barbarossa in World War II against the USSR. It was generally insufficient despite improved efficiency toward the end of the campaign.

654. Aziasski, N. O VKLADE PARTIZAN V RAZGROM GRUPPY ARMII "TSENTR" [On the contribution of the partisans to the defeat of Army Group Center]. *Voenno-Istoricheskii Zhurnal [USSR] 1980 (2): 29-35.* The partisans operating in the rear of the German Army Group Center, 1942-44, were able to pin down a large number of special troops and regular units intended for the front. By mid-October, the German command had to allocate approximately 12% of the military strength of the group to operations against the partisans. Thus partisan actions exercised a considerable influence on the course and outcome of battles at the front. Based on Soviet military and Party archives and secondary sources; 24 notes.
L. Waters

655. Bagramian, I. KHARAKTER I OSOBENNOSTI NACHAL'NOGO PERIODA VOINY [The character of the initial period of the war and its most important features]. *Voenno-Istoricheskii Zhurnal [USSR] 1981 23(10): 20-27.* The initial period of the war between Germany and the USSR, 1941-42, was highly complex and characterized by the keenness of the military struggle. Neither side achieved its strategic aims. The USSR realized that its plan of action drawn up before the commencement of hostilities was inadequate, so the plan was radically changed in order to gain time to bring up reserves to mount a counterattack. By the middle of July 1941 German headquarters realized that Operation Barbarossa was not going as planned, since the center group of armies was requiring too much time to overcome strong Soviet resistance. Directive 33 was issued to help rectify the situation. Based on a paper given at a military science conference organized by the Ministry of Defense and the Chief Directorate of the Army and Navy of the USSR to commemorate the 40th anniversary of the German attack in 1941; 17 notes.
A. Brown

656. Bagramian, Ivan Khristoforovich. KRAKH OPERATSII "TSITADEL" (POBEDA SOVETSKIKH VOISK POD ORLOM I BRIANSKOM) [The rout of Operation Citadel: the Soviet victory at Orel and Briansk]. *Novaia i Noveishaia Istoriia [USSR] 1973 (3): 91-106, (4): 78-96.* Marshall Bagramian recalls his experiences as commander of the Soviet offensive against German forces in the Orel and Briansk region of Russia during 1942-43. The Germans had mounted a major counteroffensive code-named Operation Citadel after their failure at Stalingrad, but by the summer of 1943 they were again forced into retreat by the Red Army. Two-part article based on personal recollections, and archival and published sources; 50 notes.
D. N. Collins

657. Bagramian, Ivan Khristoforovich. UDAR POD BARVENKOVO I LOZOVOI [The attack beneath Barvenkovo and Lozovaya]. *Istoriia SSSR [USSR] 1974 (6): 95-121.* Describes the organization and the military campaign against the German army in January 1942 on the southwest and southern fronts. The Soviet army broke through German lines, deep into the territory between the Donets Basin and the Azov Sea. Gives German losses in terms of men, captured equipment, and prisoners. Based on Marshall Bagramian's memoirs; 8 notes.
V. Sobeslavsky

658. Baird, Jay W. NAZI FILM PROPAGANDA AND THE SOVIET UNION. *Film & Hist. 1981 11(2): 34-41.* Anti-Soviet films made in Nazi Germany before and during World War II traced all of Germany's ills to the Jews and Bolsheviks.

659. Barr, William. OPERATION "WUNDERLAND": *ADMIRAL SCHEER* IN THE KARA SEA, AUGUST 1942. *Polar Record [Great Britain] 1975 17(110): 461-472.* Discusses the German Naval Command plan to intercept Soviet convoys, Operation Wunderland (1942), concentrating on the activities of the heavy cruiser *Admiral Scheer* and supporting U-boats in the Kara Sea.

660. Basov, A. V. BITVA ZA KRYM [The battle for the Crimea]. *Istoriia SSSR [USSR] 1975 (2): 69-84.* Details the disposition of strategic forces in the struggle for the Crimea in World War II, September 1941 to May 1944, both German and Soviet. Examines the treatment of important battles over the Crimea in various works and evaluates all these operations as part of a whole. Creates a general picture of the battle for Crimea and determines its place in the war. Primary and secondary sources; 46 notes.
L. Kalinowski

661. Bauer, Erich. DIE WALDBRANDPLÄNE DES OBERKOMMAN-DOS DER WEHRMACHT IM FRÜHJAHR 1945 [The forest fire plans of the Supreme Command of the Wehrmacht in the spring of 1945]. *Militärgeschichte [East Germany] 1982 21(4): 447-450.* A document of the Fremde Heere Ost section of the Supreme Command of the army considered the possibility of thwarting the offensive of Soviet forces against Berlin, which was expected in the spring of 1945, with the help of forest fires. The necessary preconditions (down to the required quantity of fire bombs, the weather situation, and the wind direction) are presented in great detail. This fascist document and its criminal military strategy is placed in the total framework of imperialist plans for a strategy of environmental war. 4 notes.
J/T (H. D. Andrews)

662. Benditer, J. PROPAGANDA NAZISTĂ ÎN DIRECTIVELE LUI GO-EBBELS DIN PERIOADA RĂZBOIULUI ANTISOVIETIC [Nazi propaganda: Goebbels's directives during the anti-Soviet war]. *Anuarul Institutului de Istorie și Arheologie [Rumania] 1973 (10): 385-396.* Discusses fluctuations in German propaganda during World War II. The German ministry of propaganda, led by Goebbels, at first insisted on the invincibility of the German armed forces and their leaders. After reverses on the Russian front, however, Nazi propaganda suggested that Soviet victories had no importance. In addition, management of news in Germany kept the people of that country from learning about the economic and military cooperation of the Allies or the progress of resistance in occupied lands. Repeated defeats, especially after the battle of Stalingrad, turned

Nazi propaganda to preparing the German people for the necessities of total war. 75 notes. F. Kellogg

663. Benser, Günter. KOMMUNISTISCHE PARTEIARBEIT IM KRIEGSGEFANGENENLAGER IN PIRNA JUNI/JULI 1945 [Communist Party work at the prisoner of war camp at Pirna, June-July 1945]. *Beiträge zur Geschichte der Arbeiterbewegung [East Germany] 1978 20(2): 253-260.* Describes the efforts of the German Communists to organize Party cells and study groups among the thousands of German prisoners of war at the transition camp of Pirna, June-July 1945. With the cooperation of the Soviet camp commander the German Communists addressed current political developments at the war's end, founded a camp newspaper, and discussed theoretical and ideological themes aimed at liquidating fascist attitudes among prisoners. Based on protocols, notes, and letters in the archives of the Institute for Marxism-Leninism, Berlin; 2 notes.
J. B. Street

664. Bezymenski, L. A. GENERAL'NYI PLAN *OST:* ZAMYSEL, TSELI, REZUL'TATY [The general *Ost* plan: conception, aims, results]. *Voprosy Istorii [USSR] 1978 (5): 74-94.* Discusses the *Ost* plan, conceived by the secret service and highest Nazi officials for the conquest of the nations of Eastern Europe and their subsequent political subjugation to fascist Germany. The author focuses on the involvement of the USSR, and describes and assesses the conception of the plan, the stages of its operation in particular areas, its varying successes and failures in the war years, the continuation of the underlying ideology and plan in the postwar period, its significance, and the Soviet success in overcoming its realization. Based on material in the National Archives of the United States, T 81/18, 84, and secondary works; 3 tables, 67 notes. L. Smith

665. Blank, Aleksander Solomonovitsch. BEGEGNUNGEN UND GESPRÄCHE MIT GENERALFELDMARSCHALL PAULUS [Meetings and conversations with Field Marshal Paulus]. *Militärgeschichte [East Germany] 1977 16(6): 716-724.* Field Marshal Friedrich von Paulus was captured in Krasnogorsk near Moscow in April 1943. He asked to read the works of Marx and Lenin; in *Pravda* he read of German atrocities against the Russians. Paulus gradually realized that Hitler was the cause of Germany's downfall and approved of the July 1944 plot to assassinate him. In August 1944 Paulus began broadcasting for Radio Free Germany, having willingly adopted an antifascist position. Based on archive sources and the author's conversations with Paulus; 17 notes.
A. Alcock

666. Bleyer, Wolfgang and Czollek, Roswitha. DIE VEREITELUNG DER AGGRESSIONSPLÄNE DES FASCHISTISCHEN DEUTSCHEN IMPERIALISMUS GEGENÜBER DEN BALTISCHEN STAATEN DURCH DIE SOWJETUNION IN SOMMER/HERBST 1939 [The frustration of the plans for aggression of fascist German imperialism against the Baltic States by the USSR in the summer and fall of 1939]. *Militärgeschichte [East Germany] 1980 19(4) 422-433.* Examines German plans for extending control to the Baltic states as part of the unleashing of World War II in 1939. Dilatory negotiating methods of the Western powers forced the Soviet government to conclude a treaty on 23 August 1939 with fascist Germany in which Germany agreed not to intervene in Estonia and Latvia, thus enhancing the security of those states and limiting the

sphere of German aggression. Following the German defeat of Poland, the Soviet Union sent troops into eastern Poland and established a *de facto* demarcation line that forced Germany to renounce its intention of controlling Lithuania and to sign a second treaty with the Soviet Union on 28 September 1939. Thus the Soviet Union's firm but elastic policy preserved the bourgeois Baltic states from suffering the fate of Poland. Unpublished documents in Central State Archives, Potsdam and Military Archives of the GDR, published documents; map, 68 notes.
H. D. Andrews

667. Brown, Ron. ASSAULT ON THE CRIMEA. *Marine Corps Gazette 1978 62(2): 43-47.* Examines the military strategy and tactics employed by General Erich von Mannstein in the 1941 German attack on the Soviet troops in the Crimea as a lesson in the forceful leadership of combined armed forces.

668. Brown, Ronald J. WWII GERMAN SUCCESS SHOWS HOW TO HANDLE RUSSIAN ARMOR. *Marine Corps Gazette 1977 61(8): 33-37.* Tactical analysis of the German battle plan State Farm 79, in which German forces under Eric von Manstein, who exploited Basil Liddell Hart's principles, defeated the Russian army in 1942.

669. Charisius, Albrecht and Moritz, Erhard. DOKUMENTE ZUR SUBVERSIVEN TÄTIGKEIT DES DEUTSCHEN FASCHISTISCHEN GEHEIMDIENSTES 1944 [Documents on the subversive activities of the fascist German Intelligence Service in 1944]. *Rev. Int. d'Hist. Militaire [France] 1979 (43): 199-218.* Publishes documents that reveal the content, character, and aims of the fascist system of subversion in the second half of 1944 and demonstrate a close cooperation between the Wehrmacht and the SS leadership in anti-Soviet subversion. The authors survey the organizational development of special military subversion units and the preparations for postwar intelligence activities. Based on military documents; reprint of two papers, 2 maps, 2 charts, 15 notes.
G. E. Pergl

670. Chugunov, A. I. PERVYE BOI NA GRANITSE [The first battles on the border]. *Istoriia SSSR [USSR] 1975 (2): 84-101.* Describes the situation on the border at the outbreak of World War II and vindicates the vigilance and combat behavior of Soviet border guards. Describes the first battles between the attacking German forces and the Soviet soldiers guarding the border on the Ukrainian, Belorussian, and Baltic fronts, as well as the border with East Prussia (whose guards saw combat even before the actual outbreak of war). German forces encountered heavy casualties, and Soviet soldiers fought valiantly in extremely unequal combat. When they could no longer hold the enemy back, they joined partisan units or units of the Red Army operating nearby. Primary and secondary sources; 46 notes.
L. Kalinowski

671. Ciuikov, V. I. 2 MAI 1945: GARNIZOANA BERLINULUI CAPITULEAZĂ [2 May 1945: the Berlin garrison capitulates]. *Magazin Istoric [Rumania] 1975 9(5): 28-32.* The Soviet marshal presents his view of the fall of Berlin during World War II.

672. Cousine, A. and Gourmen, P. PROKHOROVKA: 12 JUILLET 1943 [Prokhorovka, 12 July 1943]. *Rev. Hist. des Armées [France] 1980 (2): 189-223.* Prokhorovka, a tiny locality 75 kilometers south of Kursk in the territory of

Belgorod near the sources of the northern Donets on the Ukrainian border, was the site of the greatest tank battle of World War II. Between 8:30 am and 10:00 pm of 12 July 1943, 1,500 German and Russian tanks fought a decisive engagement. Describes and analyzes the battle from the strategic, tactical, moral, and psychological points of view. Based on primary material in German military archives, Freiburg im Breisgau; 7 photos, 5 maps, biblio.　　　J. V. Coutinho

673. Dallin, Alexander.　HITLER AND RUSSIA.　*Can. Slavonic Papers 1974 16(3): 460-465.* Reviews Barry A. Leach, *German Strategy Against Russia, 1939-41* (Oxford: Clarendon Press, 1973) and Barton Whaley, *Codeword BARBAROSSA* (Cambridge, Massachusetts: MIT Press, 1973).　　　　　　　S

674. Degelow, Hans J.　THE SEA OF THE MIDNIGHT SUN.　*US Naval Inst. Pro. 1978 104(12): 76-85.* Pictorial presentation of what it was like to have served with the German navy on the Baltic Sea during World War II. 27 photos.
A. N. Garland

675. Dreisziger, N. F.　CONTRADICTORY EVIDENCE CONCERNING HUNGARY'S DECLARATION OF WAR ON THE USSR IN JUNE 1941. *Can. Slavonic Papers [Canada] 1977 19(4): 481-488.* An account of the sequence of the reports and historical interpretations of the bombing raid on Kassa (now Košice) on 26 June 1941, which was followed by Hungary's declaration of war on the USSR. Examines especially the "conspiracy" theory which has usually been based on the reports of Ádám Krudy, an officer of the Royal Hungarian Air Force. He claimed that German aircraft conducted the raid. No final assignment of responsibility for the raid is attempted. Reprints Krudy's new report of February 1946. 23 notes.　　　　　　　　　　　　　　　　　　R. V. Ritter

676. Dubrovchenko, P. M.　DOPOMOHA TRANSPORTNOI AVIATSII PARTYZANAM UKRAINY　[Transport aviation's assistance to partisans in the Ukraine]. *Ukrains'kyi Istorychnyi Zhurnal [USSR] 1979 (11): 61-65.* Describes the activities of pilots and aircraft of the Soviet civil aviation assisting Soviet partisan units in the enemy's rear in the Ukraine during World War II. Types of aircraft and units involved, places and methods of building partisan airfields, and German military countermeasures are described. Communist Party and Soviet military archives; 27 notes.　　　　　　　　　　I. Krushelnyckyj

677. Eichholtz, Dietrich.　DER RAUBZUG DES FASCHISTISCHEN DEUTSCHEN IMPERIALISMUS ZU DEN ERDÖLQUELLEN DES KAUKASUS 1941-1943　[The Nazi military campaign to gain control of the Caucasus oil fields, 1941-43]. *Jahrbuch für Geschichte [East Germany] 1976 14: 445-502.* Germany lacked sufficient oil reserves to fuel its industry and war machine. As Wehrmacht divisions thrust into the USSR in 1941, a prime object was Soviet oil. In 1942, German armies launched a great offensive to the southeast to seize the oil fields of the Caucasus and Azerbaidzhan. The Maikop fields were seized and held for six months, but the Germans never reached Baku. Soviet resistance stopped them north of the Caucasus, and after Stalingrad they were obliged to retreat, thus dooming the German war machine to slow starvation. 5 documents, 79 notes.　　　　　　　　　　　　　　　J. C. Billigmeier

678. Eichholtz, Dietrich. WIRTSCHAFTSPOLITIK UND STRATEGIE DES FASCHISTISCHEN DEUTSCHEN IMPERIALISMUS IM DNEPR-DONEZ-INDUSTRIEGEBIET 1941-1943 [Economic policy and the strategy of fascist German imperialism in the Dnepr-Donets industrial area, 1941-43]. *Militärgeschichte [East Germany] 1979 18(3): 281-296.* German monopoly firms attempted to use the great raw material resources and industrial plant of the Dnepr and in the Donets basins of the USSR for the increase of their profits. Shows concrete examples of how the economic interests of a single monopoly affected the strategic and even the tactical decisions of the military command. Based on extensive archival material; 5 tables, 95 notes.

J/T (H. D. Andrews)

679. Elliott, Mark. ANDREI VLASOV: RED ARMY GENERAL IN HITLER'S SERVICE. *Military Affairs 1982 46(2): 84-87.* Approximately a million Soviet nationals served in the German army during World War II, by far the largest contingent of military collaborators in the conflict. They came to be known as the Vlasovtsi, the Vlasovites, after General Andrei Vlasov, the Red Army hero of the Battle of Moscow, who fell into German hands in July 1942. His disenchantment with the Soviet regime did not commence but rather coalesced with German captivity. He exercised no real control over his German forces, and comes down in history as a very ambiguous character, painted as a vile collaborator and Russian national hero. Primary sources; 24 notes.

A. M. Osur

680. Fastabend, David A. INITIATIVE IN COMBAT: SIX HOURS AT BALTA. *Military Rev. 1978 58(11): 13-21.* Analyzes a battle which took place 3 August 1941 at Balta in the Ukraine between a German engineer battalion and a greater Soviet force.

681. Forster, J. CROISADE DE L'EUROPE CONTRE LE BOLSHEVISME: LA PARTICIPATION D'UNITÉS DE VOLUNTAIRES EUROPÉENS A L'OPERATION BARBEROUSSE EN 1941 [Crusade of Europe against Bolshevism: the participation of European volunteer units in Operation Barbarossa in 1941]. *Rev. d'Hist. de la Deuxième Guerre Mondiale [France] 1980 30(118): 1-26.* In 1941 there were 43,000 non-German volunteers in the German armies. Spaniards, Croats, Frenchmen, Walloons, Danes, Finns and others were represented. Their motives were mixed. Some were stimulated by anti-Bolshevism, others by adventure or personal reasons. By 1942 they were disillusioned, as the character of Hitler's war became more clearly a war of conquest rather than a crusade. Based on German military archives in Freiburg, the political archives of the foreign ministry at Bonn, and published documents of *Akten zur deutschen auswärtigen Politik;* 86 notes.

G. H. Davis

682. Förster, Jürgen. HITLER'S WAR AIMS AGAINST THE SOVIET UNION AND THE GERMAN MILITARY LEADERS. *Militärhistorisk Tidskrift [Sweden] 1979: 83-93.* Analyzes the rationales for Adolf Hitler's attack on the USSR and the explanation of the lack of opposition among German military leaders to fighting a war of an ideological character. Hitler's foremost aims in the East were to exterminate the "Jewish-Bolshevik leadership cadres," decimate the inferior Slav masses and Jewry, and conquer and exploit Russian resources. The Wehrmacht played an active role in all aspects of this warfare, and

its compliance cannot sufficiently be explained by German officers being victims of their tradition of absolute obedience or a fear of jeopardizing their careers. There existed a substantial agreement between Hitler and the military leadership regarding treatment of Communists and Jews. Based on German archives, military diaries, and other primary sources. T. Parker

683. Förster, Jürgen. THE WEHRMACHT AND THE WAR OF EXTERMINATION AGAINST THE SOVIET UNION. *Yad Vashem Studies on the European Jewish Catastrophe and Resistance [Israel] 1981 14: 7-34.* Among other objectives, Hitler's invasion of the USSR in 1941 had the dual aim of simultaneously destroying Bolshevism and annihilating Judaism. Documents how this racial-ideological war was carried out by tacit and expressed agreements between special units of the SS and the German military forces. Through coordinating their efforts the task of exterminating Jews and Communists was facilitated. 72 notes. B. Reiner

684. Frolov, B. TANKOVOE SRAZHENIE V RAIONE BOGODUKHOVA (1943 G.) [Tank battle in the Bogodukhov area, 1943]. *Voenno-Istoricheskii Zhurnal [USSR] 1978 20(9): 18-24.* One of the most important battles of the Belgorod-Kharkov operation was the repulsion of the German counteroffensive near Bogodukhov, 11-17 August 1943. To prevent encirclement, the Germans reinforced their front with the Third Tank Corps comprising the *SS Totenkopf, Reich,* and *Viking* tank divisions withdrawn from the Donets Basin. They were, however, routed by the coordinated attack launched by the Soviet First Tank Army and the Fifth and Sixth Guards' Tank Armies. Based on documents of the Ministry of Defense achives; map, 24 notes. N. Frenkley

685. Gibbons, Robert. OPPOSITION GEGEN "BARBAROSSA" IM HERBST 1940. EINE DENKSCHRIFT AUS DER DEUTSCHEN BOTSCHAFT IN MOSKAU [Opposition to Barbarossa in the fall of 1940. A memorandum from the German embassy in Moscow]. *Vierteljahrshefte für Zeitgeschichte [West Germany] 1975 23(3): 332-340.* Reprints and analyzes an October 1940 memorandum about the effects on the Soviet Union of a German attack against that country, prepared by Gebhardt von Walther in the Moscow Embassy for Hasso von Etzdorf, Foreign Ministry representative to the Army High Command and thus a link between Hitler opponents Ernst von Weiszäcker in the foreign service and Chief of General Staff Franz Halder. The antiwar memorandum documents the extensive knowledge and concern about the attack six months before Hitler first informed the Foreign Ministry. Based on records at the National Archives (Microcopy T-120), memoirs, interview with Etzdorf; 28 notes. D. Prowe

686. Giesinger, Adam. THE BLACK SEA GERMANS IN 1941. *J. of the Am. Hist. Soc. of Germans from Russia 1979 2(2): 17-20.* Discusses the plight of Germans in Russia in 1941 as the invading Nazi armies found those of them who had escaped deportation.

687. Giesinger, Adam. REPORTS OF 1942-43 FROM GERMAN VILLAGES IN THE UKRAINE. *J. of the Am. Hist. Soc. of Germans from Russia 1977 (24): 19-23.* Provides reports from 80 German villages in the Ukraine, representative of the villages existing in Russia in 1942-43, which describe the

sufferings of the peasants first under Communism, then during World War II after the German occupation.

688. Gribkov, A. 40-LETIE NACHALA VELIKOI OTECHESTVENNOI VOINY [The 40th anniversary of the outbreak of World War II]. *Voenno-Istoricheskii Zhurnal [USSR] 1981 23(10): 12-19.* Outlines the course of the Great Patriotic War (1941-45) and the events that led up to the German attack in June 1941. In 1939 the Soviet Union signed a nonaggression pact with Germany in order to gain breathing space that had been denied them by the refusal of Great Britain and France to sign a mutual assistance pact with the Soviet Union. The armed forces were reorganized in readiness for war and a campaign to whip up patriotic fervor was set in motion. By November 1941 most of the western USSR was overrun but the tide began to turn in January 1942. The Battle of Stalingrad can be seen as the most important event in the whole of the war. Some 607 enemy divisions were destroyed or captured on the eastern front at a cost of 20 million Soviet dead. Based on a paper given at a military science conference organized by the Ministry of Defense and the Chief Directorate of the Army and Navy of the USSR to commemorate the 40th anniversary of the German attack in 1941; 12 notes. A. Brown

689. Groehler, Olaf. [CAUSES OF GERMAN DEFEAT]. MILITÄRISCHE URSACHEN FÜR DIE NIEDERLAGE DES FASCHISTISCHEN DEUTSCHLANDS IM ZWEITEN WELTKRIEG [Military causes for the defeat of fascist Germany in World War II]. *Militärgeschichte [East Germany] 1977 16(4): 443-455.* In summarizing the results of research on the history of World War II already produced by Soviet and East German historians, the author sketches the most important military causes for the defeat of fascist Germany. The Soviet-German front was the chief front of this war, where German imperialism suffered its decisive defeat. The author examines the role and significance of the anti-Hitler coalition and the problem of the two-front war.
DIE POLITISCH-MORALISCHE ÜBERLEGENHEIT DER VÖLKER DER ANTIHITLERKOALITION ALS URSACHE FÜR DIE NIEDERLAGE DES FASCHISTISCHEN DEUTSCHLANDS IM ZWEITEN WELTKRIEG [The political and moral superiority of the nations of the anti-Hitler coalition as cause for the defeat of fascist Germany in World War II]. *Militärgeschichte [East Germany] 1977 16(5): 561-571.* Sketches the political causes of German failure, emphasizing the international anti-fascist resistance struggle and the growing foreign policy isolation of the fascist states. Discusses how with the continuation of the war it became increasingly difficult for German monopoly capital to satisfy the growing demand for weapons and equipment with a rapidly diminishing economic base.
J/H. D. Andrews

690. Grunskis, E. LIETUVOS TSR STATYBOS ORGANIZACIJU LIKVIDAVIMAS HITLERINES OKUPACIJOS METAIS IR JU ATKURIMAS 1944-1945 M. [Liquidation of the construction organizations of the Lithuanian SSR during the Hitlerite occupation and their rehabilitation in 1944-45]. *Lietuvos TSR Mokslu Akademijos Darbai. Serija A [USSR] 1973 (45): 107-115.* Under the German occupation, state construction organizations in Lithuania were replaced by private companies. Because of shortages and military demands, civil construc-

tion stagnated. In 1944, the Lithuanian Council of People's Commissars established a Central Board of Construction which supervised the reconstruction of industrial enterprises and other projects. 63 notes.   A. E. Senn

691. Hass, Gerhart. DIE SCHLACHT BEI MOSKAU: ZU EINIGEN MILITÄRPOLITISCHEN SCHLUSSFOLGERUNGEN DER BÜRGERLICHEN HISTORIOGRAPHIE [The Battle of Moscow: on some military political conclusions of bourgeois historiography]. *Militärgeschichte [East Germany] 1981 20(5): 517-527.* The Battle of Moscow (1942) even in the 1970's, ranks among the unsurmounted problems of imperialist military historiography. With NATO's renewal of confrontation, the defeat of German troops is increasingly traced to failures and operational errors of the German military leadership, especially Hitler. Its lesson is held to be that the creation of military superiority over the USSR is both necessary and possible. 54 notes.

J/T (H. D. Andrews)

692. Haynes, Emma Schwabenland. THE DEPORTATION OF THE SOVIET GERMANS. *J. of the Am. Hist. Soc. of Germans from Russia 1977 (24): 5-18.* Discusses the experiences of Volga Germans who were deported to Siberia during World War II because Stalin feared that they were spies for the invading Germans.

693. Hohenecker, Leopold. DAS KRIEGSENDE 1945 IM RAUM FISCHBACH [The end of the war: 1945 in the Fischbach region]. *Österreich in Geschichte und Literatur [Austria] 1975 19(4): 193-225.* Describes the last months of World War II in the Fischbach region of Styria, the defensive efforts of the German forces against the Soviet advance, the occupation of Fischbach and neighboring areas by the Soviets, and the reaction of the local populace. Based on local police and parish reports, interviews, newspapers, and secondary sources; 128 notes, biblio.   J. B. Street

694. Iablochkin, Iu. N. BRATSKOE SOTRUDNICHESTVO SOVETSKIKH I NEMETSKIKH ANTIFASHISTOV-PODPOL'SHCHIKOV V UST'-LUGE (1942-1943 GG.) [Fraternal cooperation of the Soviet and German antifascist underground in Ust'-Luga, 1942-43]. *Voprosy Istorii KPSS [USSR] 1979 (2): 119-124.* Describes the life and work of Fritz Ben (1904-44), leader of a small underground antifascist group in the 301st Construction Battalion of the German Navy, stationed at Ust'-Luga near Leningrad from 1942, and of Vasili Grigor'evich Titov, who headed a Soviet underground group in Ust'-Luga. They became acquainted in 1942. This acquaintance and the similarity of objectives of their respective groups, whether the groups formally united or not, permits the conclusion that a Soviet-German underground antifascist organization existed. Based on materials in the Leningrad Party Archive; 42 notes.

L. E. Holmes

695. Ivanov, S. P. STALINGRADSKAIA BITVA I EE MEZHDUNARODNOE ZNACHENIE [The battle for Stalingrad and its international significance]. *Novaia i Noveishaia Istoriia [USSR] 1973 (1): 3-20.* The battle for Stalingrad, the most important battle of World War II, showed the heroism of the Soviet army and people. Their victory weakened the resolve of the German army, necessitating total mobilization in Germany. Before Stalingrad

Germany had diplomatic relations with 40 countries, but after with only 22, of which half were satellites. Japan abandoned the idea of attacking the USSR, and European resistance movements took heart. Thus the USSR gained tremendous international prestige, and its success still remains a potent warning to military adventurists. Based on the speeches of Leonid Brezhnev, and Soviet publications; 21 notes. A. J. Evans

696. Kahn, David. AN INTELLIGENCE CASE HISTORY: THE DEFENSE OF OSUGA. *Aerospace Hist. 1981 28(4): 242-252.* Using the German defense of Osuga on the Russian front in November 1942, demonstrates the role of military intelligence in a battle. By weaving together the various strands of information gained from high-level aerial reconnaissance, radio intelligence, deserters, and spies, the Germans predicted the date and "point of main effort" of the strongest onslaught of the "anticipated" Soviet winter offensive and successfully repulsed it. Based on German military records and interviews; 3 photos; map; 127 notes. J. K. Ohl

697. Kampe, Hans-Georg. DIE FERNMELDETECHNISCHE SICHERSTELLUNG DES FASCHISTISCHEN ÜBERFALLS AUF DIE SOWJETUNION [The establishment of technical security of communications in the fascist attack on the Soviet Union]. *Militärgeschichte [East Germany] 1981 20(3): 295-315.* In evaluating past aggression in the planning for the attack on the USSR, the Wehrmacht command devoted great attention to technical preparation for communications. The author demonstrates how the German postal service undertook strenuous efforts in 1940-41 to put a stable and extensive communications network at the disposal of the Wehrmacht. Makes clear the close interrelationship of military and civilian leadership typical of German militarism. Archives of the Ministry for Post and Communication Services, Berlin; 5 maps, table, 38 notes. J/T (H. D. Andrews)

698. Klink, Ernst. SAKSALAIS-SUOMALAISEN ASEVELJEYDEN LOPPUVAIHE POHJOIS-SUOMESSA 1944 [The final phase of German-Finnish cobelligerency in north Finland 1944]. *Hist. Aikakauskirja [Finland] 1979 77(2): 110-122.* Examines assumptions and activities of the commanders of the German 20th army in north Finland in 1944, from 1 August, when the Finnish government began to move toward a separate armistice with the USSR, until October, when Finnish troops opened hostilities to speed German withdrawal from Finland. The retreating Germans did not expect a Finnish attack and reacted with bitterness. Based on the unpublished archives of the German 20th army; map. R. G. Selleck

699. Knoll, Werner. KRIEGSSPIELE DER FASCHISTISCHEN WEHRMACHTFÜHRUNG ZUR VORBEREITUNG DES ÜBERFALLS AUF DIE UDSSR [War games of the fascist army command in preparation for the surprise attack on the USSR]. *Militärgeschichte [East Germany] 1981 20(4): 459-478.* In preparation for the surprise attack on the USSR, Germany intensively employed war games to test the feasibility of its plans for aggression. Documents of war games from November 1940 to March 1941 show how the commanders and staff officers of the operative commands as well as of the smaller units shared in the planning and preparation of the surprise attack, including the employment of means that were against international law. Military Archives of East Germany; illus., 25 notes. J/T (H. D. Andrews)

700. Kolokol'tsev, S. OPERATIVNOE PRIMENENIE TANKOVYKH VOISK VERMAKHTA (PO OPYTU BOEVYKH DEISTVII NA SOVETSKO-GERMANSKOM FRONTE) [The tactical use of the Wehrmacht's tank troops; battle experience on the Soviet-German front]. *Voenno-Istoricheskii Zhurnal [USSR] 1978 (1): 80-86.* German operations in 1941-43 were spearheaded by massive tank attacks to breach Soviet defense positions, to engage army reserves in the tactical defense zone, to force water barriers, to pursue retreating units, and to increase the range and tempo of the offensive. Though such tactics succeeded at times, the Wehrmacht's attempts to use tank concentrations to resolve large-scale strategic problems were doomed to failure. Misled by their experience in Western and Southeastern Europe, the Germans underestimated both the strength and dedication of Soviet troops and Soviet military acumen, while consistently overrating their own abilities. 18 notes. N. Frenkley

701. Komarov, N. Ia. and Orlov, A. S. "SEKRETNOE ORUZHIE" FIURERA I PROTIVOVOZDUSHNAIA OBORONA GORODOV SSSR V 1944-1945 GODAKH [The Führer's "Secret Weapon" and anti-aircraft defense of Soviet cities in 1944-45]. *Istoriia SSSR [USSR] 1975 (1): 121-128.* In February 1941 the border regions of the USSR were divided into anti-aircraft defense zones, comprised of weapons, 75 radar stations, and 39 fighter-plane squadrons. These units destroyed 7,313 enemy aircraft during the war. In 1944 the fascists planned to send planes bearing FAU-1 winged rockets manned by suicide pilots to wipe out strategic Soviet targets. FAU-1 rockets and FAU-2 rockets had been under development at Peenemunde since 1937. The first German rocket attacks of the war were directed against London on 13 June 1944. Leningrad, particularly vulnerable to such attacks due to its location, almost doubled its defenses. Training sessions in deflecting unmanned air attacks were conducted. Strategies and training were devised by Major-Generals N. D. Antonov and P. F. Rozhkov and Colonels A. P. Rysev and N. D. Gordienko. 32 notes. L. C. Moody

702. Kovalenko, I. M. TSILI I METODY NIMETS'KOI IMPERIALISTYCHNOI POLITYKY NA OKUPOVANYKH TERENAKH [The aims and methods of German imperialist policy on occupied territory]. *Sučasnist [West Germany] 1978 (2): 74-86.* Analyzes the methods of Nazi Germany's imperialist policies in the Ukraine and how they were used to justify political and economic exploitation and cultural genocide.

703. Krausnick, Helmut. KOMMISSARBEFEHL UND "GERICHTSBARKEITSERLASS BARBAROSSA" IN NEUER SICHT [Commissar Order and "Jurisdiction Decree Barbarossa" in a new perspective]. *Vierteljahrshefte für Zeitgeschichte [West Germany] 1977 25(4): 682-738.* A fresh analysis of the genesis of the 1941 German Army decrees to liquidate Red Army political commissars and to severely limit the army's jurisdiction in Soviet areas occupied by Germany. Contrary to protestations at the Nuremberg Trial and elsewhere the officer corps resisted not so much the liquidation order as the limitation of judicial authority because they feared loss of discipline in the troops, but by 1941 largely agreed with Hitler's ideological views, especially against Bolshevism. Based on recently opened Army records (OKW/WFSt/LIV) at the German Federal Military Archive (Freiburg), the Institute of Contemporary History (Munich), and Nuremberg Trial documents; 283 notes. D. Prowe

704. Kuz'michev, I. K. BOR'BA SOVETSKOGO SOIUZA ZA MIR I BEZOPASNOST' PROTIV RASPROSTRANENIIA FASHISTSKOI AGRESSII (APREL' 1940-IIUN' 1941 G.) [The struggle of the Soviet Union for peace and security and against the spread of fascist aggression, April 1940-June 1941]. *Istoriia SSSR [USSR] 1974 (1): 26-47.* Describes the USSR's foreign policy and diplomatic moves to prevent further German expansion as well as a conceivable anti-Soviet coalition between Hitler and imperialist Western powers. To gain time in the face of deteriorating Soviet-German relations and to secure its borders against German aggression, the USSR reunited Bessarabia and the Baltic republics with Russia, June-August 1940. Soviet mutual aid negotiations with Balkan countries were opposed by Britain and thwarted by German occupation of Bulgaria and Yugoslavia in Spring 1941. Abortive trade negotiations with Britain and the "moral embargo" imposed on Soviet trade by the United States, forced the USSR to sign trade agreements with Germany. Nevertheless, the USSR rejected an alliance with Germany (proposed by Hitler in November 1940) to dismember the British Empire. 88 notes.
N. Frenkley

705. Lukin, M. V SMOLENSKOM SRAZHENII [At the battle of Smolensk]. *Voenno-Istoricheskii Zhurnal [USSR] 1979 (7): 42-54.* A short background introduction precedes the author's posthumously published memoirs of the battle for Smolensk in 1941. Smolensk, always regarded as the strategic key to Moscow, was the object of German air, armor, and infantry attacks in overwhelming numbers. The defenders lacked adequate weapons to resist armored assault, and were totally without air cover. The city eventually fell after savage fighting, with heavy losses on both sides, but the German attack was so weakened that a further immediate advance on Moscow was impossible, and Hitler's blitzkrieg plans suffered a serious setback. Based on Soviet military archives; map, 10 notes.
J. S. S. Charles

706. Luther, Craig. GERMAN ARMOURED OPERATIONS IN THE UKRAINE, 1941: THE ENCIRCLEMENT BATTLE OF UMAN. *Army Q. and Defence J. [Great Britain] 1978 108(4): 454-469.* Describes the battle of encirclement fought in World War II by the German forces led by Colonel-General Paul Ludwig Ewald von Kleist against the Russians near Uman, in the Ukraine.

707. Madej, Victor and Stanton, Shelby. THE SMOLENSK CAMPAIGN 11 JULY-5 AUGUST 1941. *Strategy & Tactics 1976 (57): 4-19.* Describes the battles near Smolensk in 1941 during the German invasion of the USSR and Germany's decision made during the battles to modify Operation Barbarossa by interrupting the advance on Moscow in order to capture Kiev.

708. Mainuš, František. ROZHODUJÍCÍ PODÍL SOVĚTSKÉHO SVAZU NA VÍTĚZSTVÍ VE DRUHÉ SVĚTOVÉ VÁLCE [The decisive part in the victory in World War II]. *Sborník Prací Filosofické Fakulty Brněnské U.: Řada Hist. [Czechoslovakia] 1980 29(27): 243-252.* The sheer scale of the engagements on the Soviet-German front and the statistics for arms production and both German and Soviet losses prove that the USSR bore the brunt of the war and carries most credit for the victory.

709. Manninen, Ohto. DIE BEZIEHUNGEN ZWISCHEN DEN FINNISCHEN UND DEUTSCHEN MILITÄRBEHÖRDEN IN DER AUSARBEITUNGSPHASE DES BARBAROSSAPLANES [The relationship between the Finnish and German military authorities in the preparatory phase of the Barbarossa Plan]. *Militärgeschichtliche Mitteilungen [West Germany] 1979 (2): 79-95.* Details the liaison between German and Finnish officers in the eight months preceding the June 1941 German attack on the USSR. The early meetings dealt with simple coordination and logistical matters regarding German forces in Norway, but also considered possible measures against the Soviet Union several months in advance of the final Finnish pledge to support Operation Barbarossa. Based upon documents in German and Finnish archives; 49 notes.
K. W. Estes

710. Marolda, Edward J. THE FAILURE OF GERMAN WORLD WAR II STRATEGY IN THE BLACK SEA. *Naval War Coll. R. 1975 28(1): 39-54.* In 1942 the success of the German offensive in Russia and, indeed, the fate of Nazi Germany itself focused on the effective support of the armies in the field. Few cases can be found in history where the value of the sea as a logistic highway was so critical or the failure to recognize that fact so disastrous as in the example of the German campaign in southern Russia.
J

711. Mertsalov, A. N. STALINGRADSKAIA BITVA V OSVESHCHENII BURZHUAZNOI ISTORIOGRAFII FRG [The battle of Stalingrad in light of West German bourgeois historiography]. *Istoriia SSSR [USSR] 1978 (4): 181-192.* Reviews recent West German historiography on the battle of Stalingrad, 1942-43. On the one hand, West German historiography has devoted much more attention to the nature and significance of the battle than has American and British bourgeois historiography. On the other hand, West German historiography has displayed the same bourgeois emphasis on the role of such factors as leadership, "fatal" mistakes, and missed opportunities by which reactionary historians attempt to conceal the reasons for the Soviet victory which, in fact, are rooted in the superiority of socialist society. 59 notes.
J. W. Long

712. Müller, Norbert and Vestermanis, Margers. VERBRECHEN DER FASCHISTISCHEN WEHRMACHT AN SOWJETISCHEN KRIEGSGEFANGENEN 1941-1945 [Crimes of the fascist Wehrmacht against Soviet prisoners of war, 1941-45]. *Militärgeschichte [East Germany] 1977 16(1): 15-27.* For German imperialism, prisoners of war were for a long time objects of brutal exploitation and suppression. This conduct, which was against international law, reached its zenith in the treatment of Soviet prisoners of war during World War II. On the basis of extensive newly available sources, the authors trace this theme in special detail with the example of the prisoner of war camps in Latvia.
J/T (H. D. Andrews).

713. Mulligan, Timothy P. THE OSS AND THE NAZI OCCUPATION OF THE BALTIC STATES, 1941-1945: A NOTE ON DOCUMENTATION. *J. of Baltic Studies 1982 13(1): 53-58.* A research guide to records of the Office of Strategic Services (OSS) in the National Archives in Washington, D.C., pertaining to German military occupation policies in the Baltic area and to life under the occupation, to collaboration and resistance. The records, identified as Record Group 226, contain 319 documents. Since most original German documents were

captured by the Soviets and are not accessible to non-Marxist historians, the OSS records are especially valuable for research. Based on archival documents; 4 tables, 10 notes. R. Vilums

714. Noskova, A. F. FASHISTSKII OKKUPATSIONNYI REZHIM I POZITSII KLASSOV I SOTSIAL'NIKH GRUPP V STRANAKH TSENTRAL'NOI I IUGO-VOSTOCHNOI EVROPY [The fascist occupation regime and the position of classes and social groups in Eastern Europe]. *Sovetskoe Slavianovedenie [USSR] 1979 (3): 11-28.* Discusses the fascist occupation of the USSR and Eastern Europe during World War II. S. R. Gudgin

715. Oertel, Manfred. ZUR BETEILIGUNG DER DEUTSCHEN REICHSBANK AN DER FASCHISTISCHEN AGGRESSION GEGEN DIE SOWJETUNION [Concerning the participation of the German Reichsbank in the fascist aggression against the USSR]. *Militärgeschichte [East Germany] 1981 20(5): 579-586.* Presents a newly discovered document that proves the Reichsbank was involved concretely and at an early date in the preparation of the invasion of the Soviet Union. Describes the German banking system's role in financing the policy of aggression and pillage. An introduction sketches the degree to which the measures described in the document were effected. Document from the Central State Archives, Potsdam; map, 2 illus., chart, 27 notes.
J/T (H. D. Andrews)

716. Oseraner, Michail. DEUTSCHE ANTIFASCHISTEN IN DER PARTISANENBEWEGUNG IN DER RSFSR UND DER BELORUSSISCHEN SSR [German antifascists in the partisan movement in the RSFSR and in the Belorussian SSR]. *Militärgeschichte [East Germany] 1976 15(2): 199-205.* Provides excerpts from interviews of Soviet officers, commissars, partisans and civilians recounting numerous cases of antifascist Germans aiding the Soviet partisans in Belorussia and Western Russia during World War II. J. B. Street

717. Parham, Dave. BATTLE FOR STALINGRAD: THE STRUGGLE FOR THE CITY, SEPTEMBER-NOVEMBER 1942. *Strategy & Tactics 1980 (79): 25-31.* Detailed narrative of the German defeat at Stalingrad in the fall of 1942.

718. Patrick, Stephen B. WAR IN THE EAST, THE RUSSO-GERMAN CONFLICT, 1941-45. *Strategy & Tactics 1973 (41): 15-39.* Describes the military campaigns between the USSR and Germany during World War II.

719. Perechnev, Iu. OBORONA VOENNO-MORSKIKH BAZ V VELIKOI OTECHESTVENNOI VOINE [The defense of naval bases during World War II]. *Morskoi Sbornik [USSR] 1973 (12): 27-31.* Describes the extent to which the German military hoped to destroy the Soviet Union by taking Leningrad and other Soviet naval bases, and lists the arms and manpower on both sides during 1941-42. Contrary to the interpretation of foreign studies, Soviet naval operations were not subordinate to the army. Leningrad, Odessa, Sevastapol, Novorossiisk, and Kerch are now recognized as hero-cities with Orders of Lenin, Gold Star Medals, and special medals for the defenders of the first three cities. Based on military histories and a 1973 article by A. Khrenov and A. Basov in *Morskoi Sbornik*; 4 notes. E. Dunn

720. Perezhogin, V. A. NESOSTOIATEL'NOST' POPYTOK OBELIT' VERMAKHT [Hollow attempts to whitewash the Wehrmacht]. *Novaia i Noveishaia Istoriia [USSR] 1978 (2): 46-61.* Shows the hollowness of the attempts by the reactionary bourgeois historiography to whitewash the punitive activities of the fascist Wehrmacht on Soviet territory. He denounces the Wehrmacht's atrocities on Soviet territory and describes the heroic struggle of Soviet people who, headed by the Communist Party, launched a mighty partisan movement.
J

721. Petukhov, K. OB IZDEVATEL'STVAKH GITLEROVTSEV NAD SOVETSKIMI VOENNOPLENNYMI [Nazi abuse of Soviet prisoners of war]. *Voenno-Istoricheskii Zhurnal [USSR] 1978 20(10): 82-85.* Describes the inhuman conditions in Nazi camps for Soviet prisoners of war: starvation, exhausting labor, exposure, unchecked epidemics, lack of medical care as well as planned systematic extermination. Almost half a million Soviet war prisoners perished in Latvian and Lithuanian camps alone. Based on documents of the Nuremberg War Crimes Trials; 11 notes.
N. Frenkley

722. Pokryshkin, Aleksandr. FORMULA OF VICTORY. *Soviet Military Rev. [USSR] 1976 (2): 52-55.* Excerpt from Air Marshal Aleksandr Pokryshkin's *The Sky in the War* (Moscow, 1975) describing an episode in the air battle fought over the Kuban in the spring of 1943 in which a new "shelf" attack formation involving vertically parallel echelons of Soviet LAGG fighters swooped down from a high altitude to gain speed in order to attack the swifter German Messerschmitts, which generally cleared the skies in advance of the Junker bombers.

723. Ratley, Lonnie O. AIR POWER AT KURSK: A LESSON FOR TODAY? *Military Rev. 1978 58(4): 54-62.* The response of the Luftwaffe's Fourth Group to Soviet tank units at Kursk in 1943 demonstrates that the A10 close-support-aircraft would be highly effective against the Warsaw Pact's massive superiority in armor. Using tactics developed by Captain Bruno Meyer and new technical innovations, NATO forces should stand an excellent chance of success. 2 illus.
C. Hopkins

724. Ratley, Lonnie O., III. AIR POWER AT KURSK: THE CONFRONTATION OF AIRCRAFT AND TANKS—A LESSON FOR TODAY? *J. of the Royal United Services Inst. for Defence Studies [Great Britain] 1977 122(2): 25-29.* Analyzes the effect of tactical aircraft use against tanks by the Germans at the battle of Kursk, July 1943. Describes the German battle plans, the development of the battle, and the successful destruction of a Russian armored brigade by German ground-support aircraft. 17 notes. D. H. Murdoch

725. Riedel, Matthias. BERGBAU UND EISENHÜTTENINDUSTRIE IN DER UKRAINE UNTER DEUTSCHER BESATZUNG (1941-1944) [The mining and iron industry in the Ukraine under German occupation, 1941-44]. *Vierteljahrshefte für Zeitgeschichte [West Germany] 1973 21(3): 245-284.* Well before the German attack on the USSR the systematic economic exploitation of the country was prepared. The German steel industry relied heavily on imports of manganese ores from the USSR. The attack created a bottleneck of supply which had to be overcome quickly. For this the Mining and Forge Company East, Ltd. was founded under the management of Paul Pleiger, former director general

of the Hermann Göring works. He arranged for the reconstruction of the destroyed works in Nikopol and Krivoi Rog. In 1942 90% of German manganese requirements were satisfied by Nikopol. Subsequently, the attempt was made to meet local needs for coal from the Donets basin to relieve the overloaded transport from Germany. However, the Soviet attacks in September 1943 disrupted these plans. In February 1944 Nikopol and Krivoi Rog also had to be given up, after the works had supplied the Reich for two years. Based on the Nuremberg documents and the Federal Military Archives; 184 notes. U. Wengenroth

726. Rudenko, S. I. 1943-1944. PE CERUL DE DEASUPRA CERNIGOVULUI [In the skies over Chernigov, 1943-44]. *Magazin Istoric [Romania] 1981 15(5): 34-37.* An extract in Romanian translation from the Russian of the author's war memoirs, *Krylia Pobedy* [The wings of victory] (1976), describing air warfare between the Russians and the Germans on the central Belorussian front in 1943 and 1944.

727. Rumiantsev, N. BOI IPTAP S TANKAMI I PEKHOTOI PROTIVNIKA [An antitank artillery regiment's battle against enemy tanks and infantry]. *Voenno-Istoricheskii Zhurnal [USSR] 1978 20(11): 40-44.* The commander of the 150th Guards Anti-Tank Artillery Regiment describes the battle of 18 September 1943, near Malaia Tokmachka (southeast of Zaporozhye) against units of the German Sixth Army retreating from the Donets Basin. The Soviet victory forced the Germans to abandon this railroad junction on the Berdyansk-Zaporozhye line, a vital communication line essential if the Germans were to effectively regroup along prepared defense positions in the Ukraine. Based on Ministry of Defense archives; 4 illus., map, 12 notes. N. Frenkley

728. Rzheshevski, O. and Ivanitski, G. PRAVDA I LOZH' O ZHIZNI NEMETSKIKH VOENNOPLENNYKH V SSSR [Truth and lies about the life of German prisoners of war in the USSR]. *Voenno-Istoricheskii Zhurnal [USSR] 1978 20(10): 76-82.* A review article refuting the unjustifiable accusations in Erich Maschke's *Zur Geschichte der deutschen Kriegsgefangenen des Zweiten Weltkrieges,* 15 vols. (Bielefeld: Gieseking, 1962-74). The seven volumes on Soviet camps contain unsubstantiated accounts reflecting West German attempts to attenuate Nazi barbarity toward Russians by accusing the USSR of mistreating German prisoners in World War II. In fact, the Soviet Union treated all war prisoners humanely in accordance with Soviet military law and assiduously tried to reeducate German prisoners misled by Nazi propaganda. The truth about Soviet prisoner of war camps was published in East Germany in *Kriegsgefangene in der Sowjetunion* (Berlin: SWA-Verlag, 1949) as is demonstrated in examples of eyewitness testimonies. 19 notes. N. Frenkley

729. Salomon, Eleonore. BIOGRAPHISCHE SKIZZEN. "ICH HÄTTE DOCH SO GERN DIE NEUE ZEIT ERLEBT:" KÄTE NIEDERKIRCHNER [Biographical sketches: "I would have loved to experience the new era:" Käte Niederkirchner]. *Beiträge zur Gesch. der Arbeiterbewegung [East Germany] 1981 23(1): 94-100.* Käte Niederkirchner (1909-44), a Hungarian citizen, was born and raised in Berlin. When deported in 1933, she went to the Soviet Union. She was trained for illegal work in Germany. In October 1943, she parachuted behind German lines, but was arrested almost immediately, incarcerated, and shot in September 1944. Based largely on an unpublished autobiography and other unpublished documents; 34 notes. A. Schuetz

730. Samsons, V. BURŽUĀZISKĀ NACIONĀLISMA POLITISKĀ UN IDEJISKĀ LATVIJĀ HITLERISKĀS OKUPĀCIJAS GADOS (PIELĀGOŠANĀS NACIONĀLSOCIĀLISMA FILOZOFIJAI) [The political and ideological degeneration of bourgeois nationalism in Latvia under fascist occupation: adaptation to a national socialist philosophy]. *Latvijas PSR Zinātnu Akademijas Vestis [USSR] 1975 (8): 3-14.* Reviews the presentation of nationalist philosophies in the Latvian press of 1942-43, largely in *Izglītības Menešraksts,* and criticizes the theories of individual contributors.

731. Schechowzow, Nikolai Iwanowitsch. PROBLEME DER KRIEGSKUNST IN DER BERLINER OPERATION [Problems of the art of war in the Berlin operation]. *Militärgeschichte [East Germany] 1975 14(1): 16-31.* The battle of Berlin in 1945 confronted the Red Army with 60% of the German troops, the fighting being complicated by strong fortifications and complicated geographic conditions.

732. Scheel, Klaus. ANWEISUNGEN FÜR DIE DARSTELLUNG DER STALINGRADER SCHLACHT IN DER FASCHISTISCHEN PRESSE [Instructions for reporting the battle of Stalingrad in the fascist press]. *Zeitschrift für Geschichtswissenschaft [East Germany] 1973 21(6): 684-700.* Publication of the instructions of Otto Dietrich, the chief of the press in Germany, for the manipulation of the news about the battle of Stalingrad between August 1942 and February 1943.

733. Sella, Amnon. 'BARBAROSSA': SURPRISE ATTACK AND COMMUNICATION. *J. of Contemporary Hist. [Great Britain] 1978 13(3): 555-583.* A detailed account of the German surprise attack on the USSR on 22 June 1941 reveals the collapse of the Russian signal network, the devastating effect on command and control, the heavy losses inflicted on the Air Force and the Soviet armored units, and the utter Russian confusion of priorities and action. Based on printed primary and secondary Russian, German, and English language sources; 77 notes. M. P. Trauth

734. Sevostyanov, P. ON THE EVE OF THE GREAT BATTLE. SEPTEMBER 1939-JUNE 1941. *Int. Affairs [USSR] 1978 (6): 97-108.* Describes Germany's actions which led to its assault on the USSR in June 1941, and Soviet foreign policy during that time which tried to avoid such a confrontation.

735. Sevostyanov, P. ON THE EVE OF THE GREAT BATTLE. SEPTEMBER 1939-JUNE 1941. *Int. Affairs [USSR] 1978 (4): 106-117.* The German-Soviet Nonaggression Pact was politically necessary due to the USSR's relative weakness, but Soviet leaders certainly realized that ultimately the USSR would be forced to war with fascism. Article to be continued.

736. Shavrov, I. E. OSVOBOZHDENIE SOVETSKOI PRIBALTIKI OT GITLEROVSKIKH ZAKHVATCHIKOV [Freeing the Soviet Baltic from the Hitlerite aggressors]. *Novaia i Noveishaia Istoriia [USSR] 1974 (6): 3-19.* The Red Army penetrated the Baltic area in February 1944, and until the end of World War II fought German troops trapped there. The military campaigns may be divided into two periods. The first, July-August 1944, included nine consecutive frontal operations from south to north. The second, September-October 1944, saw a major advance in the Baltic region, one of the eight major blows against

the Germans in 1944. It was intended to annihilate Army Group North and to free Estonia, Latvia, and Lithuania, and involved four interrelated operations. Based on archival documents; 18 notes. D. N. Collins

737. Shtykov, N. TAINY KREPOSTI KENIGSHTAIN [The secrets of Königstein Fortress]. *Voenno-Istoricheskii Zhurnal [USSR] 1979 (5): 52-55.* The author, who masterminded military operations which resulted in the surrender by the Germans of Königstein Fortress in May 1945, describes how Soviet soldiers discovered hidden in the dungeons of the fortress the art treasures of the Dresden Gallery. The American officer who allegedly came to evacuate French prisoners of war intended to ship the treasures away to the US zone but was prevented from doing so by the Soviets. The invaluable treasures of the German nation were thus saved. 2 notes. V. Sobeslavsky

738. Simpson, Keith. THE GERMAN EXPERIENCE OF REAR AREA SECURITY ON THE EASTERN FRONT 1941-45. *J. of the Royal United Services Inst. for Defence Studies [Great Britain] 1976 121(4): 39-46.* Studies the problem of Germany's rear area security on the Russian front in World War II. An examination of German security organization, Soviet partisan warfare, and the problems of German rear area security after the invasion of Russia in 1941 and of home defense in 1944-45 indicates that behind-the-front security became a problem for the Germans only after they had clearly failed to achieve a rapid decisive victory. The disruption of German rear areas might have been minimized if German intelligence had achieved greater coordination and efficiency. Secondary sources; 23 notes. D. H. Murdoch

739. Stolfi, Russel H. S. BARBAROSSA REVISITED: A CRITICAL REAPPRAISAL OF THE OPENING STAGES OF THE RUSSO-GERMAN CAMPAIGN (JUNE-DECEMBER 1941). *J. of Modern Hist 1982 54(1): 27-46.* Hitler's invasion of the USSR in 1941 was not foreordained to defeat, even after the Balkan campaign delayed the spring offensive. Had Hitler continued the drive on Moscow in July instead of halting and then diverting elements of Army Group Center to the Ukraine, the Russian capital would have fallen by the end of August. Based on documents in the Bundesarchiv Freiburg and other primary sources; 31 notes. J. D. Hunley

740. Stolfi, Russel H. S. CHANCE IN HISTORY: THE RUSSIAN WINTER OF 1941-1942. *History [Great Britain] 1980 65(214): 214-228.* Discusses the severity of the European winter of 1941-42 and its effect on the German military offensive against Russia. Although Hitler diverted half the Army Group Center to the Ukraine in the summer of 1941, the Germans had remained strong enough to take Moscow, provided the autumn was mild. But the early onset of winter brought extraordinarily low temperatures and caught the ill-prepared German forces by surprise. Because this debilitating winter was so much a matter of chance, the German offensive failure and the Russian defensive achievement must both be reevaluated. Based on primary accounts by the German Army Group Center and on weather data from German and American records and journals; 3 tables, 56 notes. R. P. Sindermann, Jr.

741. Storlid, P. O. VEIEN TIL STALINGRAD [The road to Stalingrad]. *Norsk Militaert Tidsskrift [Norway] 1977 147(5): 215-219.* An account of the German offensive against the USSR, known as Operation Barbarossa, 1941-42, and the defeat of the Sixth Army at Stalingrad and its consequences.

742. Sunde, Hjalmar I. KAMPENE PÅ ISHAVSFRONTEN [The battles at the Arctic Ocean front]. *Norsk Militaert Tidsskrift [Norway] 1977 147(11): 483-496, (12): 545-558.* Part I. An account of the battles between Germany and the USSR in the Bering Strait area, 1941-45. Part II. DEN TIENDE SOVJETISKE OFFENSIV [The 10th Soviet offensive]. Describes the Soviet offensive against German troops at Petsamo, Kirkenes, and Neiden in the autumn of 1944. Article to be continued.

743. Szabó, Balázs. A SZOVJET CSAPATOK HADTÁPBIZTOSÍTÁSÁNAK SAJÁTOSSÁGAI A MAGYARORSZÁG FELSZABADÍTÁSÁÉRT VÍVOTT HADMŰVELETEKBEN 1944. SZEPTEMBER 23-1945. ÁPRILIS 4. [Details of the protection of the rear lines of Soviet troops in operations launched for the liberation of Hungary in the period 23 September 1944-4 April 1945]. *Hadtörténelmi Közlemények [Hungary] 1979 26(3): 399-424.* Examines the problems of tactics in the material, technical, and medical provision for operations conducted in Hungary, September 1944 to April 1945. German military units plundered the countryside, and their attitude toward Hungary and its troops was unscrupulous. Describes the strategic position facing Soviet forces by the time of the Debrecen and Budapest offensives and analyzes attempts to improve Soviet technical and medical supplies in the ensuing operations. Based on Soviet and German archives; 2 maps, table, 61 notes.
Gy. Foxcroft

744. Tschuikow, W. DAS ENDE DES HITLERREICHES [The end of the Hitler empire]. *Einheit [East Germany] 1975 30(4-5): 389-402.* Western historiography distorts the defensive role of the Nazi-Soviet Pact and the dominating contribution of the Red Army for the final defeat of national socialist Germany in World War II.

745. Tutkus, V. I. VIL'NIUSSKAIA NASTUPATEL'NAIA OPERATSIIA VOISK KRASNOI ARMII V IIULE 1944 G. [The Vilnius offensive by units of the Red Army, July 1944]. *Lietuvos TSR Mokslu Akademijos Darbai. Serija A: Visuomenes Mokslai [USSR] 1978 (3): 95-108.* Adds details to the accepted story of the liberation of Vilnius from German occupation. Units of the Third Belorussian Front moved on Vilnius from 6 to 13 July 1944. The author recounts stages of the battle and notes the Germans were determined to resist. The remains of the garrison surrendered on 13 July. More than 8,000 Germans were killed and 5,000 captured. Based on archival materials and interviews; 2 maps, 42 notes, 3 appendixes.
A. E. Senn

746. Ueberschaer, Gerd R. GUERRE DE COALITION OU GUERRE SÉPARÉE: CONCEPTION ET STRUCTURES DE LA STRATÉGIE GERMANO-FINLANDAISE DANS LA GUERRE CONTRE L'URSS (1941-1944) [Coalition war or separate war: the conception and structures of German-Finnish strategy in the war against the USSR, 1941-44]. *Rev. d'Hist. de la Deuxième Guerre Mondiale [France] 1980 30(118): 27-68.* Coalition warfare

is at best extremely difficult to conduct. Germany and Finland had only military motivation in common and lacked political accord from the beginning. Common strategic priorities were lacking and coordinated military operations were impossible. Hitler wanted a short, successful war without long-term alliances. He was interested in attacking Leningrad while the Finns wanted to seize the Murmansk railway. The result was uncoordinated operations. Based on German archives in Bonn, Koblenz, and Freiburg; 130 notes. G. H. Davis

747. Vasil'ev, B. RAZGROM NEMETSKO-FASHISTSKOGO MORSKOGO DESANTA U OSTROVA GOGLAND V SENTIABRE 1944 GODA [Rout of the German amphibious landing at Hogland (Suursaari) Island in September 1944]. *Voenno-Istoricheskii Zhurnal [USSR] 1978 20(12): 88-91.* Describes the successful joint Soviet-Finnish operation which foiled a German attempt to seize Hogland (Suursaari), a small island in the Finnish Gulf. Finland had abrogated its pact with Germany on 4 September 1944 and the German garrison of this island was to be evacuated by the 14th. Instead, a German flotilla attacked the island and demanded its surrender. Upon Finnish refusal to comply, the Germans succeeded in landing troops at Suurkylä Bay. However, by nightfall the bridgehead was liquidated and the German boats were sunk or badly damaged by the Soviet Baltic Naval Air Force and Finnish ground troops. 11 notes.
N. Frenkley

748. Vernon, Graham D. SOVIET COMBAT OPERATIONS IN WORLD WAR II: LESSONS FOR TODAY? *Military Rev. 1980 60(3): 30-40, (4): 42-50.* Part I. Just as the Germans underestimated the Russians before World War II, the United States may be underestimating them today. German commanders reported that Soviet commanders and soldiers had the common characteristics of toughness and discipline. Part II. Soviet World War II operations were not always imaginative or flexible, but they were well planned and executed. Intelligence operations were used mainly by the higher echelons. Based primarily on debriefings of Germans at the end of the war done by the Office of the Chief of Military History, Special Staff, US Army; 4 illus., 72 notes. D. H. Cline

749. Veryha, Wasyl. THE GALICIA UKRAINIAN DIVISION IN POLISH AND SOVIET LITERATURE. *Ukrainian Q. 1980 36(3): 253-270.* In 1943 a Ukrainian military unit known as the Galicia Division was formed under German auspices to fight against the Soviet army on the eastern front. After engaging in action in several areas, most of the Galicia unit surrendered to the British in 1945. Several Polish sources have claimed that this unit was deeply and brutally involved in the 1944 Warsaw uprising and in other Polish atrocities, but such claims have repeatedly been proven false. Soviet sources, while also ascribing crimes to the Galicia Division, minimized its role, preferring to emphasize the obvious anti-Soviet cast of the unit. Ukrainian partisans have also denigrated the role of the Galicia Division, claiming it acted only as a guerrilla unit. 47 notes.
K. N. T. Crowther

750. Voinov, A. NESOSTOIAVSHAIASIA AKTSIIA [A nonexistent action]. *Morskoi Sbornik [USSR] 1981 (3): 54-56.* The utter failure of the German attack on the Soviet base of Vayenga near Murmansk in January 1945 was a clear demonstration of the continued failure of German miniature submarines of the Biber class.

751. Wilt, Alan F. HITLER'S LATE SUMMER PAUSE IN 1941. *Military Affairs 1981 45(4): 187-191.* During the German advance into the USSR during the summer of 1941, Hitler diverted armored and motorized divisions north and south, rather than advancing swiftly toward Moscow. The northern operation was a failure, while the southern diversion, under General Heinz Guderian, was more successful. Yet, when Hitler placed emphasis on taking Moscow, the now weakened conditions of the armored and motorized forces were obviously factors in Germany's failure to sustain its offensive toward Moscow. Based on German military and other primary sources; chart, 17 notes. A. M. Osur

752. Zheltov, A. NA PRAVOM FLANGE [On the right flank]. *Voenno-Istoricheskii Zhurnal [USSR] 1979 (12): 32-40; 1980 (1): 47-54.* Part I. Describes defensive battles of 1941 on the right flank of the Soviet-German front, i.e., the Northern front. The Germans invaded from the north on 29 June 1941 and counted on taking Murmansk in three days. They were defeated in battles in July-August 1941, which led to the collapse of the German offensive in the north. On 23 August the Northern front was divided into the Leningrad and Karelian fronts. In September the Germans launched a new offensive on Murmansk but it was repelled by the Soviet army. Defensive battles were also fought to the north of Lake Ladoga. By December 1941 the line of defense had also stabilized on the left flank of the Karelian front. The way to Murmansk and Leningrad was blocked. Part II. Memoir of winter 1941-42 on the Karelian front. The front stabilized that winter, and the armies of the front received fresh reserves and military equipment. Nevertheless, the April offensive operation failed, partly because of organizational and leadership shortcomings, but mainly because of the heavy snows. By July 1942 Soviet troops had laid the groundwork for the defeat of the enemy in Karelia and the Arctic region. Based on Soviet military archives; map, 6 notes. L. Waters/L. D. Aldwinckle

753. Zhilin, P. KRUSHENIE FASHISTSKOI DOKTRINI BLITSKRIGA I EE SOVREMENNYE POSLEDOVATELI [The collapse of the fascist doctrine of blitzkrieg and its modern successors]. *Voenno-Istoricheskii Zhurnal [USSR] 1981 23(10): 42-50.* Hitler was encouraged to unleash Operation Barbarossa in 1941 because of the success of the doctrine of blitzkrieg in other areas of Europe. The German High Command clearly underestimated, however, the willingness of the Soviet people to resist attack, welded as they were into a unified whole by the activities of the Communist Party and by national pride. Ultimately it was the changeover from a defensive to an offensive strategy at Moscow in the winter of 1941-42 and the associated massive German losses that highlighted the bankruptcy of the concept of blitzkrieg. 20 notes. A. Brown

754. Ziemke, Earl F. FRANZ HALDER AT ORSHA: THE GERMAN GENERAL STAFF SEEKS A CONSENSUS. *Military Affairs 1975 39(4): 173-176.* Discusses the conference held in November 1941 of General Franz Halder and his colleagues with the chiefs of staff of the Army groups and Armies on the Eastern Front. Halder conducted a grand review of strategy to determine whether to immediately pursue a maximum effort (*Wirkungsgedanken*) or to conserve strength (*Erhaltungsgedanken*) for a later campaign when the weather improved. The consensus favored a maximum effort, in effect the only solution acceptable to Hitler. Primary and secondary sources; 16 notes. A. M. Osur

755. —. EIN BRIEFWECHSEL WILHELM PIECKS MIT DEUTSCHEN KRIEGSGEFANGENEN 1943-1944 [A correspondence of William Pieck with German prisoners of war, 1943-44]. *Beiträge zur Geschichte der Arbeiterbewegung [East Germany] 1977 19(1): 67-69.* Prints an exchange of letters between Wilhelm Pieck and German prisoners of war in a Soviet camp. The prisoners declared their support for the goals of the Communist Party of Germany and for the Free Germany Committee headed by Pieck in exile. In turn, Pieck praised their vision for a new Germany free from the tyranny of Adolf Hitler and dedicated to the principles of the international workers' movement.

G. H. Libbey

756. —. [THE KURSK BATTLE—30 YEARS]. *Soviet Military Rev. [USSR] 1973 (6): 2-39.*

—. THE KURSK BATTLE, *pp. 2-7.* The Kursk battle of July 1943 signaled the end of Nazi hopes for final victory. The German attack began on 5 July but by 10 July it had been halted. Russian troops then swung to the counterattack. On 12 July the biggest tank battle of the war began, with some 3,000 vehicles involved. The Germans suffered heavy losses in the battle, particularly to their armored units. 5 photos.

Zhukov, Georgi. DECIDES, *pp. 8-8.* Provides background to the Russian planning for the Kursk battle.

Shtemenko, S. MATTERS WERE COMING TO A HEAD, *pp. 10-11.* The former chief of the Operations Department of the General Staff recalls how intelligence was received about the time and place of the German offensive at Kursk.

Rokossovsky, K. THE ENEMY ASSAULT IS REPULSED, *pp. 12-13.* The former Central Front Commander tells how the line was held. Counterbattery fire before the German attack seriously disrupted the initial assault. The carefully prepared defensive positions in depth then prevented any complete breakthrough although the Germans advanced several kilometers in places.

Chistyakov, I. ON THE MAIN LINE OF ADVANCE, *pp. 14-15.* The former commander of the 6th Guards Army, which held part of the Voronezh front, recounts the battle from his point of view.

Zvenzlovsky, M. A. A CRUSHING BLOW, *pp. 16-19.* After absorbing the German attack, the Russian forces moved to the counteroffensive. A succession of blows was aimed at the Germans from each of the Russian groupings, and the Germans were pushed back as much as 140 kilometers, with heavy losses. The liberation of the important railway junction and industrial center of Kharkov on 23 August signaled the end of the battle. 4 photos.

Stepanov, F. STAUNCHNESS IN DEFENSE, *pp. 20-23.* The unprecedented staunchness of the Russian defense at Kursk was the result of the manysided activity of the Communist Party among the fighting men.

Matsulenko, V. NEW STAGE IN TACTICS, *pp. 24-27.* Details the Russian methods of defense and offense used at Kursk. The notable feature of the defense was the carefully prepared static positions many kilometers in depth.

Galistan, A. ENGINEER ORGANISATION OF DEFENCE, *pp. 28-30.* The engineering of the Kursk defenses began in April 1943 and continued until the battle began. There were eight defensive lines to a depth of 250-300 kilometers. The main feature was the extensive use of trenches—an average of 70 kilometers per division in the front line, allowing carefully planned fire zones. Heavy use was made of mines and tank traps.

Rabovsky, L. WHERE BATTLES RAGED, *pp. 31-34.* Looks at Kursk today, noting how some of the veterans have played a part in rebuilding it as a modern industrial city. 8 photos.

Kochetkov, A. MINES VERSUS TANKS, *pp. 36-37.* Recounts the experiences of some of the combat engineers at Kursk while laying mines in action. Photo.

Kotysh, N. UNFORGETTABLE ASSAULT, *pp. 38-39.* Tells the story of one attack made by the air attack squadron of the then Captain Georgi Beregovoi during the Kursk battle. 2 photos.   D. G. Law

7

THE HOLOCAUST

757. Adam, Uwe D. AN OVERALL PLAN FOR ANTI-JEWISH LEGISLATION IN THE THIRD REICH? *Yad Vashem Studies on the European Jewish Catastrophe and Resistance [Israel] 1976 11: 33-55.* Discusses a recently discovered draft of the 1933 law concerning Jews, and its significance for the whole question of later Nazi policy towards the Jews. Disagrees with the late Israeli historian, Shaul Esh, who unearthed the document, and who argued that the document might have been a general plan for the anti-Jewish legislation in Germany, 1933-45. Based on archival and secondary sources; 66 notes, appendix.
J. P. Fox

758. Adam, Uwe Dietrich. PERSECUTION OF THE JEWS, BUREAUCRACY AND AUTHORITY IN THE TOTALITARIAN STATE. *Leo Baeck Inst. Year Book [Great Britain] 1978 23: 139-148.* One of the last anti-Jewish measures of the Nazi regime was a top secret inquiry in November 1944 into the number of *mischlinge,* descendants of Jewish grandparents and partners in mixed marriages, still in high levels of the civil service. With the government by that time in total dissarray, the whole inquiry was a wasteful blunder, illustrating the anarchic structure and total irrationality of the Hitlerite state. 4 photos, 29 notes.
F. Rosenthal

759. Alef-Bolkowiak, Gustaw and Hoffman, Zygmunt. ŻYDZE W ANTYHITLEROWSKIM RUCHU OPORU ZBROJNEGO (NIEKTÓRE PROBLEMY BADAWCZE) [Jews in the anti-Hitler armed resistance movement]. *Biuletyn Żydowskiego Instytutu Hist. w Polsce [Poland] 1978 35(3-4): 59-63.* Characterizes the objective and subjective factors influencing the engagement of Jews in the anti-Hitler armed resistance movement. The conditions of their participation in particular countries, and even regions and periods, were different. Of essential importance was the extent of the isolation of Jews from the rest of the society in each country occupied by the Nazis.
J/S

760. Arad, Yitzhak. ALFRED ROSENBERG AND THE "FINAL SOLUTION" IN THE OCCUPIED SOVIET TERRITORIES. *Yad Vashem Studies on the European Jewish Catastrophe and Resistance [Israel] 1979 13: 263-286.* Several months before Germany invaded the USSR, Alfred Rosenberg had been appointed civil administrator of the occupied Eastern territories. Based on precedents established in Poland and contiguous areas, Rosenberg issued directives for dealing with the Jewish question. He was unaware that his less drastic plan had by then been superseded by Hitler's intention to annihilate the Jews in Europe

during the war and not afterwards, as he envisioned. Heinrich Himmler was dispatched to enlighten Rosenberg on the matter and to carry out Hitler's will. Based largely on primary sources; 36 notes.   B. Reiner

761. Arad, Yitzhak. CONCENTRATION OF REFUGEES IN VILNA ON THE EVE OF THE HOLOCAUST. *Yad Vashem Studies on the European Jewish Catastrophe and Resistance [Israel] 1973 (9): 201-214.* Describes the situation, composition, and organization of the Jews in Vilna, 1939-41. Many had fled from Polish territories which had come under German and Soviet rule, and found the city to be an island of refuge. The condition of the Jews was affected by the different stages of the city's history: 1) from the outbreak of war to the city's transfer to the Lithuanians in October 1939; 2) independent Lithuanian rule in Vilna from October 1939 to mid-June 1940; and 3) Soviet Lithuania from June 1940 to the German invasion on 22 June 1941. The repressive nature of the Soviet regime proved to be the forerunner of even worse experiences under the Nazis, the German invasion putting an end to Jewish Vilna. Based on personal testimonies, archival and published sources; 50 notes.   J. P. Fox

762. Arad, Yitzhak. THE "FINAL SOLUTION" IN LITHUANIA IN THE LIGHT OF GERMAN DOCUMENTATION. *Yad Vashem Studies on the European Jewish Catastrophe and Resistance [Israel] 1976 11: 234-272.* The implementation of the final solution in Lithuania during World War II can be divided into three periods: 1) the mass extermination of Jews by the *Einsatzkommando* units and their Lithuanian collaborators from late June to November 1941; 2) the maximum exploitation of the Jewish labor force with selective and local liquidations from December 1941 to July 1943; and 3) the dissolution and liquidation of the ghettos and transfer of exclusive control over the Jews to the SS from August 1943 to July 1944. On the eve of the German retreat the survivors of Lithuanian Jewry were liquidated or deported to camps in Germany. Based on archival and published sources; 69 notes.   J. P. Fox

763. Aran, Esther. REDIFAT YEHUDEY LUV (KEFI SHEHI MISHTAKEFET BEDIVUHEY HAKONSULIYA HAGERMANIT BETRIPOLI) [The persecution of the Libyan Jews: reports of the German consulate of Tripoli]. *Yalkut Moreshet Periodical [Israel] 1982 (33): 153-156.* Several hundred Libyan Jews were sent to concentration camps in 1940. The German army entered in 1941, and foreign nationals were expelled and the Italian authorities introduced measures against the Jews in 1942. In his reports, the German consul Dr. Gebhard Walter summed up anti-Jewish legislation adopted in Libya. 2 notes.   R. Hetzron

764. Arbitol, Michael. WAITING FOR VICHY: EUROPEANS AND JEWS IN NORTH AFRICA ON THE EVE OF WORLD WAR II. *Yad Vashem Studies on the European Jewish Catastrophe and Resistance [Israel] 1981 14: 139-166.* Traditional anti-Semitism in North Africa was exacerbated in the 1930's as the result of collusion between a minority of French colonial reactionaries and a growing number of Arab nationalists who were inflamed by German-Italian propaganda. After the Vichy regime assumed power in France, North African Jews became vulnerable to agitation and harassment by the Moslem masses, since laws protecting their civil rights were quickly abrogated by the new government. Based mainly on primary sources; 2 illus., 63 notes.
                                                                                       B. Reiner

765. Arndt, Ino and Sheffler, Wolfgang. ORGANISIERTER MASSENMORD AN JUDEN IN NATIONALSOZIALISTISCHEN VERNICHTUNGSLAGERN [Organized mass murder of Jews in Nazi extermination camps]. *Vierteljahrshefte für Zeitgeschichte [West Germany] 1976 24(2): 105-135.* Seeks to examine reliable sources and discredit current apologetic literature. In 1940 six camps in East Germany developed the methods of carbon monoxide poisoning, Action T4, later used in the six concentration camps in Poland, 1941-44: Chelmno, Belzec, Sobibor, Treblinka (the three known as Operation Reinhard), Auschwitz, and Lublin-Maidanek. The state court in Düsseldorf began investigating the Maidanek case in November 1975. The lowest possible total of deaths by gas from the other five is three million. Based on war trials and secondary works; 65 notes. A. Alcock

766. Arnon, Joseph. THE PASSION OF JANUSZ KORCZAK. *Midstream 1973 19(5): 32-53.* Biographical sketch of the renowned author, doctor, and pedagogue whose departure for Treblinka with the 200 orphans in his care was a special moment in the destruction of the Warsaw Ghetto. S

767. Aronsfeld, C. C. THE EXTERMINATION OF THE JEWS WAS NO "WAR CRIME." *Contemporary Rev. [Great Britain] 1977 231(1340): 145-148.* Analyzes the extermination of the Jews, 1941-45, arguing that it must be seen in the context of Nazi policies dating back to the mid-1920's.

768. Aronsfeld, C. C. "PERISH JUDAH": NAZI EXTERMINATION PROPAGANDA 1920-1945. *Patterns of Prejudice [Great Britain] 1978 12(5): 17-26.* Illustrates the tactics of the Nazi genocide of the Jews as a carefully organized propaganda campaign via the mass media.

769. Aronsfeld, C. C. A PROPOS OF A BRITISH "HISTORICAL REVIEW": FACTS OF THE HOLOCAUST. *Patterns of Prejudice [Great Britain] 1974 8(4): 11-16.* Gives a point-by-point refutation of a recent (1974) British publication which claims that six million Jews did not die in the World War II holocaust.

770. Avital, Zvi and Wistrich, Robert S., trans. THE POLISH GOVERNMENT IN EXILE AND THE JEWISH QUESTION. *Wiener Lib. Bull. [Great Britain] 1975 28(33/34): 43-51.* Polish anti-Semitism was as strong as ever during the Holocaust. The attempts of I. Schwarzbart, Jewish representative on the National Council of the Polish government-in-exile in London during World War II, to obtain help and publicity for the plight of Polish Jewry under the Nazis and assurances regarding their status as equal citizens in a postwar Poland met with either outright refusal or evasion. Many Poles were happy at the destruction of the Warsaw ghetto (1943) and the liquidation of Polish Jewry. Based on archival and published sources; 23 notes. J. P. Fox

771. Baird, Jay W. DAS POLITISCHE TESTAMENT JULIUS STREICHERS. EIN DOKUMENT AUS DEN PAPIEREN DES HAUPTMANNS DOLIBOIS [The political testament of Julius Streicher: a document from the papers of Captain Dolibois]. *Vierteljahrshefte für Zeitgeschichte [West Germany] 1978 26(4): 660-693.* Publication and brief analysis of the political testament of Julius Streicher, Nuremberg Nazi leader and editor of the violently anti-Semitic paper *Der Stürmer,* (1885-1946). The testament was dictated by Streicher at the

detention camp Mondorf, Luxembourg, in 1945 and given to US intelligence office Captain John E. Dolibois. Steeped in vulgar anti-Semitism, the testament is a document of self-justification not only before history, but specifically against his many enemies within the Nazi movement. Based on interviews with Captain Dolibois and printed sources; 18 notes. D. Prowe

772. Bălănică, Emilia. ERNST THÄLMANN. O VIAŢA DE EROU [Ernst Thälmann: a hero's life]. *Magazin Istoric [Rumania] 1976 10(4): 28-32.* Surveys the life of this German communist especially his continuing socialist activities whilst in concentration camps, 1933-44, as documented in the Gestapo Thälmann Dossier, and reproduces an excerpt from the memoirs of Walter Trautzch, a courier between Ernst Thälmann and the German Communist Party, written in 1964.

773. Ball-Kaduri, Kurt Jakob. BERLIN WIRD JUDENFREI. DIE JUDEN IN BERLIN IN DEN JAHREN 1942/43 [Berlin will be free of Jews: the Jews in Berlin in 1942-43]. *Jahrbuch für die Geschichte Mittel- und Ostdeutschlands [West Germany] 1973 22: 196-241.* Portrays the measures taken against Jews in 1943 and the reactions of Berlin's Jewish population. Outlines the German-Jewish experience between February 1933 and 1942. 144 notes, biblio. Reprint from *Yad Vashem Studies* 1963 5. J. A. Perkins

774. Barski, Józef. LOS DZIECI GETTA WARSZAWSKIEGO [The lot of the Warsaw ghetto children]. *Biuletyn Żydowskiego Instytutu Hist. w Polsce [Poland] 1978 35(3-4): 95-105.* Depicts the tragic lot of about 100,000 children in the ghetto, as well as the help given to them by Centos. The author discusses the actions aimed at lightening the lot of orphaned, hungry, homeless, and sick children. Before the final liquidation just the Centos, headed by the author in the Warsaw ghetto, organized help for the children, 90,000 of whom were transported to the extermination camp in Treblinka between July 22 and the middle of September 1942. J/S

775. Barski, Józef. NAZI CRIMES AGAINST CHILDREN (INTERNATIONAL SCIENTIFIC CONFERENCE IN WARSAW). *Polish Western Affairs [Poland] 1980 21(1): 149-153.* Discusses the results of the International Scientific Conference held in Warsaw, 26-28 April 1979, on the subject of the child during the years of World War II. The 66 speeches delivered at the conference by Polish and foreign contributors dealt with the various forms of oppression of children by the Nazis in the occupied territories. Based on statements of Nazi leaders and such documentary studies as *Nazi Concentration Camps in Polish Territories* and *Crimes Committed on Polish Children in the Years 1939-1945.*
D. S. Lloyd

776. Barski, Józef. ZBRODNIE HITLEROWSKIE NA DZIECIACH [Nazi crimes against children]. *Biuletyn Żydowskiego Instytutu Hist. w Polsce [Poland] 1979 (142): 121-126.* Reviews the findings of a conference on children during World War II, held in Warsaw on 26-28 April 1979. Nazi war crimes included violent abuse of children in concentration camps and ghettos, pseudoscientific experiments, robbery, removal of Polish children to Germany, and exploitation through heavy labor. J/S

777. Bartel, Walter. DIE LETZTEN ZAHN TAGE DES FASCHISTISCHEN KONZENTRATIONSLAGERS BUCHENWALD [The last ten days of the fascist concentration camp at Buchenwald]. *Beiträge zur Geschichte der Arbeiterbewegung [East Germany] 1976 18(2): 301-310.* The author's recollections of prisoner resistance in the German concentration camp Buchenwald, 1-10 April 1945. The prisoners liberated themselves before the arrival of the US army on 13 April. Based on personal recollection and secondary literature; 6 notes.
R. Wagnleitner

778. Bartelski, Lesław M. PISARZE POLSCY W GETCIE WARSZAWSKIM [Polish writers in the Warsaw ghetto]. *Biuletyn Żydowskiego Instytutu Historycznego w Polsce [Poland] 1973 (86/87): 245-252.* Polish authors including Roman Catholics of Jewish origin, who were enclosed in the ghetto, also fell victim to the Nazi occupation. Among them were Rafal Bluth—contributor to the Catholic quarterly *Verbum;* Stefan Napierski (Marek Eiger), founder of the periodical *Ateneum,* Alfred Konar, and Leo Belmont. Some survived owing to help from Polish friends, but others, including Franciszka Arnsztajnowa, Gustawa Jarecka, and Henryka Łazowertówna, Jerzy Kamil, Weintraub, and Emil Breiter were killed.
J/S

779. Bartošová, Šárka. K NACISTICKÝM PLÁNŮM KONEČNÉHO ŘEŠENÍ ČESKÉ OTÁZKY [About the Nazi plans for a final solution of the Czech question]. *Slezský Sborník [Czechoslovakia] 1976 74(1): 39-47.* With the Munich Agreement (1938) and the events of March 1939 came the end of the Czech bourgeois state. During that period the Germans—from the Reich and from the Sudetenland—began to put forward suggestions about how to deal with the Czech population in Bohemia-Moravia. Ernst Kundt believed that the Czechs should see the liquidation of the Republic as the fault of their leadership and should be made to see that prosperity would be possible through full cooperation within the Reich. He also believed that the Czechs were predisposed to the struggle against the Jews. Heinlein, the leader of the Sudeten party also commissioned Kundt to press the Slovaks to demand autonomy right after Munich. In dealing with the Czechs and Slovaks his emphasis was on propagandizing, not outright Germanization of the population. This latter approach came with the arrival of Reinhard Heydrich who set out to determine which parts of the population could be assimilated and which should be exterminated. After his assassination, leadership fell into the hands of a Sudeten German, K. H. Frank, who began closing secondary schools, sent hundreds of students to concentration camps, and began to systematically liquidate the Czech intelligentsia. Seven documents are included at the end of this article from the State Archives. 12 notes.
B. Kimmel

780. Bartoszewski, Władysław. THE GHETTO RISING 1943. *Polish Perspectives [Poland] 1978 21(4): 16-25.* Summarizes the events of the resistance in the Warsaw ghetto between 1939 and 1944 and traces the final uprising of January-May 1943.

781. Batowski, Henryk. NAZI GERMANY AND JAGIELLONIAN UNIVERSITY ("SONDERAKTION KRAKAU," 1939). *Polish Western Affairs [Poland] 1978 19(1): 113-120.* On 6 November 1939, 144 faculty members of the Jagiellonian University and 20 from the Mining Academy as well as 19 students

were arrested by the Germans and on 28 November of the same year sent to the concentration camp at Sachsenhausen-Oranienburg. Some did not survive while others were eventually released after international intervention.

M. Swiecicka-Ziemianek

782. Bauer, Yehuda. GENOCIDE: WAS IT THE NAZIS' ORIGINAL PLAN? *Ann. of the Am. Acad. of Pol. and Social Sci. 1980 (450): 35-45.* Examination of developments that led to the Final Solution raises serious questions whether the Nazis did indeed plan the mass execution even before the 1930's. Nowhere is there any pronouncement of this before 1939. The plan the Nazis did have was to evict all Jews from Germany. Although several hundred thousand did leave, those left behind as well as the millions conquered provided a dilemma. Hitler wanted them out. No one wanted them. The Schacht-Rublee negotiations and the Nisko/Madagascar plans, efforts to clear Europe of Jews, had failed dismally before 1939. The last alternative was the Final Solution, which took form in 1941 with the adoption of the Einsatzgruppen and the Wannsee plan.

J/S

783. Bauer, Yehuda. TEGUVOTEIHA SHEL HAMANHIGUT HAYEHUDIT LIMDINIYUT HANATSIM [Reactions of the Jewish leadership to Nazi policies]. *Yalkut Moreshet Periodical [Israel] 1975 20: 109-125.* Not all of the Jewish leaders in the ghettos advocated passive obedience; many refused to carry out orders if by so doing they saved Jews.

784. Bauer, Yehuda. TRENDS IN HOLOCAUST RESEARCH. *Yad Vashem Studies on the European Jewish Catastrophe and Resistance [Israel] 1977 12: 7-36.* Evaluates various theories about the origins and nature of the Holocaust in the light of recent historical studies and suggests promising areas for future research. Scholars in this field now have enough documented knowledge to finally raise the right questions, even if the answers and generalizations based on this research have thus far been inadequate and tentative. Based on a 1975 lecture at Hebrew University, Jerusalem; 38 notes.

B. Reiner

785. Ben-Shemen, Reuben. MI-TOH YOMAN GHETTO WARSHA 1941 [From the Warsaw ghetto diary 1941]. *Yalkut Moreshet Periodical [Israel] 1978 (25): 25-44.* Excerpts from a diary giving details about beggars in the Warsaw ghetto, the flea market, the Jewish New Year and the Day of Atonement, and describing an execution of 11 Jews.

786. Berman, Adolf. BLOK ANTYFASZYSTOWSKI (ZE WSPOMNIEŃ) [The Anti-Fascist Bloc: reminiscences]. *Biuletyn Żydowskiego Instytutu Hist. w Polsce [Poland] 1980 (2-3): 77-98.* The author was a participant in the resistance movement in the Warsaw ghetto. Relates motives and purposes of creation of the Anti-Fascist Bloc, embracing the Jewish Fighting Organization and the Jewish National Committee. He gives a detailed genesis of these organizations, describes their activity, mentions the most important activists, and also analyzes the activity and importance of the Bloc in the Warsaw ghetto.

J

787. Bettelheim, Bruno. THE HOLOCAUST: SOME REFLECTIONS, A GENERATION LATER. *Encounter [Great Britain] 1978 51(6): 7-19.*

788. Bialostotzki, Israel. HA-TNAYIM BE-GHETTO ŁÓDZ WE-HISULO [The conditions in the Łódz ghetto and its liquidation]. *Yalkut Moreshet Periodical [Israel] 1978 (26): 99-113.* Describes the fate of the Jews of Łódz under Nazi occupation, the internal and external factors which determined the pattern of daily life in the ghetto, April 1940-June 1944. The author also provides chronological account of the liquidation of the Łódz ghetto by the Nazis, June-August 1944.

789. Blomstedt, Yrjö. JUUTALAISPAKOLAISTEN LUOVUTTAMINEN 1942 [The expulsion of the Jewish refugees in 1942]. *Hist. Aikakauskirja [Finland] 1980 78(2): 142-146.* The expulsion to Nazi German jurisdiction of eight Jewish refugees by the Finnish government in 1942 was a single incident and not part of a Jewish extermination plan in Finland as suggested by Elina Suominen in her book *Kuolemanlaiva s/s Hohenhörn: juutalaispakolaisten kohtalo Suomessa* [Death ship S.S. *Hohenhörn:* the fate of Jewish refugees in Finland] (Porvoo, 1979). 7 notes. R. G. Selleck

790. Bolewski, Andrzej. MUZYKA POLSKA W OBOZIE KONCENTRACYJNYM W SACHSENHAUSEN [Polish music in the concentration camp of Sachsenhausen]. *Kultura i Społeczeństwo [Poland] 1975 19(2-3): 33-41.* Some 183 Polish professors were arrested by the Germans on 6 November 1939 in Cracow and taken to the concentration camp in Sachsenhausen; J. Gwiazdomorski and S. Urbańczyk wrote about their fate. The survivors owe great gratitude to Józef Klonowski who at the initiative of the Alliance of Poles in Germany brought Polish songs, carols, and music to the concentration camp. At the risk of his own life he gave strength and courage to the Polish prisoners to fight the enemy. M. A. J. Swiecicka

791. BonGherardi, Silva. UN CAMPO DI STERMINIO IN ITALIA [An extermination camp in Italy]. *Ponte [Italy] 1978 34(11-12): 1440-1453.* Examines the establishment of the Nazi extermination camp, La Risiera di San Sabba in Trieste, as part of German strategy in the Adriatic and as a manifestation of the official anti-Semitism of the Italian Social Republic, 1943-45.

792. Boozer, Jack S. CHILDREN OF HIPPOCRATES: DOCTORS IN NAZI GERMANY. *Ann. of the Am. Acad. of Pol. and Social Sci. 1980 (450): 83-97.* Examines the conduct of the doctors during the Nazi years. A brief survey of what the medical case and the Auschwitz trial revealed about the conduct of the doctors raises the question of the status and effectiveness of a professional standard like the Hippocratic oath against the power of the state. This, in turn, raises the question about the basis of the rights of man. Appeals are made for the nurture of care about human rights among international professional groups, as well as among individuals and voluntary citizen groups. Finally, a claim is made for specific kinds of social and political responsibilities of doctors in modern society. J/S

793. Boyens, Armin F. C. THE ECUMENICAL COMMUNITY AND THE HOLOCAUST. *Ann. of the Am. Acad. of Pol. and Social Sci. 1980 (450): 140-152.* The ecumenical fellowship of the churches became manifest in a special way in the work of the World Council of Churches (WCC) for all the persecuted in occupied Europe. In almost all of the churches there were minorities who tried

to help the refugees. Cooperation between Protestant member churches of the WCC and the Roman Catholic Church developed on the regional level and led to Christian-Jewish cooperation on the national and the international level. To rescue Jewish people, Christians had to act illegally. The cooperation of the WCC churches was not born out of an abstract theology of revolution, but out of the daily practice of Christian love of one's fellowman. Finally, the persecution of the Jews stimulated among Christians a theological reexamination of the role of the people of Israel, of God's revelation, and of the nature of the Church itself.

J/S

794. Braatz, Werner E. THE VÖLKISCH IDEOLOGY AND ANTI-SEMITISM IN GERMANY. *Yivo Annual of Jewish Social Sci. 1974 15: 166-187.* The believers of the "Völkisch" ideology, characterized by myths about the tribal past, desire for soil and blood, and anti-Semitism, blamed the Jews as being corruptors of the "Volk." Such people as Lagarde and von Treitschke contributed to the "Völkisch" ideology and the Nazis exploited it. 80 notes.

R. J. Wechman

795. Braham, Randolph L. THE KAMENETS PODOLSK AND DÉL-VIDÉK MASSACRES: PRELUDE TO THE HOLOCAUST IN HUNGARY. *Yad Vashem Studies on the European Jewish Catastrophe and Resistance [Israel] 1973 (9): 133-156.* Describes the background and consequences of two massacres: 1) in August 1941 at Kamenets Podolsk in territory acquired from Soviet Russia, of Jews expelled from Hungary, upon the authority of the KEOKH (National Central Alien Control Office); and 2) in the Délvidék, the Hungarian-occupied part of Yugoslavia, during January 1942, of Serbs and Jews identified as "partisans." Concludes that although the Jews of Hungary continued to enjoy the protection of the Hungarian government until the German occupation in March 1944, the two massacres were a prelude to the catastrophe that befell Hungarian Jewry in 1944. Based on published sources; 70 notes.

J. P. Fox

796. Braham, Randolph L. THE ROLE OF THE JEWISH COUNCIL IN HUNGARY: A TENTATIVE ASSESSMENT. *Yad Vashem Studies on the European Jewish Catastrophe and Resistance [Israel] 1974 10: 69-109.* Analyzes the personalities and policies of the leadership of the Jewish Council in Hungary formed by the Germans when they occupied the country in March 1944. This marked the beginning of the process leading to the annihilation of Hungarian Jewry, for the council members lulled the Jewish masses into a false sense of security and issued the orders of the Germans. Against their will and intentions, they had become one of the major instruments through which the Nazis carried out their evil designs. Based on archival and published sources; 108 notes.

J. P. Fox

797. Brenner, Hans. ZUR FRAGE DER AUSBEUTUNG VON K-Z HÄFTLINGEN DURCH DEN OSRAM-KONZERN 1944-45 [The exploitation of concentration camp prisoners by the Osram concern, 1944-45]. *Zeitschrift für Geschichtswissenschaft [East Germany] 1979 27(10): 952-965.* The armaments firm Osram GmbH maintained close contacts with the SS (Schutzstaffel) in order to obtain forced labor from the concentration camps. Newly discovered documents illuminate the firm's use of prisoners in its factory in Plaven. Osram directors were unconcerned about the lives of these workers. They were also well

informed about the central role of Auschwitz in the forced labor system. These documents also disclose the locations of Osram production facilities in other areas of Europe. Based on Berlin and Dresden city archives; 22 notes, 8 documents.

J. T. Walker

798. Broide, Frania. BABUNKER BEAZOR GRODNA [In a bunker in the Grodno area]. *Yalkut Moreshet Periodical [Israel] 1979 (27): 61-76.* Discusses experiences of a mother in the Grodno ghetto in Poland during the Nazi occupation, having to give up her daughter and to hide in a bunker in a nearby village for almost two years.

799. Bronsen, David. CHILD OF THE HOLOCAUST. *Midstream 1981 27(4): 50-56.* Reviews *The Journal of Andrew Bihaly,* edited by Anthony Tuttle (1973), the diary of a young Jew who survived the holocaust, which centers on the year 1944, the year the Nazis rounded up 760,000 Hungarian Jews for extermination.

800. Broszat, Martin. HITLER AND THE GENESIS OF THE "FINAL SOLUTION": AN ASSESSMENT OF DAVID IRVING'S THESES. *Yad Vashem Studies on the European Jewish Catastrophe and Resistance [Israel] 1979 13: 73-126.* Assesses the controversial theses propounded in David Irving's *Hitler's War* (London, 1977). Irving attempted to "normalize" Hitler based on new evidence about the National Socialist period. His revisionist interpretations of these sources are critically analyzed and rejected on the grounds that they appear to be strongly biased. His main thesis that it was Hitler's immediate subordinates who were primarily responsible for originating domestic policy, including that of extermination of Jews and others deemed social undesirables, is shown to be erroneous. 73 notes.

B. Reiner

801. Broszat, Martin. HITLER UND DIE GENESIS DER "ENDLÖSUNG." AUS ANLASS DER THESEN VON DAVID IRVING [Hitler and the genesis of the Final Solution: on the theses of David Irving]. *Vierteljahrshefte für Zeitgeschichte [West Germany] 1977 25(4): 739-775.* An extensive rebuttal to British historian David Irving's *Hitler's War* (London, 1977), whose controversial thesis that the absence of an extant written extermination order by Adolf Hitler suggests that the final solution was carried out without Hitler's consent or knowledge. Broszat argues that Irving, fascinated by Hitler as war lord, failed to understand Hitler's genocidal view of war and his methods of total control which included a preference for oral commands to trusted lieutenants, here Heinrich Himmler. 73 notes.

D. Prowe

802. Broszat, Martin. ON THE WHITEWASHERS OF NAZI CRIME. *Patterns of Prejudice [Great Britain] 1976 10(5): 11-14.* Examines attempts by some right-wing historians to cover up or cast doubt on the extermination of Jews in Poland, 1941-42.

803. Browning, Christopher R. REFERAT DEUTSCHLAND, JEWISH POLICY AND THE GERMAN FOREIGN OFFICE (1933-1940). *Yad Vashem Studies on the European Jewish Catastrophe and Resistance [Israel] 1977 12: 37-74.* After the Nazi coup d'état in 1933, the German Foreign Office reactivated the Referat Deutschland as an agency for Jewish affairs. For seven years it tried to shape a coherent Jewish policy, taking into account its effect on

domestic economics and with special consideration of foreign ramifications. Due to inept leadership and its weak position in comparison to other governmental agencies, the Referat Deutschland was relatively unsuccessful in getting its recommendations adopted. Still, its history reveals much about the rivalries and machinations of the Nazi bureaucracy that evolved to deal with the complex Jewish question. 98 notes. B. Reiner

804. Büchler, Joshua. BLOK YELADIM 66 BE-MAHANE HA-RIKUZ BUCHENWALD [The Children's Block 66 in Buchenwald concentration camp]. *Yalkut Moreshet Periodical [Israel] 1978 (25): 45-60.* An eye-witness account of daily life in the children's block of Buchenwald concentration camp in 1945, in the last three months before its liberation.

805. Burstin, Barbara Stern. THE WARSAW GHETTO: A SHATTERED WINDOW ON THE HOLOCAUST. *Hist. Teacher 1980 13(4): 531-541.* From 19 April to 16 May 1943, German troops in Warsaw methodically destroyed the Jewish community of that city. Surveys the novels, diaries, personal memoirs, official government documents, and films of the Warsaw ghetto. Secondary sources; 23 notes. S. H. Frank

806. Busse, Otto. MIHAMA BAMASHHIT—BIALYSTOK 1943 [Fighting the destroyers: Białystok 1943]. *Yalkut Moreshet Periodical [Israel] 1979 (28): 127-130.* Recollections of a German who employed Jews from Białystok ghetto in his painting enterprise and later rescued Jews and assisted the resistance fighters.

807. Cain, Seymour. COMMEMORATING THE HOLOCAUST. *Midstream 1980 26(4): 23-25.* Introduction to a series of memoirs and diaries of Jews who were victims of the concentration camps in World War II.

808. Cappelletti, Vincenzo; Fonzi, Fausto; Monticone, Alberto; and Melodia, Giovanni. IL TEMPO DEL LAGER [The time of the Lager]. *Studium [Italy] 1979 75(6): 769-782.* Four speakers reflect on the Nazi extermination camps at the round table held at the Instituto dell'Enciclopedia Italiana in June 1979 on the occasion of the publication of *Il Nazismo e i Lager* by Vittorio E. Giuntella.

809. Cargas, Harry James. HOLOCAUST PHOTOGRAPHY. *Centerpoint 1980 4(1): 141-150.* Many of the photographs taken of the Holocaust and its victims were the products of soldiers and civilians throughout Europe who refused to accept personal responsibility for ameliorating the conditions in front of their cameras.

810. Chadwick, Owen. WEIZSÄCKER, THE VATICAN, AND THE JEWS OF ROME. *J. of Ecclesiastical Hist. [Great Britain] 1977 28(2): 179-199.* The *Actes et Documents du Saint Siège relatifs à la seconde guerre mondiale*, vol. 9: *Le Saint Siège et les victimes de la guerre, janvier-décembre 1943* (Vatican City, 1975), edited by Pierre Blet et al., is the basis for a review article on Baron Ernst von Weizsäcker's embassy to the Vatican and on his exchanges with the Vatican about the SS threat to deport 8,000 Jews from Rome. When it seemed possible that the Pope would formally protest, Weizsäcker promised to do what he could. He reported to Berlin that the papacy had leaned over backwards in order not to make difficulties for the Germans, which has led some to view the Pope as weak

and insensitive, though one result was that the deportations were discontinued after the first trainload, and the church authorities were able to shelter Jews in some 155 religious houses. Based on the *Actes* and other published and unpublished primary sources. P. H. Hardacre

811. Clinton, Mark. THE MYSTICISM OF MASS MURDER: ETHICAL AND POLITICAL ISSUES IN THE AUTOBIOGRAPHY OF RUDOLF HOESS. *Centerpoint 1980 4(1): 60-69.* Probes the innate contradictions in the autobiography of the commandant of the Auschwitz death camp.

812. Conway, John S. FRÜHE AUGENZEUGENBERICHTE AUS AUSCHWITZ: GLAUBWÜRDIGKEIT UND WIRKUNGSGESCHICHTE [Early eyewitness reports from Auschwitz: credibility and the history of their impact]. *Vierteljahrshefte für Zeitgeschichte [West Germany] 1979 27(2): 260-284.* In reaction to recent sensationalist books by A. R. Butz *(The Hoax of the Twentieth Century,* 1976) and David Irving *(Hitler's War,* 1977), the author reaffirms the credibility of the first key eyewitness reports on Auschwitz and traces their history from the Auschwitz escape of Rudolf Vrba and Alfred Wetzlar in April 1944 to the report's role in breaking through the wall of silence in 1944-45 and the publication of Vrba's book *(I Cannot Forgive,* 1963). Based on interviews with Vrba, Nuremberg Trial Documents, and key Holocaust publications; 46 notes. D. Prowe

813. Conway, John S. THE HOLOCAUST AND THE HISTORIANS. *Ann. of the Am. Acad. of Pol. and Social Sci. 1980 (450): 153-164.* The impact of the Holocaust has been interpreted by historians largely according to the present needs of their audiences. Jewish historians, both in Israel and outside, see these events as the culminating tragedy of their people before the rebirth in statehood. German historians are more concerned with the attempt to overcome their knowledge of guilt and therefore concentrate, not so much on Jewish sufferings, as on Nazi rule. Christians have sought to eradicate the long tradition of Christian prejudice against Jews, which some see as culminating in the Holocaust. Historians of Nazism are divided into rival schools and have yet to reach firm conclusions on such topics as the genesis of the Final Solution. The impact of ideology in governmental policies and the weakness of the traditional barriers to the corruption of absolute power need to be reexamined in the light of the Holocaust experience. J/S

814. Conway, John S. THE LAST LETTERS OF THE BRANDT-MEYER FAMILY FROM BERLIN. *Yad Vashem Studies on the European Jewish Catastrophe and Resistance [Israel] 1976 11: 91-130.* Though the impact of the Nazi measures on the German Jews is well known, there are still gaps as to how the persecution was seen by those directly affected. This gap can be partly filled by the correspondence (reproduced in the appendix) concerning the case of the Brandt-Meyer family and their attempts to leave Germany during World War II. Based on archival, published, and private sources; 7 notes, appendix.

J. P. Fox

815. Cortey, Maria-Dolors. MAUTHAUSEN: UNA EXPERIÈNCIA INOBLIDABLE [Mauthausen: an unforgettable experience]. *Xaloc [Mexico] 1977 (90): 58-61.* Describes the author's visit to the Austrian concentration camp of

Mauthausen, which housed 335,000 prisoners, 1939-45, 7,000 of whom were Spaniards.

816. Cutter, William. LITERATURE AND THE HOLOCAUST: A REVIEW ESSAY. *Modern Judaism 1982 2(2): 213-220.* Reviews *Confronting the Holocaust: The Impact of Elie Wiesel,* edited by Alvin Rosenfeld and Irving Greenberg (1978), and Rosenfeld's *A Double Dying: Reflections on Holocaust Literature* (1980), which deal with the difficulties of confronting the Holocaust through literature and criticism without trivializing it.

817. Dańkowski, Jan. "MARSZ ŚMIERCI" WIĘŹNIÓW OŚWIĘCIMSKICH W POWIECIE NYSKIM W STYCZ-NIU I W LUTYM 1945 R [Death March of Oswięcim (Auschwitz): prisoners in the Nysa district in January and February 1945]. *Biuletyn Żydowskiego Instytutu Hist. w Polsce [Poland] 1978 (3-4): 163-181.* When the winter offensive of the Soviet Army was launched in January 1945, the Hitlerite authorities began evacuation of concentration camps and extermination camps. Over 64,000 prisoners of the main camp at Auschwitz were formed into marching columns. The same was done in other Auschwitz subcamps. The columns marched through towns and villages of the Nysa district. Exhausted through camp experiences, hunger and diseases, prisoners died or were killed by escorts. Among the participants of the march and its victims were many Jews. In Nysa at least 408 prisoners perished, determination of the exact number of them being now impossible. Based on documents from 15 Nysa district localities; 2 tables, 56 notes. J

818. Datner, Szymon. DWA DOKUMENTY [Two documents]. *Biuletyn Żydowskiego Instytutu Hist. w Polsce [Poland] 1980 (2-3): 129-134.* One document published here concerns the distinguished military service medals honoring several heroic leaders of the uprising in the Warsaw ghetto, foremost among them Mordechaj Anielewicz. The other is the detailed biography of one of the heroes of the Białystok ghetto, Edek Boraks, written by his sister, Franka Kloc, in 1946.
J

819. Datner, Szymon. OPINIA BIEGŁEGO W PROCESIE SZEFA REFERATU ŻYDOWSKIEGO W BIAŁOSTOCKIM GESTAPO (1942-1944), FRITZA GUSTAWA FRIEDLA [Opinion of an expert at the trial of Obersturmführer SS Fritz Gustav Friedel, chief of the Jewish department in Białystok Gestapo, 1942-44]. *Biuletyn Żydowskiego Instytutu Hist. w Polsce [Poland] 1976 (3): 41-58.* In October 1949 an action was taken before the Court of Appeal at Białystok against the former chief of the Jewish department in Białystok, F. G. Friedel. Doctor Szymon Datner, then a senior scientific worker of the Jewish Historical Institute in Warsaw, delivered an expert's report, describing the character of the accused and his role in the extermination of about 130,000 Jews who lived in Białystok in two successive actions in February and August 1943. The expert described the exceptional sadism of the accused against a background of the theory and practice of Nazism. Publishes an abbreviated version of Datner's report. J/S

820. Datner, Szymon. POWSTANIE W GETCIE WARSZAWSKIM [The uprising in the Warsaw ghetto]. *Biuletyn Żydowskiego Instytutu Hist. w Polsce [Poland] 1978 35(3-4): 7-16.*

821. Datner, Szymon. SONDERKOMMANDO 1005 I JEGO DZIAŁALNOŚĆ ZE SZCZEGÓLNYM UWZGLĘDNIENIEM OKRĘGU BIAŁOSTOCKIEGO [Sonderkommando 1005 and its activity, particularly in the Białystok region]. *Biuletyn Żydowskiego Instytutu Hist. w Polsce [Poland] 1976 (4): 63-78.* Sonderkommando 1005 was a Nazi cryptonym for a special staff within the framework of the Reich Central Security Office (RSHA) which was entrusted with effacing the traces of crimes perpetrated on millions of Jews, Poles, Russians, Yugoslavs, Gypsies, and other nationals from occupied Europe. This whole action, directed by SS officer Paul Blobel, was top secret. Blobel gave instructions to both extermination camps and mobile Kommandos 1005, whose task was destruction of corpses at hundreds of places of execution scattered all over the occupied areas of the USSR and Poland. Blobel had to solve two basic problems: providing labor for the exhumation and destruction of millions of corpses as well as finding methods of destruction that would leave no trace. The author exemplifies Blobel's operations at six extermination camps in Poland, Auschwitz-Birkenau, Bełżec, Chełmno, Majdanek, Sobibór, and Treblinka and of the mobile Kommandos 1005 in the Białystok Region. J/S

822. Datner, Szymon. UDZIAŁ POLSKICH JEŃCÓW WOJENNYCH W RATOWANIU ŻYDÓW W OKRESIE II WOJNY ŚWIATOWEJ [Participation of Polish prisoners of war in saving Jews during World War II]. *Biuletyn Żydowskiego Instytutu Hist. w Polsce [Poland] 1978 35(3-4): 73-86.* Jewish officers of the Polish Army constituted a loose group estimated at about 300 persons, scattered over the Polish officers' prisoner-of-war camps at Woldenberg, Doessel and Murnau. That was just a small part of a considerable group of Polish common soldier Jewish prisoners of war. In the first weeks of 1940 over 60,000 Jewish common soldiers were released by Germans from captivity and sent home to meet death in the ghettos. However, the group of officers remained in the camps and survived the war. Based on a work written by Rafał Loc, a former prisoner of war, and Second Lieutenant of the Polish Army; 35 notes. J/S

823. Datner, Szymon. ŻYDOWSKI RUCH OPORU WE SWCHODNIEJ EUROPIE W CZASIE OKUPACJI HITLEROWSKIEJ (O PRACY R. AINSZTEINA) [Jewish Resistance to the Nazi occupation in Eastern Europe (the work of R. Ainsztein)]. *Biuletyn Żydowskiego Inst. Hist. w Polsce [Poland] 1976 (2): 53-74.* Reuben Ainsztein's *Jewish Resistance in Nazi-Occupied Eastern Europe* (London, 1974) constitutes an important contribution to the study of the Jewish Resistance in the USSR and Poland. Ainsztein emphasizes the positive role of outstanding Soviet partisan commanders in the process of absorption of considerable numbers of Jews in the total partisan movement, and in the protection of those who were unfit for armed service in the so-called "family camps." The morale of Jewish partisans fighting in Soviet and Polish detachments is estimated positively. 32 notes. J/S

824. Dauzenroth, Erich. ZUM SCHICKSAL JANUSZ KORCZAKS UND SEINER KINDER [On the fate of Janusz Korczak and his children]. *Frankfurter Hefte [West Germany] 1972 27(8): 587-592.* Tells the story of Janusz Korczak, educator and director of an orphanage in the Warsaw Ghetto, who tried unsuccessfully to save his children from deportation to the Treblinka gas chambers in 1942. When he failed, he chose to die with them, though the Nazi authorities were willing to let him stay safe in Warsaw.

825. Delmaire, Danielle and Hilaire, Yves-Marie. CHRÉTIENS ET JUIFS DANS LE NORD—PAS-DE-CALAIS PENDANT LA SECONDE GUERRE MONDIALE [Christians and Jews in the Nord and the Pas-de-Calais during World War II]. *Rev. du Nord [France] 1978 60(237): 451-455.* Analyzes the situation of the Jews and their relations with Christians in the Nord and Pas-de-Calais departments during the German military occupation of France, 1940-44. The pope's stand against Hitler's and Mussolini's anti-Semitism in 1938-39 had rallied most of the regional press and an important part of Christian opinion. During the occupation, in spite of a few Christians influenced by Nazi propaganda who helped the Gestapo or denounced Jews to them, most Christians gave the Jews assistance and comfort, especially during the September 1942 "great persecution." Based on archival material, press clippings, and the oral and written statements of witnesses; 20 notes. G. P. Cleyet

826. Demps, Laurenz. DIE AUSBEUTUNG VON KZ-HÄFTLINGEN DURCH DEN OSRAM-KONZERN 1944/45 [The exploitation of concentration camp internees by the Osram factory in 1944-45]. *Zeitschrift für Geschichtswissenschaft [East Germany] 1978 26(5): 416-437.* The Allied bombing of Germany in 1944 made it necessary for factories to move from urban centers. Thereafter their greatest need was for labor, which was willingly supplied by concentration camps. Industry was not forced to accept internees, but actively colluded with the Nazis in the recruitment of such labor. In 1944 there were 165 work-camps. One camp, Richard II, had the highest death-rate among such work camps, and Osram received much of its labor from this camp. The purpose of these camps was to silence Nazi opponents and to provide cheap labor. Based on 15 documents relating to the camps; 36 notes. A. Alcock

827. Dimsdale, Joel E. THE COPING BEHAVIOR OF NAZI CONCENTRATION CAMP SURVIVORS. Dimsdale, Joel E., ed. *Survivors, Victims, and Perpetrators: Essays on the Nazi Holocaust* (Washington: Hemisphere Publ., 1980): 163-174. Identifies and describes the several strategies used by prisoners in the World War II concentration camps to meet and overcome the extraordinary stress of imprisonment. Reprinted from the *American Journal of Psychiatry* 1974 131(7): 792-797.

828. Dossa, Shiraz. HUMAN STATUS AND POLITICS: HANNAH ARENDT ON THE HOLOCAUST. *Can. J. of Pol. Sci. [Canada] 1980 13(2): 309-323.* In Hannah Arendt's *The Origins of Totalitarianism* (New York: Meridien, 1958), *The Human Condition* (New York: Doubleday Anchor, 1959), and *Eichmann in Jerusalem* (New York: Viking Pr., 1965) there is an opinion that "civilized" peoples (Europeans, Jews, Chinese, etc.) belong to an order of humanity lifted above the natural or organic *animal laborans* (e.g., Negroes and other peoples without "civilization" or "culture"). Violence against the latter may be politically unjust, but it is not immoral according to the ethnocentric view; nevertheless, the Holocaust of World War II was a unique crime. 65 notes.
S

829. Drozdowski, Marian Marek. POLONIA A POWSTANIE W GETCIE WARSZAWSKIM [Polish emigrants and the uprising in the Warsaw ghetto]. *Biuletyn Żydowskiego Instytutu Hist. w Polsce [Poland] 1978 35(3-4): 27-48.* Polish emigrants in general reacted intensely to the drama of Polish Jews and the

fighting in the Warsaw ghetto. Particularly sensitive were the communist, socialist, and liberal-democratic groups which were engaged before the war in the fight against anti-semitism. Many groups of conservative Polish emigrants, influenced by the war, gradually modified their views on the Jewish problem, departing from the historic prejudices and stereotypes; the strongest responses were elicited among Polish emigrants residing in Great Britain, the Soviet Union, the Near East, and France. The reaction was weaker among the North Americans of Polish origin. 48 notes. J/S

830. Dulnik, Shlomo. KOROTEIHA SHEL KEHILA YEHUDIT BEBRITHAMO'ATSOT [A Jewish community in the USSR]. *Yalkut Moreshet Periodical [Israel] 1976 21: 89-100.* The town of Rudnya near Smolensk had a majority of Jewish residents before the Bolshevik Revolution; the Nazis killed almost all its Jews and only in 1965 were their remains made safe from desecration.

831. Dunin-Wąsowicz, Krzysztof. DZIAŁACZE I GRUPY POLSKIEGO RUCHU ROBOTNICZEGO W HITLEROWSKICH OBOZACH KONCENTRACYJNYCH [The activists and groups of the Polish workers' movement in Nazi concentration camps]. *Z Pola Walki [Poland] 1979 22(1): 53-79.* Describes various kinds of resistance movements in concentration camps. Beyond the struggle for biological survival and the mutual aid activities of various types, there was a struggle for the preservation of human dignity, the organization of cultural, religious, and political life. Finally, there was activity directly destructive for the Third Reich, sabotage, escapes, assassinations, intelligence activities, documentation of Nazi crimes, and military organizations in camps. Describes the contribution of Polish worker activists to all forms of resistance. J/S

832. Dunin-Wąsowicz, Krzysztof. POLSKI RUCH SOCJALISTYCZNY WOBEC PROBLEMÓW GETTA WARSZAWSKIEGO [The attitude of the Polish socialist movement toward the problems of the Warsaw ghetto]. *Biuletyn Żydowskiego Instytutu Hist. w Polsce [Poland] 1978 35(3-4): 17-26.* Examines the traditions of cooperation between the Polish and the Jewish socialist movements. J

833. Dvorjetsky, M. "YEVEN METSULAH": YOMAN GETO-VILNA ME-ET HA-MOREH MOSHE ULITSKI [*Yeven Metsulah:* A Vilnius ghetto diary by the teacher Moshe Ulitski]. *Koroth [Israel] 1974 6(7-8): 427-433.* Describes contents of a small Yiddish diary kept by a school teacher in the Vilnius ghetto, 1941-42, recording the Jews' daily struggle for survival and human dignity.

834. Dzik, Leon. KOAH HA-AVODA HA-YEHUDI KE-GOREM BEMEDINIUT HA-HASHMADA HA-NAZIT [Jewish manpower as a factor in the extermination policy of the Nazis]. *Yalkut Moreshet Periodical [Israel] 1978 (25): 101-115.* Argues that the extermination policy of Nazi Germany was the result of long-term economic planning which had required that the state rid itself of surplus population after 1941, when Jewish slave labor was no longer useful.

835. Eisenbach, Artur. O NALEŻYTE ZROZUMIENIE GENEZY ZAGŁADY ŻYDÓW [Regarding proper understanding of the genesis of the extermination of Jews]. *Biuletyn Żydowskiego Instytutu Hist. w Polsce [Poland] 1977 (4): 55-69.* Disputes J. Leszczynski's supposition about the exceptional role of R.

H. Höppner in the extermination of the Jews of the Warthegau. The author attributes the misinterpretation to an incorrect reading of a German document.
J/S

836. Eisner, Joseph. YERMEI EIRMA BELWOW 1941-1944. [Days of horror in Lvov, 1941-44]. *Yalkut Moreshet Periodical [Israel] 1979 (28): 163-184.* The author, by concealing his Jewish identity, managed to survive the holocaust. Describes his experiences in Lvov under the Nazi occupation.

837. Eisner, Józef. WSPOMNIENIA Z LAT 1941-1944 [Reminiscences, 1941-44]. *Biuletyn Żydowskiego Instytutu Hist. w Polsce [Poland] 1980 (2-3): 55-76.* The author was a physics teacher at a Lvov grammar school and in 1939-41 assistant professor at the Lvov Pedagogical Institute. Eisner lost all his family in the occupation; he himself was saved by his former pupils. Describes the outbreak of the German-Soviet war and the period of occupation. Gives a dramatic picture of his hiding, and finally of the arrival of the Soviet Army.
J/S

838. Elgazi, Joseph. TIHUR HASHEREZ BEK'N TEAAMIM, O: HASIBRUT HAMAKHHISHA ET HASHOAAH [Finding excuses for wrongdoing, or: the literature which denies the Holocaust]. *Yalkut Moreshet Periodical [Israel] 1979 (28): 95-106.* Discusses the main arguments of the increasing literature that aims at denying the Holocaust, and at the purification of Nazism.

839. Eliav, Binyamin. THE HOLOCAUST IN THE "ENCYCLOPAEDIA JUDAICA". *Yad Vashem Studies on the European Jewish Catastrophe and Resistance [Israel] 1973 (9): 247-253.* Indicates the main subjects covered in the division for the History of the Holocaust in the *Encyclopaedia Judaica.* Explains that although the Holocaust period was a very short one, the editorial board of the *Encyclopaedia Judaica* decided that there was no doubt that it must take a central place in the encyclopedia. Suggests that the three main features distinguishing the new account of the Holocaust in the encyclopedia are the widening of the basis of research and bringing it up to date, the Jewish approach, and the wealth of geographical detail describing even the smallest Jewish community in Europe before its destruction. Also describes the work being undertaken on the Holocaust in the encyclopedia's Hebrew-language "Library." J. P. Fox

840. Epstein, David. HAYEHUDI HAYEHIDI (HA'AYARAH LIBISHEI BASHOAH) [The only Jew: the town of Lyubeshov in the Holocaust]. *Yalkut Moreshet Periodical [Israel] 1975 20: 7-34.* A personal account by David Epstein (1900-67) of the Nazi liquidation in August 1942 of the Jewish population of Lyubeshov, in the Ukraine, near Pinsk, and his experiences with the partisans, 1942-44.

841. Erez, Zui, ed. EDUIOT SARA BIKEL UBITA HANA ROSENSTEIN: BRINAH MITHANAT HARAKEVET SHEL AUSCHWITZ [The testimonies of Sara Bikel and her daughter Hana Rosenstein: the escape from the Auschwitz railway station]. *Yalkut Moreshet Periodical [Israel] 1980 (29): 127-133.* Sara Bikel and her daughter Hana Rosenstein escaped from Auschwitz and, after a most dangerous journey, arrived safely in Žilina, Slovakia.

842. Erez, Zvi. SHISHAH YAMIM BEYULI 1944 BEHUNGARIAH [Six days in July 1944 in Hungary]. *Yalkut Moreshet Periodical [Israel] 1975 20: 149-168.* The only attempt by an Axis power to prevent the deportation of Jews was made by Miklós Horthy (1868-1957), in Budapest in 1944.

843. Ericksen, Robert P. THEOLOGIAN IN THE THIRD REICH: THE CASE OF GERHARD KITTEL. *J. of Contemporary Hist. [Great Britain] 1977 12(3): 595-622.* Gerhard Kittel (1888-1948), well-known New Testament scholar of the University of Tübingen, joined the Nazi Party in May 1933 and became a charter member of the Reich's Institute for the History of the New Germany, begun by Walter Frank to research the Jewish question. Kittel rejected extermination, assimilation, and Zionism as solutions and proposed instead *Gastzustand*, or foreigner status, making Jews (and their Christian spouses) legally foreigners. Imprisoned by the French military government in 1945, Kittel spent his last three years trying to justify and rehabilitate himself. Based on primary sources; 94 notes. M. P. Trauth

844. Fackenheim, Emil. THE SPECTRUM OF RESISTANCE DURING THE HOLOCAUST: AN ESSAY IN DESCRIPTION AND DEFINITION. *Modern Judaism 1982 2(2): 113-130.* Describes the Nazi assault on the Jewish people, and attempts a definition of "resistance," analyzing acts of resistance that occurred.

845. Fass, Moshe. THEATRICAL ACTIVITIES IN THE POLISH GHETTOS DURING THE YEARS 1939-1942. *Jewish Social Studies 1976 38(1): 54-72.* Theatrical activities in Polish ghettos can be divided into two periods—the first lasting about a year following the German takeover of Poland, and the second until the dissolution of the ghettos. In the first period theatrical performances conducted by members of the Jewish acting community, self-help organizations, and newcomers sprang up in newly established cafes and nightclubs. Performances dealt with the Jewish heritage. This short period witnessed a revival of the legitimate theater. In the second period the Judenrats made efforts to dominate theatrical activity, including the imposition of censorship, with varying success in different ghettos. German authorities never devised a systematic overall policy regarding Jewish theatrical activities other than to encourage lowbrow productions designed to demoralize the population. Appendixes. N. Lederer

846. Fiszman, Felicja. RELACJE, WSPOMNIENIA I PAMIĘTNIKI O POWSTANIU W GETCIE WARSZAWSKIM W ARCHIWALIACH ŻYDOWSKIEGO INSTYTUTU HISTORYCZNEGO [Accounts, reminiscences, and diaries about the Warsaw ghetto uprising in the archives of the Jewish Historical Institute in Poland]. *Biuletyn Żydowskiego Instytutu Historycznego w Polsce [Poland] 1973 2/3(86/87): 227-229.* The Archives of the Jewish Historical Institute contain about 7,000 accounts concerning the martyrology of Jews. Among them about 100 accounts directly or indirectly concern the uprising in the Warsaw ghetto. There are 240 diaries, 30 of which are devoted to the uprising. These materials are mostly in Polish and Yiddish, only a few in Hebrew. Some were published in the *Bulletin,* in *Bleter far Geszichte,* or in book form. J

847. Fleming, Gerald. DIE HERKUNFT DES "BERNADOTTE-BRIEFS" AN HIMMLER VOM 10. MÄRZ 1945 [The source of the Bernadotte Letter to Himmler of 10 March 1945]. *Vierteljahrshefte für Zeitgeschichte [West Germany] 1978 26(4): 571-600.* An analysis of the probable source of an anti-Semitic letter of March 1945 alleged to be from the Swedish Red Cross representative Count Folke Bernadotte asking Nazi leader Heinrich Himmler not to release Jewish, French, Dutch and Belgian prisoners for transport to Sweden. Evidence suggests that Felix Kersten, Himmler's doctor and a key agent in the Swedish operation to save prisoners, fabricated the letter to revenge Bernadotte's callous postwar suppression of his efforts. Based on records in British, German, and Swedish archives, memoirs, personal testimonies, and document analysis; 89 notes, appendix with semantic analysis. D. Prowe

848. Flender, Harold. "I AM TRYING TO UNDERSTAND IT." *Present Tense 1973 1(1): 45-49.* Interview with Raul Hilberg about Nazi destruction of European Jewry. S

849. Freundlich, Elisabeth. MASSAKER IN STANISLAU, 1941 [Massacre in Stanislau, 1941]. *Jahrbuch des Instituts für Deutsche Geschichte [Israel] 1975 4: 423-455.* Action in Stanislau (Stanisławów, East Galicia, Poland, now Ivano-Frankovsk, USSR) a German effort to eradicate the Jewish intelligentsia as part of the "final solution" to the Jewish problem. The action in Stanislau was begun when Hans Kruger, the commander of the action, ordered all college-educated Jews to appear before him 3-4 August 1941, ostensibly to get new positions, in reality to be eliminated; this resulted in the death of hundreds of these individuals. The next step was the creation of a ghetto in the city. When the leaders of the Jews complained to the Gestapo that there were too many Jews for the area assigned them, the Gestapo promised some relief and decided on the elimination of 20,000 Jews. After a trial run in a neighboring city, Kruger was ready for the action in Stanislau. On 12 October 1941 12,000 Jews were marched to the city graveyard and shot. The firing continued the entire day, and even more would have died had daylight not run out. Based on court testimony, and published documents; 23 notes. E. F. Stocker

850. Fridman, Eva. A PERSONAL HISTORY OF LIFE UNDER THE NAZIS. *Centerpoint 1980 4(1): 74-78.* Narrates what it was like to be a Polish Jew during the Nazi occupation of Poland in 1941.

851. Friedlander, Henry. THE NAZI CONCENTRATION CAMPS. Ryan, Michael D., ed. *Human Responses to the Holocaust: Perpetrators and Victims, Bystanders and Resisters* (New York: Edwin Mellen Pr., 1981): 33-69. Traces the development and function of the Nazi concentration camps from 1933 to 1945, focusing on Theodor Eicke (1892-1943), who headed the Dachau camp and developed the model for the other camps located throughout Europe, and discusses the military careers of the commandants of the other camps.

852. Friedländer, Saül. L'EXTERMINATION DES JUIFS [The extermination of the Jews]. *Histoire [France] 1979 (11): 5-13.* Discusses the irrational dimension of the Holocaust.

853. Friedländer, Saul. L'EXTERMINATION DES JUIFS D'EUROPE: POUR UNE ÉTUDE HISTORIQUE GLOBALE [The extermination of European Jews: toward a global historical study]. *Rev. des Études Juives [France] 1976 135(1-3): 113-144.* Discusses the role of irrationality in the debate over the extermination of European Jews during World War II, in the Nazi policy of genocide, in the reaction of witnesses, and in the victims' behavior.

854. Fuks, Marian. POWSTANIE W GETCIE WARSZAWSKIM [The Warsaw ghetto uprising]. *Biuletyn Żydowskiego Instytutu Historycznego w Polsce [Poland] 1973 (86/87): 29-44.* The uprising was not improvised from desperation, but organized and led by the Jewish resistance movement which began underground activity from the first days of the occupation. The activization of the resistance movement in the Warsaw ghetto took place at the beginning of 1942 with the founding of the Jewish Antifascist Block, to which were joined the Poalei Zion leftists, Hashomer Hatsair, Dror, and Zionists-Socialists. In July 1942 the Jewish Fighting Organiztion came to life. However, the beginning of large scale deportation was witnessed passively by the Jewish resistance movement, mainly due to lack of arms and coordination of operations with the national underground organizations. The first armed resistance in the Warsaw ghetto took place in January 1943. Forced to give up the liquidation of the ghetto in January, the Nazis prepared for the final contest in April. In the meantime the Jewish Fighting Organization and the Jewish Military Union obtained certain meagre quantities of arms and made outside contacts. Fighting continued to 8 May and cost the Germans 400 dead and 1000 wounded. J/S

855. Fuks, Marian. STRATY OSOBOWE ŻYDOWSKIEGO ŚRODOWISKA MUZYCZNEGO [Personal losses of the Jewish musical milieu]. *Biuletyn Żydowskiego Instytutu Hist. w Polsce [Poland] 1978 35(3-4): 121-138.* Gives 207 names of musicians and persons professionally connected with music, who were murdered by the German occupiers, or who died in ghettos and camps. 5 illus., 29 notes. J

856. Fuks, Marian. W 40 ROCZNICĘ NAJAZDU HITLEROWSKIEGO NA POLSKĘ: ŻYDZI POLSCY W II WOJNIE ŚWIATOWEJ [The 40th anniversary of Hitler's invasion of Poland: Polish Jews in World War II]. *Biuletyn Żydowskiego Instytutu Hist. w Polsce [Poland] 1980 (1): 59-62.* Reports a symposium on the 40th anniversary of the invasion of Poland. The author lays emphasis on the traditional patriotism of Polish Jews, who more than once took part in the struggle for independence. In 1939 about 100,000 Jews served in the Polish Army, 10% of the total mobilized and proportionate to Jewish population. Some 90,000 Jews were killed and wounded during the fighting, including civilians helping the army in defense works. After defeat Jews joined partisan detachments and fought in the Warsaw Ghetto Uprising, and the 1944 Warsaw Uprising, in armed forces in the West, and in the Polish People's Army. J/S

857. Fuks, Marian. WYBÓR WAŻNIEJSZYCH PUBLIKACJI DOTYCZĄCYCH ŻYCIA MUZYCZNEGO W GETCIE WARSZAWSKIM W LATACH 1940-1942 [Publications concerning musical life in the Warsaw ghetto, 1940-42]. *Biuletyn Żydowskiego Instytutu Hist. w Polsce [Poland] 1979 (1): 77-97.* Illustrates documentary evidence for musical life in the Warsaw ghetto by examining the more important accounts and reviews in the *Jewish Gazette* which

discussed concerts, the organization of musical life, the fate of musicians, and the Jewish Symphonic Orchestra. J/S

858. Gadberry, Glen W. NAZI GERMANY'S JEWISH THEATRE. *Theatre Survey 1980 21(1): 15-32.* Discusses the formation of the Kulturbund Deutscher Juden [Cultural Union of German Jewry] in 1933 headed by Dr. Kurt Singer (1885-1944) after the Aryan Laws under Adolf Hitler forced artists, musicians, dancers, designers, and actors out of work. By 1938 the Kulturbund was responsible for 8,457 cultural events and it operated until 1941, when its last leader was gassed.

859. Garçon, François. CINÉMA ET HISTORIE: LES TROIS DISCOURS DU *JUIF SÜSS* [Cinema and history: the three messages of *The Jew Süss*]. *Ann.: Écon., Soc., Civilisations [France] 1979 34(4): 694-720.* Analyzes the form Nazi anti-Semitism took in the early 1940's, as evidenced in the film *The Jew Süss*, which Goebbels supervised throughout its production, and which was seen by 20,000,000 people. The words put into the mouths of the Jewish characters, as well as their physical appearance, manner and language, are all the product of systematic anti-Semitism. Paradoxically, though, this does not build up to an incitement to the audience to go out and murder the Jews themselves, but rather to a justification of the elimination of the Jewish elites by the state exclusively. Analysis of anti-Semitism leads in addition to the discovery of a methodological antifeminism, as well argued and cogent as the foregoing. Beneath these attacks, overt or otherwise, one can distinguish in this film a call for the domestication of Aryan youth and its authors' genuine horror of the masses when these intervene directly in the course of history. It is these obsessions and phobias, as well as specifically cinematographic factors such as montage, the scale of views, and the duration of sequences or dialogues, that make *The Jew Süss* a document of interest for what it teaches us of official ideology and Nazi sensibility. Fig., 44 notes, appendix. J

860. Gąsiorowska, Natalia. WSPOMNIENIA Z OBOZU HITLEROWESKIEGO W BERLINIE I DROGI POWROTNEJ [Reminiscences about a Nazi camp in Berlin and the return journey]. *Kwartalnik Hist. [Poland] 1981 88(3): 753-760.* The late Natalia Gąsiorowska, professor of economic history in Poland, was deported to Berlin during the Warsaw Uprising in August 1944 and sent as a forced laborer to a factory. A fragment of her memoirs for April and May 1945 covers her return journey on foot with a small group of Polish women. The journey led them through burned or abandoned German villages toward the River Odra and Warsaw. H. Heitzman-Wojcicka

861. Giard, Luce. LA HONTE [A shame]. *Esprit [France] 1979 (1): 71-78.* Discusses the 4 November 1978 interview in *L'Express* of Darquier, former Vichy Jewish affairs commissioner, 1942-44, and comments on the shameful actions of French officials who enforced the Vichy anti-Jewish legislation.

862. Gitler-Barski, Józef. "AUFENTHALTSLAGER"—BERGEN-BELSEN. DZIENNIK WIĘZNIA ["Aufenthaltslager"—Bergen-Belsen: diary of a prisoner]. *Biuletyn Żydowskiego Instytutu Historycznego W Polsce [Poland] 1975 95(3): 61-96.* The author publishes for the first time the complete text of his diary as a prisoner in Bergen-Belsen from July 1943 to April 1945. The camp

was originally intended to be the location of exchange of Jews from occupied European countries for Germans interned in some countries of the anti-Nazi coalition. The exchange was to be extended to Hungarian, Polish, Yugoslavian, Dutch, Spanish, and other Jews who expected with documents or promises of a neutral country (mainly of South American countries) citizenship status. The diary, which deals with Polish Jews, notes the living conditions of Bergen-Belsen prisoners, the constant deterioration of their health, hunger, and brutal treatment of prisoners by the SS operating personnel and commanding officers. Devotes much attention to social, cultural-educational, and mutual aid action for which he was a coorganizer. Notes the subjects of reports and discussions carried on in camp bars, and gives information about various courses, language classes, children and youth education classes conducted in difficult camp conditions, and successive "issues" of a vocally delivered camp gazette, the cryptonym of which was *Tramwaj* [Tramway]. Published in connection with the 30th anniversary of the liberation of the camp. J/S

863. Gitler-Barski, Józef. LIKWIDACJA GETTA WARSZAWSKIEGO (RELACJA ŚWIADKA) [Liquidation of the Warsaw Ghetto: account of an eyewitness]. *Biuletyn Żydowskiego Inst. Hist. w Polsce [Poland] 1976 (1): 93-108.* Describes the stages of Nazi liquidation of the Warsaw ghetto, beginning on the night of 17-18 April 1942 with the street shooting of 50 social workers. In the first stage, dangling the hope that the deportations were a temporary act soon to be terminated and merely undertaken in order to resettle Jews in other localities, the Nazis compelled the Jewish Council and the so-called Jewish Orderly Service to deliver 6,000 people a day to the *umschlagplatz*. The next stage began very intensively after the suicide of the engineer Adam Czerniaków, president of the Jewish Council. The Germans increased the daily contingent to 10,000. The Gestapo and SS took over the third stage, the one of final liquidation, assigning the Jewish Orderly Service only auxiliary functions and misleading the Jewish population to believe that some would be spared. Finally perceiving Nazi intentions clearly, the Jewish population resorted to passive and active resistance, which included the avoidance of deportation by hiding in shelters and specially prepared bunkers, escaping to the Aryan side of town, and taking up arms and organizing an uprising. The article ends with a description of the physical destruction of the ghetto in April 1943. J/S

864. Goldhagen, Erich. DER HOLOCAUST IN DER SOWJETISCHEN PROPAGANDA UND GESCHICHTSSCHREIBUNG [The Holocaust in Soviet propaganda and historiography]. *Vierteljahrshefte für Zeitgeschichte [West Germany] 1980 28(4): 502-507.* A brief commentary on the Holocaust in Soviet historiography and propaganda. In histories of the Holocaust in the Soviet Union, Jews are generally not mentioned. In propaganda, Soviets have linked Zionism with Nazism and the extermination. Based on some Soviet press commentaries and historical publications; 4 notes. D. Prowe

865. Goldhagen, Erich. OBSESSION AND REALPOLITIK IN THE "FINAL SOLUTION." *Patterns of Prejudice [Great Britain] 1978 12(1): 1-16.* Nazi anti-Semitism in the 1930's and 1940's constituted a complex and singular blend of rational calculation and unreasoning fanaticism, but most students of Nazism, including the Marxists, have been unable to account for this virulent, unreasoning hatred by means of reason or theories of class antagonism.

866. Goldhagen, Erich. THE SOVIET TREATMENT OF THE HOLOCAUST. *Midstream 1979 25(10): 5-7.* Discusses the way the USSR has dealt with the mass extermination of the Jews during World War II, accusing the Soviet of twisting the facts to make the Jews look bad.

867. Goldhagen, Erich. WELTANSCHAUUNG UND ENDLÖSUNG: ZUM ANTISEMITISMUS DER NATIONALSOZIALISTISCHEN FÜHRUNGSSCHICHT [Worldview and the Final Solution: on the anti-Semitism of the Nazi leadership]. *Vierteljahrshefte für Zeitgeschichte [West Germany] 1976 24(4): 379-405.* The central belief of Nazi anti-Semitism was that the Jews caused every misfortune. Even in May 1943 Goebbels blamed them for World War II. Hitler used anti-Semitism in his foreign policy. The author refutes the theories that Nazism defended capitalism and that the Final Solution was intended to bind the Germans to the consciousness of a "national" crime. He also asserts that though the Nazis rejected Judaeo-Christian morality, their attempts to purge society of all "sick" people encountered opposition. Based on primary sources and secondary works; 54 notes. A. Alcock

868. Gotovitch, José. QUELQUES DONÉES RELATIVES À L'EXTERMINATION DES TSIGANES DE BELGIQUE [Some data on the extermination of Belgian Gypsies]. *Cahiers d'Hist. de la Seconde Guerre Mondiale [Belgium] 1976 4: 161-180.* The Nazi extermination of the Gypsies has been little studied although they suffered the same fate as the Jews. Until October 1940 Gypsies were deported to Poland from Germany; thereafter it was decided to sterilize them. Only in December 1942 was their extermination decreed; from February 1943 the decree was systematically carried out in various concentration camps, especially in Eastern Europe. Based on Belgian police and Ministry of Health archives and secondary sources; 3 illus., 77 notes. M. K. Palat

869. Gouvrin, Joseph. HAGOREM HAYEHUDI BELLAAREKHET HAYAHASIM HAHADADIT BEIN GERMANIA HANAZIT UBRIT HAMOAAZOT BASHANIM 1933-1941 [The Jewish factor in the mutual relationship between Nazi Germany and the USSR, 1933-41]. *Yalkut Moreshet Periodical [Israel] 1979 (27): 129-154.* Although more apparent in determining the Nazi attitude toward the USSR, the Jewish factor played a part in determining the Soviet attitude toward Nazi Germany as well, and could be seen as a measurement of the closeness of the relationship between the two. Primary sources; 52 notes.

870. Graham, Robert A. THE RIGHT TO KILL IN THE THIRD REICH. PRELUDE TO GENOCIDE. *Catholic Hist. Rev. 1976 62(1): 56-76.* In 1940-41 upwards of 80,000 inmates of asylums in Germany and Austria were killed by gas or injections as "lives unworthy of being lived" *(lebensunwertes Leben).* The operation, ordered by Hitler, was carried out in secret, without legal basis and without the consent of relatives. Afterwards the same personnel, techniques, and equipment were applied to broader tasks in Poland, or in medical experiments on healthy prisoners (Russians, Poles, Jews, Gypsies, etc.). The Nuremberg Tribunal, primarily concerned with the international aspects of crimes against humanity, largely overlooked the origins of such crimes. The "German phase" of genocide is seen here in a documented review of the reactions and protests of Catholic and Protestant Church leaders. A

871. Green, Warren. THE FATE OF ORIENTAL JEWS IN VICHY FRANCE. *Wiener Lib. Bull. [Great Britain] 1979 32(49-50): 40-50.* Three Oriental Jewish communities, the Karaites, Georgian Jews, and Jugutis, had fled from Russia and Central Asia to France after the Russian Revolution. When the Germans occupied France, the leaders of these communities argued that they were not racially Jewish, an argument accepted by the Nazis. Exemptions were decreed for various reasons, as, for example, the Nazi expectation that they would need the whole Georgian community in France to help govern Georgia when it fell to German troops. Article adduces other examples of the Nazis' favoring one or another group of Slavs, Gypsies, and others, for military, political, and economic considerations. Thus one must be careful of excessive generalities when discussing Nazi racism. Based mostly on archives of the Centre de Documentation Juive Contemporaine in Paris; 45 notes. R. V. Layton

872. Green, Warren Paul. THE NAZI RACIAL POLICY TOWARD THE KARAITES. *Soviet Jewish Affairs [Great Britain] 1978 8(2): 36-44.* Emphasizes that to comprehend fully the enormity of Jewish extermination by the Nazis during World War II, the religious and racial reasons for their lenient treatment of the Karaites should be taken into consideration.

873. Greenstone, Maryann D. JERZY KOSINSKI: CHRONICLER OF THE JEWISH EXPERIENCE. *Studies in Biblio. and Booklore 1971-72 10(1-2): 53-56.* Review article on Jerzy Kosinski's novels, *The Painted Bird* (1965) and *Steps* (1968), which describe the lives of Jews during World War II in Eastern Europe. The author provides a chronology on Kosinski's life and a bibliography of his works.

874. Grosman, Ladislav. MEMORIES OF MY SERVICE IN A LABOR BATTALION. *Yad Vashem Studies on the European Jewish Catastrophe and Resistance [Israel] 1981 14: 287-302.* Recalls the years served in the Sixth Labor Battalion in Slovakia during World War II. Though the military regimen was rigorous, life in a labor battalion was preferable to being deported to a Nazi death-camp, the fate of the vast majority of Slovakian Jews. In a postscript to his memoir, the author of *The Shop On Main Street* tells how he returned to his home town, now without Jews, to make the film based on the popular book.
B. Reiner

875. Gross, Feliks. A MAN OF TWO CULTURES. *Polish Rev. 1979 24(1): 24-26.* A tribute to the Polish-Jewish physician Janusz Korczak, educator and educational philosopher. A staunch advocate of children's rights, in the orphanage that he administered he gave children responsibilities and duties that might seem beyond their years. He accompanied his children to one of Hitler's concentration camps and perished with them. J. Powell

876. Grossman, Haika. OTTO BUSSE—HAADAM, HAMAAMIN, HAMESAGEA [Otto Busse: the man, the believer, the helper]. *Yalkut Moreshet Periodical [Israel] 1979 (28): 131-134.* The author, who was rescued by Otto Busse, the German Christian, discusses the man and his actions.

877. Gruchmann, Lothar. EUTHANASIE UND JUSTIZ IM DRITTEN REICH [Euthanasia and judicial administration in the Third Reich]. *Vierteljahrshefte für Zeitgeschichte [West Germany] 1972 20(3): 235-279.* Analyzes the

interaction of the German judicial system with the Nazi euthanasia operation (January 1940-August 1941), set up by Adolf Hitler as an extralegal, secret process outside of state and party institutions. Caught in the dilemma of hiding this extralegal operation, the judicial administration first demanded written legislation and was eventually forced to spread the information to an increasing number of judges and attorneys, which contributed to Hitler's decision to abandon the operation. Based on Justice and Interior Ministry, and Nuremberg Trial documents from the *Bundesarchiv* and the *Institut für Zeitgeschichte,* letters to the author, and secondary sources; 144 notes.

D. Prowe

878. Grynberg, Henryk. THE HUMAN SPIRIT AS ORPHAN. *Polish Rev. 1979 24(1): 39-42.* Reviews Janusz Korczak's *Ghetto Diary* (1978), and *Warsaw Ghetto Memoirs of Janusz Korczak,* transl. E. P. Kulawiec (1978), which describe the suffering of Korczak, Polish Jewish educator, educational philosopher, and physician, as he awaited death with the children of his orphanage in a Jewish ghetto during World War II. Based on the works of Janusz Korczak; 32 notes.

J. Powell

879. Grynberg, Henryk. NOŚIM SHEL HASHOAH BASIFRUT HAPOLANIT [The holocaust in Polish literature]. *Shvut [Israel] 1978 6: 108-115.* Polish writers were among the first eyewitnesses of the Nazi "final solution" of the Jewish problem, and among the first to discuss the subject in their works. Polish literature is the richest of all Slavic writings on this theme, as Poland was directly affected by the holocaust and Jewish writers played a significant role in Polish literature. The author surveys many writers, including Władysław Szlengel, Zuzanna Ginczanka, Czesław Milosz, Jerzy Andrzejewski, Władysław Broniewski, Zofia Nałkowska, Stanisław Wygodski, and Adolf Rudnicki. Primary sources; 62 notes.

T. Sassoon/S

880. Grynberg, Michał. GETTA W REJENCJI CIECHANOWSKIEJ [Ghettos in Ciechanow regency]. *Biuletyn Żydowskiego Instytutu Hist. w Polsce [Poland] 1980 (4): 57-78.* Discusses the legal and material situation of Jews in the Ciechanow region, an area of 18 towns and a million inhabitants detached from occupied Poland and annexed to East Prussia. Discusses the 11 ghettos established in the area and the liquidation of the Jewish population by the end of 1942.

J/S

881. Grynberg, Michał. OBOZY W REJENCJI CIECHANOWSKIEJ [Compulsory labor camps in the Ciechanów regency]. *Biuletyn Żydowskiego Instytutu Hist. w Polsce [Poland] 1981 (1): 45-58.* In the area of the Ciechanow regency there were about 50 labor camps including 34 in which Jews were imprisoned. Prisoners worked on highway construction, land melioration, peat winning, and estates. The camps were located mostly at villages, in school buildings, barns, and the like. Unsanitary housing conditions, starvation food rations, maltreatment of prisoners at work by guards (recruited mostly from local citizens of German descent) led to the spread of contagious diseases and high mortality. In many camps hitlerites perpetrated crimes on prisoners. As a rule they murdered all Jewish prisoners when typhoid fever broke out in the camps. J/S

882. Gur, Mandy. MIBERGEN BELZEN LEBERGEN BELZEN [From Bergen-Belsen to Bergen-Belsen]. *Yalkut Moreshet Periodical [Israel] 1980 (29): 7-18.* Describes the last days of Bergen-Belsen, when prisoners were occupied in wiping out the traces of murder and torture in the death camp.

883. Gutman, Israel. AVODAT-K'FAYAH SHEL YEHUDIM B'SHERUT HA-GERMANIM B'MIZRAH EROPAH B'TEKUFAT MILHEMET-HA-OLAM HA-SHENIYAH [Forced labor in occupied countries during World War II]. *Zion [Israel] 1978 43(1-2): 119-158.* Forced labor under the Third Reich came from all occupied countries, but attitudes toward foreign workers were based on race. The Jewish population was seen as an important reservoir of skilled artisans and was efficiently exploited by the government even after the Final Solution was implemented in 1941. Before 1941 the Jewish leadership saw forced labor as a means to bolster economic life in the ghettos; after 1941, as a means of saving lives. Although the ghettos did not survive the war, most of the survivors of the concentration camps were laborers. 142 notes. R. S. Simon

884. Gutman, Yisrael. THE GENESIS OF THE RESISTANCE IN THE WARSAW GHETTO. *Yad Vashem Studies on the European Jewish Catastrophe and Resistance [Israel] 1973 (9): 29-70.* Analyzes the military and political developments in the Warsaw ghetto from a situation of apparent passivity before the great deportations of July 1942 to armed resistance during the deportations of January 1943, culminating in the uprising of April-May 1943. Discusses the role of Jewish youth in the resistance, the attitudes of the Poles toward the Jews, and the increasingly important role of the Jewish Fighting Organization (Żydowska Organizacja Bojowa—ZOB). Based on archival and published sources; 41 notes. J. P. Fox

885. Gutman, Yisrael. HEAROT VEHIRHURIM LEDIGUM AAL YIHUDA VEOFIAH HALLNIVERSALI SHEL HASHOAAH [The uniqueness and the universal character of the Holocaust]. *Yalkut Moreshet Periodical [Israel] 1979 (28): 77-94.* The Holocaust is both a universal and a unique phenomenon. It is explained not only by the general totalitarian traits of Nazism, but by European anti-Semitism, which was used by Nazi ideology for the specific and planned extermination of Jews. Based on primary sources, the Stirnberg documents and current periodicals; 26 notes.

886. Gutman, Yisrael. LEOFIAM SHEL MAHANOT RIKUZ NAZIIM [Nazi concentration camps]. *Yalkut Moreshet Periodical [Israel] 1980 (29): 29-52.* Analyzes the basic characteristics of the Nazi concentration camps, i.e., the loss of identity, humanity, and morality within them, to explain the Nazis' total control over the prisoners with almost no resistance.

887. Gutman, Yisrael. POLISH RESPONSES TO THE LIQUIDATION OF WARSAW JEWRY. *Jerusalem Q. [Israel] 1980 (17): 40-55.* The majority of the Polish population during World War II believed the Jews to be an alien population and ignored the mass removal of Jews from the Warsaw Ghetto and their liquidation in the Treblinka death camp in 1942; complicity in the genocide extended to the Polish government-in-exile in London.

888. Gutman, Yisrael. "THE WAR AGAINST THE JEWS 1939-1945." *Yad Vashem Studies on the European Jewish Catastrophe and Resistance [Israel] 1976 11: 329-343.* Reviews Lucy S. Dawidowicz's *The War against the Jews 1939-1945* (New York: Holt, Rinehart and Winston, 1975). Her section on Germany's policy toward the Jews is open to some degree of criticism, and even more so her assessment of the Jewish reaction and plight under the Nazi occupation. Nevertheless, Dawidowicz's compilation is a singular contribution to Holocaust literature. 4 notes. J. P. Fox

889. Haft, Cynthia J. L'UNION GÉNÉRALE DES ISRAËLITES DE FRANCE ET LA POLITIQUE DE "RÉDUCTION" [The General Union of Israelites of France and the politics of "reduction"]. *Contemporary French Civilization 1981 5(2): 261-274.* Describes the efforts, and the essential failure of the General Union of French Israelites (UGIF), formed in 1942, to secure the protection of Jews living in Nazi-occupied France by its concession to the Germans' demands to yield up part of the Jewish population under the pretext of saving the rest.

890. Halivni, Tzipora Hager. THE BIRKENAU REVOLT: POLES PREVENT A TIMELY INSURRECTION. *Jewish Social Studies 1979 41(2): 123-154.* Jewish attempts in Auschwitz-Birkenau to revolt in 1944 were thwarted by the refusal of the internal Polish Resistance Movement to offer significant support. The Poles, even leftists, exhibited profound anti-Semitism which allowed them to accept and put to good use tremendous sums of money and valuable goods derived from the Jews but not to aid them. Efforts by Jewish inmates to document the extermination were not aided by their fellow non-Jewish prisoners and have been largely ignored by the postwar Polish government. Contemporary Polish emphasis on the concentration camp emphasizes the prison area which contained large numbers of Poles (Auschwitz), while ignoring the death camp section (Birkenau) which primarily contained Jews. Based on primary and secondary sources, oral interviews, and participant-observation. N. Lederer

891. Heller, Paul. A CONCENTRATION CAMP DIARY. *Midstream 1980 26(4): 29-36.* The author's diary, written in January and February 1945, during the evacuation of Auschwitz before advancing Soviet armies.

892. Hilberg, Raoul and Staron, Stanislaw. MI HAYA ADAM TCHERNIAKOW? [Who was Adam Czerniakow?]. *Yalkut Moreshet Periodical [Israel] 1979 (27): 95-128.* Adam Czerniakow was head of the Warsaw Judenrat. Reproduces part of the introduction to his diary, in which he describes the different stages of German rule, from the occupation in 1939 until the beginning of the extermination in 1942, when he committed suicide. Based on microfilms in the German National Archive and newspapers; 54 notes.

893. Hilberg, Raul. CONFRONTING THE MORAL IMPLICATIONS OF THE HOLOCAUST. *Social Educ. 1978 42(4): 272-276.* German bureaucrats during the Holocaust, 1933-45, even Jewish bureaucrats such as Adam Czerniakow, learned to do what was "expected" of them without formal sanctions such as laws and ordinances or even written or oral orders. They coped with the implications of their actions by resorting to euphemism or, like German railroad officials, by adhering to routine.

894. Hilberg, Raul. GERMAN RAILROADS/JEWISH SOULS. *Society 1976 14(1): 60-74.* The active role of the German railroads, the Deutsche Reichsbaum, was crucial to the destruction of Jews in Germany, 1939-45.

895. Hilberg, Raul. THE GHETTO AS A FORM OF GOVERNMENT. *Ann. of the Am. Acad. of Pol. and Social Sci. 1980 (450): 98-112.* Isaiah Trunk's classic study of the Jewish Councils in Eastern Europe under the Nazi regime points to four major conclusions. 1) The ghetto was a captive city-state, totally subordinate to German authority while remaining a Jewish entity. The Jewish Councils faced a dilemma in that they could not follow German instructions without hurting Jews and could not help Jews without disobeying the Germans. 2) As a socioeconomic unit, the ghetto was hovering between life and death. 3) For the incarcerated Jews, the ghetto was also a mirage; it instilled thoughts of normalcy and continuity in the Jewish community when the Germans were preparing for deportations to death camps. 4) Finally, the ghetto councils and their police organs were a self-destructive mechanism insofar as they confiscated assets or recruited labor and, in the end, rounded up the people for transport.
J

896. Hilberg, Raul. HAGETO KETSURAT MIMSHAL [The ghetto as a form of government]. *Yalkut Moreshet Periodical [Israel] 1975 20: 89-108.* Analyzes Isaiah Trunk's *Judenrat—The Jewish Councils in Eastern Europe under Nazi Occupation* (New York, 1972), stressing its comprehensive portrayal of political, economic, and social life in the ghettos.

897. Hilberg, Raul. THE NATURE OF THE PROCESS. Dimsdale, Joel E., ed. *Survivors, Victims, and Perpetrators: Essays on the Nazi Holocaust* (Washington: Hemisphere Publ., 1980): 5-54. Describes German bureaucratic efficiency in overcoming administrative and psychological obstacles to the destruction of the Jews during World War II and the Jews' minimal resistance, attempts to avoid that destruction by appeals and evasion, and finally their paralysis and compliance.

898. Hilberg, Raul; Staron, Stanislaw; Kermisa, Josef, eds. THE WARSAW DIARY OF ADAM CZERNIAKOW: PRELUDE TO DOOM. *Present Tense 1979 6(2): 49-52.* Excerpts from the diary of Adam Czerniakow, chairman of the Jewish Council in Warsaw, 1939.

899. Hillebrandt, Bogdan. UDZIAŁ MŁODZIEŻY W RUCHU OPORU W GETCIE WARSZAWSKIM [Participation of youth in the resistance movement in the Warsaw ghetto]. *Biuletyn Żydowskiego Instytutu Historycznego w Polsce [Poland] 1973 (86/87): 147-154.* The leading factor that stimulated the Jewish people to organize resistance against the occupier were the young people, primarily those belonging to the organizations founded before the war. One of the new organizations was the Spartakus, founded by young Communists in November 1939. On the Bund side, a similar organization was the Zukunft. Conspiratorial youth groups were created also by Zionist organizations, such as: Hashomer Hatsair, Borochow-Jugend constituting the youth group of Poalei-Zion leftists, and Dror, the youth group of Hechaluen. The ghetto insurgents were young—mostly 17-24. The commander of the Jewish Fighting Organization was the 24-year-old Mordechai Anielewicz, of Hashomer Hatsair.
J/S

900. Hillgruber, Andreas. DIE IDEOLOGISCH-DOGMATISCHE GRUNDLAGE DER NATIONALSOZIALISTISCHEN POLITIK DER AUSROTTUNG DER JUDEN IN DEN BESETZTEN GEBIETEN DER SOWJETUNION UND IHRE DURCHFÜHRUNG 1941-1944 [The ideological-dogmatic basis for the National Socialist policy of liquidating the Jews in the occupied areas of the Soviet Union and their execution, 1941-44]. *German Studies Rev. 1979 2(3): 263-296.* Discusses Adolf Hitler's radical anti-Semitism, which was based on his conviction that Jews everywhere were determined to rule and to tyrannize the world and therefore had to be exterminated. Bolshevism to Hitler meant Jewish rule over the Slavs, and the liquidation of all Russian Jews was planned even before Germany's war with Russia started. Special squadrons successfully carried out Hitler's plans in German-occupied areas of the USSR. Based on Hitler's writings, speeches, proclamations, etc., and other primary sources; 118 notes.
G. Herritt

901. Hoess, Rudolf. EXCERPTS FROM *THE AUTOBIOGRAPHY OF RUDOLF HOESS.* Dimsdale, Joel E., ed. *Survivors, Victims, and Perpetrators: Essays on the Nazi Holocaust* (Washington: Hemisphere Publ., 1980): 289-304. Excerpts from the autobiography of the commander of Auschwitz, written in 1947 while Hoess was awaiting his war crimes trial.

902. Hoffman, Zygmunt. ARCHIWUM ŻYDOWSKIEGO INSTYTUTU HISTORYCZNEGO W POLSCE [Archive of the Jewish Historical Institute in Poland]. *Biuletyn Żydowskiego Instytutu Hist. w Polsce [Poland] 1979 (142): 101-114.* The institute's archives include diaries and reminiscences of Jews about the German occupation of Poland during World War II. It possesses the Emanuel Ringelblum archive, the underground archive of the Warsaw ghetto, as well as documents of former religious communities and Jewish institutions outside of Poland. The first additions to the archive were made in the summer of 1945 when oral history accounts of Jews relating their experiences of suffering and resistance were collected. List of documents and materials; 19 notes.
J/S

903. Hoffman, Zygmunt. Z "TEKI LWOWSKIEJ" [From the Lvov portfolio]. *Biuletyn Żydowskiego Instytutu Hist. w Polsce [Poland] 1980 (2-3): 135-148.* Publication of part of the materials that were kept in the private archive of Stefan Stasiak, professor at Lvov University and resident of that city throughout the German occupation. Besides documents and extensive fragments of the diary of a certain Gold, printed here, there are in the Stefan Stasiak "Lvov Portfolio," other documents of the Lvov Jewish Community (Council), and also records of diaries written by the well-known lawyer Maurycy Allerhand, anthropologist Salomon Czortkower, and a teacher, Berman. The whole material of the Portfolio contains many pieces of information complementing current knowledge of the martyrology of Lvov Jews in the first months of the German occupation. Article to be continued.
J/S

904. Höllen, Martin. KATHOLISCHE KIRCHE UND NS-"EUTHANISIE" [The Catholic Church and Nazi euthanasia]. *Zeits. für Kirchengeschichte [West Germany] 1980 91(1): 53-82.* The confrontation between the Catholic Church and the official euthanasia program in Nazi Germany brought a strong and determined rejection of this action by the Church and ended in Hitler's suspension of the program, which focused on Jews and opponents of the regime.

The author discusses the case of a German surgeon who was tried in Limburg in 1964 for his participation in the murder of 3,000 people and for his involvement in the killing of 70,000 euthanasia victims. The story of a Catholic priest who authored a work on lawful sterilization is also discussed. 127 notes.

G. E. Pergl

905. Horn, Maurycy. TSUM 35-STN YORTOG FUN OYFSHTAND IN VVARSHEVVER GETO [On the 35th anniversary of the Warsaw Ghetto Uprising]. *Bleter far Geszichte [Poland] 1980 19: 11-12.* Recounts the enormous toll taken by the Warsaw Ghetto Uprising in 1944 and the historical significance of the event in the struggle of the Jews and Poles against Nazi Germany in World War II.

906. Jaworski, Michał. PLAC MURANOWSKI 7 [7 Muranowski Square]. *Biuletyn Żydowskiego Instytutu Historycznego w Polsce [Poland] 1974 (90): 69-89, (91): 59-78.* The author, former member of the Jewish Fighting Organization in the Warsaw ghetto, describes the last few days spent there during bitter fighting in April 1943, which he witnessed from a bunker built in the cellars of the house at 7 Muranowski Square, assigned for defense by combat groups of the Jewish Military Union, which acted independently of the Jewish Fighting Organization. The author pictures the life of that part of the ghetto as it was just before the outbreak of the fighting and during the uprising as seen "from below," by a hundred people separated from the fighting going on above their heads. Describes his further vicissitudes in the Befehlstelle (the Gestapo agency for the Jewish quarter), Umschlag platz (reloading station at Stawki quarter) from where Jews were transported to various extermination camps, and, finally, in the railway transport train, going to Majdanek, from which he managed to escape. J/S

907. Jelinek, Yeshayahu. NATIONALITIES AND MINORITIES IN THE INDEPENDENT STATE OF CROATIA. *Nationalities Papers 1980 8(2): 195-210.* Outlines the wartime independent state of Croatia's nationalities policy. The state's Ustaši leaders "were obsessed with a heated and extreme nationalism ... permeated with racism," and anti-Jewish, anti-Gypsy, and anti-Serb purges followed. The Ustaši leaders "dreamed of creating a mononational state, with only the three accepted religions, Roman and Greek Catholicism, and Islam dividing the single national body." 83 notes.

G. F. Jewsbury

908. Jong, Louis de. SOBIBOR. *Encounter [Great Britain] 1978 51(6): 20-28.* Describes the building and operation of Sobibor, an extermination camp established in 1942 by the SS-Sonderkommando des Einsatzstabs Reinhard.

909. Kárný, Miroslav. KONCENTRAČNÍ TÁBORY, SS A NĚMECKÉ MONOPOLY [Concentration camps, the SS, and the German monopolies]. *Československý Časopis Hist. [Czechoslovakia] 1978 26(5): 676-712.* Heinrich Himmler's concentration camps were intended not only to terrorize and exterminate, but also to supply labor for a military-industrial complex to be run independently by the SS (Schutzstaffel). During World War II Himmler's ambitions collided with the maximal output demands of Albert Speer, minister of armaments, who represented the interests of the great industrial monopolies. Himmler put prisoners from his camps at the disposal of the arms industry, but Germany's defeat prevented his reaping any economic rewards. After the war German big

business repeatedly used the SS as an alibi or scapegoat to hide its involvement in Nazi crimes. Based on archival material and published sources; 153 notes.

R. E. Weltsch

910. Kárný, Miroslav. TEREZÍNSKÝ KONCENTRAČNÍ TÁBOR V PLÁNECH NACISTŮ [The Theresienstadt concentration camp in Nazi plans]. *Československý Časopis Hist. [Czechoslovakia] 1974 22(5): 673-700.* Examines the characteristics of Theresienstadt and traces Nazi plans with regard to this camp and the "final solution" by Hitler's Germany. The story of Theresienstadt is closely connected with secret negotiations to create an anti-Soviet bloc at the end of World War II. Secondary sources; 110 notes. G. E. Pergl

911. Kárný, Miroslav. TEREZÍNSKÝ RODINNÝ TÁBOR V BIRKENAU: POKUS O REKONSTRUKCI JEHO HISTORIE [The Terezín family camp in Birkenau: an attempt to reconstruct its history]. *Sborník Hist. [Czechoslovakia] 1979 26: 229-304.* Between September 1943 and July 1944 the Birkenau "family camp" near Auschwitz housed a total of 17,517 Jewish prisoners whom the Nazi authorities had sent there from the Terezin ghetto. Only 1,167 inmates survived World War II. This "model camp" is important additional evidence of Heinrich Himmler's attempts, in the later phases of the war, to barter Jewish lives for money or equipment and to disguise the Nazi holocaust while he sounded the Western Allies for a separate peace with Germany. Based on archives in Auschwitz and Prague, and on published documents and memoirs; 256 notes. R. E. Weltsch

912. Karpi, Daniel. YEHUDE YAVAN BITKUFAT HASHO'AH (1941-1943) VEYAHASAM SHEL SHILTONOT HA'ITALKIIM [The Jews of Greece in the Holocaust period (1941-43) and the behavior of the Italian occupation authorities]. *Yalkut Moreshet Periodical [Israel] 1981 (31): 7-38.* In territories conquered by them, the Italian authorities protected the Jews from German racist policy. Jews of Italian origin were claimed to be Italian citizens. Thessaloníki, which had about 56,500 of the 77,000 Jews of Greece, fell into the hands of Germans. In 1943, 45,450 of them were sent to Auschwitz and most were immediately gassed. Jews who claimed Italian citizenship were the subject of long diplomatic negotiations. Italy managed to save the Jews in its part of Greece. After Italy's surrender, however, Germany took over all of Greece and the fate of the Jews of Athens took a tragic turn. Based on contemporary official documents and secondary sources; 99 notes. R. Hetzron

913. Katz, Fred E. A SOCIOLOGICAL PERSPECTIVE TO THE HOLOCAUST. *Modern Judaism 1982 2(3): 273-296.* Discusses the large scale of the Holocaust as a way of routinizing monstrous behavior and discusses the case of Rudolf Hoess, the head of the Auschwitz concentration camp, showing how ordinary human behavior can be used in the service of extraordinary and horrible objectives.

914. Katz, Robert. L'"OLOCAUSTO" RECONSIDERATO [The Holocaust reconsidered]. *Ponte [Italy] 1978 34(11-12): 1478-1488.* Differentiates between Jewish leaders and Jews in a reexamination of the Holocaust. Collaboration with the Nazis corresponded to social class divisions; most Jews were ignorant victims, rather than martyrs defending their freedom.

915. Katz, Steven T. THE "UNIQUE" INTENTIONALITY OF THE HOLOCAUST. *Modern Judaism 1981 1(2): 161-183.* Compares the Nazi extermination of the Jews with the destruction of other populations, especially the American Indians and the Armenians in Turkey, and identifies Nazi intention, the intention to exterminate a whole "race" by destroying every individual member of it, as the factor that made Nazism and the Holocaust different from other such tragedies.

916. Kerkvliet, Gerard and Uitvlugt, Martin. DE VERNIETIGING VAN HET JOODSE WEESHUIS TE LEIDEN TIJDENS DE DUITSE BEZETTING; EEN VERSLAG [Report on the destruction of the Jewish orphanage at Leiden during the German occupation]. *Studia Rosenthaliana [Netherlands] 1974 8(2): 268-299.* The increasing anti-Semitism of Germany's occupation policy in the Netherlands during World War II led to the closing of the Jewish orphanage at Leiden in 1943.

917. Kermish, Joseph. THE WARSAW GHETTO UPRISING IN THE LIGHT OF A HITHERTO UNPUBLISHED OFFICIAL GERMAN REPORT. *Yad Vashem Studies on the European Jewish Catastrophe and Resistance [Israel] 1973 (9): 7-27.* Discusses the significance of a previously unpublished report by Wilhelm Ohlenbusch, head of the main Propaganda Department of the General-Government Administration, on the Warsaw ghetto uprising of April-May 1943. The report provides additional and significant information on the uprising, its scope, character, and the arms used, and by admitting the difficulties of suppressing the rising it pays unwilling tribute to the strength of the Jewish resistance. Based on Ohlenbusch's report, here reproduced and translated, archival and published sources; 2 photos, reproductions, 24 notes.
J. P. Fox

918. Kieval, Hillel J. LEGALITY AND RESISTANCE IN VICHY FRANCE: THE RESCUE OF JEWISH CHILDREN. *Pro. of the Am. Phil. Soc. 1980 124(5): 339-366.* Jewish organizations did not act more slowly than the general resistance movements in France. Few were active before 1942; nor was opposition to the Vichy regime widespread before 1943. The author concentrates on three of the major groups which had been caring for Jewish children in France well before the start of World War II: Oeuvre de Secours aux Enfants (OSE), the Organization for Rehabilitation through Training, and the Eclaireurs Israélites de France. A major effort of the Jewish community during the war years involved relief work with Jewish children and, ultimately, their rescue from the threat of deportation to the death camps. Of the 30,000 French Jewish children before the war, half were killed. The OSE estimates that it saved the lives of 7,500-9,000 children. Based on materials in the YIVO Institute for Jewish Research, New York, Centre de Documentation Juive Contemporaine, Paris; Consistoire Central Israélite de France, Paris; Jewish Theological Seminary of America, New York, and secondary studies; 150 notes.
H. M. Parker, Jr.

919. Kobrzyński, Stefan. STANISŁAW DUBOIS I TOWARZYSZE W OŚWIĘCIMIU [Stanisław Dubois and his friends in Auschwitz]. *Z Pola Walki [Poland] 1980 23(1): 127-145.* Stanisław Dubois (also Stanisław Dębski), a socialist and patriot, was arrested in August 1940 and sent to Auschwitz. He was transferred briefly to Pawiak (a Gestapo prison in Warsaw), then back to Ausch-

witz in September 1940 as number 3904. He was executed in 1942 and died dedicated to the cause of the working class. 　　　　　　　　　I. Lukes

920. Koenig, Pierre. LES LOIS DE NUREMBERG ET LE STATUT DES JUIFS SOUS LE IIIe REICH [The Nuremberg laws and the status of Jews under the Third Reich]. *Rev. d'Allemagne [France] 1981 13(3): 554-570.* The Nuremberg laws depriving Jews of their German citizenship and prohibiting mixed marriages placed German Jews in a dilemma, whether to seek refuge outside of Germany or, relying on the legal rights still remaining to them, to wait out the storm until the overthrow of Nazism. Many Jews believed survival possible under the racial laws, but the law ceased to limit the actions of the Nazi Party and of the Gestapo. Jews were gradually deprived of due process of law, especially in criminal cases, and finally the confiscation of their property deprived them of the means of existence. The judiciary, imbued with legal positivism, was incapable of using an ethical system which might have saved justice. Even today some jurists have retained this positivism. 53 notes. 　　　　　　　J. S. Gassner

921. Korey, William. FORTY YEARS AGO AT BABI YAR: RELIVING THE CRIME. *Present Tense 1981 9(1): 27-31.* Discusses the events surrounding the Nazi murder of over 33,000 Jews near Kiev in September 1941.

922. Krakowski, Shmuel. HASHOA BAHISTORIOGRAFIA HAPOLANIT [The Holocaust in Polish historiography]. *Yalkut Moreshet Periodical [Israel] 1982 (33): 134-144.* Though underplaying the part of Jews in the destruction, Polish historiographers provide reliable data on the Holocaust. The relation between Poles and Jews in that period is falsely presented. 9 notes.
　　　　　　　　　　　　　　　　　　　　　　　　　　　　R. Hetzron

923. Kren, George M. PSYCHOHISTORY AND THE HOLOCAUST. *J. of Psychohistory 1979 6(3): 409-417.* Surveys the modes of interpreting the Holocaust through the use of psychoanalytical insights. Most Nazi leaders responsible for the Holocaust had no symptoms of gross pathology. Rather than pathological, their actions were the logical culmination of Western culture's tendency to split emotion and reason, a product of the scientific orientation of modern society. Secondary sources; 13 notes. 　　　　　　　　R. E. Butchart

924. Kren, George M. and Rappoport, Leon. VICTIMS: THE FALLACY OF INNOCENCE. *Societas 1974 4(2): 111-129.* "The sacrificing of Jews—not least because of the anti-utilitarian aspects—was the Nazi equivalent of a religious act of faith." Almost every personal memoir of camp survivors emphasizes a strong, irrational will to live which in the camps is defined as a "defiant, perhaps transcendental resistance against reduction of the self as an object of sacrifice." In retrospect "the holocaust appears as a sequence of depersonalizing events that culminated in mass production death." 41 notes. 　　　　　　　E. P. Stickney

925. Kroszczor, Henryk. SŁUŻBA ZDROWIA W GETCIE WARSZAWSKIM [Health service in the Warsaw ghetto]. *Biuletyn Żydowskiego Instytutu Hist. w Polsce [Poland] 1978 35(3-4): 107-113.* Health service in Warsaw was inadequate from the very beginning of hostilities in September 1939 because of German orders aimed at the Jews from Doctor Kurt Schrempfon, SS officer. Organization in the health service was created by the Department of Health and the Department of Hospital Affairs, and the Judenrat. Describes the extremely

difficult conditions of the health service's work, and the activity of the hospital service, destitute of materials, medicaments, and food. J/S

926. Kugler, Victor; Shapiro, Eda, ed. THE REMINISCENCES OF VICTOR KUGLER, THE "MR. KRALER" OF ANNE FRANK'S DIARY. *Yad Vashem Studies on the European Jewish Catastrophe and Resistance [Israel] 1979 13: 353-385.* Victor Kugler worked several years for Otto Frank, the father of young Anne. Kugler helped the Frank family after they went into hiding in 1942, and he was present on the fateful day two years later when the Gestapo discovered their refuge. For his part in aiding Jews, Kugler spent eight months in various prisons and forced labor camps. His harrowing experiences in them and during the Frank ordeal are recounted. Illus. B. Reiner

927. Kühn, Günter and Weber, Wolfgang. BERICHTE ÜBER DIE ILLEGALE MILITÄRISCHE ORGANISATION IM EHEMALIGEN KONZENTRATIONSLAGER BUCHENWALD [Reports on the illegal military organization in the former concentration camp of Buchenwald]. *Militärgeschichte [East Germany] 1976 15(1): 52-61.* Presents nine documents excerpting interviews with 63 former political prisoners at the Buchenwald concentration camp, conducted 1972-74. The statements describe the tasks of building the Communist Party, formulating military policy and tactics, furthering education, and arming prisoners under conditions of imprisonment. 4 notes.

J. B. Street

928. Kühn, Günter and Weber, Wolfgang. INTERNATIONALISTISCHER CHARAKTER, AUFBAU UND TÄTIGKEIT DER ILLEGALEN MILITÄRORGANISATION IM KONZENTRATIONSLAGER BUCHENWALD [International character, make-up and activity of the illegal military organization in the concentration camp of Buchenwald]. *Militärgeschichte [East Germany] 1976 15(4): 427-439.* German and other European Communist prisoners took the lead in organizing the inmates of Buchenwald into military groups headed by an international military organization. This secret organization formed over 900 prisoners into 11 national sections, planned tactics and gathered weapons, and then led the successful uprising of April 1945 which freed the camp. This is an exemplary case of international cooperation of antifascists under conditions of extreme duress. Based on interviews and secondary works; 2 sketches, table, illus., 28 notes. J. B. Street

929. Kühne, Wolfgang. "UNVERLORENE ZEIT" [*Unverlorene Zeit*]. *Documents [France] 1973 28(4): 36-41.* Extracts from the journal of Wolfgang Kühne, *Unverlorene Zeit* ["Unlost time"], dealing with the degradation of prison life, written in a German concentration camp, 1940-45.

930. Kulka, O. D. "DA'AT HAKAHAL" BE-GERMANIAH HANATSIONAL-SOTSIALISTIT VE-"HABA'AYAH HAYEHUDIT": HAMAKOROT VEBA'AYOTEIHEM [Public opinion in Nazi Germany and the Jewish question: sources and problems]. *Zion [Israel] 1975 40(3-4): 186-290.* Discusses and reproduces a number of party and government documents concerning public opinion in the Third Reich. Also considers the methodological difficulties surrounding this subject, and examines how the documents illustrate German public opinion at three crucial stages in the Nazi treatment of the Jews, viz. 1) the

Nuremberg laws (1935), 2) the *Kristallnacht* (1938), and the Final Solution (1941-43). With rare exceptions German public opinion revealed a practical, amoral, impersonal or indifferent attitude toward what was happening to the Jews. Primary sources; 205 notes, 7 appendixes. T. Sassoon

931. Kulka, O. D. GETTO BELLAHANE HASHMADA: "HAMAHANE HAMISHPAHTI" SHEL YEHUDEI TEREZIENSTADT BEAUSCHWITZ 1943-44 [Ghetto in a concentration camp: "the family camp" of Theresienstadt Jews in Auschwitz, 1943-44]. *Yalkut Moreshet Periodical [Israel] 1980 (29): 135-141.* Examines the Nazi policy behind the unique fate of Jews from the Theresienstadt, who were brought to Birkenau (Auschwitz II) and were not subjected to selection and immediate destruction.

932. Kuperstein, Isaiah. RUMORS: A SOCIO-HISTORICAL PHENOMENON IN THE GHETTO OF ŁÓDZ. *Polish R. 1973 18(4): 63-83.*

933. Kvam, Ragnar. BLANT TO HUNDRE OVERLEVENDE FRA AUSCHWITZ [Among 200 survivors from Auschwitz]. *Samtiden [Norway] 1977 86(10): 602-611.* Emphasizes the worldwide efforts being made by writers and historians to distort the true facts about the extermination of six million Jews by the Germans in World War II.

934. Lachman, Ernest. ANATOMIST OF INFAMY: AUGUST HIRT. *Bull. of the Hist. of Medicine 1977 51(4): 594-602.* The inhumane medical experiments of August Hirt (1898-1946), the German anatomist, exemplified the barbarities of Nazi Germany. He studied at Heidelberg, where he received his medical degree in 1922. He proposed during the Nazi regime to develop a collection of Jewish skeletons, and his proposals were executed at Auschwitz. His victims were transported to the Anatomical Institute at Strassburg, where their bodies were embalmed. He also participated in live experiments at the Natzweiler concentration camp, experimenting with mustard gas and inoculation of nonimmunized prisoners with typhus. 38 notes. M. Kaufman

935. Lapomarda, Vincent A. THE JESUITS AND THE HOLOCAUST. *J. of Church and State 1981 23(2): 241-258.* Outlines the German military occupation's treatment of the Jesuits in Europe during World War II and Jesuit opposition to Hitler during this period. Based mostly on case histories of leading Jesuits; 76 notes. E. E. Eminhizer

936. Laqueur, Walter. THE MYSTERIOUS MESSENGER & THE FINAL SOLUTION. *Commentary 1980 69(3): 54-64.* An attempt to trace the identity of the German industrialist who visited Switzerland in July 1942 carrying the first report of the German decision to destroy European Jewry, what made him act as he did, and what became of him subsequently. Although the search was unsuccessful, it unearthed much information regarding the transmission of the news of the Final Solution, showing that Hitler's "secret" decision was more widespread with many different sources than earlier thought.

937. Lassen, Gilbert. AVIV 1943-KAIZ 1944 [Spring 1943-Summer 1944]. *Yalkut Moreshet Periodical [Israel] 1979 (28): 139-148.* Describes the activities of anti-Nazi resistance in Gilleleje, Denmark, among which was the rescue of Jews by helping them to get to Sweden.

938. Lavergne, Bernard and Laurière, Hervé. GENOCIDE IN THE PUPPET 'STATE' OF CROATIA. *Contemporary Rev. [Great Britain] 1974 224(1301): 291-298.* Discusses the genocidal policies toward Serbs and Jews pursued by the Nazi-created Croat state, 1941-45.

939. Lemeshchuk, N. M. PROLETARSKII INTERNATSIONALISM—VAZHNEISHEE ORUZHIE KOMMUNISTOV V BORBE PROTIV FASHIZMA V GITLEROVSKIKH ZASTENKAKH [Proletarian internationalism, the most important weapon of Communists against fascism in the Hitlerite torture chambers]. *Voprosy Istorii KPSS [USSR] 1978 (11): 91-99.* Archival sources show that the international antifascist resistance in concentration camps included Germans; this refutes the fascist and neofascist claims that the whole of the German nation stood on the side of Nazism.

940. Leszczyński, Julian. OD FORMUŁY OBOZU ZAGŁADY—HÖPPNER-CHEŁMNO N/NEREM—DO "ENDLÖSUNG" [From the extermination camp formula—Höppner's at Chełmno—to Final Solution]. *Biuletyn Żydowskiego Instytutu Hist. w Polsce [Poland] 1977 (1): 41-61.* In the process of Nazi planning for the extermination of Jews, the crucial moment was the introduction of the extermination camp as an instrument that would surpass in efficiency and economy all previous methods. It had two essential elements: concentration of victims and use of a "mechanized" killing medium—poison gas in a chamber. The first camp was established in Chełmno in the Warta region which was put into service 8 December 1941, preceded by experiments in Kazimierz Biskupi in September. According to the Nazi documents, the idea for an extermination camp for Jews in the Warta region came from the head of the local SD-Leitabschnitt SS Sturmbannführer Rolf-Heinz Höppner, who in a memorandum for the Reich Central Security Office (RSHA) of 16 July 1941 outlined the essential elements of the camp. The Endlösung der Judenfrage proclaimed 20 January 1942 in Wannsee refers to those "successful experiments in the East," and subsequently established extermination camps for Jews constituted the repetition of an already verified experiment. The total number of victims of the camps is estimated at about 4.8 million, 80 percent of the six million Jews exterminated during the Nazi occupation. J/S

941. Leszczyńska, Zofia. REKONSTRUKCJA DOKUMENTÓW BYŁEGO OBOZU KONCENTRACYJNEGO NA MAJDANKU [Reconstruction of damaged records originating from the Majdanek Concentration Camp chancery]. *Archeion [Poland] 1973 (58): 67-75.* During World War II Nazi authorities organized a concentration camp in Majdanek near Lublin. Germans abandoned the camp in the second half of 1944. Polish state authorities organized a state museum in the former camp buildings. This museum houses what has remained of the camp chancery records which the Germans had no time to destroy. These records were taken over by the Poles in a very poor condition and museum employees endeavored to do some preservation work on them. The author of the article reports on the methods used in the record reconstruction.
J

942. Leszczyński, Julian. HITLEROWSKA ADMINISTRACJA CYWILNA A ZAGŁADA GETTA WARSZAWSKIEGO [The Hitlerite civil administration and the extermination of the Warsaw ghetto]. *Biuletyn Żydow-*

skiego Instytutu Historycznego w Polsce [Poland] 1973 (86/87): 179-188. Beginning from 15 May 1941 the Warsaw ghetto and its half-million inhabitants separated from the rest of the city, as an independent "municipality" to facilitate the civil administration, draining the financial means of the ghetto, and, dividing the Jewish and Polish communities. Commissioner Auerswald directed a systematically intensified hunger régime in the ghetto, and, at the turn of 1941/42 introduced the death penalty for deserters from the ghetto. During the extermination of the Warsaw ghetto (from 22 July 1942) the civil administration received new tasks from the Sicherheitsdienst (SD), aimed at ensuring the liquidation troops free action and including the liquidation of the property left by the murdered. J/S

943. Levi, Primo. NOSTRA IGNORANZA E SCELTA [Our ignorance and choice]. *Ponte [Italy] 1978 34(11-12): 1346-1349.* Memoirs of living conditions in a community household of seven Jews from Turin, living in Milan in autumn 1942. Covers the period 1942-43 just prior to the group's arrest after the establishment of the Italian Social Republic in northern Italy in 1943. A preface describes the fate of the Jews deported to Fossoli camp: of the 650 men, women, and children deported, 14 returned.

944. Levin, Dov. DEMUT LOHEM: HAIM YELLIN [Portrait of a fighter: Chaim Yellin]. *Yalkut Moreshet Periodical [Israel] 1975 20: 169-177.* Chaim Yellin (1913-44), leader of the Jewish underground in the Kaunas ghetto in Lithuania, succeeded before his capture in bringing some 300 Jews out of the ghetto to fight as forest partisans.

945. Levin, Dov. YEHUDEI BESSARABIA BE-SHILTON HA-SOVIETI BIMEI MILHEMET HA-'OLAM HA-SHENIYAH, 1940-1945 [The Jews of Bessarabia under Soviet rule during World War II, 1940-45]. *Shvut [Israel] 1976 4: 101-118.* When Bessarabia was annexed by the USSR in 1940, the Jews there were sympathetic to the new regime, hoping for respite from Rumanian anti-Semitism and protection from German invasion. The Soviets, however, began exiling Jews to Siberia, leaving the Bessarabian community leaderless. After June 1941, many Jews fled eastwards, and those who survived Nazi occupation welcomed Soviet reconquest, March 1944. 175 notes. T. Sassoon

946. Lewin, Isaak. THE HOUR OF THE HOLOCAUST. *Polish Perspectives [Poland] 1978 21(7-8): 16-24.* During World War II two rescue agencies, the Vaad Hacala (New York) and the Hijefs (Zurich), attempted to save the Jews of Slovakia, supply South American passports to those in an internment camp in Vittel, France, and evacuate those at Theresienstadt camp to Switzerland in February 1945 after an agreement with Heinrich Himmler.

947. Lewin, Isaak. THE HOUR OF THE HOLOCAUST: ENDEAVOURS TO SAVE EUROPEAN JEWS DURING WORLD WAR II WITH THE HELP OF THE POLISH DIPLOMATIC SERVICE. *Polish Perspectives [Poland] 1978 21(12): 39-44.* An account of the endeavors of Polish diplomats during World War II to relocate Jews from concentration camps in Germany to America, based on two documents.

948. Lewin, Izaak. PRÓBY RATOWANIA ŻYDÓW EUROPEJSKICH PRZY POMOCY POLSKICH PLACÓWEK DYPLOMATYOCZNYCH PODCZAS DRUGIEJ WOJNY ŚWIATOWEJ [Attempts at saving European Jews with the help of Polish diplomatic missions during World War II. Part II]. *Biuletyn Żydowskiego Inst. Hist. w Polsce [Poland] 1979 (2): 69-87.* Continued from a previous article. See following abstract. Discusses attempts to save Jews in Shanghai. The Polish government-in-exile provided more assistance than did the United States in the rescue. The author further accounts the action of saving Romanian Jews through Turkey, and saving Hungarian Jews by supplying the Nazis with tractors. J/S

949. Lewin, Izaak. PRÓBY RATOWANIA ŻYDÓW EUROPEJSKICH PRZY POMOCY POLSKICH PLACÓWEK DYPLOMATYCZNYCH PODCZAS DRUGIEJ WOJNY ŚWIATOWEJ [Attempts at saving European Jews through Polish diplomatic agencies during the Second World War. Part I.]. *Biuletyn Żydowskiego Instytutu Hist. w Polsce [Poland] 1977 (1): 85-121.* Describes attempts to rescue Jews from occupied Europe particularly the action of saving Slovakian Jews by providing them with South American passports. Connected therewith were attempts at saving the inmates in Vittel in southern France. An agreement with Heinrich Himmler through the agency of the former president of Switzerland, Jean-Marie Musy, led to sending a train from the camp at Theresienstadt to Switzerland in February 1945. All these actions were possible owing to the help given by Polish diplomatic agencies—which had done much to mobilize public opinion in an anti-Nazi coalition to alarm the world about the Nazi crimes against Jews. Based on the files of the Union of Orthodox Rabbis of the United States, the world orthodox organization Agudath Israel, as well as aid committees in New York and Zurich. Article to be continued. See preceding abstract. J/S

950. Luchterhand, Elmer. SOCIAL BEHAVIOR OF CONCENTRATION CAMP PRISONERS: CONTINUITIES AND DISCONTINUITIES WITH PRE- AND POSTCAMP LIFE. Dimsdale, Joel E., ed. *Survivors, Victims, and Perpetrators: Essays on the Nazi Holocaust* (Washington: Hemisphere Publ., 1980): 259-282. Reports the results of interviews with survivors in 1950-51 and 1970-71, the former tending to contradict Bruno Bettelheim's description of prisoner socialization, the latter tending to put in question the notion that survivors are quite regularly psychologically impaired by their experience.

951. Luck, David. USE AND ABUSE OF HOLOCAUST DOCUMENTS: REITLINGER AND "HOW MANY?" *Jewish Social Studies 1979 41(2): 95-122.* Review article on Gerald Reitlinger's *The Final Solution,* one of the few studies of the Holocaust to deal at length with the Nazi murder of Jews in Eastern Europe during 1941-42 and in Polish slave labor camps throughout the war. Reitlinger underestimates the number of Jews who died by misusing or ignoring evidence. His errors are based in part on intellectual slovenliness and in part on personal emotion. In a larger sense Reitlinger's findings on the number of Jews killed appear to resemble similar refusals to acknowledge the enormity of the Turkish killing of Armenians during World War I. Primary sources.
N. Lederer

952. Luria, Lisa. MAMADEY HASHOA BESHITHEY BRIT-HAMOAT-SOT [The dimensions of the Holocaust in the territory of the USSR]. *Yalkut Moreshet Periodical [Israel] 1982 (33): 129-138.* During their invasion of Soviet territory, the Nazis started the systematic extermination of the Jews of the area. In the last four months of 1941, 350,000 Jews were killed. Details with geographic breakdown are given. Based on secondary documents; 66 notes. R. Hetzron

953. Mark, Ber. UPRISING IN THE WARSAW GHETTO. *Midstream 1975 21(4): 32-37.*

954. Mark, Esther. ARBA TE'UDOT ME'OSHVITS-BIRKNAU: "IN GROIL FON RETSIHE" ('IM HAKDAMA BE'IVRIT UVEYIDISH) [Four documents from the Birkenau camp: "In a nightmare of murder"]. *Gal-Ed: On the Hist. of the Jews in Poland [Israel] 1973 1: 307-332.* Reprints a diary and a list of transports of people burned in the Auschwitz crematorium kept by four prisoners who were employed in the crematoria, 1940-44.

955. Marrus, Michael R. VICHY ET LES ENFANTS JUIFS [Jewish children and the Vichy Regime]. *Histoire [France] 1980 (22): 6-15.* The Vichy government was responsible for the deportation of more than 6,000 Jewish children to Auschwitz. The French government was aware that it was sending thousands of innocent victims to their deaths. J

956. Mason, Henry L. IMPONDERABLES OF THE HOLOCAUST. *World Pol. 1981 34(1): 90-113.* Recent literature, particularly in Germany and the Netherlands, has provided insights into some of the most perplexing imponderables of the Nazi annihilation of the Jews. These are, first, the development of consensus among the various German elites for the purposes of the Final Solution; second, an incremental kind of German decisionmaking which led to the efficiently implemented mass annihilation of the Jews; and third, the passive mood toward the disasters befalling the Jews on the part of the entire universe of bystanders. (In the case of the Netherlands, this resulted, in spite of an unusually low degree of anti-Semitism, in an unusually high degree of Jewish victimization—in contrast to the so-called Danish reversal.) Fourth, because of the unimaginable predicament experienced by the victims and their "governments," the Jewish Councils (such as the Amsterdam *Joodsche Raad,)* they never had a chance to develop workable responses to such a catastrophe. J

957. Mathieu, G. Bording. THE SECRET ANTI-JUDEN-SONDERNUMMER OF 21ST MAY 1943. *Leo Baeck Inst. Year Book [Great Britain] 1981 26: 291-300.* The well-organized propaganda mills of Nazi Germany kept anti-semitism, a constant topic for newspaper and magazine editors by means of secret weekly directives contained in the *Zeitschriften-Dienst* (for periodicals) and the *Deutscher Wochendienst* (for newspapers)—together, the *Dienst*— supplied by the propaganda ministry. The anti-Jewish special number of 21 May 1943 represents a summary and culmination of the *Dienst* anti-Jewish campaign that had begun two years earlier. The campaign was orchestrated in such a way as to coincide with the various phases of Hitler's extermination of the Jews. According to Sebastian Haffner's *Anmerkungen zu Hitler* (1978) Hitler realized by 1943 that he had failed as conqueror and strategist, but he still hoped to achieve immortality by accomplishing his other goal, the mass murder of the Jews. The

dehumanizing of the Jewish people, transforming the persecuted into the persecutors, proceeded on the propaganda front without letup. 13 notes, photo.

F. Rosenthal

958. Matusak, Piotr. OBÓZ KONCENTRACYJNY DLA ŻYDÓW W WARSZAWIE [Concentration camp for Jews in Warsaw]. *Biuletyn Żydowskiego Instytutu Historycznego w Polsce [Poland] 1973 (86/87): 253-256.* The camp was located in the area of the Warsaw ghetto. The Jews imprisoned there were to be employed, among other things, in obtaining building materials and valuables from the destroyed ghetto, and in levelling the grounds which were to be changed into a park and later into a German housing estate. 2,040 camp prisoners were used in this work. The camp was to be developed and enlarged, but the plans were not realized because of the outbreak of the Warsaw insurrection in 1944.

J

959. Mayda, Giuseppe. LA PERSECUZIONE ANTISEMITA 1943-1945 [Anti-Semitic persecution, 1943-45]. *Ponte [Italy] 1978 34(11-12): 1428-1439.* Examines the period of the most extreme religious persecution of Jews in Fascist Italy, when deportations to concentration camps were most frequent, under the Italian Social Republic in northern Italy, 1943-45.

960. Melkman, J. DE BRIEFWISSELING TUSSEN MR. L. E. VISSER EN PROF. DR. D. COHEN [The correspondence between L. E. Visser and D. Cohen]. *Studia Rosenthaliana [Netherlands] 1974 8(1): 107-130.* Supplies historical and biographical background to 11 letters exchanged during 1941-42 between L. E. Visser (1871-1942) and David Cohen, who were opposed in their attitude toward the German military occupation of the Netherlands in World War II as it affected the Jews. While Cohen, president of the Jewish Council for Amsterdam that was established under German pressure, hoped that collaboration with the Germans would mitigate anti-Jewish measures; Visser, deposed by the Germans as president of the Dutch High Court of Justice, his Jewish Coordination Committee suspended, fought the German policy of isolating the Jews at the risk of his own deportation and life. Based on archival and secondary sources; 19 notes.

G. Herritt

961. Mendelsohn, John. THE HOLOCAUST: RESCUE AND RELIEF DOCUMENTATION IN THE NATIONAL ARCHIVES. *Ann. of the Am. Acad. of Pol. and Social Sci. 1980 (450): 237-249.* The National Archives is a major center for the study of the Holocaust. Records on the subject are scattered throughout its vast holdings in several locations and no general finding aid exists. Researchers have explored the records in some detail, but have neglected records dealing with rescue and relief attempts. Cites records of the War Refugee Board, which was created in early 1944 to provide avenues of rescue and relief to the Jews in Nazi-controlled Europe. Other records concern the emigration of Jews from Nazi Germany, the Evian Conference and the subsequent Schacht-Rublee negotiations, the Haavara agreements on emigration to Palestine, and the trip to Havana and return of the *St. Louis.* There are many other records, including those on the deals the SS was willing to make by trading Jewish lives for needed commodities.

J/S

962. Merians, Elaine; Merians, Melvin L.; and Dawidowicz, Lucy S. SPIRITUAL RESISTANCE ART FROM CONCENTRATION CAMPS, 1940-1945. *Present Tense 1978 5(2): 25-32.* Reproduces 11 drawings and paintings done by Jews in concentration camps during World War II in the collection of Israel's Kibbutz Lohamei Haghetaot.

963. Messerschmid, Felix. NACHÜBERLEGUNGEN ZU *HOLOCAUST* [Afterthoughts on *Holocaust*]. *Geschichte in Wissenschaft und Unterricht [West Germany] 1979 30(3): 175-178.* The film *Holocaust* had an enormous impact on the German public. Despite its combination of tragedy and commercial calculation, the film was accurate and had its place in the attempt to come to terms with the guilt of Nazism in Germany.   H. W. Wurster

964. Michaelis, Meir. LA POLITICA RAZZIALE FASCISTA VISTA DA BERLINO: L'ANTISEMITISMO ITALIANO ALLA LUCE DI DOCUMENTI INEDITI TEDESCHI (1938-1943) [Fascist racial policy as seen from Berlin: Italian anti-Semitism in the light of unpublished German documents, 1938-43]. *Storia Contemporanea [Italy] 1980 11(6): 1003-1045.* Deals with the pressures exerted by the Nazi government to move Mussolini to adopt an anti-Semitic policy and the nature and evolution of Adolf Hitler's own anti-Semitism. Corrects notions that Hitler's hatred of the Jews was so obsessive that it could in no way be manipulated, that the idea of a "final solution" was not only inherent in Nazi ideology but the fruit of a calculated design, and that the Führer's concept of anti-Semitism was essentially biological. Primary material in German, British, and Italian archives; 155 notes.   J. V. Coutinho

965. Michman, Dan. AL RADIKALIZATSIYAH BAMDINIYUT HA'ANTI-YEHUDIT SHEL HANATSIM VEAL RETSAH "HAMONI" VE "SHITATI" [On the radicalization in the anti-Jewish policy of the Nazis on systematic mass murder]. *Yalkut Moreshet Periodical [Israel] 1981 (32): 183-187.* A sequel to Isaiah Landau's comments to an article by Yisrael Gutman on the Holocaust (see entry #885). This period is to be viewed as starting not in 1939, but 1933. The idea of genocide was one of the options in dealing with the Jewish question from the beginning, but only with the outbreak of World War II did it reach a stage of realization. 22 notes.   R. Hetzron

966. Michman, Joseph. THE CONTROVERSIAL STAND OF THE *JOODSE RAAD* IN THE NETHERLANDS. *Yad Vashem Studies on the European Jewish Catastrophe and Resistance [Israel] 1974 10: 9-68.* Discusses the role and policies of Lodewijk Ernst Visser (d. 1942), chairman of the Jewish Coordination Committee, voluntarily established in December 1940 by Jewish organizations. German occupation forces created the Jewish Council in February 1941. Visser rejected the collaborationist approach of the Jewish Council and insisted that Jews demand their rights as Dutch citizens. Visser struggled with German and Dutch authorities and with the Jewish Council during the last year of his life to save those arrested and sent to Mauthausen concentration camp. Based on archival and published sources; chart, 71 notes, appendix.
                                                                                    J. P. Fox

967. Mikhman, Dan. LEBEIRUR HAMUSAG "HAZALA BITKUFAT HASHUAAH" [On clarifying the term "rescue during the Holocaust"]. *Yalkut Moreshet Periodical [Israel] 1979 (28): 55-76.* Discusses the concept of "rescue" as it was perceived by Jews in the five stages of Nazi rule: the first shock (1933), the relative relaxation (1933-38), the change of concept (1938-39), the outbreak of the war (1939), and the extermination (1941). 81 notes.

968. Miletić, Antun and Obućina, Branko. JASENOVAČKI LOGOR "GRADINA" 1941-1945 [The Gradina concentration camp at Jasenovac]. *Vojnoistorijski Glasnik [Yugoslavia] 1980 31(1): 209-230.* Describes the organization of the concentration camp at Jasenovac, in Croatia and the methods of torture and mass murder practiced there. The camp was set up in August 1941 on the same principles and with the same aims as the Nazi concentration camps in the rest of occupied Europe. Some 700,000 people, mainly Serbs, Jews, and gypsies, were killed there in the period 1941-45. The Gradina part of the camp was notorious as the site of mass extermination and the liquidation of Communists and their sympathizers among intellectuals and workers. Based on documents from the Archives of the Institute for Military History, the Jewish Historical Museum, Belgrade, and the Archives of Bosnia and Herzegovina, Sarajevo; 101 notes.
J. Bamber

969. Minei, Nicolae. BARBARIA CU FAȚĂ NAZISTĂ [The Nazi face of barbarism]. *Magazin Istoric [Rumania] 1978 12(7): 39-45.* Reprints a special article from the Rumanian newspaper *Scînteia* 29 June 1976, which describes the Nazi massacre of the Jews of Iași, Rumania, on 28-30 June 1941, and its background.

970. Moczarski, Kazimierz. THE DESTRUCTION OF THE WARSAW GHETTO. *Survey [Great Britain] 1977-78 23(4): 163-180.* Reproduces excerpts from a book published by P.I.W. in Warsaw in 1977 and written by the author of the present article, Kazimierz Moczarski, a prominent anti-Nazi resistance fighter. While imprisoned during the Stalin regime, under sentence of death, he shared a cell with two German war criminals, one of whom was an SS Gruppenführer, General Jürgen Stroop, destroyer of the Warsaw Ghetto in 1943. The author reports on nine months of conversations with Stroop.
R. V. Ritter

971. Mycak, Józef. EWAKUACJA WIĘZNIÓW OŚWIĘCIMSKICH PRZEZ TEREN POWIATU PRUDNICKIEGO [The evacuation of Auschwitz prisoners through Prudnik district]. *Biuletyn Żydowskiego Instytutu Hist. w Polsce [Poland] 1978 (2): 51-57.* In January 1945 the Germans, in fear of advancing Soviet troops, began to evacuate extermination camps throughout Poland, including Auschwitz. Liquidation of the Auschwitz camp began in mid-1944. The Germans attempted to blot out traces of crimes done in the camps as well as to remove prisoners still living. The author describes the death march of the prisoners, the majority Polish Jews, through Opole. Graves discovered after the war give evidence that thousands of prisoners died.
J/S

972. Nazarewicz, Ryszard. POLSKA PARTIA ROBOTNICZA WOBEC POWSTANIA W GETCIE WARSZAWSKIM [The attitude of the Polish Workers' Party toward the uprising in the Warsaw ghetto]. *Biuletyn Żydowskiego Instytutu Hist. w Polsce [Poland] 1978 35(3-4): 49-58.*

973. Newerly, Igor. A GOOD, WISE MAN: THE KORCZAK CENTENARY. *Polish Perspectives [Poland] 1977 20(9): 42-48.* Dr. Janusz Korczak (Henryk Goldszmit) (1878-1942) chose to go to Treblinka rather than give up the orphaned Jewish children in his care at the orphans' home in the Warsaw ghetto.

974. Noskova, A. F. ISTREBITEL'NAIA OKKUPATSIIA [Destructive occupation]. *Voprosy Istorii [USSR] 1980 (5): 86-100.* Describes a type of "destructive occupation" which was undertaken by the fascists in several countries of Central and Southeastern Europe. The fascists used these countries as storehouses of resources and cheap labor, oppressing the national consciousness of the people. Resistance hindered to some degree the oppressors and served to unite the people of many nations. Examines in particular the cases of Greece and Poland. 88 notes. S. J. Talalay

975. Oberkofler, Gerhard. BERICHT ÜBER DIE OPFER DES NATIONALSOZIALISMUS AND DER UNIVERSITÄT INNSBRUCK [Report on the victims of Nazism at the University of Innsbruck]. *Zeitgeschichte [Austria] 1981 8(4): 142-149.* Lists university teachers excluded from teaching after the Nazi occupation of Austria in 1938. Based on documents from the university archive, Innsbruck; 5 notes. M. Geyer

976. Orbach, Wila. THE DESTRUCTION OF THE JEWS IN THE NAZI-OCCUPIED TERRITORIES OF THE USSR. *Soviet Jewish Affairs [Great Britain] 1976 6(2): 14-51.* Discusses the recent discovery of Nazi documents pertaining to plans for the genocide of Jews in Nazi-occupied regions of the USSR, particularly Belorussia and the Ukraine, 1941-45.

977. Pakentreger, Aleksander. DZIEJE ŻYDÓW KALISZA I POWIATU KALISKIEGO W OKRESIE OKUPACJI HITLEROWSKIEJ (CZĘŚĆ I—DO GRUDNIA 1939) [The fate of Jews of the town and district of Kalisz during the German occupation]. *Biuletyn Żydowskiego Instytutu Hist. w Polsce [Poland] 1979 (3): 77-95.* Jews assisted in the defense of Kalisz. After the German occupation, they were harassed, and in December 1939 deported.

978. Pakentreger, Aleksander. LOSY ŻYDÓW M. KALISZA I POWIATU KALISKIEGO W OKRESIE OKUPACJI HITLEROWSKIEJ (OD 1940 DO 9 VII 1942 R.). MARTYROLOGIA I ZAGŁADA [The fate of the Jews of the town and district of Kalisz during the German occupation, January 1940 to July 1942: martyrology and extermination]. *Biuletyn Żydowskiego Instytutu Hist. w Polsce [Poland] 1980 (2-3): 3-21.* After the evacuation of the Jews from the city of Kalisz, Jews from the Kalisz district were placed in a transit camp in the town's covered market. In January 1940 the Jews in the market were loaded on trucks, taken to Łódz, refused admission, and returned to Kalisz. In February they were moved to the ghetto in Kozminek. There remained in the Kalisz Jewish hospital 598 sick and aged Jews, soon augmented by returning prisoners of war. In May the authorities ordered the destruction of both Kalisz synagogues and the Jewish cemetery. In October and November 1,100 sick and aged from the hospital and from the Kozminek ghetto were put to death in gas-chamber cars and buried nearby. In July 1942 the Kalisz camp and the Kozminek ghetto were finally liquidated and survivors moved to the Łódz ghetto. J/S

979. Pakentreger, Aleksander. POLITYKA WŁADZ NIEMIECKICH TZW. KRAJU WARTY WOBEC ŻYDÓW [The policy of the German authorities of the Warthegau with respect to Jews]. *Biuletyn Żydowskiego Instytutu Hist. W Polsce [Poland] 1977 (4): 33-48.* Germany's policy in occupied Poland was to expel or exterminate the Jewish population and to seize their property. In the Warthegau the progressively more severe stages of this policy were executed by Artur Greiser. J/S

980. Pakentreger, Aleksander. STATYSTYKA ŻYDÓW M. KALISZA, OCALAŁYCH PO II WOJNIE ŚWIATOWEJ [Statistics concerning Kalisz Jews who survived World War II]. *Biuletyn Żydowskiego Inst. Hist. w Polsce [Poland] 1975 (96): 81-92.* Depicts the martyrdom and extermination of the Jewish population of the town of Kalisz, bringing into relief the fact of internment in November 1939 of the majority of Jews in the Szrajer covered market and their resettlement in December under inhuman conditions in German-occupied Poland. Contains detailed statistical data on Kalisz Jews who survived World War II. More than 2,000 of Kalisz's former Jewish inhabitants returned to the town after the war. Includes a short review of young Kalisz Jews who joined partisan detachments, the Polish People's Army, and the Red Army to fight against Hitlerite genocide and who won fame for their heroism. J/S

981. Pätzold, Kurt. RASSISMUS UND ANTISEMITISMUS IN DER KRIEGSIDEOLOGIE DES FASCHISTISCHEN DEUTSCHEN REICHES (1939-1941) [Racism and anti-Semitism in the war ideology of fascist Germany, 1939-41]. *Zeitschrift für Geschichtswissenschaft [East Germany] 1980 28(5): 424-441.* After 1933 the new masters of Germany were able to use long-present political and spiritual reaction. National chauvinism changed to racism. Nazi racial doctrine focused on the Jews in Germany as part of the planned armed conflict. Ideological manipulation of the German people bore its first morbid fruit in the first years of World War II; it served the goals of pure aggression. 52 notes.
G. E. Pergl

982. Pawełczyńska, Anna. ADAPTATION AND SURVIVAL. *Polish Perspectives 1973 16(9): 20-29.* An attempt at an objective analysis by a former Auschwitz inmate of the Auschwitz concentration camp "experiments in social engineering."

983. Penkower, Monty N. "BELIEVE THE UNBELIEVABLE!" *Midstream 1981 27(4): 31-37.* Examines the circumstances the Jews faced before and after actually comprehending the Nazi design of total murder, from 1938 to 1944, discusses the alternatives for rescue then present, and attempts to understand the Jews' passivity.

984. Pinchuk, Ben-Cion. SOVIET MEDIA ON THE FATE OF JEWS IN NAZI-OCCUPIED TERRITORY (1939-1941). *Yad Vashem Studies on the European Jewish Catastrophe and Resistance [Israel] 1976 11: 221-233.* The efforts of the Soviet government to preserve good relations with Nazi Germany after the Nazi-soviet Pact, which indirectly affected the rescue of the Jews in Soviet territory, involved the deliberate overlooking by the Soviet media of the Nazi persecution of the Jews. This practice persisted even after Germany's attack on the USSR in June 1941. While it is difficult to determine the precise effect of

the media upon public opinion and behavior during World War II, it undoubtedly had a significant influence on the unwillingness of the Jews to flee the advancing German armies while there was still time to do so. Based on archival and published sources; 26 notes. J. P. Fox

985. Podéh (Podomski), Feivel. KEN HASHOMER HATZAIR BEGETTO LODZ [The Hashomer Hatsair cell in the Łódz ghetto]. *Yalkut Moreshet Periodical [Israel] 1979 (28): 7-36.* Describes various activities of the Hashomer Hatsair cell in the Łódz ghetto, 1939-44, among which was the establishment of the farm for Jewish youth at Maryshin. Primary sources.

986. Pommerin, Reiner. RASSENPOLITISCHE DIFFERENZEN IM VERHÄLTNIS DER ACHSE BERLIN-ROM 1938-1943 [Differences in racial policy in the relations of the Berlin-Rome Axis, 1938-43]. *Vierteljahrshefte für Zeitgeschichte [West Germany] 1979 27(4): 646-660.* Contacts between German and Italian racial policy experts existed well before Italy's first official racial policy publication, *Fascism and the Racial Question* (July 1938). But despite German pressures, Italy's anti-Semitism never came to conform to the German view, which regarded Jewry as a disease to be exterminated, but remained a policy of separation of an alien group and continued to be subordinated to other national interests. D. Prowe

987. Radlitzki, Tzvi. RESHIMOT MIMEI HAKIBUSH HAGERMANI BE-LVOV (LEMBERG), 1941-1943 [Notes from the German conquest of Lvov (Lemberg), 1941-43]. *Yalkut Moreshet Periodical [Israel] 1976 21: 7-34.* A personal account of a survivor of the Nazi occupation of Lvov, which culminated in the deaths of virtually all 130,000 Jewish residents.

988. Redlich, Shimon. THE ERLICH-ALTER AFFAIR. *Soviet Jewish Affairs [Great Britain] 1979 9(2): 24-45.* Henryk Erlich (1882-1941/2?) and Wiktor Alter (1890-1941/2?) were leading figures in the Polish Bund Central Committee who fled to the USSR. Their plan to create an anti-Nazi committee of Jews in the USSR, conceived after imprisonment and interrogation by Soviet secret police, failed in 1941. Both were executed for obscure reasons.

989. Reichman, Yehiel Meir; Bar'am, A., transl. SHANAH AHAT BETREBLINKA [One year in Treblinka]. *Yalkut Moreshet Periodical [Israel] 1981 (32): 33-70.* An account of the author's year of captivity in the Treblinka concentration camp. He escaped during the prisoner's uprising in August 1943. Based on personal memoirs. R. Hetzron

990. Rosenberg, Alan and Bardosh, Alexander. THE HOLOCAUST AND HISTORICAL CRISIS: A REVIEW ESSAY. *Modern Judaism 1981 1(3): 337-346.* Reviews and critiques George M. Kren and Leon Rappoport's *The Holocaust and the Crisis of Human Behavior* (1980), which synthesizes various insights regarding the Nazi extermination of European Jews and makes a substantial contribution to the understanding of the Holocaust and its importance to concepts of religious faith and ethical standards.

991. Rosenberg, Edgar. VANISHING ACTS. *Commentary 1982 73(5): 50-62.* Excerpt from a fictionalized family memoir of Jews in Fürth, Bavaria, 1936-41, detailing the experience of German Jews during the Nazi period, focusing on attempts to emigrate.

992. Rosenfeld, Alvin H. HIDDEN JEWS. *Midstream 1981 27(9): 49-53.* Reviews Valentin Senger's memoirs, *No. 12 Kaiserhofstrasse,* which recounts the amazing story of a Jewish family's survival through the war years in Frankfurt, Germany, undetected as Jews, owing chiefly to the mother's overpowering will and keenly developed art of subterfuge.

993. Rosensaft, Hadassah. MY JOURNEY INTO THE PAST. *Midstream 1980 26(4): 26-28.* Account of a concentration camp victim's return to the sites of her childhood and imprisonment in Poland.

994. Rosensaft, Menachem. THE HOLOCAUST: HISTORY AS ABERRATION. *Midstream 1977 28(5): 53-55.* A powerful essay on the horrors that took place during World War II outside the Polish town of Oświęcim, where, in the immense Auschwitz concentration camp, Hitler virtually destroyed European Jewry.

995. Roth, John K. HOLOCAUST BUSINESS: SOME REFLECTIONS ON *ARBEIT MACHT FREI. Ann. of the Am. Acad. of Pol. and Social Sci. 1980 (450): 68-82.* Arbeit Macht Frei, "work makes one free," framed the entry to Nazi death camps. The Nazi program included some 1,600 forced labor operations in addition to the death camps. During the 12 years of the Nazi regime, millions slaved and perished within them. If survivors were found when Allied forces arrived, it was only because the victims had somehow avoided being worked to death. Explores the links between industry, slave labor, and the Holocaust. It also examines implications for moral philosophy that spin off from Holocaust business. J/S

996. Rothchild, Sylvia. WRITING ABOUT THE HOLOCAUST: "DOESN'T IT MAKE YOU SAD TO READ THOSE STORIES?" *Present Tense 1982 9(3): 52-55.* Discusses the author's role (undertaken in 1977) in reading and editing interviews with Jewish Holocaust survivors in the United States compiled for the William E. Wiener Oral History Library of the American Jewish Committee, commenting on reactions to her work from associates and other people and on the importance of such material for understanding the Holocaust.

997. Rothkirchen, Livia. THE ZIONIST CHARACTER OF THE "SELF-GOVERNMENT" OF TEREZIN (THERESIENSTADT). A STUDY IN HISTORIOGRAPHY. *Yad Vashem Studies on the European Jewish Catastrophe and Resistance [Israel] 1976 11: 56-90.* Examines the literature on the history of Terezin, its leadership, its role in Jewish history under the Nazis, and the degree of Zionist activity in the camp. Criticizes in particular the attitudes of H. G. Adler and his contributions to the subject. There is still a great deal of work to be done which will demand the confrontation of varied and problematical sources and will require balanced and cautious inspection in order to avoid being caught up in false presumptions or, at the opposite end of the scale, creating legends and myths. Based on archival and published sources; 82 notes, biblio. J. P. Fox

998. Rousso, Henry. HOLOCAUSTE: QUI SAVAIT? [The Holocaust: who knew about it?]. *Histoire [France] 1981 (31): 92-95.* Review article of Walter Laqueur's *The Terrible Secret: An Investigation into the Suppression of Information about Hitler's "Final Solution"* (1980).

999. Rubin, Eliahu. YEHUDEI MUNKATSH BIZMAN MILHEMET HAOLAM HASHNIAH [Munkács Jews during World War II]. *Yalkut Moreshet Periodical [Israel] 1979 (28): 149-162.* Describes the deteriorating situation of the Jews in Munkacs (Mukachevo), Ruthenia, in 1944, from their concentration in the ghetto to their final expulsion to Auschwitz.

1000. Ryszka, Franciszek. ZAGŁADA WARSZAWSKIEGO GETTA A DOKTRYNA I PROGRAM LUDOBÓJSTWA [Extermination of the Warsaw ghetto and the doctrine and program of genocide]. *Biuletyn Żydowskiego Instytutu Historycznego w Polsce [Poland] 1973 (86/87): 7-27.* The reply to the question of the sources of this tragedy cannot be given without introducing threads from the field of social psychology. Otherwise it would be difficult to explain why such a great number of people belonging to a nation having beautiful cultural traditions and a high standard of civilization proved to be capable of falling into barbarism, what was not however a freak of one-time psychosis but an organized action carried out unswervingly. The liquidation of the Warsaw ghetto was the logical epilogue of the doctrine and program created by the social phenomenon called Nazism. The doctrine and program grew in force over a period of years. Preparations for the decision of mass killing and full consciousness of participation in the crime were initiated the moment Hitler founded his party in Munich in 1919. A new stage began with the 9 November *Kristallnacht,* when the Jewish question first came within the province of the SS and the first deportations of Jews, "Ostjude," let the world see that limitations of the law. In June 1941 the killing machine was set into motion and it did not stop until the last day of the war. The heroism of the members of the Jewish Fighting Organization was the negation of life; therefore it was the voice of truth. J/S

1001. Sabini, John P. and Silver, Maury. DESTROYING THE INNOCENT WITH A CLEAR CONSCIENCE: A SOCIOPSYCHOLOGY OF THE HOLOCAUST. Dimsdale, Joel E., ed. *Survivors, Victims, and Perpetrators: Essays on the Nazi Holocaust* (Washington: Hemisphere Publ., 1980): 329-358. Applies the results of recent research in the social sciences to the circumstances of the guards and bureaucrats who ran the World War II concentration camps to show that their inhumanity "could have been the product not only of deranged individuals but of normal people placed in deranged and degrading circumstances."

1002. Sakowska, Ruta. ARCHIWUM RINGELBLUMA [Ringelblum Archive]. *Biuletyn Żydowskiego Instytutu Hist. w Polsce [Poland] 1978 35(3-4): 115-119.* Discusses the work of Doctor Emanuel Ringelblum and a group of Jewish historians from the Warsaw ghetto in attempting to preserve records of Hitler's genocide. The author describes the research in the Ringelblum Archive and the methodology of Dr. Ringelblum, gained from his experiences with the Jewish Scientific Institute in Vilna. J/S

1003. Sakowska, Ruta. OPÓR CYWILNY GETTA WARSZAWSKIEGO [Civil resistance of the Warsaw ghetto]. *Biuletyn Żydowskiego Instytutu Historycznego w Polsce [Poland] 1973 (86/87): 67-83.* Despite serious differences in the occupier policy with respect to Polish and Jewish population, there appeared in the ghettos certain phenomena similar to those on the "Aryan" side of the wall. The various forms of resistance overlapped, but to get better knowledge of them one should isolate the particular components. One of them was the civil resistance. Standing face to face with biological extermination and seeing its cultural values in danger of being annihilated, society set a number of defense mechanisms in motion: civil resistance embraced secret teaching, secret cultural training, artistic, scientific, archival, and documentary activities, secret futurological work, social self-aid, hiding of the persecuted, and forming of citizen attitudes. Civil resistance among the Jewish population sprung up in the first months of the occupation. The struggle for life of the ghetto's inhabitants concentrated in the cells of the Jewish Social Self-Aid (ŻSS). The civil resistance movement rested on the protection societies, house committees, and associations of compatriots of displaced persons united by ŻSS. Under the protection of ŻSS secret meetings were held by the political parties embracing the left wings and liberal-bourgeoisie and conservative-religious parties. The prewar antagonisms lost much of their sharpness. Polish underground organizations were the natural allies of the Jewish people and the victories won by the Soviet Army kindled the hope for liberation. The social help cells performed protective, cultural, and educational as well as self-government functions. There was a peculiar dualism in the ghetto—the social help cells doubled and fought the *Judenrat* in many fields of life. A special role in the system of civil resistance fell to the team taking care of the underground archive (Ringelblum). Only the so-called great extermination action (22 July-21 September 1942) shattered the attempt to save the ghetto's population. After the great extermination action, those who remained started ardently to prepare for armed resistance. Civil resistance action is inseparably connected with the genesis of the Jewish Fighting Organization—the main force in the ghetto uprising.

J

1004. Sakowska, Ruta, comp. SPRAWOZDANIA ŚWIETLICZANEK Z GETTA WARSZAWSKIEGO (Z DZIEJÓW TAJNEGO NAUCZANIA): Z ARCHIWUM RINGELBLUMA [Reports of club room managers from the Warsaw ghetto (from the records of secret instruction): from the Ringelblum Archive]. *Biuletyn Żydowskiego Inst. Hist. w Polsce [Poland] 1975 94(2): 57-70.* At the beginning of 1941, in the period of highest intensification of transfer of Jews to the Warsaw ghetto, a Commission for Care of Children of Displaced Persons was formed at Centos (Head Office of Societies for Care of Orphans and Desolate Children, which acted during the occupation under cover of the Jewish Mutual Aid Society). In larger hospices club rooms were organized, and to smaller ones "flying" managers were appointed. These women took care of several rooms every day. The club rooms fed and educated the children. Club room managers ran the risk of losing their lives, spending much time with children who suffered from infectious diseases. The activity of club managers was one of the manifestations of the civil resistance in the ghetto. Publishes 19 reports in Ring II, Number 110 of the Underground Archive of the Warsaw ghetto, the Ringelblum Archive.

J/S

1005. Sakowska, Ruta. WSPOMNIENIA PRACOWNIKA GMINY I JUDENRATU W WARSZAWIE (WRZESIEŃ-PAZDZIERNIK 1939) [Reminiscences of an employee of the community and the *Judenrat* in Warsaw]. *Biuletyn Żydowskiego Inst. Hist. w Polsce [Poland] 1976 (2): 97-102.* The reminiscences of an unknown author, found in the second part of the Ringelblum Archive, were written probably at the end of 1942, and cover the siege of Warsaw in September 1939 and the first several months of the Nazi occupation. The author was a young man connected with the *halutz* movement. It is supposed that the reminiscences were written by Nachum Remba, one of the few *Judenrat* employees connected with the conspiracy. J

1006. Sakowska, Ruta. Z ARCHIWUM RINGELBLUMA. *GŁOS DOMU CHŁOPCÓW* [From the Ringelblum Archive: the *Voice of Boys' Home*]. *Biuletyn Żydowskiego Inst. Hist. w Polsce [Poland] 1976 97(1): 77-87.* Presents one issue of *Głos Domu Chłopców*, a magazine issued by the orphans housed in the orphanage on Gęsia Street and found in the Underground Archive of the Warsaw Ghetto (Ringelblum Archive). The issue covers the first months after the establishment of the enclosed quarter, from the period of the violent breakdown of social foundations, both of individual families and social protective institutions. The organization of help for Jewish children in occupied Warsaw centered in the Centos Society which functioned under cover of the Jewish Mutual Aid Society. The dramatic struggle for a child's life was one of the elements of civil resistance of the Jewish population during the occupation. Of momentous importance in this struggle were the educational solutions. The Warsaw ghetto applied the modern ideas of Korczak and Makarenko concerning collective education. One piece of evidence of the efforts of the ghetto pedagogues is *The Voice of Boys' Home*.
J/S

1007. Schlesinger, Wilhelm. A REAPPRAISAL OF THE "SHTADLAN" DURING THE HOLOCAUST: THE ACTIVITY AND CORRESPONDENCE OF DR. WILHELM FILDERMAN ON BEHALF OF ROUMANIA'S JEWS. *Centerpoint 1980 4(1): 113-121.* Discusses the key role played by Wilhelm Filderman, the leader of Romania's Jewish population during World War II, in saving large segments of that population by interceding directly with the anti-Semitic Marshal Antonescu, leader of the pro-Nazi Romanian government.

1008. Schorsch, Ismar. GERMAN ANTISEMITISM IN THE LIGHT OF POST-WAR HISTORIOGRAPHY. *Leo Baeck Inst. Y. [Great Britain] 1974 19: 257-272.* A growing literature endeavors to explore the roots of German anti-Semitism and its connection with the traditional Christian perception of the Jew. It appears now that Christian anti-Semitism deserves to be considered only as one component of a complex matrix. Eva Reichmann and Hannah Arendt point out that the decline of Christianity during the early modern period and the rise of the nation state produced the roots of the modern totalitarian state in which extermination of the Jewish minority became a reality. Other major contributions were made by Paul Massing and Eleonore Sterling in their examination of 19th-century political and social anti-Semitic attitudes. F. Rosenthal

1009. Sendlerowa, Irena. O DZIAŁALNOŚCI KÓŁ MŁODZIEŻY PRZY KOMITETACH DOMOWYCH W GETCIE WARSZAWSKIM [The activity of youth organizations at the house committees in the Warsaw ghetto]. *Biuletyn Żydowskiego Instytutu Hist. w Polsce [Poland] 1981 (2): 89-118.* Depicts the author's experiences, and work, particularly with children, in the Warsaw ghetto. After the first phase of liquidation of the ghetto, from July 1942 to autumn of that year, the activity of the youth organizations in the ghetto ceased. A considerable number of these young people later joined the fighting groups in the Warsaw ghetto uprising. J/S

1010. Shavit, David. JEWISH LIBRARIES IN THE POLISH GHETTOS DURING THE NAZI ERA. *Lib. Q. 1982 52(2): 103-121.* During the Nazi occupation of Poland in World War II a large proportion of the Jewish population was incarcerated in ghettos. Even in the most adverse conditions the Jews in the ghettos developed an extensive educational and cultural life. Libraries were established in several of the ghettos, and these libraries were used by many of the residents. This article deals with the Jewish libraries in the ghettos of Łódz, Warsaw, and Vilna, their readers, and the books they read during the years of the holocaust.　　　　　　　　　　　　　　　　　　　　　　　　　　　　　　　J

1011. Shirman, Israël. UN ASPECT DE LA "SOLUTION FINALE": LA SPOLIATION ÉCONOMIQUE DES JUIFS DE BELGIQUE [An aspect of the Final Solution: the economic plunder of Belgian Jews]. *Cahiers d'Hist. de la Seconde Guerre Mondiale [Belgium] 1974 (3): 65-83.* From November 1940 all movable and immovable Jewish property in Belgium was systematically aryanized with special provision for the diamond industry in Antwerp, almost entirely Jewish. The property of refugees and deportees was confiscated, that of remaining Jews compulsorily sold at fixed prices, and concerns with Jewish participation removed the Jews. Based on archives with detailed statistics; 77 notes.
M. K. Palat

1012. Shneiderman, S. L. THE BLACK BOOK OF SOVIET JEWRY. *Midstream 1981 27(10): 49-52.* Discusses Ilya Ehrenburg's *The Black Book* (1980), a compilation of documents and personal memoirs dealing with the Nazi extermination of Soviet Jews during World War II, and the suppression of this work in the USSR.

1013. Shneiderman, S. L. THE WARSAW GHETTO STRUGGLE. *Midstream 1978 24(6): 18-27.* A 35th anniversary account of the Warsaw Ghetto Uprising during World War II.

1014. Šijački, Ljubica. O ZATVORIMA, LOGORIMA I LOGORSKIM RADIONICAMA U BANATU 1941-1944. GODINE [Prisons, concentration camps, and work camps in Banat, 1941-45]. *Vojnoistorijski Glasnik [Yugoslavia] 1979 30(1): 175-190.* Surveys the penal institutions in Banat set up by the German occupying authorities and points out that most atrocities were committed by the local German minority (Volksdeutsche) aided by the Hungarian sympathizers of the Horthy regime and Serbian quislings. During the period 1941-44, camps and prisons in Banat processed 10,000 people. In the camp of Gross Vetschkerek (Veliki Bečkerek, now Zrenjanin) alone, 2,500 people were executed. Primary sources; 40 notes.
S. Košak

1015. Silberner, Edmund. DIE KOMMUNISTISCHE PARTEI DEUTSCHLANDS ZUR JUDENFRAGE [The Communist Party of Germany and the Jewish question]. *Jahrbuch des Inst. für Deutsche Geschichte [Israel] 1979 8: 283-334.* Contemporary Communist documents for the years 1933-45, originally related to Communist Party matters, cast considerable and varied light on the problems of German Jews during these years. Various aspects of Jewish history are discussed along with the effects they had on the Jewish people. The Communists are seen to seek the aid of Jews to mobilize the proletarians. During the Hitler years the situation of the Jews is so serious that no political group could save them. 149 notes.
M. Faissler

1016. Smith, Bradley F. TWO ALIBIES FOR THE INHUMANITIES: A. R. BUTZ, *THE HOAX OF THE TWENTIETH CENTURY* AND DAVID IRVING, *HITLER'S WAR. German Studies Rev. 1978 1(3): 327-335.* A. R. Butz, a professor of electrical engineering in the United States, has produced *The Hoax of the Twentieth Century,* in which he argues that the Nazis killed no Jews during World War II. They merely sent them to "labor camps" whence, at the close of the war, Zionists and Communists spirited them away to Israel or the USSR, while creating the myth of the six million martyrs. This book is simply another sleazy anti-Semitic tract, filled with lies and omissions. David Irving's *Hitler's War* is more serious stuff, and therefore more dangerous. He tries to prove that the Holocaust, which he admits took place, was the work of Himmler and Heydrich, without Hitler's knowledge and against his wishes. This ignores the fact that Himmler was devoted to Hitler, and would not have taken initiative on so important a question. And it was Hitler, not Himmler, who was the great anti-Semite. 11 notes. J. C. Billigmeier

1017. Spicehandler, Arnold. TEACHING THE HOLOCAUST. *Midstream 1980 26(4): 37-39.* Recounts a session of a class in the Holocaust at City University of New York, taught by Elie Wiesel and devoted to a guest lecture by Leon W. Wells, author of *The Janowoska Road,* an early and classic survivor account.

1018. Steinmetz, Selma. EMIL ALPHONS RHEINHARDT (1889-1945). AUS DEM LEBEN EINES EXILSCHRIFTSTELLERS [Emil Alphons Rheinhardt (1889-1945): From the life of an exiled writer]. *Zeitgeschichte [Austria] 1977 4(4): 109-122.* Emil Alphons Rheinhardt's death in the Dachau concentration camp in February 1945 closed prematurely a productive literary career. Friend and contemporary of such authors as Thomas Mann, Arthur Schnitzler, and Alfred Kantorowicz, Rheinhardt carried on extensive correspondence with exiled and soon-to-be-exiled writers of the 1930's. His letters are compelling testimony to the struggle of German and Austrian authors for free expression and for the basic political freedoms lost to the Nazi regime of Adolf Hitler. Among his literary works are several historical or biographical dramas and several volumes of poetry. Includes four of Rheinhardt's poems, one previously unpublished. Primary sources; 32 notes. G. H. Libbey

1019. Strauss, Herbert A. JEWISH EMIGRATION FROM GERMANY: NAZI POLICIES AND JEWISH RESPONSES (I). *Leo Baeck Inst. Year Book [Great Britain] 1980 25: 313-361.* Presents data on Jewish emigration during the Nazi period. Interpretation of this raw data includes consideration of the anti-Semitic tradition, resistance, demographic aspects of German Jewry, Nazi persecution and its effects, economic impact, international migration restrictions, and the European response to this problem. 10 tables. F. Rosenthal

1020. Sultanik, Kalman. THE WARSAW GHETTO UPRISING. *Midstream 1979 25(5): 49-52.* An account of the human force behind the Warsaw Ghetto resistance uprising of 1943.

1021. Suominen, Elina. REHELLISYYS VAI "SUOMEN KUNNIA" [Honesty or "Finland's honor"]. *Hist. Aikakauskirja [Finland] 1980 78(3): 251-255.* Defends the research in the author's *Kuolemanlaiva s/s Hohenhörn: juutalaispakolaisten kohtalo Suomessa* [Death ship s/s *Hohenhörn:* the fate of

Jewish refugees in Finland] (Porvoo: 1979) against the criticisms made by Yrjö Blomstedt in "Juutalaispakolaisten luovuttaminen 1942" [The expulsion of the Jewish refugees in 1942] *Hist. Aikakauskirja* 1980 78(2): 142-146.

R. G. Selleck

1022. Szczechura, Tomasz. ŻYCIE I ZAGŁADA SPOŁECZNOŚCI ŻYDOWSKIEJ W POWIECIE WĘGROWSKIM W LATACH 1939-1944 [Jews and the extermination of the Jewish community in the Węgrów district, 1939-44]. *Biuletyn Żydowskiego Instytutu Hist. w Polsce [Poland] 1978 (1): 39-52*. Węgrów district Jews were first ordered to wear white armbands with stars, then their property was confiscated and Poles were forbidden to employ them, and finally they were herded into ghettos in Węgrów, Stoczek, and Łochów. In September 1942 the ghettos were surrounded and their inhabitants driven onto trains to the extermination camp at Treblinka. A few Jews succeeded in hiding, saved by Poles. A ghetto was later reestablished at Węgrów, but those few Jews who deluded themselves that they could survive in it were murdered several months later.

J/S

1023. Szewdowski, Stanisław. HITLEROWSKIE OBOZY PRACY DLA ŻYDÓW NA OPOLSCZYZNIE [The Nazi labor camps for Jews in Opole Region]. *Biuletyn Żydowskiego Inst. Hist. w Polsce [Poland] 1975 (96): 67-80*. Notes the various locations in Poland of labor camps for Jews, the number of inmates, their countries of origin, the work performed, and the number who died, 1942-44.

J/S

1024. Szulfried, Stanisław. WSPOMNIENIA Z OKRESU OKUPACJI [Reminiscences of the occupation years]. *Biuletyn Żydowskiego Instytutu Hist. w Polsce [Poland] 1980 (1): 63-83*. Part I. Describes the living conditions of Jews in occupied Warsaw, both in the ghetto and outside it. Especially emphasized are the economic matters and the manner of expropriating the Jewish entrepreneurs and merchants. Describes corrupt practices, lawlessness, and predatory behavior in these actions, which were regarded as felonious even under German regulations.

J

1025. Szulkin, Michał. DR. EMANUEL RINGELBLUM—HISTORYK I ORGANIZATOR PODZIEMNEGO ARCHIWUM GETTA WARSZAWSKIEGO [Doctor Emanuel Ringelblum—a historian and organizer of the Warsaw ghetto's underground archive]. *Biuletyn Żydowskiego Instytutu Historycznego w Polsce [Poland] 1973 (86/87): 111-125*. Emanuel Ringelblum founded and organized the Underground Archive of the Warsaw Ghetto in October 1939. The archive was recovered after the war, in 1946 and 1950. It is now a valuable source of information on the history of Jewish people during the Nazi occupation. In that time Ringelblum was universally active and managed to write *Notatki z getta warszawskiego* [Notes from the Warsaw Ghetto] and *Stosunki polsko-żydowskie w czasie II wojny światowej* [Polish-Jewish Relations during the World War II] which appeared after the war and were translated into many languages. After the liquidation of the ghetto Ringelblum hid in a bunker built in the garden of a villa near Warsaw. Betrayed, he, together with the family of Marczak who kept him in hiding, was killed in the prison of Pawiak, 7 March 1944.

J/S

1026. Tal, Uriel. NAZISM AS A "POLITICAL FAITH." *Jerusalem Q. [Israel] 1980 (15): 70-90.* Discusses Nazism as a messianic belief system and world view which depended upon the elimination of the Jews for its culmination.

1027. Tal, Uriel. ON THE STUDY OF THE HOLOCAUST AND GENOCIDE. *Yad Vashem Studies on the European Jewish Catastrophe and Resistance [Israel] 1979 13: 7-52.* Defines and analyzes the term genocide, especially in reference to the Jewish Holocaust. Compares similarities and differences in particular cases of mass extermination. Discovers a remarkable consistency of purpose in the Nazi policy of extermination of the Jewish people, and contrasts it to the shifts in genocidal policy directed toward non-Jews. Though mass annihilation of human groups has been a universal phenomenon, concludes that the Holocaust was unique in its symbolic rejection of monotheism and the values of Western Civilization. Based on archival and published sources; 89 notes, appendix. B. Reiner

1028. Talmon, J. L. EUROPEAN HISTORY—SEEDBED OF THE HOLOCAUST. *Midstream 1973 19(5): 3-25.* The Final Solution had deeper historical roots than Nazism or Hitler. S

1029. Tillion, Germaine. CUPTOARELE-CREMATORII DE LA RAVENSBRÜCK [The furnace-crematoria of Ravensbrück]. *Magazin Istoric [Romania] 1980 14(1): 52-56.* An extract from the forthcoming Romanian translation of the author's *Ravensbrück* (Paris, 1973), a republication of three earlier memoirs. Chronicles life in Ravensbrück concentration camp during March and April 1945.

1030. Tregenza, Michael. BELZEC DEATH CAMP. *Wiener Lib. Bull. [Great Britain] 1977 30(41-42): 8-25.* Belzec was the first death camp on Polish territory. The author reconstructs the history of the camp and the life stories of its personnel. Today nothing remains of the camp, save an inscription in several languages: "Remember the 600,000 victims of the Nazi death camp at Belzec murdered during the years 1942-43." In 1975 the Polish authorities removed the Yiddish inscription. 3 photos, 2 diagrams, 31 notes. R. V. Layton

1031. Tubin, Yehuda. BEDEREKH ELEIHEM (MIYOMANO SHEL ISH HABRIGADA, 1945-1946) [En route to them: from the diary of a Jewish Brigade soldier, 1945-46]. *Yalkut Moreshet Periodical [Israel] 1976 21: 57-88.* Excerpts from the diary of a Jewish Palestinian soldier in the British army, telling about the Jewish Brigade, its combat experience, meetings with Holocaust survivors, and visits to Belsen and Polish towns, 1945-46.

1032. Tyszka, Leon. FRAGMENT WSPOMNIEŃ (1939-1942) [A fragment of reminiscences, 1939-42]. *Biuletyn Żydowskiego Instytutu Hist. w Polsce [Poland] 1981 (4): 61-64.* The author, former secretary of the president of the Jewish community in the Warsaw ghetto, Adam Czerniakow, describes the period preceding his return to Warsaw from evacuation to the outbreak of war. He then lived and worked in Lvov. J/S

1033. Tyszka, Leon. FRAGMENTY WSPOMNIEŃ Z OSTATNIEJ WOJNY. ROK 1943 [Fragments of reminiscences from the last war: 1943]. *Biuletyn Żydowskiego Instytutu Hist. w Polsce [Poland] 1980 (2-3): 99-111.*

Discusses the displacement of Jews from the Warsaw ghetto on 18-19 January 1943. After the author managed to take out his family (with the help of Poles, his friends) from the Umschlagplatz, he succeeded in hiding his next of kin in the Aryan part of the city. With changed identification documents, he and, separately, also his wife, were deported to a compulsory work camp, where they were fortunate in surviving the last period of war. The camp was liberated by the Soviet Army. After his return home, he also recovered his daughter. J

1034. Tyszka, Leon. WSPOMNIENIA Z GETTA WARSZAWSKIEGO [Reminiscences from the Warsaw ghetto]. *Biuletyn Żydowskiego Instytutu Historycznego w Polsce [Poland] 1974 (89): 109-126.* The author, who during the occupation was personal secretary of the chairman of the Council of Elders in the Warsaw ghetto, writes in his reminiscences about the relations which dominated in the administration of the Jewish Council (*Judenrat*) and outlines the character of the chairman—engineer Adam Czerniakow. Particularly interesting are the reminiscences concerning the period of the deportation and its course. The author devotes much space to Czerniakow, trying to show how difficult a role he had to play both with respect to the people imprisoned in the ghetto as well as in his official contacts with the German authorities. The tragedy of the chairman reached its summit in August 1942 when, refusing to reconcile himself to the mass deportation and extermination of Jews—he committed suicide. J

1035. Vidal-Naquet, Pierre. UN EICHMANN DE PAPIER [A paper Eichmann]. *Esprit [France] 1980 (9): 8-52.* Analyzes the debate on the reality of Nazi genocide; answers Faurisson's and other historical argumentation used to dispute the credibility of the events connected with the Nazi persecution of the Jews.

1036. Volk, Ludwig. EPISKOPAT UND KIRCHENKAMPF IM ZWEITEN WELTKRIEG: II. JUDENVERFOLGUNG UND ZUSAMMENBRUCH DES NS-STAATS [Episcopacy and church conflict in World War II: II. The persecution of the Jews and the collapse of the Nazi state]. *Stimmen der Zeit [West Germany] 1980 198(10): 687-702.* Continued from an earlier article. In contrast to the open opposition of leading German bishops against the National Socialist program of euthanasia, the deportation and mass murder of the Jews caused only four secret protests between 1942 and 1944.

1037. Voutey, Maurice. LES PERSECUTIONS RACIALES EN COTE-D'OR: CONTRIBUTION A L'ETUDE DES ARRESTATIONS [Racial persecution in the Côte-d'Or department: a contribution to the study of the arrests]. *Rev. d'Hist. de la Deuxième Guerre Mondiale [France] 1981 31(123): 17-30.* Of the 185 French and foreign Jews arrested in the department of Côte-d'Or (Burgundy) between 1941 and 1944, 93% failed to return. Almost half came from outside France. A surprisingly high percentage came from Alsace-Lorraine. Chronological development reveals the role of political hostage-taking and the presence of refugees from the combat zones. Analysis of procedures shows some lines of responsibility. Based on private archives. G. H. Davis

1038. Wachtel, Nathan. LE TEMPS DU SOUVENIR [The time for memory]. *Ann.: Écon., Soc., Civilisations [France] 1980 35(1): 146-148.* A critical appraisal of Claudine Vegh's *Je ne lui ai pas dit au revoir: Des enfants de déportés parlent* [I did not tell him good-bye: children of the deported speak] (Paris:

Gallimard, 1979), a series of autobiographical recollections of people whose parents died in Nazi concentration camps during World War II. It is a unique document which allows one to analyze a trauma affecting one or more generations. Primary sources; 4 notes. G. P. Cleyet

1039. Wagman Eshkoly, Hava. TAKHNIT TRANSNISTRIA—HIZDAMNUT HAZALA O HANAAH [The Transdniester Plan: an opportunity for life or a deceit?]. *Yalkut Moreshet Periodical [Israel] 1979 (27): 155-171.* Discusses the factors responsible for the nonrealization of the 1942 Transdniester Plan to save Romanian Jews. Based on protocols from Sokhnut management meetings; 70 notes.

1040. Wahlen, Verena. SELECT BIBLIOGRAPHY ON JUDENRAETE UNDER NAZI RULE. *Yad Vashem Studies on the European Jewish Catastrophe and Resistance [Israel] 1974 10: 277-294.* Isaiah Trunk's monumental work, *Judenrat: The Jewish Councils in Eastern Europe Under Nazi Occupation* (New York: Macmillan, 1972), brings renewed interest in the controversial activities of the Judenräte in Nazi-occupied Europe. Once again the question is being asked: Were the Jewish Councils a positive or negative factor in the final outcome of the Holocaust? In order to assist researchers and students of the Holocaust, a select bibliography with 214 entries is presented, covering Western as well as Eastern European sources. J. P. Fox

1041. Waite, Robert G. L. THE PERPETRATOR: HITLER AND THE HOLOCAUST. Ryan, Michael D., ed. *Human Responses to the Holocaust: Perpetrators and Victims, Bystanders and Resisters* (New York: Edwin Mellen Pr., 1981): 15-31. Discusses Adolf Hitler and the Holocaust from a psychological perspective, focusing on the personal sources of Hitler's anti-Semitism, and examines the revisionist views of David Irving, espoused in his book, *Hitler's War* (1977), in which Irving argues that Hitler never ordered the extermination of the Jews, which was due instead to the overzealousness of Heinrich Himmler (1900-45) and Adolf Eichmann (1906-62).

1042. Wallach, Jehuda L. FELDMARSCHALL ERICH VON MANSTEIN UND DIE DEUTSCHE JUDENAUSROTTUNG IN RUSSLAND [Field Marshal Erich von Manstein and the German Jewish exterminations in Russia]. *Jahrbuch des Instituts für Deutsche Geschichte [Israel] 1975 4: 457-472.* Discusses Manstein's policy toward the Jews in Russia during his command there in World War II. Attempts to answer two basic questions: 1) did Manstein take an active part in ordering the extermination of Russian Jews? and 2) Why did the British courtmartial acquit him of these charges? Manstein must have been acquainted with the actions of the SD (Sicherheitsdienst) against the Jews in his command area. His protestations of innocence were merely excuses and not explanations. The British acquitted Manstein because they did not know the full extent of Nazi brutality and because they thought Manstein was an example of the old German soldier with purely military interests. Primary and secondary sources; 28 notes. E. F. Stocker

1043. Wallach, Jehuda L. PROBLEMS DER ZWANGSARBEIT IN DER DEUTSCHEN KRIEGSWIRTSCHAFT [Problems of forced labor in the German war economy]. *Jahrbuch des Inst. für Deutsche Geschichte [Israel] 1977 6:*

477-512. Contrary to international covenants agreed to by the imperial German government, the Germans in World War II forced captured military personnel and millions of civilian men and women of occupied countries to work in German fields, mines, and factories. Ever more devious methods were employed to secure these forced laborers, and their treatment became more brutal as the needs of the German armies increased. Destruction of the Jews had been determined before the war, and the greatest excesses occurred where they were incarcerated. The author pays particular attention to Mauthausen and Auschwitz concentration camps and to the responsibility of high officials for forced labor. Based on *Das Urteil von Nürnberg;* 85 notes. M. Faissler

1044. Weinrib, Abrasha. ZIKHRONOT SHEL ROFE MIGETTO VILNA [Memories of a doctor from Vilnius Ghetto]. *Yalkut Moreshet Periodical [Israel] 1979 (27): 7-60.* Describes experiences as a doctor in the ghetto hospital of Vilnius, Lithuania during the Nazi occupation and records impressions of the role of the Judenrat, centering on such moral dilemmas as the right to determine the fate of others and the nature of resistance.

1045. Weiss, Aharon. HA-"13" BEGETO VARSHAH [The Warsaw ghetto 13]. *Yalkut Moreshet Periodical [Israel] 1976 21: 157-180.* Avraham Ganzweich headed a unique organization in the Warsaw ghetto, equivalent to the Jewish council (Judenrat), which had close ties with the Gestapo.

1046. Weiss, Aharon. IYUN NOSAF BENOSE HA"YUDENRATIM" [Further insight into the problem of the Judenrats]. *Gal-Ed: On the Hist. of the Jews in Poland [Israel] 1976 (3): 279-294.* Describes changing concepts in the duties and organization of Judenräte (Jewish Councils) during World War II.

1047. Weiss, Aharon. JEWISH LEADERSHIP IN OCCUPIED POLAND —POSTURES AND ATTITUDES. *Yad Vashem Studies on the European Jewish Catastrophe and Resistance [Israel] 1977 12: 335-366.* From 1939 to 1941 Poland was occupied jointly by the Soviet Union and Germany. The author describes Jewish attitudes and behavior during this period, with emphasis on the changing role of the Nazi-imposed Jewish Councils *(Judenräte).* As German policy toward the Jews became more stringent, most of the original *Judenräte* found it impossible to serve the interests of the Jewish communities, and they were replaced by more compliant "representatives." During the Soviet administration of Eastern Galicia, communal life centered in religious institutions, where, despite incessant harassment, Jewish leadership was exerted effectively. 4 tables, 77 notes. B. Reiner

1048. Weiss, Aharon. QUANTITATIVE MEASUREMENT OF FEATURES OF THE HOLOCAUST. *Yad Vashem Studies on the European Jewish Catastrophe and Resistance [Israel] 1981 14: 319-334.* Presents critical notes on Helen Fein's *Accounting for Genocide* (1979). Fein attempted to account for the differences in numbers of Jewish casualties in European countries that were dominated by the Nazis. The extensive sociological model she constructed is criticized on the grounds that it is insensitive to the complexity of the historical data. Quantitative methods are a useful tool in understanding the Holocaust, but a more precise and refined methodogy is required. 5 notes. B. Reiner

1049. Wiesel, Elie. THEN AND NOW: THE EXPERIENCES OF A TEACHER. *Social Educ. 1978 42(4): 266-271.* Since 1945 there have been efforts to deny the reality of the Holocaust, to obliterate the memories of the survivors, and to exonerate Adolf Hitler and his subordinates.

1050. Winick, Myron. THE WARSAW GHETTO STARVATION STUDIES. *Centerpoint 1980 4(1): 70-73.* Summarizes the historical context, methodology, and findings of the hunger and disease research documenting the planned starvation of the Jewish population of the Warsaw ghetto, 1941-42.

1051. Woodman, Gayle M. BIBLIOGRAPHY OF PERIODICALS: THE HOLOCAUST, 1939-1945. Ryan, Michael D., ed. *Human Responses to the Holocaust: Perpetrators and Victims, Bystanders and Resisters* (New York: Edwin Mellen Pr., 1981): 261-278. A bibliography of historical and theological writings on the Holocaust period, 1939-45, published between 1960 and 1978.

1052. Zahn, Gordon C. CATHOLIC RESPONSES TO THE HOLOCAUST. *Thought 1981 56(221): 153-162.* Christian communities within Germany and outside failed to meet their moral obligation to witness against the Holocaust. The official silence of the Catholic Church was due only in part to theological and cultural anti-Semitism. More important were Church leaders' fear of reprisals and policy of neutrality to support possible papal intervention and mediation. Also, formal condemnation of Third Reich policies toward Jews would have exposed Jews in Vatican safe-keeping to immediate arrest. What has received little attention to date, largely due to its necessary secrecy, is the institutional support of the Church in sheltering individual Jews and ushering them to safe countries. 8 notes.
R. D. Rahmes

1053. Zerner, Ruth. GERMANY'S CONFESSING CHURCH LEADERS AND THE JEWS IN THE 1930S: A COMMENT. *Centerpoint 1980 4(1): 101-112.* Discusses the acceptance by most of the German Protestant clergy of popular prejudices against the Jews, the actions of those few church leaders who worked actively against German anti-Semitism, and the excesses of the Nazi regime.

1054. Zimandt, Roman. "BALEILAH MI-12 'AD 5 BABOKER LO YASHNANTI" (AL YOMANO SHEL ADAM CZERNIAKOV) ["From midnight to 5 a.m. I did not sleep": Adam Czerniakow's diary]. *Yalkut Moreshet Periodical [Israel] 1975 20: 51-88; 1976 21: 139-156.* Adam Czerniakow, head of the Warsaw Jewish Council (Judenrat), 1939-42, kept a diary because he expected to survive and save many Jews. His diary details the living conditions of the Warsaw ghetto Jewish community and shows his state of mind, leading to his eventual suicide, when ordered to organize death camp deportations.

1055. Zuckerman, Itzhak. HA'IRGUN HAYEHUDI HALOHEM [The Jewish Fighting Organization]. *Yalkut Moreshet Periodical [Israel] 1981 (32): 5-32.* The posthumous publication of an interview held in 1973 with Itzhak Zuckerman (d. 1981), the last leader of the Jewish Fighting Organization of Warsaw. Details the opposition to the Nazis, the role of youth movements, the cooperation and differences of opinion, the timing of the Warsaw ghetto uprising, and the fate of some of its leaders. Based on personal memoirs; 10 notes.
R. Hetzron

1056. Zuroff, Efraim. CONFERENCES AND SYMPOSIA ON THE HOLOCAUST (1973-1974). *Yad Vashem Studies on the European Jewish Catastrophe and Resistance [Israel] 1974 10: 295-306.* The year 1973 marked the 30th anniversary of the ghetto uprisings in Nazi-occupied Europe and 25 years since the founding of Israel. These events were commemorated by many conferences and symposia on the Holocaust. Attention was focused on the execution of the Final Solution, efforts to rescue Jews, the lessons of the Holocaust, and the impact of the disaster in Europe on the establishment of Israel.   J. P. Fox

1057. —. DID HITLER EVER LIVE? *Patterns of Prejudice [Great Britain] 1977 11(3): 10-12.* Questions David Irving's account of Hitler's World War II years in *Hitler's War* (London: Hodder and Stoughton: 1977), especially the contention that Hitler was ignorant of the genocide of European Jews.

1058. —. DISTORTING HISTORICAL EVIDENCE. *Patterns of Prejudice [Great Britain] 1978 12(2): 8-10, 11.* David Irving, a British historian and author of *Hitler's War,* which alleges Adolf Hitler's ignorance of the extermination of German Jewry, not only distorts evidence but also is guilty of misinterpretation and partisanship.

1059. —. NEO-NAZI VIEW OF THE HOLOCAUST. *Patterns of Prejudice [Great Britain] 1973 7(5): 19-21.* Discusses the publication of Reich Ministry of Propaganda directives dealing with crimes against Jews by Nazis in Germany from 1939-45, and its relationship to the current rightist movement in West Germany.

1060. —. THIRD INTERNATIONAL HISTORICAL CONFERENCE. *Yad Vashem Studies on the European Jewish Catastrophe and Resistance [Israel] 1977 12: 367-369.* Lists speakers and lectures at a conference organized by the Yad Vashem Scientific Advisory Board, 4-7 April 1977, on "The *Judenräte* and the Patterns of Jewish Leadership in Nazi Europe—1933-45."   B. Reiner

1061. —. WALTER SPITZER: THE ARTIST AS WITNESS. *Centerpoint 1980 4(1): 87-94.* Describes the wartime experiences of a Jewish artist incarcerated in German concentration camps; includes drawings of camp life never before published.

SUBJECT INDEX

Subject Profile Index (ABC-SPIndex) carries both generic and specific index terms. Begin a search at the general term but also look under more specific or related terms. Cross-references also appear in this index.

Each string of index descriptors is intended to present a profile of a given article; however, no particular relationship between any two terms in the profile is implied. Terms within the profile are listed alphabetically after the leading term. The variety of punctuation and capitalization reflects production methods and has no intrinsic meaning; e.g., there is no difference in meaning between "History, study of" and "History (study of)."

Cities, towns, counties, and other small geographical subdivisions are normally listed in parentheses following their respective countries, e.g., "France (Paris)." However, certain regions of divided, disputed, changed, or indeterminate sovereignty do appear as leading terms listed alphabetically in the index, e.g., "Alsace-Lorraine," "Danzig (Free City 1919-39)," "Kashmir." Both "Great Britain" and "England" are indexed, the latter primarily when followed by geographical modifiers, e.g., "England (London)." The constituent republics of the USSR, e.g., "Ukraine," "Tadzhikistan," as well as its major regions, e.g., "Asia, Central," "Siberia," also appear as leading terms.

Terms beginning with an arabic numeral are listed after the letter Z. Chronology of a particular article appears at the end of the string of index descriptors. In the chronological descriptor, 'c' stands for century, e.g., "19c" means "19th century."

The last number in the index string, in italics, refers to the bibliographic entry number.

A

Aachen (battle). Military Strategy. 1944. *479*
Abs, Hermann J. Deutsche Bank. Goering, Hermann. 1940. *339*
Abwehr. Intelligence services. Military Organization (fusion). SD (Sicherheitsdienst). 1944. *29*
Admiral Scheer (cruiser). Kara Sea. Naval Strategy. Operation Wunderland. 1942. *659*
Aesthetics. Industrial Relations. Labor. Nazism. Symbolism. 1933-39. *210*
—. Nazism. 1920-45. *84*
Affiche Rouge. France. Psychological Warfare. Resistance. Trials. 1944. *495*
Afghanistan. Foreign Relations. Weizsäcker, Ernst von. 1940. *351*
Africa. Armies (Supreme Command; documents). Middle East. Military campaigns, plans for. 1941-45. *513*
—. Nazi Party (Colonial Political Office). Pacific Area. War aims memorandum. Weigelt, Kurt. 1940. *55*
—. War aims. 1939-45. *116*
Africa, North. Afrika Corps. Armored Vehicles and Tank Warfare. Great Britain. 1940-42. *521*
—. Egypt. Libya. Rommel, Erwin. 1941-42. *520*
—. Hitler, Adolf. Logistics. Military Strategy. Rommel, Erwin. 1941-42. *555*
—. Jews. Vichy regime. World War II (antecedents). 1930-40. *764*
—. Tobruk (battle). 1942. *532*
Afrika Corps. Prisoners of War. USA (Louisiana). 1943-46. *544*
—. Africa, North. Armored Vehicles and Tank Warfare. Great Britain. 1940-42. *521*
Agricultural labor. 1942-45. *158*
Agricultural Policy. Backe, Herbert. Nazism. 1936-42. *157*
—. Czechoslovakia (Moravia; Silesia). Military occupation. 1938-45. *590*
Ainsztein, Reuben. Europe, Eastern. Jews (review article). Resistance. 1939-45. *823*

Air Forces. Armies. Europe. Great Britain. Greece. Italy. 1940-41. *640*
—. Armored Vehicles and Tank Warfare. Meyer, Bruno. USSR (Kursk). 1943. *723*
—. Eastern front. 1939-45. *77*
—. Economic Policy. Military Occupation. 1939-45. *334*
—. Hungary. 1938-44. *317*
—. Irving, David. Milch, Erhard (review article). 1933-45. *156*
—. Military Strategy. 1939-41. *188*
Air transport forces. Military strategy. 1936-44. *151*
Air warfare. Architecture. World War II (antecedents). 1933-45. *31*
—. Arnhem (battle). Operation Market-Garden. Ryan, Cornelius (review article). 1944. *501*
—. Belorussia. Memoirs. Ukraine (Chernigov). 1943-44. *726*
—. Bombing, strategic. Military Strategy. 1934-45. *198*
—. Hitler, Adolf. Military Strategy. 1941-45. *199*
—. Kursk, battle of. Tactics. Tanks. 1943. *724*
—. Military Strategy. 1918-45. *254*
—. Military Strategy. Pokryshkin, Aleksandr (memoir). USSR (Kuban). 1943. *722*
—. Netherlands (Rotterdam). 1940. *550*
Air Warfare (personal accounts). Europe. USA. 1942. *24*
Airborne troops. 1887-1945. *201*
—. Crete (battle). 1941. *551*
—. Crete (battle). Freyberg, Bernard Cyril. Military Campaigns. Student, Kurt. 1941. *473*
—. Partisans. Street, Lieutenant Colonel (report). Yugoslavia (Drvar). 1944. *571*
Aircraft carriers. Submarine Warfare. 1939-45. *534*
Airplane Industry and Trade. France. Vichy regime. 1940-43. *297*
—. Germany (Rostock). Social organization. 1939-45. *70*

Airplane Industry

—. Ostmark Aircraft Motor Works. Yugoslavia (Maribor). 1940-45. *118*
Airplanes. Espinosa, Manuel (memoirs). Spain. Travel. ca 1944. *296*
Airplanes, Military. Technology, development of. 1939-45. *75*
Airplanes, Military (heavy bomber; development). Goering, Hermann. Milch, Erhard. 1932-37. *102*
Air-sea rescue operations. *Seenotdienst*. 1937-41. *253*
Albania. Atrocities. Military Occupation. 1939-44. *609*
—. Communism. Military Occupation. 1943. *565*
—. Economic Conditions. Military Occupation. 1943-44. *586*
—. Military Occupation. Resistance. 1943. *564*
Alliances. 1939-45. *303*
—. Axis pact. Bulgaria. 1941-45. *633*
—. Italy. Military Strategy. 1927-45. *345*
Allied collapse. Military Strategy. 1940. *453*
Allied invasion, expected. France. Military Strategy. Rommel, Erwin. Rundstedt, Gerd von. 1942-44. *561*
Allies. Bibliographies. Italy. Military occupation. Resistance. 1939-45. *474*
—. Boundaries. Military Occupation. 1943-45. *28*
—. France. Military campaigns. Operation Dragoon. Operation Overlord. USA. 1944. *562*
—. France (Paris). Liberation. Resistance. 1944. *545*
—. Historiography. Italy. Military occupation. Resistance. 1939-45. *455*
—. Italy, North. Operation Sunrise. 1944-45. *464*
—. Military Campaigns. Norway, Northern. 1940. *514*
—. Military intelligence. Military strategy. Scandinavia. 1939-40. *441*
—. Military intelligence. Ultra. 1920's-45. *115*
—. Military Occupation. Sudetenland. 1945. *595*
Alsace-Lorraine. France. Germanization. Kettenbacher, Lothar. 1940-44. *497*
—. France. Iron Industry. 1940-44. *364*
Alter, Wiktor. Anti-Nazi Movements. Erlich, Henryk. Jews. USSR. 1939-41. *988*
American Jewish Committee (William E. Wiener Oral History Library). Genocide. Jews. Oral History. 1941-45. 1977-82. *996*
Amt Schrifttumspflege. Censorship. Literature. Nazism. 1932-45. *218*
Anielewicz, Mordechai. Jewish Fighting Organization. People's Guard. Poland. Warsaw ghetto uprising. Youth groups. 1930's-42. *899*
Annexation. Czechoslovakia (Eastern Sudetenland). Daily Life. 1938-45. *570*
—. France (Briey, Longwy, Nancy). Klein Commission. Mining industry. War aims. 1911-42. *295*
Anschluss. Austria. Resistance. 1938-45. *278*
Anti-aircraft defense. Cities. Rockets. USSR. 1937-45. *701*
Anti-Communism. Germany, West. Nazism. Political Education. Propaganda. Youth. 1933-78. *260*
Anti-Communist Movements. Brandt, Willi. Goebbels, Joseph. Propaganda. Taubert, Eberhard. 1931-60. *2*
—. Foreign Auxiliaries. USSR. 1941. *681*
Anti-Fascism. Communist Party. Sweden. 1933-43. *203*
—. Paulus, Friedrich von. 1943-44. *665*

Anti-Fascist Bloc. Memoirs. Poland (Warsaw ghetto). Resistance. 1941-44. *786*
Anti-Fascist Movements. Communist Party. Concentration camps. Resistance. 1933-45. *939*
—. Nazism. Political Factions. Resistance. 1933-45. *171*
Anti-Nazi Movements. Alter, Wiktor. Erlich, Henryk. Jews. USSR. 1939-41. *988*
—. Assassination. Bonhoeffer, Dietrich. Hitler, Adolf. Moltke, Helmuth James von. 1940-45. *195*
—. Communist Party. Manouchian group. Resistance. 1939-45. *32*
—. Jews. Poland (Warsaw ghetto). Socialist movement. 1939-44. *832*
—. Kreisau Circle. 1938-44. *131*
—. Kreisau Circle. Moltke, Helmuth James von. 1929-44. *169*
—. Scholl, Hans and Sophie (commemoration). 1940-43. *268*
—. Trott, Adam von. 1929-44. *160*
Anti-Nazi movements (conference). Poland. 1933-45. ca 1977. *145*
Anti-Semitism *See also* Jews.
—. Auschwitz-Birkenau. Concentration Camps. Historiography. Poland. Resistance. 1939-78. *890*
—. Bernadotte, Folke (letter). Forgery. Himmler, Heinrich. Kersten, Felix. 1944-45. *847*
—. Christianity. Historiography. 19c-20c. *1008*
—. Clergy. Confessing Church. Resistance. 1930's-45. *1053*
—. Darwinism. Europe. Nietzsche, Friedrich. 1800-1945. *1028*
—. Expansionism. Genocide. Nazism. 1919-45. *94*
—. Expansionism. Hitler, Adolf. Nationalism. 1919-40. *17*
—. Films. *Jew Süss* (film). Nazism. Propaganda. 1940's. *859*
—. Genocide. Jews. 1933-77. *1049*
—. Genocide. Jews. Nazism. 1939-45. *885*
—. Genocide. Jews. Nazism. Political Theory. 1917-45. *1026*
—. Genocide. Press. Propaganda. 1943. *957*
—. Government-in-exile, London. Poland. Schwarzbart, I. 1933-45. *770*
—. Hitler, Adolf. Italy. 1938-43. *964*
—. Ideology. Nazism. Racism. World War II (antecedents). 1933-45. *981*
—. Jews. Netherlands (Leiden). Orphanage. 1940-43. *916*
—. Nazism. 1930's-40's. *865*
—. Nazism. Political Leadership. ca 1929-45. *867*
—. "Völkisch" ideology. 19c-20c. *794*
Antonescu, Ion. Foreign Relations. Romania. 1944. *289*
Arab States. Foreign Relations. Hussein, Muhammad Amin al-. 1941-45. *44*
Archaeology. Espionage. Middle East. Oppenheim, Max von. 1890's-1946. *327*
—. Nazism. Schnapp, Alain. 1933-44. *227*
Architecture. Air warfare. World War II (antecedents). 1933-45. *31*
Archival Catalogs and Inventories. Jewish Historical Institute. Poland. 1940-47. *902*
Archives. Czechoslovakia (Slovakia). Military Occupation. ca 1943-45. *600*
—. France (Vincennes). Historical Service of the Army (Military History Center). 1939-78. *43*
—. Genocide. Jews. Poland (Warsaw ghetto). Ringelblum, Emanuel. 1942-43. *1002*
—. Heike, Otto. Military Occupation. Poland (Łódz). 1939-45. *388*

—. Jewish Historical Institute. Poland. Warsaw ghetto uprising. 1942. *846*
—. Military Occupation. Poland (Lublin). 1939-44. *439*
—. Military Occupation. Poland (Pszczyna). 1939-45. *427*
—. Military Occupation. Public Administration. Yugoslavia (Slovenia). 1941-45. *583*
—. Nazism (documents). 1933-45. *109*
—. Poland (Wroclaw). Prisoners of War. 1939-45. *401*
Archives, National. Genocide. Jews. Rescue. USA. War Refugee Board. 1918-52. *961*
Archives, provincial. Documents. Poland (Rzeszów). War crimes. 1939-45. *378*
Archives (records preservation). Majdanek Concentration Camp chancery. Poland. 1941-44. *941*
Archives, underground. Historians. Jews. Military Occupation. Poland (Warsaw ghetto). Ringelblum, Emanuel. 1939-50. *1025*
Arctic Ocean. Battles. USSR. 1941-45. *742*
Arendt, Hannah. Ethnocentrism. Genealogy. Jews. Political Theory. 1958-65. *828*
Armaments. Infantry. Statistics. 1939-44. *148*
Armaments industry. Austria. Economic Policy. Nazism. 1939-44. *312*
—. Documents. Labor, forced. 1943. *45*
Armies. Air Forces. Europe. Great Britain. Greece. Italy. 1940-41. *640*
—. Eastern Front. General staff. Halder, Franz. Military Strategy (review). 1941. *754*
—. Poles. Psychological Warfare. 1939-45. *546*
—. Psychological warfare. 1939-45. *42*
Armies (Supreme Command; documents). Africa. Middle East. Military campaigns, plans for. 1941-45. *513*
Armistice. Finland (Lapland). Roads. USSR. 1940-45. *310*
Armored Vehicles and Tank Warfare See also Tanks.
—. 1939-79. *106*
—. Afrika Corps. Africa, North. Great Britain. 1940-42. *521*
—. Air Forces. Meyer, Bruno. USSR (Kursk). 1943. *723*
—. Eastern front. 1941-45. *587*
—. Eastern front. Ukraine (Bogodukhov). 1943. *684*
—. Military Strategy. USSR. 1941-43. *700*
—. Prokhorovka (battle). USSR. 1943. *672*
—. Tactics (battle plan State Farm 79). 1942-77. *668*
Army. Assassination. Hitler, Adolf. July 20 plot. 1944. *61*
—. Bamler, Rudolf. Military Occupation (preparation). Sweden. 1940-44. *272*
—. Belgium. Collaboration movements. Himmler, Heinrich. Reeder, Eggert. SS (Schutzstaffel; appointments). 1941-44. *462*
—. Military Supplies. 1941-45. *241*
—. National Socialist Leadership Officers. Political education. 1943-45. *209*
—. Veterinary service. 1932-45. *134*
Army Group Center. Partisans. USSR. 1942-44. *654*
Army officer (capture). Romania. 1944. *620*
Army, 2d. Poland (Horka). SS (Schutzstaffel). War Crimes. 1945. *420*
Army, 20th. Finland, north. 1944. *698*
Arnhem (battle). Air Warfare. Operation Market-Garden. Ryan, Cornelius (review article). 1944. *501*
Art. Concentration camps. Daily Life. Spitzer, Walter. 1939-45. *1061*
—. Concentration camps. Jews. Resistance, spiritual. 1940-45. *962*
—. Culture. Military Occupation. Poland. 1939-45. *433*

Art, seizures of. Military Occupation. 1940-44. *233*
Art treasures. Germany (Dresden). Königstein Fortress. Staatliche Kunstsammlungen Dresden. USSR. 1945. *737*
Artillery. V3 Rocket. Weapons. 1943-44. *76*
Asia, East. Electrical industry. Felten & Guilleaume. North German Ocean Cable Works. 1850-1939. *298*
Assassination. Anti-Nazi Movements. Bonhoeffer, Dietrich. Hitler, Adolf. Moltke, Helmuth James von. 1940-45. *195*
—. Army. Hitler, Adolf. July 20 plot. 1944. *61*
—. Fascism. Nazism. 1933-44. *207*
—. Kutschera, Franz. Poland (Warsaw). Resistance. 1944. *422*
Assassination attempts. Hitler, Adolf. Stauffenberg, Claus von. 1938-44. *185*
Asylums, inmates of. Church leaders. Genocide. 1940-41. *870*
Atlantic, North. Communications. Norway. Shipping. 1940. *554*
—. Submarine warfare. 1939-43. *459*
Atomic energy. Research. 1935-45. *19*
Atrocities. Albania. Military Occupation. 1939-44. *609*
—. Babi Yar (massacre). Jews. 1941-43. *921*
—. Blobel, Paul. Concentration Camps. Poland (Białystok). Sonderkommando 1005. 1940-45. *821*
—. Communists. Jews. USSR. 1939-41. *683*
—. Concentration camps. Veliki Bečerek. Yugoslavia (Banat). 1941-45. *1014*
—. Galicia Division. Historiography. Poland. Ukrainians. USSR. 1943-45. *749*
—. Germans. Poland. 1939. *417*
—. Nazism (review article). Psychohistory. ca 1930's-45. *138*
—. Ukraine (Czech Malín). USSR. 1943. *597*
Attitudes. Emigrants. Poles. Warsaw ghetto uprising. 1942-43. *829*
—. Germans. Military occupation. Poland. Propaganda, underground. 1939-45. *431*
—. Jewish Councils. Military Occupation. Poland. USSR. 1939-41. *1047*
—. Tito, Josip (personality, documents). 1941-44. *617*
Auflockerung Räumung Lähmung Zerstörung (ARLZ). Czechoslovakia. Documents. Evacuation. Germans. 1944-45. *634*
Augustus II, code name. People's Army. People's Guard. Poland (Miechów; Mniszek). Resistance. 1939-45. *409*
Auschwitz. Autobiography. Concentration Camps. Hoess, Rudolf. Nazism. 1939-45. *811*
—. Autobiography. Concentration Camps. Hoess, Rudolf. War crimes. 1906-47. *901*
—. Children. Deportation. France. Jews. Vichy Regime. 1942-44. *955*
—. Concentration Camps. Diaries. 1940-44. *954*
—. Concentration Camps. Dubois, Stanisław (pseud. Dębski). Poland. 1940-42. *919*
—. Concentration Camps. Genocide. Hoess, Rudolf. Sociology. 1942-45. *913*
—. Concentration Camps. Jews. Poland. 1940-45. *994*
—. Concentration Camps. Jews. Theresienstadt camp. 1943-44. *931*
—. Concentration camps. Labor, forced. Mauthausen. 1935-45. *1043*
—. Concentration Camps. Poland. 1939-45. *982*
—. Concentration Camps. Vrba, Rudolf. 1933-45. *812*
Auschwitz (escape). Bikel, Sara. Concentration Camps. Jews. Rosenstein, Hana. 1944. *841*

Auschwitz (evacuation). Concentration Camps. Diaries. Heller, Paul. 1945. *891*
—. Concentration camps. Poland (Nysa district). 1945. *817*
—. Concentration Camps. Poland (Opole; Prudnik). 1944-45. *971*
Auschwitz-Birkenau. Anti-Semitism. Concentration Camps. Historiography. Poland. Resistance. 1939-78. *890*
Australia. *Kormoran* (warship). Naval Battles. *Sydney* (warship). 1941. *153*
Australia (Hay). *Dunera* (vessel). Prisoners of War (memoirs). 1940-41. *498*
Austria. Anschluss. Resistance. 1938-45. *278*
—. Armaments industry. Economic Policy. Nazism. 1939-44. *312*
—. Authors. Exiles. Rheinhardt, Emil Alphons (letters). 1930's-45. *1018*
—. Concentration Camps. Cortey, Maria-Dolors (memoirs). Mauthausen. 1939-45. *815*
—. Foreign Relations. Italy. South Tyrol. 1938-45. *290*
—. Germany, West. Neo-Nazism. Propaganda. 1960's-70's. *149*
—. Italy. South Tyrol. 1938-45. *355*
Austria (Lower Austria; Zwettl). Jury, Hugy. 1945. *614*
Austria (Styria). Political Conditions. Social Conditions. 1940-45. *604*
Austria (Styria; Fischbach). World War II (end). 1945. *693*
Austria (Styria; Hochschwab). Resettlement. South Tyrol (Gröden valley). SS (Schutzstaffel). 1940-41. *119*
Austria (Vienna). Foreign policy. Munich crisis. Nazism. Neubacher, Hermann. 1938-40. *282*
Authors. Austria. Exiles. Rheinhardt, Emil Alphons (letters). 1930's-45. *1018*
—. Jews. Poland (Warsaw ghetto). 1939-45. *778*
Autobiography. Auschwitz. Concentration Camps. Hoess, Rudolf. Nazism. 1939-45. *811*
—. Auschwitz. Concentration Camps. Hoess, Rudolf. War crimes. 1906-47. *901*
Avant-garde (term). Expressionism. 20c. *270*
Aviation, civil. Partisans. Ukraine. 1941-45. *676*
Axis, defection from. War aims. 1939-45. *346*
Axis pact. Alliances. Bulgaria. 1941-45. *633*
—. Italy. Japan. Oshima Hiroshi. World War II (antecedents). 1934-40. *283*
Axis powers. Diplomacy. Tripartite Pact. Yugoslavia. 1939-41. *363*
—. Horthy, Miklós. Hungary. Kallay, Miklós. Negotiations. 1943. *311*
—. Neutrality. World War II (antecedents). Yugoslavia. 1939. *284*
Axis powers (defeat). 1943-45. *249*

B

Babi Yar (massacre). Atrocities. Jews. 1941-43. *921*
Backe, Herbert. Agricultural Policy. Nazism. 1936-42. *157*
Badoglio, Pietro. Foreign Relations. Italy. Keitel, Wilhelm. Marras, Luigi (papers). 1936-43. *286*
Bagramian, Ivan (memoirs). Military Campaigns. Ukraine. USSR. 1942. *657*
—. Operation Citadel. USSR (Briansk, Orel). 1942-43. *656*
Balance of power. Europe. 1800-1945. *135*
Balkans. Coups d'Etat (August 1944). Resistance. Romania. Yugoslavia. 1944. *567*
—. Europe, Central. Propaganda (conference). 1939-45. *580*
—. Expansionism. Ideology. 1938-44. *599*
—. Foreign Policy. 1933-41. *601*
—. Hitler, Adolf. Italians. Lanz, Hubert. Military Command. Surrender. 1943. *502*
—. Military Intelligence. Military Strategy. 1944. *568*
—. Propaganda. 1939-45. *630*
Balkans (documents). Historiography, East German. 1939-45. *632*
Balkans policy. Macedonia. 1878-1945. *648*
Ball-bearings. SKF. Sweden. War economy. 1939-45. *301*
Balta (battle). USSR. 1941. *680*
Baltic Area. Baltic German Church (removal). Clergy. Poland (Łódz, Poznań). 1939-44. *435*
—. Military campaigns. USSR. 1944-45. *736*
—. Minelaying operations. USSR. 1941. *650*
Baltic German Church (removal). Baltic Area. Clergy. Poland (Łódz, Poznań). 1939-44. *435*
Baltic Sea. Degelow, Hans J. (photographs). Navies. 1943-45. *674*
Baltic States. Documents. Military occupation. Office of Strategic Services. 1941-45. *713*
—. USSR. 1939. *666*
Bamler, Rudolf. Army. Military Occupation (preparation). Sweden. 1940-44. *272*
Banking. Documents. Reichsbank. USSR. World War II (antecedents). 1941. *715*
Bar association. Lawyers. Nazism. 1928-45. *273*
Bartel, Walter (memoirs). Buchenwald. Concentration Camps. Resistance. 1945. *777*
Bartoszewski, Władysław. Military Occupation (review article). Poland (Warsaw). 1939-45. *429*
Battles *See also* names of specific battles, e.g., Arnhem, Balta, and names of specific operations, e.g., Operation Hercules; Military Campaigns.
—. Arctic Ocean. USSR. 1941-45. *742*
—. Germany, western. Netherlands. 1944-45. *527*
—. Military Strategy. USSR. Vistula-Oder campaign. 1945. *652*
—. Morale. 1944-45. *478*
Behavior. Hitler, Adolf. 1939-45. *38*
Belgians. Prisoners of war. Protestants. Religious life. 1940-45. *482*
—. Prisoners of war. Religious life. 1940-45. *483*
Belgium. Army. Collaboration movements. Himmler, Heinrich. Reeder, Eggert. SS (Schutzstaffel; appointments). 1941-44. *462*
—. Buchenwald. Concentration camps. Evacuation. Labor camps. Military Occupation. 1944. *541*
—. Catholic Church. Labor Unions and Organizations. Military Occupation. 1940-42. *476*
—. Charles, J. L. Dasney, F. Geheime Feldpolizei (reports). Jews. Resistance. 1940-42. *457*
—. Christian Workers Youth. Resistance. 1942-44. *543*
—. Collaboration. Degrelle, Léon. Rexist Party. World War II (antecedents). 1933-40. *493*
—. Collaboration. Economic Conditions (review article). Gillingham, John. Nazis. 1936-44. *556*
—. Conferences. Foreign policy. 1940. *362*
—. Confiscation. Jews. Property. 1940-44. *1011*
—. Diplomacy. Netherlands. Peace. 1939-40. *559*
—. Diplomatic representation. Government-in-exile. Switzerland. 1940-45. *343*
—. Genocide. Gypsies. 1940-45. *868*
—. Invasion (threat). Military Intelligence. 1939-40. *558*

Bulgarians 227

—. Military Strategy (attack planes). World War II (antecedents). 1939-40. *557*
Belgium (Brussels). Collaboration. Himmler, Heinrich. Military Occupation. Reeder, Eggert. SS (Schutzstaffel; appointments). 1942-43. *461*
Belgium (Kortrijk). Conscription, Civilian. Labor. 1940-45. *528*
Belorussia. Air warfare. Memoirs. Ukraine (Chernigov). 1943-44. *726*
—. Genocide (documents). Jews. Military Occupation. Ukraine. USSR. 1941-45. *976*
—. Germans. Partisans. USSR. 1942-45. *716*
Belorussia (Grodno ghetto). Family. Memoirs. Military Occupation. 1941-45. *798*
Belzec. Concentration Camps. Poland. 1939-45. *1030*
Ben, Fritz. Resistance. Titov, Vasilj. USSR (Ust'-Luga). 1942-43. *694*
Beneš, Eduard. Jaksch, Wenzel (correspondence). Sudeten Germans (expulsion). 1939-43. *637*
Berberova, Nina. Memoirs. Turgenev Library. 1880-1945. *446*
Bergen-Belsen. Concentration Camps. 1945. *882*
—. Concentration Camps. Gitler-Barski, Józef (diary). 1943-45. *862*
Berger, Gottlob. Military Recruitment. Waffen-SS. 1939-40. *212*
Berlin (battle). Tactics. USSR. 1945. *731*
Berlin, fall of. Chuikov, Vasili (memoirs). 1945. *671*
Bernadotte, Folke (letter). Anti-Semitism. Forgery. Himmler, Heinrich. Kersten, Felix. 1944-45. *847*
Bessarabia. Jews. USSR. 1940-45. *945*
Bibliographies. Allies. Italy. Military occupation. Resistance. 1939-45. *474*
—. Danzig. Poland. Westerplatte, battle of. 1939. *387*
—. Denmark. Military Occupation. 1940-43. *560*
—. Domestic policy. Foreign policy. 1933-45. *95*
—. Domestic policy. Foreign policy. 1933-45. *96*
—. France. Hitler, Adolf. 1919-39. *25*
—. Genocide. Jews. 1939-45. 1960-78. *1051*
—. Germany, West. Historiography. 1939-75. *107*
—. Germany, West. Militärgeschichtliches Forschungsamt. Military history. 1648-1974. *219*
—. Historiography. Netherlands. 1939-75. *480*
—. Hitler, Adolf. Political Leadership. 1919-80. *123*
—. Jewish Councils. Trunk, Isaiah. 1939-44. *1040*
—. *Jewish Gazette*. Music. Poland (Warsaw Ghetto). 1940-42. *857*
—. Nazism. Psychohistory. 1933-45. *177*
Bihaly, Andrew. Diaries (review article). Genocide. Hungary. Jews. 1944. *799*
Bikel, Sara. Auschwitz (escape). Concentration Camps. Jews. Rosenstein, Hana. 1944. *841*
Biography. Davidson, Eugene. Historiography. Hitler, Adolf (review article). Irving, David. Toland, John. 1930's-77. *163*
Birkenau. Concentration Camps. Czechoslovakia (Terezin ghetto). Genocide. Jews. 1943-44. *911*
Birth rate. Nazi Party. Population policy. Reichsbund der Kinderreichen. 1930-44. *245*
Bishops. Genocide. Jews. 1942-44. *1036*
Bismarck (battleship). Military Intelligence. Naval Vessels (spy ships). 1939-45. *113*
—. Naval Strategy. 1941. *487*
Black Sea. Eastern front. Logistics. Military Strategy. 1942. *710*

Blitzkrieg. Military strategy. 1939-45. *179*
—. Military Strategy. 1941-42. *753*
—. Military Strategy. Nazism. USSR. World War II (antecedents). 1914-45. *66*
Blobel, Paul. Atrocities. Concentration Camps. Poland (Białystok). Sonderkommando 1005. 1940-45. *821*
Bloch, Eduard. Hitler, Adolf (review article). Jews. Psychohistory. Stierlin, Helm. 1907-45. 1973-76. *114*
Blohm & Voss. Germany (Hamburg). Shipbuilding. 1877-1977. *315*
Bock, Franz Heinrich (diary). Military Occupation. Poland (Poddębice). 1940-42. *416*
Bohemia. Political Integration. 1938-45. *594*
Bombing. Fuller, J. F. C. Germany (Freiburg). Military history. 1940-61. *481*
—. Memoirs. Speer, Albert. 1944. *547*
Bombing, strategic. Air Warfare. Military Strategy. 1934-45. *198*
Bonhoeffer, Dietrich. Anti-Nazi Movements. Assassination. Hitler, Adolf. Moltke, Helmuth James von. 1940-45. *195*
Bonnard, Abel. Collaboration. France. Ideology. Vichy regime. 1928-42. *512*
Border guards, Soviet. Eastern front (first battles). USSR. 1941. *670*
Boundaries. Allies. Military Occupation. 1943-45. *28*
—. Czechoslovakia. Historiography, Czech. Nationalities. 1938-45. *579*
—. Hungary. Romania. Transylvania, partition of. Vienna Diktat. 1940. *352*
Brand, Hans. Military Occupation. Yugoslavia (Kras). 1942-44. *581*
Brand, Joel, mission. Grosz, Bandi. Hungary. Military Intelligence. Peace negotiations. 1944. *361*
Brandt, Willi. Anti-Communist Movements. Goebbels, Joseph. Propaganda. Taubert, Eberhard. 1931-60. *2*
Brandt-Meyer family (correspondence). Germany (Berlin). Jews. 1941-43. *814*
Bräutigam, Otto (memorandum). Military occupation policy. USSR. 1941. *588*
Brecht, Alfred (memoirs). Protestantism. Urach Theological Seminary. 20c. *26*
Brett-Smith, Richard. Military strategy (review article). 1938-44. *112*
Britain, Battle of. 1940. *445*
Brown, Anthony Cave. Great Britain. Kahn, David. Military Intelligence (review article). USA. 1939-45. *155*
Buch, Walter. Nazism. 1922-49. *175*
Buchenwald. Bartel, Walter (memoirs). Concentration Camps. Resistance. 1945. *777*
—. Belgium. Concentration camps. Evacuation. Labor camps. Military Occupation. 1944. *541*
—. Concentration Camps. Military organization. 1942-45. *928*
—. Concentration Camps (interviews). Military organization. 1937-45. *927*
Buchenwald (Block 66). Büchler, Joshua (memoirs). Children. Concentration Camps. Daily life. 1945. *804*
Büchler, Joshua (memoirs). Buchenwald (Block 66). Children. Concentration Camps. Daily life. 1945. *804*
Bulgaria. Alliances. Axis pact. 1941-45. *633*
—. Business. Erz mining corporation. 1938-44. *627*
—. Hungary. Propaganda. Romania. 1941-43. *645*
—. Intervention. USSR. 1944. *598*
Bulgarians. Greece (central Macedonia). Merten, Dr. Military occupation. Tendzos, Christos. 1943. *643*

Bulge (battle). 1944. *525*
Bumke, Erwin. Gürtner, Franz. Judicial Administration (review article). Law. Nazism. 1933-45. *71*
Burckhardt, Carl Jacob. Danzig. Hitler, Adolf (interview). 1938-40. *341*
—. Diplomacy. Great Britain. Mediation. World War II (antecedents). 1937-39. *323*
Bureaucracies. Concentration camps. Psychology. 1941-45. *1001*
—. Genocide. Jews. 1932-45. *897*
—. Genocide. Jews. Morality. 1933-45. *893*
—. Jews *(mischlinge)*. Persecution. 1944. *758*
Business. Bulgaria. Erz mining corporation. 1938-44. *627*
—. Concentration camps. Himmler, Heinrich. SS (Schutzstaffel). 1933-45. *909*
—. Economic Planning (postwar). 1943-45. *231*
—. Gotha Life Insurance Company. 1927-77. *359*
—. Himmler, Heinrich. Interest Groups. SS (Schutzstaffel). 1930-45. *121*
Busse, Otto. Jews. Memoirs. Military Occupation. Poland (Białystok). Rescue. 1943. *806*
—. Jews. Memoirs. Rescue. 1943-79. *876*
Butz, A. R. Genocide (review article). Irving, David. Jews. 1941-45. *1016*

C

Cabinet (dissolution). Denmark. Military occupation. Resistance. 1940-45. *440*
Canada. Germans. Prisoners of war. 1940-47. *490*
Canada (Labrador). Weather stations. 1943. 1981. *466*
Capitalism. Fascism. Foreign Policy. Historiography (West German, Soviet). 1930-45. *329*
Case Yellow. Military (troop concentration). Neutrality. Switzerland. 1939-40. *524*
Casualties. Military Occupation. Partisans. War Crimes. Yugoslavia. 1941-45. *628*
Catholic Church. Belgium. Labor Unions and Organizations. Military Occupation. 1940-42. *476*
—. Church and State. Galen, Clemens August von (letter). Germany (Münster diocese). 1941. *65*
—. Church and State. Historiography. Nazism. 1933-76. *305*
—. Euthanasia. Nazism. 1933-45. *904*
—. France. Military Occupation. 1940-45. *553*
—. Genocide. Jews. 1939-45. *1052*
—. Hlond, August. Poland. 1939-45. *425*
Caucasus. Military Campaigns. Oil fields. USSR. 1941-43. *677*
Censorship. Amt Schriftumspflege. Literature. Nazism. 1932-45. *218*
—. Comédie-Française. France. Military Occupation. Theater. 1939-45. *504*
—. Communist Party. Documents. France. *Humanité* (newspaper). Military Occupation. 1940. *529*
—. Dietrich, Otto. Journalism. Stalingrad (battle). 1942-43. *732*
—. Literature. Nazism. 1933-45. *86*
Censuses. Germany (Berlin). Poles. 1810-1946. *402*
Centos Society. Children. Poland (Warsaw ghetto). 1942-45. *774*
—. Education. *Głos Domu Chłopców* (magazine). Jews. Orphans. Poland (Warsaw Ghetto). 1940-41. *1006*
Central Station for Volksdeutsche. Germans. Military Occupation. Poland (Galicia). ca 1930's-40's. *390*

Central Union of the Polish Industry. Poland (Warsaw). Resistance. Wachowiak, Stanislaw (memoirs). 1939-45. *434*
Champagne. Confiscations, agricultural. France. Military occupation. 1940-42. *450*
Charles, J. L. Belgium. Dasney, F. Geheime Feldpolizei (reports). Jews. Resistance. 1940-42. *457*
Chełmno concentration camp. Genocide. Höppner, Rolf-Heinz. 1941-42. *940*
Chemical and Biological Warfare (poison gas). 1916-45. *186*
Chetniks. Collaboration. Ethnic Groups. Nedić, Milan. Yugoslavia (Banat). 1941-44. *618*
—. Collaboration. Yugoslavia (Serbia). 1943-44. *608*
—. Collaborators. Communications. Counterinsurgency. Industry. Ustaši. Yugoslavia. 1941-42. *573*
—. Italy. Yugoslavia (Croatia; Lika). 1943-44. *607*
Children. Auschwitz. Deportation. France. Jews. Vichy Regime. 1942-44. *955*
—. Buchenwald (Block 66). Büchler, Joshua (memoirs). Concentration Camps. Daily life. 1945. *804*
—. Centos Society. Poland (Warsaw ghetto). 1942-45. *774*
—. Concentration camps. Education. Jews. Korczak, Janusz. Poland. 1930's-40's. *875*
—. Concentration Camps. Korczak, Janusz. Poland (Warsaw ghetto). Treblinka. 1942. *824*
—. Concentration Camps (review article). Memoirs. Vegh, Claudine. 1939-45. *1038*
—. France. Jews. Rescue. Vichy regime. 1939-45. *918*
—. Jews. Korczak, Janusz. Poland (Warsaw ghetto). 1900-42. *973*
—. Korczak, Janusz (review article). Poland (Warsaw ghetto). 1940's. *878*
—. Nazism. Poland. War Crimes. 1939-1945. *775*
Children (conference). Poland. War crimes. 1939-45. *776*
China (Shanghai). Diplomatic missions, Polish. Europe, Eastern. Jews. Rescue. 1942-44. *948*
Christian Workers Youth. Belgium. Resistance. 1942-44. *543*
Christianity. Anti-Semitism. Historiography. 19c-20c. *1008*
Christians. France (Nord, Pas-de-Calais). Jews. 1938-44. *825*
Chuikov, Vasili (memoirs). Berlin, fall of. 1945. *671*
—. Germany (Berlin). Krebs, Hans. Military Campaigns. Negotiation attempts. 1945. *288*
Church and State. Catholic Church. Galen, Clemens August von (letter). Germany (Münster diocese). 1941. *65*
—. Catholic Church. Historiography. Nazism. 1933-76. *305*
—. Confessing Church. Nazism. 1933-45. *264*
—. Luther, Martin (use and misuse of). Lutheran Church. Nazism. 1933-39. *252*
Church leaders. Asylums, inmates of. Genocide. 1940-41. *870*
Cities. Anti-aircraft defense. Rockets. USSR. 1937-45. *701*
City University of New York. Genocide. History Teaching. Jews. 1941-45. 1979. *1017*
Civil religion. Nazism. 1923-45. *47*
Civil resistance. Club rooms. Poland (Warsaw ghetto). 1941. *1004*
—. Jewish Fighting Organization. Jewish Social Self-Aid. Military Occupation. Poland (Warsaw ghetto). Resistance. 1939-42. *1003*

Concentration camps   229

Civil-Military Relations. Commissar Order. Military Occupation. USSR. War crimes. 1941. *703*
—. Europe, Eastern. Military Government. 1942-44. *137*
Clausewitz, Karl von. Nazism. 1939-45. *5*
Clauss, Edgar. Kleist, Peter. Peace, separate. USSR. 1942-44. *316*
Clergy. Anti-Semitism. Confessing Church. Resistance. 1930's-45. *1053*
—. Baltic Area. Baltic German Church (removal). Poland (Łódz, Poznań). 1939-44. *435*
—. Germanization. Poland. 1939-45. *393*
Club rooms. Civil resistance. Poland (Warsaw ghetto). 1941. *1004*
Coal. Fuel, synthetic. 1938-43. *9*
Coal Mines and Mining. Exploitation. Iron Industry. Ukraine. 1941-44. *725*
—. Germany (Ruhr). Nazism. Resistance. 1933-45. *205*
Cohen, David (correspondence). Jews. Military occupation. Visser, Lodewijk Ernst. 1941-42. *960*
Collaboration. Belgium. Degrelle, Léon. Rexist Party. World War II (antecedents). 1933-40. *493*
—. Belgium. Economic Conditions (review article). Gillingham, John. Nazis. 1936-44. *556*
—. Belgium (Brussels). Himmler, Heinrich. Military Occupation. Reeder, Eggert. SS (Schutzstaffel; appointments). 1942-43. *461*
—. Bonnard, Abel. France. Ideology. Vichy regime. 1928-42. *512*
—. Chetniks. Ethnic Groups. Nedić, Milan. Yugoslavia (Banat). 1941-44. *618*
—. Chetniks. Yugoslavia (Serbia). 1943-44. *608*
—. Darnand, Joseph. France. *Milice.* 1914-45. *475*
—. Elites. France. Military Occupation. Netherlands. Poland. 1940-44. *181*
—. Flemish. France. Nationalism. 1940-42. *511*
—. France. Légion des Volontaires Français contre le Bolchevisme. Volunteers. Waffen-SS (Charlemagne division). 1941-45. *508*
Collaboration movements. Army. Belgium. Himmler, Heinrich. Reeder, Eggert. SS (Schutzstaffel; appointments). 1941-44. *462*
Collaborators. Chetniks. Communications. Counterinsurgency. Industry. Ustaši. Yugoslavia. 1941-42. *573*
—. Ganzweich, Avraham. Jews. Poland (Warsaw ghetto). 1940-43. *1045*
—. Military Officers. USSR. Vlasov, Andrei. 1939-46. *679*
Collaborators, Belgian. *Vlaamse Landsleiding.* 1944-45. *510*
Colleges and Universities. Looting. Military Occupation. Poland. 1939-45. *399*
Colleges and Universities (closing of). Czechoslovakia. Military Occupation. Resistance. 1939-45. *605*
Comédie-Française. Censorship. France. Military Occupation. Theater. 1939-45. *504*
Commissar Order. Civil-Military Relations. Military Occupation. USSR. War crimes. 1941. *703*
Communications. Atlantic, North. Norway. Shipping. 1940. *554*
—. Chetniks. Collaborators. Counterinsurgency. Industry. Ustaši. Yugoslavia. 1941-42. *573*
Communications, Military. Operation Barbarossa. USSR. 1941. *733*
—. USSR. World War II (antecedents). 1940-41. *697*
Communism. 1918-44. *772*
—. Albania. Military Occupation. 1943. *565*
Communist Party. Anti-Fascism. Sweden. 1933-43. *203*

—. Anti-Fascist Movements. Concentration camps. Resistance. 1933-45. *939*
—. Anti-Nazi Movements. Manouchian group. Resistance. 1939-45. *32*
—. Censorship. Documents. France. *Humanité* (newspaper). Military Occupation. 1940. *529*
—. Documents. Resistance. 1944. *142*
—. Documents. Resistance. 1944. *144*
—. Economic policy. 1944-45. *127*
—. France. Military Occupation. 1940-41. *443*
—. Germany, East. Resistance. Social Democratic Party. 1933-45. *225*
—. Germany (Hamburg). Resistance. Sacke, Georg (documents). 1933-45. *257*
—. Germany (Pirna). Prisoners of war. Propaganda. 1945. *663*
—. Jews. 1933-45. *1015*
—. Military Occupation. Political Change. 1945. *11*
—. Military policy. 1919-45. *88*
Communists. Atrocities. Jews. USSR. 1939-41. *683*
—. Denmark. Germans. Resistance. 1933-45. *237*
—. Pożywiłek, Michał (memoirs). 1939-45. *208*
Concentration camps *See also* names of specific camps, e.g., Auschwitz, etc.
—. Anti-Fascist Movements. Communist Party. Resistance. 1933-45. *939*
—. Anti-Semitism. Auschwitz-Birkenau. Historiography. Poland. Resistance. 1939-78. *890*
—. Art. Daily Life. Spitzer, Walter. 1939-45. *1061*
—. Art. Jews. Resistance, spiritual. 1940-45. *962*
—. Atrocities. Blobel, Paul. Poland (Białystok). Sonderkommando 1005. 1940-45. *821*
—. Atrocities. Veliki Bečerek. Yugoslavia (Banat). 1941-45. *1014*
—. Auschwitz. Autobiography. Hoess, Rudolf. Nazism. 1939-45. *811*
—. Auschwitz. Autobiography. Hoess, Rudolf. War crimes. 1906-47. *901*
—. Auschwitz. Diaries. 1940-44. *954*
—. Auschwitz. Dubois, Stanisław (pseud. Dębski). Poland. 1940-42. *919*
—. Auschwitz. Genocide. Hoess, Rudolf. Sociology. 1942-45. *913*
—. Auschwitz. Jews. Poland. 1940-45. *994*
—. Auschwitz. Jews. Theresienstadt camp. 1943-44. *931*
—. Auschwitz. Labor, forced. Mauthausen. 1935-45. *1043*
—. Auschwitz. Poland. 1939-45. *982*
—. Auschwitz. Vrba, Rudolf. 1933-45. *812*
—. Auschwitz (escape). Bikel, Sara. Jews. Rosenstein, Hana. 1944. *841*
—. Auschwitz (evacuation). Diaries. Heller, Paul. 1945. *891*
—. Auschwitz (evacuation). Poland (Nysa district). 1945. *817*
—. Auschwitz (evacuation). Poland (Opole; Prudnik). 1944-45. *971*
—. Austria. Cortey, Maria-Dolors (memoirs). Mauthausen. 1939-45. *815*
—. Bartel, Walter (memoirs). Buchenwald. Resistance. 1945. *777*
—. Belgium. Buchenwald. Evacuation. Labor camps. Military Occupation. 1944. *541*
—. Belzec. Poland. 1939-45. *1030*
—. Bergen-Belsen. 1945. *882*
—. Bergen-Belsen. Gitler-Barski, Józef (diary). 1943-45. *862*
—. Birkenau. Czechoslovakia (Terezin ghetto). Genocide. Jews. 1943-44. *911*
—. Buchenwald. Military organization. 1942-45. *928*

—. Buchenwald (Block 66). Büchler, Joshua (memoirs). Children. Daily life. 1945. *804*
—. Bureaucracies. Psychology. 1941-45. *1001*
—. Business. Himmler, Heinrich. SS (Schutzstaffel). 1933-45. *909*
—. Children. Education. Jews. Korczak, Janusz. Poland. 1930's-40's. *875*
—. Children. Korczak, Janusz. Poland (Warsaw ghetto). Treblinka. 1942. *824*
—. Croatia (Jasenovac). Gradina concentration camp. 1941-45. *968*
—. Dachau. Eicke, Theodor. 1933-45. *851*
—. Genocide. Italy (Trieste). Jews. Nazism. Risiera di San Sabba. 1943-45. *791*
—. Genocide. Jews. 1939-44. *807*
—. Genocide. Jews. 1941-44. *765*
—. Germany (Berlin). Poland. 1945. *860*
—. Hijefs. Jews. Rescue agencies. Slovakia. Vaad Hacala. 1941-45. *946*
—. Hirt, August. Jews. Medical experiments. 1941-44. *934*
—. Historiography. Theresienstadt camp. Zionism. 1941-45. *997*
—. Jews. Memoirs. Poland. Rosensaft, Hadassah. 1940's. *993*
—. Jews. Memoirs. Poland (Warsaw ghetto). 1943-47. *1033*
—. Jews. Poland (Ciechanów). 1940's. *881*
—. Jews. Poland (Warsaw ghetto). 1941-44. *958*
—. Klonowski, Józef. Music. Poland. Sachsenhausen. 1939. *790*
—. Kühne, Wolfgang (journal). 1940-45. *929*
—. Labor, forced. Osram factory. 1944-45. *826*
—. Memoirs. Ravensbrück. Tillion, Germaine. 1945. *1029*
—. Memoirs. Reichman, Yehiel Meir. Treblinka. 1942-43. *989*
—. Nazism. 1936-45. *886*
—. Poland. Sobibor. 1942. *908*
—. Psychology. Survivors (interviews). 1941-71. *950*
—. Psychology (stress). 1941-74. *827*
—. Resistance. Socialists. 1939-45. *831*
—. Theresienstadt camp. 1939-45. *910*
Concentration Camps (interviews). Buchenwald. Military organization. 1937-45. *927*
Concentration Camps (review article). Children. Memoirs. Vegh, Claudine. 1939-45. *1038*
Concentration Camps (symposium). 1935-45. *808*
Conferences. Belgium. Foreign policy. 1940. *362*
—. Genocide. Jews. 1933-45. 1973-74. *1056*
—. Historiography. 1939-73. *69*
Confessing Church. Anti-Semitism. Clergy. Resistance. 1930's-45. *1053*
—. Church and State. Nazism. 1933-45. *264*
Confiscation. Belgium. Jews. Property. 1940-44. *1011*
Confiscations, agricultural. Champagne. France. Military occupation. 1940-42. *450*
Conscription, Civilian. Belgium (Kortrijk). Labor. 1940-45. *528*
Conservatism. Hitler, Adolf. Poland. Political opposition. 1940-44. *258*
Conspiracy. Germany (Berlin). Hitler, Adolf. Prisoners of war, American. 1945. *238*
Construction industry. Territory, occupied. USSR (Lithuania). 1941-45. *690*
Consular Reports. Jews. Libya. Walther, Gebhardt von. 1940-43. *763*
Convoys (PQ13, QP9). Great Britain. Naval Battles. North Sea. 1942. *509*
—. Great Britain. Submarines. *U-585* (submarine). 1942. *488*
Cortey, Maria-Dolors (memoirs). Austria. Concentration Camps. Mauthausen. 1939-45. *815*
Counterinsurgency. Chetniks. Collaborators. Communications. Industry. Ustaši. Yugoslavia. 1941-42. *573*
Coups d'Etat (August 1944). Balkans. Resistance. Romania. Yugoslavia. 1944. *567*
Courts. Documents. Navies. 1939-45. *79*
Crete (battle). Airborne troops. 1941. *551*
—. Airborne troops. Freyberg, Bernard Cyril. Military Campaigns. Student, Kurt. 1941. *473*
Crimea, battle for the. Military Strategy. USSR. 1941-44. *660*
Croatia. Diplomacy. Hitler, Adolf. Pavelić, Ante. 1942. *336*
—. Diplomacy. Hitler, Adolf. Pavelić, Ante. 1943. *335*
—. Diplomacy. Mandić (prime minister). 1944. *337*
—. Documents. Hitler, Adolf. 1941-42. *374*
—. Genocide. Jews. Nazism. Serbs. 1941-45. *938*
—. Nationalities policy. 1940-45. *907*
—. Operation Schach. Partisans. Yugoslavia (Bosnia). 1944. *575*
Croatia (Jasenovac). Concentration camps. Gradina concentration camp. 1941-45. *968*
Cultural policy. Press conferences. Propaganda Ministry. 1933-45. *64*
Cultural Union of German Jewry. Jews. Nazism. Singer, Kurt. Theater. 1933-41. *858*
Culture. Art. Military Occupation. Poland. 1939-45. *433*
Curricula. Higher Education. Military Occupation. Ukraine (Lvov). 1942-45. *438*
Customs union (proposed). Denmark. Monetary Systems. 1940. *347*
Czechoslovakia. Auflockerung Räumung Lähmung Zerstörung (ARLZ). Documents. Evacuation. Germans. 1944-45. *634*
—. Boundaries. Historiography, Czech. Nationalities. 1938-45. *579*
—. Colleges and Universities (closing of). Military Occupation. Resistance. 1939-45. *605*
—. Diplomacy. Prague Uprising. Resistance. 1945. *606*
—. Education. Military Occupation. Sudetenland. 1938-45. *592*
—. Germanization. Military Occupation. 1938-45. *569*
—. Germans. Partisan movement. Poland. USSR. 1939-45. *197*
—. Military Campaigns (letters). Resistance. Slovak National Uprising. 1944. *591*
—. Military Occupation. 1939-45. *779*
—. Military Strategy. 1945. *623*
—. Prisoners of war. Resistance. USSR. 1941-45. *611*
Czechoslovakia (Bratislava). Economic relations. Gebert, Erich. 1939-44. *626*
Czechoslovakia (Eastern Sudetenland). Annexation. Daily Life. 1938-45. *570*
Czechoslovakia (Moravia, Northern). Germanization. 1939-45. *563*
Czechoslovakia (Moravia; Silesia). Agricultural policy. Military occupation. 1938-45. *590*
Czechoslovakia (Náchod). Military Occupation. Textile industry. 1938-48. *596*
Czechoslovakia (Ostrava). Germanization. Military Occupation. Poland (Upper Silesia). 1939-45. *589*
Czechoslovakia (Prague). Demonstrations. Frank, Karl Hermann. Military occupation policy. 1939. *574*
Czechoslovakia (Slovakia). Archives. Military Occupation. ca 1943-45. *600*
Czechoslovakia (Terezin ghetto). Birkenau. Concentration Camps. Genocide. Jews. 1943-44. *911*

Diplomacy 231

Czechoslovakia (Teschen). Military Occupation. Nationalities policy. Social status. 1939-45. *593*
Czerniakow, Adam. Diaries. Jewish Councils (Judenrat). Military Occupation. Poland (Warsaw ghetto). 1939-42. *892*
—. Diaries. Jewish Councils (Judenrat). Poland (Warsaw ghetto). 1939. *898*
—. Jewish Councils (Judenrat). Military Occupation. Poland (Warsaw ghetto). Tyszka, Leon (reminiscence). 1939-42. *1034*
Czerniakow, Adam (diary). Jewish Councils (Judenrat). Poland (Warsaw ghetto). 1939-42. *1054*

D

Dachau. Concentration camps. Eicke, Theodor. 1933-45. *851*
Dahlerus, Jean Birger Essen. Diplomacy. Great Britain. 1939. *285*
Daily Life. Annexation. Czechoslovakia (Eastern Sudetenland). 1938-45. *570*
—. Art. Concentration camps. Spitzer, Walter. 1939-45. *1061*
—. Buchenwald (Block 66). Büchler, Joshua (memoirs). Children. Concentration Camps. 1945. *804*
—. Genocide. Jews. Poland (Łódz ghetto). 1940-44. *788*
—. Italy (Milan). Jews. Levi, Primo (memoirs). 1942-43. *943*
—. Jews. Military Occupation. Nazism. Poland. 1941-44. *850*
Daitz, Werner. Economic Planning, postwar. Nazism. 1939-44. *7*
Danube River. Minesweepers. 1939-45. *39*
Danzig. Bibliographies. Poland. Westerplatte, battle of. 1939. *387*
—. Burckhardt, Carl Jacob. Hitler, Adolf (interview). 1938-40. *341*
Darlan, Jean. Diplomacy. France. Great Britain. 1940-41. *328*
Darnand, Joseph. Collaboration. France. *Milice*. 1914-45. *475*
Darwinism. Anti-Semitism. Europe. Nietzsche, Friedrich. 1800-1945. *1028*
Dasney, F. Belgium. Charles, J. L. Geheime Feldpolizei (reports). Jews. Resistance. 1940-42. *457*
Datner, Szymon (report). Friedel, Fritz Gustav. Poland (Białystok). Trials. War crimes. 1942-49. *819*
Davidson, Eugene. Biography. Historiography. Hitler, Adolf (review article). Irving, David. Toland, John. 1930's-77. *163*
Dawidowicz, Lucy S. Jews (review article). 1939-45. *888*
Decisionmaking (chance). Navies. 1923-80. *167*
DeGaulle, Charles. Press campaign. 1936-45. *448*
Degelow, Hans J. (photographs). Baltic Sea. Navies. 1943-45. *674*
Degrelle, Léon. Belgium. Collaboration. Rexist Party. World War II (antecedents). 1933-40. *493*
Demonstrations. Czechoslovakia (Prague). Frank, Karl Hermann. Military occupation policy. 1939. *574*
—. Romania. Vienna conference. 1939-40. *333*
Denmark. Bibliographies. Military Occupation. 1940-43. *560*
—. Cabinet (dissolution). Military occupation. Resistance. 1940-45. *440*
—. Communists. Germans. Resistance. 1933-45. *237*
—. Customs union (proposed). Monetary Systems. 1940. *347*
—. Diplomacy. Germany (Berlin). Mohr, O. C. (conversation). 1940-45. *375*
—. Military occupation. Prisoners of war. Russians. 1943-45. *537*
—. Mohr, Otto (memoirs). Trade. 1940. *354*
Denmark (Gilleleje). Jews. Rescue. Resistance. 1943-44. *937*
Deportation. Auschwitz. Children. France. Jews. Vichy Regime. 1942-44. *955*
—. Finland. Jews. Refugees. 1942. *789*
—. Germans, Volga. USSR. 1941. *692*
—. Horthy, Miklós. Hungary (Budapest). Jews. 1944. *842*
—. Labor, forced. Plenipotentiary for Labor Allocation. Sauckel, Fritz. 1941-42. *56*
—. Slovenes. Yugoslavia (Lower Styria). 1919-48. *602*
Deutsche Arbeitsfront. Nazism. Social security. 1918-45. *250*
Deutsche Bank. Abs, Hermann J. Goering, Hermann. 1940. *339*
Deutsches Volkliste. Military Occupation. Nationalities policy. Poland. Silesia, Upper. 1939-45. *414*
Diaries. Auschwitz. Concentration Camps. 1940-44. *954*
—. Auschwitz (evacuation). Concentration Camps. Heller, Paul. 1945. *891*
—. Czerniakow, Adam. Jewish Councils (Judenrat). Military Occupation. Poland (Warsaw ghetto). 1939-42. *892*
—. Czerniakow, Adam. Jewish Councils (Judenrat). Poland (Warsaw ghetto). 1939. *898*
—. Frank, Hans. Military Occupation. Poland. 1939-41. *382*
—. Gîrbea, Titus. Memoirs. Romania. Steflea, Ilie. 1942-44. *636*
—. Goebbels, Joseph. Trevor-Roper, Hugh R. 1925-45. *90*
—. Jews. Poland (Warsaw ghetto). 1941. *785*
Diaries (review article). Bihaly, Andrew. Genocide. Hungary. Jews. 1944. *799*
Diem, Carl. Sports. 1940. *503*
Dietrich, Otto. Censorship. Journalism. Stalingrad (battle). 1942-43. *732*
Diplomacy. Axis powers. Tripartite Pact. Yugoslavia. 1939-41. *363*
—. Belgium. Netherlands. Peace. 1939-40. *559*
—. Burckhardt, Carl Jacob. Great Britain. Mediation. World War II (antecedents). 1937-39. *323*
—. Croatia. Hitler, Adolf. Pavelić, Ante. 1942. *336*
—. Croatia. Hitler, Adolf. Pavelić, Ante. 1943. *335*
—. Croatia. Mandić (prime minister). 1944. *337*
—. Czechoslovakia. Prague Uprising. Resistance. 1945. *606*
—. Dahlerus, Jean Birger Essen. Great Britain. 1939. *285*
—. Darlan, Jean. France. Great Britain. 1940-41. *328*
—. Denmark. Germany (Berlin). Mohr, O. C. (conversation). 1940-45. *375*
—. Espionage. USA (Washington). 1940. *332*
—. Etzdorf, Hasso von. Operation Barbarossa (opposition to). Walther, Gebhardt von (memorandum). 1940-41. *685*
—. Foreign Policy. Yugoslavia. 1939-41. *319*
—. France. Vichy Regime. 1940. *292*
—. Honduras. Zinsser, Christian (memoir). 1940-41. *372*
—. Italy (Rome). Jews. Vatican. Weizsäcker, Ernst von. 1943. *810*

232 Diplomacy

—. Jews. Poland. Rescue agencies. 1939-45. *947*
—. Mirošević-Sorgo, Niko H. (expulsion). Vatican. Yugoslavia. 1941-42. *624*
—. Norway. Sweden. 1940. *324*
—. Peace discussions, secret. Weissauer, Ludwig. 1940-43. *326*
Diplomacy (advisers). Slovakia. 1939-41. *639*
Diplomacy (private). Finland. Foreign policy. Kallia, Rauno. 1940. *360*
Diplomacy, secret. Dulles, Allen. Hohenlohe-Langenburg, Maximilian. USA. 1939-44. *281*
—. Lithuanian strip. Treaties. USSR. 1939-41. *313*
Diplomatic missions, Polish. China (Shanghai). Europe, Eastern. Jews. Rescue. 1942-44. *948*
—. Europe. Jews (rescue). 1930's-40's. *949*
Diplomatic representation. Belgium. Government-in-exile. Switzerland. 1940-45. *343*
Documents. Archives, provincial. Poland (Rzeszów). War crimes. 1939-45. *378*
—. Armaments industry. Labor, forced. 1943. *45*
—. Auflockerung Räumung Lähmung Zerstörung (ARLZ). Czechoslovakia. Evacuation. Germans. 1944-45. *634*
—. Baltic States. Military occupation. Office of Strategic Services. 1941-45. *713*
—. Banking. Reichsbank. USSR. World War II (antecedents). 1941. *715*
—. Censorship. Communist Party. France. *Humanité* (newspaper). Military Occupation. 1940. *529*
—. Communist Party. Resistance. 1944. *142*
—. Communist Party. Resistance. 1944. *144*
—. Courts. Navies. 1939-45. *79*
—. Croatia. Hitler, Adolf. 1941-42. *374*
—. Foreign Auxiliaries. SS-Panzer Corps, 3d ("Germanic"). 1939-44. *265*
—. Genealogy. Jews. Poland (Warsaw Ghetto). 1943. *805*
—. Heroes. Jews. Military Decorations, Flags, and Symbols. Poland (Białystok, Warsaw ghettos). Resistance. 1944. *818*
—. Historiography, Yugoslav. Yugoslavia. 1940's. 1950's-73. *613*
—. Jews. Lvov portfolio. Military Occupation. Poland. Ukraine (Lvov). 1941. *903*
—. Military. 1920-45. *59*
—. Military Law. Military Occupation. Norway. Surrender. 1945. *489*
—. Papen, Franz von. Peace initiative. USA. 1942-45. *325*
—. Rebellions. Romania. 1944. *622*
Documents (memoir). Jewish Councils (Judenrat). Poland (Warsaw ghetto). Ringelblum Archive. 1939-42. *1005*
Documents on German foreign policy. Foreign policy. 1919-45. *344*
Documents (review article). Foreign Relations. Italy. Japan. 1941-42. *365*
Dolibois, John E. Nazism. Streicher, Julius (memoirs). 1933-45. *771*
Domestic policy. Bibliographies. Foreign policy. 1933-45. *95*
—. Bibliographies. Foreign policy. 1933-45. *96*
—. Goebbels, Joseph (directives). 1939-45. *10*
Dubois, Stanisław (pseud. Dębski). Auschwitz. Concentration Camps. Poland. 1940-42. *919*
Duerlein, E. Fest, I. C. Hitler, Adolf (biographies; review article). Maser, Werner. 1890-1945. *16*
Dulles, Allen. Diplomacy, secret. Hohenlohe-Langenburg, Maximilian. USA. 1939-44. *281*

Dunera (vessel). Australia (Hay). Prisoners of War (memoirs). 1940-41. *498*

E

Eastern front. Air forces. 1939-45. *77*
—. Armies. General staff. Halder, Franz. Military Strategy (review). 1941. *754*
—. Armored Vehicles and Tank Warfare. 1941-45. *587*
—. Armored Vehicles and Tank Warfare. Ukraine (Bogodukhov). 1943. *684*
—. Black Sea. Logistics. Military Strategy. 1942. *710*
—. Europe. Political Change. USSR. 1933-45. *146*
—. Germany, East. Historiography. USSR. 1943-45. *689*
—. Goebbels, Joseph. Nazism. Propaganda. 1941-43. *662*
—. Intelligence service. 1941-45. *653*
—. Kleist, Paul Ludwig Ewald von. Military Strategy. Ukraine. Uman (battle). 1941. *706*
—. Military Strategy (rear area security). 1941-45. *738*
Eastern front (first battles). Border guards, Soviet. USSR. 1941. *670*
Economic Conditions. Albania. Military Occupation. 1943-44. *586*
—. France (Marseilles). Military occupation. 1943. *444*
—. France (Vienne). Military Occupation. 1940-44. *530*
Economic Conditions (review article). Belgium. Collaboration. Gillingham, John. Nazis. 1936-44. *556*
Economic development. Slovakia. 1939-40. *638*
Economic History. Fascism. Kehrl, Hans. Krosigk, Lutz Schwerin von. Memoirs (review article). Nazism. 1933-45. *277*
Economic penetration. Europe, Southeastern. 1933-40. *635*
Economic planning. Genocide. Jews. Manpower. 1939-45. *834*
—. Rubber, synthetic. War. 1915-45. *255*
Economic Planning (postwar). Business. 1943-45. *231*
—. Daitz, Werner. Nazism. 1939-44. *7*
—. Europe. Planungs-Stab Europa. 1943-45. *230*
Economic Policy. Air Forces. Military Occupation. 1939-45. *334*
—. Armaments industry. Austria. Nazism. 1939-44. *312*
—. Communist Party. 1944-45. *127*
—. Funk, Walther. Japan. Matsuoka, Yosuke. 1941-45. *322*
—. Hitler, Adolf. World War II (antecedents). 1939-41. *200*
—. Military Strategy. USSR (Donets basin). 1941-43. *678*
—. Natural gas. Pipe Lines. 1938-44. *73*
Economic preparations. Kontinentale Oel AG. Oil. 1937-45. *314*
Economic Regulations. Monopolies. Reichsgruppe Industrie. 1933-45. *294*
Economic relations. Czechoslovakia (Bratislava). Gebert, Erich. 1939-45. *626*
—. Sweden. 1939-45. *300*
Ecumenism. Jews. Rescue. World Council of Churches. 1939-45. *793*
Edelmann, Moritz. History teaching. Klagge, Dietrich. Nazism. Textbooks. 1938-45. *213*
Education. Centos Society. *Głos Domu Chłopców* (magazine). Jews. Orphans. Poland (Warsaw Ghetto). 1940-41. *1006*

Expansionism 233

—. Children. Concentration camps. Jews. Korczak, Janusz. Poland. 1930's-40's. *875*
—. Czechoslovakia. Military Occupation. Sudetenland. 1938-45. *592*
—. Germany, West. Military officers. Social Classes. 1900-79. *4*
—. Hitler Jugend. 1933-45. *104*
—. Nazism. Social mobility. 1930-40. *110*
Education, clandestine. Military occupation. Poland. 1940-45. *408*
Egypt. Africa, North. Libya. Rommel, Erwin. 1941-42. *520*
Ehrenburg, Ilya *(The Black Book)*. Jews. USSR. 1941-80. *1012*
Eichmann, Adolf. Genocide. Himmler, Heinrich. Hitler, Adolf. Irving, David *(Hitler's War)*. Jews. 1939-45. *1041*
Eicke, Theodor. Concentration camps. Dachau. 1933-45. *851*
—. Waffen-SS (Death's Head division). 1939-45. *248*
Electrical industry. Asia, East. Felten & Guilleaume. North German Ocean Cable Works. 1850-1939. *298*
Elites. Collaboration. France. Military Occupation. Netherlands. Poland. 1940-44. *181*
Elster, General (surrender). France. Military Campaigns. Resistance. 1944. *516*
—. France (Issoudun). 1944. *519*
Emigrants. Attitudes. Poles. Warsaw ghetto uprising. 1942-43. *829*
—. Latin America. Nazism. 1933-45. *338*
Emigration. Germany (Fürth). Jews. Memoirs. 1936-41. *991*
—. Jews. Nazism. 1933-45. *1019*
Employment (seasonal). Forests and Forestry. Hungarians. 1937-44. *40*
Encyclopaedia Judaica. Genocide. Jews. 1939-45. *839*
Encyclopedia of World War II. Poland. 1939-45. *236*
Enigma (security of). Military Intelligence. 1928-45. *216*
Epstein, David (memoirs). Genocide. Jews. Partisans. Ukraine (Lyubeshov). 1941-44. *840*
Erlich, Henryk. Alter, Wiktor. Anti-Nazi Movements. Jews. USSR. 1939-41. *988*
Erz mining corporation. Bulgaria. Business. 1938-44. *627*
Esh, Shaul. Historiography. Legislation, anti-Jewish. Nazism. 1933. *757*
Espinosa, Manuel (memoirs). Airplanes. Spain. Travel. ca 1944. *296*
Espionage. Archaeology. Middle East. Oppenheim, Max von. 1890's-1946. *327*
—. Diplomacy. USA (Washington). 1940. *332*
—. Ireland. Schütz, Günther. 1941-42. *452*
—. Niederkirchner, Käte. 1909-44. *729*
Estonia. Germans. Latvia. Poland. Racism. Resettlement. 1939. *389*
Ethnic Groups. Chetniks. Collaboration. Nedić, Milan. Yugoslavia (Banat). 1941-44. *618*
Ethnocentrism. Arendt, Hannah. Genealogy. Jews. Political Theory. 1958-65. *828*
Etzdorf, Hasso von. Diplomacy. Operation Barbarossa (opposition to). Walther, Gebhardt von (memorandum). 1940-41. *685*
Europe. Air Forces. Armies. Great Britain. Greece. Italy. 1940-41. *640*
—. Air Warfare (personal accounts). USA. 1942. *24*
—. Anti-Semitism. Darwinism. Nietzsche, Friedrich. 1800-1945. *1028*
—. Balance of power. 1800-1945. *135*
—. Diplomatic missions, Polish. Jews (rescue). 1930's-40's. *949*
—. Eastern front. Political Change. USSR. 1933-45. *146*
—. Economic Planning (postwar). Planungs-Stab Europa. 1943-45. *230*
—. Fascism. Greece. Military Occupation. Poland. 1940-45. *974*
—. Genocide. Hilberg, Raul (interview). Jews. 1930's-40's. *848*
—. Genocide. Jews. 1938-45. *914*
—. Genocide. Jews. Photography. 1939-45. *809*
—. Jesuits. Military occupation. 1933-45. *935*
—. Jewish Councils (conference). Nazism. 1933-45. *1060*
—. Military Occupation. Radio. 1940-42. *159*
—. Military Occupation (comparative). Nazism. Resistance. 1940-44. *610*
—. Preservation. 1940-46. *82*
Europe, Central. Balkans. Propaganda (conference). 1939-45. *580*
—. Expansionism. Poland. World War II (antecedents). 1934-40. *380*
Europe, East Central. Historiography. Horthy, Miklós. 1939-45. *649*
Europe, Eastern. Ainsztein, Reuben. Jews (review article). Resistance. 1939-45. *823*
—. China (Shanghai). Diplomatic missions, Polish. Jews. Rescue. 1942-44. *948*
—. Civil-Military Relations. Military Government. 1942-44. *137*
—. Ghettos. Government. Jewish Councils (Judenrat). Military Occupation. 1941-43. *895*
—. Ghettos. Jewish Councils (Judenrat; review article). 1939-44. *896*
—. Ideology. Military Occupation. 1941-45. *57*
—. Jews (review article). Kosinski, Jerzy. Novels. 1933-71. *873*
—. Military Occupation. Propaganda. 1939-45. *629*
—. Military Occupation. Social Classes. 1941-45. *714*
—. Military Planning. *Ost* plan. USSR. 1915-77. *664*
—. Research. Silesia. 1938-45. *72*
Europe, Northern. Military Strategy. Trade. 1900-45. *331*
Europe, Southeastern. Economic penetration. 1933-40. *635*
—. Expansionism. World War II (antecedents). 1933-45. *603*
Euthanasia. Catholic Church. Nazism. 1933-45. *904*
—. Hitler, Adolf. Judicial system. Public Administration. 1940-41. *877*
Evacuation. Auflockerung Räumung Lähmung Zerstörung (ARLZ). Czechoslovakia. Documents. Germans. 1944-45. *634*
—. Belgium. Buchenwald. Concentration camps. Labor camps. Military Occupation. 1944. *541*
Exiles. Austria. Authors. Rheinhardt, Emil Alphons (letters). 1930's-45. *1018*
Expansionism. Anti-Semitism. Genocide. Nazism. 1919-45. *94*
—. Anti-Semitism. Hitler, Adolf. Nationalism. 1919-45. *17*
—. Balkans. Ideology. 1938-44. *599*
—. Europe, central. Poland. World War II (antecedents). 1934-40. *380*
—. Europe, Southeastern. World War II (antecedents). 1933-45. *603*
—. Romania. World War II (antecedents). 1938-39. *356*
Expansionism (explanation of). Labor policy. 1939-43. *172*

Exploitation. Coal Mines and Mining. Iron Industry. Ukraine. 1941-44. *725*
Exports. Iran. 1939-41. *308*
Expressionism. Avant-garde (term). 20c. *270*
Expropriation. Jews. Memoirs. Military Occupation. Poland (Warsaw). Szulfried, Stanisław. 1939-42. *1024*

F

Family. Belorussia (Grodno ghetto). Memoirs. Military Occupation. 1941-45. *798*
Farben, I. G. Fuel supply. Hydrogenation techniques. 1930-45. *133*
Fascism. Assassination. Nazism. 1933-44. *207*
—. Capitalism. Foreign Policy. Historiography (West German, Soviet). 1930-45. *329*
—. Economic History. Kehrl, Hans. Krosigk, Lutz Schwerin von. Memoirs (review article). Nazism. 1933-45. *277*
—. Europe. Greece. Military Occupation. Poland. 1940-45. *974*
Fein, Helen. Genocide. Jews. Quantitative methods. 1939-45. *1048*
Feldherrnhalle regiment. SA (Sturmabteilung). 1933-45. *276*
Felten & Guilleaume. Asia, East. Electrical industry. North German Ocean Cable Works. 1850-1939. *298*
Fest, I. C. Duerlein, E. Hitler, Adolf (biographies; review article). Maser, Werner. 1890-1945. *16*
Fest, Joachim. Hitler, Adolf (review article). 1889-1945. *170*
—. Hitler, Adolf (review article). ca 1918-45. *100*
Filderman, Wilhelm. Jews. Letters. Military Occupation. Romania. 1940-44. *1007*
Films. Anti-Semitism. *Jew Süss* (film). Nazism. Propaganda. 1940's. *859*
—. France. Military Occupation. 1940-44. *224*
—. July 20 Plot. Trials. 1944-45. 1979-80. *220*
—. Propaganda. USSR. 1930's-45. *658*
—. Propaganda. Wessel, Horst (myth). 1930's. *83*
Finland. 1944. *330*
—. Deportation. Jews. Refugees. 1942. *789*
—. Diplomacy (private). Foreign policy. Kallia, Rauno. 1940. *360*
—. Foreign Policy. Mannerheim, Carl Gustav. USSR. 1940-41. *373*
—. Foreign Relations. 1939-45. *287*
—. Foreign Relations. 1941-44. *342*
—. Hogland (battle). USSR. 1944. *747*
—. *Hohenhörn* (vessel). Jews. Refugees. 1942. *1021*
—. Military. Operation Barbarossa. World War II (antecedents). 1939-41. *709*
—. Military Strategy. 1939-42. *161*
—. Military Strategy. USSR. 1941-44. *746*
—. Neutrality. Norway. 1940. *340*
Finland (Lapland). Armistice. Roads. USSR. 1940-45. *310*
Finland, north. Army, 20th. 1944. *698*
Fischer, Ludwig (report). Poland. Warsaw Uprising. 1939-44. *386*
Flemish. Collaboration. France. Nationalism. 1940-42. *511*
Foreign Auxiliaries. Anti-Communist Movements. USSR. 1941. *681*
—. Documents. SS-Panzer Corps, 3d ("Germanic"). 1939-44. *265*
Foreign office. Luther, Martin. Ribbentrop, Joachim von. 1933-45. *27*
Foreign policy. Austria (Vienna). Munich crisis. Nazism. Neubacher, Hermann. 1938-40. *282*
—. Balkans. 1933-41. *601*
—. Belgium. Conferences. 1940. *362*
—. Bibliographies. Domestic policy. 1933-45. *95*
—. Bibliographies. Domestic policy. 1933-45. *96*
—. Capitalism. Fascism. Historiography (West German, Soviet). 1930-45. *329*
—. Diplomacy. Yugoslavia. 1933-41. *319*
—. Diplomacy (private). Finland. Kallia, Rauno. 1940. *360*
—. Documents on German foreign policy. 1919-45. *344*
—. Finland. Mannerheim, Carl Gustav. USSR. 1940-41. *373*
—. Germany (review article). Nazism. Resistance. 1933-45. *97*
—. Great Britain. Hitler, Adolf. 1921-45. *306*
—. Great Britain. Pius XII, Pope. 1939-40. *500*
—. Gustavus V (abdication threat). Midsummer crisis. Sweden. 1941. *358*
—. Historiography. 1930-45. *291*
—. Historiography. Hitler, Adolf. Nazism. 1933-45. *357*
—. Historiography, Bulgarian. 1944. *619*
—. Historiography (East German). 1933-45. *321*
—. Hitler, Adolf. 1933-45. *92*
—. Hitler, Adolf. Military Strategy (grand). 1933-45. *307*
—. Military History. Politics. World War II (review article). 1933-45. *34*
—. Neutrality. Sweden. 1939-45. *369*
—. Poland. 1939-45. *426*
—. USSR. World War II (antecedents). 1939-41. *734*
—. USSR. World War II (antecedents). 1940-41. *704*
Foreign Relations. Afghanistan. Weizsäcker, Ernst von. 1940. *351*
—. Antonescu, Ion. Romania. 1944. *289*
—. Arab States. Hussein, Muhammad Amin al-. 1941-45. *44*
—. Austria. Italy. South Tyrol. 1938-45. *290*
—. Badoglio, Pietro. Italy. Keitel, Wilhelm. Marras, Luigi (papers). 1936-43. *286*
—. Documents (review article). Italy. Japan. 1941-42. *365*
—. Finland. 1939-45. *287*
—. Finland. 1941-44. *342*
—. Hungary. Poland. 1938-44. *396*
—. Italy. Racial policy. 1938-43. *986*
—. Jews. USSR. 1933-41. *869*
—. Kumlin, Ragnar (memoranda). Sweden. 1941-43. *320*
—. Poland. 1939. *403*
—. Sweden. 1941. *370*
Forest fires. Military strategy. 1945. *661*
Forests and Forestry. Employment (seasonal). Hungarians. 1937-44. *40*
Forgery. Anti-Semitism. Bernadotte, Folke (letter). Himmler, Heinrich. Kersten, Felix. 1944-45. *847*
France. *Affiche Rouge*. Psychological Warfare. Resistance. Trials. 1944. *495*
—. Airplane Industry and Trade. Vichy regime. 1940-43. *297*
—. Allied invasion, expected. Military Strategy. Rommel, Erwin. Rundstedt, Gerd von. 1942-44. *561*
—. Allies. Military campaigns. Operation Dragoon. Operation Overlord. USA. 1944. *562*
—. Alsace-Lorraine. Germanization. Kettenbacher, Lothar. 1940-44. *497*
—. Alsace-Lorraine. Iron Industry. 1940-44. *364*
—. Auschwitz. Children. Deportation. Jews. Vichy Regime. 1942-44. *955*
—. Bibliographies. Hitler, Adolf. 1919-39. *25*

—. Bonnard, Abel. Collaboration. Ideology. Vichy regime. 1928-42. *512*
—. Catholic Church. Military Occupation. 1940-45. *553*
—. Censorship. Comédie-Française. Military Occupation. Theater. 1939-45. *504*
—. Censorship. Communist Party. Documents. *Humanité* (newspaper). Military Occupation. 1940. *529*
—. Champagne. Confiscations, agricultural. Military occupation. 1940-42. *450*
—. Children. Jews. Rescue. Vichy regime. 1939-45. *918*
—. Collaboration. Darnand, Joseph. *Milice.* 1914-45. *475*
—. Collaboration. Elites. Military Occupation. Netherlands. Poland. 1940-44. *181*
—. Collaboration. Flemish. Nationalism. 1940-42. *511*
—. Collaboration. Légion des Volontaires Français contre le Bolchevisme. Volunteers. Waffen-SS (Charlemagne division). 1941-45. *508*
—. Communist Party. Military Occupation. 1940-41. *443*
—. Darlan, Jean. Diplomacy. Great Britain. 1940-41. *328*
—. Diplomacy. Vichy Regime. 1940. *292*
—. Elster, General (surrender). Military Campaigns. Resistance. 1944. *516*
—. Films. Military Occupation. 1940-44. *224*
—. General Union of Israelites. Jews. Military Occupation. 1942-43. *889*
—. Great Britain. Stalingrad (Battle). USSR. 1939-45. *688*
—. Historiography. Military collapse. 1940. *454*
—. Jews. Legislation. Persecution. 1942-44. *861*
—. Jews (Oriental). Nazism. 1940-45. *871*
—. National Characteristics. Nazism. Propaganda. 1939-45. *484*
France (Alsace-Lorraine). Jews. Military occupation. Nazism. Negroes. Racism. 1939-42. *485*
France (Ariège). Labor, forced. *Service du Travail Obligatoire.* 1942-44. *494*
France (Briey, Longwy, Nancy). Annexation. Klein Commission. Mining industry. War aims. 1911-42. *295*
France (Burgundy; Dijon). World War II (antecedents). 1939-40. *477*
France (Côte-d'Or). Genocide. Jews. 1941-44. *1037*
France (Douai). Military Occupation. Political Systems. 1939-45. *539*
France (Issoudun). Elster, General (surrender). 1944. *519*
France (Lyons). Military Occupation. 1942-44. *517*
France (Marseilles). Economic Conditions. Military occupation. 1943. *444*
France (Massif Central). Military Campaigns. 1942-44. *505*
France (Moselle department). Germanization. Military Occupation. Political repression. 1940-45. *518*
France (Nord, Pas-de-Calais). Christians. Jews. 1938-44. *825*
France (northern). Military Occupation. Public opinion. 1940-42. *463*
France (Paris). Allies. Liberation. Resistance. 1944. *545*
—. July 20 Plot. 1943-46. *130*
France (Strasbourg). Liberation. Military Occupation. 1940-44. *496*
France (Vienne). Economic Conditions. Military Occupation. 1940-44. *530*

France (Vincennes). Archives. Historical Service of the Army (Military History Center). 1939-78. *43*
Frank, Anne. Kugler, Victor. Memoirs. Netherlands. 1942-44. *926*
Frank, Hans. Diaries. Military Occupation. Poland. 1939-41. *382*
Frank, Karl Hermann. Czechoslovakia (Prague). Demonstrations. Military occupation policy. 1939. *574*
Freyberg, Bernard Cyril. Airborne troops. Crete (battle). Military Campaigns. Student, Kurt. 1941. *473*
Friedel, Fritz Gustav. Datner, Szymon (report). Poland (Białystok). Trials. War crimes. 1942-49. *819*
Fuel supply. Farben, I. G. Hydrogenation techniques. 1930-45. *133*
Fuel, synthetic. Coal. 1938-43. *9*
Fuller, J. F. C. Bombing. Germany (Freiburg). Military history. 1940-61. *481*
Funk, Walther. Economic policy. Japan. Matsuoka, Yosuke. 1941-45. *322*

G

Galbraith, John Kenneth. Memoirs. Strategic Bombing Survey. USA. 1944-45. *470*
Galen, Clemens August von (letter). Catholic Church. Church and State. Germany (Münster diocese). 1941. *65*
Galicia Division. Atrocities. Historiography. Poland. Ukrainians. USSR. 1943-45. *749*
Gangs. Resistance. Youth. 1936-45. *105*
Ganzweich, Avraham. Collaborators. Jews. Poland (Warsaw ghetto). 1940-43. *1045*
Gebert, Erich. Czechoslovakia (Bratislava). Economic relations. 1939-44. *626*
Geheime Feldpolizei. Partisans. USSR. 1939-45. *68*
Geheime Feldpolizei (reports). Belgium. Charles, J. L. Dasney, F. Jews. Resistance. 1940-42. *457*
Geheime Meldedienst (recruitment). Intelligence Service. 1944-45. *78*
Genealogy. Arendt, Hannah. Ethnocentrism. Jews. Political Theory. 1958-65. *828*
—. Documents. Jews. Poland (Warsaw Ghetto). 1943. *805*
General Plan East. Germanization. Poland. USSR. 1939-43. *120*
General staff. Armies. Eastern Front. Halder, Franz. Military Strategy (review). 1941. *754*
General Union of Israelites. France. Jews. Military Occupation. 1942-43. *889*
Generals, German. Guderian, Heinz. Liddell Hart, B. H. (influence). Military Strategy. 1920's-40's. *23*
Genocide. American Jewish Committee (William E. Wiener Oral History Library). Jews. Oral History. 1941-45. 1977-82. *996*
—. Anti-Semitism. Expansionism. Nazism. 1919-45. *94*
—. Anti-Semitism. Jews. 1933-77. *1049*
—. Anti-Semitism. Jews. Nazism. 1939-45. *885*
—. Anti-Semitism. Jews. Nazism. Political Theory. 1917-45. *1026*
—. Anti-Semitism. Press. Propaganda. 1943. *957*
—. Archives. Jews. Poland (Warsaw ghetto). Ringelblum, Emanuel. 1942-43. *1002*
—. Archives, National. Jews. Rescue. USA. War Refugee Board. 1918-52. *961*
—. Asylums, inmates of. Church leaders. 1940-41. *870*
—. Auschwitz. Concentration Camps. Hoess, Rudolf. Sociology. 1942-45. *913*

236 Genocide

—. Belgium. Gypsies. 1940-45. *868*
—. Bibliographies. Jews. 1939-45. 1960-78. *1051*
—. Bihaly, Andrew. Diaries (review article). Hungary. Jews. 1944. *799*
—. Birkenau. Concentration Camps. Czechoslovakia (Terezin ghetto). Jews. 1943-44. *911*
—. Bishops. Jews. 1942-44. *1036*
—. Bureaucracies. Jews. 1932-45. *897*
—. Bureaucracies. Jews. Morality. 1933-45. *893*
—. Catholic Church. Jews. 1939-45. *1052*
—. Chełmno concentration camp. Höppner, Rolf-Heinz. 1941-42. *940*
—. City University of New York. History Teaching. Jews. 1941-45. 1979. *1017*
—. Concentration Camps. Italy (Trieste). Jews. Nazism. Risiera di San Sabba. 1943-45. *791*
—. Concentration camps. Jews. 1939-44. *807*
—. Concentration camps. Jews. 1941-44. *765*
—. Conferences. Jews. 1933-45. 1973-74. *1056*
—. Croatia. Jews. Nazism. Serbs. 1941-45. *938*
—. Daily life. Jews. Poland (Łódz ghetto). 1940-44. *788*
—. Economic planning. Jews. Manpower. 1939-45. *834*
—. Eichmann, Adolf. Himmler, Heinrich. Hitler, Adolf. Irving, David *(Hitler's War)*. Jews. 1939-45. *1041*
—. *Encyclopaedia Judaica*. Jews. 1939-45. *839*
—. Epstein, David (memoirs). Jews. Partisans. Ukraine (Lyubeshov). 1941-44. *840*
—. Europe. Hilberg, Raul (interview). Jews. 1930's-40's. *848*
—. Europe. Jews. 1938-45. *914*
—. Europe. Jews. Photography. 1939-45. *809*
—. Fein, Helen. Jews. Quantitative methods. 1939-45. *1048*
—. France (Côte-d'Or). Jews. 1941-44. *1037*
—. Germany (Berlin). Jews. 1933-43. *773*
—. Government-in-exile, London. Jews. Poland. Public Opinion. 1942. *887*
—. Historiography. Jews. 1939-45. *956*
—. Historiography. Jews. 1939-77. *933*
—. Historiography. Jews. Nazism. 1940-44. *1035*
—. Historiography. Jews. Nazism. 1946-79. *838*
—. Historiography. Jews. Nazism. 1952-79. *813*
—. Historiography. Jews. Poland. 1939-45. 1939-71. *879*
—. Historiography. Jews. Poland. 1941-42. *802*
—. Historiography. Jews. USSR. 1940-45. *866*
—. Historiography, Polish. Jews. Poland. 1939-45. *922*
—. Historiography, Soviet. Jews. 1938-78. *864*
—. Hitler, Adolf. Irving, David. Jews. 1933-45. *801*
—. Hitler, Adolf *(Mein Kampf)*. Poland. 1928-45. *407*
—. Höppner, Rolf-Heinz. Jews. Leszczynski, J. Poland (Warta region). 1940-42. *835*
—. Ideology. Jews. Military Occupation. USSR. 1941-44. *900*
—. Intellectuals. Jews. Poland (Stanisławów). 1941. *849*
—. Intellectuals. Military occupation. Poland. Theater. 1939-45. *421*
—. Jews. 1919-43. *782*
—. Jews. 1933-45. *784*
—. Jews. 1938-45. *853*
—. Jews. 1939-45. *769*
—. Jews. 1939-45. *787*
—. Jews. 1940-45. *852*
—. Jews. 1941-45. *924*
—. Jews. 1942-43. *936*
—. Jews. Leadership. Nazism. Psychohistory. 1938-45. *923*
—. Jews. Lithuania. 1941-44. *762*
—. Jews. Manstein, Erich von. USSR. 1939-45. *1042*
—. Jews. Mass media. Nazism. Propaganda. 1920-45. *768*
—. Jews. Military Occupation. Poland (Kalisz). 1940-42. *978*
—. Jews. Nazism. 1920-45. *1027*
—. Jews. Nazism. 1924-45. *767*
—. Jews. Nazism. 1933-45. *965*
—. Jews. Nazism. 2c BC-20c. *915*
—. Jews. Poland (Ciechanów region). 1941-45. *880*
—. Jews. Poland (Węgrów). 1939-44. *1022*
—. Jews. Psychology. 1938-44. *983*
—. Jews. Radlitzki, Tzvi (memoirs). Ukraine (Lvov). 1941-45. *987*
—. Jews. Railroads. 1939-45. *894*
—. Jews. Romania (Iași). 1941. *969*
—. Jews. USSR. 1941-42. *952*
—. Jews. USSR (Rudnya). 1939-45. *830*
—. Military Occupation. Poland (Warsaw ghetto). Public Administration. 1941-43. *942*
—. Nazism. Poland (Warsaw ghetto). 1919-45. *1000*
Genocide (documents). Belorussia. Jews. Military Occupation. Ukraine. USSR. 1941-45. *976*
Genocide (review article). Butz, A. R. Irving, David. Jews. 1941-45. *1016*
—. Hitler, Adolf. Irving, David. Jews. 1939-45. *800*
—. Hitler, Adolf. Irving, David. Jews. 1940-45. 1977. *1058*
—. Jews. Kren, George M. Rappoport, Leon. ca 1939-45. *990*
—. Jews. Laqueur, Walter. 1941-45. *998*
—. Jews. Literature. 1941-45. *816*
—. Jews. Methodology. 1939-45. *951*
German Resettlement Fiduciary Company. Germanization. War aims. 1939-41. *50*
German-American Bund. Kuhn, Fritz. USA. 1936-41. *309*
Germanization. Alsace-Lorraine. France. Kettenbacher, Lothar. 1940-44. *497*
—. Clergy. Poland. 1939-45. *393*
—. Czechoslovakia. Military Occupation. 1938-45. *569*
—. Czechoslovakia (Moravia, Northern). 1939-45. *563*
—. Czechoslovakia (Ostrava). Military Occupation. Poland (Upper Silesia). 1939-45. *589*
—. France (Moselle department). Military Occupation. Political repression. 1940-45. *518*
—. General Plan East. Poland. USSR. 1939-43. *120*
—. German Resettlement Fiduciary Company. War aims. 1939-41. *50*
—. Germany (Lusatia). Nazism. Sorbs. 1933-45. *585*
Germans. Atrocities. Poland. 1939. *417*
—. Attitudes. Military occupation. Poland. Propaganda, underground. 1939-45. *431*
—. Auflockerung Räumung Lähmung Zerstörung (ARLZ). Czechoslovakia. Documents. Evacuation. 1944-45. *634*
—. Belorussia. Partisans. USSR. 1942-45. *716*
—. Canada. Prisoners of war. 1940-47. *490*
—. Central Station for Volksdeutsche. Military Occupation. Poland (Galicia). ca 1930's-40's. *390*
—. Communists. Denmark. Resistance. 1933-45. *237*
—. Czechoslovakia. Partisan movement. Poland. USSR. 1939-45. *197*

Great Britain 237

—. Estonia. Latvia. Poland. Racism. Resettlement. 1939. *389*
—. Hungary (Bac). Minorities. 1942-45. *621*
—. Lutheran Church. Missionaries. New Guinea. 1914-44. *190*
—. Repatriation. USSR. 1939. *384*
—. Ukraine. Villages. 1942-43. *687*
—. USSR. 1941. *686*
Germans, Baltic. Nazism. Settlement. Warta River. 1940-45. *259*
Germans, Volga. Deportation. USSR. 1941. *692*
Germany, battle for. Military Strategy. Weapons. 1944-45. *526*
Germany (Bavaria). Nazism (review article). 1933-45. *168*
—. Research. Resistance. 1972-76. *108*
Germany (Belsen). Jewish Brigade. Liberation. Poland. Tubin, Yehuda (memoirs). 1945-46. *1031*
Germany (Berlin). Brandt-Meyer family (correspondence). Jews. 1941-43. *814*
—. Censuses. Poles. 1810-1946. *402*
—. Chuikov, Vasili (memoirs). Krebs, Hans. Military Campaigns. Negotiation attempts. 1945. *288*
—. Concentration Camps. Poland. 1945. *860*
—. Conspiracy. Hitler, Adolf. Prisoners of war, American. 1945. *238*
—. Denmark. Diplomacy. Mohr, O. C. (conversation). 1940-45. *375*
—. Genocide. Jews. 1933-43. *773*
—. Military Intelligence. Radio broadcasts (monitoring). 1939-45. *22*
Germany (Dresden). Art treasures. Königstein Fortress. Staatliche Kunstsammlungen Dresden. USSR. 1945. *737*
Germany, East. Communist Party. Resistance. Social Democratic Party. 1933-45. *225*
—. Eastern front. Historiography. USSR. 1943-45. *689*
—. Historiography. 1939-75. *150*
Germany (Freiburg). Bombing. Fuller, J. F. C. Military history. 1940-61. *481*
Germany (Fürth). Emigration. Jews. Memoirs. 1936-41. *991*
Germany (Hamburg). Blohm & Voss. Shipbuilding. 1877-1977. *315*
—. Communist Party. Resistance. Sacke, Georg (documents). 1933-45. *257*
Germany (Lamsdorf). Jews. Prisoners of war. 1941-45. *471*
Germany (Lusatia). Germanization. Nazism. Sorbs. 1933-45. *585*
Germany (Münster diocese). Catholic Church. Church and State. Galen, Clemens August von (letter). 1941. *65*
Germany (Pirna). Communist Party. Prisoners of war. Propaganda. 1945. *663*
Germany (review article). Foreign policy. Nazism. Resistance. 1933-45. *97*
Germany (Rhineland, Westphalia). Persecution. Poles. 1933-45. *379*
Germany (Rostock). Airplane Industry and Trade. Social organization. 1939-45. *70*
Germany (Ruhr). Coal Mines and Mining. Nazism. Resistance. 1933-45. *205*
Germany (Thuringia). Nazism. Political Parties (development). 1924-30. *256*
Germany, West. Anti-Communism. Nazism. Political Education. Propaganda. Youth. 1933-78. *260*
—. Austria. Neo-Nazism. Propaganda. 1960's-70's. *149*
—. Bibliographies. Historiography. 1939-75. *107*

—. Bibliographies. Militärgeshichtliches Forschungsamt. Military history. 1648-1974. *219*
—. Education. Military officers. Social Classes. 1900-79. *4*
—. Historiography. Nazism. 1946-74. *178*
—. History teaching. Military Occupation. Poland. 1939-44. *385*
—. *Holocaust* (television film). 1979. *963*
Germany, western. Battles. Netherlands. 1944-45. *527*
Ghettos. Europe, Eastern. Government. Jewish Councils (Judenrat). Military Occupation. 1941-43. *895*
—. Europe, Eastern. Jewish Councils (Judenrat; review article). 1939-44. *896*
—. Jews. Leadership. Resistance. 1939-44. *783*
—. Jews. Poland. Theater. 1939-42. *845*
Gillingham, John. Belgium. Collaboration. Economic Conditions (review article). Nazis. 1936-44. *556*
Gîrbea, Titus. Diaries. Memoirs. Romania. Steflea, Ilie. 1942-44. *636*
Gitler-Barski, Józef (diary). Bergen-Belsen. Concentration Camps. 1943-45. *862*
Głos Domu Chłopców (magazine). Centos Society. Education. Jews. Orphans. Poland (Warsaw Ghetto). 1940-41. *1006*
Goebbels, Joseph. Anti-Communist Movements. Brandt, Willi. Propaganda. Taubert, Eberhard. 1931-60. *2*
—. Diaries. Trevor-Roper, Hugh R. 1925-45. *90*
—. Eastern front. Nazism. Propaganda. 1941-43. *662*
—. *Great King* (film). *Kolberg* (film). Myths, historical. Propaganda. 1942-45. *89*
—. Music. Nazism. Propaganda ministry. Racism (biological aesthetic). Rosenberg, Alfred. 1920's-45. *58*
Goebbels, Joseph (directives). Domestic policy. 1939-45. *10*
Goering, Hermann. Abs, Hermann J. Deutsche Bank. 1940. *339*
—. Airplanes, Military (heavy bomber; development). Milch, Erhard. 1932-37. *102*
Gotha Life Insurance Company. Business. 1927-77. *359*
Gothic Line. Italy. Partisans. 1943-45. *447*
Gottwaldt, Alfred B. Kreidler, Eugen. Railroads (review article). 1919-45. *214*
Government. Europe, Eastern. Ghettos. Jewish Councils (Judenrat). Military Occupation. 1941-43. *895*
Government enterprise. Reichswerke AG Hermann Göring. 1936-43. *126*
Government-in-exile. Belgium. Diplomatic representation. Switzerland. 1940-45. *343*
Government-in-exile, London. Anti-Semitism. Poland. Schwarzbart, I. 1933-45. *770*
—. Genocide. Jews. Poland. Public Opinion. 1942. *887*
Gradina concentration camp. Concentration camps. Croatia (Jasenovac). 1941-45. *968*
Graphic arts. Lanauve, Cluseau. Military Museum Art Collection. Prisoners of war. 1941-42. *247*
Great Britain. Afrika Corps. Africa, North. Armored Vehicles and Tank Warfare. 1940-42. *521*
—. Air Forces. Armies. Europe. Greece. Italy. 1940-41. *640*
—. Brown, Anthony Cave. Kahn, David. Military Intelligence (review article). USA. 1939-45. *155*
—. Burckhardt, Carl Jacob. Diplomacy. Mediation. World War II (antecedents). 1937-39. *323*

238   Great Britain

—. Convoys (PQ13, QP9). Naval Battles. North Sea. 1942. *509*
—. Convoys (PQ13, QP9). Submarines. *U-585* (submarine). 1942. *488*
—. Dahlerus, Jean Birger Essen. Diplomacy. 1939. *285*
—. Darlan, Jean. Diplomacy. France. 1940-41. *328*
—. Foreign policy. Hitler, Adolf. 1921-45. *306*
—. Foreign policy. Pius XII, Pope. 1939-40. *500*
—. France. Stalingrad (Battle). USSR. 1939-45. *688*
—. Historical theory. USA. 1939-45. *211*
—. Military Strategy. Operation Sea Lion. 1939-40. *458*
—. Morale. Propaganda. Retaliation. 1943-45. *491*
—. Railroads. Sweden. Transportation policy. 1940-43. *304*
—. Rocket defense. 1944-45. *548*
—. Shipping. Submarine Warfare. 1939-45. *540*
Great King (film). Goebbels, Joseph. *Kolberg* (film). Myths, historical. Propaganda. 1942-45. *89*
Greece. Air Forces. Armies. Europe. Great Britain. Italy. 1940-41. *640*
—. Europe. Fascism. Military Occupation. Poland. 1940-45. *974*
—. Invasion. Italy. Military Strategy. 1940-41. *641*
—. Italy. Jews. Military Occupation. 1940-43. *912*
Greece (central Macedonia). Bulgarians. Merten, Dr. Military occupation. Tendzos, Christos. 1943. *643*
Greiser, Artur. Jews. Poland (Warta region). 1939-43. *979*
Grosman, Ladislav *(Shop on Main Street)*. Labor, forced. Memoirs. Slovakia. 1941-44. *874*
Grosz, Bandi. Brand, Joel, mission. Hungary. Military Intelligence. Peace negotiations. 1944. *361*
Guards Anti-Tank Artillery Regiment, 150th. Malaia Tokmachka (battle). Rumiantsev, N. (memoir). USSR. 1943. *727*
Guderian, Heinz. Generals, German. Liddell Hart, B. H. (influence). Military Strategy. 1920's-40's. *23*
—. Military officers. Military Strategy. 1939-44. *81*
Guerrilla Warfare (Polish). Military Strategy (German). Warsaw Uprising. 1944. *437*
Gürtner, Franz. Bumke, Erwin. Judicial Administration (review article). Law. Nazism. 1933-45. *71*
Gustavus V (abdication threat). Foreign Policy. Midsummer crisis. Sweden. 1941. *358*
Gypsies. Belgium. Genocide. 1940-45. *868*

H

Halder, Franz. Armies. Eastern Front. General staff. Military Strategy (review). 1941. *754*
Hansa company. Merchant Marine. Shipbuilding. 1939-45. *275*
Harrower, Molly. Psychohistory. War criminals. 1939-45. *232*
Hashomer Hatsair. Military Occupation. Poland (Łódz ghetto, Maryshin). 1939-44. *985*
Heike, Otto. Archives. Military Occupation. Poland (Łódz). 1939-45. *388*
Heller, Paul. Auschwitz (evacuation). Concentration Camps. Diaries. 1945. *891*
Heroes. Documents. Jews. Military Decorations, Flags, and Symbols. Poland (Białystok, Warsaw ghettos). Resistance. 1944. *818*

Hess, Rudolf. 1941. *506*
—. Nazism. 1920-41. *101*
—. Spandau prison. 1946-80. *18*
Higher Education. Curricula. Military Occupation. Ukraine (Lvov). 1942-45. *438*
Higher Middle School. Military Occupation. Netherlands. Public Administration. 1940-44. *549*
Hijefs. Concentration Camps. Jews. Rescue agencies. Slovakia. Vaad Hacala. 1941-45. *946*
Hilberg, Raul (interview). Europe. Genocide. Jews. 1930's-40's. *848*
Himmler, Heinrich. Anti-Semitism. Bernadotte, Folke (letter). Forgery. Kersten, Felix. 1944-45. *847*
—. Army. Belgium. Collaboration movements. Reeder, Eggert. SS (Schutzstaffel; appointments). 1941-44. *462*
—. Belgium (Brussels). Collaboration. Military Occupation. Reeder, Eggert. SS (Schutzstaffel; appointments). 1942-43. *461*
—. Business. Concentration camps. SS (Schutzstaffel). 1933-45. *909*
—. Business. Interest Groups. SS (Schutzstaffel). 1930-45. *121*
—. Eichmann, Adolf. Genocide. Hitler, Adolf. Irving, David *(Hitler's War)*. Jews. 1939-45. *1041*
—. Kersten, Felix. Resistance. 1941-44. *125*
Hirschfeld, G. Kettenacker, L. Nazism. Political Systems (review article). 1933-45. *30*
Hirt, August. Concentration Camps. Jews. Medical experiments. 1941-44. *934*
Historians. Archives, underground. Jews. Military Occupation. Poland (Warsaw ghetto). Ringelblum, Emanuel. 1939-50. *1025*
—. Meinecke, Friedrich. Nazism. 1923-35. *235*
Historical Service of the Army (Military History Center). Archives. France (Vincennes). 1939-78. *43*
Historical theory. Great Britain. USA. 1939-45. *211*
Historiography. 1937-45. 1971-74. *279*
—. 1939-45. *154*
—. Allies. Italy. Military occupation. Resistance. 1939-45. *455*
—. Anti-Semitism. Auschwitz-Birkenau. Concentration Camps. Poland. Resistance. 1939-78. *890*
—. Anti-Semitism. Christianity. 19c-20c. *1008*
—. Atrocities. Galicia Division. Poland. Ukrainians. USSR. 1943-45. *749*
—. Bibliographies. Germany, West. 1939-75. *107*
—. Bibliographies. Netherlands. 1939-75. *480*
—. Biography. Davidson, Eugene. Hitler, Adolf (review article). Irving, David. Toland, John. 1930's-77. *163*
—. Catholic Church. Church and State. Nazism. 1933-76. *305*
—. Concentration Camps. Theresienstadt camp. Zionism. 1941-45. *997*
—. Conferences. 1939-73. *69*
—. Eastern front. Germany, East. USSR. 1943-45. *689*
—. Esh, Shaul. Legislation, anti-Jewish. Nazism. 1933. *757*
—. Europe, East Central. Horthy, Miklós. 1939-45. *649*
—. Foreign Policy. 1930-45. *291*
—. Foreign policy. Hitler, Adolf. Nazism. 1933-45. *357*
—. France. Military collapse. 1940. *454*
—. Genocide. Jews. 1939-45. *956*
—. Genocide. Jews. 1939-77. *933*
—. Genocide. Jews. Nazism. 1940-44. *1035*
—. Genocide. Jews. Nazism. 1946-79. *838*

—. Genocide. Jews. Nazism. 1952-79. *813*
—. Genocide. Jews. Poland. 1939-45. 1939-71. *879*
—. Genocide. Jews. Poland. 1941-42. *802*
—. Genocide. Jews. USSR. 1940-45. *866*
—. Germany, East. 1939-75. *150*
—. Germany, West. Nazism. 1946-74. *178*
—. Hitler, Adolf. 1940's-70's. *98*
—. Hitler, Adolf. Nazism. ca 1910-45. *54*
—. Hitler, Adolf. Nazism (conference). 1933-45. *93*
—. Hitler, Adolf. Resistance. 1930-49. *183*
—. Hungary. Košice (air raid). USSR. War, declaration of. 1941-46. *675*
—. Irving, David. Nazism. Resistance. Rommel, Erwin. 1941-45. *53*
—. Nazism. Psychohistory. ca 1940-78. *139*
—. Taylor, A. J. P. World War II (antecedents). 1919-39. 1945-79. *33*
Historiography, bourgeois. Military Occupation. USSR. 1940-45. *720*
—. Moscow (battle). 1941-42. *691*
Historiography, Bulgarian. Foreign Policy. 1944. *619*
Historiography, Czech. Boundaries. Czechoslovakia. Nationalities. 1938-45. *579*
Historiography, East German. Balkans (documents). 1939-45. *632*
—. Foreign policy. 1933-45. *321*
Historiography, Polish. Genocide. Jews. Poland. 1939-45. *922*
Historiography (review article). War aims. World War I (antecedents). 1897-1945. *13*
Historiography (revisionist). Hitler, Adolf. 1933-45. *1*
Historiography, Soviet. Genocide. Jews. 1938-78. *864*
Historiography, West German. Stalingrad, battle. 1942-43. *711*
Historiography (West German, Soviet). Capitalism. Fascism. Foreign Policy. 1930-45. *329*
Historiography, Western. Nazi-Soviet Pact. USSR. 1939-45. *744*
Historiography, Yugoslav. Documents. Yugoslavia. 1940's. 1950's-73. *613*
History Teaching. City University of New York. Genocide. Jews. 1941-45. 1979. *1017*
—. Edelmann, Moritz. Klagge, Dietrich. Nazism. Textbooks. 1938-45. *213*
—. Germany, West. Military Occupation. Poland. 1939-44. *385*
Hitler, Adolf. Africa, North. Logistics. Military Strategy. Rommel, Erwin. 1941-42. *555*
—. Air Warfare. Military Strategy. 1941-45. *199*
—. Anti-Nazi Movements. Assassination. Bonhoeffer, Dietrich. Moltke, Helmuth James von. 1940-45. *195*
—. Anti-Semitism. Expansionism. Nationalism. 1919-40. *17*
—. Anti-Semitism. Italy. 1938-43. *964*
—. Army. Assassination. July 20 plot. 1944. *61*
—. Assassination attempts. Stauffenberg, Claus von. 1938-44. *185*
—. Balkans. Italians. Lanz, Hubert. Military Command. Surrender. 1943. *502*
—. Behavior. 1939-45. *38*
—. Bibliographies. France. 1919-39. *25*
—. Bibliographies. Political Leadership. 1919-80. *123*
—. Conservatism. Poland. Political opposition. 1940-44. *258*
—. Conspiracy. Germany (Berlin). Prisoners of war, American. 1945. *238*
—. Croatia. Diplomacy. Pavelić, Ante. 1942. *336*
—. Croatia. Diplomacy. Pavelić, Ante. 1943. *335*
—. Croatia. Documents. 1941-42. *374*
—. Economic Policy. World War II (antecedents). 1939-41. *200*
—. Eichmann, Adolf. Genocide. Himmler, Heinrich. Irving, David *(Hitler's War)*. Jews. 1939-45. *1041*
—. Euthanasia. Judicial system. Public Administration. 1940-41. *877*
—. Foreign policy. 1933-45. *92*
—. Foreign policy. Great Britain. 1921-45. *306*
—. Foreign policy. Historiography. Nazism. 1933-45. *357*
—. Foreign policy. Military Strategy (grand). 1933-45. *307*
—. Genocide. Irving, David. Jews. 1933-45. *801*
—. Genocide (review article). Irving, David. Jews. 1939-45. *800*
—. Genocide (review article). Irving, David. Jews. 1940-45. 1977. *1058*
—. Historiography. 1940's-70's. *98*
—. Historiography. Nazism. ca 1910-45. *54*
—. Historiography. Nazism (conference). 1933-45. *93*
—. Historiography. Resistance. 1930-49. *183*
—. Historiography (revisionist). 1933-45. *1*
—. July 20 Plot. 1944. *60*
—. July 20 Plot. Stauffenberg, Claus von. 1939-46. *132*
—. Langer, Walter C. Psychohistory. 1930's-45. *162*
—. Lebensraum theory. ca 1925-45. *87*
—. Medical history. 1889-1945. *239*
—. Military. USSR. War aims. 1939-41. *682*
—. National Characteristics. Public Opinion. 1940-44. *243*
—. Nazism. 1928-45. *192*
—. Nazism. Nuremberg trials. Speer, Albert (interview). 1945-76. *193*
—. Nazism. Rauschning, Hermann. 1940-73. *36*
—. Political opposition (handbill). 1943. *234*
—. Psychohistory. 20c. *228*
—. Psychohistory. Research (interdisciplinary). 1981. *262*
—. USSR. World War II (antecedents). 1933-42. *651*
—. Yugoslavia. 1939-41. *615*
Hitler, Adolf (biographies; review article). Duerlein, E. Fest, I. C. Maser, Werner. 1890-1945. *16*
Hitler, Adolf (biography, letters—review article). Maser, Werner. 1920-45. *263*
Hitler, Adolf (interview). Burckhardt, Carl Jacob. Danzig. 1938-40. *341*
Hitler, Adolf *(Mein Kampf)*. Genocide. Poland. 1928-45. *407*
Hitler, Adolf (review article). Biography. Davidson, Eugene. Historiography. Irving, David. Toland, John. 1930's-77. *163*
—. Bloch, Eduard. Jews. Psychohistory. Stierlin, Helm. 1907-45. 1973-76. *114*
—. Fest, Joachim. 1889-1945. *170*
—. Fest, Joachim. ca 1918-45. *100*
—. Irving, David. Jews. 1939-45. *1057*
—. Irving, David. Nuremberg Trials. Smith, Bradley F. 1941-45. 1977. *136*
—. Payne, Robert. Political Science. Pridham, Geoffrey. 1920's-33. *215*
—. Rich, Norman. War aims 1936-45. *91*
Hitler Jugend. Education. 1933-45. *104*
Hitler Youth. National Socialist Teachers League. Schools. 1933-45. *124*
Hlond, August. Catholic Church. Poland. 1939-45. *425*

Hoess, Rudolf. Auschwitz. Autobiography. Concentration Camps. Nazism. 1939-45. *811*
—. Auschwitz. Autobiography. Concentration Camps. War crimes. 1906-47. *901*
—. Auschwitz. Concentration Camps. Genocide. Sociology. 1942-45. *913*
Hogland (battle). Finland. USSR. 1944. *747*
Hohenhörn (vessel). Finland. Jews. Refugees. 1942. *1021*
Hohenlohe-Langenburg, Maximilian. Diplomacy, secret. Dulles, Allen. USA. 1939-44. *281*
Holocaust (television film). Germany, West. 1979. *963*
Honduras. Diplomacy. Zinsser, Christian (memoir). 1940-41. *372*
Höppner, Rolf-Heinz. Chełmno concentration camp. Genocide. 1941-42. *940*
—. Genocide. Jews. Leszczynski, J. Poland (Warta region). 1940-42. *835*
Horthy, Miklós. Axis powers. Hungary. Kallay, Miklós. Negotiations. 1943. *311*
—. Deportation. Hungary (Budapest). Jews. 1944. *842*
—. Europe, East Central. Historiography. 1939-45. *649*
Humanité (newspaper). Censorship. Communist Party. Documents. France. Military Occupation. 1940. *529*
Hungarians. Employment (seasonal). Forests and Forestry. 1937-44. *40*
Hungary. Air Forces. 1938-44. *317*
—. Axis powers. Horthy, Miklós. Kallay, Miklós. Negotiations. 1943. *311*
—. Bihaly, Andrew. Diaries (review article). Genocide. Jews. 1944. *799*
—. Boundaries. Romania. Transylvania, partition of. Vienna Diktat. 1940. *352*
—. Brand, Joel, mission. Grosz, Bandi. Military Intelligence. Peace negotiations. 1944. *361*
—. Bulgaria. Propaganda. Romania. 1941-43. *645*
—. Foreign Relations. Poland. 1938-44. *396*
—. Historiography. Košice (air raid). USSR. War, declaration of. 1941-46. *675*
—. Jewish Councils (Judenrat). Military Occupation. 1944. *796*
—. Jews. Massacres. USSR (Kamenets Podolsk). Yugoslavia (Délvidék). 1941-42. *795*
—. Logistics. USSR. 1944-45. *743*
—. Military Occupation. USSR. 1944-45. *625*
Hungary (Bac). Germans. Minorities. 1942-45. *621*
Hungary (Budapest). Deportation. Horthy, Miklós. Jews. 1944. *842*
Hungary (Újvidék). Military Occupation. 1944. *578*
Hussein, Muhammad Amin al-. Arab States. Foreign Relations. 1941-45. *44*
Hydrogenation techniques. Farben, I. G. Fuel supply. 1930-45. *133*

I

Ideology. Anti-Semitism. Nazism. Racism. World War II (antecedents). 1933-45. *981*
—. Balkans. Expansionism. 1938-44. *599*
—. Bonnard, Abel. Collaboration. France. Vichy regime. 1928-42. *512*
—. Europe, Eastern. Military Occupation. 1941-45. *57*
—. Genocide. Jews. Military Occupation. USSR. 1941-44. *900*
Imperialism. Military Occupation. Ukraine. 1941-45. *702*
Imports. Iron ore. Steel production. Sweden. 1938-40. *302*

Industrial conditions. Research sources. Zentrale Planung. 1942-45. *194*
Industrial Relations. Aesthetics. Labor. Nazism. Symbolism. 1933-39. *210*
Industry. Chetniks. Collaborators. Communications. Counterinsurgency. Ustaši. Yugoslavia. 1941-42. *573*
Infantry. Armaments. Statistics. 1939-44. *148*
Innsbruck, University of. Nazism. 1938-45. *975*
Intellectuals. Genocide. Jews. Poland (Stanisławów). 1941. *849*
—. Genocide. Military occupation. Poland. Theater. 1939-45. *421*
—. Nazism. 1933-45. *122*
—. Poland. 1939-45. *412*
Intelligence service. Eastern front. 1941-45. *653*
—. Geheime Meldedienst (recruitment). 1944-45. *78*
—. Subversive activities. USSR. 1944. *669*
—. USA. 1933-41. *468*
Intelligence services. Abwehr. Military Organization (fusion). SD (Sicherheitsdienst). 1944. *29*
Interest Groups. Business. Himmler, Heinrich. SS (Schutzstaffel). 1930-45. *121*
International law, principles of. Racism. Schmitt, Carl. Walz, Gustav. 1919-45. *111*
Intervention. Bulgaria. USSR. 1944. *598*
Invasion. Greece. Italy. Military Strategy. 1940-41. *641*
—. Military Strategy. Operation Barbarossa. USSR. 1941. *739*
Invasion (threat). Belgium. Military Intelligence. 1939-40. *558*
Iran. Exports. 1939-41. *308*
Ireland. Espionage. Schütz, Günther. 1941-42. *452*
Iron Industry. Alsace-Lorraine. France. 1940-44. *364*
—. Coal Mines and Mining. Exploitation. Ukraine. 1941-44. *725*
Iron ore. Imports. Steel production. Sweden. 1938-40. *302*
—. Neutrality. Sweden. Trade. 1939-45. *368*
Irving, David. Air Forces. Milch, Erhard (review article). 1933-45. *156*
—. Biography. Davidson, Eugene. Historiography. Hitler, Adolf (review article). Toland, John. 1930's-77. *163*
—. Butz, A. R. Genocide (review article). Jews. 1941-45. *1016*
—. Genocide. Hitler, Adolf. Jews. 1933-45. *801*
—. Genocide (review article). Hitler, Adolf. Jews. 1939-45. *800*
—. Genocide (review article). Hitler, Adolf. Jews. 1940-45. 1977. *1058*
—. Historiography. Nazism. Resistance. Rommel, Erwin. 1941-45. *53*
—. Hitler, Adolf (review article). Jews. 1939-45. *1057*
—. Hitler, Adolf (review article). Nuremberg Trials. Smith, Bradley F. 1941-45. 1977. *136*
Irving, David *(Hitler's War)*. Eichmann, Adolf. Genocide. Himmler, Heinrich. Hitler, Adolf. Jews. 1939-45. *1041*
Italian Social Republic. Jews. Persecution. 1943-45. *959*
Italians. Balkans. Hitler, Adolf. Lanz, Hubert. Military Command. Surrender. 1943. *502*
Italy. Air Forces. Armies. Europe. Great Britain. Greece. 1940-41. *640*
—. Alliances. Military Strategy. 1927-45. *345*
—. Allies. Bibliographies. Military occupation. Resistance. 1939-45. *474*
—. Allies. Historiography. Military occupation. Resistance. 1939-45. *455*
—. Anti-Semitism. Hitler, Adolf. 1938-43. *964*

—. Austria. Foreign Relations. South Tyrol. 1938-45. *290*
—. Austria. South Tyrol. 1938-45. *355*
—. Axis Pact. Japan. Oshima Hiroshi. World War II (antecedents). 1934-40. *283*
—. Badoglio, Pietro. Foreign Relations. Keitel, Wilhelm. Marras, Luigi (papers). 1936-43. *286*
—. Chetniks. Yugoslavia (Croatia; Lika). 1943-44. *607*
—. Documents (review article). Foreign Relations. Japan. 1941-42. *365*
—. Foreign Relations. Racial policy. 1938-43. *986*
—. Gothic Line. Partisans. 1943-45. *447*
—. Greece. Invasion. Military Strategy. 1940-41. *641*
—. Greece. Jews. Military Occupation. 1940-43. *912*
—. Malta. Operation Hercules. 1935-42. *486*
—. Military control. 1943. *542*
—. Military Defeat. Operation Sunrise. 1945. *350*
Italy (Milan). Daily Life. Jews. Levi, Primo (memoirs). 1942-43. *943*
Italy, North. Allies. Operation Sunrise. 1944-45. *464*
Italy (Rome). Diplomacy. Jews. Vatican. Weizsäcker, Ernst von. 1943. *810*
Italy (Sicily). Military Strategy. 1943. *522*
Italy (Trieste). Concentration Camps. Genocide. Jews. Nazism. Risiera di San Sabba. 1943-45. *791*

J

Jagiellonian University. Poland. Political Imprisonment. ca 1939-45. *781*
Jaksch, Wenzel (correspondence). Beneš, Eduard. Sudeten Germans (expulsion). 1939-43. *637*
Japan. Axis Pact. Italy. Oshima Hiroshi. World War II (antecedents). 1934-40. *283*
—. Documents (review article). Foreign Relations. Italy. 1941-42. *365*
—. Economic policy. Funk, Walther. Matsuoka, Yosuke. 1941-45. *322*
—. Peace mediation. USSR. 1941-45. *318*
Jesuits. Europe. Military occupation. 1933-45. *935*
Jew Süss (film). Anti-Semitism. Films. Nazism. Propaganda. 1940's. *859*
Jewish Antifascist Block. Jewish Fighting Organization. Warsaw ghetto uprising. 1940-43. *854*
Jewish Brigade. Germany (Belsen). Liberation. Poland. Tubin, Yehuda (memoirs). 1945-46. *1031*
Jewish Councils (conference). Europe. Nazism. 1933-45. *1060*
Jewish Councils (Judenrat). Attitudes. Military Occupation. Poland. USSR. 1939-41. *1047*
—. Bibliographies. Trunk, Isaiah. 1939-44. *1040*
—. Czerniakow, Adam. Diaries. Military Occupation. Poland (Warsaw ghetto). 1939-42. *892*
—. Czerniakow, Adam. Diaries. Poland (Warsaw ghetto). 1939. *898*
—. Czerniakow, Adam. Military Occupation. Poland (Warsaw ghetto). Tyszka, Leon (reminiscence). 1939-42. *1034*
—. Czerniakow, Adam (diary). Poland (Warsaw ghetto). 1939-42. *1054*
—. Documents (memoir). Poland (Warsaw ghetto). Ringelblum Archive. 1939-42. *1005*
—. Europe, Eastern. Ghettos. Government. Military Occupation. 1941-43. *895*
—. Hungary. Military Occupation. 1944. *796*

Jews   *241*

—. Lithuania (Vilnius ghetto). Medicine (practice of). Memoirs. Military Occupation. 1939-45. *1044*
—. Military Occupation. 1930's-40's. *1046*
—. Netherlands. Visser, Lodewijk Ernst. 1940-42. *966*
Jewish Councils (Judenrat; review article). Europe, Eastern. Ghettos. 1939-44. *896*
Jewish Fighting Organization. Anielewicz, Mordechai. People's Guard. Poland. Warsaw ghetto uprising. Youth groups. 1930's-42. *899*
—. Civil resistance. Jewish Social Self-Aid. Military Occupation. Poland (Warsaw ghetto). Resistance. 1939-42. *1003*
—. Jewish Antifascist Block. Warsaw ghetto uprising. 1940-43. *854*
—. Poland. Warsaw ghetto uprising (origins). 1942-43. *884*
—. Warsaw ghetto uprising. Zuckerman, Itzhak (interview). 1933-44. *1055*
Jewish Gazette. Bibliographies. Music. Poland (Warsaw Ghetto). 1940-42. *857*
Jewish Historical Institute. Archival Catalogs and Inventories. Poland. 1940-47. *902*
—. Archives. Poland. Warsaw ghetto uprising. 1942. *846*
Jewish Military Union. Poland. Warsaw ghetto uprising. World War II (personal narratives). 1942. *906*
Jewish Social Self-Aid. Civil resistance. Jewish Fighting Organization. Military Occupation. Poland (Warsaw ghetto). Resistance. 1939-42. *1003*
Jews *See also* Anti-Semitism.
—. Africa, North. Vichy regime. Word War II (antecedents). 1930-40. *764*
—. Alter, Wiktor. Anti-Nazi Movements. Erlich, Henryk. USSR. 1939-41. *988*
—. American Jewish Committee (William E. Wiener Oral History Library). Genocide. Oral History. 1941-45. 1977-82. *996*
—. Anti-Nazi Movements. Poland (Warsaw ghetto). Socialist movement. 1939-44. *832*
—. Anti-Semitism. Genocide. 1933-77. *1049*
—. Anti-Semitism. Genocide. Nazism. 1939-45. *885*
—. Anti-Semitism. Genocide. Nazism. Political Theory. 1917-45. *1026*
—. Anti-Semitism. Netherlands (Leiden). Orphanage. 1940-43. *916*
—. Archives. Genocide. Poland (Warsaw ghetto). Ringelblum, Emanuel. 1942-43. *1002*
—. Archives, National. Genocide. Rescue. USA. War Refugee Board. 1918-52. *961*
—. Archives, underground. Historians. Military Occupation. Poland (Warsaw ghetto). Ringelblum, Emanuel. 1939-50. *1025*
—. Arendt, Hannah. Ethnocentrism. Genealogy. Political Theory. 1958-65. *828*
—. Art. Concentration camps. Resistance, spiritual. 1940-45. *962*
—. Atrocities. Babi Yar (massacre). 1941-43. *921*
—. Atrocities. Communists. USSR. 1939-41. *683*
—. Auschwitz. Children. Deportation. France. Vichy Regime. 1942-44. *955*
—. Auschwitz. Concentration Camps. Poland. 1940-45. *994*
—. Auschwitz. Concentration Camps. Theresienstadt camp. 1943-44. *931*
—. Auschwitz (escape). Bikel, Sara. Concentration Camps. Rosenstein, Hana. 1944. *841*
—. Authors. Poland (Warsaw ghetto). 1939-45. *778*

242 Jews

—. Belgium. Charles, J. L. Dasney, F. Geheime Feldpolizei (reports). Resistance. 1940-42. *457*
—. Belgium. Confiscation. Property. 1940-44. *1011*
—. Belorussia. Genocide (documents). Military Occupation. Ukraine. USSR. 1941-45. *976*
—. Bessarabia. USSR. 1940-45. *945*
—. Bibliographies. Genocide. 1939-45. 1960-78. *1051*
—. Bihaly, Andrew. Diaries (review article). Genocide. Hungary. 1944. *799*
—. Birkenau. Concentration Camps. Czechoslovakia (Terezin ghetto). Genocide. 1943-44. *911*
—. Bishops. Genocide. 1942-44. *1036*
—. Bloch, Eduard. Hitler, Adolf (review article). Psychohistory. Stierlin, Helm. 1907-45. 1973-76. *114*
—. Brandt-Meyer family (correspondence). Germany (Berlin). 1941-43. *814*
—. Bureaucracies. Genocide. 1932-45. *897*
—. Bureaucracies. Genocide. Morality. 1933-45. *893*
—. Busse, Otto. Memoirs. Military Occupation. Poland (Białystok). Rescue. 1943. *806*
—. Busse, Otto. Memoirs. Rescue. 1943-79. *876*
—. Butz, A. R. Genocide (review article). Irving, David. 1941-45. *1016*
—. Catholic Church. Genocide. 1939-45. *1052*
—. Centos Society. Education. *Głos Domu Chłopców* (magazine). Orphans. Poland (Warsaw Ghetto). 1940-41. *1006*
—. Children. Concentration camps. Education. Korczak, Janusz. Poland. 1930's-40's. *875*
—. Children. France. Rescue. Vichy regime. 1939-45. *918*
—. Children. Korczak, Janusz. Poland (Warsaw ghetto). 1900-42. *973*
—. China (Shanghai). Diplomatic missions, Polish. Europe, Eastern. Rescue. 1942-44. *948*
—. Christians. France (Nord, Pas-de-Calais). 1938-44. *825*
—. City University of New York. Genocide. History Teaching. 1941-45. 1979. *1017*
—. Cohen, David (correspondence). Military occupation. Visser, Lodewijk Ernst. 1941-42. *960*
—. Collaborators. Ganzweich, Avraham. Poland (Warsaw ghetto). 1940-43. *1045*
—. Communist Party. 1933-45. *1015*
—. Concentration camps. Genocide. 1939-44. *807*
—. Concentration camps. Genocide. 1941-44. *765*
—. Concentration Camps. Genocide. Italy (Trieste). Nazism. Risiera di San Sabba. 1943-45. *791*
—. Concentration Camps. Hijefs. Rescue agencies. Slovakia. Vaad Hacala. 1941-45. *946*
—. Concentration Camps. Hirt, August. Medical experiments. 1941-44. *934*
—. Concentration Camps. Memoirs. Poland. Rosensaft, Hadassah. 1940's. *993*
—. Concentration Camps. Memoirs. Poland (Warsaw ghetto). 1943-47. *1033*
—. Concentration Camps. Poland (Ciechanów). 1940's. *881*
—. Concentration camps. Poland (Warsaw ghetto). 1941-44. *958*
—. Conferences. Genocide. 1933-45. 1973-74. *1056*
—. Consular Reports. Libya. Walther, Gebhardt von. 1940-43. *763*
—. Croatia. Genocide. Nazism. Serbs. 1941-45. *938*

—. Cultural Union of German Jewry. Nazism. Singer, Kurt. Theater. 1933-41. *858*
—. Daily life. Genocide. Poland (Łódz ghetto). 1940-44. *788*
—. Daily Life. Italy (Milan). Levi, Primo (memoirs). 1942-43. *943*
—. Daily Life. Military Occupation. Nazism. Poland. 1941-44. *850*
—. Denmark (Gilleleje). Rescue. Resistance. 1943-44. *937*
—. Deportation. Finland. Refugees. 1942. *789*
—. Deportation. Horthy, Miklós. Hungary (Budapest). 1944. *842*
—. Diaries. Poland (Warsaw ghetto). 1941. *785*
—. Diplomacy. Italy (Rome). Vatican. Weizsäcker, Ernst von. 1943. *810*
—. Diplomacy. Poland. Rescue agencies. 1939-45. *947*
—. Documents. Genealogy. Poland (Warsaw Ghetto). 1943. *805*
—. Documents. Heroes. Military Decorations, Flags, and Symbols. Poland (Białystok, Warsaw ghettos). Resistance. 1944. *818*
—. Documents. Lvov portfolio. Military Occupation. Poland. Ukraine (Lvov). 1941. *903*
—. Economic planning. Genocide. Manpower. 1939-45. *834*
—. Ecumenism. Rescue. World Council of Churches. 1939-44. *793*
—. Ehrenburg, Ilya *(The Black Book)*. USSR. 1941-80. *1012*
—. Eichmann, Adolf. Genocide. Himmler, Heinrich. Hitler, Adolf. Irving, David *(Hitler's War)*. 1939-45. *1041*
—. Emigration. Germany (Fürth). Memoirs. 1936-41. *991*
—. Emigration. Nazism. 1933-45. *1019*
—. *Encyclopaedia Judaica*. Genocide. 1939-45. *839*
—. Epstein, David (memoirs). Genocide. Partisans. Ukraine (Lyubeshov). 1941-44. *840*
—. Europe. Genocide. 1938-45. *914*
—. Europe. Genocide. Hilberg, Raul (interview). 1930's-40's. *848*
—. Europe. Genocide. Photography. 1939-45. *809*
—. Expropriation. Memoirs. Military Occupation. Poland (Warsaw). Szulfried, Stanisław. 1939-42. *1024*
—. Fein, Helen. Genocide. Quantitative methods. 1939-45. *1048*
—. Filderman, Wilhelm. Letters. Military Occupation. Romania. 1940-44. *1007*
—. Finland. *Hohenhörn* (vessel). Refugees. 1942. *1021*
—. Foreign Relations. USSR. 1933-41. *869*
—. France. General Union of Israelites. Military Occupation. 1942-43. *889*
—. France. Legislation. Persecution. 1942-44. *861*
—. France (Alsace-Lorraine). Military occupation. Nazism. Negroes. Racism. 1939-42. *485*
—. France (Côte-d'Or). Genocide. 1941-44. *1037*
—. Genocide. 1919-43. *782*
—. Genocide. 1933-45. *784*
—. Genocide. 1938-45. *853*
—. Genocide. 1939-45. *769*
—. Genocide. 1939-45. *787*
—. Genocide. 1940-45. *852*
—. Genocide. 1941-45. *924*
—. Genocide. 1942-43. *936*
—. Genocide. Germany (Berlin). 1933-43. *773*
—. Genocide. Government-in-exile, London. Poland. Public Opinion. 1942. *887*
—. Genocide. Historiography. 1939-45. *956*
—. Genocide. Historiography. 1939-77. *933*

—. Genocide. Historiography. Nazism. 1940-44. *1035*
—. Genocide. Historiography. Nazism. 1946-79. *838*
—. Genocide. Historiography. Nazism. 1952-79. *813*
—. Genocide. Historiography. Poland. 1939-45. 1939-71. *879*
—. Genocide. Historiography. Poland. 1941-42. *802*
—. Genocide. Historiography. USSR. 1940-45. *866*
—. Genocide. Historiography, Polish. Poland. 1939-45. *922*
—. Genocide. Historiography, Soviet. 1938-78. *864*
—. Genocide. Hitler, Adolf. Irving, David. 1933-45. *801*
—. Genocide. Höppner, Rolf-Heinz. Leszczynski, J. Poland (Warta region). 1940-42. *835*
—. Genocide. Ideology. Military Occupation. USSR. 1941-44. *900*
—. Genocide. Intellectuals. Poland (Stanisławów). 1941. *849*
—. Genocide. Leadership. Nazism. Psychohistory. 1938-45. *923*
—. Genocide. Lithuania. 1941-44. *762*
—. Genocide. Manstein, Erich von. USSR. 1939-45. *1042*
—. Genocide. Mass media. Nazism. Propaganda. 1920-45. *768*
—. Genocide. Military Occupation. Poland (Kalisz). 1940-42. *978*
—. Genocide. Nazism. 1920-45. *1027*
—. Genocide. Nazism. 1924-45. *767*
—. Genocide. Nazism. 1933-45. *965*
—. Genocide. Nazism. 2c BC-20c. *915*
—. Genocide. Poland (Ciechanów region). 1941-45. *880*
—. Genocide. Poland (Węgrów). 1939-44. *1022*
—. Genocide. Psychology. 1938-44. *983*
—. Genocide. Radlitzki, Tzvi (memoirs). Ukraine (Lvov). 1941-45. *987*
—. Genocide. Railroads. 1939-45. *894*
—. Genocide. Romania (Iași). 1941. *969*
—. Genocide. USSR. 1941-42. *952*
—. Genocide. USSR (Rudnya). 1939-45. *830*
—. Genocide (review article). Hitler, Adolf. Irving, David. 1939-45. *800*
—. Genocide (review article). Hitler, Adolf. Irving, David. 1940-45. 1977. *1058*
—. Genocide (review article). Kren, George M. Rappoport, Leon. ca 1939-45. *990*
—. Genocide (review article). Laqueur, Walter. 1941-45. *998*
—. Genocide (review article). Literature. 1941-45. *816*
—. Genocide (review article). Methodology. 1939-45. *951*
—. Germany (Lamsdorf). Prisoners of war. 1941-45. *471*
—. Ghettos. Leadership. Resistance. 1939-44. *783*
—. Ghettos. Poland. Theater. 1939-42. *845*
—. Greece. Italy. Military Occupation. 1940-43. *912*
—. Greiser, Artur. Poland (Warta region). 1939-43. *979*
—. Hitler, Adolf (review article). Irving, David. 1939-45. *1057*
—. Hungary. Massacres. USSR (Kamenets Podolsk). Yugoslavia (Délvidék). 1941-42. *795*
—. Italian Social Republic. Persecution. 1943-45. *959*
—. Karaites. Nazism. Racism. 1939-45. *872*
—. Kittel, Gerhard. Nazi Party. Theology. 1888-1948. *843*

—. Korczak, Janusz (biography). Poland (Warsaw Ghetto). 1899-1942. *766*
—. Labor camps. Poland (Opole region). 1942-44. *1023*
—. Labor (forced). 1939-45. *883*
—. Libraries. Lithuania (Vilnius). Poland (Łódz, Warsaw). 1930-45. *1010*
—. Lithuania (Kaunas ghetto). Partisans. Yellin, Chaim. 1913-44. *944*
—. Lithuania (Vilna). Military Occupation. Refugees. 1939-41. *761*
—. Lithuania (Vilnius ghetto). Ulitski, Moshe (diary). 1941-42. *833*
—. Madajczyk, Czesław (review article). Military Occupation. Poland. 1939-45. *398*
—. Memoirs. Military Occupation. Ukraine (Lvov). 1941-44. *836*
—. Memoirs. Military Occupation. Ukraine (Lvov). 1941-44. *837*
—. Memoirs. Senger, Valentin. Survivors (review article). 1940's. *992*
—. Military. Poland. 1939. *856*
—. Military Occupation. Modrzewska, Krystyna (memoirs). Poland (Lublin). 1942-45. *410*
—. Military Occupation. Poland (Warsaw ghetto). Research. Starvation. 1941-42. *1050*
—. Military occupation. Poland (Złoczów). 1939-45. *415*
—. Military Occupation. Rosenberg, Alfred. USSR. 1941-44. *760*
—. Military Occupation. Ukraine (Mukachevo). 1938-44. *999*
—. Military Occupation. USSR. 1939-41. *984*
—. Musicians (deaths). Poland. 1939-44. *855*
—. Nazism. Nuremberg laws. 1933-45. *920*
—. Neo-Nazism. Rightist movement. 1939-45. 1969-73. *1059*
—. Ohlenbusch, Wilhelm (report). Poland. Warsaw ghetto uprising. 1943. *917*
—. Periodization of History. Rescue. 1933-45. *967*
—. Poland. Prisoners of war. 1939-45. *397*
—. Poland. Prisoners of war. 1939. *392*
—. Poland. Prisoners of war. 1940-45. *822*
—. Poland. Warsaw Ghetto Uprising. 1943. *953*
—. Poland. Warsaw Ghetto Uprising. 1943. *1013*
—. Poland (Kalisz). 1939-45. *980*
—. Poland (Kalisz). 1939. *977*
—. Poland (Łódz ghetto). Rumors. Social Psychology. 1939-44. *932*
—. Poland (Warsaw Ghetto; liquidation). 1942-43. *863*
—. Poles. Resistance. Warsaw Ghetto Uprising. 1944. *905*
—. Public opinion. 1935-43. *930*
—. Referat Deutschland. 1933-40. *803*
—. Rescue. Romania. Transdniester Plan. 1942-44. *1039*
—. Resistance. 1939-45. *759*
—. Resistance. 1941-45. *844*
Jews *(mischlinge)*. Bureaucracies. Persecution. 1944. *758*
Jews (Oriental). France. Nazism. 1940-45. *871*
Jews (rescue). Diplomatic missions, Polish. Europe. 1930's-40's. *949*
Jews (review article). Ainsztein, Reuben. Europe, Eastern. Resistance. 1939-45. *823*
—. Dawidowicz, Lucy S. 1939-45. *888*
—. Europe, Eastern. Kosinski, Jerzy. Novels. 1933-71. *873*
Jong, Louis de. Netherlands. Resistance. World War II (review article). 20c. *536*
Journalism. Censorship. Dietrich, Otto. Stalingrad (battle). 1942-43. *732*
—. Memoirs. Peterson, Jürgen. 1936-43. *204*

244 Judicial Administration

Judicial Administration (review article). Bumke, Erwin. Gürtner, Franz. Law. Nazism. 1933-45. *71*
Judicial system. Euthanasia. Hitler, Adolf. Public Administration. 1940-41. *877*
July 20 plot. Army. Assassination. Hitler, Adolf. 1944. *61*
—. Films. Trials. 1944-45. 1979-80. *220*
—. France (Paris). 1943-46. *130*
—. Hitler, Adolf. 1944. *60*
—. Hitler, Adolf. Stauffenberg, Claus von. 1939-46. *132*
—. Mertz von Quirnheim, Albrecht (family; papers). National Committee "Free Germany". 1941-44. *266*
—. Stauffenberg, Claus von. 1944. *48*
Jury, Hugy. Austria (Lower Austria; Zwettl). 1945. *614*

K

Kahn, David. Brown, Anthony Cave. Great Britain. Military Intelligence (review article). USA. 1939-45. *155*
Kallay, Miklós. Axis powers. Horthy, Miklós. Hungary. Negotiations. 1943. *311*
Kallia, Rauno. Diplomacy (private). Finland. Foreign policy. 1940. *360*
Kara Sea. *Admiral Scheer* (cruiser). Naval Strategy. Operation Wunderland. 1942. *659*
Karaites. Jews. Nazism. Racism. 1939-45. *872*
Katyn massacre. Poland. USSR. 1939-43. *430*
—. Poland. USSR. 1939-45. *377*
Kehrl, Hans. Economic History. Fascism. Krosigk, Lutz Schwerin von. Memoirs (review article). Nazism. 1933-45. *277*
Keitel, Wilhelm. Badoglio, Pietro. Foreign Relations. Italy. Marras, Luigi (papers). 1936-43. *286*
Kersten, Felix. Anti-Semitism. Bernadotte, Folke (letter). Forgery. Himmler, Heinrich. 1944-45. *847*
—. Himmler, Heinrich. Resistance. 1941-44. *125*
Kettenacker, L. Hirschfeld, G. Nazism. Political Systems (review article). 1933-45. *30*
Kettenbacher, Lothar. Alsace-Lorraine. France. Germanization. 1940-44. *497*
Kittel, Gerhard. Jews. Nazi Party. Theology. 1888-1948. *843*
Klagge, Dietrich. Edelmann, Moritz. History teaching. Nazism. Textbooks. 1938-45. *213*
Klein Commission. Annexation. France (Briey, Longwy, Nancy). Mining industry. War aims. 1911-42. *295*
Kleist, Paul Ludwig Ewald von. Eastern front. Military Strategy. Ukraine. Uman (battle). 1941. *706*
Kleist, Peter. Clauss, Edgar. Peace, separate. USSR. 1942-44. *316*
Klonowski, Józef. Concentration Camps. Music. Poland. Sachsenhausen. 1939. *790*
Kolberg (film). Goebbels, Joseph. *Great King* (film). Myths, historical. Propaganda. 1942-45. *89*
Königstein Fortress. Art treasures. Germany (Dresden). Staatliche Kunstsammlungen Dresden. USSR. 1945. *737*
Kontinentale Oel AG. Economic preparations. Oil. 1937-45. *314*
Korczak, Janusz. Children. Concentration camps. Education. Jews. Poland. 1930's-40's. *875*
—. Children. Concentration Camps. Poland (Warsaw ghetto). Treblinka. 1942. *824*
—. Children. Jews. Poland (Warsaw ghetto). 1900-42. *973*
Korczak, Janusz (biography). Jews. Poland (Warsaw Ghetto). 1899-1942. *766*
Korczak, Janusz (review article). Children. Poland (Warsaw ghetto). 1940's. *878*
Kormoran (warship). Australia. Naval Battles. *Sydney* (warship). 1941. *153*
Košice (air raid). Historiography. Hungary. USSR. War, declaration of. 1941-46. *675*
Kosinski, Jerzy. Europe, Eastern. Jews (review article). Novels. 1933-71. *873*
Krebs, Hans. Chuikov, Vasili (memoirs). Germany (Berlin). Military Campaigns. Negotiation attempts. 1945. *288*
Kreidler, Eugen. Gottwaldt, Alfred B. Railroads (review article). 1919-45. *214*
Kreisau Circle. Anti-Nazi Movements. 1938-44. *131*
—. Anti-Nazi Movements. Moltke, Helmuth James von. 1929-44. *169*
Kren, George M. Genocide (review article). Jews. Rappoport, Leon. ca 1939-45. *990*
Krosigk, Lutz Schwerin von. Economic History. Fascism. Kehrl, Hans. Memoirs (review article). Nazism. 1933-45. *277*
Kuckhoff, Greta (memoirs). Resistance. Schulze-Boysen-Harnack organization. 1935-43. *141*
Kugler, Victor. Frank, Anne. Memoirs. Netherlands. 1942-44. *926*
Kuhn, Fritz. German-American Bund. USA. 1936-41. *309*
Kühne, Wolfgang (journal). Concentration Camps. 1940-45. *929*
Kumlin, Ragnar (memoranda). Foreign Relations. Sweden. 1941-43. *320*
Kursk (battle). 1943. *756*
—. Air Warfare. Tactics. Tanks. 1943. *724*
Kutschera, Franz. Assassination. Poland (Warsaw). Resistance. 1944. *422*

L

Labor. Aesthetics. Industrial Relations. Nazism. Symbolism. 1933-39. *210*
—. Belgium (Kortrijk). Conscription, Civilian. 1940-45. *528*
—. Nazism. Social Policy. Women. 1925-40. *173*
—. Public Policy. Winkler, Dörte. Women (review article). 1930-45. *174*
—. Social Classes. Women. 1938-44. *221*
—. Social Classes. Women. 1939-45. *223*
Labor camps. Belgium. Buchenwald. Concentration camps. Evacuation. Military Occupation. 1944. *541*
—. Jews. Poland (Opole region). 1942-44. *1023*
Labor force. Nazism. Women. 1918-45. *274*
Labor, forced. Armaments industry. Documents. 1943. *45*
—. Auschwitz. Concentration camps. Mauthausen. 1935-45. *1043*
—. Concentration Camps. Osram factory. 1944-45. *826*
—. Deportation. Plenipotentiary for Labor Allocation. Sauckel, Fritz. 1941-42. *56*
—. France (Ariège). *Service du Travail Obligatoire*. 1942-44. *494*
—. Grosman, Ladislav *(Shop on Main Street)*. Memoirs. Slovakia. 1941-44. *874*
—. Jews. 1939-45. *883*
—. Nazism. 1933-45. *995*
—. Osram (company). 1944-45. *797*
Labor (imported). Prisoners of war. Working conditions. 1939-45. *166*
Labor policy. Expansionism (explanation of). 1939-43. *172*

Labor Service. Women. 1931-43. *3*
Labor Unions and Organizations. Belgium. Catholic Church. Military Occupation. 1940-42. *476*
Lanauve, Cluseau. Graphic arts. Military Museum Art Collection. Prisoners of war. 1941-42. *247*
Langer, Walter C. Hitler, Adolf. Psychohistory. 1930's-45. *162*
Langlade Tactical Group. Panzer, Brigade, 112th (destruction). 1944. *469*
Lanz, Hubert. Balkans. Hitler, Adolf. Italians. Military Command. Surrender. 1943. *502*
Laqueur, Walter. Genocide (review article). Jews. 1941-45. *998*
Latin America. Emigrants. Nazism. 1933-45. *338*
Latvia. Estonia. Germans. Poland. Racism. Resettlement. 1939. *389*
—. Lithuania. Prisoners of War (Soviet). 1941-45. *721*
—. Nationalism. Nazism. Political Theory. 1942-43. *730*
—. Prisoners of war. USSR. 1941-45. *712*
Law. Bumke, Erwin. Gürtner, Franz. Judicial Administration (review article). Nazism. 1933-45. *71*
Law Enforcement. Nazi Party. SS (Schutzstaffel). 1933-45. *62*
Lawyers. Bar association. Nazism. 1928-45. *273*
Leach, Barry A. Military Strategy (review article). Operation Barbarossa. Whaley, Barton. 1939-41. *673*
Leadership. Genocide. Jews. Nazism. Psychohistory. 1938-45. *923*
—. Ghettos. Jews. Resistance. 1939-44. *783*
—. Political parties. 1900-45. *269*
—. Submarines. 1939-45. *41*
Lebensraum theory. Hitler, Adolf. ca 1925-45. *87*
Leeb, Wilhelm von. Public Finance. 1941-44. *267*
Légion des Volontaires Français contre le Bolchevisme. Collaboration. France. Volunteers. Waffen-SS (Charlemagne division). 1941-45. *508*
Legislation. France. Jews. Persecution. 1942-44. *861*
Legislation, anti-Jewish. Esh, Shaul. Historiography. Nazism. 1933. *757*
Lemberg University. Murder. Nazis. Poland. Teachers. 1941. *383*
Leszczynski, J. Genocide. Höppner, Rolf-Heinz. Jews. Poland (Warta region). 1940-42. *835*
Letters. Filderman, Wilhelm. Jews. Military Occupation. Romania. 1940-44. *1007*
—. National Committee "Free Germany". Pieck, Wilhelm. Prisoners of war, German. 1943-44. *755*
—. Prisons. Thälmann, Ernst. 1944. *251*
Levi, Primo (memoirs). Daily Life. Italy (Milan). Jews. 1942-43. *943*
Libby, Frederick J. Malmédy massacre. National Council for the Prevention of War. War Crime Trial. 1944-49. *465*
Liberation. Allies. France (Paris). Resistance. 1944. *545*
—. France (Strasbourg). Military Occupation. 1940-44. *496*
—. Germany (Belsen). Jewish Brigade. Poland. Tubin, Yehuda (memoirs). 1945-46. *1031*
Libraries. Jews. Lithuania (Vilnius). Poland (Łódz, Warsaw). 1930-45. *1010*
—. Poland. Warsaw University Library. 1939-45. *376*
Libya. Africa, North. Egypt. Rommel, Erwin. 1941-42. *520*
—. Consular Reports. Jews. Walther, Gebhardt von. 1940-43. *763*

Liddell Hart, B. H. (influence). Generals, German. Guderian, Heinz. Military Strategy. 1920's-40's. *23*
Literature. Amt Schrifttumspflege. Censorship. Nazism. 1932-45. *218*
—. Censorship. Nazism. 1933-45. *86*
—. Genocide (review article). Jews. 1941-45. *816*
Lithuania. Genocide. Jews. 1941-44. *762*
—. Latvia. Prisoners of War (Soviet). 1941-45. *721*
Lithuania (Kaunas ghetto). Jews. Partisans. Yellin, Chaim. 1913-44. *944*
Lithuania (Vilna). Jews. Military Occupation. Refugees. 1939-41. *761*
Lithuania (Vilnius). Jews. Libraries. Poland (Łódz, Warsaw). 1930-45. *1010*
—. Military Campaigns. USSR. 1944. *745*
Lithuania (Vilnius ghetto). Jewish Councils (Judenrat). Medicine (practice of). Memoirs. Military Occupation. 1939-45. *1044*
—. Jews. Ulitski, Moshe (diary). 1941-42. *833*
Lithuanian strip. Diplomacy, secret. Treaties. USSR. 1939-41. *313*
Logistics. Africa, North. Hitler, Adolf. Military Strategy. Rommel, Erwin. 1941-42. *555*
—. Black Sea. Eastern front. Military Strategy. 1942. *710*
—. Hungary. USSR. 1944-45. *743*
Looting. Colleges and Universities. Military Occupation. Poland. 1939-45. *399*
Lukin, M. Memoirs. Smolensk (battle). 1941. *705*
Luther, Martin. Foreign office. Ribbentrop, Joachim von. 1933-45. *27*
Luther, Martin (use and misuse of). Church and State. Lutheran Church. Nazism. 1933-39. *252*
Lutheran Church. Church and State. Luther, Martin (use and misuse of). Nazism. 1933-39. *252*
—. Germans. Missionaries. New Guinea. 1914-44. *190*
Lvov portfolio. Documents. Jews. Military Occupation. Poland. Ukraine (Lvov). 1941. *903*

M

Macedonia. Balkans policy. 1878-1945. *648*
Madajczyk, Czeslaw (review article). Jews. Military Occupation. Poland. 1939-45. *398*
Majdanek Concentration Camp chancery. Archives (records preservation). Poland. 1941-44. *941*
Malaia Tokmachka (battle). Guards Anti-Tank Artillery Regiment, 150th. Rumiantsev, N. (memoir). USSR. 1943. *727*
Malmédy massacre. Libby, Frederick J. National Council for the Prevention of War. War Crime Trial. 1944-49. *465*
Malta. Italy. Operation Hercules. 1935-42. *486*
—. Military supplies. Operation Hercules. 1940-43. *492*
Mandić (prime minister). Croatia. Diplomacy. 1944. *337*
Mannerheim, Carl Gustav. Finland. Foreign Policy. USSR. 1940-41. *373*
Mannstein, Erich von. Military strategy. USSR (Crimea). 1941. *667*
Manouchian group. Anti-Nazi Movements. Communist Party. Resistance. 1939-45. *32*
Manpower. Economic planning. Genocide. Jews. 1939-45. *834*
Manstein, Erich von. Genocide. Jews. USSR. 1939-45. *1042*

Marras, Luigi (papers). Badoglio, Pietro. Foreign Relations. Italy. Keitel, Wilhelm. 1936-43. *286*
Maschke, Erich (review article). Prisoners of War (German). USSR. 1941-45. *728*
Maser, Werner. Duerlein, E. Fest, I. C. Hitler, Adolf (biographies; review article). 1890-1945. *16*
—. Hitler, Adolf (biography, letters—review article). 1920-45. *263*
Mass media. Genocide. Jews. Nazism. Propaganda. 1920-45. *768*
Massacres. Hungary. Jews. USSR (Kamenets Podolsk). Yugoslavia (Délvidék). 1941-42. *795*
Matsuoka, Yosuke. Economic policy. Funk, Walther. Japan. 1941-45. *322*
Mauthausen. Auschwitz. Concentration camps. Labor, forced. 1935-45. *1043*
—. Austria. Concentration Camps. Cortey, Maria-Dolors (memoirs). 1939-45. *815*
Mediation. Burckhardt, Carl Jacob. Diplomacy. Great Britain. World War II (antecedents). 1937-39. *323*
Medical experiments. Concentration Camps. Hirt, August. Jews. 1941-44. *934*
Medical history. Hitler, Adolf. 1889-1945. *239*
Medicine (practice of). Jewish Councils (Judenrat). Lithuania (Vilnius ghetto). Memoirs. Military Occupation. 1939-45. *1044*
—. Trials. War Crimes. Women. 1941-48. *176*
Mediterranean Sea and area. Military Strategy. 1939-44. *229*
—. Naval Vessels. Submarine lighters. 1943-44. *538*
Meinecke, Friedrich. Historians. Nazism. 1923-35. *235*
Memoirs. Air warfare. Belorussia. Ukraine (Chernigov). 1943-44. *726*
—. Anti-Fascist Bloc. Poland (Warsaw ghetto). Resistance. 1941-44. *786*
—. Belorussia (Grodno ghetto). Family. Military Occupation. 1941-45. *798*
—. Berberova, Nina. Turgenev Library. 1880-1945. *446*
—. Bombing. Speer, Albert. 1944. *547*
—. Busse, Otto. Jews. Military Occupation. Poland (Białystok). Rescue. 1943. *806*
—. Busse, Otto. Jews. Rescue. 1943-79. *876*
—. Children. Concentration Camps (review article). Vegh, Claudine. 1939-45. *1038*
—. Concentration Camps. Jews. Poland. Rosensaft, Hadassah. 1940's. *993*
—. Concentration Camps. Jews. Poland (Warsaw ghetto). 1943-47. *1033*
—. Concentration Camps. Ravensbrück. Tillion, Germaine. 1945. *1029*
—. Concentration Camps. Reichman, Yehiel Meir. Treblinka. 1942-43. *989*
—. Diaries. Gîrbea, Titus. Romania. Steflea, Ilie. 1942-44. *636*
—. Emigration. Germany (Fürth). Jews. 1936-41. *991*
—. Expropriation. Jews. Military Occupation. Poland (Warsaw). Szulfried, Stanisław. 1939-42. *1024*
—. Frank, Anne. Kugler, Victor. Netherlands. 1942-44. *926*
—. Galbraith, John Kenneth. Strategic Bombing Survey. USA. 1944-45. *470*
—. Grosman, Ladislav *(Shop on Main Street).* Labor, forced. Slovakia. 1941-44. *874*
—. Jewish Councils (Judenrat). Lithuania (Vilnius ghetto). Medicine (practice of). Military Occupation. 1939-45. *1044*
—. Jews. Military Occupation. Ukraine (Lvov). 1941-44. *836*

—. Jews. Military Occupation. Ukraine (Lvov). 1941-44. *837*
—. Jews. Senger, Valentin. Survivors (review article). 1940's. *992*
—. Journalism. Peterson, Jürgen. 1936-43. *204*
—. Lukin, M. Smolensk (battle). 1941. *705*
—. Merkl, Peter H. Nazism (review article). Quantitative Methods. 1919-34. *85*
—. Military General Staff. Poland. Stachiewicz, Wacław. 1939. *428*
—. Nazism. Speer, Albert (interview). 1930's-60's. 1977. *15*
—. Poland. Poland (Warsaw ghetto). Tyszka, Leon. 1939-42. *1032*
—. Poland (Warsaw ghetto). Resistance. Sendlerowa, Irena. Youth groups. 1942. *1009*
Memoirs (review article). Economic History. Fascism. Kehrl, Hans. Krosigk, Lutz Schwerin von. Nazism. 1933-45. *277*
Merchant Marine. Hansa company. Shipbuilding. 1939-45. *275*
Merkl, Peter H. Memoirs. Nazism (review article). Quantitative Methods. 1919-34. *85*
Merten, Dr. Bulgarians. Greece (central Macedonia). Military occupation. Tendzos, Christos. 1943. *643*
Mertz von Quirnheim, Albrecht (family; papers). July 20 Plot. National Committee "Free Germany". 1941-44. *266*
Messerschmidt, M. World War II (review article). 1979. *12*
Methodology. Genocide (review article). Jews. 1939-45. *951*
Meyer, Bruno. Air Forces. Armored Vehicles and Tank Warfare. USSR (Kursk). 1943. *723*
Middle classes. Nazism. Political attitudes. *Simplicissimus* (journal). 1920's-44. *191*
Middle East. Africa. Armies (Supreme Command; documents). Military campaigns, plans for. 1941-45. *513*
—. Archaeology. Espionage. Oppenheim, Max von. 1890's-1946. *327*
Midsummer crisis. Foreign Policy. Gustavus V (abdication threat). Sweden. 1941. *358*
Milch, Erhard. Airplanes, Military (heavy bomber; development). Goering, Hermann. 1932-37. *102*
Milch, Erhard (review article). Air Forces. Irving, David. 1933-45. *156*
Milice. Collaboration. Darnand, Joseph. France. 1914-45. *475*
Militärgeshichtliches Forschungsamt. Bibliographies. Germany, West. Military history. 1648-1974. *219*
Military. Documents. 1920-45. *59*
—. Finland. Operation Barbarossa. World War II (antecedents). 1939-41. *709*
—. Hitler, Adolf. USSR. War aims. 1939-41. *682*
—. Jews. Poland. 1939. *856*
—. Nazism. Propaganda. 1939-43. *240*
Military Aid. Romania. World War II (antecedents). 1938-41. *299*
Military Biography. Rommel, Erwin. 1911-44. *449*
Military Campaigns *See also* names of specific operations, e.g., Operation Hercules.
—. Airborne troops. Crete (battle). Freyberg, Bernard Cyril. Student, Kurt. 1941. *473*
—. Allies. France. Operation Dragoon. Operation Overlord. USA. 1944. *562*
—. Allies. Norway, Northern. 1940. *514*
—. Bagramian, Ivan (memoirs). Ukraine. USSR. 1942. *657*
—. Baltic area. USSR. 1944-45. *736*
—. Caucasus. Oil fields. USSR. 1941-43. *677*

Military occupation 247

—. Chuikov, Vasili (memoirs). Germany (Berlin). Krebs, Hans. Negotiation attempts. 1945. *288*
—. Elster, General (surrender). France. Resistance. 1944. *516*
—. France (Massif Central). 1942-44. *505*
—. Lithuania (Vilnius). USSR. 1944. *745*
—. USSR. 1941-45. *718*
Military Campaigns (letters). Czechoslovakia. Resistance. Slovak National Uprising. 1944. *591*
Military campaigns, plans for. Africa. Armies (Supreme Command; documents). Middle East. 1941-45. *513*
Military collapse. France. Historiography. 1940. *454*
Military Command. Balkans. Hitler, Adolf. Italians. Lanz, Hubert. Surrender. 1943. *502*
Military control. Italy. 1943. *542*
Military Decorations, Flags, and Symbols. Documents. Heroes. Jews. Poland (Białystok, Warsaw ghettos). Resistance. 1944. *818*
Military Defeat. Italy. Operation Sunrise. 1945. *350*
Military effectiveness. 1941-44. *165*
Military General Staff. Memoirs. Poland. Stachiewicz, Wacław. 1939. *428*
Military Government. Civil-Military Relations. Europe, Eastern. 1942-44. *137*
Military history. Bibliographies. Germany, West. Militärgeshichtliches Forschungsamt. 1648-1974. *219*
—. Bombing. Fuller, J. F. C. Germany (Freiburg). 1940-61. *481*
—. Foreign Policy. Politics. World War II (review article). 1933-45. *34*
Military intelligence. Allies. Military strategy. Scandinavia. 1939-40. *441*
—. Allies. Ultra. 1920's-45. *115*
—. Balkans. Military Strategy. 1944. *568*
—. Belgium. Invasion (threat). 1939-40. *558*
—. *Bismarck* (battleship). Naval Vessels (spy ships). 1939-45. *113*
—. Brand, Joel, mission. Grosz, Bandi. Hungary. Peace negotiations. 1944. *361*
—. Enigma (security of). 1928-45. *216*
—. Germany (Berlin). Radio broadcasts (monitoring). 1939-45. *22*
—. Military offensives. Osuga (battle). USSR. 1942. *696*
—. Military Operations. USSR. 1941-45. *748*
Military Intelligence (review article). Brown, Anthony Cave. Great Britain. Kahn, David. USA. 1939-45. *155*
Military Law. Documents. Military Occupation. Norway. Surrender. 1945. *489*
Military Museum Art Collection. Graphic arts. Lanauve, Cluseau. Prisoners of war. 1941-42. *247*
Military occupation. Agricultural policy. Czechoslovakia (Moravia; Silesia). 1938-45. *590*
—. Air Forces. Economic Policy. 1939-45. *334*
—. Albania. Atrocities. 1939-44. *609*
—. Albania. Communism. 1943. *565*
—. Albania. Economic Conditions. 1943-44. *586*
—. Albania. Resistance. 1943. *564*
—. Allies. Bibliographies. Italy. Resistance. 1939-45. *474*
—. Allies. Boundaries. 1943-45. *28*
—. Allies. Historiography. Italy. Resistance. 1939-45. *455*
—. Allies. Sudetenland. 1945. *595*
—. Archives. Czechoslovakia (Slovakia). ca 1943-45. *600*

—. Archives. Heike, Otto. Poland (Łódz). 1939-45. *388*
—. Archives. Poland (Lublin). 1939-44. *439*
—. Archives. Poland (Pszczyna). 1939-45. *427*
—. Archives. Public Administration. Yugoslavia (Slovenia). 1941-45. *583*
—. Archives, underground. Historians. Jews. Poland (Warsaw ghetto). Ringelblum, Emanuel. 1939-50. *1025*
—. Art. Culture. Poland. 1939-45. *433*
—. Art, seizures of. 1940-44. *233*
—. Attitudes. Germans. Poland. Propaganda, underground. 1939-45. *431*
—. Attitudes. Jewish Councils. Poland. USSR. 1939-41. *1047*
—. Baltic States. Documents. Office of Strategic Services. 1941-45. *713*
—. Belgium. Buchenwald. Concentration camps. Evacuation. Labor camps. 1944. *541*
—. Belgium. Catholic Church. Labor Unions and Organizations. 1940-42. *476*
—. Belgium (Brussels). Collaboration. Himmler, Heinrich. Reeder, Eggert. SS (Schutzstaffel; appointments). 1942-43. *461*
—. Belorussia. Genocide (documents). Jews. Ukraine. USSR. 1941-45. *976*
—. Belorussia (Grodno ghetto). Family. Memoirs. 1941-45. *798*
—. Bibliographies. Denmark. 1940-43. *560*
—. Bock, Franz Heinrich (diary). Poland (Poddębice). 1940-42. *416*
—. Brand, Hans. Yugoslavia (Kras). 1942-44. *581*
—. Bulgarians. Greece (central Macedonia). Merten, Dr. Tendzos, Christos. 1943. *643*
—. Busse, Otto. Jews. Memoirs. Poland (Białystok). Rescue. 1943. *806*
—. Cabinet (dissolution). Denmark. Resistance. 1940-45. *440*
—. Casualties. Partisans. War Crimes. Yugoslavia. 1941-45. *628*
—. Catholic Church. France. 1940-45. *553*
—. Censorship. Comédie-Française. France. Theater. 1939-45. *504*
—. Censorship. Communist Party. Documents. France. *Humanité* (newspaper). 1940. *529*
—. Central Station for Volksdeutsche. Germans. Poland (Galicia). ca 1930's-40's. *390*
—. Champagne. Confiscations, agricultural. France. 1940-42. *450*
—. Civil resistance. Jewish Fighting Organization. Jewish Social Self-Aid. Poland (Warsaw ghetto). Resistance. 1939-42. *1003*
—. Civil-Military Relations. Commissar Order. USSR. War crimes. 1941. *703*
—. Cohen, David (correspondence). Jews. Visser, Lodewijk Ernst. 1941-42. *960*
—. Collaboration. Elites. France. Netherlands. Poland. 1940-44. *181*
—. Colleges and Universities. Looting. Poland. 1939-45. *399*
—. Colleges and Universities (closing of). Czechoslovakia. Resistance. 1939-45. *605*
—. Communist Party. France. 1940-41. *443*
—. Communist Party. Political Change. 1945. *11*
—. Curricula. Higher Education. Ukraine (Lvov). 1942-45. *438*
—. Czechoslovakia. 1939-45. *779*
—. Czechoslovakia. Education. Sudetenland. 1938-45. *592*
—. Czechoslovakia. Germanization. 1938-45. *569*
—. Czechoslovakia (Náchod). Textile industry. 1938-48. *596*
—. Czechoslovakia (Ostrava). Germanization. Poland (Upper Silesia). 1939-45. *589*

248 Military occupation

—. Czechoslovakia (Teschen). Nationalities policy. Social status. 1939-45. *593*
—. Czerniakow, Adam. Diaries. Jewish Councils (Judenrat). Poland (Warsaw ghetto). 1939-42. *892*
—. Czerniakow, Adam. Jewish Councils (Judenrat). Poland (Warsaw ghetto). Tyszka, Leon (reminiscence). 1939-42. *1034*
—. Daily Life. Jews. Nazism. Poland. 1941-44. *850*
—. Denmark. Prisoners of war. Russians. 1943-45. *537*
—. Deutsches Volkliste. Nationalities policy. Poland. Silesia, Upper. 1939-45. *414*
—. Diaries. Frank, Hans. Poland. 1939-41. *382*
—. Documents. Jews. Lvov portfolio. Poland. Ukraine (Lvov). 1941. *903*
—. Documents. Military Law. Norway. Surrender. 1945. *489*
—. Economic Conditions. France (Marseilles). 1943. *444*
—. Economic Conditions. France (Vienne). 1940-44. *530*
—. Education, clandestine. Poland. 1940-45. *408*
—. Europe. Fascism. Greece. Poland. 1940-45. *974*
—. Europe. Jesuits. 1933-45. *935*
—. Europe. Radio. 1940-42. *159*
—. Europe, Eastern. Ghettos. Government. Jewish Councils (Judenrat). 1941-43. *895*
—. Europe, Eastern. Ideology. 1941-45. *57*
—. Europe, eastern. Propaganda. 1939-45. *629*
—. Europe, Eastern. Social Classes. 1941-45. *714*
—. Expropriation. Jews. Memoirs. Poland (Warsaw). Szulfried, Stanisław. 1939-42. *1024*
—. Filderman, Wilhelm. Jews. Letters. Romania. 1940-44. *1007*
—. Films. France. 1940-44. *224*
—. France. General Union of Israelites. Jews. 1942-43. *889*
—. France (Alsace-Lorraine). Jews. Nazism. Negroes. Racism. 1939-42. *485*
—. France (Douai). Political Systems. 1939-45. *539*
—. France (Lyons). 1942-44. *517*
—. France (Moselle department). Germanization. Political repression. 1940-45. *518*
—. France (northern). Public opinion. 1940-42. *463*
—. France (Strasbourg). Liberation. 1940-44. *496*
—. Genocide. Ideology. Jews. USSR. 1941-44. *900*
—. Genocide. Intellectuals. Poland. Theater. 1939-45. *421*
—. Genocide. Jews. Poland (Kalisz). 1940-42. *978*
—. Genocide. Poland (Warsaw ghetto). Public Administration. 1941-43. *942*
—. Germany, West. History teaching. Poland. 1939-44. *385*
—. Greece. Italy. Jews. 1940-43. *912*
—. Hashomer Hatsair. Poland (Łódz ghetto, Maryshin). 1939-44. *985*
—. Higher Middle School. Netherlands. Public Administration. 1940-44. *549*
—. Historiography, bourgeois. USSR. 1940-45. *720*
—. Hungary. Jewish Councils (Judenrat). 1944. *796*
—. Hungary. USSR. 1944-45. *625*
—. Hungary (Újvidék). 1944. *578*
—. Imperialism. Ukraine. 1941-45. *702*
—. Jewish Councils. 1930's-40's. *1046*

—. Jewish Councils (Judenrat). Lithuania (Vilnius ghetto). Medicine (practice of). Memoirs. 1939-45. *1044*
—. Jews. Lithuania (Vilna). Refugees. 1939-41. *761*
—. Jews. Madajczyk, Czeslaw (review article). Poland. 1939-45. *398*
—. Jews. Memoirs. Ukraine (Lvov). 1941-44. *836*
—. Jews. Memoirs. Ukraine (Lvov). 1941-44. *837*
—. Jews. Modrzewska, Krystyna (memoirs). Poland (Lublin). 1942-45. *410*
—. Jews. Poland (Warsaw ghetto). Research. Starvation. 1941-42. *1050*
—. Jews. Poland (Złoczów). 1939-45. *415*
—. Jews. Rosenberg, Alfred. USSR. 1941-44. *760*
—. Jews. Ukraine (Mukachevo). 1938-44. *999*
—. Jews. USSR. 1939-41. *984*
—. Minorities. Poland. USSR. 1939-45. *436*
—. Nazism. 1939-45. *164*
—. Physicians. Poland (Poznan). 1939-45. *418*
—. Poland. Resistance. 1939-45. *391*
—. Raw materials. Yugoslavia. 1934-44. *631*
—. Resistance (losses). Yugoslavia (Šalek Valley). 1942. *647*
—. Tunisia. 1942-43. *467*
—. Yugoslavia (Slovenia). 1941-45. *582*
Military Occupation (comparative). Europe. Nazism. Resistance. 1940-44. *610*
Military occupation policy. Bräutigam, Otto (memorandum). USSR. 1941. *588*
—. Czechoslovakia (Prague). Demonstrations. Frank, Karl Hermann. 1939. *574*
Military Occupation (preparation). Army. Bamler, Rudolf. Sweden. 1940-44. *272*
Military Occupation (review article). Bartoszewski, Władysław. Poland (Warsaw). 1939-45. *429*
Military offensives. Military intelligence. Osuga (battle). USSR. 1942. *696*
—. USSR. Weather. 1941. *740*
Military Officers. Collaborators. USSR. Vlasov, Andrei. 1939-46. *679*
—. Education. Germany, West. Social Classes. 1900-79. *4*
—. Guderian, Heinz. Military Strategy. 1939-44. *81*
Military Operations. Military Intelligence. USSR. 1941-45. *748*
—. Northern front. USSR (Leningrad, Murmansk). 1941-42. *752*
—. Romania (Black Sea coast). 1944. *566*
Military organization. Buchenwald. Concentration Camps. 1942-45. *928*
—. Buchenwald. Concentration Camps (interviews). 1937-45. *927*
Military Organization (fusion). Abwehr. Intelligence services. SD (Sicherheitsdienst). 1944. *29*
Military Planning. Europe, Eastern. Ost plan. USSR. 1915-77. *664*
Military policy. Communist Party. 1919-45. *88*
Military Recruitment. Berger, Gottlob. Waffen-SS. 1939-40. *212*
Military Service. Youth. 1943-45. *21*
Military Strategy. 1939-45. *49*
—. 1944. *552*
—. Aachen (battle). 1944. *479*
—. Africa, North. Hitler, Adolf. Logistics. Rommel, Erwin. 1941-42. *555*
—. Air Forces. 1939-41. *188*
—. Air transport forces. 1936-44. *151*
—. Air Warfare. 1918-25. *254*
—. Air Warfare. Bombing, strategic. 1934-45. *198*
—. Air Warfare. Hitler, Adolf. 1941-45. *199*
—. Air Warfare. Pokryshkin, Aleksandr (memoir). USSR (Kuban). 1943. *722*

National Characteristics 249

—. Alliances. Italy. 1927-45. *345*
—. Allied collapse. 1940. *453*
—. Allied invasion, expected. France. Rommel, Erwin. Rundstedt, Gerd von. 1942-44. *561*
—. Allies. Military intelligence. Scandinavia. 1939-40. *441*
—. Armored Vehicles and Tank Warfare. USSR. 1941-43. *700*
—. Balkans. Military Intelligence. 1944. *568*
—. Battles. USSR. Vistula-Oder campaign. 1945. *652*
—. Black Sea. Eastern front. Logistics. 1942. *710*
—. Blitzkrieg. 1939-45. *179*
—. Blitzkrieg. 1941-42. *753*
—. Blitzkrieg. Nazism. USSR. World War II (antecedents). 1914-45. *66*
—. Crimea, battle for the. USSR. 1941-44. *660*
—. Czechoslovakia. 1945. *623*
—. Eastern front. Kleist, Paul Ludwig Ewald von. Ukraine. Uman (battle). 1941. *706*
—. Economic policy. USSR (Donets basin). 1941-43. *678*
—. Europe, Northern. Trade. 1900-45. *331*
—. Finland. 1939-42. *161*
—. Finland. USSR. 1941-44. *746*
—. Forest fires. 1945. *661*
—. Generals, German. Guderian, Heinz. Liddell Hart, B. H. (influence). 1920's-40's. *23*
—. Germany, battle for. Weapons. 1944-45. *526*
—. Great Britain. Operation Sea Lion. 1939-40. *458*
—. Greece. Invasion. Italy. 1940-41. *641*
—. Guderian, Heinz. Military officers. 1939-44. *81*
—. Invasion. Operation Barbarossa. USSR. 1941. *739*
—. Italy (Sicily). 1943. *522*
—. Mannstein, Erich von. USSR (Crimea). 1941. *667*
—. Mediterranean Sea and area. 1939-44. *229*
—. Narvik (battles). Norway. 1940. *515*
—. Operation Barbarossa. Smolensk campaign. USSR. 1941. *707*
—. Phoney war. 1939-40. *189*
—. Phoney War. Scandinavia. 1939-40. *523*
—. Scandinavia. 1939-45. *507*
—. Skorzeny, Otto. 1941-45. *217*
—. Sweden. 1939-45. *472*
—. Sweden. 1941-42. *456*
—. *Tirpitz* (battleship). Warships. 1941-44. *152*
—. USSR. 1941-42. *655*
—. USSR. 1941. *751*
—. USSR. War games. World War II (antecedents). 1940-41. *699*
Military Strategy (attack planes). Belgium. World War II (antecedents). 1939-40. *557*
Military Strategy (documents). Resistance. Romania. 1944. *576*
Military Strategy (German). Guerrilla Warfare (Polish). Warsaw Uprising. 1944. *437*
Military Strategy (grand). Foreign policy. Hitler, Adolf. 1933-45. *307*
Military Strategy (rear area security). Eastern front. 1941-45. *738*
Military Strategy (review). Armies. Eastern Front. General staff. Halder, Franz. 1941. *754*
Military strategy (review article). Brett-Smith, Richard. 1938-44. *112*
—. Leach, Barry A. Operation Barbarossa. Whaley, Barton. Military strategy. 1939-41. *673*
Military Strategy *(Weserübung* directive). Scandinavia. 1939-40. *499*
Military Supplies. Army. 1941-45. *241*
—. Malta. Operation Hercules. 1940-43. *492*
Military (troop concentration). Case Yellow. Neutrality. Switzerland. 1939-40. *524*

Minelaying operations. Baltic Area. USSR. 1941. *650*
Minesweepers. Danube River. 1939-45. *39*
Mining industry. Annexation. France (Briey, Longwy, Nancy). Klein Commission. War aims. 1911-42. *295*
Minorities. Germans. Hungary (Bac). 1942-45. *621*
—. Military Occupation. Poland. USSR. 1939-45. *436*
Mirošević-Sorgo, Niko H. (expulsion). Diplomacy. Vatican. Yugoslavia. 1941-42. *624*
Missiles. 1941-45. *196*
Missionaries. Germans. Lutheran Church. New Guinea. 1914-44. *190*
Moczarski, Kazimierz. Nazism (review article). Political Imprisonment. Stroop, Jürgen. 1949. *63*
—. Stroop, Jürgen (interviews). War criminals. Warsaw Ghetto Uprising. 1943. *970*
Modrzewska, Krystyna (memoirs). Jews. Military Occupation. Poland (Lublin). 1942-45. *410*
Mohr, O. C. (conversation). Denmark. Diplomacy. Germany (Berlin). 1940-45. *375*
Mohr, Otto (memoirs). Denmark. Trade. 1940. *354*
Moltke, Helmuth James von. Anti-Nazi Movements. Assassination. Bonhoeffer, Dietrich. Hitler, Adolf. 1940-45. *195*
—. Anti-Nazi Movements. Kreisau Circle. 1929-44. *169*
Moltke, Helmuth von (letter). Resistance. 1943. *182*
Monetary Systems. Customs union (proposed). Denmark. 1940. *347*
Monopolies. Economic Regulations. Reichsgruppe Industrie. 1933-45. *294*
Morale. Battles. 1944-45. *478*
—. Great Britain. Propaganda. Retaliation. 1943-45. *491*
Morality. Bureaucracies. Genocide. Jews. 1933-45. *893*
Moscow (battle). Historiography, bourgeois. 1941-42. *691*
Munich crisis. Austria (Vienna). Foreign policy. Nazism. Neubacher, Hermann. 1938-40. *282*
Murder. Lemberg University. Nazis. Poland. Teachers. 1941. *383*
Music. Bibliographies. *Jewish Gazette.* Poland (Warsaw Ghetto). 1940-42. *857*
—. Concentration Camps. Klonowski, Józef. Poland. Sachsenhausen. 1939. *790*
—. Goebbels, Joseph. Nazism. Propaganda ministry. Racism (biological aesthetic). Rosenberg, Alfred. 1920's-45. *58*
—. Poland (Western Territories). Theater. 1939-44. *381*
Musicians (deaths). Jews. Poland. 1939-44. *855*
Musicology. Myths and Symbols. Nazism. 1933-45. *180*
Myths and Symbols. Musicology. Nazism. 1933-45. *180*
Myths, historical. Goebbels, Joseph. *Great King* (film). *Kolberg* (film). Propaganda. 1942-45. *89*

N

Narvik (battles). Military Strategy. Norway. 1940. *515*
Narvik (operations). Submarines. Tactics. 1940. *460*
National Characteristics. France. Nazism. Propaganda. 1939-45. *484*
—. Hitler, Adolf. Public Opinion. 1940-44. *243*
—. Poland. Propaganda. Public opinion. 1939-45. *432*

National Committee "Free Germany". July 20 Plot. Mertz von Quirnheim, Albrecht (family; papers). 1941-44. *266*
—. Letters. Pieck, Wilhelm. Prisoners of war, German. 1943-44. *755*
—. Paulus, Friedrich von. Pieck, Wilhelm. Propaganda. 1939-45. *261*
National Council for the Prevention of War. Libby, Frederick J. Malmédy massacre. War Crime Trial. 1944-49. *465*
National liberation army. Operation Schwartz. Operation Weiss. Yugoslavia. 1942-43. *572*
National liberation movements. Yugoslavia. 1941. *616*
National People's Party. 1925-44. *280*
National Reich Church. Propaganda campaign. Roosevelt, Franklin D. USA. 1941. *37*
National Socialist Leadership Officers. Army. Political education. 1943-45. *209*
National Socialist Teachers League. Hitler Youth. Schools. 1933-45. *124*
National Socialist Women's Groups. Nazism. Social Classes. Women. 1933-42. *244*
Nationalism. Anti-Semitism. Expansionism. Hitler, Adolf. 1919-40. *17*
—. Collaboration. Flemish. France. 1940-42. *511*
—. Latvia. Nazism. Political Theory. 1942-43. *730*
Nationalities. Boundaries. Czechoslovakia. Historiography, Czech. 1938-45. *579*
Nationalities policy. Croatia. 1940-45. *907*
—. Czechoslovakia (Teschen). Military Occupation. Social status. 1939-45. *593*
—. Deutsches Volkliste. Military Occupation. Poland. Silesia, Upper. 1939-45. *414*
—. Poland (Upper Silesia). 1938-45. *413*
Natural gas. Economic policy. Pipe Lines. 1938-44. *73*
Naval Battles. Australia. *Kormoran* (warship). *Sydney* (warship). 1941. *153*
—. Convoys (PQ13, QP9). Great Britain. North Sea. 1942. *509*
—. Submarines (Biber class). USSR (Vayenga-Severomorsk). 1944-45. *750*
Naval operations. USSR. 1939-45. *719*
Naval Strategy. *Admiral Scheer* (cruiser). Kara Sea. Operation Wunderland. 1942. *659*
—. *Bismarck* (battleship). 1941. *487*
Naval Vessels. Mediterranean Sea and Area. Submarine lighters. 1943-44. *538*
—. Operation Sea Lion. 1940. *535*
Naval Vessels (spy ships). *Bismarck* (battleship). Military Intelligence. 1939-45. *113*
Navies. Baltic Sea. Degelow, Hans J. (photographs). 1943-45. *674*
—. Courts. Documents. 1939-45. *79*
—. Decisionmaking (chance). 1923-80. *167*
Nazarewicz, Ryszard (memoir). Poland. Resistance. 1944-45. *411*
Nazi Party. Birth rate. Population policy. Reichsbund der Kinderreichen. 1930-44. *245*
—. Jews. Kittel, Gerhard. Theology. 1888-1948. *843*
—. Law Enforcement. SS (Schutzstaffel). 1933-45. *62*
Nazi Party (Colonial Political Office). Africa. Pacific Area. War aims memorandum. Weigelt, Kurt. 1940. *55*
Nazis. Belgium. Collaboration. Economic Conditions (review article). Gillingham, John. 1936-44. *556*
—. Lemberg University. Murder. Poland. Teachers. 1941. *383*
Nazism. 1923-45. *140*
—. Aesthetics. 1920-45. *84*
—. Aesthetics. Industrial Relations. Labor. Symbolism. 1933-39. *210*

—. Agricultural Policy. Backe, Herbert. 1936-42. *157*
—. Amt Schrifttumspflege. Censorship. Literature. 1932-45. *218*
—. Anti-Communism. Germany, West. Political Education. Propaganda. Youth. 1933-78. *260*
—. Anti-Fascist Movements. Political Factions. Resistance. 1933-45. *171*
—. Anti-Semitism. 1930's-40's. *865*
—. Anti-Semitism. Expansionism. Genocide. 1919-45. *94*
—. Anti-Semitism. Films. *Jew Süss* (film). Propaganda. 1940's. *859*
—. Anti-Semitism. Genocide. Jews. 1939-45. *885*
—. Anti-Semitism. Genocide. Jews. Political Theory. 1917-45. *1026*
—. Anti-Semitism. Ideology. Racism. World War II (antecedents). 1933-45. *981*
—. Anti-Semitism. Political Leadership. ca 1929-45. *867*
—. Archaeology. Schnapp, Alain. 1933-44. *227*
—. Armaments industry. Austria. Economic Policy. 1939-44. *312*
—. Assassination. Fascism. 1933-44. *207*
—. Auschwitz. Autobiography. Concentration Camps. Hoess, Rudolf. 1939-45. *811*
—. Austria (Vienna). Foreign policy. Munich crisis. Neubacher, Hermann. 1938-40. *282*
—. Bar association. Lawyers. 1928-45. *273*
—. Bibliographies. Psychohistory. 1933-45. *177*
—. Blitzkrieg. Military Strategy. USSR. World War II (antecedents). 1914-45. *66*
—. Buch, Walter. 1922-49. *175*
—. Bumke, Erwin. Gürtner, Franz. Judicial Administration (review article). Law. 1933-45. *71*
—. Catholic Church. Church and State. Historiography. 1933-76. *305*
—. Catholic Church. Euthanasia. 1933-45. *904*
—. Censorship. Literature. 1933-45. *86*
—. Children. Poland. War Crimes. 1939-1945. *775*
—. Church and State. Confessing Church. 1933-45. *264*
—. Church and State. Luther, Martin (use and misuse of). Lutheran Church. 1933-39. *252*
—. Civil religion. 1923-45. *47*
—. Clausewitz, Karl von. 1939-45. *5*
—. Coal Mines and Mining. Germany (Ruhr). Resistance. 1933-45. *205*
—. Concentration camps. 1936-45. *886*
—. Concentration Camps. Genocide. Italy (Trieste). Jews. Risiera di San Sabba. 1943-45. *791*
—. Croatia. Genocide. Jews. Serbs. 1941-45. *938*
—. Cultural Union of German Jewry. Jews. Singer, Kurt. Theater. 1933-41. *858*
—. Daily Life. Jews. Military Occupation. Poland. 1941-44. *850*
—. Daitz, Werner. Economic Planning, postwar. 1939-45. *7*
—. Deutsche Arbeitsfront. Social security. 1918-45. *250*
—. Dolibois, John E. Streicher, Julius (memoirs). 1933-45. *771*
—. Eastern front. Goebbels, Joseph. Propaganda. 1941-43. *662*
—. Economic History. Fascism. Kehrl, Hans. Krosigk, Lutz Schwerin von. Memoirs (review article). 1933-45. *277*
—. Edelmann, Moritz. History teaching. Klagge, Dietrich. Textbooks. 1938-45. *213*
—. Education. Social mobility. 1930-40. *110*
—. Emigrants. Latin America. 1933-45. *338*
—. Emigration. Jews. 1933-45. *1019*

North Sea   251

—. Esh, Shaul. Historiography. Legislation, anti-Jewish. 1933. *757*
—. Europe. Jewish Councils (conference). 1933-45. *1060*
—. Europe. Military Occupation (comparative). Resistance. 1940-44. *610*
—. Foreign policy. Germany (review article). Resistance. 1933-45. *97*
—. Foreign policy. Historiography. Hitler, Adolf. 1933-45. *357*
—. France. Jews (Oriental). 1940-45. *871*
—. France. National Characteristics. Propaganda. 1939-45. *484*
—. France (Alsace-Lorraine). Jews. Military occupation. Negroes. Racism. 1939-42. *485*
—. Genocide. Historiography. Jews. 1940-44. *1035*
—. Genocide. Historiography. Jews. 1946-79. *838*
—. Genocide. Historiography. Jews. 1952-79. *813*
—. Genocide. Jews. 1920-45. *1027*
—. Genocide. Jews. 1924-45. *767*
—. Genocide. Jews. 1933-45. *965*
—. Genocide. Jews. 2c BC-20c. *915*
—. Genocide. Jews. Leadership. Psychohistory. 1938-45. *923*
—. Genocide. Jews. Mass media. Propaganda. 1920-45. *768*
—. Genocide. Poland (Warsaw ghetto). 1919-45. *1000*
—. Germanization. Germany (Lusatia). Sorbs. 1933-45. *585*
—. Germans, Baltic. Settlement. Warta River. 1940-45. *259*
—. Germany (Thuringia). Political Parties (development). 1924-30. *256*
—. Germany, West. Historiography. 1946-74. *178*
—. Goebbels, Joseph. Music. Propaganda ministry. Racism (biological aesthetic). Rosenberg, Alfred. 1920's-45. *58*
—. Hess, Rudolf. 1920-41. *101*
—. Hirschfeld, G. Kettenacker, L. Political Systems (review article). 1933-45. *30*
—. Historians. Meinecke, Friedrich. 1923-35. *235*
—. Historiography. Hitler, Adolf. ca 1910-45. *54*
—. Historiography. Irving, David. Resistance. Rommel, Erwin. 1941-45. *53*
—. Historiography. Psychohistory. ca 1940-78. *139*
—. Hitler, Adolf. 1928-45. *192*
—. Hitler, Adolf. Nuremberg trials. Speer, Albert (interview). 1945-76. *193*
—. Hitler, Adolf. Rauschning, Hermann. 1940-73. *36*
—. Innsbruck, University of. 1938-45. *975*
—. Intellectuals. 1933-45. *122*
—. Jews. Karaites. Racism. 1939-45. *872*
—. Jews. Nuremberg laws. 1933-45. *920*
—. Labor. Social Policy. Women. 1925-40. *173*
—. Labor force. Women. 1918-45. *274*
—. Labor, forced. 1933-45. *995*
—. Latvia. Nationalism. Political Theory. 1942-43. *730*
—. Memoirs. Speer, Albert (interview). 1930's-60's. 1977. *15*
—. Middle classes. Political attitudes. *Simplicissimus* (journal). 1920's-44. *191*
—. Military. Propaganda. 1939-45. *240*
—. Military occupation. 1939-45. *164*
—. Musicology. Myths and Symbols. 1933-45. *180*
—. National Socialist Women's Groups. Social Classes. Women. 1933-42. *244*
—. Persecution. Poland (Poznan). Teachers. 1939-45. *424*
—. Physicians. 1933-45. *792*
—. Poland. Radio recordings. Warsaw Mechanical Documentation Archives. 1939-45. *117*
—. Racism. Science. 1933-45. *20*
—. Resistance. 1933-44. *52*
—. Resistance. 1933-45. *99*
—. Speer, Albert (interview). ca 1932-45. *6*
—. Territorial claims (memoranda). 1940. *584*
—. Women. 1930's-40's. *129*
Nazism (conference). Historiography. Hitler, Adolf. 1933-45. *93*
Nazism (documents). Archives. 1933-45. *109*
Nazism (review article). Atrocities. Psychohistory. ca 1930's-45. *138*
—. Germany (Bavaria). 1933-45. *168*
—. Memoirs. Merkl, Peter H. Quantitative Methods. 1919-34. *85*
—. Moczarski, Kazimierz. Political Imprisonment. Stroop, Jürgen. 1949. *63*
Nazi-Soviet Pact. Historiography, Western. USSR. 1939-45. *744*
Nedić, Milan. Chetniks. Collaboration. Ethnic Groups. Yugoslavia (Banat). 1941-44. *618*
Negotiation attempts. Chuikov, Vasili (memoirs). Germany (Berlin). Krebs, Hans. Military Campaigns. 1945. *288*
Negotiations. Axis powers. Horthy, Miklós. Hungary. Kallay, Miklós. 1943. *311*
Negroes. France (Alsace-Lorraine). Jews. Military occupation. Nazism. Racism. 1939-42. *485*
Neo-Nazism. Austria. Germany, West. Propaganda. 1960's-70's. *149*
—. Jews. Rightist movement. 1939-45. 1969-73. *1059*
Netherlands. Battles. Germany, western. 1944-45. *527*
—. Belgium. Diplomacy. Peace. 1939-40. *559*
—. Bibliographies. Historiography. 1939-75. *480*
—. Collaboration. Elites. France. Military Occupation. Poland. 1940-44. *181*
—. Frank, Anne. Kugler, Victor. Memoirs. 1942-44. *926*
—. Higher Middle School. Military Occupation. Public Administration. 1940-44. *549*
—. Jewish Councils (Judenrat). Visser, Lodewijk Ernst. 1940-42. *966*
—. Jong, Louis de. Resistance. World War II (review article). 20c. *536*
Netherlands (Leiden). Anti-Semitism. Jews. Orphanage. 1940-43. *916*
Netherlands (Rotterdam). Air Warfare. 1940. *550*
Neubacher, Hermann. Austria (Vienna). Foreign policy. Munich crisis. Nazism. 1938-40. *282*
Neutrality. Axis powers. World War II (antecedents). Yugoslavia. 1939. *284*
—. Case Yellow. Military (troop concentration). Switzerland. 1939-40. *524*
—. Finland. Norway. 1940. *340*
—. Foreign Policy. Sweden. 1939-45. *369*
—. Iron ore. Sweden. Trade. 1939-45. *368*
—. Railroads. Sweden. Transit rights. 1939-45. *371*
Neutrality (disregard of). War. 1890's-1945. *349*
New Guinea. Germans. Lutheran Church. Missionaries. 1914-44. *190*
Niederkirchner, Käte. Espionage. 1909-44. *729*
Nietzsche, Friedrich. Anti-Semitism. Darwinism. Europe. 1800-1945. *1028*
North German Ocean Cable Works. Asia, East. Electrical industry. Felten & Guilleaume. 1850-1939. *298*
North Sea. Convoys (PQ13, QP9). Great Britain. Naval Battles. 1942. *509*

252 Northern front

Northern front. Military operations. USSR (Leningrad, Murmansk). 1941-42. *752*
Norway. Atlantic, North. Communications. Shipping. 1940. *554*
—. Diplomacy. Sweden. 1940. *324*
—. Documents. Military Law. Military Occupation. Surrender. 1945. *489*
—. Finland. Neutrality. 1940. *340*
—. Military Strategy. Narvik (battles). 1940. *515*
—. Stanghelle (battle). 1940. *451*
Norway (Narvik). Sweden. Transportation, Military. 1940. *366*
Norway, Northern. Allies. Military Campaigns. 1940. *514*
Novels. Europe, Eastern. Jews (review article). Kosinski, Jerzy. 1933-71. *873*
Nuremberg laws. Jews. Nazism. 1933-45. *920*
Nuremberg trials. Hitler, Adolf. Nazism. Speer, Albert (interview). 1945-76. *193*
—. Hitler, Adolf (review article). Irving, David. Smith, Bradley F. 1941-45. 1977. *136*

O

Office of Strategic Services. Baltic States. Documents. Military occupation. 1941-45. *713*
Ohlenbusch, Wilhelm (report). Jews. Poland. Warsaw ghetto uprising. 1943. *917*
Oil. Economic preparations. Kontinentale Oel AG. 1937-45. *314*
—. Trade. USSR. 1940-41. *348*
Oil fields. Caucasus. Military Campaigns. USSR. 1941-43. *677*
Operation Barbarossa. Communications, Military. USSR. 1941. *733*
—. Finland. Military. World War II (antecedents). 1939-41. *709*
—. Invasion. Military Strategy. USSR. 1941. *739*
—. Leach, Barry A. Military Strategy (review article). Whaley, Barton. 1939-41. *673*
—. Military Strategy. Smolensk campaign. USSR. 1941. *707*
—. Stalingrad (battle). USSR. 1941-42. *741*
Operation Barbarossa (opposition to). Diplomacy. Etzdorf, Hasso von. Walther, Gebhardt von (memorandum). 1940-41. *685*
Operation Citadel. Bagramian, Ivan (memoirs). USSR (Briansk, Orel). 1942-43. *656*
Operation Dragoon. Allies. France. Military campaigns. Operation Overlord. USA. 1944. *562*
Operation Hercules. Italy. Malta. 1935-42. *486*
—. Malta. Military supplies. 1940-43. *492*
Operation Maigewitter. Yugoslavia (Bosnia). 1945. *642*
Operation Market-Garden. Air Warfare. Arnhem (battle). Ryan, Cornelius (review article). 1944. *501*
Operation Overlord. Allies. France. Military campaigns. Operation Dragoon. USA. 1944. *562*
Operation Rösselsprung. Yugoslavia (Drvar). 1944. *646*
Operation Schach. Croatia. Partisans. Yugoslavia (Bosnia). 1944. *575*
Operation Schwartz. National liberation army. Operation Weiss. Yugoslavia. 1942-43. *572*
Operation Sea Lion. Great Britain. Military Strategy. 1939-40. *458*
—. Naval vessels. 1940. *535*
Operation Sunrise. Allies. Italy, North. 1944-45. *464*
—. Italy. Military Defeat. 1945. *350*

Operation Weiss. National liberation army. Operation Schwartz. Yugoslavia. 1942-43. *572*
Operation Wunderland. *Admiral Scheer* (cruiser). Kara Sea. Naval Strategy. 1942. *659*
Oppenheim, Max von. Archaeology. Espionage. Middle East. 1890's-1946. *327*
Oral History. American Jewish Committee (William E. Wiener Oral History Library). Genocide. Jews. 1941-45. 1977-82. *996*
Orphanage. Anti-Semitism. Jews. Netherlands (Leiden). 1940-43. *916*
Orphans. Centos Society. Education. *Głos Domu Chłopców* (magazine). Jews. Poland (Warsaw Ghetto). 1940-41. *1006*
Oshima Hiroshi. Axis Pact. Italy. Japan. World War II (antecedents). 1934-40. *283*
Osram (company). Labor, forced. 1944-45. *797*
Osram factory. Concentration Camps. Labor, forced. 1944-45. *826*
Ost plan. Europe, Eastern. Military Planning. USSR. 1915-77. *664*
Ostmark Aircraft Motor Works. Airplane Industry and Trade. Yugoslavia (Maribor). 1940-45. *118*
Osuga (battle). Military intelligence. Military offensives. USSR. 1942. *696*

P

Pacific Area. Africa. Nazi Party (Colonial Political Office). War aims memorandum. Weigelt, Kurt. 1940. *55*
Panzer, Brigade, 112th (destruction). Langlade Tactical Group. 1944. *469*
Papen, Franz von. Documents. Peace initiative. USA. 1942-45. *325*
Partisan movement. Czechoslovakia. Germans. Poland. USSR. 1939-45. *197*
Partisans *See also* Resistance.
—. Airborne troops. Street, Lieutenant Colonel (report). Yugoslavia (Drvar). 1944. *571*
—. Army Group Center. USSR. 1942-44. *654*
—. Aviation, civil. Ukraine. 1941-45. *676*
—. Belorussia. Germans. USSR. 1942-45. *716*
—. Casualties. Military Occupation. War Crimes. Yugoslavia. 1941-45. *628*
—. Croatia. Operation Schach. Yugoslavia (Bosnia). 1944. *575*
—. Epstein, David (memoirs). Genocide. Jews. Ukraine (Lyubeshov). 1941-44. *840*
—. Geheime Feldpolizei. USSR. 1939-45. *68*
—. Gothic Line. Italy. 1943-45. *447*
—. Jews. Lithuania (Kaunas ghetto). Yellin, Chaim. 1913-44. *944*
Paulus, Friedrich von. Anti-Fascism. 1943-44. *665*
—. National Committee "Free Germany". Pieck, Wilhelm. Propaganda. 1939-45. *261*
Pavelić, Ante. Croatia. Diplomacy. Hitler, Adolf. 1942. *336*
—. Croatia. Diplomacy. Hitler, Adolf. 1943. *335*
Payne, Robert. Hitler, Adolf (review article). Political Science. Pridham, Geoffrey. 1920's-33. *215*
Peace. Belgium. Diplomacy. Netherlands. 1939-40. *559*
Peace discussions, secret. Diplomacy. Weissauer, Ludwig. 1940-43. *326*
Peace initiative. Documents. Papen, Franz von. USA. 1942-45. *325*
Peace mediation. Japan. USSR. 1941-45. *318*
Peace negotiations. Brand, Joel, mission. Grosz, Bandi. Hungary. Military Intelligence. 1944. *361*

Poland 253

Peace, separate. Clauss, Edgar. Kleist, Peter. USSR. 1942-44. *316*
People's Army. Augustus II, code name. People's Guard. Poland (Miechów; Mniszek). Resistance. 1939-45. *409*
People's Guard. Anielewicz, Mordechai. Jewish Fighting Organization. Poland. Warsaw ghetto uprising. Youth groups. 1930's-42. *899*
—. Augustus II, code name. People's Army. Poland (Miechów; Mniszek). Resistance. 1939-45. *409*
Periodization of History. 1939-45. *35*
—. 1943. *577*
—. Jews. Rescue. 1933-45. *967*
Persecution. Bureaucracies. Jews *(mischlinge)*. 1944. *758*
—. France. Jews. Legislation. 1942-44. *861*
—. Germany (Rhineland, Westphalia). Poles. 1933-45. *379*
—. Italian Social Republic. Jews. 1943-45. *959*
—. Nazism. Poland (Poznan). Teachers. 1939-45. *424*
Peterson, Jürgen. Journalism. Memoirs. 1936-43. *204*
Petroleum. 1938-45. *8*
Phoney war. Military Strategy. 1939-40. *189*
—. Military Strategy. Scandinavia. 1939-40. *523*
Photography. Europe. Genocide. Jews. 1939-45. *809*
Physicians. Military Occupation. Poland (Poznan). 1939-45. *418*
—. Nazism. 1933-45. *792*
Pieck, Wilhelm. Letters. National Committee "Free Germany". Prisoners of war, German. 1943-44. *755*
—. National Committee "Free Germany". Paulus, Friedrich von. Propaganda. 1939-45. *261*
Pipe Lines. Economic policy. Natural gas. 1938-44. *73*
Pius XII, Pope. Foreign policy. Great Britain. 1939-40. *500*
Planungs-Stab Europa. Economic Planning (postwar). Europe. 1943-45. *230*
Plenipotentiary for Labor Allocation. Deportation. Labor, forced. Sauckel, Fritz. 1941-42. *56*
Pokryshkin, Aleksandr (memoir). Air Warfare. Military Strategy. USSR (Kuban). 1943. *722*
Poland. Anielewicz, Mordechai. Jewish Fighting Organization. People's Guard. Warsaw ghetto uprising. Youth groups. 1930's-42. *899*
—. Anti-Nazi movements (conference). 1933-45. ca 1977. *145*
—. Anti-Semitism. Auschwitz-Birkenau. Concentration Camps. Historiography. Resistance. 1939-78. *890*
—. Anti-Semitism. Government-in-exile, London. Schwarzbart, I. 1933-45. *770*
—. Archival Catalogs and Inventories. Jewish Historical Institute. 1940-47. *902*
—. Archives. Jewish Historical Institute. Warsaw ghetto uprising. 1942. *846*
—. Archives (records preservation). Majdanek Concentration Camp chancery. 1941-44. *941*
—. Art. Culture. Military Occupation. 1939-45. *433*
—. Atrocities. Galicia Division. Historiography. Ukrainians. USSR. 1943-45. *749*
—. Atrocities. Germans. 1939. *417*
—. Attitudes. Germans. Military occupation. Propaganda, underground. 1939-45. *431*
—. Attitudes. Jewish Councils. Military Occupation. USSR. 1939-41. *1047*
—. Auschwitz. Concentration Camps. 1939-45. *982*
—. Auschwitz. Concentration Camps. Dubois, Stanisław (pseud. Dębski). 1940-42. *919*
—. Auschwitz. Concentration Camps. Jews. 1940-45. *994*
—. Belzec. Concentration Camps. 1939-45. *1030*
—. Bibliographies. Danzig. Westerplatte, battle of. 1939. *387*
—. Catholic Church. Hlond, August. 1939-45. *425*
—. Children. Concentration camps. Education. Jews. Korczak, Janusz. 1930's-40's. *875*
—. Children. Nazism. War Crimes. 1939-1945. *775*
—. Children (conference). War crimes. 1939-45. *776*
—. Clergy. Germanization. 1939-45. *393*
—. Collaboration. Elites. France. Military Occupation. Netherlands. 1940-44. *181*
—. Colleges and Universities. Looting. Military Occupation. 1939-45. *399*
—. Concentration Camps. Germany (Berlin). 1945. *860*
—. Concentration Camps. Jews. Memoirs. Rosensaft, Hadassah. 1940's. *993*
—. Concentration Camps. Klonowski, Józef. Music. Sachsenhausen. 1939. *790*
—. Concentration Camps. Sobibor. 1942. *908*
—. Conservatism. Hitler, Adolf. Political opposition. 1940-44. *258*
—. Czechoslovakia. Germans. Partisan movement. USSR. 1939-45. *197*
—. Daily Life. Jews. Military Occupation. Nazism. 1941-44. *850*
—. Deutsches Volkliste. Military Occupation. Nationalities policy. Silesia, Upper. 1939-45. *414*
—. Diaries. Frank, Hans. Military Occupation. 1939-41. *382*
—. Diplomacy. Jews. Rescue agencies. 1939-45. *947*
—. Documents. Jews. Lvov portfolio. Military Occupation. Ukraine (Lvov). 1941. *903*
—. Education, clandestine. Military occupation. 1940-45. *408*
—. *Encyclopedia of World War II.* 1939-45. *236*
—. Estonia. Germans. Latvia. Racism. Resettlement. 1939. *389*
—. Europe. Fascism. Greece. Military Occupation. 1940-45. *974*
—. Europe, central. Expansionism. World War II (antecedents). 1934-40. *380*
—. Fischer, Ludwig (report). Warsaw Uprising. 1939-44. *386*
—. Foreign policy. 1939-45. *426*
—. Foreign Relations. 1939. *403*
—. Foreign Relations. Hungary. 1938-44. *396*
—. General Plan East. Germanization. USSR. 1939-43. *120*
—. Genocide. Government-in-exile, London. Jews. Public Opinion. 1942. *887*
—. Genocide. Historiography. Jews. 1939-45. 1939-71. *879*
—. Genocide. Historiography. Jews. 1941-42. *802*
—. Genocide. Historiography, Polish. Jews. 1939-45. *922*
—. Genocide. Hitler, Adolf *(Mein Kampf)*. 1928-45. *407*
—. Genocide. Intellectuals. Military occupation. Theater. 1939-45. *421*
—. Germany (Belsen). Jewish Brigade. Liberation. Tubin, Yehuda (memoirs). 1945-46. *1031*
—. Germany, West. History teaching. Military Occupation. 1939-45. *385*
—. Ghettos. Jews. Theater. 1939-42. *845*
—. Intellectuals. 1939-45. *412*
—. Jagiellonian University. Political Imprisonment. ca 1939-45. *781*

254 Poland

—. Jewish Fighting Organization. Warsaw ghetto uprising (origins). 1942-43. *884*
—. Jewish Military Union. Warsaw ghetto uprising. World War II (personal narratives). 1942. *906*
—. Jews. Madajczyk, Czeslaw (review article). Military Occupation. 1939-45. *398*
—. Jews. Military. 1939. *856*
—. Jews. Musicians (deaths). 1939-44. *855*
—. Jews. Ohlenbusch, Wilhelm (report). Warsaw ghetto uprising. 1943. *917*
—. Jews. Prisoners of war. 1939-45. *397*
—. Jews. Prisoners of war. 1939. *392*
—. Jews. Prisoners of war. 1940-45. *822*
—. Jews. Warsaw Ghetto Uprising. 1943. *953*
—. Jews. Warsaw Ghetto Uprising. 1943. *1013*
—. Katyn massacre. USSR. 1939-43. *430*
—. Katyn massacre. USSR. 1939-45. *377*
—. Lemberg University. Murder. Nazis. Teachers. 1941. *383*
—. Libraries. Warsaw University Library. 1939-45. *376*
—. Memoirs. Military General Staff. Stachiewicz, Wacław. 1939. *428*
—. Memoirs. Poland (Warsaw ghetto). Tyszka, Leon. 1939-42. *1032*
—. Military Occupation. Minorities. USSR. 1939-45. *436*
—. Military occupation. Resistance. 1939-45. *391*
—. National Characteristics. Propaganda. Public opinion. 1939-45. *432*
—. Nazarewicz, Ryszard (memoir). Resistance. 1944-45. *411*
—. Nazism. Radio recordings. Warsaw Mechanical Documentation Archives. 1939-45. *117*
—. Resistance. Warsaw ghetto uprising. 1939-44. *780*
—. War, defensive. World War II (antecedents). 1939. *404*
—. War Victims. 1939-45. *423*
—. Warsaw ghetto uprising. 1942-43. *820*
—. Warsaw ghetto uprising. Workers' Party. 1942-43. *972*
—. World War II (antecedents). 1919-39. *395*
Poland (Białystok). Atrocities. Blobel, Paul. Concentration Camps. Sonderkommando 1005. 1940-45. *821*
—. Busse, Otto. Jews. Memoirs. Military Occupation. Rescue. 1943. *806*
—. Datner, Szymon (report). Friedel, Fritz Gustav. Trials. War crimes. 1942-49. *819*
Poland (Białystok, Warsaw ghettos). Documents. Heroes. Jews. Military Decorations, Flags, and Symbols. Resistance. 1944. *818*
Poland (Ciechanów). Concentration Camps. Jews. 1940's. *881*
Poland (Ciechanów region). Genocide. Jews. 1941-45. *880*
Poland (Galicia). Central Station for Volksdeutsche. Germans. Military Occupation. ca 1930's-40's. *390*
Poland (Horka). Army, 2d. SS (Schutzstaffel). War Crimes. 1945. *420*
Poland (Kalisz). Genocide. Jews. Military Occupation. 1940-42. *978*
—. Jews. 1939-45. *980*
—. Jews. 1939. *977*
Poland (Kłodzko). Prisons. Resistance. 1939-45. *394*
Poland (Łódź). Archives. Heike, Otto. Military Occupation. 1939-45. *388*
Poland (Łódź ghetto). Daily life. Genocide. Jews. 1940-44. *788*
—. Jews. Rumors. Social Psychology. 1939-44. *932*
Poland (Łódź ghetto, Maryshin). Hashomer Hatsair. Military Occupation. 1939-44. *985*

Poland (Łódź, Poznań). Baltic Area. Baltic German Church (removal). Clergy. 1939-44. *435*
Poland (Łódź, Warsaw). Jews. Libraries. Lithuania (Vilnius). 1930-45. *1010*
Poland (Lublin). Archives. Military Occupation. 1939-44. *439*
—. Jews. Military Occupation. Modrzewska, Krystyna (memoirs). 1942-45. *410*
—. Resistance (review article). 1939-44. *400*
Poland (Miechów; Mniszek). Augustus II, code name. People's Army. People's Guard. Resistance. 1939-45. *409*
Poland (Nysa district). Auschwitz (evacuation). Concentration camps. 1945. *817*
Poland (Opole; Prudnik). Auschwitz (evacuation). Concentration Camps. 1944-45. *971*
Poland (Opole region). Jews. Labor camps. 1942-45. *1023*
Poland (Poddębice). Bock, Franz Heinrich (diary). Military Occupation. 1940-42. *416*
Poland (Poznan). Military Occupation. Physicians. 1939-45. *418*
—. Nazism. Persecution. Teachers. 1939-45. *424*
Poland (Pszczyna). Archives. Military Occupation. 1939-45. *427*
Poland (Rzeszów). Archives, provincial. Documents. War crimes. 1939-45. *378*
Poland (Stanisławów). Genocide. Intellectuals. Jews. 1941. *849*
Poland (Upper Silesia). Czechoslovakia (Ostrava). Germanization. Military Occupation. 1939-45. *589*
—. Nationalities policy. 1938-45. *413*
Poland (Warsaw). Assassination. Kutschera, Franz. Resistance. 1944. *422*
—. Bartoszewski, Władysław. Military Occupation (review article). 1939-45. *429*
—. Central Union of the Polish Industry. Resistance. Wachowiak, Stanislaw (memoirs). 1939-45. *434*
—. Expropriation. Jews. Memoirs. Military Occupation. Szulfried, Stanisław. 1939-42. *1024*
—. Popular Culture. Resistance. 1939-44. *405*
—. War aims. 1939-45. *406*
Poland (Warsaw ghetto) *See also* Warsaw ghetto uprising.
—. Anti-Fascist Bloc. Memoirs. Resistance. 1941-44. *786*
—. Anti-Nazi Movements. Jews. Socialist movement. 1939-44. *832*
—. Archives. Genocide. Jews. Ringelblum, Emanuel. 1942-43. *1002*
—. Archives, underground. Historians. Jews. Military Occupation. Ringelblum, Emanuel. 1939-50. *1025*
—. Authors. Jews. 1939-45. *778*
—. Bibliographies. *Jewish Gazette.* Music. 1940-42. *857*
—. Centos Society. Children. 1942-45. *774*
—. Centos Society. Education. *Głos Domu Chłopców* (magazine). Jews. Orphans. 1940-41. *1006*
—. Children. Concentration Camps. Korczak, Janusz. Treblinka. 1942. *824*
—. Children. Jews. Korczak, Janusz. 1900-42. *973*
—. Children. Korczak, Janusz (review article). 1940's. *878*
—. Civil resistance. Club rooms. 1941. *1004*
—. Civil resistance. Jewish Fighting Organization. Jewish Social Self-Aid. Military Occupation. Resistance. 1939-42. *1003*
—. Collaborators. Ganzweich, Avraham. Jews. 1940-43. *1045*
—. Concentration camps. Jews. 1941-44. *958*

Prisoners 255

—. Concentration Camps. Jews. Memoirs. 1943-47. *1033*
—. Czerniakow, Adam. Diaries. Jewish Councils (Judenrat). 1939. *898*
—. Czerniakow, Adam. Diaries. Jewish Councils (Judenrat). Military Occupation. 1939-42. *892*
—. Czerniakow, Adam. Jewish Councils (Judenrat). Military Occupation. Tyszka, Leon (reminiscence). 1939-42. *1034*
—. Czerniakow, Adam (diary). Jewish Councils (Judenrat). 1939-42. *1054*
—. Diaries. Jews. 1941. *785*
—. Documents. Genealogy. Jews. 1943. *805*
—. Documents (memoir). Jewish Councils (Judenrat). Ringelblum Archive. 1939-42. *1005*
—. Genocide. Military Occupation. Public Administration. 1941-43. *942*
—. Genocide. Nazism. 1919-45. *1000*
—. Jews. Korczak, Janusz (biography). 1899-1942. *766*
—. Jews. Military Occupation. Research. Starvation. 1941-42. *1050*
—. Memoirs. Poland. Tyszka, Leon. 1939-42. *1032*
—. Memoirs. Resistance. Sendlerowa, Irena. Youth groups. 1942. *1009*
—. Public Health. 1939-45. *925*
Poland (Warsaw Ghetto; liquidation). Jews. 1942-43. *863*
Poland (Warta region). Genocide. Höppner, Rolf-Heinz. Jews. Leszczynski, J. 1940-42. *835*
—. Greiser, Artur. Jews. 1939-43. *979*
Poland (Węgrów). Genocide. Jews. 1939-44. *1022*
Poland (Western Territories). Music. Theater. 1939-44. *381*
Poland (Wroclaw). Archives. Prisoners of War. 1939-45. *401*
Poland (Złoczów). Jews. Military occupation. 1939-45. *415*
Poles. Armies. Psychological Warfare. 1939-45. *546*
—. Attitudes. Emigrants. Warsaw ghetto uprising. 1942-43. *829*
—. Censuses. Germany (Berlin). 1810-1946. *402*
—. Germany (Rhineland, Westphalia). Persecution. 1933-45. *379*
—. Jews. Resistance. Warsaw Ghetto Uprising. 1944. *905*
Political attitudes. Middle classes. Nazism. Simplicissimus (journal). 1920's-44. *191*
Political Change. Communist Party. Military Occupation. 1945. *11*
—. Eastern front. Europe. USSR. 1933-45. *146*
Political Conditions. Austria (Styria). Social Conditions. 1940-45. *604*
Political Education. Anti-Communism. Germany, West. Nazism. Propaganda. Youth. 1933-78. *260*
—. Army. National Socialist Leadership Officers. 1943-45. *209*
Political Factions. Anti-Fascist Movements. Nazism. Resistance. 1933-45. *171*
Political Imprisonment. Jagiellonian University. Poland. ca 1939-45. *781*
—. Moczarski, Kazimierz. Nazism (review article). Stroop, Jürgen. 1949. *63*
Political Integration. Bohemia. 1938-45. *594*
Political Leadership. Anti-Semitism. Nazism. ca 1929-45. *867*
—. Bibliographies. Hitler, Adolf. 1919-80. *123*
Political opposition. Conservatism. Hitler, Adolf. Poland. 1940-44. *258*

Political opposition (handbill). Hitler, Adolf. 1943. *234*
Political parties. Leadership. 1900-45. *269*
Political Parties (development). Germany (Thuringia). Nazism. 1924-30. *256*
Political repression. France (Moselle department). Germanization. Military Occupation. 1940-45. *518*
Political Science. Hitler, Adolf (review article). Payne, Robert. Pridham, Geoffrey. 1920's-33. *215*
Political Systems. France (Douai). Military Occupation. 1939-45. *539*
Political Systems (review article). Hirschfeld, G. Kettenacker, L. Nazism. 1933-45. *30*
Political Theory. Anti-Semitism. Genocide. Jews. Nazism. 1917-45. *1026*
—. Arendt, Hannah. Ethnocentrism. Genealogy. Jews. 1958-65. *828*
—. Latvia. Nationalism. Nazism. 1942-43. *730*
Politics. Foreign Policy. Military History. World War II (review article). 1933-45. *34*
—. Romania (Transylvania). Territorial cessions. Vienna, Treaty of. 1940. *353*
—. World War II (antecedents). 1938-45. *184*
Popular Culture. Poland (Warsaw). Resistance. 1939-44. *405*
—. Propaganda. 1933-45. *226*
Population policy. Birth rate. Nazi Party. Reichsbund der Kinderreichen. 1930-44. *245*
Pożywiłek, Michał (memoirs). Communists. 1939-45. *208*
Prague Uprising. Czechoslovakia. Diplomacy. Resistance. 1945. *606*
Preservation. Europe. 1940-46. *82*
Press. Anti-Semitism. Genocide. Propaganda. 1943. *957*
Press campaign. DeGaulle, Charles. 1936-45. *448*
Press conferences. Cultural policy. Propaganda Ministry. 1933-45. *64*
Pridham, Geoffrey. Hitler, Adolf (review article). Payne, Robert. Political Science. 1920's-33. *215*
Prisoners of War. Afrika Corps. USA (Louisiana). 1943-46. *544*
—. Archives. Poland (Wroclaw). 1939-45. *401*
—. Belgians. Protestants. Religious life. 1940-45. *482*
—. Belgians. Religious life. 1940-45. *483*
—. Canada. Germans. 1940-47. *490*
—. Communist Party. Germany (Pirna). Propaganda. 1945. *663*
—. Czechoslovakia. Resistance. USSR. 1941-45. *611*
—. Denmark. Military occupation. Russians. 1943-45. *537*
—. Germany (Lamsdorf). Jews. 1941-45. *471*
—. Graphic arts. Lanauve, Cluseau. Military Museum Art Collection. 1941-42. *247*
—. Jews. Poland. 1939-45. *397*
—. Jews. Poland. 1939. *392*
—. Jews. Poland. 1940-45. *822*
—. Labor (imported). Working conditions. 1939-45. *166*
—. Latvia. USSR. 1941-45. *712*
—. Stalag I B Hohenstein. 1939-45. *147*
Prisoners of war, American. Conspiracy. Germany (Berlin). Hitler, Adolf. 1945. *238*
Prisoners of war, German. Letters. National Committee "Free Germany". Pieck, Wilhelm. 1943-44. *755*
—. Maschke, Erich (review article). USSR. 1941-45. *728*
Prisoners of War (memoirs). Australia (Hay). Dunera (vessel). 1940-41. *498*
Prisoners of War (Soviet). Latvia. Lithuania. 1941-45. *721*

256 Prisons

Prisons. Letters. Thälmann, Ernst. 1944. *251*
—. Poland (Kłodzko). Resistance. 1939-45. *394*
Prokhorovka (battle). Armored Vehicles and Tank Warfare. USSR. 1943. *672*
Proletarian Division, 1st. Resistance. Yugoslavia (Sanjak). 1944. *644*
Propaganda. 1939-45. *206*
—. Anti-Communism. Germany, West. Nazism. Political Education. Youth. 1933-78. *260*
—. Anti-Communist Movements. Brandt, Willi. Goebbels, Joseph. Taubert, Eberhard. 1931-60. *2*
—. Anti-Semitism. Films. *Jew Süss* (film). Nazism. 1940's. *859*
—. Anti-Semitism. Genocide. Press. 1943. *957*
—. Austria. Germany, West. Neo-Nazism. 1960's-70's. *149*
—. Balkans. 1939-45. *630*
—. Bulgaria. Hungary. Romania. 1941-43. *645*
—. Communist Party. Germany (Pirna). Prisoners of war. 1945. *663*
—. Eastern front. Goebbels, Joseph. Nazism. 1941-43. *662*
—. Europe, eastern. Military Occupation. 1939-45. *629*
—. Films. USSR. 1930's-45. *658*
—. Films. Wessel, Horst (myth). 1930's. *83*
—. France. National Characteristics. Nazism. 1939-45. *484*
—. Genocide. Jews. Mass media. Nazism. 1920-45. *768*
—. Goebbels, Joseph. *Great King* (film). *Kolberg* (film). Myths, historical. 1942-45. *89*
—. Great Britain. Morale. Retaliation. 1943-45. *491*
—. Military. Nazism. 1939-43. *240*
—. National Characteristics. Poland. Public opinion. 1939-45. *432*
—. National Committee "Free Germany". Paulus, Friedrich von. Pieck, Wilhelm. 1939-45. *261*
—. Popular culture. 1933-45. *226*
—. USA. Women. 1939-45. *80*
—. USA. Women. 1939-45. *222*
Propaganda campaign. National Reich Church. Roosevelt, Franklin D. USA. 1941. *37*
Propaganda (conference). Balkans. Europe, Central. 1939-45. *580*
Propaganda Ministry. Cultural policy. Press conferences. 1933-45. *64*
—. Goebbels, Joseph. Music. Nazism. Racism (biological aesthetic). Rosenberg, Alfred. 1920's-45. *58*
Propaganda, underground. Attitudes. Germans. Military occupation. Poland. 1939-45. *431*
Property. Belgium. Confiscation. Jews. 1940-44. *1011*
Protestantism. Brecht, Alfred (memoirs). Urach Theological Seminary. 20c. *26*
Protestants. Belgians. Prisoners of war. Religious life. 1940-45. *482*
Psychohistory. Atrocities. Nazism (review article). ca 1930's-45. *138*
—. Bibliographies. Nazism. 1933-45. *177*
—. Bloch, Eduard. Hitler, Adolf (review article). Jews. Stierlin, Helm. 1907-45. 1973-76. *114*
—. Genocide. Jews. Leadership. Nazism. 1938-45. *923*
—. Harrower, Molly. War criminals. 1939-45. *232*
—. Historiography. Nazism. ca 1940-78. *139*
—. Hitler, Adolf. 20c. *228*
—. Hitler, Adolf. Langer, Walter C. 1930's-45. *162*
—. Hitler, Adolf. Research (interdisciplinary). 1981. *262*
Psychological Warfare. *Affiche Rouge*. France. Resistance. Trials. 1944. *495*
—. Armies. 1939-45. *42*
—. Armies. Poles. 1939-45. *546*
Psychology. Bureaucracies. Concentration camps. 1941-45. *1001*
—. Concentration Camps. Survivors (interviews). 1941-71. *950*
—. Genocide. Jews. 1938-44. *983*
Psychology (stress). Concentration camps. 1941-74. *827*
Public Administration. Archives. Military Occupation. Yugoslavia (Slovenia). 1941-45. *583*
—. Euthanasia. Hitler, Adolf. Judicial system. 1940-41. *877*
—. Genocide. Military Occupation. Poland (Warsaw ghetto). 1941-43. *942*
—. Higher Middle School. Military Occupation. Netherlands. 1940-44. *549*
Public Finance. Leeb, Wilhelm von. 1941-44. *267*
Public Health. Poland (Warsaw ghetto). 1939-45. *925*
Public opinion. France (northern). Military Occupation. 1940-42. *463*
—. Genocide. Government-in-exile, London. Jews. Poland. 1942. *887*
—. Hitler, Adolf. National Characteristics. 1940-44. *243*
—. Jews. 1935-43. *930*
—. National Characteristics. Poland. Propaganda. 1939-45. *432*
Public Policy. Labor. Winkler, Dörte. Women (review article). 1930-45. *174*
Public welfare. Rearmament. 1930's. *46*

Q

Quantitative methods. Fein, Helen. Genocide. Jews. 1939-45. *1048*
—. Memoirs. Merkl, Peter H. Nazism (review article). 1919-34. *85*

R

Racial policy. Foreign Relations. Italy. 1938-43. *986*
Racism. Anti-Semitism. Ideology. Nazism. World War II (antecedents). 1933-45. *981*
—. Estonia. Germans. Latvia. Poland. Resettlement. 1939. *389*
—. France (Alsace-Lorraine). Jews. Military occupation. Nazism. Negroes. 1939-42. *485*
—. International law, principles of. Schmitt, Carl. Walz, Gustav. 1919-45. *111*
—. Jews. Karaites. Nazism. 1939-45. *872*
—. Nazism. Science. 1933-45. *20*
Racism (biological aesthetic). Goebbels, Joseph. Music. Nazism. Propaganda ministry. Rosenberg, Alfred. 1920's-45. *58*
Radio. Europe. Military Occupation. 1940-42. *159*
Radio broadcasts (monitoring). Germany (Berlin). Military Intelligence. 1939-45. *22*
Radio recordings. Nazism. Poland. Warsaw Mechanical Documentation Archives. 1939-45. *117*
Radlitzki, Tzvi (memoirs). Genocide. Jews. Ukraine (Lvov). 1941-45. *987*
Railroads. Genocide. Jews. 1939-45. *894*
—. Great Britain. Sweden. Transportation policy. 1940-45. *304*
—. Neutrality. Sweden. Transit rights. 1939-45. *371*
Railroads (review article). Gottwaldt, Alfred B. Kreidler, Eugen. 1919-45. *214*
Rappoport, Leon. Genocide (review article). Jews. Kren, George M. ca 1939-45. *990*

Rauschning, Hermann. Hitler, Adolf. Nazism. 1940-73. *36*
Ravensbrück. Concentration Camps. Memoirs. Tillion, Germaine. 1945. *1029*
Raw materials. Military Occupation. Yugoslavia. 1934-44. *631*
Rearmament. Public welfare. 1930's. *46*
Rebellions. Documents. Romania. 1944. *622*
—. Romania. 1944. *612*
Reeder, Eggert. Army. Belgium. Collaboration movements. Himmler, Heinrich. SS (Schutzstaffel; appointments). 1941-44. *462*
—. Belgium (Brussels). Collaboration. Himmler, Heinrich. Military Occupation. SS (Schutzstaffel; appointments). 1942-43. *461*
Referat Deutschland. Jews. 1933-40. *803*
Refugees. Deportation. Finland. Jews. 1942. *789*
—. Finland. *Hohenhörn* (vessel). Jews. 1942. *1021*
—. Jews. Lithuania (Vilna). Military Occupation. 1939-41. *761*
Reichman, Yehiel Meir. Concentration Camps. Memoirs. Treblinka. 1942-43. *989*
Reichsbank. Banking. Documents. USSR. World War II (antecedents). 1941. *715*
Reichsbund der Kinderreichen. Birth rate. Nazi Party. Population policy. 1930-44. *245*
Reichsgruppe Industrie. Economic Regulations. Monopolies. 1933-45. *294*
Reichswerke AG Hermann Göring. Government enterprise. 1936-43. *126*
Religion. Resistance, conservative. 1933-45. *128*
—. SD (Sicherheitsdienst). USSR. 1919-44. *271*
Religious life. Belgians. Prisoners of war. 1940-45. *483*
—. Belgians. Prisoners of war. Protestants. 1940-45. *482*
Repatriation. Germans. USSR. 1939. *384*
Rescue. Archives, National. Genocide. Jews. USA. War Refugee Board. 1918-52. *961*
—. Busse, Otto. Jews. Memoirs. 1943-79. *876*
—. Busse, Otto. Jews. Memoirs. Military Occupation. Poland (Białystok). 1943. *806*
—. Children. France. Jews. Vichy regime. 1939-45. *918*
—. China (Shanghai). Diplomatic missions, Polish. Europe, Eastern. Jews. 1942-44. *948*
—. Denmark (Gilleleje). Jews. Resistance. 1943-44. *937*
—. Ecumenism. Jews. World Council of Churches. 1939-44. *793*
—. Jews. Periodization of History. 1933-45. *967*
—. Jews. Romania. Transdniester Plan. 1942-44. *1039*
Rescue agencies. Concentration Camps. Hijefs. Jews. Slovakia. Vaad Hacala. 1941-45. *946*
—. Diplomacy. Jews. Poland. 1939-45. *947*
Research. Atomic energy. 1935-45. *19*
—. Europe, Eastern. Silesia. 1938-45. *72*
—. Germany (Bavaria). Resistance. 1972-76. *108*
—. Jews. Military Occupation. Poland (Warsaw ghetto). Starvation. 1941-42. *1050*
—. Resistance, anti-Fascist. 1940-75. *143*
Research (interdisciplinary). Hitler, Adolf. Psychohistory. 1981. *262*
Research sources. Industrial conditions. Zentrale Planung. 1942-45. *194*
Resettlement. Austria (Styria; Hochschwab). South Tyrol (Gröden valley). SS (Schutzstaffel). 1940-41. *119*
—. Estonia. Germans. Latvia. Poland. Racism. 1939. *389*
Resistance *See also* Partisans.
—. *Affiche Rouge*. France. Psychological Warfare. Trials. 1944. *495*

Resistance   *257*

—. Ainsztein, Reuben. Europe, Eastern. Jews (review article). 1939-45. *823*
—. Albania. Military Occupation. 1943. *564*
—. Allies. Bibliographies. Italy. Military occupation. 1939-45. *474*
—. Allies. France (Paris). Liberation. 1944. *545*
—. Allies. Historiography. Italy. Military occupation. 1939-45. *455*
—. Anschluss. Austria. 1938-45. *278*
—. Anti-Fascist Bloc. Memoirs. Poland (Warsaw ghetto). 1941-44. *786*
—. Anti-Fascist Movements. Communist Party. Concentration camps. 1933-45. *939*
—. Anti-Fascist Movements. Nazism. Political Factions. 1933-45. *171*
—. Anti-Nazi Movements. Communist Party. Manouchian group. 1939-45. *32*
—. Anti-Semitism. Auschwitz-Birkenau. Concentration Camps. Historiography. Poland. 1939-78. *890*
—. Anti-Semitism. Clergy. Confessing Church. 1930's-45. *1053*
—. Assassination. Kutschera, Franz. Poland (Warsaw). 1944. *422*
—. Augustus II, code name. People's Army. People's Guard. Poland (Miechów; Mniszek). 1939-45. *409*
—. Balkans. Coups d'Etat (August 1944). Romania. Yugoslavia. 1944. *567*
—. Bartel, Walter (memoirs). Buchenwald. Concentration Camps. 1945. *777*
—. Belgium. Charles, J. L. Dasney, F. Geheime Feldpolizei (reports). Jews. 1940-42. *457*
—. Belgium. Christian Workers Youth. 1942-44. *543*
—. Ben, Fritz. Titov, Vasili. USSR (Ust'-Luga). 1942-43. *694*
—. Cabinet (dissolution). Denmark. Military occupation. 1940-45. *440*
—. Central Union of the Polish Industry. Poland (Warsaw). Wachowiak, Stanislaw (memoirs). 1939-45. *434*
—. Civil resistance. Jewish Fighting Organization. Jewish Social Self-Aid. Military Occupation. Poland (Warsaw ghetto). 1939-42. *1003*
—. Coal Mines and Mining. Germany (Ruhr). Nazism. 1933-45. *205*
—. Colleges and Universities (closing of). Czechoslovakia. Military Occupation. 1939-45. *605*
—. Communist Party. Documents. 1944. *142*
—. Communist Party. Documents. 1944. *144*
—. Communist Party. Germany, East. Social Democratic Party. 1933-45. *225*
—. Communist Party. Germany (Hamburg). Sacke, Georg (documents). 1933-45. *257*
—. Communists. Denmark. Germans. 1933-45. *237*
—. Concentration camps. Socialists. 1939-45. *831*
—. Czechoslovakia. Diplomacy. Prague Uprising. 1945. *606*
—. Czechoslovakia. Military Campaigns (letters). Slovak National Uprising. 1944. *591*
—. Czechoslovakia. Prisoners of war. USSR. 1941-45. *611*
—. Denmark (Gilleleje). Jews. Rescue. 1943-44. *937*
—. Documents. Heroes. Jews. Military Decorations, Flags, and Symbols. Poland (Białystok, Warsaw ghettos). 1944. *818*
—. Elster, General (surrender). France. Military Campaigns. 1944. *516*
—. Europe. Military Occupation (comparative). Nazism. 1940-44. *610*
—. Foreign policy. Germany (review article). Nazism. 1933-45. *97*

258 Resistance

—. Gangs. Youth. 1936-45. *105*
—. Germany (Bavaria). Research. 1972-76. *108*
—. Ghettos. Jews. Leadership. 1939-44. *783*
—. Himmler, Heinrich. Kersten, Felix. 1941-44. *125*
—. Historiography. Hitler, Adolf. 1930-49. *183*
—. Historiography. Irving, David. Nazism. Rommel, Erwin. 1941-45. *53*
—. Jews. 1939-45. *759*
—. Jews. 1941-45. *844*
—. Jews. Poles. Warsaw Ghetto Uprising. 1944. *905*
—. Jong, Louis de. Netherlands. World War II (review article). 20c. *536*
—. Kuckhoff, Greta (memoirs). Schulze-Boysen-Harnack organization. 1935-43. *141*
—. Memoirs. Poland (Warsaw ghetto). Sendlerowa, Irena. Youth groups. 1942. *1009*
—. Military occupation. Poland. 1939-45. *391*
—. Military Strategy (documents). Romania. 1944. *576*
—. Moltke, Helmuth von (letter). 1943. *182*
—. Nazarewicz, Ryszard (memoir). Poland. 1944-45. *411*
—. Nazism. 1933-44. *52*
—. Nazism. 1933-45. *99*
—. Poland. Warsaw ghetto uprising. 1939-44. *780*
—. Poland (Kłodzko). Prisons. 1939-45. *394*
—. Poland (Warsaw). Popular Culture. 1939-44. *405*
—. Proletarian Division, 1st. Yugoslavia (Sanjak). 1944. *644*
—. Weisse Rose. 1943. *51*
Resistance, anti-Fascist. Research. 1940-75. *143*
Resistance, conservative. Religion. 1933-45. *128*
Resistance (losses). Military Occupation. Yugoslavia (Šalek Valley). 1942. *647*
Resistance (review article). Poland (Lublin). 1939-44. *400*
Resistance, spiritual. Art. Concentration camps. Jews. 1940-45. *962*
Retaliation. Great Britain. Morale. Propaganda. 1943-45. *491*
Rexist Party. Belgium. Collaboration. Degrelle, Léon. World War II (antecedents). 1933-40. *493*
Rheinhardt, Emil Alphons (letters). Austria. Authors. Exiles. 1930's-45. *1018*
Ribbentrop, Joachim von. Foreign office. Luther, Martin. 1933-45. *27*
Rich, Norman. Hitler, Adolf (review article). War aims. 1936-45. *91*
Rightist movement. Jews. Neo-Nazism. 1939-45. 1969-73. *1059*
Ringelblum Archive. Documents (memoir). Jewish Councils (Judenrat). Poland (Warsaw ghetto). 1939-42. *1005*
Ringelblum, Emanuel. Archives. Genocide. Jews. Poland (Warsaw ghetto). 1942-43. *1002*
—. Archives, underground. Historians. Jews. Military Occupation. Poland (Warsaw ghetto). 1939-50. *1025*
Risiera di San Sabba. Concentration Camps. Genocide. Italy (Trieste). Jews. Nazism. 1943-45. *791*
Roads. Armistice. Finland (Lapland). USSR. 1940-45. *310*
Rocket defense. Great Britain. 1944-45. *548*
Rockets. Anti-aircraft defense. Cities. USSR. 1937-45. *701*
Romania. Antonescu, Ion. Foreign Relations. 1944. *289*
—. Army officer (capture). 1944. *620*
—. Balkans. Coups d'Etat (August 1944). Resistance. Yugoslavia. 1944. *567*
—. Boundaries. Hungary. Transylvania, partition of. Vienna Diktat. 1940. *352*
—. Bulgaria. Hungary. Propaganda. 1941-43. *645*
—. Demonstrations. Vienna conference. 1939-40. *333*
—. Diaries. Gîrbea, Titus. Memoirs. Steflea, Ilie. 1942-44. *636*
—. Documents. Rebellions. 1944. *622*
—. Expansionism. World War II (antecedents). 1938-39. *356*
—. Filderman, Wilhelm. Jews. Letters. Military Occupation. 1940-44. *1007*
—. Jews. Rescue. Transdniester Plan. 1942-44. *1039*
—. Military Aid. World War II (antecedents). 1938-41. *299*
—. Military Strategy (documents). Resistance. 1944. *576*
—. Rebellions. 1944. *612*
Romania (Black Sea coast). Military operations. 1944. *566*
Romania (Iași). Genocide. Jews. 1941. *969*
Romania (Transylvania). Territorial cessions. Vienna, Treaty of. 1940. *353*
Rommel, Erwin. Africa, North. Egypt. Libya. 1941-42. *520*
—. Africa, North. Hitler, Adolf. Logistics. Military Strategy. 1941-42. *555*
—. Allied invasion, expected. France. Military Strategy. Rundstedt, Gerd von. 1942-44. *561*
—. Historiography. Irving, David. Nazism. Resistance. 1941-45. *53*
—. Military Biography. 1911-44. *449*
Roosevelt, Franklin D. National Reich Church. Propaganda campaign. USA. 1941. *37*
Rosenberg, Alfred. Goebbels, Joseph. Music. Nazism. Propaganda ministry. Racism (biological aesthetic). 1920's-45. *58*
—. Jews. Military Occupation. USSR. 1941-44. *760*
Rosensaft, Hadassah. Concentration Camps. Jews. Memoirs. Poland. 1940's. *993*
Rosenstein, Hana. Auschwitz (escape). Bikel, Sara. Concentration Camps. Jews. 1944. *841*
Rubber, synthetic. Economic Planning. War. 1915-45. *255*
Rumiantsev, N. (memoir). Guards Anti-Tank Artillery Regiment, 150th. Malaia Tokmachka (battle). USSR. 1943. *727*
Rumors. Jews. Poland (Łódz ghetto). Social Psychology. 1939-44. *932*
Rundstedt, Gerd von. Allied invasion, expected. France. Military Strategy. Rommel, Erwin. 1942-44. *561*
Russians. Denmark. Military occupation. Prisoners of war. 1943-45. *537*
Ryan, Cornelius (review article). Air Warfare. Arnhem (battle). Operation Market-Garden. 1944. *501*

S

SA (Sturmabteilung). Feldherrnhalle regiment. 1933-45. *276*
Sachsenhausen. Concentration Camps. Klonowski, Józef. Music. Poland. 1939. *790*
Sacke, Georg (documents). Communist Party. Germany (Hamburg). Resistance. 1933-45. *257*
Sauckel, Fritz. Deportation. Labor, forced. Plenipotentiary for Labor Allocation. 1941-42. *56*
Scandinavia. Allies. Military intelligence. Military strategy. 1939-40. *441*
—. Military Strategy. 1939-45. *507*

—. Military Strategy. Phoney War. 1939-40.
523
—. Military Strategy *(Weserübung* directive).
1939-40. *499*
Schmitt, Carl. International law, principles of.
Racism. Walz, Gustav. 1919-45. *111*
Schnapp, Alain. Archaeology. Nazism. 1933-44.
227
Scholl, Hans and Sophie (commemoration).
Anti-Nazi Movements. 1940-43. *268*
Schools. Hitler Youth. National Socialist Teachers
League. 1933-45. *124*
Schulze-Boysen-Harnack organization. Kuckhoff,
Greta (memoirs). Resistance. 1935-43. *141*
Schütz, Günther. Espionage. Ireland. 1941-42.
452
Schwarzbart, I. Anti-Semitism.
Government-in-exile, London. Poland. 1933-45.
770
Science. Nazism. Racism. 1933-45. *20*
SD (Sicherheitsdienst). Abwehr. Intelligence
services. Military Organization (fusion). 1944.
29
—. Religion. USSR. 1919-44. *271*
Seenotdienst. Air-sea rescue operations. 1937-41.
253
Sendlerowa, Irena. Memoirs. Poland (Warsaw
ghetto). Resistance. Youth groups. 1942.
1009
Senegal (Dakar). Thierry d'Argenlieu, Admiral
(review article). 1940. *442*
Senger, Valentin. Jews. Memoirs. Survivors (review
article). 1940's. *992*
Serbs. Croatia. Genocide. Jews. Nazism. 1941-45.
938
Service du Travail Obligatoire. France (Ariège).
Labor, forced. 1942-44. *494*
Settlement. Germans, Baltic. Nazism. Warta River.
1940-45. *259*
Shipbuilding. Blohm & Voss. Germany (Hamburg).
1877-1977. *315*
—. Hansa company. Merchant Marine. 1939-45.
275
Shipping. Atlantic, North. Communications.
Norway. 1940. *554*
—. Great Britain. Submarine Warfare. 1939-45.
540
Silesia. Europe, Eastern. Research. 1938-45.
72
Silesia, Upper. Deutsches Volksliste. Military
Occupation. Nationalities policy. Poland.
1939-45. *414*
Simplicissimus (journal). Middle classes. Nazism.
Political attitudes. 1920's-44. *191*
Singer, Kurt. Cultural Union of German Jewry.
Jews. Nazism. Theater. 1933-41. *858*
SKF. Ball-bearings. Sweden. War economy.
1939-45. *301*
Skorzeny, Otto. Military Strategy. 1941-45. *217*
Slovak National Uprising. Czechoslovakia. Military
Campaigns (letters). Resistance. 1944. *591*
Slovakia. Concentration Camps. Hijefs. Jews.
Rescue agencies. Vaad Hacala. 1941-45. *946*
—. Diplomacy (advisers). 1939-41. *639*
—. Economic development. 1939-40. *638*
—. Grosman, Ladislav *(Shop on Main Street).*
Labor, forced. Memoirs. 1941-44. *874*
Slovenes. Deportation. Yugoslavia (Lower Styria).
1919-48. *602*
Smith, Bradley F. Hitler, Adolf (review article).
Irving, David. Nuremberg Trials. 1941-45.
1977. *136*
Smolensk (battle). Lukin, M. Memoirs. 1941.
705
Smolensk campaign. Military Strategy. Operation
Barbarossa. USSR. 1941. *707*
Sobibor. Concentration Camps. Poland. 1942.
908

Social Classes. Education. Germany, West.
Military officers. 1900-79. *4*
—. Europe, Eastern. Military Occupation. 1941-45.
714
—. Labor. Women. 1938-44. *221*
—. Labor. Women. 1939-45. *223*
—. National Socialist Women's Groups. Nazism.
Women. 1933-42. *244*
Social Conditions. Austria (Styria). Political
Conditions. 1940-45. *604*
Social Democratic Party. Communist Party.
Germany, East. Resistance. 1933-45. *225*
Social mobility. Education. Nazism. 1930-40.
110
Social organization. Airplane Industry and Trade.
Germany (Rostock). 1939-45. *70*
Social Policy. Labor. Nazism. Women. 1925-40.
173
Social Psychology. Jews. Poland (Łódz ghetto).
Rumors. 1939-44. *932*
Social security. Deutsche Arbeitsfront. Nazism.
1918-45. *250*
Social status. Czechoslovakia (Teschen). Military
Occupation. Nationalities policy. 1939-45.
593
Socialist movement. Anti-Nazi Movements. Jews.
Poland (Warsaw ghetto). 1939-44. *832*
Socialists. Concentration camps. Resistance.
1939-45. *831*
Sociology. Auschwitz. Concentration Camps.
Genocide. Hoess, Rudolf. 1942-45. *913*
Sonderkommando 1005. Atrocities. Blobel, Paul.
Concentration Camps. Poland (Białystok).
1940-45. *821*
Sorbs. Germanization. Germany (Lusatia). Nazism.
1933-45. *585*
South Tyrol. Austria. Foreign Relations. Italy.
1938-45. *290*
—. Austria. Italy. 1938-45. *355*
South Tyrol (Gröden valley). Austria (Styria;
Hochschwab). Resettlement. SS (Schutzstaffel).
1940-41. *119*
Spain. Airplanes. Espinosa, Manuel (memoirs).
Travel. ca 1944. *296*
Spandau prison. Hess, Rudolf. 1946-80. *18*
—. Speer, Albert (interview). 1930's-78. *14*
Speer, Albert. Bombing. Memoirs. 1944. *547*
Speer, Albert (interview). Hitler, Adolf. Nazism.
Nuremberg trials. 1945-76. *193*
—. Memoirs. Nazism. 1930's-60's. 1977. *15*
—. Nazism. ca 1932-45. *6*
—. Spandau Prison. 1930's-78. *14*
Spitzer, Walter. Art. Concentration camps. Daily
Life. 1939-45. *1061*
Sports. Diem, Carl. 1940. *503*
SS (Schutzstaffel). Army, 2d. Poland (Horka).
War Crimes. 1945. *42d*
—. Austria (Styria; Hochschwab). Resettlement.
South Tyrol (Gröden valley). 1940-41. *119*
—. Business. Concentration camps. Himmler,
Heinrich. 1933-45. *909*
—. Business. Himmler, Heinrich. Interest Groups.
1930-45. *121*
—. Law Enforcement. Nazi Party. 1933-45.
62
SS (Schutzstaffel; appointments). Army. Belgium.
Collaboration movements. Himmler, Heinrich.
Reeder, Eggert. 1941-44. *462*
—. Belgium (Brussels). Collaboration. Himmler,
Heinrich. Military Occupation. Reeder, Eggert.
1942-43. *461*
SS-Panzer Corps, 3d ("Germanic"). Documents.
Foreign Auxiliaries. 1939-44. *265*
Staatliche Kunstsammlungen Dresden. Art treasures.
Germany (Dresden). Königstein Fortress.
USSR. 1945. *737*
Stachiewicz, Wacław. Memoirs. Military General
Staff. Poland. 1939. *428*

260 Stalag I

Stalag I B Hohenstein. Prisoners of War. 1939-45. *147*
Stalingrad (battle). Censorship. Dietrich, Otto. Journalism. 1942-43. *732*
—. France. Great Britain. USSR. 1939-45. *688*
—. Historiography, West German. 1942-43. *711*
—. Operation Barbarossa. USSR. 1941-42. *741*
—. USSR. 1942-43. *695*
—. USSR. 1942. *717*
Stanghelle (battle). Norway. 1940. *451*
Starvation. Jews. Military Occupation. Poland (Warsaw ghetto). Research. 1941-42. *1050*
Statistics. Armaments. Infantry. 1939-44. *148*
Stauffenberg, Claus von. Assassination attempts. Hitler, Adolf. 1938-44. *185*
—. Hitler, Adolf. July 20 Plot. 1939-46. *132*
—. July 20 Plot. 1944. *48*
Steel production. Imports. Iron ore. Sweden. 1938-40. *302*
Steflea, Ilie. Diaries. Gîrbea, Titus. Memoirs. Romania. 1942-44. *636*
Stierlin, Helm. Bloch, Eduard. Hitler, Adolf (review article). Jews. Psychohistory. 1907-45. 1973-76. *114*
Strategic Bombing Survey. Galbraith, John Kenneth. Memoirs. USA. 1944-45. *470*
Street, Lieutenant Colonel (report). Airborne troops. Partisans. Yugoslavia (Drvar). 1944. *571*
Streicher, Julius (memoirs). Dolibois, John E. Nazism. 1933-45. *771*
Stroop, Jürgen. Moczarski, Kazimierz. Nazism (review article). Political Imprisonment. 1949. *63*
Stroop, Jürgen (interviews). Moczarski, Kazimierz. War criminals. Warsaw Ghetto Uprising. 1943. *970*
Student, Kurt. Airborne troops. Crete (battle). Freyberg, Bernard Cyril. Military Campaigns. 1941. *473*
Stumpf, Richard (diary). 1914-54. *103*
Submarine lighters. Mediterranean Sea and Area. Naval Vessels. 1943-44. *103*
Submarine Warfare. Aircraft carriers. 1939-45. *534*
—. Atlantic, North. 1939-43. *459*
—. Great Britain. Shipping. 1939-45. *540*
Submarines. Convoys (PQ13, QP9). Great Britain. U-585 (submarine). 1942. *488*
—. Leadership. 1939-45. *41*
—. Narvik (operations). Tactics. 1940. *460*
Submarines (Biber class). Naval Battles. USSR (Vayenga-Severomorsk). 1944-45. *750*
Subversive activities. Intelligence Service. USSR. 1944. *669*
Sudeten Germans (expulsion). Beneš, Eduard. Jaksch, Wenzel (correspondence). 1939-43. *637*
Sudetenland. Allies. Military Occupation. 1945. *595*
—. Czechoslovakia. Education. Military Occupation. 1938-45. *592*
Surrender. Balkans. Hitler, Adolf. Italians. Lanz, Hubert. Military Command. 1943. *502*
—. Documents. Military Law. Military Occupation. Norway. 1945. *489*
Survivors (interviews). Concentration Camps. Psychology. 1941-71. *950*
Survivors (review article). Jews. Memoirs. Senger, Valentin. 1940's. *992*
Sweden. Anti-Fascism. Communist Party. 1933-43. *203*
—. Army. Bamler, Rudolf. Military Occupation (preparation). 1940-44. *272*
—. Ball-bearings. SKF. War economy. 1939-45. *301*
—. Diplomacy. Norway. 1940. *324*
—. Economic relations. 1939-45. *300*
—. Foreign Policy. Gustavus V (abdication threat). Midsummer crisis. 1941. *358*
—. Foreign Policy. Neutrality. 1939-45. *369*
—. Foreign Relations. 1941. *370*
—. Foreign Relations. Kumlin, Ragnar (memoranda). 1941-43. *320*
—. Great Britain. Railroads. Transportation policy. 1940-43. *304*
—. Imports. Iron ore. Steel production. 1938-40. *302*
—. Iron ore. Neutrality. Trade. 1939-45. *368*
—. Military Strategy. 1939-45. *472*
—. Military Strategy. 1941-42. *456*
—. Neutrality. Railroads. Transit rights. 1939-45. *371*
—. Norway (Narvik). Transportation, Military. 1940. *366*
—. Trade. 1940-44. *367*
Switzerland. Belgium. Diplomatic representation. Government-in-exile. 1940-45. *343*
—. Case Yellow. Military (troop concentration). Neutrality. 1939-40. *524*
Sydney (warship). Australia. *Kormoran* (warship). Naval Battles. 1941. *153*
Symbolism. Aesthetics. Industrial Relations. Labor. Nazism. 1933-39. *210*
Szulfried, Stanisław. Expropriation. Jews. Memoirs. Military Occupation. Poland (Warsaw). 1939-42. *1024*

T

Tactics. Air Warfare. Kursk, battle of. Tanks. 1943. *724*
—. Berlin (battle). USSR. 1945. *731*
—. Narvik (operations). Submarines. 1940. *460*
Tactics (battle plan State Farm 79). Armored Vehicles and Tank Warfare. 1942-77. *668*
Tanks *See also* Armored Vehicles and Tank Warfare.
—. Air Warfare. Kursk, battle of. Tactics. 1943. *724*
Taubert, Eberhard. Anti-Communist Movements. Brandt, Willi. Goebbels, Joseph. Propaganda. 1931-60. *2*
Taylor, A. J. P. Historiography. World War II (antecedents). 1919-39. 1945-79. *33*
Teachers. Lemberg University. Murder. Nazis. Poland. 1941. *383*
—. Nazism. Persecution. Poland (Poznan). 1939-45. *424*
Technology, development of. Airplanes, Military. 1939-45. *75*
Tendzos, Christos. Bulgarians. Greece (central Macedonia). Merten, Dr. Military occupation. 1943. *643*
Territorial cessions. Politics. Romania (Transylvania). Vienna, Treaty of. 1940. *353*
Territorial claims (memoranda). Nazism. 1940. *584*
Territory, occupied. Construction industry. USSR (Lithuania). 1941-45. *690*
Textbooks. Edelmann, Moritz. History teaching. Klagge, Dietrich. Nazism. 1938-45. *213*
Textile industry. Czechoslovakia (Náchod). Military Occupation. 1938-48. *596*
Thälmann, Ernst. Letters. Prisons. 1944. *251*
Theater. Censorship. Comédie-Française. France. Military Occupation. 1939-45. *504*
—. Cultural Union of German Jewry. Jews. Nazism. Singer, Kurt. 1933-41. *858*
—. Genocide. Intellectuals. Military occupation. Poland. 1939-45. *421*
—. Ghettos. Jews. Poland. 1939-42. *845*
—. Music. Poland (Western Territories). 1939-44. *381*
Theology. Jews. Kittel, Gerhard. Nazi Party. 1888-1948. *843*

Theresienstadt camp. Auschwitz. Concentration Camps. Jews. 1943-44. *931*
—. Concentration camps. 1939-45. *910*
—. Concentration Camps. Historiography. Zionism. 1941-45. *997*
Thierry d'Argenlieu, Admiral (review article). Senegal (Dakar). 1940. *442*
Tillion, Germaine. Concentration Camps. Memoirs. Ravensbrück. 1945. *1029*
Tirpitz (battleship). Military Strategy. Warships. 1941-44. *152*
Tito, Josip (personality, documents). Attitudes. 1941-44. *617*
Titov, Vasili. Ben, Fritz. Resistance. USSR (Ust'-Luga). 1942-43. *694*
Tobruk (battle). 1939-43. *533*
—. 1941-42. *531*
—. Africa, North. 1942. *532*
Toland, John. Biography. Davidson, Eugene. Historiography. Hitler, Adolf (review article). Irving, David. 1930's-77. *163*
Trade. Denmark. Mohr, Otto (memoirs). 1940. *354*
—. Europe, Northern. Military Strategy. 1900-45. *331*
—. Iron ore. Neutrality. Sweden. 1939-45. *368*
—. Oil. USSR. 1940-41. *348*
—. Sweden. 1940-44. *367*
Transdniester Plan. Jews. Rescue. Romania. 1942-44. *1039*
Transit rights. Neutrality. Railroads. Sweden. 1939-45. *371*
Transportation, Military. Norway (Narvik). Sweden. 1940. *366*
Transportation policy. Great Britain. Railroads. Sweden. 1940-43. *304*
Transylvania, partition of. Boundaries. Hungary. Romania. Vienna Diktat. 1940. *352*
Travel. Airplanes. Espinosa, Manuel (memoirs). Spain. ca 1944. *296*
Treaties. Diplomacy, secret. Lithuanian strip. USSR. 1939-41. *313*
Treblinka. Children. Concentration Camps. Korczak, Janusz. Poland (Warsaw ghetto). 1942. *824*
—. Concentration Camps. Memoirs. Reichman, Yehiel Meir. 1942-43. *989*
Trevor-Roper, Hugh R. Diaries. Goebbels, Joseph. 1925-45. *90*
Trials. *Affiche Rouge*. France. Psychological Warfare. Resistance. 1944. *495*
—. Datner, Szymon (report). Friedel, Fritz Gustav. Poland (Białystok). War crimes. 1942-49. *819*
—. Films. July 20 Plot. 1944-45. 1979-80. *220*
—. Medicine (practice of). War Crimes. Women. 1941-48. *176*
Tripartite Pact. Axis powers. Diplomacy. Yugoslavia. 1939-41. *363*
Trott, Adam von. Anti-Nazi Movements. 1929-44. *160*
Trunk, Isaiah. Bibliographies. Jewish Councils. 1939-44. *1040*
Tubin, Yehuda (memoirs). Germany (Belsen). Jewish Brigade. Liberation. Poland. 1945-46. *1031*
Tunisia. Military occupation. 1942-43. *467*
Turgenev Library. Berberova, Nina. Memoirs. 1880-1975. *446*
Tyszka, Leon. Memoirs. Poland. Poland (Warsaw ghetto). 1939-42. *1032*
Tyszka, Leon (reminiscence). Czerniakow, Adam. Jewish Councils (Judenrat). Military Occupation. Poland (Warsaw ghetto). 1939-42. *1034*

U

U-boats. *See* Naval Vessels; Submarines.
Ukraine. Aviation, civil. Partisans. 1941-45. *676*
—. Bagramian, Ivan (memoirs). Military Campaigns. USSR. 1942. *657*
—. Belorussia. Genocide (documents). Jews. Military Occupation. USSR. 1941-45. *976*
—. Coal Mines and Mining. Exploitation. Iron Industry. 1941-44. *725*
—. Eastern front. Kleist, Paul Ludwig Ewald von. Military Strategy. Uman (battle). 1941. *706*
—. Germans. Villages. 1942-43. *687*
—. Imperialism. Military Occupation. 1941-45. *702*
Ukraine (Bogodukhov). Armored Vehicles and Tank Warfare. Eastern front. 1943. *684*
Ukraine (Chernigov). Air warfare. Belorussia. Memoirs. 1943-44. *726*
Ukraine (Czech Malín). Atrocities. USSR. 1943. *597*
Ukraine (Lvov). Curricula. Higher Education. Military Occupation. 1942-45. *438*
—. Documents. Jews. Lvov portfolio. Military Occupation. Poland. 1941. *903*
—. Genocide. Jews. Radlitzki, Tzvi (memoirs). 1941-45. *987*
—. Jews. Memoirs. Military Occupation. 1941-44. *836*
—. Jews. Memoirs. Military Occupation. 1941-44. *837*
Ukraine (Lyubeshov). Epstein, David (memoirs). Genocide. Jews. Partisans. 1941-44. *840*
Ukraine (Mukachevo). Jews. Military Occupation. 1938-44. *999*
Ukrainians. Atrocities. Galicia Division. Historiography. Poland. USSR. 1943-45. *749*
Ulitski, Moshe (diary). Jews. Lithuania (Vilnius ghetto). 1941-42. *833*
Ultra. Allies. Military intelligence. 1920's-45. *115*
Uman (battle). Eastern front. Kleist, Paul Ludwig Ewald von. Military Strategy. Ukraine. 1941. *706*
Urach Theological Seminary. Brecht, Alfred (memoirs). Protestantism. 20c. *26*
USA (Louisiana). Afrika Corps. Prisoners of War. 1943-46. *544*
USA (Washington). Diplomacy. Espionage. 1940. *332*
USSR. 1939-45. *202*
—. 1941-45. *708*
—. Alter, Wiktor. Anti-Nazi Movements. Erlich, Henryk. Jews. 1939-41. *988*
—. Anti-aircraft defense. Cities. Rockets. 1937-45. *701*
—. Anti-Communist Movements. Foreign Auxiliaries. 1941. *681*
—. Arctic Ocean. Battles. 1941-45. *742*
—. Armistice. Finland (Lapland). Roads. 1940-45. *310*
—. Armored Vehicles and Tank Warfare. Military Strategy. 1941-43. *700*
—. Armored Vehicles and Tank Warfare. Prokhorovka (battle). 1943. *672*
—. Army Group Center. Partisans. 1942-44. *654*
—. Art treasures. Germany (Dresden). Königstein Fortress. Staatliche Kunstsammlungen Dresden. 1945. *737*
—. Atrocities. Communists. Jews. 1939-41. *683*
—. Atrocities. Galicia Division. Historiography. Poland. Ukrainians. 1943-45. *749*

262 USSR

—. Atrocities. Ukraine (Czech Malín). 1943. *597*
—. Attitudes. Jewish Councils. Military Occupation. Poland. 1939-41. *1047*
—. Bagramian, Ivan (memoirs). Military Campaigns. Ukraine. 1942. *657*
—. Balta (battle). 1941. *680*
—. Baltic area. Military campaigns. 1944-45. *736*
—. Baltic Area. Minelaying operations. 1941. *650*
—. Baltic States. 1939. *666*
—. Banking. Documents. Reichsbank. World War II (antecedents). 1941. *715*
—. Battles. Military Strategy. Vistula-Oder campaign. 1945. *652*
—. Belorussia. Genocide (documents). Jews. Military Occupation. Ukraine. 1941-45. *976*
—. Belorussia. Germans. Partisans. 1942-45. *716*
—. Berlin (battle). Tactics. 1945. *731*
—. Bessarabia. Jews. 1940-45. *945*
—. Blitzkrieg. Military Strategy. Nazism. World War II (antecedents). 1914-45. *66*
—. Border guards, Soviet. Eastern front (first battles). 1941. *670*
—. Bräutigam, Otto (memorandum). Military occupation policy. 1941. *588*
—. Bulgaria. Intervention. 1944. *598*
—. Caucasus. Military Campaigns. Oil fields. 1941-43. *677*
—. Civil-Military Relations. Commissar Order. Military Occupation. War crimes. 1941. *703*
—. Clauss, Edgar. Kleist, Peter. Peace, separate. 1942-44. *316*
—. Collaborators. Military Officers. Vlasov, Andrei. 1939-46. *679*
—. Communications, Military. Operation Barbarossa. 1941. *733*
—. Communications, Military. World War II (antecedents). 1940-41. *697*
—. Crimea, battle for the. Military Strategy. 1941-44. *660*
—. Czechoslovakia. Germans. Partisan movement. Poland. 1939-45. *197*
—. Czechoslovakia. Prisoners of war. Resistance. 1941-45. *611*
—. Deportation. Germans, Volga. 1941. *692*
—. Diplomacy, secret. Lithuanian strip. Treaties. 1939-41. *313*
—. Eastern front. Europe. Political Change. 1933-45. *146*
—. Eastern front. Germany, East. Historiography. 1943-45. *689*
—. Ehrenburg, Ilya *(The Black Book)*. Jews. 1941-80. *1012*
—. Europe, Eastern. Military Planning. Ost plan. 1915-77. *664*
—. Films. Propaganda. 1930's-45. *658*
—. Finland. Foreign Policy. Mannerheim, Carl Gustav. 1940-41. *373*
—. Finland. Hogland (battle). 1944. *747*
—. Finland. Military Strategy. 1941-44. *746*
—. Foreign policy. World War II (antecedents). 1939-41. *734*
—. Foreign policy. World War II (antecedents). 1940-41. *704*
—. Foreign Relations. Jews. 1933-41. *869*
—. France. Great Britain. Stalingrad (Battle). 1939-45. *688*
—. Geheime Feldpolizei. Partisans. 1939-45. *68*
—. General Plan East. Germanization. Poland. 1939-43. *120*
—. Genocide. Historiography. Jews. 1940-45. *866*
—. Genocide. Ideology. Jews. Military Occupation. 1941-44. *900*

—. Genocide. Jews. 1941-42. *952*
—. Genocide. Jews. Manstein, Erich von. 1939-45. *1042*
—. Germans. 1941. *686*
—. Germans. Repatriation. 1939. *384*
—. Guards Anti-Tank Artillery Regiment, 150th. Malaia Tokmachka (battle). Rumiantsev, N. (memoir). 1943. *727*
—. Historiography. Hungary. Košice (air raid). War, declaration of. 1941-46. *675*
—. Historiography, bourgeois. Military Occupation. 1940-45. *720*
—. Historiography, Western. Nazi-Soviet Pact. 1939-45. *744*
—. Hitler, Adolf. Military. War aims. 1939-41. *682*
—. Hitler, Adolf. World War II (antecedents). 1933-42. *651*
—. Hungary. Logistics. 1944-45. *743*
—. Hungary. Military Occupation. 1944-45. *625*
—. Intelligence Service. Subversive activities. 1944. *669*
—. Invasion. Military Strategy. Operation Barbarossa. 1941. *739*
—. Japan. Peace mediation. 1941-45. *318*
—. Jews. Military Occupation. 1939-41. *984*
—. Jews. Military Occupation. Rosenberg, Alfred. 1941-44. *760*
—. Katyn massacre. Poland. 1939-43. *430*
—. Katyn massacre. Poland. 1939-45. *377*
—. Latvia. Prisoners of war. 1941-45. *712*
—. Lithuania (Vilnius). Military Campaigns. 1944. *745*
—. Maschke, Erich (review article). Prisoners of War (German). 1941-45. *728*
—. Military campaigns. 1941-45. *718*
—. Military intelligence. Military offensives. Osuga (battle). 1942. *696*
—. Military Intelligence. Military Operations. 1941-45. *748*
—. Military Occupation. Minorities. Poland. 1939-45. *436*
—. Military Offensives. Weather. 1941. *740*
—. Military Strategy. 1941-42. *655*
—. Military Strategy. 1941. *751*
—. Military Strategy. Operation Barbarossa. Smolensk campaign. 1941. *707*
—. Military Strategy. War games. World War II (antecedents). 1940-41. *699*
—. Naval operations. 1939-45. *719*
—. Oil. Trade. 1940-41. *348*
—. Operation Barbarossa. Stalingrad (battle). 1941-42. *741*
—. Religion. SD (Sicherheitsdienst). 1919-44. *271*
—. Stalingrad (battle). 1942-43. *695*
—. Stalingrad (battle). 1942. *717*
—. World War II (antecedents). 1939-40. *735*
USSR (Briansk, Orel). Bagramian, Ivan (memoirs). Operation Citadel. 1942-43. *656*
USSR (Crimea). Mannstein, Erich von. Military strategy. 1941. *667*
USSR (Donets basin). Economic policy. Military Strategy. 1941-43. *678*
USSR (Kamenets Podolsk). Hungary. Jews. Massacres. Yugoslavia (Délvidék). 1941-42. *795*
USSR (Kuban). Air Warfare. Military Strategy. Pokryshkin, Aleksandr (memoir). 1943. *722*
USSR (Kursk). Air Forces. Armored Vehicles and Tank Warfare. Meyer, Bruno. 1943. *723*
USSR (Leningrad, Murmansk). Military operations. Northern front. 1941-42. *752*
USSR (Lithuania). Construction industry. Territory, occupied. 1941-45. *690*
USSR (Rudnya). Genocide. Jews. 1939-45. *830*

USSR (Ust'-Luga). Ben, Fritz. Resistance. Titov, Vasili. 1942-43. *694*
USSR (Vayenga-Severomorsk). Naval Battles. Submarines (Biber class). 1944-45. *750*
Ustaši. Chetniks. Collaborators. Communications. Counterinsurgency. Industry. Yugoslavia. 1941-42. *573*
U-585 (submarine). Convoys (PQ13, QP9). Great Britain. Submarines. 1942. *488*

V

Vaad Hacala. Concentration Camps. Hijefs. Jews. Rescue agencies. Slovakia. 1941-45. *946*
Vatican. Diplomacy. Italy (Rome). Jews. Weizsäcker, Ernst von. 1943. *810*
—. Diplomacy. Mirošević-Sorgo, Niko H. (expulsion). Yugoslavia. 1941-42. *624*
Vegh, Claudine. Children. Concentration Camps (review article). Memoirs. 1939-45. *1038*
Veliki Bečerek. Atrocities. Concentration camps. Yugoslavia (Banat). 1941-45. *1014*
Veterinary service. Army. 1932-45. *134*
Vichy regime. Africa, North. Jews. World War II (antecedents). 1930-40. *764*
—. Airplane Industry and Trade. France. 1940-43. *297*
—. Auschwitz. Children. Deportation. France. Jews. 1942-44. *955*
—. Bonnard, Abel. Collaboration. France. Ideology. 1928-42. *512*
—. Children. France. Jews. Rescue. 1939-45. *918*
—. Diplomacy. France. 1940. *292*
Vienna conference. Demonstrations. Romania. 1939-40. *333*
Vienna Diktat. Boundaries. Hungary. Romania. Transylvania, partition of. 1940. *352*
Vienna, Treaty of. Politics. Romania (Transylvania). Territorial cessions. 1940. *353*
Villages. Germans. Ukraine. 1942-43. *687*
Visser, Lodewijk Ernst. Cohen, David (correspondence). Jews. Military occupation. 1941-42. *960*
—. Jewish Councils (Judenrat). Netherlands. 1940-42. *966*
Vistula-Oder campaign. Battles. Military Strategy. USSR. 1945. *652*
Vlaamse Landsleiding. Collaborators, Belgian. 1944-45. *510*
Vlasov, Andrei. Collaborators. Military Officers. USSR. 1939-46. *679*
"Völkisch" ideology. Anti-Semitism. 19c-20c. *794*
Volkssturm. 1944-45. *74*
Volunteers. Collaboration. France. Légion des Volontaires Français contre le Bolchevisme. Waffen-SS (Charlemagne division). 1941-45. *508*
Vrba, Rudolf. Auschwitz. Concentration Camps. 1933-45. *812*
V2 rocket. 1939-45. *246*
V3 Rocket. Artillery. Weapons. 1943-44. *76*

W

Wachowiak, Stanislaw (memoirs). Central Union of the Polish Industry. Poland (Warsaw). Resistance. 1939-45. *434*
Waffen-SS. Berger, Gottlob. Military Recruitment. 1939-40. *212*
Waffen-SS (Charlemagne division). Collaboration. France. Légion des Volontaires Français contre le Bolchevisme. Volunteers. 1941-45. *508*
Waffen-SS (Death's Head division). Eicke, Theodor. 1939-45. *248*

Walther, Gebhardt von (memorandum). Diplomacy. Etzdorf, Hasso von. Operation Barbarossa (opposition to). 1940-41. *685*
Walther, Gebhardt von. Consular Reports. Jews. Libya. 1940-43. *763*
Walz, Gustav. International law, principles of. Racism. Schmitt, Carl. 1919-45. *111*
War. Economic Planning. Rubber, synthetic. 1915-45. *255*
—. Neutrality (disregard of). 1890's-1945. *349*
War aims. 1939-40. *242*
—. 1940-43. *187*
—. Africa. 1939-45. *116*
—. Annexation. France (Briey, Longwy, Nancy). Klein Commission. Mining industry. 1911-42. *295*
—. Axis, defection from. 1939-45. *346*
—. German Resettlement Fiduciary Company. Germanization. 1939-41. *50*
—. Historiography (review article). World War I (antecedents). 1897-1945. *13*
—. Hitler, Adolf. Military. USSR. 1939-41. *682*
—. Hitler, Adolf (review article). Rich, Norman. 1936-45. *91*
—. Poland (Warsaw). 1939-45. *406*
War aims memorandum. Africa. Nazi Party (Colonial Political Office). Pacific Area. Weigelt, Kurt. 1940. *55*
War Crime Trial. Libby, Frederick J. Malmédy massacre. National Council for the Prevention of War. 1944-49. *465*
War crimes. Archives, provincial. Documents. Poland (Rzeszów). 1939-45. *378*
—. Army, 2d. Poland (Horka). SS (Schutzstaffel). 1945. *420*
—. Auschwitz. Autobiography. Concentration Camps. Hoess, Rudolf. 1906-47. *901*
—. Casualties. Military Occupation. Partisans. Yugoslavia. 1941-45. *628*
—. Children. Nazism. Poland. 1939-1945. *775*
—. Children (conference). Poland. 1939-45. *776*
—. Civil-Military Relations. Commissar Order. Military Occupation. USSR. 1941. *703*
—. Datner, Szymon (report). Friedel, Fritz Gustav. Poland (Białystok). Trials. 1942-49. *819*
—. Medicine (practice of). Trials. Women. 1941-48. *176*
War criminals. Harrower, Molly. Psychohistory. 1939-45. *232*
—. Moczarski, Kazimierz. Stroop, Jürgen (interviews). Warsaw Ghetto Uprising. 1943. *970*
War, declaration of. Historiography. Hungary. Košice (air raid). USSR. 1941-46. *675*
War, defensive. Poland. World War II (antecedents). 1939. *404*
War economy. Ball-bearings. SKF. Sweden. 1939-45. *301*
War games. Military Strategy. USSR. World War II (antecedents). 1940-41. *699*
War Refugee Board. Archives, National. Genocide. Jews. Rescue. USA. 1918-52. *961*
War Victims. Poland. 1939-45. *423*
Warsaw ghetto uprising *See also* Poland (Warsaw ghetto).
—. 1943. *1020*
—. Anielewicz, Mordechai. Jewish Fighting Organization. People's Guard. Poland. Youth groups. 1930's-42. *899*
—. Archives. Jewish Historical Institute. Poland. 1942. *846*
—. Attitudes. Emigrants. Poles. 1942-43. *829*
—. Jewish Antifascist Block. Jewish Fighting Organization. 1940-43. *854*
—. Jewish Fighting Organization. Zuckerman, Itzhak (interview). 1933-44. *1055*

Warsaw ghetto

—. Jewish Military Union. Poland. World War II (personal narratives). 1942. *906*
—. Jews. Ohlenbusch, Wilhelm (report). Poland. 1943. *917*
—. Jews. Poland. 1943. *953*
—. Jews. Poland. 1943. *1013*
—. Jews. Poles. Resistance. 1944. *905*
—. Moczarski, Kazimierz. Stroop, Jürgen (interviews). War criminals. 1943. *970*
—. Poland. 1942-43. *820*
—. Poland. Resistance. 1939-44. *780*
—. Poland. Workers' Party. 1942-43. *972*
Warsaw ghetto uprising (origins). Jewish Fighting Organization. Poland. 1942-43. *884*
Warsaw Mechanical Documentation Archives. Nazism. Poland. Radio recordings. 1939-45. *117*
Warsaw University Library. Libraries. Poland. 1939-45. *376*
Warsaw Uprising. Fischer, Ludwig (report). Poland. 1939-44. *386*
—. Guerrilla Warfare (Polish). Military Strategy (German). 1944. *437*
Warships. Military Strategy. *Tirpitz* (battleship). 1941-44. *152*
Warta River. Germans, Baltic. Nazism. Settlement. 1940-45. *259*
Weapons. Artillery. V3 Rocket. 1943-44. *76*
—. Germany, battle for. Military Strategy. 1944-45. *526*
Weather. Military Offensives. USSR. 1941. *740*
Weather stations. Canada (Labrador). 1943. 1981. *466*
Weigelt, Kurt. Africa. Nazi Party (Colonial Political Office). Pacific Area. War aims memorandum. 1940. *55*
Weissauer, Ludwig. Diplomacy. Peace discussions, secret. 1940-43. *326*
Weisse Rose. Resistance. 1943. *51*
Weizsäcker, Ernst von. Afghanistan. Foreign Relations. 1940. *351*
—. Diplomacy. Italy (Rome). Jews. Vatican. 1943. *810*
Wessel, Horst (myth). Films. Propaganda. 1930's. *83*
Westerplatte, battle of. Bibliographies. Danzig. Poland. 1939. *387*
Whaley, Barton. Leach, Barry A. Military Strategy (review article). Operation Barbarossa. 1939-41. *673*
Winkler, Dörte. Labor. Public Policy. Women (review article). 1930-45. *174*
Women. Labor. Nazism. Social Policy. 1925-40. *173*
—. Labor. Social Classes. 1938-44. *221*
—. Labor. Social Classes. 1939-45. *223*
—. Labor force. Nazism. 1918-45. *274*
—. Labor Service. 1931-43. *3*
—. Medicine (practice of). Trials. War Crimes. 1941-48. *176*
—. National Socialist Women's Groups. Nazism. Social Classes. 1933-42. *244*
—. Nazism. 1930's-40's. *129*
—. Propaganda. USA. 1939-45. *80*
—. Propaganda. USA. 1939-45. *222*
Women (review article). Labor. Public Policy. Winkler, Dörte. 1930-45. *174*
Workers' Party. Poland. Warsaw ghetto uprising. 1942-43. *972*
Working conditions. Labor (imported). Prisoners of war. 1939-45. *166*
World Council of Churches. Ecumenism. Jews. Rescue. 1939-44. *793*
World War I (antecedents). Historiography (review article). War aims. 1897-1945. *13*
World War II (antecedents). 1938-80. *67*
—. Africa, North. Jews. Vichy regime. 1930-40. *764*
—. Air warfare. Architecture. 1933-45. *31*
—. Anti-Semitism. Ideology. Nazism. Racism. 1933-45. *981*
—. Axis Pact. Italy. Japan. Oshima Hiroshi. 1934-40. *283*
—. Axis powers. Neutrality. Yugoslavia. 1939. *284*
—. Banking. Documents. Reichsbank. USSR. 1941. *715*
—. Belgium. Collaboration. Degrelle, Léon. Rexist Party. 1933-40. *493*
—. Belgium. Military Strategy (attack planes). 1939-40. *557*
—. Blitzkrieg. Military Strategy. Nazism. USSR. 1914-45. *66*
—. Burckhardt, Carl Jacob. Diplomacy. Great Britain. Mediation. 1937-39. *323*
—. Communications, Military. USSR. 1940-41. *697*
—. Economic Policy. Hitler, Adolf. 1939-41. *200*
—. Europe, central. Expansionism. Poland. 1934-40. *380*
—. Europe, Southeastern. Expansionism. 1933-45. *603*
—. Expansionism. Romania. 1938-39. *356*
—. Finland. Military. Operation Barbarossa. 1939-41. *709*
—. Foreign policy. USSR. 1939-41. *734*
—. Foreign policy. USSR. 1940-41. *704*
—. France (Burgundy; Dijon). 1939-40. *477*
—. Historiography. Taylor, A. J. P. 1919-39. 1945-79. *33*
—. Hitler, Adolf. USSR. 1933-42. *651*
—. Military Aid. Romania. 1938-41. *299*
—. Military Strategy. USSR. War games. 1940-41. *699*
—. Poland. 1919-39. *395*
—. Poland. War, defensive. 1939. *404*
—. Politics. 1938-45. *184*
—. USSR. 1939-40. *735*
World War II (antecedents; review article). 1930-39. *419*
World War II (end). Austria (Styria; Fischbach). 1945. *693*
World War II (personal narratives). Jewish Military Union. Poland. Warsaw ghetto uprising. 1942. *906*
World War II (review article). Foreign Policy. Military History. Politics. 1933-45. *34*
—. Jong, Louis de. Netherlands. Resistance. 20c. *536*
—. Messerschmidt, M. 1979. *12*

Y

Yellin, Chaim. Jews. Lithuania (Kaunas ghetto). Partisans. 1913-44. *944*
Youth. Anti-Communism. Germany, West. Nazism. Political Education. Propaganda. 1933-78. *260*
—. Gangs. Resistance. 1936-45. *105*
—. Military Service. 1943-45. *21*
Youth groups. Anielewicz, Mordechai. Jewish Fighting Organization. People's Guard. Poland. Warsaw ghetto uprising. 1930's-42. *899*
—. Memoirs. Poland (Warsaw ghetto). Resistance. Sendlerowa, Irena. 1942. *1009*
Yugoslavia. Axis powers. Diplomacy. Tripartite Pact. 1939-41. *363*
—. Axis powers. Neutrality. World War II (antecedents). 1939. *284*
—. Balkans. Coups d'Etat (August 1944). Resistance. Romania. 1944. *567*
—. Casualties. Military Occupation. Partisans. War Crimes. 1941-45. *628*

—. Chetniks. Collaborators. Communications. Counterinsurgency. Industry. Ustaši. 1941-42. *573*
—. Diplomacy. Foreign Policy. 1939-41. *319*
—. Diplomacy. Miroševic-Sorgo, Niko H. (expulsion). Vatican. 1941-42. *624*
—. Documents. Historiography, Yugoslav. 1940's. 1950's-73. *613*
—. Hitler, Adolf. 1939-41. *615*
—. Military Occupation. Raw materials. 1934-44. *631*
—. National liberation army. Operation Schwartz. Operation Weiss. 1942-43. *572*
—. National liberation movements. 1941. *616*
Yugoslavia (Banat). Atrocities. Concentration camps. Veliki Bečerek. 1941-45. *1014*
—. Chetniks. Collaboration. Ethnic Groups. Nedić, Milan. 1941-44. *618*
Yugoslavia (Bosnia). Croatia. Operation Schach. Partisans. 1944. *575*
—. Operation Maigewitter. 1945. *642*
Yugoslavia (Croatia; Lika). Chetniks. Italy. 1943-44. *607*
Yugoslavia (Délvidék). Hungary. Jews. Massacres. USSR (Kamenets Podolsk). 1941-42. *795*
Yugoslavia (Drvar). Airborne troops. Partisans. Street, Lieutenant Colonel (report). 1944. *571*
—. Operation Rösselsprung. 1944. *646*
Yugoslavia (Kras). Brand, Hans. Military Occupation. 1942-44. *581*
Yugoslavia (Lower Styria). Deportation. Slovenes. 1919-48. *602*
Yugoslavia (Maribor). Airplane Industry and Trade. Ostmark Aircraft Motor Works. 1940-45. *118*
Yugoslavia (Šalek Valley). Military Occupation. Resistance (losses). 1942. *647*
Yugoslavia (Sanjak). Proletarian Division, 1st. Resistance. 1944. *644*
Yugoslavia (Serbia). Chetniks. Collaboration. 1943-44. *608*
Yugoslavia (Slovenia). Archives. Military Occupation. Public Administration. 1941-45. *583*
—. Military occupation. 1941-45. *582*

Z

Zentrale Planung. Industrial conditions. Research sources. 1942-45. *194*
Zinsser, Christian (memoir). Diplomacy. Honduras. 1940-41. *372*
Zionism. Concentration Camps. Historiography. Theresienstadt camp. 1941-45. *997*
Zuckerman, Itzhak (interview). Jewish Fighting Organization. Warsaw ghetto uprising. 1933-44. *1055*

AUTHOR INDEX

A

Achkasov, V. 650
Adam, Uwe D. 757 758
Alef-Bolķowiak, Gustaw 759
Amort, Čestmír 651
Andersen, William D. 440
Andrae, Anders J. 441
Antsiz, B. 652
Arad, Yitzhak 760 761 762
Aran, Esther 763
Arbitol, Michael 764
Arimia, Vasile 622
Ark, O. I. 653
Arndt, Ino 765
Arndtova, Veronika 563
Arnon, Joseph 766
Aronsfeld, C. C. 1 767 768 769
Auphan, Amiral 442
Avakoumovitch, Ivan 443
Avital, Zvi 770
Aziasski, N. 654

B

Bagramian, I. 655 656 657
Baird, Jay W. 2 658 771
Bajohr, Stefan 3
Bălănică, Emilia 772
Bald, Detlef 4
Baldwin, P. M. 5
Ball-Kaduri, Kurt Jakob 773
Ballvora, Shyqri 564 565
Bantea, Eugen 566 567 568 576
Bar'am, A. 989
Bardosh, Alexander 990
Barkas, Janet 6
Barr, William 659
Barrett, Michael 7 176
Barski, Józef 774 775 776
Bartel, Walter 777
Bartelski, Lesław M. 778
Bartoš, Josef 569 570
Bartošová, Šárka 779
Bartoszewski, Władysław 780
Basov, A. V. 660
Batowski, Henryk 781
Bauer, Erich 661
Bauer, Yehuda 782 783 784
Beauquier, J. P. 444
Becker, Peter 7 176
Becker, Peter W. 8 9
Bednarski, Hanna J. 376
Benditer, J. 10 662
Bennett, Neville 445
Benser, Günter 11 663
Ben-Shemen, Reuben 785
Berberova, Nina 446
Berkin, Carol R. 221 222
Berman, Adolf 786
Bernbaum, John A. 278
Bettelheim, Bruno 787
Beumer, P. M. 377
Bezymenski, L. 12 281 664
Bialostotzki, Israel 788
Bianchi, Gerardo 447
Biddiss, Michael D. 13
Bieda, Tadeusz 378
Billson, Marc K., III 14 15
Binion, Rudolph 16 17
Binoche, Jacques 448
Bird, Eugene K. 18

Blank, Aleksander S. 665
Blankestein, Herbert 19 20
Bleistein, Roman 21
Bleyer, Wolfgang 666
Blomstedt, Yrjö 789
Bobocescu, Vasile 333
Boelcke, Willi A. 22
Bogdanović, Rade 571
Bojić, Mehmedalija 572
Bolewski, Andrzej 790
Bond, Brian 23
BonGherardi, Silva 791
Boozer, Jack S. 792
Borgen, Thom G. 449
Bošnjak, Ljubomir 573
Botz, Gerhard 278 282
Boussard, Isabel 450
Bowers, Ray L. 24
Boyd, Carl 283
Boyens, Armin F. C. 793
Braatz, Werner E. 794
Braham, Randolph L. 795 796
Brandes, Detlev 574
Branica, Vinko 575
Braubach, Max 25
Breccia, Alfredo 284
Brecht, Alfred 26
Brenner, Hans 797
Bridenthal, Renate 129
Brinkmann, August, Jr. 451
Broide, Frania 798
Bronsen, David 799
Broszat, Martin 800 801 802
Brown, Ron 667
Brown, Ronald J. 668
Browning, Christopher R. 27 803
Brügel, Johann Wolfgang 285
Brunn, Hans Henrik 375
Büchler, Joshua 804
Burian, Peter 278
Burstin, Barbara Stern 805
Busse, Otto 806

C

Cain, Seymour 807
Cappelletti, Vincenzo 808
Cargas, Harry James 809
Carlgren, W. M. 320
Carter, Carolle J. 452
Caspar, Gustav-Adolf 28
Ceva, Lucio 286
Chabert, Henry 453 454
Chadwick, Owen 810
Charisius, Albrecht 29 669
Charnitzky, Jürgen 30
Chernaia, L. B. 329
Chistyakov, I. 756
Choldkovskij, Victor M. 287
Chugunov, A. I. 670
Ciukov, V. I. 288 671
Clinton, Mark 811
Cluet, Marc 31
Cogniot, Georges 32
Cole, C. Robert 33
Collotti, Enzo 34 455
Columbeanu, Sergiu 576
Constantiniu, Florin 35 289 577
Conway, J. S. 36
Conway, John S. 37 812 813 814
Cortey, Maria-Dolors 815
Cousine, A. 672
Creveld, M. van 38

Csikos, Stefan 39
Csonkaréti, Károly 578
Csöppüs, István 40
Cutter, William 816
Cygański, Mirosław 379
Czollek, Roswitha 666
Czubiński, Antoni 380

D

Dahlgren, Tore 456
Dallin, Alexander 673
Dańkowski, Jan 817
Dar, E. H. 41
Datner, Szymon 457 818 819 820 821 822 823
Dauzenroth, Erich 824
Davis, Frank 458 459
Dawidowicz, Lucy S. 962
De Felice, Renzo 290
Defrasne, J. 42
Degelow, Hans J. 674
Dehnert, Hans 460
DeJonghe, Albert 461 462
Dejonghe, Etienne 463
Delmaire, Danielle 825
Delmas, J. 43
DeLuca, Anthony R. 44
Demps, Laurenz 45 826
DeWitt, Thomas E. J. 46
Diephouse, David J. 47
Dimsdale, Joel E. 827 897 901 950 1001
DiNolfo, Ennio 464
Doenecke, Justus D. 465
Dossa, Shiraz 828
Douglas, Alec 466
Dow, James Elstone 48
Drechsler, Karl 49 50
Dreisziger, N. F. 675
Drewniak, Bogusław 381
Driss, Rachid 467
Drobisch, Klaus 50
Drobish, K. 51
Droz, Jacques 52
Drozdowski, Marian Marek 829
Dubrovchenko, P. M. 676
Dülffer, Jost 53
Dulnik, Shlomo 830
Dunin-Wąsowicz, Krzysztof 831 832
Dunk, H. W. von der 54
Dupeux, Louis 291
Durad, Arthur A. 238
Durand, Yves 292 293
Dvorjetsky, M. 833
Dzik, Leon 834

E

Eckert, Rainer 294
Eichholtz, Dietrich 55 56 57 295 677 678
Eisenbach, Artur 835
Eisner, Joseph 836
Eisner, Józef 837
Elgazi, Joseph 838
Eliav, Binyamin 839
Elliott, Mark 679
Ellis, Donald W. 58
Epstein, David 840
Erez, Zui 841 842

Author Index

Ericksen, Robert P. 843
Ernst, Volker 59
Espinosa, Manuel 296
Etzold, Thomas H. 468

F

Fackenheim, Emil 844
Facon, Patrick 297
Faitys, Antonin 579
Fass, Moshe 845
Fastabend, David A. 680
Fekete, Edit 580
Feldenkirchen, Wilfried von 298
Ferenc, Tone 581 582 583 584
Fiedor, Karol 585
Finker, Kurt 60
Fishta, Iljaz 586
Fiszman, Felicja 846
Fjaerli, Eystein O. 61
Fleischer, Hans-Otto 62
Fleming, Gerald 847
Flender, Harold 848
Fonde, J.-J 469
Fonzi, Fausto 808
Forišković, Aleksandar 63
Forster, J. 681
Förster, Jürgen 299 682 683
Frank, Hans 382
Freundlich, Elisabeth 383 849
Fridman, Eva 850
Friedlander, Henry 851
Friedländer, Saül 852 853
Fritz, Martin 300 301 302
Fröhlich, Elke 64
Frolov, B. 684
Frolow, B. 587
Fuks, Marian 854 855 856 857

G

Gadberry, Glen W. 858
Galbraith, John Kenneth 470
Galen, Clemens August von 65
Galistan, A. 66 756
Garçon, François 859
Gąsiorowska, Natalia 860
Gelber, Yoav 471
Gemzell, Carl-Axel 472
Genri, Ernst 67
Gessner, Klaus 68
Giard, Luce 861
Gibbons, Robert 588 685
Giesinger, Adam 384 686 687
Gîrbea, Titus 636
Gitler-Barski, Józef 862 863
Glatz, Ferenc 69
Golczewski, Frank 385
Goldberg, Eric 473
Goldhagen, Erich 864 865 866 867
Gollert, Friedriech 386
Gollotti, Enzi 474
Gordon, Bertram 475
Gotovitch, José 476 868
Gottwald, Herbert 269
Gounand, Pierre 477
Gourmen, P. 672
Gouvrin, Joseph 869
Graham, Robert A. 870
Grammdorf, Gerda 70
Green, Warren 871 872
Greenstone, Maryann D. 873
Gribkov, A. 688
Gritschneder, Otto 71

Grobelný, Anděĺin 72 73 589 590 591 592
Grobelný, Antonín 593 594
Grobosch, Werner 74
Groehler, Olaf 49 75 76 77 78 303 478 479 689
Groeneveld, Eduard G. 480
Grosman, Ladislav 874
Gross, Feliks 875
Grossman, Haika 876
Gruchmann, Lothar 79 877
Gruggel, Bogumila 387
Grunskis, E. 690
Grynberg, Henryk 878 879
Grynberg, Michał 880 881
Gur, Mandy 882
Gutman, Yisrael 883 884 885 886 887 888
Gyarmati, György 580
Gyllenstierna, Ebbe 304

H

Hackman, W. Kent 481
Haft, Cynthia J. 889
Halivni, Tzipora Hager 890
Hamerow, Theodore S. 80
Hammond, Keith 81
Hammond, Mason 82
Hanisch, Ernst 278 305
Hanlon, Lindley P. 83
Hanson, John H. 84
Harris, James F. 85
Hass, Gerhart 49 50 691
Hass, Kurt 86
Hauge, Andreas 515
Hauner, Milan 87
Hautecler, Georges 482 483
Haynes, Emma Schwabenland 692
Heider, Paul 88
Heike, Otto 388
Heller, Paul 891
Herget, Toni 595
Herzstein, Robert E. 7 89 90 484 485
Hilaire, Yves-Marie 825
Hilberg, Raul 892 893 894 895 896 897 898
Hildebrand, Klaus 91 92 93
Hillebrandt, Bogdan 899
Hillgruber, Andreas 94 95 96 97 98 306 307 900
Hirschfeld, Yair 308
Hladký, Ladislav 596
Hoess, Rudolf 901
Hoffman, Zygmunt 759 902 903
Hoffmann, Marhild 99
Hoffmann, Peter 100
Hofman, J. 101
Hofsten, Gustaf von 486
Hohenecker, Leopold 693
Höllen, Martin 904
Holmén, Hans 487
Homze, Edward L. 102
Hoover, Karl D. 389
Horejsek, Jaroslav 597
Horn, Daniel 103 104 105
Horn, Maurycy 390 905
Huan, Claude 488
Hürten, Heinz 489

I

Iablochkin, Iu. N. 694
Ilel, I. 598
Ionescu, Mihail E. 576
Isby, David C. 106
Ivanitski, G. 728
Ivanov, S. P. 695

J

Jacobmeyer, Wolfgang 391
Jacobsen, Hans-Adolf 107
Jaeger, Harald 108 109
Janner, William, Jr. 110
Jaworski, Michał 906
Jelinek, Yeshayahu 907
Johnson, Ronald W. 309
Jokipii, Mauno 310 373 373
Jonca, K. 111 599
Jong, Louis de 908
Juhász, Gyula 311 396 649
Jukes, Geoffrey 112
Jung, Dieter 113

K

Kafka, John S. 114
Kahn, David 115 696
Kaiser, Hans 600
Kalbe, Ernstgert 601
Kam'a N'dumbe III, Alexandre 116
Kampe, Hans-Georg 697
Karchmer, Naphtali 392
Karczowa, Halina 117
Karner, Stefan 118 119 312 602
Kárný, Miroslav 120 121 909 910 911
Karp, Hans-Jürgen 393
Karpi, Daniel 912
Kaslas, Bronis J. 313
Kasper, Hanns-Heinz 314
Kater, Michael H. 122 123 124
Katz, Fred E. 913
Katz, Robert 914
Katz, Steven T. 915
Kaun, Anita 59
Kelly, John Joseph 490
Kerkvliet, Gerard 916
Kermisa, Josef 898
Kermish, Joseph 917
Kessel, Joseph 125
Kibata, Kazuko 126
Kieval, Hillel J. 918
Kirste, Peter 127
Kirwin, Gerald 491
Klemperer, Klemens von 128
Klink, Ernst 698
Kludas, Arnold 315
Knoll, Werner 699
Kobrzyński, Stefan 919
Koch, H. W. 316
Koch, Karl W., Jr. 492
Kochetkov, A. 756
Koenig, Pierre 920
Kolokol'tsev, S. 700
Komarov, N. Ia 701
Konieczny, Alfred 394
Koonz, Claudia 129 129
Korey, William 921
Korotyński, Henryk 395
Korthals Altes, A. 130
Kotysh, N. 756
Kovalenko, I. M. 702
Kováts, Lajos 317

Kozeński, Jerzy 131 132 603 604
Kozmiński, Maciej 396
Kráčmarová, Hana 605
Krakowski, Shmuel 397 398 922
Král, Václav 606
Krammer, Arnold 133 318
Krantz, G. T. 134
Krasuski, Jerzy 135
Krause, Michael D. 136
Krausnick, Helmut 703
Kreidel, Hellmuth 137
Kren, George M. 138 139 923 924
Krieger, Leonard 140
Krier, Emile 493
Krimper, Ronald L. 319
Król, Eugeniusz, C. 399
Kroszczor, Henryk 925
Krzyżanowski, Jerzy R. 400
Kuckhoff, Greta 141
Kugler, Victor 926
Kühn, Günter 927 928
Kühne, Wolfgang 929
Kühnrich, Heinz 142 143 144
Kulak, Zbigniew 145
Kulikov, V. G. 146
Kulka, O. D. 930 931
Kumlin, Ragnar 320
Kuperstein, Isaiah 932
Kuz'michev, I. K. 704
Kvam, Ragnar 933
Kwiatkowska, Celestyna 401

L

Lachman, Ernest 934
Łagodziński, Stanisław 147
Lakowski, Richard 148
Lammers, Karl Christian 321
Langbein, Herrmann 149
Lange, Dieter 150
Lange, Wolfgang 151
Langenberg, William H. 152 153
Lapomarda, Vincent A. 935
Laqueur, Walter 154 936
Larson, Arthur D. 155
Lassen, Gilbert 937
Latas, Branko 607 608
Laurens, André 494
Laurière, Hervé 938
Lavergne, Bernard 938
Leci, Thanas 609
Lee, Asher 156
Lehmann, Hans Georg 322
Lehmann, Joachim 157 158
Lemeshchuk, N. M. 939
Leszczyńska, Zofia 941
Leszczyński, Julian 940 942
Levi, Primo 943
Levin, Dov 944 945
Levine, Herbert S. 323
Lévy, Claude 495
Levy, Gilles 516
Levy, Paul M. G. 159
Lewin, Isaak 946 947 948 949
L'Huillier, Fernand 496 497
Liman, Stefan 402
Loewald, K. G. 498
Loock, Hans-Dietrich 499
Lovett, Clara M. 221
Luchterhand, Elmer 950
Luck, David 951
Ludlow, Peter 500
Lukens, Nancy 160
Lukin, M. 705

Lukkes, J. R. 377
Lunt, J. D. 501
Luria, Lisa 952
Luther, Craig 502 706
Luttwak, E. N. 161
Lutzhöft, Hans-Jürgen 324

M

Macartney, C. A. 649
MacDonald, William W. 162 163
Madajczyk, Czesław 164 403 404 405 610
Madej, Victor 165 707
Mainuš, František 166 611 708
Makhrov, N. 167
Małczużyński, Karol 406
Mal'kov, Viktor Leonidovich 325
Mandell, Richard D. 503
Mann, Golo 168 169 170
Mann, Reinhard 171
Manninen, Ohto 326 373 709
Marcu, Paraschiv 612
Marczewski, Jerzy 407
Marjanović, Jovan 613
Mark, Ber 953
Mark, Esther 954
Marolda, Edward J. 710
Marrus, Michael R. 955
Marsh, Patrick 504
Martres, M. 505
Mason, Henry L. 956
Mason, T. W. 172
Mason, Tim 173 174
Mathieu, G. Bording 957
Matsulenko, V. 756
Matthews, Kenneth 506
Matusak, Piotr 958
Mayda, Giuseppe 959
McKale, Donald 175 176
Melka, R. L. 327 328
Melkman, J. 960
Mel'nikov, D. E. 329
Melodia, Giovanni 808
Mendelsohn, John 961
Menger, Manfred 330 331 507
Mensch, Terry G. 177
Merglen, Albert 508
Merians, Elaine 962
Merians, Melvin L. 962
Merinsky, Karl 614
Mertsalov, A. N. 178 711
Messerschmid, Felix 963
Messerschmidt, M. 179
Meyer, Michael 180
Meyer-Brenkhoff, Heinz-Jürgen 509
Meyers, Peter 99 385
Meyers, Willem C. M. 510 511
Mięso, Józef 408
Michaelis, Meir 964
Michman, Dan 965
Michman, Joseph 966
Michta, Norbert 409
Mievre, J. 512
Mikhman, Dan 967
Milak, Enes 615
Miletić, Antun 616 617 968
Milošević, Slobodan 618
Milova, Chr 619
Mindru, Costachi 620
Minei, Nicolae 332 969
Mirnić, Josip 621
Mitchell, Alan 181
Moczarski, Kazimierz 970
Modrzewska, Krystyna 410
Moltke, Helmuth von 182

Mommsen, Hans 183
Monticone, Alberto 808
Moritz, Erhard 29 78 513 669
Morozov, V. 184
Mulholland, Virginia 185
Müller, Norbert 712
Müller, Rolf-Dieter 186 187
Mulligan, Timothy P. 713
Munthe-Kaas, O. U. 514
Munthe-Kaas, Otto H. 515
Murray, Williamson 188 189
Mușat, Mircea 333 622
Mycak, Józef 971
Myllyniemi, Seppo 373

N

Nanteuil, Hughes de 516
Natali, Jacques 517
Nazarewicz, Ryszard 411 972
Neigert, Marcel 518
Nejedlý, Miloslav 623
Nelson, H. N. 190
Nelson, Otto M. 191
Newerly, Igor 973
Nicault, Maurice 519
Nitzsche, Gerhard 261
Noakes, Jeremy 192
Nofi, A. A. 520 521 522
Norton, Mary Beth 222
Noskova, A. F. 714 974

O

Oberdörfer, Lutz 523
Oberkofler, Gerhard 975
Obućina, Branko 968
O'Donnell, James P. 193
Oertel, Manfred 715
Olsson, Sven-Olof 194
Olszewski, Marian 412
Oppen, Beate Ruhm von 195
Orbach, Wila 976
Orlov, A. S. 196 701
Oseraner, Michail 197 716
Overy, R. J. 198 199 200 334

P

Pakentreger, Aleksander 977 978 979 980
Pallas, Ladislav 413 414 589
Palm, Thede 524
Parham, Dave 717
Parker, Harold T. 33
Patrick, Stephen B. 201 525 526 527 718
Pätzold, Kurt 981
Pavlović, Konstantin 335 336 337
Pawełczyńska, Anna 982
Pawlowitch, Stevan K. 624
Pech, Karlheinz 142 144
Penkower, Monty N. 983
Perechnev, Iu 719
Perezhogin, V. A. 720
Perski, Jakub 415
Pertz, Erik 528
Peša, Václav 202
Peschanski, Denis 529
Peters, Jan 203
Petersen, Jürgen 204
Petrick, Fritz 331 507
Petukhov, K. 721
Peukert, Detlev 205

Author Index

Picard, Roger 530
Pinchuk, Ben-Cion 984
Pitt, Barrie 531 532 533
Pliacheko, P. 625
Podéh (Podomski), Feivel 985
Pokryshkin, Aleksandr 722
Pommerin, Reiner 338 986
Popescu-Puțuri, Ion 206
Pospieszalski, Karol Marian 416 417
Potra, George G. 207
Pożywiłek, Michał 208
Pritchett, Merrill R. 544
Przychodzki, Michal 418
Pushkin, A. 534

Q

Quinnett, Robert L. 209

R

Rabinbach, Anson G. 210
Rabovsky, L. 756
Racault, Gaston 530
Radandt, Hans 339 626 627
Radlitzki, Tzvi 987
Ránki, György 649
Rappoport, Leon 924
Rastelli, Achille 535
Ratley, Lonnie O. 723
Ratley, Lonnie O., III 724
Rauchensteiner, Manfried 211
Redlich, Shimon 988
Reichman, Yehiel Meir 989
Reimaa, Markku 340
Reisenberger, Dieter 385
Rempel, Gerhard 212
Renner, H. J. 377
Riedel, Matthias 725
Riel, H. van 536
Riemenschneider, Rainer 213
Riesenberger, Dieter 99
Robbins, Michael 214
Roberts, Geoffrey 215
Robertson, James C. 419
Roche, Emile 341
Rohwer, Jürgen 216
Rokossovsky, K. 756
Romano, Jaša 628
Rosenberg, Alan 990
Rosenberg, Edgar 991
Rosenfeld, Alvin H. 992
Rosensaft, Hadassah 993
Rosensaft, Menachem 994
Roslyng-Jensen, Palle 537
Rossetto, L. 217
Rössler, Eberhard 538
Rostowski, Dieter 420
Roth, John K. 995
Rothchild, Sylvia 996
Rothfeder, Herbert P. 218
Rothkirchen, Livia 997
Rousseau, Michel 539
Rousso, Henry 998
Rubin, Eliahu 999
Rudenko, S. I. 726
Ruffray, Françoise de 297
Ruge, Friedrich 219
Rühle, Jürgen 220
Rumiantsev, N. 727
Rumschöttel, Hermann 108
Rupp, Leila J. 221 222 223
Rutkowska, Maria 421
Ryan, Michael D. 160 195 851 1041 1051

Ryszka, Franciszek 1000
Rzheshevski, O. 728

S

Sabini, John P. 1001
Saint-Jours, Frédéric 224
Sakowska, Ruta 1002 1003 1004 1005 1006
Salecki, Jerzy A. 422
Salewski, Michael 342
Salomon, Eleonore 729
Samsons, V. 730
Saroka, Waclaw W. 400
Schärer, Martin R. 343
Schechowzow, Nikolai 731
Scheel, Heinrich 225
Scheel, Klaus 226 629 630 732
Schickel, Alfred 423
Schieder, Theodor 344
Schlesinger, Wilhelm 1007
Schnapp, Alain 227
Schofield, B. B. 540
Schöllgen, Gregor 228
Scholliers, Peter 541
Schönfeld, Roland 631
Schorsch, Ismar 1008
Schreiber, Gerhard 229 345
Schröder, Josef 346 542
Schumann, Wolfgang 50 230 231 303 347 632
Schustereit, Hartmut 348
Schützle, Kurt 349
Sella, Amnon 733
Selleslagh, F. 543
Selzer, Michael 232
Sendlerowa, Irena 1009
Sergeev, F. 350
Serwański, Edward 421 424
Sevostyanov, P. 734 735
Seydewitz, Max 233
Seydewitz, Ruth 233
Shamir, Haim 234 351
Shapiro, Eda 926
Shavit, David 1010
Shavrov, I. E. 736
Shea, William L. 544
Sheffler, Wolfgang 765
Shirman, Israël 1011
Shneiderman, S. L. 1012 1013
Shtemenko, S. 756
Shtykov, N. 737
Sijački, Ljubica 1014
Silberner, Edmund 1015
Silver, Maury 1001
Simion, A. 352 353
Simpson, Keith 738
Sims, Amy R. 235
Sirkov, Dimităr 633
Sjøqvist, Viggo 354 375
Sládek, Oldřich 634
Sládek, Zdeněk 635
Smirnov, V. P. 545
Smith, Bradley F. 1016
Sobczak, Janusz 425 426 546
Sobczak, Kazimierz 236
Spangenberg, Max 237
Speer, Albert 547
Spicehandler, Arnold 1017
Spivey, Delmar T. 238
Spyra, Bronisława 427
Stachiewicz, Wacław 428
Stam, A. 101 239
Stanca, Horia 251
Stang, Werner 240 241
Stanton, Shelby 707
Staron, Stanislaw 892 898

Ştefan, M. 352
Şteflea, Ilie 636
Stegemann, Bernd 242
Steiner, Herbert 278
Steinert, Marlis G. 243
Steinmetz, Selma 1018
Stepanov, F. 756
Stephenson, Jill 244 245
Stich, Karl 246 548
Stolfi, Russel H. S. 739 740
Storlid, P. O. 741
Strauss, Herbert A. 1019
Strzembosz, Tomasz 429
Ştuhlpfarrer, Karl 355
Šuica, Nada 247
Sultanik, Kalman 1020
Sunde, Hjalmar I. 742
Suominen, Elina 1021
Suppan, Arnold 637
Suško, Ladislav 638 639
Suttorp, L. C. 549
Swianiewicz, Stanislaw 430
Swint, William A. 550
Sydnor, Charles W., Jr. 248
Szabó, Balázs 743
Szarota, Tomasz 431 432
Szczechura, Tomasz 1022
Szewdowski, Stanisław 1023
Szulfried, Stanisław 1024
Szulkin, Michał 1025

T

Takashi, Saito 249
Tal, Uriel 1026 1027
Talmon, J. L. 1028
Talpeş, Ioan 356
Tejchman, Miroslav 635 640
Teppe, Karl 250
Terej, Jerzy Janusz 433
Thackrah, J. R. 641
Thälmann, Ernst 251
Thies, Jochen 357
Thulstrup, Åke 358
Tiefel, Hans 252
Tilford, Earl H., Jr. 253
Tillion, Germaine 1029
Timokhovich, I. 254
Toçi, Veniamin 586
Todd, Douglas 255
Toshkova, Vitka 619
Tracey, Donald R. 256
Tregenza, Michael 1030
Treue, Wilhelm 359
Tschuikow, W. 744
Tubin, Yehuda 1031
Tugwell, Maurice A. J. 551
Turkenburg, Wim C. 19
Turkenburg, Wim C. 20
Tutkus, V. I. 745
Tyszka, Leon 1032 1033 1034

U

Ueberschaer, Gerd R. 746
Uitvlugt, Martin 916
Umbreit, Hans 552 553
Underwood, G. L. 554
Unger, Manfred 257
Uola, Mikko 360
Uzelac, Dušan 642

V

Vago, Bela 361

Van Crefeld, M. 555
VanderWee, Herman 556
Vanwelkenhuyzen, Jean 362 557 556 558
Vasdravelles, I. 643
Vasil'ev, B. 747
Vedovato, Giuseppe 363
Vernon, Graham D. 748
Veryha, Wasyl 749
Vestermanis, Margers 712
Viault, Birdsall S. 559
Vidal-Naquet, Pierre 1035
Vigne, Eric 227
Višnjić, Petar 644
Voinov, A. 750
Voitsekhovski, Marian 258
Volk, Ludwig 65 1036
Volkmann, Hans-Erich 259 364
Volkov, N. 260
Voorhis, Jerry L. 560
Vosske, Heinz 261
Voutey, Maurice 1037

W

Wachowiak, Stanislaw 434
Wachtel, Nathan 1038
Wagman Eshkoly, Hava 1039
Wahlen, Verena 1040
Waite, Robert G. L. 262 263 1041
Walczak, Maria 424
Wall, Donald D. 264
Wallach, Jehuda L. 1042 1043
Wappler, Anke 632
Warner, Geoffrey 365
Weber, Wolfgang 927 928
Wegner, Bernd 265
Wegner-Korfes, Sigrid 266
Weinberg, Gerhard L. 267
Weinrib, Abrasha 1044
Weiss, Aharon 1045 1046 1047 1048
Weissbecker, Manfred 268 269
Weisstein, Ulrich 270
West, John M. 366
Wette, Wolfram 645
Wiesel, Elie 1049
Wilhelm, Hans-Heinrich 271
Wilhelmus, Wolfgang 272 331 367 368 369 370 507
Williams, Maurice 278
Willig, Kenneth C. H. 273
Wilson, Craig A. 446
Wilt, Alan F. 561 562 751
Winick, Myron 1050
Winkler, Dörte 274
Wistrich, Robert S. 770
Witthöft, Hans Jürgen 275
Wittram, Heinrich 435
Woche, Klaus 276
Woodman, Gayle M. 1051
Wynot, Edward D., Jr. 436

Z

Zahn, Gordon C. 1052
Zawodny, J. K. 437
Zeidler, Hans-Jürgen 59
Zelenin, V. V. 646
Zeleński, Władysław 438
Zerner, Ruth 1053
Zetterberg, Kent 371
Ževart, Milan 582 647
Zheltov, A. 752
Zhilin, P. 753
Zhukov, Georgi 756
Ziemke, Earl F. 754
Zimandt, Roman 1054
Zinsser, Christian 372
Zografski, Dancho 648
Zuckerman, Itzhak 1055
Zumpe, Lotte 277
Zuroff, Efraim 1056
Zvenzlovsky, M. A. 756
Zyśko, Wojciech 439

Ref.
Z
6207
W8
T46
1984